THE OXFORD BOOK OF
CARIBBEAN
SHORT STORIES

Stewart Brown is a poet and critic who teaches African and Caribbean literature at the Centre of West African Studies, University of Birmingham. He worked as a teacher in Jamaica in the early 1970s, lectured at Bayero University, Kano in Nigeria in the 1980s, and later taught at the University of the West Indies in Barbados. He has edited several anthologies of Caribbean writing and published many books and essays on aspects of West Indian culture.

John Wickham is one of the most respected figures in Caribbean literature. His essays and short stories have been widely published and anthologized. Born and educated in Barbados, he worked for several years at the World Meteorological Organisation in Geneva before returning to the island, where he has been Literary Editor of the *Nation* newspaper since 1979. He is editor of *Bim*, the Caribbean's longest-established literary journal, and served for several years as a Senator in the Barbados parliament.

D0228052

'This has to be the best anthology of Caribbean stories of all time, and if a better one appears some time in the future, it will be edited by Stewart Brown and John Wickham.'

Benjamin Zephaniah

'breathtakingly rich and diverse'
Elleke Boehmer
University of Leeds

'[W]hat we have here is a stunning collection of writers representing almost every region that is touched by the Caribbean Sea . . . some of the best writing to have appeared in this century has come from this archipelago of complex histories and diverse traditions.'

Kwame Dawes
University of South Carolina

'a wonderfully varied but integrated flow of writing from, or about, the Caribbean, over almost a hundred years. Brown's brilliant, long introduction defends and explains his and Wickham's selection and arrangement—and far, far more'

Anne Walmsley
Caribbean arts researcher and writer, London

'An important feature is its inclusion of authors from the French, Spanish and Dutch-speaking Caribbean, including Alejo Carpentier and René Depestre. Generous in its expanse, and imaginative in its selection, the book can serve as both introduction and consolidation to this vivid and varied literature.'

Louis James
University of Kent

Also available from Oxford Paperbacks

The Oxford Book of American Short Stories
Edited by Joyce Carol Oates

The Oxford Book of Irish Short Stories
Edited by William Trevor

The Oxford Book of Japanese Short Stories
Edited by Ted Goossen

The Oxford Book of New Zealand Short Stories
Edited by Vincent O'Sullivan

The Oxford Book of Scottish Short Stories
Edited by Douglas Dunn

THE OXFORD BOOK OF

CARIBBEAN

SHORT STORIES

Edited by

Stewart Brown and John Wickham

OXFORD
UNIVERSITY PRESS

OXFORD
UNIVERSITY PRESS

Great Clarendon Street, Oxford OX2 6DP

Oxford University Press is a department of the University of Oxford.
It furthers the University's objective of excellence in research,
scholarship, and education by publishing worldwide in

Oxford New York

Auckland Cape Town Dar es Salaam Hong Kong Karachi
Kuala Lumpur Madrid Melbourne Mexico City Nairobi
New Delhi Shanghai Taipei Toronto

With offices in

Argentina Austria Brazil Chile Czech Republic France Greece
Guatemala Hungary Italy Japan Poland Portugal Singapore
South Korea Switzerland Thailand Turkey Ukraine Vietnam

Oxford is a registered trade mark of Oxford University Press
in the UK and in certain other countries

Published in the United States
by Oxford University Press Inc., New York

Selection and editorial matter © Stewart Brown and John Wickham 1999

The moral rights of the author have been asserted
Database right Oxford University Press (maker)

First published 1999
Reissued 2001

British Library Cataloguing in Publication Data

Data available

Library of Congress Cataloging in Publication Data
The Oxford book of Caribbean short stories / edited by Stewart Brown
and John Wickham.
1. Short stories. Caribbean (English) 2. Caribbean Area—Social
Life and customs—Fiction. 3. West Indies—Social life and customs—Fiction.
4. Short stories, West Indian (English) I. Brown, Stewart. 1951– .
II. Wickham, John.
PR9205.8.094 1999 813´.01089729—DC21 98–29731

ISBN 978–0–19–280229–3

10

Typeset by Best-set Typesetter Ltd., Hong Kong
Printed in Great Britain by the MPG Books Group,
Bodmin and King's Lynn

Contents

Contents

Contents

Contents

Contents

ix

Contents

x

Contents

Introduction

Cutting the Ground

Our ambition for this anthology is that it will engage, entertain, and inspire its readers, whether they are new to Caribbean writing or already committed to the literature of the region. To that end we have chosen stories from across the wider Caribbean—though predominantly from 'the cricket playing West Indies'[1]—which seem to us both distinctly 'of' the region and yet accessible to a wide readership. The collection contains sufficient surprises to keep even the most avid student of West Indian writing turning the pages while including enough excellent stories from the other language traditions to remind readers that the Caribbean is a multilingual, multicultural space.

It is traditional to relegate an account of the hows and whys of making anthology selections to a brief paragraph at the end of the Introduction but I feel it is important to foreground what we have tried to do with this anthology.* Our original brief was to compile a truly pan-Caribbean collection that would 'fairly' represent the short-story traditions in the four major languages of the region: English, Spanish, French, and Dutch. The five-hundred-page extent of this collection would surely be generous enough to accommodate such a selection. And so it seemed to us . . . until, that is, we really got down to making those selections and realized how distorted a picture such a collection would give of each of those traditions, while implying that there was one Caribbean cultural entity which over-rode those linguistic and cultural differences. The more we struggled with such a selection the more dissatisfied we became with that implicit, homogenizing agenda. For while everyone agrees that the different linguistic territories of the region share much in common—'the unity is submarine' as Kamau Brathwaite puts

* I should explain here the elision between 'we' and 'I' in this Introduction: John Wickham was very much involved in the selection of stories for the anthology but, as the academic in the editorial team, the responsibility for writing this Introduction has fallen to me.

[1] The usage is Professor Gordon Rohlehr's in personal correspondence, elegantly distinguishing the linguistic boundaries of the Caribbean while at the same time giving a little spin to the debate around whether the language used in the places where cricket is played is adequately covered by the description 'English'.

it[2]—it is also true that—notwithstanding their geographical proximity—the culture of, say, Cuba differs in fundamental ways from that of Haiti or Jamaica. At least, within the English language region, British colonialism provided—for better or worse—some degree of shared cultural values, some parameters within which it is possible to compare the achievement of individual writers from places as otherwise distinct as Jamaica and Trinidad, Barbados and Guyana. We decided then that we would try to let the anthology tell the story of that one linguistic tradition while including major writers and favourite stories from the other languages in the general chronological sequence of the selection so that readers would be continually alerted to those other strands in the Caribbean experience and the fact that collections which began with, say, a Spanish bias would look very different from the one we have produced.

For all sorts of reasons, not least the linguistic insularity of the British, there was little cultural interchange between the different language communities of the Caribbean through most of this century. In terms of literature there was some contact between the poets—Derek Walcott, on the already linguistically complex ground of Saint Lucia, acknowledges the influence of the Martiniquan writers Saint-John Perse and Aimé Césaire, Kamau Brathwaite comes to admire the work of the Cuban Nicholás Guillén—but the difficulties of travel between the islands, the problems of translation and accessibility, made such cultural exchange very much the exception rather than the rule. The short story in particular suffered from the lack of translations, so it is unlikely that very many Jamaican writers would have known what was being written just across the horizon in Cuba, or even that any aspiring prose writer in Dominica could know what was being written in Guadeloupe, even though, on a clear day, you can see the one island from the other. That relative insularity is another reason why the notion of an 'all-a-we-is-one' Caribbean literary tradition is problematic, at least as we look back through the twentieth century. It may well be that with the end of colonialism, with much improved communication and travel technologies enabling easier interchange between the islands and territories across the region, with so much more being published and translated—and in various ways broadcast—and with the eclectic conventions of a post-

---

[2] Edward Brathwaite, *Contradictory Omens* (Savacou Publications, Mona, Jamaica, 1974). See also Bridget Jones's essay ' "The unity is submarine": aspects of a pan-Caribbean consciousness in the work of Kamau Brathwaite', in S. Brown (ed.), *The Art of Kamau Brathwaite* (Seren, Bridgend, 1995).

modern sensibility gaining sway, it may be that in another generation the notion of a pan-Caribbean tradition will be a much more viable proposition. So who counts as a Caribbean writer? If we take a fairly conventional notion of 'nationality' as someone born in the region, and/or who lived and worked for most of their lives there, then a significant percentage of the writers we have included would not have been eligible. Migration has been a fact of Caribbean life—indeed, it is arguably the defining experience of Caribbean 'being'. Historically, with the exception of the few surviving Amerindian communities in the islands (and, of course, in the mainland South American territories) all the peoples of the Caribbean are 'incomers', whether from Africa, Europe, India, China, or the Middle East. So a sense of being 'half home' is perhaps part of what it means to be a West Indian. That being so it is not surprising that so many Caribbean people have been willing to uproot themselves 'again' to pursue economic opportunities or other ambitions. All through this century West Indians have migrated in significant numbers; to Panama, to England, to Canada, and the USA. Many writers were among them, most famously the group who ventured to Britain in the 1950s and collectively drew attention to the region's literary ambitions—Naipaul, Lamming, Selvon, Salkey, Mittelholzer, Harris, etc. Hardly any of those writers returned to live in the Caribbean but all continued to write about the region throughout their careers.

Many contemporary writers also spend much of their lives 'elsewhere'—settling particularly in recent years in Florida and New York and in Toronto where they have some opportunity to establish their literary reputations. But today such migrations are not so absolute, do not entail such a breaking of ties as they did for the emigrants of the forties and fifties who literally crossed the seas; many of today's migrants are able to maintain close links with home and to travel back and forth quite regularly. So we have been fairly flexible as regards our definition of a Caribbean writer, considering work by any writer with Caribbean connections whose work somehow 'spoke to' Caribbean experience—as broad and vague an idea as that is. Consequently we have no doubts about including a story by the great Colombian writer Gabriel García Márquez, who spent much of his childhood on the Caribbean coast. We chose it first of all because it is such a memorable story but also as a way of acknowledging that wonderful richness of the wider Caribbean's literary gumbo! Writers such as the Cuban Benítez Rojo and the Trinidadian/Bahamian

Introduction

Robert Antoni, both based now in the USA, have theorized notions of a late twentieth-century Caribbean aesthetic which depends less on a lived geography than on a distinctive perspective on history, a perspective which reflects the creole nature of Caribbean societies and is understood in relation to those other—conflicting—versions of history that have served the interests of the dominant empires—initially of Europe and latterly the USA.[3] All that said though it comes down in the end to how the writers think of themselves. One writer whose story we wanted to include in this selection refused permission because he did not want to be categorized as a Caribbean writer!

Roots

Caribbean literature has grown in both volume and stature through this century from something that hardly existed—at least as far as the literary mainstream was concerned—into a body of word-culture (embracing both oral and written dimensions) that is generally acknowledged to be one of the richest, most accessible, and yet technically adventurous libraries of contemporary world literature. Across the region major writers such as Derek Walcott, Kamau Brathwaite, V. S. Naipaul, Jean Rhys, Sam Selvon, Wilson Harris—to name just a few of the English language writers—have produced poetry, drama, and fiction that offers both an account of a particular Caribbean experience and speaks to a wider notion of 'the contemporary world'. Indeed, West Indian literature is essentially a twentieth-century phenomenon, for while there were, of course, writers and some interesting pieces of writing produced in the five hundred years or so between the European occupation of the region and the turn of the twentieth century, with a few exceptions that material is more interesting now to the literary anthropologist and antiquarian than to a general reader.

Of course there was an alternative 'word culture' existing and developing in the region throughout that period—the oral tradition of songs and stories, prayers and performances, versions of history and mythology passed down the generations and remade—adapted and added to—each generation. Obviously much of that material would have derived

---

[3] See Antonio Benítez-Rojo, *The Repeating Island: The Caribbean and the Postmodern Perspective* (Duke University Press, Durham, North Carolina, 1992), and the editors' introduction to *The Archipelago: New Caribbean Writing* (Conjunctions: 27), eds. Robert Antoni and Bradford Morrow (Bard College, Annandale-on-Hudson, New York State, 1996).

from African sources during the period of slavery, but there are also Amerindian and European inputs and later the influx of peoples from the Indian sub-continent added to the range and substance of those oral traditions. Through the nineteenth century, after the abolition of slavery, various other forms of oral presentation developed—ranging from the great West Indian preachers at one level, through to the formalization of various kinds of word-play and verbal contestation into calypso and other popular forms, at another. Perhaps combining the skills of both the pulpit orator and the calypsonian were generations of political leaders who used the spoken word as a powerful agent in galvanizing a still largely illiterate population in the struggle for democracy and independence.

Over the same period the collection of more traditional 'folk stories' as literary texts was begun and there are by now many such collections from across the geographical and cultural spread of the region. Many, probably most, West Indian short-story writers have been conscious of and to some extent influenced by those oral forms and the stories spun around figures like Anancy, the West African trickster or Amerindian spirits like Ol' Higue or Mantop. We considered including some such folk stories here but decided not to—both for reasons of space and because it seems to us that the 'folk story' and the literary short story really are very different entities. Certain writers have taken stories and characters out of the oral tradition and re-imagined them in a literary context—Andrew Salkey's adaptation of Anancy is the most sustained example and we include one of his stories here, but perhaps the more significant impact of the oral tradition on the West Indian short story has been in the movement towards the language of speech becoming the language of narration and action—a journey charted in this collection from the experiments of Eric Walrond in the early years of the century through to the fluid handling of voices by contemporary writers such as Robert Antoni and Sasenarine Persaud. The device of the literary short story pretending to be a 'told tale' has real political and cultural resonance in the Caribbean context. The historical experience of the region through most of that five hundred years was hardly conducive to the cultivation of a literary sensibility; the decimation of the indigenous peoples, the institution and gradual decline of transatlantic slavery with its concomitant brutalities and the obscenities of the contrasting life styles of Great House and slave yard. And after abolition the mass indenture of East Indian labourers, their presence further complicating the evolution of a colonialism characterized by the poison of what Edgar Mittelholzer memorably called the 'spite of shade' mentality,[4] an outlook which for so long distorted West Indian society. However, with the end of the Victorian era, with slavery—at least in most places—more than a generation gone and access to education gradually more widespread, it perhaps became possible to think of a literature produced by writers who felt themselves identified by their experience as Caribbean people, which could in some sense be both a commentary on that past and an exploration of its resonances into the contemporary society that would inevitably be the essential subject of a West Indian literature.

Certainly it seems fitting to open this anthology with a story by Frank Collymore, born in 1893, regarded by many writers as the father of modern West Indian writing in English. Collymore was very much a man of Barbados, superficially at least that most English of the West Indian islands, but he was also a man committed to the idea of Caribbean creativity. That commitment is evident in his own literary work—as poet, short-story writer, and actor—but it is particularly evident in his work as editor of *BIM*, the major literary magazine in the region for 40 years and particularly active under Collymore's editorship in the late forties and through the 1950s. Just about every West Indian writer of that period published early work in *BIM* and took encouragement from Collymore's enthusiasm and vision. In some ways the possibility of this present anthology is the fruit of Collymore's vision.

In shaping the anthology we have divided the century's writing in the West Indies into four 'generations'; the Pioneer group born before the First World War and publishing in the years before the Second; the Nationalist generation of writers born before the mid-1930s who were writing most vigorously in the decades approaching the independence period in the Caribbean; the Independence generation of writers born in the late thirties and through the 1940s who established their writing careers in the sixties around and after that independence period; and the Contemporary flowering of post-colonial writers, born around 1950 or later, who came to prominence in the seventies and eighties, and are writing into the 1990s. These categories do not really bear too much scrutiny in terms of trying to define attitudes or styles and of course individual writers straddle those 'generations'—many of those 'Nationalist' and 'Independence' generation writers are still very much part of the contem-

---

[4] See Mittelholzer's poem 'Island Tints' in the anthology *Caribbean Voices*, edited by John Figueroa (Evans, London, 1971). See also Mittelholzer's autobiography of a Guyanese childhood, *A Swarthy Boy* (Putnam, London, 1963).

porary literary scene, but in terms of structuring our selection this seemed a useful armature.

Of course there were many fine stories and accomplished writers we were unable to include in this collection. We have included suggestions for further reading in a bibliography at the end of the collection which we hope will direct readers new to Caribbean writing to explore the range and extent of the short-story traditions of the region.

Pioneers

Frank Collymore's writing in some ways represents the qualities of that conventional, high-colonial period. His prose is self-consciously 'fine'— linguistically and grammatically correct, aspiring to a universal rather than a local character—and he does it well enough. His story here, at the beginning of the anthology, works as a traditional 'strange tale', with murder, muddled moralities, and a tale within a tale. There is little that is obviously Caribbean except a few details of the setting like the references to jalousies and whistling frogs and while we can admire its particular qualities this story also serves to remind us of the cultural assumptions many of the other writers in the anthology have striven to break away from. Jean Rhys came from the same kind of social world as Collymore and there is a colonial middle-class ambiance to her story of Dominica's white-creole milieu of the turn of the century. The stories share some themes too, the effects of isolation, rumours of murder in the community, social disgrace. But in other ways Rhys's sensuous, haunting, and in places very funny tale of the eccentric English incomer who 'goes native' could not be more different from Collymore's restrained and well-mannered tale. The reader has an immediate sense of the importance of class and colour in that society and there is a sense of history too in the references to the black characters—still essentially bit-part players in this story. When the newspaper article that precipitates the final catastrophe asserts that 'black people bear much' it is invoking dangerous memories of the historical relationship between black and white on the island. This story is no celebration of that colonial world; both the substance of the story and the manner of its telling represent a challenge to its smug, hypocritical self-righteousness.

If the stories by Rhys and Collymore are saying something about middle-class creole values and manners around the turn of the century but only obliquely commenting on the lives of the majority of West Indian people, then the next group of writers represented in the anthology go some way to redress that balance. Eric Walrond, Alfred Mendes, and

C. L. R. James, were each, in different ways, setting out to represent in literature a cultural experience which had hardly been the subject of such scrutiny before, at least not in any informed or sympathetic way.

One crucial element of that 'other life' is heard in the language the characters in such stories speak. In Walrond's story 'Drought' we have the first intimation of a different 'way of saying', of a speech that is distinctively West Indian. Immediately we are confronted by a vocabulary that is non-standard, that the author sometimes feels the need to translate for non-West Indian readers—so 'buckra johnny—English white' and 'cookoo—cornmeal, okras and butter stewed'. Walrond's representation of his characters' language also gives readers a sense of the rhythms of a spoken West Indian vernacular, albeit that it seems somewhat tentative when compared with the rendering of Caribbean voices by contemporary writers. The cultural domain Walrond's characters inhabit seems a world away from the genteel drawing rooms of the characters drawn in Collymore and Rhys's stories. The 'black peons', as he calls the country people, eke a subsistence living from their labour despite the cruelties of the climate and the economic structure of their society.

Walrond's literary representation of the Caribbean's rural poor has obvious political resonances but for the Trinidadians Alfred Mendes and C. L. R. James, imaginative writing was just one element of their primary concern with the struggle to address the injustices of colonial society. Both writers are associated with 'the Beacon group', a community of intellectuals involved in the proto-independence movement in Trinidad— Mendes wrote the important early novels *Pitch Lake* and *Black Fauns*, while James is one of the great Caribbean men-of-letters. Both were associated with *Trinidad* and *The Beacon*, short-lived but influential cultural journals which appeared in the 1920s and early 1930s.[5] Mendes's story here reveals much about race and class relationships within the community and confirms the importance of notions of status and dignity right across the society.

James's story 'Triumph' is also concerned with issues of pride and dignity among people who have little material wealth or social status. Much of the work associated with *The Beacon* was set in the barrack-yard slum tenements of Port of Spain. James's story describes them very well in its opening paragraph, where we notice the social historian is at work:

---

[5] See Reinhard Sander's critical anthology *From Trinidad* (Hodder and Stoughton, London, 1978).

Introduction

Every street in Port of Spain proper could show you numerous examples of the type: a narrow gateway leading into a fairly big yard, on either side of which run long, low buildings, consisting of anything from four to eighteen rooms, each about twelve feet square. In these lived the porters, the prostitutes, carter-men, washerwomen and domestic servants of the city.

James goes on to chronicle the 'squalid adversity' of the living conditions that prevail in the barrack-yard, but also to acknowledge that the lives of the people who live there are complex, that his characters have their rituals and their superstitions, but they also have their pride. Like Walrond he is interested in representing the language those characters would speak which adds greatly to the credibility of his story . . . their voices convince us that these are 'real' characters.

All five of those early stories, no matter the social milieu in which they are set, employ essentially conventional devices of story-telling, plot their tales in a familiar way, develop their characters through dialogue and the details of description, move through time more or less sequentially—in short, they display the formal characteristics of the English short story. With the Cuban Alejo Carpentier's 'Journey to the Seed'—the first of our stories from the wider Caribbean—we are suddenly conscious of a different manner of writing and representing the world. Carpentier, of course, is recognized now as one of the great novelists of the Americas, his work including *The Lost Steps* and *The Kingdom of This World*. He was perhaps the earliest exponent of the way of writing that has become known as magical realism. We can find the roots of it in this story; dream and reality are blurred, image and metaphor—the traditional devices of poetry—are here the storyteller's primary tools rather than a concern with verisimilitude or the poignancy of 'captured moments'. The power of writing to actually change a person's circumstances is itself a powerful image in the story:

He thought of the mysteries of the written word, of those black threads which, raveling and unraveling over wide, filigrained balance sheets, had raveled and unraveled agreements, oaths, covenants, testimonies . . . a web of threads extracted from the ink-well, threads in which a man's legs became fouled . . . they formed a noose pressing at his throat and muffling his voice.

This is a different texture of writing; to compare those last two extracts— from C. L. R. James and Carpentier—is to understand the fundamental difference in approach that characterizes the English language and the Spanish (and to some extent the French) short-story traditions in the Caribbean. There are, of course, exceptions to that general distinction between the naturalistic tradition in the English language territories—writers such as Wilson Harris and E. A. Markham and, among a younger generation, Lawrence Scott, Erna Brodber, and Robert Antoni have all moved towards more abstracted manners of narrative—while in Cuba, the Russian/Soviet model of naturalistic 'social realism' was a powerful influence for many years and a writer like Juan Bosh in the Dominican Republic was nothing if not committed to the cause of the peasant and working classes. Indeed, it would be foolish to pretend that the magical realism of writers such as Carpentier, Cabrera Infante, or Márquez was in any sense 'above' the political and historical struggles of the Caribbean people, only that their manner of addressing those concerns is less direct than their English language contemporaries.

Perhaps it is enough to observe that many of the English language writers in the period before political independence—particularly those who stayed in the region rather than venturing overseas to pursue literary careers—were very much conscious of the place of literary activity as an aspect of a kind of cultural nationalism. Roger Mais, for example, was associated with the journal *Focus* in Jamaica in the 1940s, which was founded by the sculptress Edna Manley, wife of Norman Manley, the future Prime Minister of Jamaica. Both Edna and Norman Manley were loud in their assertion of the importance of culture as an aspect of the nationalist/independence movement across the Caribbean. The writers associated with *Focus*, like the *Beacon* writers in Trinidad a decade earlier, were determined to use their writing to bring their political concerns 'to life' as it were. As we see in Mais's story 'Red Dirt Don't Wash', he was very interested in questions of class and ingrained attitudes left over from the time of slavery.

But if any Caribbean writer has been driven by his commitment to the peasant class, both in terms of his writing and his political practice, then it has been Juan Bosch of the Dominican Republic. Indeed, he was briefly President of that perennially troubled nation. His story here—translated into English for the first time—reveals both Bosh's characteristic sympathy for the poorest in his society, the victims of economic, political, and even psychological oppression, and his great skill as a storyteller. This short story (though quite long for a Bosch story) employs so many elements of the storyteller's art with such unobtrusive craft—a deprived child's innocent delight in a mongrel puppy's playfulness sparks a series of events which culminate in an act of intense cruelty on the part of the local agent of 'justice' and a terrible burden of betrayal falling on the child. Along the way we have a chase, a tale of revenge, a wonderful sense of suspense, a love story, a moment of terrible horror and, in the final twisting of the story's tail, a tragic moment of recognition. The terrible irony of all this taking place on Christmas Eve, with the implicit suggestion that other children, elsewhere, are waiting in anticipation for the joyous surprises that the following morning might bring, just emphasizes the bleakness of Bosch's vision of an unjust, cruel world. There is no romancing of the peasant life in Bosch's work, though individual peasant characters may act with dignity and strength and honour; fate, he seems to suggest, is stacked against them.

I have discussed the stories by these pioneer figures from across the Caribbean in some detail because both in terms of their concerns and in the stylistic range of these stories—from gritty naturalism to magical realism—this group of writers set the stage, as it were, for the writers who emerge through the rest of the century.

The 'Nationalist' Generation

Except perhaps in their interest in rendering the dialogue of their characters' speech with some authenticity there is little evidence, in those early stories, of a relationship between the oral storytelling traditions of the Caribbean and the developing literary tradition. An interest in exploring connections between the 'folk-story' and the mythologies that inform those oral traditions is one concern that links many of the writers represented here as belonging to that nationalist generation who were writing most forcefully in the years leading up to the period of political independence in the British Caribbean. A desire to focus on the inequalities of the prevailing social order was one strand of that linkage the *Focus* and *Beacon* writers understood between cultural and political nationalism. But the recognition and incorporation of that alternative word-culture which the West African derived Anancy stories, the borrowed Amerindian mythologies, and the echoes of Hindu mysticism represent—especially as they were all modified and 'creolized' by a West Indian experience—is another important element in that cultural nationalism. Such concerns are important elements in the stories by—among others—Jan Carew, Ismith Khan, and Andrew Salkey, and the liberation from the naturalistic mode that an engagement with such further dimensions of experience and imagination represents perhaps helps explain the shift to a 'magic-realist' mode of narration in stories like Kamau Brathwaite's 'Dream Haiti' and, of course, Márquez's 'The Last Voyage of the Ghost Ship'.

However, it is the issue of migration and its consequences—both economic and psychological—that most concerns the Anglophone writers of this generation. Many of those writers were themselves migrants—leaving home in the islands, as George Lamming said, for the same reason that so many other West Indians left home, to find work—to pursue the dream of making a career of their particular calling. Sam Selvon, the Trinidadian novelist and master storyteller, is represented here by his wonderful comedy of manners, 'The Cricket Match', a story of West Indian bold-face boast and bluff meeting English stereotyping and reserve. On first reading this may seem a slight, whimsical piece but in fact, as in most of Selvon's lonely Londoner stories, beneath the laughter is the most insightful commentary on the psychological nuances of that immigrant experience to be found anywhere in the literature.

Other writers examine different aspects of that experience; John Stewart, Paule Marshall, and Earl Lovelace explore the emotional cost of migration for so many of those who dared to leave and the effects on those left behind, while the young man at the centre of Austin Clarke's 'Leaving this Island Place' is desperate to escape the ties that seem to bind him to the island. For him and others of his generation the tiny island seems a kind of prison—as his girlfriend Cynthia puts it:

this island stifles me . . . Sometimes I feel like a crab in a crab hole with a pile o sand in front.

That wish to escape, and the sense of *possibilities* that emigration offered such bright and determined young men, is an aspect of the story not so often explored.

The other English language stories in this section might be read as reinforcing that sense of claustrophobia the characters in Austin Clarke's story acknowledge. V. S. Naipaul's story 'The Night Watchman's Occurrence Book', for example, while it is marvellously witty and linguistically very clever, also reveals much about class and race relations in the Trinidad of the period—differences of attitude and expectation, the rigidities of a kind of 'them and us' society where both privileged and exploited 'know their place'. Michael Anthony points up a similar tension between the perspectives of the ruling elite in colonial Trinidad and that of the 'mas man'—represented by the calypsonian Lord Invader—in his story 'They Better Don't Stop the Carnival'. But the frustrations of British colonial rule pale in comparison with the dreadful privations endured by many Haitians in more recent times and Kamau

Introduction

Brathwaite's 'Dream Haiti' is a harrowing engagement with the experience of those 'boat-people' who set sail from the poverty and fear of their lives to try to reach a dream of America in all manner of frail and unseaworthy craft. It is also—as I read it—a comment on the role and responsibility of Caribbean writers to respond to such events and their underlying causes.

With the exception of Brathwaite, whose fragmented poetic-prose in some ways serves as a kind of bridge between the Anglophone and the wider Caribbean traditions, it is perhaps in this section of the anthology that the divide between the English language writers and their contemporaries writing in French and Spanish is most marked. Of course in some ways it makes little sense to think of Haiti's René Depestre as belonging to a 'nationalist generation' in that Haiti was hardly 'approaching independence' in the 1950s, nor were the Cuba of G. Cabrera Infante and Antonio Benítez Rojo or the Columbia of Gabriel García Márquez colonies in at all the same way that Jamaica, Barbados, and Guyana were. In a more general sense though the region as a whole was caught up in the global movements that precipitated the end of Empire and those questions around identity, history, and society were very much live issues for the wider Caribbean. Indeed, it may be that those differences in the nature of political structures in societies like Haiti, Cuba, and Columbia in this period—none of their governments exactly open to dissent or reasoned socialistic argument—does help to explain the very different style and texture of the stories by writers from those countries when contrasted with that predominantly naturalistic and direct style that characterizes the English language writing.

The one long sentence that is the opening paragraph of Infante's story 'The Doors Open at Three' bombards the reader with impressionistic detail, with colour, with sensations, setting the scene with an intensity that is unlike anything an Anglophone writer of this period would dare. In its concern with class, insecurity, and notions of self-worth, however, this story is not so far from a piece like Roger Mais's 'Red Dirt Don't Wash' although in Infante's story it is a young medical student who tells the tale of his sudden and intense love for Virginia, the beautiful daughter of an impoverished gravedigger.

There is a tragic sensuousness about both the matter and the manner of Infante's writing which links it to that of his Haitian contemporary René Depestre and his younger Cuban compatriot Antonio Benítez Rojo.

Both are represented here by rather mysterious stories that revolve around ideas of 'forbidden fruit' and sexual awakening but seem to operate at several levels—enclosed worlds, a web of complicated relationships, an island that is penetrated by dangerous strangers. . . . The end of Rojo's story has a dream-like quality and raises all sorts of questions about the status of the preceding narrative. Where—how—do we 'locate' this story? Similar questions are raised by Márquez's 'The Last Voyage of the Ghost Ship', a fantastical account of a young man's premonition or dream that seems to come true. Almost incidentally the story evokes the cosmopolitan vigour and threat of the Colombian-Caribbean coastal towns—like the one in which Márquez grew up—with wonderful energy and detail. This is a world known and 'celebrated', if only in the extent to which the story catches its particular spirit and style. Where dream ends and the reality of the beached liner, lured into the coastal village of the people who mocked the youth for his earlier visions, begins is a moot point.

Is Márquez raising issues about the way individuals with vision are regarded in such a society? Can we read the Depestre and Rojo stories as political fables? Few of these writers could be described as 'nationalist' in the narrow sense that term might be ascribed to some of the Anglophone writers, but perhaps a more sophisticated notion of the relationship between political and cultural nationalism emerges from a reading of these stories, implying a greater trust in their readers' capacity to make connections, to unpack the laughter, to understand the way stories, whether political fable or poetic metaphor, can work in the imagination as well as on the social conscience.

The Independence Generation

The most striking difference in the cast of voices that make up this 'independence generation' is that suddenly the majority of the writers are women. That fact is particularly striking when one considers that there are only two—Jean Rhys and Paule Marshall—included in the earlier sections. This is not mere chance or editorial whim—among the English language writers at least there were few women who might have been included in the earlier selections, while with this generation we have had to leave out several women writers whose work we might well have selected.

There are several factors that may help explain this apparent upsurge in women's writing—most obviously to do with access to formal education for girls which, until the 1950s, was not widely available. Of the girls who did get a secondary education, very few had access to university study. The few scholarships available to send students to study abroad were rarely given to girls. So the development of the regional University of the West Indies through the 1950s, which made access to higher education much more available to women, must have contributed to the climate which made some of those women feel that becoming a writer was a real possibility. The University of the West Indies only came to its full flowering with the advent of political independence for the former British colonies, through the 1960s, and it is no coincidence that women emerge as writers in such numbers in the following decades, when the direction of the new social order was being formulated. These young, well-educated women clearly felt empowered to contribute to those fundamental debates about moral and social values, and fiction—especially the short story—was a powerful medium with which to address those issues. This was also the period when the Feminist movement was gaining ground internationally and the impact of those ideas—albeit modulated to address Caribbean realities—both gave women a subject and encouraged them in their ambitions to become writers.

It would be a mistake, however, to think that this sudden 'visibility' of women, *as writers*, means that there had been no women involved in 'the verbal arts' before. Quite the contrary, in fact, the oral traditions of the Caribbean have been nurtured over generations by the region's women. The image of the grandmother telling tales out of their folk heritage to an enthralled audience of her young charges may be a stereotype but, as many of the region's writers have suggested, there is significant truth in it. But it was not just as a conduit of myth and legend that women functioned within the oral tradition; one of the earliest records in the literature of songs composed and sung by female slaves in the eighteenth century suggests that they were using the voiced word both for solace and as weapon in their struggle against their oppression.[6] Contemporary women writers have taken on many of those historical roles, indeed an acknowledgement of the importance of the oral tradition in the broad sweep of Caribbean life is a feature of many of these writers'

---

[6] The reference is to songs collected by J. B. Moreton in *West India Customs and Manners*, 2nd edn. (London, 1793). For a perceptively subversive and transgressive reading of those songs see Carolyn Cooper's essay, 'Me know no law, me know no sin' in her book *Noises in the Blood: Orality, Gender and the 'vulgar' body of Jamaican popular culture* (Macmillan, Basingstoke, 1993).

work. So we find stories here exploring the power of verbal wit, the subversive potential of asking 'innocent' questions, the ability of characters to improvise and inspire with the spoken word, and the importance ascribed to stories of the supernatural—both as gossip and prayer.

Do these women share other concerns in common as writers? Is there a discernible women's style that links this otherwise very disparate group? The answer to each of those questions is both yes and no!

The themes which dominate Caribbean fiction—history, race, social justice, childhood, questions of allegiance—are the same themes that these women writers address, although their perspectives on those issues are often very different. To begin with, almost all of these stories are focused around girls or women as their central characters. Even in those few that seem to tell a story 'about' a man, like Velma Pollard's sympathetic portrait of the adulterous 'Altamont Jones', it seems to be the women in the story who act. Girls looking for life models and the strong women who might provide them are the major characters in many of the stories by this group of women writers. Across the Caribbean the economic and spiritual struggle of such women—particularly in the rural communities—constitutes a story that has not been told in the official, male, histories of the region. Writers such as Maryse Condé in Guadeloupe, Olive Senior in Jamaica, Astrid Roemer in Surinam, and Ana Lydia Vega in Puerto Rico have been engaged in fleshing out the bones of that *herstory* which other women, as scholars in the History departments of Caribbean universities, have been uncovering in recent years.

Such an agenda could make for a litany of harrowing tales that focus only on the suffering and exploitation of female characters, but in fact the tone of many of these stories is celebratory, with writers such as Olive Senior, Jean 'Binta' Breeze, and Rosario Ferré employing humour and comedy as key agents of that celebration. The moment when Becka, the 11-year-old girl at the centre of Olive Senior's story, asks the visiting Archdeacon, 'do angels wear brassieres?' has to be one of the finest comic moments in the whole literature. Of course there is a serious side to Senior's story of an intelligent girl child who refuses to accept the conventional expectations of her elders and insists on asking embarrassing questions; that refusal to be silenced is another aspect of the *herstory*.

Implicit in that engagement with the oral tradition—and indeed in the concern to tell the region's *herstory*—is an awareness that stories are inherently untrustworthy, are biased, partial. Indeed, the need to acknowledge, in Jean Rhys's words, that 'there is always the other side of the story'[7] is arguably the single idea that has most engaged and inspired Caribbean women writers in every genre from poetry to the novel and across the generations. Two stories here from writers representing the 'wider Caribbean' illustrate that this is another concern that is not necessarily tied to the political history of the different linguistic territories of the region. Astrid Roemer from Surinam is perhaps the leading Caribbean writer in Dutch and much of her work dwells on such issues of race, gender, and history. Her story here, 'The Inheritance of my Father', is just such a retelling or recovery of history, not so much from a feminist perspective but with an acknowledgement that ancient prejudices and animosities run deep and that in such contexts there will always be conflicting versions of stories, whether of a family or a whole region. Rosario Ferré has been exploring similar issues in the context of Puerto Rico and her story here, 'When Women Love Men', is at one level a marvellously sensual thriller, the reader left uncertain at the end of the story as to quite what has happened—has a murder been committed or some accommodation been reached between the two women who tell their story from such differing perspectives? That uncertainty is emphasized in the way the story is told—the narrating voice shifts without warning and so further disrupts that idea of a fixed, definitive account of events.

So how to answer those questions about the impact of this sudden emergence of women as authors of Caribbean short fiction? In so far as we might notice shared concerns that link them *as writers*, an interest in exploring the spaces in the prevailing versions of history, domestic as well as 'national', by giving female characters opportunity to speak and so drawing attention to the partial character of all storytelling—oral or written, academic history or science fiction—is perhaps as near as we can get to identifying a common agenda. As far as looking for stylistic similarities in terms of the ways these women writers tell their stories, it is interesting perhaps that there is not that great divide, in terms of style and technique, between the Anglophone and the Spanish, Dutch, and French language writers that we notice in the earlier generation of male writers, and as a logical extension of their shared concern with ideas about exploring 'other versions' of events we see several of these writers using a range of voices and shifting narrative perspectives within a single story. Beyond that observation it would be difficult, and perhaps foolish, to generalize about a 'women's style'.

[7] Jean Rhys, '*Wide Sargasso Sea*' (Andre Deutsch, 1966).

Introduction

The stories by the male writers of this 'independence generation' included here are linked in their concern with difference, with characters who never feel that they quite belong to the society in which they must live out their lives. The central characters in these five stories are as diverse and cosmopolitan a West Indian crew as one could come up with, from Lawrence Scott's bittersweet lament for a lost strand in Trinidadian society—the elite French Creole class which thrived in the era 'when cocoa was king'—to Mammie, in Archie Markham's classic story out of that first generation of West Indian migrants in England, 'Mammie's Form at the Post Office', who is a very different kind of exile. Her concern is to send money 'home' to the West Indies to pay for the upkeep of family graves. The confusions, racism, and just plain crossed cultural wires of her encounter with the young Post Office clerk are beautifully observed by Markham:

the boy pretended he didn't understand what she was saying, and then asked if she wanted to send money ABROAD. She had to correct him and tell him she was sending money HOME: that's where she was from. She was indignant that first they treated you like a foreigner, and then they denied you your home.

The linguistic and psychological twists and turns of that brief passage say much about the experience of migration for Mammie's generation.

Perhaps this interest by so many of the writers of what we have called this 'Independence generation' in figures who are somehow marginalized—by gender, by race or religion, or by the processes of history—is the concern that most characterizes the period. For this generation questions of identity—'who are we?', 'how is *we* defined?', 'where is our place', 'what happens when we must take responsibility for our own futures?'—are the crucial dilemmas which fiction as much as politics, history, and social science needed to address.

Contemporary Voices

Although in terms of our chronology she only just scrapes into this section of the anthology, in her attitude to language, to the foregrounding of the *fictionality* of her writing, and the complexity of her narrative style in stories like 'Blackness', included here, the Antiguan Jamaica Kincaid seems very much a 'contemporary' writer. Kincaid further blurs that distinction between the Anglophone and the French and Spanish traditions that we suggested existed in relation to earlier generations. In 'Blackness' the narrative shifts from a poetic and philosophical evocation of the experience and significance of 'blackness', through dream and fantasy to engage the underlying political resonances of a story which at no point seems to address 'blackness' in an obvious political sense. That resistance to limitations in terms of style or indeed subject matter is a feature of the writers we have included to represent this 'contemporary generation', writers who have roots in and strong connections with the Caribbean and for whom that Caribbean dimension to their self-identity is fundamental, but who are much less self-consciously fixed to that 'small place', that experience, that Caribbean *locus* than were the earlier generations of West Indian writers. Or perhaps another way of thinking of it is that this generation inevitably sees the Caribbean and the concerns that have dominated the work of Caribbean writers in more complex terms. Only three—at most—of these dozen writers actually live and work in the Caribbean now, though all maintain those strong ties. But living in Florida or Toronto or Europe as 'home'—not now isolated migrants but as part of established 'Caribbean' communities, their 'take' on Caribbean issues is inevitably complicated by those other perspectives. That difference in attitudes to 'home' is evident here as a kind of stylistic liberation in writers such as Kincaid, Robert Antoni, and Edwidge Danticat—and the young Cuban writer Edgardo Sanabria Santaliz but it is also the apparent subject matter of some stories here—Zoila Ellis's 'The Waiting Room' or Makeda Silvera's 'Caribbean Chameleon' dealing with different ends, as it were, of that journey between the Caribbean and 'elsewhere'.

But a concern with the politics of exile, or identity, or race is not a dominant motif in the work of contemporary writers in the way that it was for that earlier generation of writers involved in the first wave of mass migration and immigration in the 1950s. At least as many of the stories in this section of the anthology might be termed love stories, though they are very different in tone and all, interestingly enough, are written by men. Edgardo Sanabria Santaliz's fantastical story of the capture of a mermaid has the quality of fairy tale while Patrick Chamoiseau's 'Red Hot Peppers' is a more down-to-earth story of seduction, callous betrayal, and revenge. Robert Antoni's 'A World of Canes' combines elements of both romance and cruelty, but is particularly interesting as a 'told tale', Antoni giving the narrative over to the poorly educated girl who speaks her story as if to a friend. The fluent, confident, unapologetic way he uses that creole voice is a measure of the journey West Indian writers have made from the tentativeness of Eric Walrond's experimentation with language in the early years of the century. Sasenarine Persaud's story, written in a creolized Canadian/Indo-Guyanese voice, full of local references—local to both Toronto and to Georgetown—adds another dimension to that continuum of voices contemporary Caribbean writers have drawn on.

Some of the other stories by writers from the 'cricket-playing Caribbean' included here may seem comparatively traditional; naturalistic in both setting and manner of narration, concerned with the poor and their routes out of the kinds of struggle that define their lives and essentially told from a child's perspective. Each is included because it is a fine story in its own right and it is that very diversity of styles, voices, and concerns that characterizes the contemporary Caribbean short story—it will not be contained in any convenient linguistic, geographical, or thematic definition.

The kinds of question about identity, allegiance, and notions of audience that such diversity implies come to the fore when we consider the work of the youngest writer in this collection, Edwidge Danticat. Born in Haiti she has lived most of her life in the USA and she writes in English, though much of her work is a reflection back on Haiti and indeed into Haitian history. But whom is she writing for? Is her work part of Haitian/Caribbean literature or more properly part of the multiplicity of voices that must make up modern American literature? Of course it belongs to both—is part of the multiplicity of voices that must make up modern *Caribbean* literature—for in so far as those lines of demarcation were ever clear or useful, they have been now irredeemably blurred. Perhaps the most we can say is that Danticat's background provides her with the emotional connection to characters in Haiti's story that speak through her imagination in ways not accessible to writers without those connections. Her story here touches on that notion of finding a way to escape the cruelties of one life for another, elsewhere, and also offer another angle on that process by which the Caribbean *herstory* is brought to life. It is a story about witchcraft, in a sense, about women's 'secret' powers, powers to defy all sorts of laws—the least significant being those made and administered by men. It is a story about the oppression of women and male fear of those powers they believe certain women to have. But it is also a story about metaphor and the power of stories . . . whether of the tears of the Madonna or the capacity of some women to fly. Danticat straddles many traditions—the folk and religious oral traditions of Haiti, the literature of the wider Caribbean, and the modern American short story. By her drawing of them into a style that is both personal and yet accessible to her readers, whether in Haiti or Handsworth, Harlem or Halfway Tree in

Introduction

Jamaica, she points the way forward for 'Caribbean writing' into the twenty-first century.

DR STEWART BROWN

Centre of West African Studies
University of Birmingham
May 1998

FRANK COLLYMORE (1893–1980)

Some People are Meant to Live Alone

Some people are meant to live alone. Take, for instance, Uncle Arthur.
We called him Uncle Arthur, all of us, but he wasn't our uncle. He was
really some sort of elderly cousin and he was almost a legend in the family.
'I'll send you to live with Uncle Arthur,' was Mother's threat when
one of us had been particularly unruly, or 'A week with Uncle Arthur'll
do you good.' Not that Uncle Arthur was especially ogre-like or repulsive
to our childish eyes. Far from it—a milder little man I never saw, although
his visits to our home in those days were few and far between. No, it
was the fact that he lived all alone; alone in the old, dilapidated house
on the hill, a house we could see when the canes were cut, a house that
loomed gaunt and cockeyed against the brooding background of the two
huge twisted evergreens that added their touch of mystery to his unac-
countable isolation. None of us had ever been there. Uncle Arthur never
invited anyone to his home. So the threat of being sent to Uncle Arthur's
never lost its sting, even though at Christmas time we could always expect
a large, clumsily wrapped box of toffee or butterscotch from the house on
the hill.

Uncle Arthur's visits grew fewer and fewer till there was no in between,
and it wasn't till I'd grown up that I ever gave him a thought again.

I was convalescing from an attack of 'flu, and I must have been a bit curt
in replying to Mother who was fussing around my room before wishing
me goodnight.

'Naughty boy, I think a week at Uncle Arthur's is what you really want.'

'A week at Uncle Arthur's!' What childhood memories the old phrase
brought back.

'By the way, Mother,' I asked, 'whatever is the mystery about the old
man?'

'Mystery! I really can't say there was ever any mystery. He's just one of
those unfortunate souls that can't manage to live with anybody.'

'Why not?'

Mother, only too glad of an excuse to remain a little longer, sat at the foot of my bed.

'Well, he got married when he was quite young. They lived rather a cat and dog life. Eventually she disappeared. Ran off with a travelling agent, I believe. She wasn't much good, anyway. Fortunately there weren't any children. Then . . . well, I'm afraid he grew too fond of his cook. Then *she* skedaddled one day with most of the spare cash. It was quite a scandal. After that I suppose he decided to remain a bachelor. From time to time one or other of his sisters went to keep house for him, but none of them stayed very long. Then an old school friend appeared on the scene. They seemed to get on very well together. Might have been a couple of years. Then the friend . . . another of life's failures, he was . . . got drowned. People said it was suicide. Since then Uncle Arthur has lived by himself.'

'How long ago was that?'

'That was the year you had the mumps. Dear me, how time flies!'

'How old is he now?'

'Let me see.' Mother did a bit of complicated calculation on her fingers. 'Nineteen sixteen. Ethel died in nineteen o two. About sixty, I should think.'

'Good Lord, he looked that when I last saw him. And that was years ago.'

'Yes, he aged rather early, poor dear.'

'But whatever does he do up there all by himself?'

'Oh, he has an old woman to cook his meals. And he reads a great deal. And he's interested in painting, I think.'

'Have you ever been there?'

'Have I ever been there? Why, I was born there, silly. But I haven't been there since . . . since that business with the cook. I often wonder what the old place looks like now. I hear the carriage house has completely tumbled down . . .'

We didn't talk any more about Uncle Arthur, but that night I dreamt of him. One of those long, rambling dreams you have when you're convalescing. Uncle Arthur showing me his paintings. They were all done on the ceiling, and I had to lie on the dining-table to look at them. I couldn't get him out of my mind for the next few days. As soon as I was up and about I decided I'd pay him a visit. It wasn't more than three miles away up the short cut by the hill, so I strolled over one afternoon.

Climbing up the hill was harder going than I'd thought. I hadn't quite got back into the swing of living yet. I sat on the guard-wall at the entrance and had a look at the old house. It was an old-fashioned two-storeyed building with a low open verandah facing the road. The evergreens on either side of the doorway merged their bushy branches overhead so that the upper storey was hardly visible. All the doors and windows I could see were closed. A white cat lay curled on the verandah. Why on earth had I come? Perhaps it was the books, perhaps because I too happened to be interested in painting. I didn't know. Well, here I was. I rose to my feet and approached the house. Beneath the evergreens was moss-grown and damp, and although it couldn't have been later than five, whistling frogs were tuning up. The cat rose as I approached and stretched herself encouragingly. I mounted the weather-worn steps, knocked at the door and stroked her. She looked remarkably well-fed and contented. I waited a few moments and then knocked again. Presently I was aware of two eyes peering at me through a broken flap of the jalousies. I pretended not to notice and turned so that the afternoon sun might show me up more clearly. After a brief interval I heard a key turn in the lock and the door grated open. Though I hadn't seen him for so many years I recognized him at once. He didn't seem to have changed at all. He was barefooted and was wearing a pair of old flannels and a faded pyjama jacket. His untidy grey hair fell about his forehead just as it always did, and his meek, rather plaintive features were screwed up into an unasked question.

'Hello, Uncle Arthur! It's Bill. I don't suppose you remember me.'

'Bill . . . Bill . . .' His eyes blinked and he frowned. 'I'm sorry, but I'm afraid you've got the better of me.'

'I'm Bill . . . Bill Church.'

'You mean . . . you mean you're Rosie's son? Come in, come in! I *am* glad to see you. Well, well, I'd never have recognized you.'

I followed him through a very cheerless looking hallway and up a rickety flight of stairs.

'Careful, son. I don't use this part of the house very much. Mind out . . . that one's missing. Well, here we are.'

I was altogether surprised on entering the room at the top of the stairs. But for a large table littered with a miscellany of papers, books, cardboard boxes and empty cigarette tins in its further corner, the room was well furnished and comparatively tidy. Low bookshelves skirted the walls; there were a couple of comfortable armchairs and a divan, a rug that had seen better days but which was still full of warm colour, and an up-to-date Victrola with stacks of records. The late afternoon sunlight struggled through the evergreen branches that almost thrust themselves into the room and lit up the two pictures that hung over the largest of the bookshelves.

Uncle Arthur watched me closely as I took my bearings.

'Like it?'

'I should say. Why, this is what I always thought a room should be.'

Uncle Arthur grinned. I noticed for the first time that his face took on an impish, delightfully humorous expression when he smiled. I felt thoroughly at ease.

'Did you paint those?'

'Those? Dear me, no . . . That one's a Cézanne, the other a Gauguin. Reproductions, of course . . . German . . . but aren't they exquisite?'

Well, he started off on painting . . . Impressionism, the Pre-Raphaelites, the Post-Impressionists . . . Though I didn't understand half of what he was trying to tell me, I found it all fascinating. By degrees I discovered he'd done some painting himself, but he wouldn't show me any of his pictures. He gave me the impression of being extremely shy and sensitive. He went on to make excuses for the shabbiness of the house. He intended doing something . . . sometime. Of course he remembered Mother as a little girl. In fact, this had been her bedroom in the old days. He recalled how one day he had been summoned to make her come in off the roof. 'I'm afraid it wouldn't hold her up now,' he added ruefully. 'I mean, if she was still a little girl.' I laughed. Mother's size was a family joke.

We talked of all sorts of things. He played some records for me, a Beethoven concerto, and while I listened he brought in a decanter of rum and we had a couple of drinks. 'You must stay on and have pot luck. Tell you what I'll do: I'll send the cook's boy over to your mother's so she won't be anxious. There'll be a lovely moon to light your way down the hill.'

I stayed on. We ate at an old claw-footed mahogany table in the adjoining room, and the cook, an agreeable but unusually deaf old soul, served us. She wore brass ear-rings and a large floppy straw hat. The dinner was quite good, and after a great deal of shouting and gesticulation on Uncle Arthur's part, she brought in a liqueur which he served in cracked pony-glasses. Afterwards we returned to the living room. The moon, round and full, flooded the room with light. 'Shall I switch on, or is this good enough?'

'It's good enough,' I replied. I felt unusually serene and happy. The moonlight fell in a broad cool band across the rug, and a gentle breeze supplied a final touch of satisfaction to the scene.

'You know, I almost envy you, Uncle Arthur.' I was feeling particularly grown up . . . the rum and the liqueur, I suppose . . . and now, watching the blue haze of my cigarette smoke curling away mysteriously into the dim shadows of the room, I felt as though Uncle Arthur and I were two pals together. There was a singular charm and lightness of heart about the old man that appealed to me. The things he liked and talked about . . . music, painting, whimsical anecdotes of this and that . . . struck a responsive chord somewhere in me. Everybody I'd ever talked to was so confoundedly practical. As I sat there I wondered . . . perhaps some day I, like Uncle Arthur, might come to find a life like this all satisfying . . . Who could tell?

'Uncle Arthur, are you ever lonely? Really lonely, I mean?'

The old man sighed. 'No. I don't think so. Not really, honest to God lonely. No, I can't say that. Some people are meant to live alone. I'm one of them, I guess.' He paused and lit a cigarette. 'I'm really much happier when I'm alone.'

I thought of Betty, of football, of next week's dance . . . 'I wonder!'

'When you're young perhaps, no. But later on . . . Well . . .' He sighed again. 'I've tried both ways. I don't think I've ever been really happy with anyone for long. No. I prefer it this way.'

He was silent for a while. Suddenly I was overwhelmed by a feeling of intense affection for the old man. I resolved this was to be the first of many evenings in his company. I felt I was somehow on the threshold of a different existence, far more exciting, far more real than the sort I'd led; and I felt that despite all he'd said, he wasn't averse to my company.

'I knew a man once . . .' he began, then broke off. 'But I'm not good at telling stories.'

'Please!'

'It will only show you what some people will do to . . . Yes, some people are meant to live alone. This man . . . I'll call him Jones . . .' He broke off and chuckled. 'You know, it might be my own story. Ah well . . . Jones, when my story begins, had been married four or five years and he was desperately unhappy. His wife was one of the nagging sort. And a passion for doing this and doing that when this was finished. No sooner had poor Jones finished tidying up the garden beds than the furniture had to be polished. You know the type, I expect?'

I nodded with all the sagacity of my twenty-two years.

'And then one day she left him . . . or he left her . . . I'm not rightly sure which, but he was free, free to do as he liked. He decided marriage wasn't meant for him. No, sir. He could do just as he pleased. No wife to nag him, no people dropping in to talk and talk when he wanted to be left alone, nobody to remind him of what he had to do, what he ought to do, what he must do. It was delightful. He was irresponsible, gay, free. And then one day a dreadful thing happened. An old school chum of his turned up. Let's call him Smith. Smith was one of those unfortunate people who aren't satisfied unless they're *doing* things . . . dancing somewhere, eating somewhere, making love to someone, and so unhappy if left up to their own resources for five minutes, they begin to disintegrate. It so happened he'd done a little too much. First he'd helped himself to somebody else's money . . . that was smoothed over. Then he was arrested for murder. They hadn't enough evidence to convict him, but he was *fini*. Disowned by all his former friends, he could go nowhere, do nothing. The shock and the scandal had killed his poor old mother. He was desperate. He sought out his old friend, Jones. Would he let him stay with him? He was frantic. If only he had someone to keep him company . . . Jones was rather a sympathetic sort; besides, he didn't have the guts to say no. So Smith came to stay.

'At first it wasn't so bad. Smith was so glad to feel he wasn't altogether an outcast, he was fairly agreeable. That is to say, he kept out of Jones's way most of the time. At dinner he was apt to be rather a nuisance talking of what he'd done from time to time at cricket or football or some such, and then sometimes he'd drink a bit too much. And now that he couldn't go around with the society girls, he discovered that the girls in the village were quite flattered by his advances. Jones didn't mind: Smith's way of life was Smith's. But then unfortunately Smith went one night, for want of something to do, and poked his silly head into a revivalist tent and got his soul saved. Let me tell you, sonny, there's nothing worse than living in a house with a saved soul, that is, if it happens to be one like Smith's. Smith's soul gave him no rest. It was always reminding him of all his past sins. Now that was all right as far as Smith was concerned, but when Smith's soul began worrying about Jones's, then the trouble started.

'Smith would come in on Sundays all dressed up from prayer meeting and looking as though he'd had a personal interview with Old Nick, and find Jones in his shirt sleeves, a rum and ginger at his elbow, smoking his pipe and reading. He'd just sit and look at him and groan. After a while he'd go upstairs and then he'd begin to pray. Pray aloud. Jones told me that of all the things on earth that are likely to rouse thoughts of murder in a man's heart, there is nothing to equal the sound of a voice you do not particularly care for, praying on your behalf. After two or three Sundays of this Jones couldn't stand it any longer. He told him he'd either have to quit praying or quit the house. He'd been there well over a year; his soul was saved. Knowing that, he could now start life afresh.'

Uncle Arthur paused to hunt for his cigarette tin.

'And did he?'

'Not much. Smith cried like a child. He couldn't, he couldn't go and live somewhere all by himself. And then . . . then he confessed to having committed that murder. He couldn't live alone with the knowledge of that. If he woke in the night and felt there was nobody near him, nobody he really knew, he was certain he'd either go mad or kill himself. Would you believe it, he actually swore he'd never go to another prayer meeting if only Jones would let him stay. So again Jones gave way to his better and more cowardly feelings.'

He paused to light up.

'Wasn't he afraid Jones might tell on him?'

'If he did, that fear was overwhelmed by a far greater fear . . . the fear of being alone. He just couldn't come to terms with the reality of loneliness, the essential loneliness of humanity.

'So Smith stayed on. He didn't worry so much about his soul now. He seemed to have only one aim in life . . . to show Jones how much he appreciated his kindness in allowing him to stay on. Jones would be reading or writing or trying to doze off or something or other, and he'd be conscious that Smith was watching him. Not with any evil intent, you know. No, just watching him with a sort of dog-like devotion. It was embarrassing. It was horrible. Sometimes Jones would lose his temper and ask him for God's sake to leave him alone, and off he'd go meekly enough. And of an evening, after dinner, when Jones wanted to read and enjoy a pipe, Smith would walk up and down, up and down, just outside the window, solemn and silent, for all the world just like some Praetorian guard. It's an awful thing to listen to anyone pacing up and down like that. The confounded monotony of the thing, the soullessness of it, eats into your very core.

'One evening Jones couldn't stand it any longer. "God damn it, Smith," he said, "I can't stand this any longer. You've got to get out of here or I won't be responsible. You've got to go. First thing tomorrow morning. If you can't live alone, why don't you get married or something? Go and live with a woman. I'll give you the money. Any one of the girls in the village . . ." But Smith shrieked in horror and ran off. When Jones went to bed he hadn't yet returned. Jones went to sleep. In the middle of the night he woke and heard him in his room which was next door. He was praying again, praying earnestly and loudly that the soul of his dear friend, Jones, might be washed clean of all such lewd and sinful thoughts. Over and over, over and over the voice went on.

'Jones was a very quiet little fellow . . . I knew him well . . . but he told me something just went off pop inside him. He got up and went straight into Smith's room and strangled him.'

'He what?'

'Strangled him.'

'You mean, he murdered him?'

'Yes. He murdered him. He was sorry afterwards, of course, but he couldn't undo what he'd done.

'Well, poor Jones was in a very awkward position. He had to move and move quickly. In those days he had a car . . . it was the day of the old "upstairs" Ford, so he managed to haul the body downstairs and prop it up somehow in the car. It was two or three o'clock in the morning and there wasn't a soul stirring. Jones drove down to the cliff by Threecorner and dropped Smith overboard.'

'They never found the body?' I had suddenly gone very cold.

'About a week after. The fish had got at it. It was identified. Indeed I was one of the persons who identified it.'

I had to say it. I don't know why. 'And . . . and nobody ever suspected you, Uncle Arthur?'

He sighed. 'I told you I wasn't much good at telling a story. Ah well, I suppose I had to tell somebody sometime. Strange, you know, I've never felt the slightest twinge of conscience. I'd do exactly the same tomorrow in such circumstances. Only it didn't seem fair that nobody should know.'

I rose and switched on the light.

'Do you think you've been fair to me to tell me this?'

'Sorry, son. Perhaps not. But I don't know. I took a liking to you the moment I saw you through the jalousies. And I wanted to see you again. And I didn't want you to be under any misapprehensions as regards my character. But I see it's no go. Some people are meant to live alone. I will show you down the stairs. The moon's high now and you can get down the cliff easily.'

I couldn't say a word; I followed him down the stairs and with a mumbled goodbye I left him.

I never saw him again. The next year I proposed to Betty and we got married shortly afterwards. Our marriage was a failure from the first. Last year we got our divorce. And a week ago old Uncle Arthur died. He has left me his sole heir. He had some money. I think I shall repair the old house and go and live there. The thought fascinates me.

Some people, I suppose, are meant to live alone.

Pioneers, Oh, Pioneers

As the two girls were walking up yellow-hot Market Street, Irene nudged her sister and said: 'Look at her!'

They were not far from the market, they could still smell the fish.

When Rosalie turned her head the few white women she saw carried parasols. The black women were barefooted, wore gaily striped turbans and highwaisted dresses. It was still the nineteenth century, November 1899.

'There she goes,' said Irene.

And there was Mrs Menzies, riding up to her house on the Morne for a cool weekend.

'Good morning,' Rosalie said, but Mrs Menzies did not answer. She rode past, clip-clop, clip-clop, in her thick, dark riding habit brought from England ten years before, balancing a large dripping parcel wrapped in flannel on her knee.

'It's ice. She wants her drinks cold,' said Rosalie.

'Why can't she have it sent up like everybody else? The black people laugh at her. She ought to be ashamed of herself.'

'I don't see why,' Rosalie said obstinately.

'Oh, you,' Irene jeered. 'You like crazy people. You like Jimmy Longa and you like old maman Menzies. You liked Ramage, nasty beastly horrible Ramage.'

Rosalie said: 'You cried about him yesterday.'

'Yesterday doesn't count. Mother says we were all hysterical yesterday.'

By this time they were nearly home so Rosalie said nothing. But she put her tongue out as they went up the steps into the long, cool gallery.

Their father, Dr Cox, was sitting in an armchair with a three-legged table by his side.

On the table were his pipe, his tin of tobacco and his glasses. Also *The Times* weekly edition, the *Cornhill Magazine*, the *Lancet*, and a West Indian newspaper, the *Dominica Herald and Leeward Islands Gazette*.

He was not to be spoken to, as they saw at once though one was only eleven and the other nine.

'Dead as a doornail,' he muttered as they went past him into the next room so comfortably full of rocking chairs, a mahogany table, palm leaf fans, a tigerskin rug, family photographs, view of Bettws-y-Coed, and a large picture of wounded soldiers in the snow, Napoleon's Retreat from Moscow.

The doctor had not noticed his daughters, for he too was thinking about Mr Ramage. He had liked the man, stuck up for him, laughed off his obvious eccentricities, denied point blank that he was certifiable. All wrong. Ramage, probably a lunatic, was now as dead as a doornail. Nothing to be done.

Ramage had first arrived in the island two years before, a handsome man in tropical kit, white suit, red cummerbund, solar topee. After he grew tired of being followed about by an admiring crowd of negro boys he stopped wearing the red sash and the solar topee but he clung to his white suits though most of the men wore dark trousers even when the temperature was ninety in the shade.

Miss Lambton, who had been a fellow passenger from Barbados, reported that he was certainly a gentleman and also a king among men when it came to looks. But he was very unsociable. He ignored all invitations to dances, tennis parties, and moonlight picnics. He never went to church and was not to be seen at the club. He seemed to like Dr Cox, however, and dined with him one evening. And Rosalie, then aged seven, fell in love.

After dinner, though the children were not supposed to talk much when guests were there, and were usually not allowed downstairs at all, she edged up to him and said: 'Sing something.' (People who came to dinner often sang afterwards, as she well knew.)

'I can't sing,' said Ramage.

'Yes you can.' Her mother's disapproving expression made her insist the more. 'You can. You can.'

He laughed and hoisted her on to his knee. With her head against his chest she listened while he rumbled gently: 'Baa baa black sheep, have you any wool? Yes sir, yes sir, three bags full.'

Then the gun at the fort fired for nine o'clock and the girls, smug in their stiff white dresses, had to say goodnight nicely and go upstairs to bed.

After a perfunctory rubber of whist with a dummy, Mrs Cox also departed. Over his whisky and soda Ramage explained that he'd come to the island with the intention of buying an estate. 'Small, and as remote as possible.'

'That won't be difficult here.'

'So I heard,' said Ramage.

'Tried any of the other islands?'

'I went to Barbados first.'

'Litttle England,' the doctor said. 'Well?'

'I was told that there were several places going along this new Imperial Road you've got here.'

'Won't last,' Dr Cox said. 'Nothing lasts in this island. Nothing will come of it. You'll see.'

Ramage looked puzzled.

'It's all a matter of what you want the place for,' the doctor said without explaining himself. 'Are you after a good interest on your capital or what?'

'Peace,' Ramage said. 'Peace, that's what I'm after.'

'You'll have to pay for that,' the doctor said.

'What's the price?' said Ramage, smiling. He put one leg over the other. His bare ankle was hairy and thin, his hands long and slender for such a big man.

'You'll be very much alone.'

'That will suit me,' Ramage said.

'And if you're far along the road, you'll have to cut the trees down, burn the stumps and start from scratch.'

'Isn't there a half-way house?' Ramage said.

The doctor answered rather vaguely: 'You might be able to get hold of one of the older places.'

He was thinking of young Errington, of young Kellaway, who had both bought estates along the Imperial Road and worked hard. But they had given up after a year or two, sold their land cheap and gone back to England. They could not stand the loneliness and melancholy of the forest.

A fortnight afterwards Miss Lambton told Mrs Cox that Mr Ramage had bought Spanish Castle, the last but one of the older properties. It was beautiful but not prosperous—some said bad luck, others bad management. His nearest neighbour was Mr Eliot, who owned *Malgré Tout*. Now called Twickenham.

For several months after this Ramage disappeared and one afternoon at croquet Mrs Cox asked Miss Lambton if she had any news of him.

'A strange man,' she said, 'very reserved.'

'Not so reserved as all that,' said Miss Lambton. 'He got married several weeks ago. He told me that he didn't want it talked about.'

'No!' said Mrs Cox. 'Who to?'

Then it all came out. Ramage had married a coloured girl who called herself Isla Harrison, though she had no right to the name of Harrison. Her mother was dead and she'd been brought up by her godmother, old Miss Myra, according to local custom. Miss Myra kept a sweetshop in Bay Street and Isla was very well known in the town—too well known.

'He took her to Trinidad,' said Miss Lambton mournfully, 'and when they came back they were married. They went down to Spanish Castle and I've heard nothing about them since.'

'It's not as though she was a nice coloured girl,' everybody said.

So the Ramages were lost to white society. Lost to everyone but Dr Cox. Spanish Castle estate was in a district which he visited every month, and one afternoon as he was driving past he saw Ramage standing near his letter box which was nailed to a tree visible from the road. He waved. Ramage waved back and beckoned.

While they were drinking punch on the verandah, Mrs Ramage came in. She was dressed up to the nines, smelt very strongly of cheap scent and talked loudly in an aggressive voice. No, she certainly wasn't a nice coloured girl.

The doctor tried—too hard perhaps—for the next time he called at Spanish Castle a door banged loudly inside the house and a grinning boy told him that Mr Ramage was out.

'And Mrs Ramage?'

'The mistress is not at home.'

At the end of the path the doctor looked back and saw her at a window peering at him.

He shook his head, but he never went there again, and the Ramage couple sank out of sight, out of mind.

It was Mr Eliot, the owner of Twickenham, who started the trouble. He was out with his wife, he related, looking at some young nutmeg trees near the boundary. They had a boy with them who had lighted a fire and put on water for tea. They looked up and saw Ramage coming out from under the trees. He was burnt a deep brown, his hair fell to his shoulders, his beard to his chest. He was wearing sandals and a leather belt, on one side of which hung a cutlass, on the other a large pouch. Nothing else.

'If,' said Mr Eliot, 'the man had apologized to my wife, if he'd shown the slightest consciousness of the fact that he was stark naked, I would have overlooked the whole thing. God knows one learns to be tolerant in this wretched place. But not a bit of it. He stared hard at her and came out with: "What an uncomfortable dress—and how ugly!" My wife got very red. Then she said: "Mr Ramage, the kettle is just boiling. Will you have some tea?"'

'Good for her,' said the doctor. 'What did he say to that?'

'Well, he seemed rather confused. He bowed from the waist, exactly as if he had clothes on, and explained that he never drank tea. "I have a stupid habit of talking to myself. I beg your pardon," he said, and off he went. We got home and my wife locked herself in the bedroom. When she came out she wouldn't speak to me at first, then she said that he was quite right, I didn't care what she looked like, so now she didn't either. She called me a mean man. A mean man. I won't have it,' said Mr Eliot indignantly. 'He's mad, walking about with a cutlass. He's dangerous.'

'Oh, I don't think so,' said Dr Cox. 'He'd probably left his clothes round the corner and didn't know how to explain. Perhaps we do cover ourselves up too much. The sun can be good for you. The best thing in the world. If you'd seen as I have. . . .'

Mr Eliot interrupted at once. He knew that when the doctor started talking about his unorthodox methods he went on for a long time.

'I don't know about all that. But I may as well tell you that I dislike the idea of a naked man with a cutlass wandering about near my place. I dislike it very much indeed. I've got to consider my wife and my daughter. Something ought to be done.'

Eliot told his story to everyone who'd listen and the Ramages became the chief topic of conversation.

'It seems,' Mrs Cox told her husband, 'that he does wear a pair of trousers as a rule and even an old coat when it rains, but several people have watched him lying in a hammock on the verandah naked. You ought to call there and speak to him. They say,' she added, 'that the two of them fight like Kilkenny cats. He's making himself very unpopular.'

So the next time he visited the district Dr Cox stopped near Spanish Castle. As he went up the garden path he noticed how unkempt and deserted the place looked. The grass on the lawn had grown very high and the verandah hadn't been swept for days.

The doctor paused uncertainly, then tapped on the sitting-room door, which was open. 'Hello,' called Ramage from inside the house, and he appeared, smiling. He was wearing one of his linen suits, clean and pressed, and his hair and beard were trimmed.

'You're looking very well,' the doctor said.

'Oh, yes, I feel splendid. Sit down and I'll get you a drink.'

There seemed to be no one else in the house.

'The servants have all walked out,' Ramage explained when he appeared with the punch.

'Good Lord, have they?'

'Yes, but I think I've found an old woman in the village who'll come up and cook.'

'And how is Mrs Ramage?'

At this moment there was a heavy thud on the side of the house, then another, then another.

'What was that?' asked Dr Cox.

'Somebody throwing stones. They do sometimes.'

'Why, in heaven's name?'

'I don't know. Ask them.'

Then the doctor repeated Eliot's story, but in spite of himself it came out as trivial, even jocular.

'Yes, I was very sorry about that,' Ramage answered casually. 'They startled me as much as I startled them. I wasn't expecting to see anyone. It was a bit of bad luck but it won't happen again.'

'It was bad luck meeting Eliot,' the doctor said.

And that was the end of it. When he got up to go, no advice, no warning had been given.

'You're sure you're all right here?'

'Yes, of course,' said Ramage.

'It's all rubbish,' the doctor told his wife that evening. 'The man's as fit as a fiddle, nothing wrong with him at all.'

'Was Mrs Ramage there?'

'No, thank God. She was out.'

'I hear this morning,' said Mrs Cox, 'that she's disappeared. Hasn't been seen for weeks.'

The doctor laughed heartily. 'Why can't they leave those two alone? What rubbish!'

'Well,' said Mrs Cox without smiling, 'it's odd, isn't it?'

'Rubbish,' the doctor said again some days later, for, spurred on by Mr Eliot, people were talking venomously and he could not stop them. Mrs Ramage was not at Spanish Castle, she was not in the town. Where was she?

Old Myra was questioned. She said that she had not seen her god-daughter and had not heard from her 'since long time'. The Inspector of Police had two anonymous letters—the first writer claimed to know 'all what happen at Spanish Castle one night': the other said that witnesses were frightened to come forward and speak against a white man.

The *Gazette* published a fiery article:

'The so-called "Imperial Road" was meant to attract young Englishmen with capital who would buy and develop properties in the interior. This costly experiment has not been a success, and one of the last of these gentlemen planters has seen himself as the king of the cannibal islands ever since he landed. We have it, on the best authority, that his very eccentric behaviour has been the greatest possible annoyance to his neighbour. Now the whole thing has become much more serious. . . .'

It ended: 'Black people bear much; must they also bear beastly murder and nothing done about it?'

'You don't suppose that I believe all these lies, do you?' Dr Cox told Mr Eliot, and Mr Eliot answered: 'Then I'll make it my business to find out the truth. That man is a menace, as I said from the first, and he should be dealt with.'

'Dear Ramage,' Dr Cox wrote. 'I'm sorry to tell you that stupid and harmful rumours are being spread about your wife and yourself. I need hardly say that no one with a grain of sense takes them seriously, but people here are excitable and very ready to believe mischiefmakers, so I strongly advise you to put a stop to the talk at once and to take legal action if necessary.'

But the doctor got no answer to this letter, for in the morning news reached the town of a riot at Spanish Castle the night before.

A crowd of young men and boys, and a few women, had gone up to Ramage's house to throw stones. It was a bright moonlight night. He had come on to the verandah and stood there facing them. He was dressed in white and looked very tall, they said, like a zombi. He said something that nobody heard, a man shouted 'white zombi' and thrown a stone which hit him. He went into the house and came out with a shotgun. Then stories differed wildly. He had fired and hit a woman in the front of the crowd. . . . No, he'd hit a little boy at the back. . . . He hadn't fired at all, but had threatened them. It was agreed that in the rush to get away people had been knocked down and hurt, one woman seriously.

It was also rumoured that men and boys from the village planned to burn down Spanish Castle house, if possible with Ramage inside. After this there was no more hesitation. The next day a procession walked up the garden path to the house—the Inspector of Police, three policemen and Dr Cox.

'He must give some explanation of all this', said the Inspector.

The doors and windows were all open, and they found Ramage and the shotgun, but they got no explanation. He had been dead for some hours.

His funeral was an impressive sight. A good many came out of curiosity, a good many because, though his death was said to be 'an accident', they felt guilty. For behind the coffin walked Mrs Ramage, sent for post-haste by old Myra. She'd been staying with relatives in Guadeloupe. When asked why she had left so secretly—she had taken a fishing boat from the other side of the island—she answered sullenly that she didn't want anyone to know her business, she knew how people talked. No, she'd heard no rumours about her husband, and the *Gazette*—a paper written in English—was not read in Guadeloupe.

'Eh-eh,' echoed Myra. 'Since when the girl obliged to tell everybody where she go and what she do chapter and verse. . . .'

It was lovely weather, and on their way to the Anglican cemetery many had tears in their eyes.

But already public opinion was turning against Ramage.

'His death was really a blessing in disguise', said one lady. 'He was evidently mad, poor man—sitting in the sun with no clothes on—much worse might have happened.'

'This is All Souls Day,' Rosalie thought, standing at her bedroom window before going to sleep. She was wishing that Mr Ramage could have been buried in the Catholic cemetery, where all day the candles burnt almost invisible in the sunlight. When night came they twinkled like fireflies. The graves were covered with flowers—some real, some red or yellow paper or little gold cut-outs. Sometimes there was a letter weighted by a stone and the black people said that next morning the letters had gone. And where? Who would steal letters on the night of the dead? But the letters had gone.

The Anglican cemetery, which was not very far away, down the hill, was deserted and silent. Protestants believed that when you were dead, you were dead.

If he had a letter . . . she thought.

'My dear darling Mr Ramage,' she wrote, then felt so sad that she began to cry.

Two hours later Mrs Cox came into the room and found her daughter in bed and asleep; on the table by her side was the unfinished letter. Mrs

Cox read it, frowned, pressed her lips together, then crumpled it up and threw it out of the window.

There was a stiff breeze and she watched it bouncing purposefully down the street. As if it knew exactly where it was going.

Pablo's Fandango

Pablo had worked hard, but now that he could look upon his ten acres of healthy cocoa trees, he was satisfied. From earliest days, he could remember himself aspiring towards being salaamed by the coolie labourers and being referred to by the villagers as a cocoa proprietor. Both stages he had now reached and passed, and although he was not as young as he was, he could still find time and strength once in a while to go down into the village of Arima and there gossip, have a drink with a friend or two and perhaps visit Rosita, who lived near to the racecourse savannah.

His smallholding lay in a hollow on the heights of D'Abadie. To get to it from Arima, you took the old main road and walked along, if you were so minded, until you came to the De Gannes trace. Three miles up the trace, the land rising all the time, was Pablo's holding; and because the soil was not cocoa soil, Pablo had had to work very hard before he was able to squeeze a living out of it. Many a night he had sat in his little shanty, a mile away from any other habitation, wondering if he would ever succeed in subduing the land to his will; but because his will was strong, and his body too, even in such moments of depression there would come stealing into his mind the vision of success. It had been a long time in coming, but now that it had come, all the sweat and toil had been worthwhile. Had not his crops increased from three fanegas to twenty-three, and was that not something to be proud of? For a cocoa estate is, after all, like a child: it needs care and attention, and what mother's pride does not glow in her face when she sees her strong grown boy standing before her? And, too, what made matters worse for Pablo was that all his ten acres spread down into a large hollow of land, so that when cocoa was picked in the higher reaches of it, the pods would roll down until they settled at the bottom. That meant paying his pickers more, and putting more manure into the soil than he would otherwise have done, for hilly land is coconut-land and not good for cocoa.

Pablo had always lived alone. In crop-time, when it was necessary for him to have as many as six labourers—all East Indians, because they were docile and hardworking—he would house them in the two barrack-rooms that supported the drying-shed, which was about a hundred yards from his shanty; but when the crop was over, he always insisted on their returning to the places from which they had come. He liked to be alone. Alone, he was happy. He disliked people around him because they put him out of temper when they did anything wrong. Talking to men of his own class—small proprietors and overseers—in a rum-shop was all right; a man wanted that sort of thing now and again.

Pablo, like all men of his class, was superstitious. He believed that if you did not show the Holy Mother that you sometimes thought of God, you were bound to be unsuccessful in the worldly affairs of life. So once in a blue moon Pablo, astride his mule, rode into Arima on a Sunday morning to attend mass. He had been brought up in the Catholic faith; but having all these years lived so far away from any church, he had grown out of the habit of attending mass regularly. On such occasions you would see him wearing as fine a pair of leggings as the whole country side could show, prominent spurs, a huge khaki helmet on his head to match the newly starched khaki suit. Then, indeed, he looked the true cocoa-proprietor, so that the coolies and black people he passed on the way would 'sahib' and 'boss' him respectful greetings of the day. His beard would flow in the wind as he passed on his mule, ambling down the serpentining road with a slow rhythmic motion, and Pablo's keen grey eyes would view, every five minutes or so in a clearing, the broad stretch of country rolling before him in green undulations. Everywhere was green, especially in the rainy season. He rode well, his trunk straight, his chest thrown out, his head thrown back, a clay pipe in his mouth. You wouldn't have thought he was already past fifty; his age showed only in the greyness of his beard.

Hidden away in his shanty were all his savings. By frugal living he had managed to save over six hundred dollars, and every crop saw the little hoard increased by thirty or forty dollars. Seldom did Pablo eat meat. For one thing, it was difficult to get, even by way of hunting; for another, it was expensive. From his vegetable garden, cultivated but a stone's throw from his shanty, he got all he wanted: tannias and yams and plantains and sweet potatoes; and sometimes he boiled himself a plate of dumplings. At such times he would eat himself sick, for what else can a man do when he is fond of a particular dish? Never a drop of liquor did he keep up in his shanty: there was time enough for that when he rode down into Arima to sell his cocoa and gossip with friends. As long as a man was on his estate, he was once heard to say, he was at work, and work and liquor were enemies and always would be.

Pablo liked to think over his success: it gave him the satisfaction of feeling himself wiser than other men of his acquaintance. There was, for instance, Augustus Jack, the negro who was once his neighbour. But Augustus Jack was typical of his race: improvident and fond of pleasure. When he, Pablo, was struggling with his few acres of land, Augustus Jack's property was already full-bearing, yielding a crop of fifty bags a year: but Augustus Jack liked to go into Arima, and sometimes into Port of Spain, where he would squander his money in sprees with men and women; so that the time came when Augustus Jack found himself short of money to pay his labourers and was forced into mortgaging his land to Sing Lee & Co., the rich Chinese shopkeepers who had shops in almost every village along the Northern main road. Once you got into the clutches of Sing Lee & Co., people said, you were as good as lost. Augustus Jack's interest lagged; then it stopped altogether and Sing Lee & Co. put him up for sale and themselves bought him out before the doors of the court, and that was the last of Augustus Jack in D'Abadie.

Pablo liked to think over Augustus Jack's failure: it gave him a sense of victory and superiority.

There were others, too, who had gone the way of Augustus Jack, but never would Pablo go that way. All his cocoa he sold to Sing Lee & Co., and time and again Mr Sing Lee, perhaps thinking him in difficulties, would say: 'You know Mr Paplo, if you in trouple any time I help you,' and Pablo would say nothing, just look at Mr Sing Lee and feel triumph in leaving him in the dark about his affairs.

Pablo had had his mule for several years, ever since his crop had reached ten fanegas. Its job was to crook the cocoa out from the estate to the old main road where Monir, the East Indian carterman, would load the bags on to his cart and take them into Arima to Sing Lee's shop. And, too, whenever Pablo wanted to go into the village, he rode; it wouldn't do for a proprietor of his standing to walk; riding gave him prestige. Always he followed the cocoa into Arima on mule-back.

'I bring you about six fanegas today, Mr Sing Lee,' Pablo would say, standing before the counter, his huge frame towering above it. 'How is the price today?'

'Eight tollar faneg,' Sing Lee would say, cutting open one of the bags to examine the fruit.

'I suppose price in town about ten dollars?' Pablo would say, a teasing twinkle in his grey eyes.

'Ten tollar, Mr Paplo, ten tollar? No get lich so quick. Plice in tong, Mr

Paplo, no more eight a quart an' lailway fleight an' cart an' bag—all cos' money, Mr Paplo.'

Actually, the market in Port of Spain would be nearer ten dollars than eight dollars; and knowing that, you were silly if you wondered how Sing Lee, after ten years of business in a small place like Arima, could go to China on a three-year holiday, taking with him bank drafts to the value of perhaps thirty thousand dollars.

Pablo, having received his money and checked it, would sit in the shop and chat with Sing Lee until some friends arrived for a round of drinks. Sing Lee would say: 'How weat'er, Mr Paplo?'

'Weather not so bad, a little too much sun.'

'And clop, goot?'

'All the *chirelles* gone in the sun. We wan' a little rain. And what about the market, Mr Sing Lee? You think it going up?'

'Pe'haps yes, pe'haps no.'

Pablo would puff blue smoke into the fetid atmosphere of the shop.

'Money scarce now, Mr Sing Lee.' Immediately the Chinaman would say, his little yellow eyes blinking: 'You know Mr Paplo, if you in trouple, I help you.' And Pablo would say nothing, just look into Sing Lee's eyes and feel triumphant.

When he arrived home, night already fallen into the hollow of his land, he would carefully recount the money given him for his cocoa and add it to his savings. Then he would light his pipe, stroll about the yard and feel himself a happy and wise man. In bed, he would sleep the sleep of the just.

And then the War came. People in Arima began to talk about it, and Pablo, standing one day in Sing Lee's shop seeing after the weighing of his cocoa, overheard the talk of the War. He rode home, wondering. All the tortuous way up the mountain trace, seated on his mule with his pipe in his mouth, he wondered. He didn't know what to make of it, but in a vague way it worried him, for he thought that perhaps after all these years of struggle with the soil his little reapings would be taken away from him. He went to mass on the following Sunday. Kneeling as the host was elevated by the priest, all he could think of was the roll of notes that lay hidden away in a corner of his shanty, and he prayed that the Holy Mother would preserve it for him. He couldn't bear the thought of losing it. When he got home, a lighter mood coming upon him, he laughed at himself for imagining that a war, thousands of miles away, could harm him. In what way could it harm him? Was he not alone, cut off from even the people in the village around? And what had he done that the good Mother of God should be vexed with him and want to take away from him what he had won by so much self-sacrifice and labour? And he laughed at himself and said to his mule aloud, 'War . . . hell!'

But in the evening, smoking his pipe as he strolled about his yard, he began to fear something again. What it was, he could not have said if he had been asked. It was in the dusk, in the screech of the crickets, in the croaking of the frogs, in the lights of the few fireflies searing the dark; and during the night he heard it in the doleful song of a distant poor-me-one.

Time passed and Pablo worked harder than ever, for soon the crop would be in and he expected to make at least three fanegas more than the previous year. The War had been raging for four years now; and although he was not quite at peace with himself, so far it had done him no harm, and he was beginning to think that perhaps after all, his fears were groundless. However, he was more careful and more parsimonious than ever. Prices had remained almost the same as they were before the War, but Pablo saved more than he had ever done before. His mule had died and he had not even made up his mind as yet to buy another: he himself shouldered the cocoa when it was ready and bag by bag trudged down the mountain trace with it to Monir, waiting on the road. And when he was in the village, he avoided Carmeno and his other boon companions, so that he might not be put to the expense of paying for drinks.

The income-tax authorities, after desperate efforts at finding him, gave up the search in despair. One day in the village Sing Lee told Pablo about this. Pablo, not knowing what income tax meant, thought that Sing Lee was trying to tease him. Sing Lee explained as best he could.

'But that isn't right!' Pablo said at last, involuntarily looking around to make sure that no one was searching for him at that moment. 'That isn't right. A man work hard for his money and the government must take it away from him? For what?'

'The War, Mr Paplo, the War,' Sing Lee said, blinking. 'But if effer you in trouple I help you.'

Pablo was in no mood to hear this offer now. He gave Sing Lee a quick indignant look, then mounted the mule, which he had bought earlier in the year, and rode off at a canter.

His feelings were all mixed up. He was vexed with Sing Lee, he was afraid of something: what it was, he could not tell. The day was a fine cloudless one, the sun riding high, but it could not drive his fears away. He was already cantering down the old main road, the pipe cold between his teeth, when he glanced up and saw the green heights in which, somewhere, his ten acres of cocoa nestled. Up there was very far from everywhere and everybody. And he was alone. It was folly to be alone up there. He would have to have somebody share his shanty with him now. But who? He thought of Rosita, living near the racecourse savannah, and tugging at one rein, turned the unwilling mule round and cantered back into Arima.

Pablo greeted the half-caste Rosita affectionately. She was a tall, thin woman in her early thirties. Although her skin was brown, there was an undercurrent of a rich red tint in it. She was not bad looking. Her hair was long and straight and black. Her upper lip held the suspicion of a moustache.

Rosita said yes, she would be glad to stay with Pablo for a few days. Although she said nothing, she wondered what had caused him to make this strange request of her, but she went willingly—first, because Pablo was one of her oldest flames in the village; and secondly, because he was reported to be rich (wasn't he a cocoa proprietor?) and this, she thought, would be her opportunity for getting a tidy sum of money out of him.

Two days later they quarrelled, and when she left, stamping down the trace in a fine frenzy, Pablo said aloud to his mule that Rosita was all right to visit now and again, but an impossible woman to live with.

And then the War came to an end. Pablo, in his mountain retreat, heard nothing, for it was about four months since he had gone into the village with cocoa to sell. For some reason or another he was afraid to leave his shanty, but now that the crop was in full swing and his trees burdened with fruit as never before, in a fortnight or so he would have to be going down with the first picking—six or seven fanegas. He had six East Indian women picking and sweating and drying. All day long he was in the field, swearing and bossing as was his wont.

So far, no ill-fortune had befallen him and he put that down to the fact that he prayed to the Virgin Mary every night before retiring. At times he would wake in the middle of the night; and his old fear pouncing upon him with a perspiring intensity, he would rise, go to his hoard and count it over carefully, to assure himself that no evil spirit had tampered with it.

One fine morning saw Pablo riding into Arima with his first picking on Monir's cart. He was trembling in every limb: had he not dreamed the night before that this day's visit would be fraught with misfortune for him? The dream was so real, so convincing. He had dreamed that as he halted before Sing Lee's shop, the Chinaman had appeared at the threshold of one of the shop doors and laughed loud and long at him. At first he was angry to have a Chinaman laughing at him like that, until Sing Lee had said in his squeaky voice, 'Trow all dat cocoa away, Mr Paplo. Cocoa wort' not'ing now. All cocoa estate bus'. De bags wort' more dan de cocoa'. And that had awakened him in a cold sweat.

And now he was more frightened than ever, so frightened that he did not dare to ask Monir if he had heard anything about the price of cocoa.

He puffed at his pipe violently as they neared Sing Lee's shop, and there, right enough, just as he had seen him in the dream, was the Chinaman standing at one of his doors. He took his eyes away from Sing Lee, but as he dismounted he heard, as in the dream, the loud and long laugh.

'What you laughing at?' he asked, walking up to Sing Lee while Monir was unloading the cocoa.

'Come, come, Mr Paplo,' Sing Lee said, shaking Pablo by the hand, 'I no see you long time. You no hear?'

Pablo's heart sank. He pulled at his beard, a habit of his when he was losing his temper.

'You no hear, Mr Paplo, dat de War f'nish?' Sing Lee said. 'An' you no hear abou' cocoa-plice?'

Pablo shook his head, unable to speak.

'Cocoa plice now eighteen tollar faneg,' Sing Lee said, his face wrinkled in glee. 'Eperypody make money now, eperypody,' and he rubbed one hand against the other rapidly.

Pablo took his pipe from his mouth and threw it out into the street. He was no longer pulling at his beard. He said, 'Gie me a good pipe, Mr Sing Lee. You got good pipes here? An' what about a drink?'

Sing Lee said no, he wasn't drinking, so Pablo swallowed, at one gulp, a stiff shot of rum and refused the water with which to wash it down.

When he received his money he counted it over carefully: one hundred and twenty-six dollars and forty three cents.

'This is too much, Mr Sing Lee, too much for that cocoa,' he said, shaking his head sorrowfully. 'Before-time I get only fifty, sixty dollars for that cocoa; now more than twice as much. This too much, Mr Sing Lee, too much', and in an undertone he added, 'Holy Mary, Mother of God!'

Later that day, Pablo was entertaining with drink a huge crowd of the villagers at Sing Lee's shop. He called for rum, for whisky, for beer, for wine. When night fell he suggested a feed, so with all the crowd at his heels, he went across to old Ma Nainty's house and ordered pelau. Ma Nainty killed nine fowls that night and there were six dishes, piled mountain high with pelau, for Pablo and his guests. They ate and drank again. Pablo kept murmuring drunkenly: 'Eighteen dollars a fanega: Holy Mary, Mother of God! Eighteen dollars a fanega: too much, Holy Mary,

Mother of God, too much!' And everybody was patting him on the back and saying how they had misjudged him in the past and what a fine fellow he was.

At midnight he staggered over to Rosita's house with twenty dollars and a few cents in his pockets. Rosita received him with open arms.

The next morning, he rode up the mountain trace sober; and although his pockets were empty, he was happy.

Drought*

I

The whistle blew for eleven o'clock. Throats parched, grim, sun-crazed blacks cutting stone on the white burning hillside dropped with a clang the hot, dust-powdered drills and flew up over the rugged edges of the horizon to descend into a dry, waterless gut. Hunger—pricks at stomachs inured to brackish coffee and cassava pone—pressed on folk, joyful as rabbits in a grassy ravine, wrenching themselves free of the lure of the white earth. Helter-skelter dark, brilliant, black faces of West Indian peasants moved along, in pain—the stiff tails of blue denim coats, the hobble of chigger-cracked heels, the rhythm of a stride . . . dissipating into the sun-stuffed void the radiant forces of the incline.

The broad road—a boon to constables moping through the dusk or on hot, bright mornings plowing up the thick, adhesive marl on some seasonal chore, was distinguished by a black, animate dot upon it.

It was Coggins Rum. On the way down he had stopped for a tot—ziga-boo word for tin cup—of water by the rock engine. The driver, a buckra johnny—English white—sat on the waste box scooping with a fork handle the meat out of a young water cocoanut. An old straw hat, black, and its rim saggy by virtue of the moisture of sweating sun-fingers, served as a calabash for a ball of 'cookoo'—corn meal, okras and butter stewed—roundly poised in its crown. By the buckra's side, a black girl stood, her lips pursed in an indifferent frown, paralyzed in the intense heat.

Passing by them Coggins' bare feet kicked up a cloud of the white marl dust and the girl shouted, 'Mistah Rum, you gwine play de guitah tee nite, no?' Visions of Coggins—the sky a vivid crimson or blackly star-gemmed—on the stone step picking the guitar, picking it 'with all his hand . . . .'

Promptly Coggins answered, 'Come down and dance de fango fo' Coggins Rum and he are play for you.'

> Bajan gal don't wash 'ar skin
> Till de rain come down. . . .

---

* I wish to thank the editor of *The New Age* for permission to reprint *Drought*.

Grumblings. Pitch-black, to the 'washed-out' buckra she was more than a bringer of victuals. The buckra's girl. It wasn't Sepia, Georgia, but a backwoods village in Barbadoes. 'Didn't you bring me no molasses to pour in the rain-water?' the buckra asked, and the girl, sucking in her mouth, brought an ungovernable eye back to him.

Upon which Coggins, swallowing a hint, kept on his journey—noon-day pilgrimage—through the hot creeping marl.

Scorching—yet Coggins gayly sang:

> O! you come with yo' cakes
> Wit' yo' cakes an' yo' drinks
> Ev'y collection boy ovah deah!—
> An' we go to wah—
> We shall carry de name,
> Bajan boys for—evah!

'It are funny,' mused Coggins, clearing his throat, 'Massa Braffit an' dat chiggah-foot gal. . . .'

He stopped and picked up a fern and pressed the back of it to his shiny ebon cheek. It left a white ferny imprint. Grown up, according to the ethics of the gap, Coggins was yet to it a 'queer saht o' man', given to the picking of a guitar, and to cogitations, on the step after dark—indulging in an avowed juvenility.

Drunk with the fury of the sun Coggins carelessly swinging along cast an eye behind him—more of the boys from the quarry—overalled, shoeless, caps whose peaks wiggled on red, sun-red eyes . . . the eyes of the black sunburnt folk.

He always cast an eye behind him before he turned off the broad road into the gap.

Flaring up in the sun were the bright new shingles on the Dutch-style cottage of some Antigua folk. Away in a clump of hibiscus was a mansion, the color of bilgy water, owned by two English dowager maidens. In the gap rock-stones shot up—obstacles for donkey carts to wrestle over at dusk. Rain-worms and flies gathered in muddy water platoons beside them.

'Yo' dam vagabond yo'!'

Coggins cursed his big toe. His big toe was blind. Helpless thing . . . a blind big toe in broad daylight on a West Indian road gap.

He paused, and gathered up the blind member. 'Isn't this a hell of a case fo' yo', sah?' A curve of flesh began to peel from it. Pree-pree-pree. As if it were frying. Frying flesh. The nail jerked out of place, hot, bright blood began to stream from it. Around the spot white marl dust clung in grainy cakes. Now, red, new blood squirted—spread over the whole toe—and the dust became crimson.

Gently easing the toe back to the ground, Coggins avoided the grass sticking up in the road and slowly picked his way to the cabin.

'I stump me toe,' he announced, 'I stump me toe . . . woy . . . woy.'

'Go bring yo' pappy a tot o' water . . . Ada . . . quick.'

Dusky brown Sissie took the gored member in her lap and began to wipe the blood from it.

'Pappy stump he toe.'

'Dem rocks in de gap . . .'

'Mine ain't got better yet, needer . . .'

'Hurry up, boy, and bring de lotion.'

'Bring me de scissors, an' tek yo' fingers out o' yo' mout' like yo' is starved out! Hey, yo', sah!'

'. . . speakin' to you. Big boy lik' yo' suckin' yo' fingers. . . .'

Zip! Onion-colored slip of skin fluttered to the floor. Rattah Grinah, the half-dead dog, cold dribbling from his glassy blue eyes on to his freckled nose, moved inanimately towards it. Fox terrier . . . shaggy . . . bony . . . scarcely able to walk.

'Where is dat Beryl?' Coggins asked, sitting on the floor with one leg over the other, and pouring the salt water over the crimsoning wadding.

'Outside, sah.'

'Beryl!'

'Wha' yo' dey?'

'Wha' yo' doin' outside?'

'Answer me, girl!'

'. . . Hey, yo' miss, answer yo' pappy!'

'Hard-ears girl! She been eatin' any mo' marl, Sissie?'

'She, Ada?'

'Sho', gal eatin' marl all de haftah-noon. . . .'

Pet, sugar—no more terms of endearment for Beryl. Impatient, Coggins, his big toe stuck up cautiously in the air,—inciting Rattah to indolent curiosity—moved past Sissie, past Ada, past Rufus, to the rear of the cabin.

II

Yesterday, at noon . . . a roasting sun smote Coggins. Liquid . . . fluid . . . drought. Solder. Heat and juice of fruit . . . juice of roasting *cashews*.

Drought

It whelmed Coggins. The dry season was at its height. Praying to the Lord to send rain, black peons gathered on the rumps of breadfruit or cherry trees in abject supplication.

Crawling along the road to the gap, Coggins gasped at the consequences of the sun's wretched fury. There, where canes spread over with their dark rich foliage into the dust-laden road, the village dogs, hunting for eggs to suck, fowls to kill, paused amidst the yellow stalks of cork-dry canes to pant, or drop, exhausted, sun-smitten.

The sun had robbed the land of its juice, squeezed it dry. Star apples, sugar apples, husks, transparent on the dry sleepy trees. Savagely prowling through the orchards blackbirds stopped at nothing. . . . Turtle doves rifled the pods of green peas and purple beans and even the indigestible Brazilian *bonavis*. Potato vines, yellow as the leaves of autumn, severed from their roots by the pressure of the sun, stood on the ground, the wind's eager prey. Undug, stemless—peanuts, carrots— seeking balm, relief, the caress of a passing wind, shot dead unlustered eyes up through sun-etched cracks in the hard, brittle soil. The sugar corn went to the birds. Ripening prematurely, breadfruits fell swiftly on the hard naked earth, half ripe, good only for fritters. . . . Fell in spatters . . . and the hungry dogs, elbowing the children, lapped up the yellow-mellow fruit.

His sight impaired by the livid sun, Coggins turned hungry eyes to the soil. Empty corn stalks . . . blackbirds at work. . . .

Along the water course, bushy palms shading it, frogs gasped for air, their white breasts like fowls, soft and palpitating. The water in the drains sopped up, they sprang at flies, mosquitoes . . . wrangled over a mite.

It was a dizzy spectacle and the black peons were praying to God to send rain. Coggins drew back. . . .

Asking God to send rain . . . why? Where was the rain? Barreled up there in the clouds? Odd! Invariably, when the ponds and drains and rivers dried up they sank on their knees asking God to pour the water out of the sky. . . . Odd . . . water in the sky. . . .

The sun! It wrung toll of the earth. It had its effect on Coggins. It made the black stone cutter's face blacker. Strong tropic suns make black skins blacker. . . .

At the quarry it became whiter and the color of dark things generally grew darker. Similarly, with white ones—it gave them a whiter hue. Coggins and the quarry. Coggins and the marl. Coggins and the marl road.

Beryl in the marl road. Six years old; possessing a one-piece frock, no hat, no shoes.

29

Brown Beryl . . . the only one of the Rum children who wasn't black as sin. Strange . . . Yellow Beryl. It happens that way sometimes. Both Coggins and Sissie were unrelievably black. Still Beryl came a shade lighter. 'Dat am nuttin',' Sissie had replied to Coggins' intimately naïve query, 'is yo' drunk dat yo' can't fomembah me sistah-in-law what had a white picknee fo' 'ar naygeh man? Yo' don't fomembah, no?' Light-skinned Beryl. . . .

It happens that way sometimes.

Victim of the sun—a bright spot under its singeing mask—Beryl hesitated at Coggins' approach. Her little brown hands flew behind her back.

'Eatin' marl again,' Coggins admonished, 'eatin' marl again, you little vagabon'!'

Only the day before he had had to chastise her for sifting the stone dust and eating it.

'You're too hard ears,' Coggins shouted, slapping her hands, 'you're too hard ears.'

Coggins turned into the gap for home, dragging her by the hand. He was too angry to speak . . . too agitated.

Avoiding the jagged rocks in the gap, Beryl, her little body lost in the crocus bag frock jutting her skinny shoulders, began to cry. A gulping sensation came to Coggins when he saw Beryl crying. When Beryl cried, he felt like crying, too. . . .

But he sternly heaped invective upon her. 'Marl'll make yo' sick . . . tie up yo' guts, too. Tie up yo' guts like green guavas. Don't eat it, yo' hear, don't eat no mo' marl. . . .'

No sooner had they reached home than Sissie began. 'Eatin' marl again, like yo' is starved out,' she landed a clout on Beryl's uncombed head. 'Go under de bed an' lay down befo' I crack yo' cocoanut. . . .'

Running a house on a dry-rot herring bone, a pint of stale, yellowless corn meal, a few spuds, yet proud, thumping the children around for eating scraps, for eating food cooked by hands other than hers . . . Sissie. . . .

'Don't talk to de child like dat, Sissie.'

'Oh, go 'long you, always tryin' to prevent me from beatin' them. When she get sick who gwine tend she? Me or you? Man, go 'bout yo' business.'

Beryl crawled meekly under the bed. Ada, a bigger girl—fourteen and 'ownwayish'—shot a look of composed neutrality at Rufus—a sulky, cry-cry, suck-finger boy nearing twenty—Big Head Rufus.

'Serve she right,' Rufus murmured.

'Nobody ain't gwine beat me with a hairbrush. I know dat.' One leg on top of the other, Ada, down on the floor, grew impatient at Sissie's languor in preparing the food. . . .

Coggins came in at eleven to dinner. Ada and Rufus did likewise. The rest of the day they spent killing birds with stones fired from slingshots; climbing neighbors' trees in search of birds' nests; going to the old French ruins to dig out, with the puny aid of Rattah Grinah, a stray mongoose or to rob of its prize some canary-catching cat; digging holes in the rocky gap or on the brink of drains and stuffing them with paper and gunpowder stolen from the Rum canister and lighting it with a match. Dynamiting! Picking up hollow pieces of iron pipe, scratching a hole on top of them, towards one end, and ramming them with more gunpowder and stones and brown paper, and with a pyramid of gunpowder moistened with spit for a squib, leveling them at snipes or sparrows. Touch bams.

'Well, Sissie, what yo' got fo' eat to-day?'

'Cookoo, what yo' think Ah are have?'

'Lawd, mo' o' dat corn mash. Mo' o' dat prison gruel. People would t'ink a man is a horse!' . . . a restless crossing of scaly, marl-white legs in the corner.

'Any salt fish?'

'Wha' Ah is to get it from?'

'Herrin'?'

'You t'ink I muss be pick up money. Wha' you expect mah to get it from, wit' butter an' lard so dear, an' sugar four cents a pound. Yo' must be expect me to steal.'

'Well, I ain't mean no harm. . . .'

'Hey, this man muss be crazy. You forget I ain't workin' ni, yo' forget dat I can't even get water to drink, much mo' grow onions or green peas. Look outside. Look in the yard. Look at the parsley vines.'

Formerly things grew under the window or near the tamarind trees, fed by the used water or the swill, yams, potatoes, lettuce. . . .

Going to the door, Coggins paused. A 'forty-leg' was working its way into the craw of the last of the Rum hens. 'Lahd 'a' massie. . . .' Leaping to the rescue, Coggins slit the hen's craw—undigested corn spilled out—and ground the surfeited centipede underfoot.

'Now we got to eat this,' and he strung the bleeding hen up on a nail by the side of the door, out of poor Rattah Grinah's blinking reach. . . .

Unrestrained rejoicing on the floor.

Coggins ate. It was hot—hot food. It fused life into his body. It rammed the dust which had gathered in his throat at the quarry so far down into his stomach that he was unaware of its presence. And to eat food that had butter on it was a luxury. Coggins sucked up every grain of it.

'Hey, Ada.'

'Rufus, tek this.'

'Where is dat Miss Beryl?'

'Under de bed, m'm.'

'Beryl. . . .'

'Yassum. . . .'

Unweeping, Beryl, barely saving her skull, shot up from underneath the bed. Over Ada's obstreperous toes, over Rufus' by the side of Coggins, she had to pass to get the proffered dish.

'Take it quick!'

Saying not a word, Beryl took it and, sliding down beside it, deposited it upon the floor beside Coggins.

'You mustn't eat any more marl, yo' hear?' he turned to her. 'It will make yo' belly hard.'

'Yes . . . pappy.'

Throwing eyes up at him—white, shiny, appealing—Beryl guided the food into her mouth. The hand that did the act was still white with the dust of the marl. All up along the elbow. Even around her little mouth the white, telltale marks remained.

Drying the bowl of the last bit of grease, Coggins was completely absorbed in his task. He could hear Sissie scraping the iron pot and trying to fling from the spoon the stiff, overcooked corn meal which had stuck to it. Scraping the pan of its very bottom, Ada and Rufus fought like two mad dogs.

'You, Miss Ada, yo' better don't bore a hole in dat pan, gimme heah!'

'But, Mahmie, I ain't finish.'

Picking at her food, Beryl, the dainty one, ate sparingly. . . .

Once a day the Rums ate. At dusk, curve of crimson gold in the sensuous tropic sky, they had tea. English to a degree, it was a rite absurdly regal. Pauperized native blacks clung to the utmost vestiges of the Crown. Too, it was more than a notion for a black cane hole digger to face the turmoil of a hoe or fork or 'bill'—zigaboo word for cutlass—on a bare cup of molasses coffee.

III

'Lahd 'a' massie. . . .'

'Wha' a mattah, Coggins?'

'Say something, no!'

'Massie, come hay, an' see de gal picknee.'

'. . . open yo' mout' no, what's a mattah?'

Coggins flew to the rainwater keg. Knocked the swizzle stick—relic of Sissie's pop manufactures—behind it, tilting over the empty keg.

'Get up, Beryl, get up, wha' a mattah, sick?'

'Lif' she up, pappy.'

'Yo' move out o' de way, Mistah Rufus, befo'. . . .'

'Don't, Sissie, don't lick she!'

'Gal playin' sick! Gal only playin' sick, dat what de mattah wit' she. Gal only playin' sick. Get up, yo' miss!'

'God—don't, Sissie, leave she alone.'

'Go back, every dam one o' yo', all yo' gwine get in de way.'

Beryl, little naked brown legs apart, was flat upon the hard, bare earth. The dog, perhaps, or the echo of some fugitive wind had blown up her little crocus bag dress. It lay like a cocoanut flap-jack on her stomach. . . .

'Bring she inside, Coggins, wait I gwine fix de bed.'

Mahogany bed . . . West Indian peasants sporting a mahogany bed; canopied with a dusty grimy slice of cheesecloth. . . .

Coggins stood up by the lamp on the wall, looking on at Sissie prying up Beryl's eyelids.

'Open yo' eyes . . . open yo' eyes . . . betcha the little vagabon' is playin' sick.'

Indolently Coggins stirred. A fist shot up—then down. 'Move, Sissie, befo' Ah hit yo.' The women dodged.

'Always wantin' fo' hit me fo' nuttin', like I is any picknee.'

'. . . anybody hear this woman would think. . . .'

'I ain't gwine stand for it, yes, I ain't gwine. . . .'

'Shut up, yo' old hard-hearted wretch! Shut up befo' I tump yo' down!'

. . . Swept aside, one arm in a parrying attitude . . . backing, backing toward the larder over the lamp. . . .

Coggins peered back at the unbreathing child. A shade of compassion stole over Sissie. 'Put dis to 'er nose, Coggins, and see what'll happen.' Assafetida, bits of red cloth. . . .

Last year Rufus, the sickliest of the lot, had had the measles and the parish doctor had ordered her to tie a red piece of flannel around his neck. . . .

She stuffed the red flannel into Coggins' hand. 'Try dat,' she said, and stepped back.

Brow wrinkled in cogitation, Coggins—space cleared for action—denuded the child. 'How it ah rise! How 'er belly a go up in de year!' Bright wood; bright mahogany wood, expertly shellacked and laid out in the sun to dry, not unlike it. Beryl's stomach, a light brown tint, grew bit by bit shiny. It rose; round and bright, higher and higher. They had never seen one so none of them thought of wind filling balloons. Beryl's stomach resembled a wind-filling balloon.

Then—

'She too hard ears,' Sissie declared, 'she won't lissen to she pappy, she too hard ears.'

Dusk came. Country folk, tired, soggy, sleepy, staggering in from 'town'—depressed by the market quotations on Bantam cocks—hollowed howdy-do to Coggins, on the stone step, waiting.

Rufus and Ada strangely forgot to go down to the hydrant to bathe their feet. It had been a passion with Coggins. 'Nasty feet breed disease,' he had said, 'you Mistah Rufus, wash yo' foots befo' yo' go to sleep. An' yo', too, Miss Ada, I'm speaking to yo', gal, yo' hear me? Tak' yo' mout' off o' go 'head, befo' Ah box it off. . . .'

Inwardly glad of the escape, Ada and Rufus sat, not by Coggins out on the stone step, but down below the cabin, on the edge of a stone overlooking an empty pond, pitching rocks at the frogs and crickets screaming in the early dusk.

The freckled-face old buckra physician paused before the light and held up something to it. . . .

'Marl . . . marl . . . dust. . . .'

It came to Coggins in swirls. Autopsy. Noise comes in swirls. Pounding, pounding—dry Indian corn pounding. Ginger. Ginger being pounded in a mortar with a bright, new pestle. Pound, pound. And. Sawing. Butcher shop. Cow foot is sawed that way. Stew—or tough hard steak. Then the drilling—drilling—drilling to a stone cutter's ears! Ox grizzle. Drilling into ox grizzle. . . .

'Too bad, Coggins,' the doctor said, 'too bad, to lose yo' dawtah. . . .'

In a haze it came to Coggins. Inertia swept over him. He saw the old duffer climb into his buggy, tug at the reins of his sickly old nag and slowly drive down the rocky gap and disappear into the night.

Inside, Sissie, curious, held things up to the light. 'Come,' she said to Coggins, 'and see what 'im take out a' ar. Come an' see de marl. . . .'

And Coggins slowly answered, 'Sissie—if yo' know what is good fo' yo'self, you bes' leave dem stones alone.'

C. L. R. JAMES (1901–1989)

Triumph

Where people in England and America say slums, Trinidadians said barrack-yards. Probably the word is a relic of the days when England relied as much on garrisons of soldiers as on her fleet to protect her valuable sugar-producing colonies. Every street in Port-of-Spain proper could show you numerous examples of the type: a narrow gateway leading into a fairly big yard, on either side of which run long, low buildings, consisting of anything from four to eighteen rooms, each about twelve feet square. In these lived the porters, the prostitutes, cartermen, washerwomen, and domestic servants of the city.

In one corner of the yard is the hopelessly inadequate water-closet, unmistakable to the nose if not to the eye; sometimes there is a structure with the title of bathroom, a courtesy title, for he or she who would wash in it with decent privacy must cover the person as if bathing on the banks of the Thames; the kitchen happily presents no difficulty; never is there one and each barrack-yarder cooks before her door. In the centre of the yard is a heap of stones. On these the half-laundered clothes are bleached before being finally spread out to dry on the wire lines which in every yard cross and recross each other in all directions. Not only to Minerva have these stones been dedicated. Time was when they would have had an honoured shrine in a local temple to Mars, for they were the major source of ammunition for the homicidal strife which so often flared up in barrack-yards.

No longer do the barrack-yarders live the picturesque life of twenty-five years ago. Then, practising for the carnival, rival singers, Willie, Jean, and Freddie, porter, wharf-man or loafer in ordinary life, were for that season ennobled by some such striking sobriquet as the Duke of Normandy or the Lord Invincible, and carried with dignity homage such as young aspirants to literature had paid to Mr Kipling or Mr Shaw. They sang in competition from seven in the evening until far into the early morning, stimulated by the applause of their listeners and the excellence and copiousness of the rum; night after night the stickmen practised their dangerous and skilful game, the 'pierrots', after elaborate preface of complimentary speech, belaboured each other with riding whips; while around the performers the spectators pressed thick and good-humoured until mimic warfare was transformed into real, and stones from 'the bleach' flew thick. But today that life is dead. All carnival practice must cease at ten o'clock. The policeman is to the stick-fighter and 'pierrot' as the sanitary inspector to mosquito larvae. At nights the streets are bright with electric light, the arm of the law is longer, its grip stronger. Gone are the old lawlessness and picturesqueness. Barrack-yard life has lost its savour. Luckily, prohibition in Trinidad is still but a word. And life, dull and drab as it is in comparison, can still offer its great moments.

On a Sunday morning in one of the rooms of the barrack in Abercromby Street sat Mamitz. Accustomed as is squalid adversity to reign unchallenged in these quarters, yet in this room it was more than usually triumphant, sitting, as it were, high on a throne of regal state, so depressed was the woman and so depressing her surroundings.

The only representatives of the brighter side of life were three full-page pictures torn from illustrated periodicals, photographs of Lindbergh, Bernard Shaw, and Sargent's 'Portrait of a Woman', and these owed their presence solely to the fact that no pawnshop would have accepted them. They looked with unseeing eyes upon a room devoid of furniture save for a few bags spread upon the floor to form a bed. Mamitz sat on the door step talking to, or rather being talked to by her friend, Celestine, who stood astride the concrete canal, which ran in front of the door.

'Somebody do you something,' said Celestine with conviction. 'Nobody goin' to change my mind from that. An' if you do what I tell you, you will t'row off this black spirit that on you. A nice woman like you, and you carn't get a man to keep you! You carn't get nothing to do!'

Mamitz said nothing. Had Celestine said the exact opposite, Mamitz's reply would have been the same.

She was a black woman, too black to be pure Negro, probably with some Madrasi East Indian blood in her, a suspicion which was made a certainty by the long thick plaits of her plentiful hair. She was shortish and fat, voluptuously developed, tremendously developed, and as a creole loves development in a woman more than any other extraneous allure, Mamitz (like the rest of her sex in all stations of life) saw to it when she moved that you missed none of her charms. But for the last nine weeks she had been 'in derricks', to use Celestine's phrase. First of all the tram conductor who used to keep her (seven dollars every Saturday night, out of which Mamitz usually got three) had accused her of infidelity and beaten her. Neither the accusation nor the beating had worried Mamitz. To her and her type those were minor incidents of existence, from their knowledge of life and men, the kept woman's inevitable fate. But after a temporary reconciliation he had beaten her once more, very badly indeed, and left her. Even this was not an irremediable catastrophe. But thenceforward, Mamitz, from being the most prosperous woman in the yard, had sunk gradually to being the most destitute. Despite her very obvious attractions, no man took notice of her. She went out asking for washing or for work as a cook. No success. Luckily, in the days of her prosperity she had been generous to Celestine who now kept her from actual starvation. One stroke of luck she had had. The agent for the barracks had suddenly taken a fancy to her, and Mamitz had not found it difficult to persuade him to give her a chance with the rent. But that respite was over: he was pressing for the money, and Mamitz had neither money to pay nor hope of refuge when she was turned out. Celestine would have taken her in, but Celestine's keeper was a policeman who visited her three or four nights a week, and to one in that position a fifteen-foot room does not offer much scope for housing the homeless. Yet Celestine was grieved that she could do nothing to help Mamitz in her trouble which she attributed to the evil and supernatural machinations of Irene, their common enemy.

'Take it from me, that woman do you something. Is she put Nathan against you. When was the quarrel again?'

'It was two or three days after Nathan gave me the first beating.'

Nathan then had started on his evil courses before the quarrel with Irene took place, but Celestine brushed away objection.

'She musta had it in her mind for you from before. You didn't see how she fly out at you . . . As long as you livin' here an' I cookin' I wouldn't see you want a cup o' tea an' a spoonful o' rice. But I carn't help with the rent. . . . An' you ain't have nobody here.'

Mamitz shook her head. She was from Demerara.

'If you could only cross the sea—that will cut any spirit that on you . . . Look the animal!'

Irene had come out of her room on the opposite side of the yard. She could not fail to see Celestine and Mamitz and she called loudly to a neighbour lower down the yard:

'Hey Jo-jo! What is the time? Ten o'clock a'ready? Le' me start to cook me chicken that me man buy for me—even if 'e have a so' foot . . . I don't know how long it will last before 'e get drunk and kick me out o' here. Then I will have to go dawg'n round other po' people to see if I could pick up what they t'row 'way.'

She fixed a box in front of her door, put her coal-pot on it, and started to attend to her chicken.

Sunday morning in barrack-yards is pot-parade. Of the sixteen tenants in the yard twelve had their pots out, and they lifted the meat with long iron forks to turn it, or threw water into the pot so that it steamed to the heavens and every woman could tell what her neighbour was cooking—beef, or pork, or chicken. It didn't matter what you cooked in the week, if you didn't cook at all. But to cook salt fish, or hog-head, or pig-tail on a Sunday morning was a disgrace. You put your pot inside your house and cooked it there.

Mamitz, fat, easy-going, and cowed by many days of semi-starvation, took little notice of Irene. But Celestine, a thin little whip of a brown-skinned woman, bubbled over with repressed rage.

'By Christ, if it wasn't for one t'ing I'd rip every piece o' clothes she have on off 'er.'

'Don' bother wid 'er. What is the use o' gettin' you'self in trouble with Jimmy?'

Jimmy was the policeman. He was a steady, reliable man but he believed in discipline and when he spoke, he spoke. He had made Celestine understand that she was not to fight: he wasn't going to find himself mixed up in court as the keeper of any brawling woman. Celestine's wrath, deprived of its natural outlet, burned none the less implacably.

'I tell you something, Mamitz, I goin' to talk to the agent in the morning. I goin' to tell 'im to give you to the end of the month. Is only five days . . . I goin' to give you a bath. Try and see if you could get some gully-root and so on this afternoon . . . Tonight I goin' give you . . . An' I will give you some prayers to read. God stronger than the devil. We gon' break this t'ing that on you. Cheer up. I goin' send you a plate with you' chicken an' rice as soon as it finish. Meanwhile burn you' little candle, say you' little prayers, console you' little mind. I goin' give you that bath tonight. You ain' kill priest. You ain' cuss you' mudder. So you ain' have cause to 'fraid nothin'.'

Celestine would never trust herself to indulge in abuse with Irene; the chances that it would end in a fight were too great. So she contented herself with casting a look of the most murderous hate and scorn and defiance at her enemy, and then went to her own pot which was calling for attention.

And yet three months before Mamitz, Celestine and Irene had been good friends. They shared their rum and their joys and troubles: and on Sunday afternoons they used to sit before Mamitz's room singing hymns:

'Abide With Me', 'Jesu, Lover of My Soul', 'Onward! Christian Soldiers'. Celestine and Irene sang soprano and Irene sang well. Mamitz was a naturally fine contralto and had a fine ear, while Nathan, who was a Barbadian and consequently knew vocal music, used to sing bass whenever he happened to be in. The singing would put him in a good mood and he would send off to buy more rum and everything would be peaceful and happy. But Irene was a jealous woman, not only jealous of Mamitz's steady three dollars a week and Celestine's policeman with his twenty-eight dollars at the end of the month. She lived with a cab-man, whose income though good enough was irregular. And he was a married man, with a wife and children to support. Irene had to do washing to help out, while Mamitz and Celestine did nothing, merely cooked and washed clothes for their men. So gradually a state of dissatisfaction arose. Then one damp evening, Mamitz, passing near the bamboo pole which supported a clothes line overburdened with Irene's clothes, brought it down with her broad, expansive person. The line burst, and nightgowns, sheets, pillow-cases, white suits, and tablecloths fluttered to the mud. It had been a rainy week with little sun, and already it would have been difficult to get the clothes ready in time for Saturday morning: after this it was impossible. And hot and fiery was the altercation. Celestine who tried to make peace was drawn into the quarrel by Irene's comprehensive and incendiary invective.

'You comin' to put you' mouth in this. You think because you livin' with a policeman you is a magistrate. Mind you' business, woman, min' you' business. The two o' all you don't do nothing for you' livin'. You only sittin' down an' eatin' out the men all you livin' wid. An' I wo'k so hard an' put out me clo's on the line. And this one like some cab-horse knock it down, and when I tell 'er about it you comin' to meddle! Le' me tell you . . .'

So the wordy warfare raged, Celestine's policeman coming in for rough treatment at the tongue of Irene. Celestine, even though she was keeping herself in check, was a match for any barrack-yard woman Port of Spain could produce, but yet it was Mamitz who clinched the victory.

'Don't mind Celestine livin' with a policeman. You will be glad to get 'im for you'self. An' it better than livin' with any stinkin' so'-foot man.'

For Irene's cab-man had a sore on his foot, which he had had for thirty years and would carry with him to the grave even if he lived for thirty years more. Syphilis, congenital and acquired, and his copious boozing would see to it that there was no recovery. Irene had stupidly hoped that nobody in the yard knew. But in Trinidad when His Excellency the Governor and his wife have a quarrel the street boys speak of it the day after, and Richard's bad foot had long been a secret topic of conversation in the yard.

But it was Mamitz who had made it public property, and Irene hated Mamitz with a virulent hatred, and had promised to 'do' for her. Three days before, Nathan, the tram-conductor, had given Mamitz the first beating; but even at the time of the quarrel there was no hint of his swift defection and Mamitz's rapid descent to her present plight. So that Celestine, an errant but staunch religionist, was convinced that Mamitz's troubles were due to Irene's trafficking with the devil, if not personally, at least through one of his numerous agents who ply their profitable trade in every part of Port of Spain. Secure in her own immunity from anything that Irene might 'put on her', she daily regretted that she couldn't rip the woman to pieces. 'Oh Jesus! If it wasn't for Jimmy I'd tear the wretch limb from limb!' But the energy that she could not put into the destruction of Irene she spent in upholding Mamitz. The fiery Celestine had a real affection for the placid Mamitz, whose quiet ways were so soothing. But, more than this, she was determined not to see Mamitz go down. In the bitter antagonism she nursed against Irene, it would have been a galling defeat if Mamitz went to the wall. Further, her reputation as a woman who knew things and could put crooked people straight was at stake. Once she had seen to Jimmy's food and clothes and creature comforts she set herself to devise ways and means of supporting the weak, easily crushed Mamitz.

Celestine's policeman being on duty that night, she herself was off duty and free to attend to her own affairs. At midnight, with the necessary rites and ceremonies, Ave Marias and Pater Nosters, she bathed Mamitz in a large bath pan full of water prepared with gully root, fever grass, lime leaves, *guerin tout, herbe a femmes,* and other roots, leaves and grasses noted for their efficacy (when properly applied) against malign plots and influences. That was at twelve o'clock the Sunday night. On Monday morning at eight o'clock behold Popo des Vignes walking into the yard, with a little bag in his hand.

Popo is a creole of creoles. His name is des Vignes, but do not be misled into thinking that there flows in his veins blood of those aristocrats who found their way to Trinidad after '89. He is a Negro, and his slave ancestor adopted the name from his master. Popo is nearing forty, medium-sized, though large about the stomach, with a longish moustache. He is dressed in a spotless suit of white with tight-fitting shoes of a particularly yellowish brown (no heavy English brogues or fantastic American shoes for him). On his head he wears his straw hat at a jaunty angle, and his manner of smoking his cigarette and his jacket always flying open (he wears no waistcoat) will give the impression that Popo is a man of pleasure rather than a man of work. And that impression would be right. He has never done a week's honest work in his life. He can get thirty dollars for you if you are in difficulties (at one hundred per cent); or three thousand dollars if you have a house or a cocoa estate. During the cocoa crop he lurks by the railway station with an unerring eye for peasant proprietors who have brought their cocoa into town and are not quite certain where they will get the best price. This is his most profitable business, for he gets commission both from the proprietors and from the big buyers. But he is not fastidious as to how he makes money, and will do anything that does not bind him down, and leaves him free of manual or clerical labour. For the rest, after he has had a good meal at about half past seven in the evening he can drink rum until six o'clock the next morning without turning a hair; and in his own circle he has a wide reputation for his connoisseurship in matters of love and his catholicity of taste in women.

'Eh, Mr des Vignes! How you?' said Celestine. The inhabitants of every barrack-yard, especially the women, knew Popo.

'Keeping fine.'

'Who you lookin' for roun' this way?'

'I come roun' to see you. How is Jimmy? When you getting married?'

'Married!' said Celestine with fine scorn. 'Me married a police! I wouldn't trust a police further than I could smell him. Police ain't have no regard. A police will lock up 'is mudder to get a stripe. An' besides I ain' want to married the man in the house all the time, you go'n be a perfect slave. I all right as I be.'

'Anyway, I want you to buy a ring.'

'Rings you sellin' in the bag? I ain' have no money, but le' me see them.'

Popo opened his bags and displayed the rings—beautiful gold of American workmanship, five dollars cash and six dollars on terms. They had cost an Assyrian merchant in Park Street ten dollars the dozen, and Popo was selling them on commission. He was doing good business, especially with those who paid two dollars down and gave promises of monthly or weekly instalments. If later the merchant saw trouble to collect his instalments or to get back his rings, that wouldn't worry Popo much for by that time he would have chucked up the job.

'So you wouldn't take one,' said he, getting ready to put away his treasures again.

'Come roun' at the end o' the month. But don't shut them up yet. I have a friend I want to see them.'

She went to the door.

'Mamitz!' she called. 'Come see some rings Mr des Vignes sellin'.'

Mamitz came into Celestine's room, large, slow-moving, voluptuous, with her thick, smooth hair neatly plaited and her black skin shining. She took Popo's fancy at once.

'But you have a nice friend, Celestine,' said Popo. 'And she has a nice name too: Mamitz! Well, how many rings you are going to buy from me?'

Celestine answered quickly: 'Mamitz can't buy no rings. The man was keepin' her, they fall out, an' she lookin' for a husband now.'

'A nice woman like you can't stay long without a husband,' said des Vignes. 'Let me give you some luck . . . Choose a ring and I will make you a present.'

Mamitz chose a ring and des Vignes put it on her finger himself.

'Excuse me, I comin' back now,' said Celestine. 'The Sanitary Inspector comin' just now, an' I want to clean up some rubbish before he come.'

When she came back des Vignes was just going.

'As we say, Mamitz,' he smiled. 'So long, Celestine!'

He was hardly out of earshot when Celestine excitedly tackled Mamitz. 'What 'e tell you?'

''E say that 'e comin' round here about ten o'clock tonight or little later . . . An' 'e give me this.' In her palm reposed a red two-dollar note.

'You see what I tell you?' said Celestine triumphantly. 'That bath. But don't stop. Read the prayers three times a day for nine days . . . Buy some stout, Mitz, to nourish up you'self . . . 'E ain't a man you could depend on. If you dress a broomstick in a petticoat 'e will run after it. But you goin' to get something out o' 'im for a few weeks or so . . . An' you see 'e is a nice man.'

Mamitz smiled her lazy smile.

Celestine knew her man. For four weeks Popo was a more or less regular visitor to Mamitz's room. He paid the rent, he gave her money to get her bed and furniture out of the pawnshop, and every Sunday morning Mamitz was stirring beef or pork or chicken in her pot. More than that, whenever Popo said he was coming to see her, he gave her money to prepare a meal so that sometimes late in the week, on a Thursday night, Mamitz's pot smelt as if it was Sunday morning. Celestine shared in the prosperity and they could afford to take small notice of Irene who prophesied early disaster.

'All you flourishin' now. But wait little bit. I know that Popo des Vignes well. 'E don't knock round a woman no more than a month. Just now all that high livin' goin' shut down an' I going see you Mamitz eatin' straw.'

But Mamitz grew fatter than ever, and when she walked down the road in a fugi silk dress, tight fitting and short, which exposed her noble calves to the knee and accentuated the amplitudes of her person, she created a sensation among those men who took notice of her.

On Sunday morning she went into the market to buy beef. She was passing along the stalls going to the man she always bought from, when a butcher called out to her.

'Hey, Mamitz! Come this way.'

Mamitz went. She didn't know the man, but she was of an acquiescent nature and she went to see what he wanted.

'But I don't know you,' she said, after looking at him. 'Where you know my name?'

'Ain't was you walkin' down Abercromby Street last Sunday in a white silk dress?'

'Yes,' smiled Mamitz.

'Well, I know a nice woman when I see one. An' I find out where you livin' too. Ain't you livin' in the barrack just below Park Street? . . . Girl, you did look too sweet. You mustn't buy beef from nobody but me. How much you want? A pound? Look a nice piece. Don't worry to pay me for that. You could pay me later. Whenever you want beef, come round this way.'

Mamitz accepted and went. She didn't like the butcher too much, but he liked her. And a pound of beef was a pound of beef. Nicholas came to see her a day or two after and brought two pints of stout as a present. At first Mamitz didn't bother with him. But des Vignes was a formidable rival. Nicholas made Mamitz extravagant presents and promises. What helped him was that Popo now began to slack off. A week would pass and Mamitz would not see him. And no more money was forthcoming. So, after a while she accepted Nicholas, and had no cause to regret her bargain. Nicholas made a lot of money as a butcher. He not only paid the rent, but gave her five dollars every Saturday night, and she could always get a dollar or two out of him during the week. Before long he loved her to distraction, and was given to violent fits of jealousy which, however, were always followed by repentance and lavish presents. Still Mamitz hankered after Popo. One day she wrote him a little note telling him that she was sorry she had to accept Nicholas but that she would be glad to see him any time he came round. She sent it to the Miranda Hotel where Popo took his meals. But no answer came and after a while Mamitz ceased actively to wish to see Popo. She was prosperous and pretty happy. She and Celestine were thicker than ever, and were on good terms with the neighbours in the yard. Only Irene they knew would do them mischief, and on mornings when Mamitz got up, on Celestine's advice, she looked carefully before the door lest she should unwittingly set foot on any churchyard bones, deadly powders, or other satanic agencies guaranteed to make the victim go mad, steal, or commit those breaches of good conduct which are punishable by law. But nothing untoward happened. As Celestine pointed out to Mamitz, the power of the bath held good, 'and as for me,' concluded she, 'no powers Irene can handle can touch my little finger'.

Easter Sunday came, and with it came Popo. He walked into the yard early, about seven in the morning, and knocked up Mamitz who was still sleeping.

'I t'ought you had given me up for good,' said Mamitz. 'I write you and you didn't answer.'

'I didn't want any butcher to stick me with his knife,' laughed Popo. 'Anyway, that is all right . . . I was playing baccarat last night and I made a good haul, so I come to spend Easter with you. Look! Here is five dollars. Buy salt fish and sweet oil and some greens and tomatoes. Buy some pints of rum. And some stout for yourself. I am coming back about nine o'clock. Today is Easter Saturday, Nicholas is going to be in the market the whole day. Don't be afraid for him.'

Mamitz became excited. She gave the five dollars to Celestine and put her in charge of the catering, while she prepared for her lover. At about half past nine Popo returned. He, Mamitz and Celestine ate in Mamitz's room, and before they got up from the table, much more than two bottles of rum had disappeared. Then Celestine left them and went to the market to Nicholas. She told him that Mamitz wasn't feeling too well and had sent for beef and pork. The willing Nicholas handed over the stuff and sent a shilling for his lady love. He said he was rather short of money but at the end of the day he was going to make a big draw. Celestine cooked, and at about half past one, she, Popo and Mamitz had lunch. Celestine had to go out again and buy more rum. The other people in the yard didn't take much notice of what was an everyday occurrence, were rather pleased in fact, for after lunch Celestine had a bottle and a half of rum to herself and ostentatiously invited all the neighbours to have drinks, all, of course, except Irene.

At about three o'clock Irene felt that she could bear it no longer and that if she didn't take this chance it would be throwing away a gift from God. She put on her shoes, took her basket on her arm, and left the yard. It was the basket that aroused the observant Celestine's suspicions for she knew that Irene had already done all her shopping that morning. She sat thinking for a few seconds, then she knocked at Mamitz's door.

'Look here, Mamitz,' she called. 'It's time for Mr des Vignes to go.

Irene just gone out with a basket, I think she gone to the market to tell Nicholas.'

'But he can't get away today,' called Mamitz.

'You know how the man jealous and how 'e bad,' persisted Celestine. 'Since nine o'clock Mr des Vignes, is time for you to go.'

Celestine's wise counsel prevailed. Popo dressed himself with his usual scrupulous neatness and cleared off. The rum bottles were put out of the way and Mamitz's room was made tidy. She and Celestine had hardly finished when Irene appeared with the basket empty.

'You see,' said Celestine. 'Now look out!'

Sure enough, it wasn't five minutes after when a cab drew up outside, and Nicholas still in his bloody butcher's apron, came hot foot into the yard. He went straight up to Mamitz and seized her by the throat.

'Where the hell is that man you had in the room with you—the room I payin' rent for?'

'Don't talk dam' foolishness, man, lemme go,' said Mamitz.

'I will stick my knife into you as I will stick it in a cow. You had Popo des Vignes in that room for the whole day. Speak the truth, you dog.'

'You' mother, you' sister, you' aunt, you' wife was the dog,' shrieked Mamitz, quoting one of Celestine's most brilliant pieces of repartee.

'It's the wo'se when you meddle with them common low-island people,' said Celestine. Nicholas was from St Vincent, and Negroes from St Vincent, Grenada, and the smaller West Indian islands are looked down upon by the Trinidad Negro as low-island people.

'You shut you' blasted mouth and don't meddle with what don' concern you. Is you encouragin' the woman. I want the truth, or by Christ I'll make beef o' one o' you here today.'

'Look here, man, lemme tell you something.' Mamitz, drunk with love and rum and inspired by Celestine, was showing spirit. 'That woman over there come and tell you that Mr des Vignes was in this room. The man come in the yard, 'e come to Celestine to sell 'er a ring she did promise to buy from 'im long time. Look in me room,' she flung the half doors wide, 'you see any signs of any man in there? Me bed look as if any man been lyin' down on it? But I had no right to meddle with a low brute like you. You been botherin' me long enough. Go live with Irene. Go share she wid she so' foot cab-man. Is woman like she men like you want. I sorry the day I ever see you. An' I hope I never see you' face again.'

She stopped, panting, and Celestine, who had only been waiting for an opening, took up the tale.

'But look at the man! The man leave 'is work this bright Easter Saturday because this nasty woman go and tell 'im that Mr des Vignes in the room with Mamitz! Next thing you go'n say that 'e livin' with me. But man, I never see such a ass as you. Bertha, Olive, Josephine,' she appealed to some of the other inhabitants of the yard. 'Ain't all you been here the whole day an' see Mr des Vignes come here after breakfast? I pay 'im two dollars I had for 'im. 'E sen' and buy a pint o' rum an' I call Mamitz for the three o' we to fire a little liquor for the Easter. Next thing I see is this one goin' out—to carry news: and now this Vincelonian fool leave 'e work—But, man, you drunk.'

Bertha, Olive, and Josephine, who had shared in the rum, confirmed Celestine's statement. Irene had been sitting at the door of her room cleaning fish and pretending to take no notice, but at this she jumped up.

'Bertha, you ought to be ashame' o' you'self. For a drink o' rum you lyin' like that? Don't believe them, Nicholas. Whole day—'

But here occurred an unlooked for interruption. The cabby, hearing the altercation and not wishing to lose time on a day like Easter Saturday, had put a little boy in charge of his horse and had been listening for a minute or two. He now approached and held Nicholas by the arm.

'Boss,' he said, 'don't listen to that woman. She livin' with Richard the cab-man an' 'e tell me that all women does lie but 'e never hear or know none that does lie like she—'

There was a burst of laughter.

'Come go, boss,' said the cabby, pulling the hot, unwilling Nicholas by the arm.

'I have to go back to my work, but I am comin' back tonight and I am goin' to lick the stuffin' out o' you.'

'An' my man is a policeman,' said Celestine. 'An' 'e goin' to be here tonight. An' if you touch this woman, you spend you' Easter in the lock-up sure as my name is Celestine an' you are a good-for-nothing Vincelonian fool of a butcher.'

Nicholas drove away, leaving Celestine mistress of the field, but for the rest of the afternoon Mamitz was depressed. She was tired out with the day's excitement, and after all Nicholas had good money. On a night like this he would be drawing quite a lot of money and now it seemed that she was in danger of losing him. She knew how he hated Popo. She liked Popo more than Nicholas, much more, but after all people had to live.

Celestine, however, was undaunted. 'Don't min' what 'e say. 'E comin' back. 'E comin' back to beg. When you see a man love a woman like he love you, she could treat 'im how she like, 'e still comin' back like a dog to eat 'is vomit. But you listen to me, Mamitz. When 'e come back cuss 'im a little bit. Cuss 'im plenty. Make 'im see that you ain't goin' to stand too much nonsense from 'im.'

Mamitz smiled in her sleepy way, but she was not hopeful. And all the rest of the afternoon Irene worried her by singing ballads appropriate to the occasion.

> Though you belong to somebody else
> Tonight you belong to me.
>
> Come, come, come to me, Thora,
> Come once again and be . . .
>
> How can I live without you!
> How can I let you go!

Her voice soared shrill over the babel of clattering tongues in the yard. And as the voice rose so Mamitz's heart sank.

'Don' forget,' were Celestine's last words before they parted for the night. 'If 'e come back tonight, don't open the door for 'im straight. Le' 'im knock a little bit.'

'All right,' said Mamitz dully. She was thinking that she had only about thirty-six cents left over from the money des Vignes had given her. Not another cent.

But Celestine was right. The enraged Nicholas went back to work and cut beef and sawed bones with a ferocity that astonished his fellow-butchers and purchasers. But at seven o'clock, with his pocket full of money and nothing to do, he felt miserable. He had made his plans for the Easter: Saturday night he had decided to spend with Mamitz, and all Easter Sunday after he knocked off at nine in the morning. Easter Monday he had for himself and he had been thinking of taking Mamitz, Celestine, and Jimmy down to Carenage in a taxi to bathe. He mooned about the streets for a time. He took two or three drinks, but he didn't feel in the mood for running a spree and getting drunk. He was tired from the strain of the day and he felt for the restful company of a woman, especially the woman he loved—the good-looking, fat, agreeable Mamitz. At about half past ten he found his resolution never to look at her again wavering.

'Damn it,' he said to himself. 'That woman Irene is a liar. She see how I am treatin' Mamitz well and she want to break up the livin'.'

He fought the question out with himself.

'But the woman couldn't lie like that. The man musta been there.'

He was undecided. He went over the arguments for and against, the testimony of Bertha and Olive, the testimony of the cab-man. His reason inclined him to believe that Mamitz had been entertaining des Vignes for the whole day in the room he was paying for, while he, the fool, was working hard for money to carry to her. But stronger powers than reason were fighting for Mamitz, and eleven o'clock found him in the yard knocking at the door.

'Mamitz! Mamitz! Open. Is me—Nicholas.' There was a slight pause. Then he heard Mamitz's voice sounding a little strange.

'What the devil you want!'

'I sorry for what happen today. Is that meddlin' woman, Irene. She come to the market an' she lie on you. Open the door, Mamitz . . . I have something here for you.'

Celestine next door was listening closely, pleased that Mamitz was proving herself so obedient to instruction.

'Man, I 'fraid you. You have a knife out there an' you come here to cut me up as Gorrie cut up Eva.'

'I have no knife. I brought some money for you.'

I don't believe you. You want to treat me as if I a cow.'

'I tell you I have no knife . . . open the door, woman, or I'll break it in. You carn't treat me like that.'

Nicholas's temper was getting the better of him, he hadn't expected this. The watchful Celestine here interfered.

'Open the door for the man, Mamitz. 'E say 'e beg pardon and, after all, is he payin' the rent.'

So Mamitz very willingly opened the door and Nicholas went in. He left early the next morning to go to work but he promised Mamitz to be back by half past nine.

Irene, about her daily business in the yard, gathered that Nicholas had come 'dawgin'' back to Mamitz the night before and Mamitz was drivin' him dog and lance, but Celestine beg for him and Mamitz let 'im come in. Mamitz, she noticed, got up that morning much later than usual. In fact Celestine (who was always up at five o'clock) knocked her up and went into the room before she came out. It was not long before Irene knew that something was afoot. First of all, Mamitz never opened her door as usual, but slipped in and out closing it after her. Neither she nor Celestine went to the market. They sent out Bertha's little sister who returned with beef and pork and mutton, each piece of which Mamitz held up high in the air and commented upon. Then Bertha's sister went out again and returned with a new coal-pot. Irene could guess where it came from— some little store, in Charlotte Street probably, whose owner was not afraid to run the risk of selling on Sundays. In and out the yard went Bertha's little sister, and going and coming the clutched something tightly in her hand. Irene, her senses tuned by resentment and hate to their highest pitch, could not make out what was happening. Meanwhile Celestine was inside Mamitz's room, and Mamitz, outside, had started to cook in three coal-pots.

Every minute or so Mamitz would poke her head inside the room and talk to Celestine. Irene could see Mamitz shaking her fat self with laughter while she could hear Celestine's shrill cackle inside. Then Bertha's sister returned for the last time and after going into the room to deliver whatever her message was, came and stood a few yards away, opposite Mamitz's door, expectantly waiting. Think as she would, Irene could form no idea as to what was going on inside.

Then Mamitz went and stood near to Bertha's sister; and, a second after, the two halves of the door were flung open and Irene saw Celestine standing in the doorway with arms akimbo. But there was nothing to—and then she saw. Both halves of the door were plastered with notes, green five-dollar notes, red two-dollar notes, and blue dollar notes, with a pin at a corner of each to keep it firm. The pin-heads were shining in the sun. Irene was so flabbergasted that for a second or two she stood with her mouth open. Money Nicholas had given Mamitz. Nicholas had come back and begged pardon, and given her all this money. The fool! So that was what Celestine had been doing inside there all the time. Bertha's sisters had been running up and down to get some of the notes changed. There must be about forty, no, fifty dollars, spread out on the door. Mamitz and Bertha's sister were sinking with laughter and the joke was spreading, for other people in the yard were going up to see what the disturbance was about. What a blind fool that Nicholas was! Tears of rage and mortification rushed to Irene's eyes.

'Hey, Irene, come see a picture Nicholas bring for Mamitz last night! An' tomorrow we goin' to Carenage. We don't want you, but we will carry you' husband, the sea-water will do 'is so'-foot good.' Celestine's voice rang across the yard.

Bertha, Josephine, the fat Mamitz and the rest were laughing so that they could hardly hold themselves up. Irene could find neither spirit nor voice to reply. She trembled so that her hands shook. The china bowl in which she was washing rice slipped from her fingers and broke into a dozen pieces while the rice streamed into the dirty water of the canal.

ALEJO CARPENTIER (1904–1983)

Journey to the Seed

Translated by Jean Franco

I

'What do you want, old 'un?'

The question fell several times from the top of the scaffolding. But the old man did not reply. He went from one spot to another, poking about, a long monologue of incomprehensible phrases issuing from his throat. They had already brought down the roof-tiles which covered the faded pavings with their earthenware mosaic. Up above, the picks were loosening the masonry, sending the stones rolling down wooden channels in a great cloud of lime and chalk. And through each one of the embrasures which had been cut into the battlements appeared (their secret uncovered) smooth oval or square ceilings, cornices, garlands, denticles, mouldings and wallpaper which hung down from the friezes like old, cast-off snake skins. Watching the demolition, a Ceres with a broken nose, a discoloured robe and with a blackened crown of maize upon her head stood in her back court upon her fountain of faded masks. Visited by the sun in the dusky hours, the grey fish in her basin yawned in mossy, warm water, their round eyes watching those black workmen in the gap in the skyline who were gradually reducing the age-old height of the house. The old man had seated himself at the foot of the statue with his stick pointing at his chin. He watched the raising and lowering of buckets in which valuable remains were carried away. There was the sound of muffled street noises and, up above, the pulleys harmonized their disagreeable and grating bird-songs in a rhythm of iron upon stone.

Five o'clock struck. The cornices and entablatures emptied of people. There only remained the hand-ladders ready for the next day's assault. The breeze turned fresher, now that it was relieved of its load of sweat, curses, rope-creakings, axles shrieking for the oil-can, and the slapping of greasy bodies. Twilight arrived earlier for the denuded house. It was clothed in shadows at an hour when the now-fallen upper parapets had

50

been wont to regale the façade with a sparkle of sunlight. Ceres tightened her lips. For the first time, the rooms slept without window-blinds, open on to a landscape of ruins.

Contrary to their wishes, several capitals lay in the grass. Their acanthus leaves revealed their vegetable condition. A climbing plant, attracted by the family resemblance, ventured to stretch its tendrils towards the Ionic scrolls. When night fell, the house was nearer the ground. A door-frame still stood on high with planks of shade hanging from its bewildered hinges.

II

Then the dark old man who had not moved from that place, gestured strangely and waved his stick over a cemetery of tiles.

The black and white marble squares flew back and covered the floors again. With sure leaps, stones closed the gaps in the battlements. The walnut panels, garnished with nails, fitted themselves into their frames whilst, with rapid rotations, the screws of the hinges buried themselves in their holes. Raised up by an effort from the flowers, the tiles on the faded pavings put together their broken fragments and in a noisy whirlwind of clay fell like rain upon the roof-tree. The house grew, returned again to its usual proportions, clothed and modest. Ceres was less grey. There were more fish in the fountain. And the murmur of water invoked forgotten begonias.

The old man put a key into the lock of the main door and began to open windows. His heels sounded hollow. When he lit the brass lamps, a yellow tremor ran along the oil of the family portraits and black-robed people murmured in all the galleries to the rhythm of spoons stirred in chocolate bowls.

Don Marcial, Marquis of Capellanías lay on his deathbed, his breast clad in medals, and with an escort of four candles with long beards of melted wax.

III

The candles grew slowly and lost their beads of sweat. When they regained their full height, a nun put them out and drew away her taper. The wicks became white and threw off their snuff. The house emptied of visitors and the carriages departed into the night. Don Marcial played on an invisible keyboard and opened his eyes.

The blurred and jumbled roof-beams fell gradually back into place. The flasks of medicine, the damask tassels, the scapulary over the head of the bed, the daguerrotypes and the palms of the balcony grille emerged from the mists. Whilst the doctor shook his head with professional condolence, the sick man felt better. He slept for a few hours and awoke with the black beetle-browed regard of Father Anastasio upon him. The confession changed from being frank, detailed, and full of sins to being reticent, halting, and full of concealments. And after all, what right had that Carmelite friar to interfere in his life? Suddenly Don Marcial felt himself drawn into the middle of the room. The weight on his forehead lifted and he got up with surprising speed. The naked woman who was lounging upon the brocade of the bed searched for her petticoats and bodices and took away with her, soon afterwards, the sound of crushed silk and perfume. Below, in the closed carriage, covering the seat studs, there was an envelope containing gold coins.

Don Marcial did not feel well. As he arranged his tie in front of the pierglass he found that he looked bloated. He went down to the office where legal men, solicitors and notaries were waiting for him to settle the auctioning of the house. It had all been useless. His belongings would go bit by bit to the highest bidder to the rhythm of hammer-blows upon the table. He greeted them and they left him alone. He thought of the mysteries of the written word, of those black threads which, ravelling and unravelling over wide, filigrained balance sheets, had ravelled and unravelled agreements, oaths, covenants, testimonies, declarations, surnames, titles, dates, lands, trees, and stones—a web of threads extracted from the inkwell, threads in which a man's legs became fouled and which formed barriers across the paths, access to which was denied by law; they formed a noose pressing at his throat and muffling his voice as he perceived the dreadful sound of words which floated free. His signature had betrayed him, getting involved in knots and tangles of parchments. Bound by it, the man of flesh became a man of paper.

It was dawn. The dining-room clock had just struck six in the afternoon.

IV

Months of mourning passed, overshadowed by a growing feeling of remorse. At first the idea of bringing another woman into that bedroom seemed almost reasonable to him. But, little by little, the need for a new body was replaced by increasing scruples which reached the point of flagellation. One night, Don Marcial drew blood from his flesh with a strap and immediately felt a more intense desire, though of short duration. It was then that the Marchioness returned, one afternoon, from her ride along the banks of the Almendares. The horses of the calash had no moisture on their manes other than that of their own sweat. But all the rest of the day, they kicked at the panels of the stable as if irritated by the stillness of the low clouds.

At twilight, a basin full of water fell in the Marchioness' bath and broke. Then the May rains made the tank overflow. And the dark old woman who had a touch of the tar-brush and who kept doves under her bed walked through the yard muttering: 'Beware of rivers, child, beware of the running green.' There wasn't a day on which water did not betray its presence. But this presence was finally nothing more than a bowlful spilled upon a Paris gown when they came back from the anniversary ball given by the Captain General of the colony.

Many relatives reappeared. Many friends returned. The chandeliers of the great drawing-room now sparkled very brightly. The cracks in the façades gradually closed. The piano again became a clavichord. The palm trees lost some rings. The climbing plants let go of the first cornice. The rings under Ceres' eyes grew whiter and the capitals seemed newly-carved. Marcial grew livelier and would spend whole afternoons embracing the Marchioness. Crowsfeet, frowns, and double chins were erased and the flesh regained its firmness. One day the smell of fresh paint filled the house.

V

The blushes were genuine. Every night the leaves of screens opened wider, skirts fell in the darker corners and there were new barriers of lace. Finally the Marchioness blew out the lamps. Only he spoke in the darkness.

They left for the sugar-mill in a great train of calashes—a shining of sorrel croups, of silver bits and of varnish in the sun. But in the shade of the poinsettias which made the inner portico of the house glow red, they realized that they hardly knew one another. Marcial gave permission for Negro tribal dances and drums in order to divert them a little on those days which were odorous with Cologne perfume, baths of benzoin, with loosened hair and sheets taken from the cupboards which, when opened, spilled out bunches of vetiver herb on to the tiles. A whiff of cane liquor whirled in the breeze with the prayer-bell. The low breezes wafted tidings of reluctant rains whose first, big, noisy drops were sucked in by roofs so dry that they gave out the sound of copper. After a dawn lengthened by an awkward embrace, their disagreements made up, the wound healed, they both went back to the city. The Marchioness changed her travelling dress for a bridal gown and as usual, the couple went to church to recover their liberty. They gave the presents back to relatives and friends and in a flurry of bronze bells, a parade of harnesses, each one took the road back to his own home. Marcial went on visiting María de las Mercedes for some time until the day when the rings were taken to the goldsmith's to be disengraved. There began a new life for Marcial. In the house with the high balconies, Ceres was replaced by an Italian Venus and the masks of the fountain almost imperceptibly pushed out their reliefs on seeing the flames of the oil-lamps still alight when dawn already dappled the sky.

VI

One night when he had been doing a lot of drinking and felt dizzied by the smell of stale tobacco left by his friends, Marcial had the strange sensation that all the clocks in the house were striking five, then half-past four, then half-past three. It was like a distant recognition of other possibilities. Just as one imagines oneself during the lassitude of a sleepless night able to walk on the smooth ceiling among furniture placed amidst the roof-beams and with the floor as a smooth ceiling above. It was a fleeting impression that left not the slightest trace in his mind which was now little inclined to meditation.

And there was a big party in the music-room on the day when he reached his minority. He was happy when he thought that his signature no longer had any legal value and that the moth-eaten registers and the notaries were erased from his world. He was reaching the stage where law courts were no longer to be feared by those whose persons were not held in any regard by the law codes. After getting tipsy on full-bodied wines, the young men took down from the wall a guitar encrusted with mother-of-pearl, a psaltery and a trombone. Someone wound up the clock which played the Tyrolean Cow Song and the Ballad of the Scottish Lakes. Another blew on the hunting horn that had lain coiled in its copper case upon the scarlet felt of a show-case alongside the transverse flute brought from Aránjuez. Marcial who was boldly courting the Campoflorido girl joined in the din and picked out the tune of Trípili-Trápala on the bass notes of the keyboard. Then they all went up into the attic, suddenly remembering that there, under the beams which were once again covered with plaster, were hoarded the dresses and liveries of the

House of Capellanías. Along shelves frosted with camphor lay court-gowns, an Ambassador's sword, several braided military jackets, the cloak of a Prince of the Church, and long dress-coats with damask buttons and with damp marks in the folds. The shadows were tinted with amaranth ribbons, yellow crinolines, faded tunics, and velvet flowers. A thinker's costume with a tasselled hair-net made for a Carnival masquerade won applause. The Campoflorido rounded her shoulders underneath a shawl which was the colour of creole flesh and which had been used by a certain grandmother on a night of momentous family decision, in order to receive the waning fires of a rich treasurer of the Order of St Clare.

The young people returned to the music-room in fancy dress. Wearing an alderman's tricorne hat on his head, Marcial struck the floor three times with his stick, and started off the waltz which the mothers found terribly improper for young ladies with that clasping around the waist and the man's hand touching the whalebone supports of their corsets which they had all made from the latest pattern in the 'Garden of Fashion'. The doors were obscured by maidservants, stable-boys, servants who came from their far-off outbuildings and from stifling basements to marvel at such a riotous party. Later, they played blind man's buff and hide-and-seek. Marcial hid with the Campoflorido girl behind the Chinese screen and imprinted a kiss on her neck and in return received a perfumed handkerchief whose Brussels lace still held the soft warmth from her décolleté. And when, in the twilight, the girls went off to the watchtowers and fortresses which were silhouetted grey-black against the sea, the young men left for the Dance Hall where mulatto girls with huge bracelets swayed so gracefully without ever losing their little high-heeled shoes however agitated the dance. And from behind a neighbouring wall in a yard full of pomegranate trees the men of the Cabildo Arará Tres Ojos band beat out a drum roll just as if it were carnival time. Standing on tables and stools, Marcial and his friends applauded the grace of a Negress with greyish kinky hair who was beautiful, almost desirable again when she looked over her shoulder and danced with a proud gesture of defiance.

VII

The visits of Don Abundio, the family notary and executor, grew more frequent. He sat down gravely at the head of Marcial's bed, letting his stick of acana wood fall to the floor in order to wake him up before time.

When he opened his eyes, they met an alpaca coat covered with dandruff, a coat whose shining sleeves gathered up titles and rents. There was finally only a small allowance left, one designed to put a check on any folly. It was then that Marcial resolved to enter the Royal Seminary of San Carlos.

After passing his examinations indifferently, he began to frequent the cloisters where he understood less and less of the teachers' explanations. The world of ideas was slowly becoming empty. What had first been a universal assembly of togas, doublets, ruffs and wigs, debaters and sophists took on the immobility of a waxworks museum. Marcial was now content with the scholastic exposition of system and accepted as true what was said in the text book. Over the copper engravings of Natural History were inscribed Lion, Ostrich, Whale, Jaguar. In the same way, Aristotle, Saint Thomas, Bacon, and Descartes headed the black pages on which boring catalogues of interpretations of the universe appeared in the margins of the lengthy chapters. Little by little, Marcial left off studying them and found that a great weight was lifted from him. His mind became light and happy when he accepted only an instinctive knowledge of things. Why think of the prism when the clear winter light gave added detail to the fortress of the door? An apple falling from the tree was only an incitement to the teeth. A foot in a bathtub was only a foot in a bathtub. The day on which he left the Seminary, he forgot his books. The gnomon recovered its fairy character; the spectrum became synonymous with the word spectre; the octander was an armour-plated insect with spines on its back.

Several times, he had walked quickly with an anxious heart to visit women who whispered behind blue doors at the foot of the battlements. The memory of one of them who wore embroidered shoes and basil leaves over her ear pursued him like a toothache on hot afternoons. But one day, the anger and threats of his confessor made him weep with fear. He fell for the last time between the sheets of hell and renounced forever his wanderings along quiet streets, and his last-minute cowardice which made him return home angrily after turning his back on a certain cracked pavement (the sign, when he was walking with his eyes lowered, of the half-turn he must make in order to enter the perfumed threshold).

Now he was living his religious crisis, full of amulets, paschal lambs and china doves, Virgins in sky-blue cloaks, angels with swan's wings, the Ass, the Ox, and a terrible Saint Dionysius who appeared to him in dreams with a big hollow between his shoulders and the hesitant walk of one who seeks for something he has lost. He stumbled against the bed and Marcial awoke in fear, grasping the rosary of muffled beads. The wicks in their oil vessels gave a sad light to the images which were recovering their pristine colours.

VIII

The furniture grew. It became more and more difficult to keep his arms on the edge of the dining-room table. The cupboards with carved cornices became wider at the front. Stretching their bodies, the Moors on the staircase brought their torches up to the balustrades of the landing. The armchairs were deeper and the rocking chairs tended to go over backwards. He no longer needed to bend his legs when he lay down at the bottom of the bathtub which had marble rings.

One morning, whilst reading a licentious book, Marcial suddenly felt like playing with the lead soldiers which lay in their wooden boxes. He hid the book again under the washbasin and opened a drawer covered with spiders' webs. The study table was too small to fit so many persons. For this reason, Marcial sat on the floor. He placed the grenadiers in lines of eight, then the officers on horseback, clustered round the standard-bearer and behind, the artillery with their cannons, gunwads, and matchstaffs. Bringing up the rear came fifes and kettledrums and an escort of drummers. The mortars were provided with a spring which enabled them to shoot glass marbles from a yard away.

Bang! Bang! Bang!

Horses fell, standard-bearers fell, drums fell. He had to be called three times by the Negro Eligio before he made up his mind to wash his hands and go down to the dining-room.

From then on, Marcial retained the habit of sitting on the tile floor. When he realized the advantages, he was surprised at not having thought of it before. Grown-ups with their addiction to velvet cushions sweat too much. Some smell of notary—like Don Abundio—because they know nothing of the coolness of marble (whatever the temperature) when one is lying full-length on the floor. It is only from the floor that all the angles and perspectives of a room can be appreciated. There are beauties of wood, mysterious insect paths, shadowy corners which are unknown from a man's height. When it rained, Marcial hid under the clavichord. Each roll of thunder made the box tremble and all the notes sang. From the sky fell thunderbolts which created a cavern full of improvisations—the sounds of an organ, of a pine grove in the wind, of a cricket's mandoline.

IX

That morning, they shut him in his room. He heard murmurs all over the house and the lunch they served him was too succulent for a weekday. There were six cakes from the confectioner's shop on the Alameda when only two could be eaten on Sundays after mass. He amused himself by looking at the travel engravings until the rising buzz which came from under the doors caused him to peep out between the Venetian blinds. Men dressed in black were arriving, carrying a box with bronze handles. He felt like crying but at that moment, Melchor the coachman appeared, displaying a toothy smile over his squeaky boots. They began to play chess. Melchor was knight. He was King. With the floor-tiles as the board, he could advance one at a time whilst Melchor had to jump one to the front and two sideways or vice versa. The game went on until nightfall when the Chamber of Commerce's Fire Brigade went past.

When he got up, he went to kiss the hand of his father who lay on his sick-bed. The Marquis was feeling better and spoke to his son with his normal looks and phrases. His 'Yes, father' and 'No, father' were fitted in between each bead in the rosary of questions like the responses of the acolyte in mass. Marcial respected the Marquis but for reasons which nobody would have guessed. He respected him because of his great height and because he appeared on ball nights with decorations sparkling across his breast; because he envied his sabre and his militia officer's epaulets, because at Christmas he had eaten a whole turkey stuffed with almonds and raisins to win a bet; because, on one occasion, perhaps because he wanted to beat her, he seized one of the mulatto girls who was sweeping in the rotunda and carried her in his arms to his room. Hidden behind a curtain, Marcial saw her emerge a short time later weeping and with her dress unbuttoned, and he was glad she had been punished because she was the one who always emptied the jam-pots that were returned to the larder.

His father was a terrible, magnanimous being whom he ought to love first after God. Marcial felt that he was more God than God because his gifts were daily and tangible. But he preferred the God of heaven because he interfered with him less.

X

When the furniture grew taller and Marcial knew better than anyone else what there was underneath beds, cupboards, and escritoires, he had a big secret; life held no charm away from Melchor, the coachman. Neither God nor his father, nor the gilded bishop in the Corpus processions were as important as Melchor.

Melchor came from far away. He was the grandson of conquered princes. In his kingdom, there were elephants, hippopotamus, tigers, and giraffes. There men did not work in dark rooms full of parchments like Don Abundio. They lived by being cleverer than the animals. One of them had caught a great crocodile in a blue lake by piercing it with a hook concealed in the tightly-packed bodies of twelve roast geese. Melchor knew songs that were easy to learn because the words had no meaning and were repeated a great deal. He stole sweets from the kitchen, got out at night through the stable door, and on one occasion had thrown stones at the police and then had disappeared into the shadows of Amargura street.

On rainy days, his boots were put to dry in front of the kitchen fire. Marcial would have liked to have had feet to fill such boots. The right-hand one was called Calambín. The left-hand one was called Calambán. The man who tamed unbroken horses just by putting his fingers on their lips, this lord of velvet and spurs who wore such tall top hats also knew how cool the marble floor was in summer and hid under the furniture a fruit or cake snatched from the trays which were destined for the big drawing-room. Marcial and Melchor had a secret store full of fruit and almonds which they held in common and called Urí, urí, urá, with understanding laughs. Both of them had explored the house from top to bottom and were the only ones who knew of the existence of a small basement full of Dutch flasks underneath the stables and of twelve dusty butterflies which had just lost their wings in a broken glass box in a disused attic over the maids' rooms.

XI

When Marcial acquired the habit of breaking things, he forgot about Melchor and drew closer to the dogs. There were several of them in the house. There was a big, striped one, a hound with dragging teats, a greyhound who was too old to play with, a woolly dog which the rest chased at certain periods and which the housemaids had to lock up.

Marcial liked Canelo best because he took shoes from out of the bedrooms and dug up the rose-bushes in the garden. He was always black from charcoal or covered with red earth and he used to devour the other dogs' meals, whine without reason, and hide stolen bones by the fountain. Occasionally he would finish off a newly-laid egg after sending the hen flying into the air with a swift levering movement of the muzzle. Everyone would kick Canelo. But Marcial fell ill when they took him away. And the dog returned in triumph, wagging its tail after having been abandoned at the other side of the Charity Hospital and recovered a position in the house which the other dogs with their skill at hunting or their alertness as watchdogs never occupied.

Canelo and Marcial used to pee together. Sometimes, they chose the Persian carpet in the drawing-room and upon the wool pile, they outlined the shapes of clouds which would grow slowly bigger. For this they were given the strap. But the beating did not hurt as much as the grown-ups thought. On the contrary, it was an excellent excuse for setting up a concert of howls and of arousing the sympathy of the neighbours. When the cross-eyed woman in the attic called his father a 'savage', Marcial looked at Canelo and laughed with his eyes. They cried a bit more to get a biscuit and all was forgotten. Both of them used to eat earth, roll in the sun, drink from the fish-pond, and look for shade and perfume under the sweet basil. In hours of the greatest heat, the damp paving-stones were crowded. There was a grey goose with a bag hanging between its bow-legs; there was the old hen with a bare behind and the lizard that croaked and shot out a tongue like a pink tie issuing from its throat; there was the juba snake born in a city without females, and the mouse which walled up its hole with the seed of the carey bush. One day they showed Marcial a dog.

'Bow, wow,' he said.

He spoke his own language. He had attained the supreme freedom. He already wanted to reach with his hands things which were out of reach of his hands.

XII

Hunger, thirst, heat, pain, cold. When Marcial had reduced his perception to these essential realities, he renounced light which was now incidental to him. He did not know his name. The baptism with its unpleasant salt was taken away from him and he did not now need smell, hearing, or sight. His hands brushed against pleasing forms. He was a totally sentient and tactile being. The universe entered him through all his pores. Then he closed his eyes which only perceived nebulous giants and penetrated into a warm, damp body full of shadows in which he died. The body, on feeling him wrapped in its own substance, slipped towards life.

But now time sped more rapidly and lessened its last hours. The minutes sounded like the slipping of cards under a gambler's thumb.

The birds returned to the egg in a rush of feathers. The fish coagulated into spawn leaving a snowstorm of scales at the bottom of the tank. The palms folded their fronds and disappeared into the earth like closed fans. Stalks sucked in the leaves and the ground drew in all that belonged to it. Thunder resounded in the corridors. Hair grew on the suède of gloves. Woollen shawls lost their dye and plumped out the fleece of distant sheep. Cupboards, escritoires, beds, crucifixes, tables, blinds flew into the night seeking their ancient roots in the jungles. Everything which had nails in it crumbled. A brig anchored (heaven knows where) hurriedly took the marble of the floor-tiles and the fountain back to Italy. The collection of arms, ironwork, the keys, copper-pans, horse-bits from the stables melted, swelling the river of metal which was channelled along roofless galleries into the earth. All was metamorphosed and went back to its primitive condition. The clay became clay again leaving a desert in place of a house.

XIII

When the workmen came at daybreak to continue the demolition, they found their work finished. Someone had taken away the statue of Ceres which had been sold the day before to an antique-dealer. After lodging a complaint with the Union, the men went and sat on the benches of the city park. Then one of them recalled the very vague story of a Marchioness of Capellanías who had been drowned one May afternoon among the lilies of the Almendares. But nobody paid any attention to the tale, because the sun was travelling from East to West and the hours which grow on the right-hand of clocks must become longer out of laziness since they are those which lead most surely to death.

Red Dirt Don't Wash

He stood awkwardly, shifting his weight from one foot to the other, looking through the open pantry window with the dancing eyes of a boy about to receive a treat of good things. But it wasn't the jam tarts that the maid, Miranda, was taking hot from the oven and putting in a dish that held his gaze, rapt. It was Miranda herself, flicking her fingers smartly and putting them to her mouth as the hot baking tin burnt them.

Her trim figure in her blue uniform, chic, neat-fitting, made his eyes swim in his head. It was as though whenever she was in sight he couldn't take his eyes off her. She ravished his senses. And simple country yokel that he was he didn't know how to set about making a girl like Miranda. For Miranda was city-bred, and house-broke, and all the things that he wasn't. She had training. She had refinement, culture. She knew how to lay a table all by herself. Things like that. She knew all the tableware, all the silver, by name. She could tell them over to you, without even stumbling once. He had often helped her polish them, so he knew.

She knew which was a cake fork from a fish fork. She knew a cake server from a cheese server. She knew a tea plate from a breakfast plate, and which one of the shiny mugs was a coffee percolator, and which was for hot water, and which for cream. There wasn't anything she didn't know.

And she had let him help her after his work in the garden was over. She had let him stand near as near to her over the kitchen sink and wash dishes . . . and feel the presence of her, the delicious, maddening nearness of her go through him like sharp knives, like red hot needles. He could get the smell of her in his nostrils, standing that near to her; like you get the smell of a ripe fruit in your nostrils when you bite it! She smelt like a lady. Just like any lady. He wondered what it was that gave her that delicious, wonderful, ravishing perfume to her body; and so he had been tempted to stand on tiptoe outside the crack in the window of her room, where the gummed paper just didn't cover it quite, and take a good long look at her . . . one day after she had come out from the servants' shower bath. What he had seen had devastated him. He had come away feeling dizzy, faint; as though something was happening inside him, in his stomach.

He had seen all her loveliness in the nude. For one devastating instant he had held within his dull, unimaginative eye, all her loveliness that was without blemish; and his heart was like a leaping fish held in the hand.

But he knew now what it was that gave her body that delicious smell, that mounted to his nostrils like incense, and held his senses within a hazy sort of swoon, and gave him that dry feeling in his throat, and that queer feeling in his stomach. It was powder!

She took powder from a large red tin and dusted it all over her body. Not just dabbing it on her face alone, like other girls did, but all over her body!

Such luxury! Such expensiveness! It made his head reel.

Made him aware of his own grossness, his own inferiority, his own lack of polish and refinement. Made him aware of his own soiled and patched clothes, and his own large bare feet, his own rough red skin, which seemed as though the red dirt of his native Clarendon hills had come there to stay, and couldn't ever wash off.

When his work was done in the garden, when he had washed down the car, and rubbed it down with a chamois cloth until it shone, she would let him carry the pan in which she washed napkins and doilies and table-runners and handkerchiefs, and small things like that (for you must understand that Miranda was no ordinary servant, but a lady's maid. She was not a cook, though she made delicious pastries. Not a washer-woman, although she was entrusted with the washing of doilies and the table-runners and the cushion covers and the table napkins and the handkerchiefs and the silk stockings, and dainty things like that). She would let him carry the pan with its heaping foam of white suds from the sink under the standpipe in the backyard to the deal table on the back verandah; and he would just stand and watch her, her arms up to the elbows in suds. Now and then she would look up from her work and smile at him, and he grinned back at her all the time.

He learnt a lot from just standing around talking and joking with her; and helping her through her pantry chores sometimes.

He told her about the place he came from. All about his people up in the mountains. And the ways in which their ways were different from the ways of the people who lived in towns. And she laughed a lot. She was a great one for laughing.

'They are simple, jealous folk, but really the kindest people in the world. We understand each other. We know what makes a man or a woman happy, and what makes them mad. All the people in my district get along together like one big family.'

'My! And I suppose all the girls and the men work together in the fields? Don't tell me that! Really?'

'It just come natural for everybody to pitch in and do whatever work there is to be done—whether in the fields, or about the yard, or in the house—it's all the same. But mostly the men do the heavier work. And women in the family way don't do any but the slightest things.'

'You don't say!' She squealed with laughter.

'They say,' she remarked, twinkling up at him, provocatively, 'that all the people are red—like you. Is that true?'

He just grinned back at her for answer.

'Even the dirt is red. All red dirt. They say the people's skins take its colour from the dirt, if they live there long enough—all their lives, I suppose.' She frowned a little, flicking soapsuds from her forearms and hands. 'They say the red dirt gets on them, and even *inside* them, under their skins, and just stays there.

She looked at him quizzically.

'Don't know 'bout that. I 'spects it's so! Never give it no thought before.'

'It's true. For no matter where you meet a mountain man you can always know him. I guess it must be true—that red dirt don't wash.'

Once or twice she let him walk home with her, where she stayed with her cousin who was another kind of maid—an office maid—because she got along better with gentlemen, they said.

But always she led him through back lanes, and down through a dry gully course, and always she parted with him at a certain spot some little way from the house. And he never questioned her. He never thought to question anything she did.

He knew this girl was right—just right in everything she did or said. Almost a lady. Much too good for him, just a country boy. Big and clumsy and awkward and halting in speech and gestures. Almost a living carica-ture of a country boy, he was so bad. But he knew also that he wanted her, even though she was miles too good for him. And at first it didn't trouble him at all, the thought of wanting her so badly. But after a bit it got to haunting him at nights. Days and nights, so that he got no rest from the thought of her that was sweet torture to him.

He would lie in his bed and remember every sprightly word and vivid gesture of hers. How she looked at him, looking up sideways, like a little bird, and laughing in his face. Well, a girl didn't look at a fellow like that unless she—she kind of liked him. A bit.

He remembered how she put out her hand once and touched his arm—and grabbed hard hold of his arm around the bicep muscles and said 'My!', admiringly. Meaning how hard and strong he was. He remembered how she let a clothes-pin fall down his back once, and laughing that squealing laugh of hers, ran her hand down after it, and fetched it up slowly from way down at his waist—skylarking—while he just sat still and let her do what she would with him. He remembered all that; and it was as though things were going on inside him all the time, in his blood, secretly.

Once or twice he saw her walking out with nice looking young men—chauffeurs, and such. He envied them. Not alone because she was walking out with them, but because of something they had that he lacked. A poise, a certain assurance that was almost swagger. Shoes on their feet. The way they wore their clothes.

He had never worn shoes in his life, but once. Once, when he was about seventeen, his Gran'pa had bought him a pair of yellow boots to wear Sundays. They were grand boots. They must have cost a pile of money. He wore them once to church. And that was enough. His feet inside boots didn't feel like his at all. He lost possession of them, and they behaved as though they knew it.

He let them go cheap to a boy he knew from the neighbouring district, about his size. The other fellow got a real bargain. They were grand boots. But he didn't care. He bought him a goat with the money. Now there were six goats the last time he heard from home, and more coming along. He didn't care about the boots. Boots wore out and got old so you had to throw them away. But a goat gave you more and more goats. He liked goats. Now there was something he knew about.

One evening as he walked home with her—they were halfway through the dry gully course when he made bold enough to carry out the desperate scheme he had been turning over slowly, methodically in his mind all along—he suddenly blurted out:

'I seen you walking out with fellows.'

She looked up at him quickly.

Her eyes, he noticed, were bright like stars, her lips slightly parted, as though she were panting from walking too fast; but they had been coming along slowly, saying nothing, mostly; their bodies just touching, or almost touching, in the dark.

He said, stopping suddenly and looking down at her face.

'I would like for you to come out with me, once in a while. Eh?'

'How? Where?'

'Movies?' It was a bold gesture. He had never been to a movie in his life . . . now he was asking this girl to go with him. Just like that.

Unconsciously he was taking on to himself some of the easy swagger of the young men he'd seen Miranda with.

He said, coming closer to her, 'What say we go to a movie Sat'day night? You'n me. Eh?'

She looked up at his face . . . and away . . . and down at his feet.

Suddenly, unexpectedly, she burst out laughing. She just fell on the bank and squealed with laughter. She *was* a one for laughing!

But it did something to him. For one thing it made him lose all his recently acquired swagger; for another it made him all of a sudden fiercely resolved within his mind to make her take it all back. To make her look at him as she looked at her natty young men. Plus the special look she gave *him*—that said as plain as anything that she could like him—and more than a bit.

'All right,' he said, in a terrible, calm voice. 'I know I'm not good enough for you. But all the same I love you, see.'

She stopped laughing immediately. She put the back of her hand to her mouth.

'Adrian,' she said. 'I—I'm not laughing—at what you think. I'm just laughing like—oh you don't understand about women, or you would know.'

He was silent for a while, chewing on this. Of course she was right. He didn't understand about women, either. Not her kind. She was miles above him. She would take *some* understanding. Of a sudden he felt great humility, standing before her . . . great humility, and with it a great resolve.

The very next day he put the first part of his resolve into effect. He asked for time off in the afternoon and went to town to one of the big stores where they sold shoes and things.

'How much for the yellow ones in the window?' he asked, after the man at the store had showed him half-a-dozen pairs from the shelves.

'Now there's a pair of shoes for you! Genuine vici kid. You can't do better than that at any price, anywhere. It's marked twenty-five shillings. We sold the lot before this at twenty-seven and six. But I tell you what. Now I'm doing the best I can for you. It isn't like I'd do this for everyone. But I'll put them in for you—special—for twenty-two and elevenpence.

'I'll take them,' said Adrian, without hesitation.

All that money for a pair of shoes. But he didn't mind that a bit. They were genuine vici kid. Goat skin leather, he knew that too. You could buy two goats, let alone the skins, for twenty-two and eleven. But he didn't mind that a bit. She put powder on all over her. He seen it himself. He knew!

Came Saturday night; and to Adrian it seemed none too soon, either.

He put on his best Sunday clothes of blue serge, and his yellow shoes. He looked down at his feet and admired the gleaming shine of them.

He went round by the back of the tennis court from the garage, through the little enclosed vegetable garden, to the back porch, where he knew he would find her, his shoes creaking faintly across the grass. His feet felt as though they were taking him places. This was different to just walking. Just walking you set your feet down, one before the other, without thinking about it. He'd heard about a man walking on a clothes-line wire high above the ground. He'd often thought about it, wondering how it felt. He didn't anymore after that night. He knew.

The family had dined, and had gone out in the car. He knew just where she would be, what doing, and that she would be alone.

When she saw him, she just stood looking at him for a time. Then she suddenly burst out laughing, as though she wouldn't stop.

She said: 'Where you all dressed up going to, Adrian?' Like that.

He said, coming up close to her: 'We're steppin' out.'

'My! Who an' you?'

'You an' me. Remember? You said if I got myself some shoes . . . remember? Well, I got them. They cost a heap of money too. But I don't give it a thought.'

He swelled out his chest. He was almost as big as a barrel around. For a moment she looked at him with slightly troubled eyes. His body looked so strong and fine, beneath all the marks of the country lad on him. The awkwardness. You could see at a glance his flesh was good and strong. Her eyes sort of misted over a bit. For a moment though. And then they dropped to his feet again.

'What's the matter, don't they look all right?'

'Sure. They're swell. They must have cost a pile of money, I bet.'

And she burst out laughing.

At first he didn't understand, and he started laughing too, with his hearty country lad's guffaw. And then he saw her face; saw how she looked at his feet, and looked up and laughed again. And suddenly the laughter died out of him. Leaving him, as it were, standing there foolishly, with his mouth open, staring at her.

She said, curiously enough: 'Don't make me laugh!' gasping.

'But what—why—what's the matter with them?'

'Nothing, big boy. The shoes are fine. But they're not yours, that's all. They don't fit you, see?'

'They's a bit tight. But my feet'll get used to them after a spell.'

'That's where you are wrong. They never will. They'll always look just what they are—a pair of shoes carrying your feet around. All your life you've never worn shoes. You know that's true.'

He nodded.

'You can't educate them feet to shoes, big boy. Not as long as you live. You'll always *feel* as though you were wearing shoes, and you'll *look* just the way you feel. Always. No, it's no good. Better take them off now. Perhaps if you clean the soles a bit they might even take them back from you at the store where you bought them.'

'But I don't want them to take them back. They're mine. You know why I got them,' he said, looking down at them self-consciously. 'It was all for you.'

At that she burst out laughing again.

'Do you think I'm going out with you, in *them*?' she demanded scornfully. It was no use. No use at all thinking about sparing his feelings. He just didn't have sense enough for a child. Nothing short of this could make him understand. It was a pity, but none of her cooking, she was sure.

'I get you,' he said, slowly. 'I'm not good enough for you. Oh I know it. Still, you said if I got myself some shoes, like . . .'

'Don't take it hard, big boy.' She laid a hand on his arm. But for a moment only, then she took it away. 'I tell you what,' she said in a low, husky voice. Perversely the firm, strong, clean touch of his flesh stung her like nettles; went driving with sharp pangs through her, stirring something in her blood. 'Tomorrow night we'll go for a walk. I know a place we can go where nobody'll be around.' A pause. 'That's a promise, now.'

But he remained for a space, looking away, saying nothing. Then he turned slowly, painfully away, with the unaccustomed pain of walking in tight shoes. But he was resolved upon this thing. He was going to walk them in . . . going to walk those darned feet of his in. He'd do it if it broke his heart, if it killed him. After walking about a mile, he came to a lonely spot on the road. He didn't even know where he was, but he didn't care.

He sat down on the side of the road and pulled off his shoes. He took each foot between his hands and chafed it gently, wriggling his toes until they felt like his own again.

She was leading him on, she was. Playing him for a sucker . . . all the time laughing at him, and carrying on with other fellows . . . and laughing at him behind his back.

He felt in his pocket for his clasp knife and opened and tested the blade passing it along the ball of his thumb. There was a cold, still, sullen look in his eyes. Deadly like anger burned down the glowing coals of a still white heat.

What she wanted to make of him a blooming Cinderella for? Just so she could laugh at him.

He lifted his head and stared blankly up at the cold stars. There was nothing there. Beyond them the sombre mountains. They reminded him of his own mountains that seemed so far away, almost unreal—veiled as with a mist—and the mist was in his own eyes—trying to see beyond the St Andrew hills, beyond the stars, horizon; space limitless like that.

He tested the edge of the blade against the ball of his thumb. And it was right. What she want to make of him a blooming Cinderella for?

He took the shoes, one at a time, and cut them into thin strips—all but the soles, which, because of their toughness he just cut anyway.

Back there he belonged, where there was red dirt everywhere, and people didn't go around wearing shoes. Red dirt everywhere, on the tilled land as far as the eyes could see, and on the faces and bare arms and legs of men and women. Good, clean red dirt that he loved, that was the symbol of home to him, and more. Clean, happy faces that he loved, that were all frankness and homeliness. All that went for cleanness and wholeness. It was clean, the red dirt of his land, the place of his birth.

He looked down at the jagged strips of leather in his hand, and his face became wonderfully luminous. He even smiled.

They were good shoes. Genuine vici kid. He paid twenty-two and elevenpence for them at the store.

JUAN BOSCH (b. 1910)

Encarnación Mendoza's Christmas Eve

Translated by John Gilmore

With the keen eye of a fugitive, Encarnación Mendoza had made out the
outline of a tree at twenty paces, which led him to think the night was coming to an end. He was right enough; where he began to go wrong was in
drawing conclusions from this observation. Since daylight was coming,
he had to find somewhere to hide, and he asked himself whether
he should go into the hills on his right or into the canefield on the left.
Unfortunately for him, he chose the canefield. An hour and a half later, the
sun of the 24th December was lighting up the countryside and gently
warming Encarnación Mendoza, who was lying face up, stretched out on
the cane-trash.

At seven in the morning, things seemed to be turning out just as the
fugitive had expected, nobody had passed along the nearby cart-roads.
Besides, there was a cool breeze and perhaps it would rain, like it did most
years at Christmas Eve. Whether it rained or not, the men weren't going
to come out of the shop, where they had been drinking rum from early,
talking at the top of their voices and trying to enjoy themselves like they
were supposed to. He wouldn't have felt as safe if he had headed into the
hills instead. He knew the place well; the families who lived in the valleys
produced firewood, cassava, and corn. If any of the men who lived in the
shacks up there came down that day to sell provisions in the shop at the
batey[1] and happened to see him, he would be done for. For miles around

---

[1] *Batey* is a word of Amerindian origin, which originally meant a ceremonial ball-court.
In the Hispanic Caribbean it has come to mean the area on a large plantation occupied by
living accommodation for workers and shops for their use, as well as the sugar factory and
related buildings. The nearest equivalent in the Anglophone Caribbean would be 'plantation
yard', but this is not quite the same thing as, after the end of slavery, workers in the Eastern
Caribbean islands did not normally live in the immediate vicinity of the mill or factory.

there was no one who would have dared to keep quiet about the encounter. There would never be any forgiveness for someone who sheltered Encarnación Mendoza: and even if he said nothing about it, everyone in the district knew that whoever saw him must report it at once to the nearest guardhouse.

Encarnación Mendoza was beginning to feel nice and comfortable that he had chosen the best place to hide himself in for the day, when fate began to work against him.

For just then, Mundito's mother was thinking the same thing as the runaway, nobody would be going along the cart-roads in the morning, and if Mundito got a move on, he could make the trip to the shop before the usual daytime drunks of Christmas Eve began to wander the roads. Mundito's mother had a few cents which she had been keeping out of the little she earned washing clothes and selling fowls at the crossroads which lay half a day's walk to the west. With these same cents she could send Mundito to the shop to buy flour, salt-fish, and a little butter. She wanted to celebrate Christmas Eve with her six little children, however poorly, even if it just meant eating a few fish-cakes.

The village where they lived—beside the hills, on the road that divided the canefields from the uncultivated lands—might have had fourteen or fifteen poor dwellings, mostly thatched with palm leaves. Coming out of his, entrusted with the task of going to the shop, Mundito stopped for a moment in the middle of the dried mud along which the cane-carts passed in crop-time. The sky was clear, blazing with light all the way to the cane-tops on the horizon; the breeze was pleasant and there was a sweet sadness in the silence. Why go alone, getting bored with walking along cart-roads which were always the same? For all of ten seconds Mundito thought about going into the neighbouring shack, where six weeks before a black bitch had given birth to six puppies. The animal's owners had given away five, but one remained 'to suckle the mother', and on this one Mundito heaped all the affection which was piled up in his love-starved little soul. His nine years burdened with a precocious wisdom, the child knew that if he took the puppy-dog, he would have to carry it most of the time, since it wouldn't be able to make such a journey on its own. Mundito felt his knowing that more or less entitled him to do what he felt like with the little dog. Suddenly, without thinking more about it, he ran to the hovel yelling, 'Doña Ofelia, lend me Blackie, so I can take him along with me!'

Whether they'd heard him or not, he had asked permission, and that was enough. He went in like a whirlwind, snatched up the little brute and ran off at top speed, until he was lost in the distance. And that was how fate began to interfere with Encarnación Mendoza's plans.

For it happened that when, a little before nine, the child Mundito was passing along in front of the cane-piece where the fugitive was hidden, Blackie—whether he was bored, or just stirred by that kind of indifference to what is going on and curiosity about what might happen next which is the privilege of small animals—Blackie went into the canefield. Encarnación Mendoza heard the child's voice ordering the little dog to stop. For a second he was afraid that the boy was the vanguard of a search party. It was broad daylight. Even with his runaway's sharp eyes, he could only see as far as the confusion of stalks and leaves would let him. Over there, as far as his gaze would reach, there was no child. Encarnación Mendoza was no fool. Quickly he decided that if they found him peeking out like that, he was done for; the best thing would be to pretend to be asleep, turning his back to the direction from which he heard the noise. To be on the safe side, he covered his face with his hat.

The little black puppy-dog ran around, playing with the cane-trash, trying to jump, clumsy in its movements. When it saw the fugitive lying stretched out, it began to let out funny little barks. Shouting after it and creeping through the canes, Mundito was getting closer, when suddenly he stopped, paralysed with fright: he had seen the man. But for him it wasn't just a man, but something startling and terrible; it was a corpse. There was no other explanation for its being there at all, much less the way it was lying. He was frozen with terror. At first, he thought of running away, quietly, so the corpse wouldn't notice. But it seemed to him that it would be a crime to leave Blackie abandoned, exposed to the danger that the dead man would be annoyed by his barking, and grab hold of him and squeeze him to death. Unable to go without the little animal, and unable to stay where he was, the child felt he was going to faint. Involuntarily he raised a hand and stared at the deceased, trembling while the doggy backed away, letting out its little barks. Mundito was sure the corpse was going to get up right then. In his fright, he tried to move forward in the direction of the dead man: he took a jump at the puppy-dog, grabbed it with nervous violence by the neck, and at once, bumping into the canes which cut his face and hands, driven by terror, suffocating, he ran away towards the village. Getting there, on the point of fainting from exhaustion and fright, he called out, waving in the direction of the far-off place of his adventure, 'There's a dead man on the Adela Plantation!'

A harsh deep voice answered, shouting, 'What that boy saying?'

And since it was the voice of Sergeant Rey, chief of the guardhouse at the Central Factory, it got the greatest possible attention from those present, as did the information he demanded from the boy.

The day before Christmas one couldn't expect the judge from La Romana to do anything about having the corpse removed, since he'd be on his way to the capital for his end-of-year vacation. But the sergeant was on the ball; fifteen minutes after having heard what Mundito had to say, Sergeant Rey was on his way with two of his men and ten or twelve curiosity-seekers to where the alleged corpse was lying. This had not entered into Encarnación Mendoza's plans.

Encarnación Mendoza's intention was to spend Christmas Eve with his wife and children. Hiding by day and travelling by night, he had covered miles and miles, all the way from the first spurs of the Cordillera, in the province of Seybo, shunning all human contact and avoiding shacks, farms, and places where trees had been cut or the earth burnt. The whole region knew he had killed Corporal Pomares and nobody was unaware that he was a condemned man wherever he was found. He couldn't allow himself to be seen by anybody except Nina and his children. And he would see them only for an hour or two, on Christmas Eve. He had already been on the run for six months, because it had been on St John's Day that those things had happened which had cost Corporal Pomares his life.

Of course he had to see his wife and children. It was an animal impulse which drove him on, a blind force he couldn't resist. In spite of that, and being so free of regrets, Encarnación Mendoza understood that with the urge to embrace his wife and tell the children a story, there was mixed a hint of jealousy. But besides, he had to see the hovel, the light of the lamp lighting up the room where they were reunited when he came back from work and the children crowded round him so he could make them laugh with his stories. His whole being demanded he see the dirty track which turned into mud when it rained. He had to go, or the terrible yearning would kill him.

Encarnación Mendoza was accustomed to doing whatever he wanted; he never wanted anything bad, and he had self-respect. It was because of self-respect that what had happened on St John's Day had happened, when Corporal Pomares had insulted him by hitting him in the face. Him, who hadn't been drinking so as not to cause any trouble, and whose only concern was his family. No matter what, even if the Devil himself got in his way, Encarnación Mendoza would be spending Christmas Eve in his own shack. Just imagining how Nina and the children would be sad, without a peso with which to celebrate the festival, perhaps crying for him, broke his heart and made him curse with sorrow.

But his plans had got fouled up. It was important to think whether the boy would have talked or kept quiet. Encarnación could tell he had run away from the speed of his footsteps, and perhaps he had thought it was just some field-hand asleep. It might be wise to move away from there, go into another cane-piece. However, it was worth thinking twice about it, because if somebody chanced to be going or coming along the cart-road and saw him crossing the road and recognized him, he would be done for. He mustn't rush things, he was safe there for now. At nine o'clock at night he could leave, going cautiously along the edge of the hills, and he would be home by eleven, perhaps quarter past eleven. He knew what he was going to do; he would call softly at the window of the room and tell Nina to open up, that it was him, her husband. Already he could imagine coming to Nina, with her black hair falling over her cheeks, her eyes dark and shining, her full lips, her upturned face . . . That moment of getting home was his reason for living, he couldn't risk being caught first. It would be risky to change from one field to another in broad daylight; the best thing to do would be to rest, to sleep . . .

He woke up to the rush of footsteps and the child's voice saying 'He did be there, sergeant.'

'But in which field—this one here or the one over there?'

'In that one,' the child assured him.

'In that one' might mean that the boy was pointing to the one Encarnación was in, one next to it, or the one opposite. Because to judge from their voices, the child and the sergeant were standing in the cart-road, perhaps at a point midway between several cane-fields. It depended on where the child was pointing to when he said 'that one'. The situation was really serious, because what there could be no question about was that right now there were people tracking down the runaway. So it was no time to be asking questions, it was time to act. Making up his mind quickly, Encarnación Mendoza began to creep away with the utmost caution, taking care that whatever noise he made could be confused with the sound of the cane-blades rustling in the breeze. He had to get out of there right away, without a moment to lose. He heard the sergeant's harsh voice:

'Go long over there, Nemesio, while I go through here. You! Solito—you stop here!'

He could hear whispers and remarks. While he was moving off stealthily, crouched down, Encarnación could gather that there were several men in the group which was looking for him. There was no question but that things were beginning to look ugly.

Ugly for him and ugly for the boy, whoever he was. Because when Sergeant Rey and Private Nemesio Arroyo had been through the cane piece they'd gone into, trampling the young shoots and cutting their hands and arms on the blades, and didn't see any corpse, they would begin to think the story about the dead man on the Adela Plantation was just a prank.

'You sure it was here, boy?' asked the sergeant.

'Yes, he was here,' Mundito insisted, frightened enough already.

'The boy making sport, sergeant, nobody there,' chipped in Private Arroyo.

The sergeant transfixed the child with a chilling stare which filled him with terror.

'Look, I did be coming along here with Blackie,' Mundito began to explain, 'and I put he to run along so'—he put the little dog on the ground as he spoke—'and he go 'long and go through there.'

But Private Solito Ruiz interrupted Mundito's dramatization, asking 'What the dead man look like?'

'I din't see he face,' the boy said, trembling with fear. 'I only see he clothes. He got a hat over he face. He stop so, pon he side . . .'

'What colour pants?' the sergeant asked.

'Blue, and the shirt like it yellow, and he got a black hat pon top he face . . .'

But poor Mundito could scarcely talk; he stood there terrified, wanting to cry. To his childish way of thinking, the dead man must have gone off by himself to take revenge for being reported, and to make him look like a liar. Surely he was going to appear to him at home at night and haunt him for the rest of his life.

Anyway, whether Mundito knew it or not, they weren't going to find the corpse in that cane-piece. Encarnación Mendoza had crossed over with astonishing swiftness to another field, and then to yet another, and he was already crossing the cart-road to go into a third when the child, sent packing by the sergeant, came running along with the puppy-dog under his arm. Fear brought him up short when he caught sight of the torso and one leg of the deceased disappearing into the canefield. It couldn't be anybody else, since the clothes were the same he had seen that morning.

'Look he there, sergeant, look he there!' he called out, indicating the place where the runaway had disappeared. 'Inside there!'

And since he was very frightened he carried on running home, ready to pass out and full of pity for himself because of the trouble he'd got himself into. The sergeant, and the soldiers and the curiosity-seekers who were with him, were going back when they heard the boychild's voice.

'The boy making sport,' said Nemesio Arroyo calmly.

But the sergeant, who'd been in his job a long time, was suspicious, 'Look, something there. Lewwe surround this field right now!' he shouted.

And so the hunt began, without the hunters knowing what quarry they were pursuing.

It was a little after mid-morning. They were divided into groups, each soldier followed by three or four field-hands, searching here and there, running along the cart-roads, all of them a bit drunk and all of them excited. Slowly the little dark blue clouds resting on a level with the horizon began to get bigger and climb the sky. Encarnación Mendoza knew already that he was more or less encircled. Except that, unlike his pursuers—who didn't know who they were looking for—he thought that the searching of the cane-piece was in order to arrest him and make him pay for what had happened on St John's Day.

Without knowing for sure where the soldiers were, the fugitive obeyed his instinct and his wish to escape; and he was running from one cane-piece to another, avoiding the soldiers. He was already so far away from them that if he had stayed quiet he could have waited until dusk without danger of being tracked down. But he didn't feel safe and kept on moving from field to field. While crossing a cart-road he was seen from a distance, and someone called out at the top of his voice:

'He going long there, sergeant! And it look like Encarnación Mendoza!'

Encarnación Mendoza! Everyone froze at once. Encarnación Mendoza!

'Come along!' shouted the sergeant, who immediately began to run, revolver in hand, towards where the field-hand who had seen the runaway was signalling.

It was already getting on for noon, and the growing piles of clouds were making the atmosphere hot and suffocating, but the man-hunters hardly noticed. They were running and running, yelling, zig-zagging, firing into the canes. Encarnación let himself be seen for just a moment on a distant cart-road, running as fast as a fleeing shadow, and he didn't give Private Solito Ruiz time to aim his gun.

The sergeant shouted an order: 'Someone go to the *batey* and tell them from me, to send me two mo' men!'

Nervous, excited, breathing heavily, trying to look in all directions at once, the pursuers ran about yelling at each other and advising caution whenever anyone showed signs of actually going into the canes. Noon came and went. Not two, but three soldiers and nine or ten more field-hands arrived. They scattered in groups and the hunt spread out over several cane-pieces. In the distance a soldier and four or five field-hands were seen to pass without warning, something which slowed down their movements, because it was risky to fire if your own people were in the way. Men were coming out from the *batey*, and even some of the women. Only the helper was left in the rum-shop, busy asking every blessed person who went by if 'they catch him yet'.

Encarnación Mendoza was not an easy man. But at three o'clock, as he was on the road which divided the canefields from the hills, crossing to go into the scrub—that is to say, more than two hours' distance from the *batey*, a well-aimed shot broke his spine. He was rolling about on the ground, running with blood, when he took four more shots, for the soldiers kept on firing as they surrounded him. And just then the first drops of the rain which had looked as though it was coming since mid-morning began to fall.

Encarnación Mendoza was dead. His features were still there, even though his teeth had been destroyed by a Mauser bullet. It was the day before Christmas and he had left the Cordillera in order to spend Christmas Eve at home, not in the *batey*, alive or dead. It was beginning to rain, if not very hard for the moment. And the sergeant was thinking of something else. If he took the corpse to the highway which lay towards the west, he could carry it that same day to Macorís and give it to the captain as a Christmas present. If he took it to the *batey*, he would have to get a train from the sugar factory to go to La Romana, and since it might be a long time before the train left, he would arrive in the city late at night, perhaps too late to change for Macorís. On the highway things were different; vehicles went by often, he could stop a car, make the people get out and put the corpse in, or put it on top of the load some truck was carrying.

'Go look for a horse right now an' lewwe take this vagabond to the highway!' he ordered whoever was standing closest.

It wasn't a horse that appeared but a donkey, and that was at gone four o'clock, when the downpour was sounding heavily and without stopping on the young canes. The sergeant didn't want to lose any time. Several field-hands, getting in each other's way, put the corpse across the ass's back and tied it on as best they could. Followed by two soldiers and three of the curious whom he had picked to urge the donkey along, the sergeant ordered them to set off in the rain.

It did not prove an easy journey. Three times, before they got to the first village, the dead man slipped and ended up under the ass's stomach. The animal was snorting and making efforts to trot through the mud which was already beginning to form. At first covered only by their regulation hats, the soldiers grabbed pieces of palm, big leaves snatched from the trees, or sheltered themselves in the canefield from time to time, whenever the rain got worse. The mournful procession walked on without stopping, most of the time in silence, though from time to time the voice of one of the soldiers would comment, 'Look at that wretch', or simply refer to Corporal Pomares, whose blood had been avenged at last.

It got completely dark, definitely earlier than usual as a result of the rain, and with the darkness the journey became more difficult, and so the procession slowed down. It must have been after seven, and it was scarcely raining any more, when one of the field-hands said, 'There's a bit of light over there.'

'Yes, in the village,' the sergeant explained, and right then he thought up a plan which gave him enormous satisfaction.

For the death of Encarnación Mendoza wasn't enough for the sergeant. The sergeant wanted something more. And so, when another quarter of an hour found him in front of the first hovel they came to in the district, he ordered in his rough voice, 'Untie that dead fellow and throw him inside there—we can't carry on getting wet.'

He said this when the rain had thinned out so much it looked as though it was about to stop, and as he spoke he was watching the men who were struggling to free the corpse from its ropes. When the body was untied, he knocked on the door of the hovel just in time for the woman who came to open up, to receive, thrown down at her feet like that of a dog, the body of Encarnación Mendoza. The dead man was soaked in water, blood, and mud, and had his teeth destroyed by a bullet, which made his once serene and kindly face look as though it was making a horrible grimace.

The woman looked at that inert mass, and at once her eyes took on the expressionless stare of madness. Raising a hand to her mouth, she began to move back slowly, until after three steps she stopped and rushed forward onto the corpse, stricken with grief and yelling, 'Oh me children! They gone an' left you orphans! They gone an' kill Encarnación!'

Falling over each other with fright, the children ran out of the house and threw themselves at their mother's skirts.

And then came a childish voice mingled with tears and horror: 'Mummy! Mummy! That was the dead man I did see today in the cane-field!'

The Doors Open at Three

Above the sun was a hole in the sky through which midday fell to the earth: the yellow more than yellow of the buildings painted yellow and the burning white of the pavements and the mauve of the asphalt melting into the gutters and the black of the blacks asleep in the thin shade and the fashionable girls dressed in a hue of blue bluer than the china blue apples of their eyes and the sour smell of squashed onions from the armpits of the bright boys (with bright faces full of pimples and scratch marks, clumsy with words and with razors but always bragging of both, with bright shining hair on heads filled with not one single bright idea, bragging also about their *cojones* as they scratched or caressed their groins) drinking Cokes in the nearby cafeterias and the fragrance of the girls of the day rustling their skirts noisily as they walked and the sweet scent in their hair blending with the nearing noises of kissing in the total dark of the night clubs in daytime and the fast furious flight of the swallows and the gabble of the kids playing *pitén* baseball in the parking lots among parked cars, the ball a pentagon made with layers of cardboard cups and the silence of the old people swaying to and fro in old squeaking rocking chairs and the quivering of little old ladies, nice and clean and slightly mad, and the rattle of spoons against false teeth at lunch: the haziness of warm, damp rooms and the indecent inside of urban buses and of underpants hung out in the sun at noon: the unbearable stink of the stockyard and all butcher's shops and of consulting rooms and funeral homes and graves and of all the butchers and all the doctors and all the medical students and of all undertakers and gravediggers: everything cadaverous: death or the killers or those who live off the dead or those who profane the dead by adorning them to look as they never looked alive for burial and maggots and corruption of the flesh or those who habitually move among the dead: Death and those who use or serve it—this I did not feel or sense (because I refused to) but I knew it was in the air as sure as I sensed the movement of the breeze among the *areca* leaves right behind me in the courtyard.

The sound of the wind in the palm trees and the fragrance of fedoras brought back that pervading memory. It came to me on the wind, laced with the diffuse rumours of the city below, and although it was not in the air I could feel its smell palpitating in the cavities of my nose and a bittersweet sting came to my lips while an agreeable pain climbed over the walls of the bone up my nose (as when I used to eat ice-creams all at once, without going up for air, only lifting the enormous spoon from those cold dollops into the warm hole of my face and back again, without stopping to breathe, afraid that the ice-cream might melt or that somebody would come uninvited to ask, Little Boy, can I have some of your delicious: so come-along-eat-it-up-eatitup, without unblocking your nose and without closing your mouth ever, without, in fact, breathing) and the agreeable pain sneaked through the sinuses to move up as far as the tearduct, doctor, and I felt my ears getting as red as a traffic-light on red and my eyes, two too, were hurting in the ravishing afternoon.

That memory in the murmur of the brittle breeze was also in the vicarias and the cosmos and in the smell of salt and sea-spray that came mingled with the evanescent or silent sound of the pines that was like the rumour of the grave cypress and the weeping of the willow that usually grows aslant a brook. But it was in the flight of flocks of pigeons in the still sky occasionally and in the smoothness of warm marble of the bench I was stroking with my fingertips ever so intimately, and even in the taste of salt from the sea that came into my lungs with each gulp of air, I, almost, gasping. It was all in the afternoon but also in myself: in my eyes that beheld all that unnecessary beauty. It was in the life around me struggling to get in, outside, and in the life that was pushing to get out, inside. Death was the referee.

I was still sitting in the swivel-chair, unmoved, as I sharpened my pencil by rubbing it on the sole of my left shoe to doodle a set of flat funny faces on the back of the receipt that was an extreme unction ready already half an hour earlier. Then I rubbed out one more time because true time had stopped. I was bored. Just waiting for the deceased to depart, waiting for the last of the bereaved to leave, so that I could go home, but they wouldn't leave. It wasn't that they didn't want to go, they simply couldn't.

I didn't try, truly, to understand when someone appeared in the doorway near my desk to stretch out his hand and put it out insistently and even turn it around as if handling a loaf in reverse out of the oven but really putting it out in the rain, foolishly but ceremoniously. I looked at him or her as straight as a reproach and he or she walked back quickly and didn't come back again. But all of them had followed the same moronic pattern, one after the other. Or rather almost all of them. The obvious mother had not budged even for a moment and the little girl stayed huddled in a corner, her eyes reddened, her mouth closed. Neither had the old man who wasn't weeping because behind his dark glasses he had no eyes, although he masked his blindness well in the darkness and didn't use a white stick or a seeing-eye dog. He was the only one to go out. Outside he looked at the obviously overcast sky as if he could really see and the rain ran down over his dark glasses and all over his face and over his body. Then he came back all drenched and a woman said to him, 'But Papa.' I wouldn't err if I say she was his daughter.

Inside there was the cloying smell of the flowers and the colours and noises to go with the ceremony of death: wreaths of red and white roses and:

> yellow roses
> dahlias
> hydrangeas
> cannas or *calas*
> amaranths
> gardenias
> petunias
> peonies
> and stacks and stacks of red and white gladioli.

Then there were the whispers and hushed voices, and even gagged laughter and suppressed desire, both whipped up by alcohol from the open bar but checked by respect and remorse. And the sighing and the sobbing and the stifled shouts, the contained wailing and the cries. Outside or rather at the door there was the hugging noise of people trying to get in and being prevented by others already standing in the doorway. Dolorous gatecrashers? Hardly. They were pedestrians trying to flee from the rain and into the chapel. Out there was the noise of splashing wheels and the honking of klaxons and the people running almost as fast as the water amid the anonymous cries and the rubbery splash of fast footsteps. Walking on water like latter-day imitators of Christ in the inclement, intense rain.

Outside the rain was falling as noisily as ever. Inside the women went on crying as in the beginning, though weakly now. The men continued to sing the same dirty ditties about the woman who, half an hour before, had had a bout with numerous, invisible spirits and in a seizure had torn her black blouse and exposed her breasts to the pain rather than to the rain. They grinned and ground as if nobody had covered her up with a black shawl. By now the women had no more gossip to exchange and the men no more jokes to tell and there was no longer a spirit of the wake in them. All of us wanted the definitive affair to come to an end—the men to take a rest from the dead and the women to take a rest from the men and the dead.

But the rainstorm only let up to gather momentum: a tropical rain is just an unending show where the curtain is constantly falling.

The unbearable sweet smell of the flowers (I should not have been able to smell them any more but despite the long lapse they plagued me still) made thicker by late-arriving wreaths, plus the growing stench of a decaying body, what with the delay caused by the rain and the heatwave, bombed my brain to spread its sharp shrapnel all over my face. I closed my eyes for they were covered with—what else?—water and it stuffed itself into my nose, stopping me breathing. I was allergic to wakes. I had to leave! Now! I got up and hurried to the door, leaning against the frame to breathe some fresh air. But the air was so damp that it was not fit to breathe—though at least I could breathe out. I saw how really heavily it was raining. The rain ran now down all the gutters and fell down every wall and gushed down the street, towards the corner, to rush into the manhole and down the drains. Bits of paper and rubbish and even a movie programme paraded in front of the door and yellow rings of orange peel and the skin of a banana were floating in the water, never still but clearer now, transparent even—and so swift that it created whirlpools here and there. It rained all over Havana, all over the world.

I turned to some recent death moves in the chapel but before realizing what was happening, an odd, old feeling that was somehow inspiring shot through me. Piercing not only my mind but my body too. It was agreeably disturbing: a canzonet, a sentiment, a rosy riot now within me but responding to something that occurred outside: it was like lightning made of slow light, a soft bolt. Without knowing what it was (was it the rainstorm being echoed by a brainstorm or had I been struck by a silent thunderbolt?) I stood there rooted to the spot for a few seconds without being able to move. Then, motion restored, I began to look around the room of the dead and I found nothing new. I turned back to the street: I could look across for the first time in the afternoon. Then—I saw her! Clearly defined against the soaked wall, her feet making tiny timid twists in the rain, visibly vexed, there *she* was. She was sheltered by the awful awning of the Radio & Record Shop, closed for the duration, and the never-ending waterfall formed around her a fluid full circle. She became totally motionless and I looked at her but she wasn't looking at me.

The rain thinned out so soon that it was suddenly, as I looked at her, all over. The sky began to clear and then there was light. People were beginning to move about in the street and the pavement was rapidly covered with unwanted newspapers nobody ever read because they were bought to be tailored into instant raincoats. She ventured away from the wall—but inside, damn it, the cries were starting up again. Inevitably she was going to vanish as irretrievably as the deceased. I had to go.

I had to go in to hand over the receipt and I stopped to cover up the coffin and help carry it, *him* to the hearse. Abruptly the people rushed to the door and pushed me back. When I finally managed to come out all the cars, including the hearse, had started up—and she was gone. Gone! Slowly they all went the way of all flesh (and bones too) and now the street was empty. It was then, just then, that I saw her purple dress in the distance. She was walking away fast and in the opposite direction from the mourners. Before going back inside I saw on the wet pavement, a dark mirror, the neon sign that said: EMOH LARENUF. The name of a Russian rabbi no doubt.

Not very far away, down the street or perhaps somewhere around here in some café, a radio or a juke-box (the music had that rainy sound that comes only from a record being played for ever), a septet and a single voice incessantly crooned a balmy *bolero*, slightly heady. Just like the afternoon:

> Remember me
> when the clock strikes three
> and I'll remember you
> when the clock strikes two.

The wind picked up both words and music to carry it away and then I could hear the swaying of the trees like rustling skirts. It all swooned my soul as I held my breath—and before long came back the same sound, the same song:

> When evening starts to fall
> and the sun goes down fast
> the moon will find me moved
> talking of love to last!

The lovely fragrance of the *madreselva*, feminine flower, was everywhere as it began to open now, mingling with the scent of honeysuckle, its silly translation, with the jasmine and the reseda in bloom like dier's rocker. Sparrows, urban chatterboxes, came out of their hiding among the bougainvilleas, scarlet red, to alight on the grass, venturing right to my feet to peck at the crumbs of a few peanuts spilling out of a torn paper cornet. The theme song here should be that rowdy rumba, 'The Peanut Vendor'. But sparrows are not musical birds. Dressed just like her—for a moment I thought it was her!—a girl came walking towards me, closer and closer. But when I almost got up to greet her like my lost lover, a man came from behind, obviously hidden in the hedge, and she hurried forward with arms outstretched: the universal language of love that for me was an unlearned Esperanto. Then he took both her hands in his and they walked off together.

The second time I was at the public library, with Gray in front of me, heavily resting on his anatomy, and she was reading a cheap novel by M. Delly or perhaps by the ubiquitous Tellado or something or other. Who knows what feelings lurk in the heart of women? I lifted my head, what Gray's calls the skull—and my eyes met hers! Two marvellous marbles chatoyant playing with the deep shadow of lashes all around them. I could not read Gray's grey matter any more. I picked up my pencil though and began to sketch her face. When I completed the drawing I passed her the piece of paper that became a message then.

She looked at me with the misgiving of somebody reading an anonymous letter (and so it was, so it was: an anonymous letter of love I wanted, desired it to become eponymous), but as soon as she saw the drawing (I must call it something) she smiled, she *smiled at me*! But she said in the sweetest voice in the Western world:

'You're being too kind. I don't look like that.'

Of course she didn't look like that—nobody looks like *that*!

'That was the best I could do.' That strangled voice was my modest self struggling to get through. 'It's a pale reflection.'

'Thank you,' she said with the second sweetest voice in the whole world. The first sweetest voice was when she spoke for the first time. To me, ladies and gentlemen, to *me*!

I must confess to a passion for chess, second only to my passion for girls. I moved to the seat next to her and we made it look (for the sake of the stern, old, one-eyed librarian everybody in the library called Polyphemus, the ever-vigilant Cyclops) as though we were discussing classes in whispers or (that's me) dissecting a body. Vivisecting rather. But beneath the customary words there was an undercurrent of something deeper than words. For me but even for her too, I believed.

When she got up to return her book (Polyphemus's desk blocking the way out of the book-cavern), I went with her—but not before I carried my heavy volume of forgotten lore to deposit on the desk, with whimsy in the form of a bang. Outside the library there was a splendid sunny evening to greet us. I was looking at her hair, sometimes gold, sometimes yellow, then like beer, then like urine. She was looking at the sandals covering her small and surprisingly perfect feet. It's very difficult, believe me, to find feet out of shoes in a city—and not all of them are fine feet. Women's I mean. Shoes are for men, sandals for women. She walked in sandals like the evening. We walked together for some time, although at the time it seemed to me that we had gone only around the corner.

'It looks as if we're both going the same way,' she said.

'Oh no! I'm not going anywhere. Do you live around here?'

'I'm going to my aunt's, just around the corner,' she said meaning a real corner. 'What about you?'

'I'm working—' My tongue stopped by my feet carried on, my arms trying to become familiar, my body close to hers. Then I looked at her closely and it occurred to me that I had seen her before. Not outside the funeral home but before that, a long time before. But I made no attempt to remember. I went on looking at her features other than her feet. Not tall and perhaps a trifle plump, with hips wide for a girl and round breasts (with a bra on) and that pretty almost perfect face so close to mine now. Only the forehead was too broad, masculine even (as a matter of fact it looked like the balding head of Nietzsche but blond), breaking that oscillating oval and my heart. Her mouth, that was at first part pert, part perfect, turned out to be totally charming and almost shy. (But not her deep voice.) And the small nose and her arms and hands so fine and smooth and gentle: her beautiful body. She was small but so was I.

Already on the staircase, inside the house, when she climbed a step or two, turning to me before going up (though I didn't, know then that she was going down), I said to her:

'You haven't told me your name yet.'

'Virginia.'

'Silvestre, that's me!'

She smiled, I don't know if out of a sense of humour or out of shyness. I drew close not to her but to the banister, gripping the shining wooden rail to leave a dark mark on the polished surface with my hands, wet with sweat. And I asked her:

'When will we see each other again?' I almost added, like a witch, 'in thunder or in rain?' Luckily I didn't add anything.

'I come here every day at the same time.'

'Till then,' I said. 'I mean tomorrow.'

I left without waiting to listen to her goodbye. Timid people always arrive late and leave early. Or vice versa. Be that as it may, I left with my hands in my pockets, juggling my change, all silver and one nickel or two thrown in for good measure. I did not even wait to hear the footsteps of a well-dressed girl going upstairs. Stupid I am.

The next day I went to meet her but I arrived too early (what did I tell you?) and had to wait at the door. Nobody but Chinamen came out. I did not understand how there could be so many people squeezed into a house of only two floors, one of them occupied by a freemason's lodge. (Saw the sign.) Her aunt must have lived on the other floor because I never heard of Chinese masons—a triad perhaps? But when I was about to go, having waited the longest wait, I saw her at the corner, coming towards me though not yet to me—and nothing else mattered any more.

Two pigeons flew over the square holding hands in midflight and a dog passed arm in arm with a cat. Then a rat. It was already some time since the doors and the *damas de noche*, ladies of the night, and the jasmine and the honey*sucker*—

I heard footsteps and when I raised my head I saw a couple walking alone along the main path of the square, going towards the benches under the sick sycamore. Just at that moment a red-painted truck passed by and I looked at their faces (before I had only looked at her feet shoddily shod) and I saw them both blush. But when the truck had gone they were still blushing. I looked at the truck leaving the square and I realized it was a garbage truck painted white.

To my chagrin some clock struck four.

The third time—or rather the fourth, counting the time before the first— I saw her, I was in my uncle's butcher shop and I was embarrassed to be found there by her. So I went out quickly and stood by the lamp-post on the corner making as if I was waiting for the streetcar. But I realized that I was putting my uncle down unfairly and that the same feeling made me hide where I worked from her. I even regretted having told her I was studying medicine—though it was true.

Then we went for a walk and finally, she probably being tired of walking in the same sandals all the time, and I surely waiting to be able to talk with her face, we sat in the square—this stupid square. But when I was about to speak she put one hand over my mouth (I could feel her fragrant fingers on my lips) and she asked me not to say anything yet, because she wanted to look at me, all she wanted was to look at me. No girl, believe me, had said this to me before. So I sat there giving her my best profile. She kept looking at me for some time—and then some. Afterwards, she moved away from me a little or perhaps more than a little to tip back her head, her face turned up to the sky, her eyes closed. She stayed like that, motionless and mum. After a while I thought that she was truly asleep and I bent over her, silently. But before my face reached her, before I could kiss her cheek, she said, almost in a whisper, without opening her eyes: 'Keep still.' That's all she said and she said no more until she got up to go.

'Wait for me,' she said then, meaning perhaps this bench, surely meaning this square more square than my behaviour. 'The doors open at three.'

The squarest thing is that I pretended to understand. Even more, I believed her. That is why I kept waiting for her. But it was already five o'clock and she had not come back. She knew I had to be somewhere else (I didn't say to her that somewhere else was the funeral home) before five and I simply could not afford not to be. 'Three o'clock' she said when she told me to wait. But she had not come. I had to go but I needed to see her badly. For I foresaw that I would be unable to tell her another day what I wanted to tell her today. But she was not coming. The doors had been open for hours and soon they would be closing the square. But she did not come.

I knew she did not even know that I knew she had no aunt in that house nor perhaps even the other side of the walls of the cemetery. She had only made it up so that I should not know where she lived. But I was not unaware that she did not even guess I was aware that she was the daughter of one of the gravediggers and she lived in a wooden shack at one end of the cemetery, beyond the plot where they bury the paupers, those who have no land to be buried in. That is why I sensed I had seen her before even before I saw her in the rain. One day I went to a funeral and then, to get away from the loudest mourners ever, I walked towards the house beyond the wall and among the palpitating pines when a flock of white pigeons flew off. In their shadow I saw her. She was washing her hair under a pine-tree. She didn't see me because she was crying and her tears were rolling down her face and falling in a round wooden washtub to be finally lost in the water she was washing her blond hair in—though her hair looked darker then. But she wore a flimsy blouse that the water made transparent and I could see her breasts, her big boobs, nipples and all. Then I went away.

I went away because a dog was sitting in the doorway and then the suspicious dog stood up and began to growl, even to bark. Besides, the insufferable cries of the female mourners meant that they were lowering the coffin into the grave and I had to get back so as not to miss my ride back to town. I remembered all I saw but I could only really remember her tears.

The sun was a hole in the sky where the afternoon was now on its way out.

The pleasant breeze had slackened and a rough trade wind had already begun to blow, full of the cloying smell of lilies and jasmine and honey-suckle opening up to the evening. The square was empty and I was alone. But I said to myself, you've still got all your ribs.

Nor far away, down the street or even closer in some café, there was a stolid juke-box playing (the music had that time-bent sound that only comes from a record-player), a septet and one vocalist, nasal and unbear-able, tirelessly singing over and over the same stupid song, as pointless as my being there:

> The date is
> when the clock strikes six

And the reedy, sometimes cracked voice went on, dragging out the vowels and distorting the words, the clown:

> The date finally is
> when the clock strikes six

And the wind of madness came my way to make the words louder:

> I have things in my mouth
> that I want to say now

And the March wind of mad dogs and the twanging voice making all unbearable:

> Don't be late please
> when the clock strikes six.

But nothing changed a bit when the wind and the voice and the music and the square stayed behind. Except my life, except my life, except my life.

Actually I went away with the sun. A shrivelled sun that went down behind the flat rooftops. Looking behind I saw the bench: a boy and a girl were sitting on *my* bench very close together, talking, almost without giv-ing words a chance to cross through the space between their faces, as if they could hear each other through the mouth and the lips were ears. Who the hell said that the square is ever closed?

I went on my way. The stink of the slaughterhouses and consulting rooms and holes in the ground, whether they are called graves or tombs, and all the doctors and all the medical students and all the gravediggers and all the undertakers suffocated me, and although I did not want to smell any of it (all I wanted was memory, the fragrance of my memory), it all crawled into my nostrils, forcing me to smell its stench every time I breathed. My shoes were squeaking.

Down the street a man with a long pole in his hands was lighting the lamps one by one. As I watched him I understood. It was then that I realized that I was quite alone, all alone rather, and that I would never see Virginia again. Never again would I feel what I felt when she said to me: 'Wait for me. The doors open at three. I'll be there.' The idea of loneliness horrified me more than loneliness itself. But it was inevitable and I accepted it: I knew because two big tears were clouding my eyes. I could make nothing out but the yellow glare of the yellow lamps lighting the street ahead.

The Cricket Match

The time when the West Indies cricket eleven come to England to show the Englishmen the finer points of the game, Algernon was working in a tyre factory down by Chiswick way, and he lambast them English fellars for so.

'That is the way to play the game,' he tell them, as the series went on and West Indies making some big score and bowling out them English fellars for duck and thing, 'you thought we didn't know how to play the game, eh? That is cricket, lovely cricket.'

And all day he singing a calypso that he make up about the cricket matches that play, ending up by saying that in the world of sport, is to wait until the West Indies report.

Well in truth and in fact, the people in this country believe that everybody who come from the West Indies at least like the game even if they can't play it. But you could take it from me that it have some tests that don't like the game at all, and among them was Algernon. But he see a chance to give the Nordics tone and he get all the gen on the matches and players, and come like an authority in the factory on cricket. In fact, the more they ask him the more convinced Algernon get that perhaps he have the talent of a Walcott in him only waiting for a chance to come out.

They have a portable radio hide away from the foreman and they listening to the score every day. And as the match going on you should hear Algernon: 'Yes, lovely stroke,' and 'That should have been a six,' and so on. Meanwhile, he picking up any round object that near to hand and making demonstration, showing them how Ramadhin does spin the ball.

'I bet you used to play a lot back home,' the English fellars tell him.

'Who, me?' Algernon say. 'Man, cricket is breakfast and dinner where I come from. If you want to learn about the game you must go down there. I don't want to brag,' he say, hanging his head a little, 'but I used to live next door to Ramadhin, and we used to teach one another the fine points.'

But what you think Algernon know about cricket in truth? The most he ever play was in the street, with a bat make from a coconut branch, a dry mango seed for ball, and a pitchoil tin for wicket. And that was when he was a boy, and one day he get lash with the mango seed and since that time he never play again.

But all day long in the factory, he and another West Indian fellar name Roy getting on as if they invent the game, and the more the West Indies eleven score, the more they getting on. At last a Englisher name Charles, who was living in the suburbs, say to Algernon one morning:

'You chaps from the West Indies are really fine cricketers. I was just wondering . . . I play for a side where I live, and the other day I mentioned you and Roy to our captain, and he said why don't you organize an eleven and come down our way one Saturday for a match? Of course,' Charles went on earnestly, 'we don't expect to be good enough for you, but still, it will be fun.'

'Oh,' Algernon say airily, 'I don't know. I uses to play in first-class matches, and most of the boys I know accustom to a real good game with strong opposition. What kind of pitch you have?'

'The pitch is good,' Charles say. 'Real English turf.'

Algernon start to hedge. He scratch his head. He say, 'I don't know. What you think about the idea, Roy?'

Roy decide to hem and leave Algernon to get them out of the mooch. He say, 'I don't know, either. It sound like a good idea, though.'

'See what you can do,' Charles say, 'and let me know this week.'

Afterwards in the canteen having elevenses Roy tell Algernon: 'You see what your big mouth get us into.'

'*My* big mouth!' Algernon say. 'Who it is say he bowl four top bats for duck one after the other in a match in Queen's Park oval in Port of Spain? Who it is say he score two hundred and fifty not out in a match against Jamaica?'

'Well to tell you the truth Algernon,' Roy say, now that they was down to brass tacks, 'I ain't play cricket for a long time. In fact, I don't believe I could still play.'

'Me too, boy,' Algernon say. 'I mean, up here in England you don't get a chance to practise or anything. I must be out of form.'

They sit down there in the canteen cogitating on the problem.

'Anyway,' Roy say, 'it look as if we will have to hustle an eleven somehow. We can't back out of it now.'

'I studying,' Algernon say, scratching his head. 'What about Eric, you think he will play?'

'You could ask him, he might. And what about Williams? And Wilky? And Heads? Those boys should know how to play.'

'Yes, but look at trouble to get them! Wilky working night and he will want to sleep. Heads is a man you can't find when you want. And Williams—I ain't see him for a long time, because he owe me a pound and he don't come my way these days.'

'Still,' Roy say, 'we will have to manage to get a side together. If we back out of this now them English fellars will say we are only talkers. You better wait for me after work this evening, and we will go around by some of the boys and see what we could do.'

That was the Monday, and the Wednesday night about twelve of the boys get together in Algernon room in Kensal Rise, and Algernon boiling water in the kettle and making tea while they discuss the situation.

'Algernon always have big mouth, and at last it land him in trouble.'

'Cricket! I never play in my life!'

'I uses to play a little "pass-out" in my days, but to go and play against a English side! Boy, them fellars like this game, and they could play, too!'

'One time I hit a ball and it went over a fence and break a lady window and . . .'

'All right, all right, ease up on the good old days, the problem is right now. I mean, we have to rally.'

'Yes, and then when we go there everybody get bowl for duck, and when them fellars batting we can't get them out, Not me.'

But in the end, after a lot of blague and argument, they agree that they would go and play.

'What about some practice?' Wilky say anxiously. Wilky was the only fellar who really serious about the game.

'Practice!' Roy say. 'It ain't have time for that. I wonder if I could still hold a bat?' And he get up and pick up a stick Algernon had in the corner and begin to make stance.

'Is not that way to hold a bat, stupid. Is so.'

'And there in Algernon room the boys begin to remember what they could of the game, and Wilky saying he ain't playing unless he is captain, and Eric saying he ain't playing unless he get pads because one time a cork ball nearly break his shinbone, and a fellar name Chips pull a cricket cap from his back pocket and trying it on in front a mirror.

So everything was arranged in a half-hearted sort of way. When the great day come, Algernon had hopes that they might postpone the match, because only eight of the boys turn up, but the English captain say it was a shame for them to return without playing, that he would make his side eight, too.

Well that Saturday on the village green was a historic day. Whether cold feet take the English side because of the licks the West Indies eleven was sharing at Lord's I can't say, but the fact is that they had to bowl first and they only coming down with some nice hop-and-drop that the boys lashing for six and four.

When Algernon turn to bat he walk out like a veteran. He bend down and inspect the pitch closely and shake his head, as if he ain't too satisfied with the condition of it but had to put up with it. He put on gloves, stretch out his hands as if he about to shift a heavy tyre in the factory, and take up the most unorthodox stance them English fellars ever did see. Algernon legs wide apart as if he doing the split and he have the bat already swing over his shoulder although the bowler ain't bowl yet. The umpire making sign to him that he covering the wicket but Algernon do as if he can't see. He make up his mind that he rather go for l.b.w. than for the stumps to fly.

No doubt an ordinary ball thrown with ease would have had him out in two-twos, but as I was saying, it look as if the unusual play of the boys have the Englishers in a quandary, and the bowler come down with a nice hop-and-drop that a baby couldn't miss.

Algernon close his eyes and he make a swipe at the ball, and he swipe so hard that when the bat collide the ball went right out of the field and fall in the road.

Them Englishers never see a stroke like that in their lives. All heads turn up to the sky watching the ball going.

Algernon feel like a king: only thing, when he hit the ball the bat went after it and nearly knock down a English fellar who was fielding silly-mid-on-square-leg.

Well praise the lord, the score was then sixty-nine and one set of rain start to fall and stop the match.

Later on, entertaining the boys in the local pub, the Englishers asking all sort of questions, like why they stand so and so and why they make such and such a stroke, and the boys talking as if cricket so common in the West Indies that the babies born either with a bat or a ball, depending on if it would be a good bowler or batsman.

'That was a wonderful shot,' Charles tell Algernon grudgingly. Charles still had a feeling that the boys was only talkers, but so much controversy raging that he don't know what to say.

'If my bat didn't fly out my hand,' Algernon say, and wave his hand in the air dramatically, as if to say he would have lost the ball in the other county.

'Of course, we still have to see your bowling,' the English captain say. 'Pity about the rain—usual English weather, you know.'

'Bowling!' Algernon echo, feeling as if he is a Walcott and a Valentine roll into one. 'Oh yes, we must come back some time and finish off the match.'

'What about next Saturday?' the captain press, eager to see the boys in action again, not sure if he was dreaming about all them wild swipe and crazy strokes.

'Sure, I'll get the boys together,' Algernon say.

Algernon say that, but it wasn't possible, because none of them wanted to go back after batting, frighten that they won't be able to bowl the Englishers out.

And Charles keep reminding Algernon all the time, but Algernon keep saying how the boys scatter about, some gone Birmingham to live, and others move and gone to work somewhere else, and he can't find them anywhere.

'Never mind,' Algernon tell Charles, 'next cricket season I will get a sharp eleven together and come down your way for another match. Now, if you want me to show you how I make that stroke . . .'

JOHN WICKHAM (b. 1923)

The Light on the Sea

Two elderly women were sitting in the room with their backs to the sea when I stepped through the front door. They were sitting at opposite ends of the room, which was large enough, but looked even larger because it was so sparsely furnished: three or four chairs in dully grey upholstery and a table or two, but no flowers on them and no pictures on the walls. I said, 'Good Morning,' and they looked in my direction, blinking but not speaking. I guessed that they could not make me out with my figure silhouetted against the bright light of the doorway and they must have been a trifle alarmed at my sudden appearance. I stepped further into the room and then they spoke, both of them together and both of them pleasantly, as if they were glad to see me, although they had never seen me before.

I asked whether there was a Mr Farley in the house and they both shook their heads and looked as if they were sorry for my sake that there was no Mr Farley to offer me. Then one of them said that, perhaps if I went downstairs, someone might be able to tell me, because the truth was that they didn't really know the names of all the guests. Both of them brightened up at this and one of them got out of her chair to show me where the staircase was. I told her that she needn't have bothered, but she came with me all the same, anxious to help.

At the bottom of the stairs, an old man, gaunt, bony-faced, with thin white hair, was sitting at a small table which was covered with a check tablecloth frayed at the edges. A small yellow plastic bowl was before him and he was staring at its contents with an expression of disgust amounting to revulsion. With a silver teaspoon, he began to stir an egg yolk which had separated from its accompanying white, and he let the yellow viscous liquid drip off the spoon back into the bowl and emitted a series of heavy, forlorn sighs. He was quite unaware of my presence and paid not the slightest attention to me. Opposite the table, a door opened on a kitchen, and as I pushed my head inside the room, a woman in a blue apron looked up from what she was doing and I asked her whether she had a Mr Farley living there. She wiped her hands in her apron and told me that she would go to let him know that he had a visitor.

The white-haired old man at the table was still sighing and stirring the yellow mess in his bowl while I waited. Another woman, whom I had not seen before, came out of the kitchen and stopped by the old man's table and asked him, solicitously, I thought, whether there was something wrong with his egg. The question irritated him and it was clear that his irritation puzzled the woman. There was nothing wrong with the egg, so far as she could see. And, indeed, from where I stood, the egg, as an egg, seemed perfectly good. But what the woman could not understand was that the old man's disgust had nothing to do with the egg, as an egg.

'Oh, my God,' he half-muttered, half-whispered. 'Look at this.' He rapped the plastic bowl with his spoon and then tilted it as if he would empty it of its yellow contents. 'But look at this, couldn't you ... ?' But words failed him, and with something like a mixture of resolve and resignation, he plunged the spoon into the bowl and raised it to his mouth. But his hand was trembling and the spoon, when it reached his mouth, was empty. And still the woman was watching him, concerned and, it seemed to me, anxious to help, could not understand what was wrong.

Mr Farley came forward to see me. He was wearing a scarlet dressing gown and deep red carpet slippers, and he smiled broadly when I moved out of the light of the doorway and he was able to see me. I had taken some fruit for him, a hand of bananas, a pawpaw and a shaddock, and when he took the bag from me, he smiled even more. He sat in a chair beside the bed and motioned me to make myself comfortable on the bed.

'I am so glad to see you,' he said.

I told him that I had been wondering how he was getting on. I had heard only a few days before that he had gone into the home.

'I am as well as an old man can be,' he said, and grinned broadly.

I had known Mr Farley ever since I was a child; he had taught me in my first class at the elementary school and I was fond of him in a pitying sort of way. He was not a good teacher of small boys: he could not keep them in order and did not really try to, and I used to feel sorry for him when the boys teased him by asking silly questions which he took seriously and to which he always tried to give considered replies. I never understood how he could not see through the questions. He never lost his temper and I used often to be angry with him, because he didn't seem to see how ineffectual he was.

It did not surprise me that Mr Farley never succeeded in his career, never became talked about but always remained a kind of butt, outside the swim of things, a harmless figure of fun. Until one evening, at his invitation, some of us who had already graduated from his class, went to his house to look at his pictures.

He lived near our school in an old house set back from the main road to town and behind what seemed to us a thick forest of trees—breadfruit, sugar apple, hog plum, soursop. The possibilities of such a house and such a forest were enormous to us, and Mr Farley immediately went up in our estimation.

That afternoon we sat around a room full of dark mahogany furniture—what-not, an old sideboard with a lion's head carved on its back panel and an assortment of rocking chairs. An old oil lamp stood on the sideboard. The room smelt of dust and mildew, but it was cosy. Mr Farley gave us lemonade and sweet biscuits, and when we had finished eating, he brought some of his pictures for us to look at: water colours and a few oils and some sketches in ink.

I did not like the sketches and remember thinking that they were childish; the outlines were weak. But the water colours were like Mr Farley himself, muted and shy. Some of them were of the sea, which he made look like an inland lake of quiet dappled water. He took us into a dark cellar under the house where hundreds of canvases were stacked carelessly on the floor around the walls. It was too dark to see them very clearly, but many of them looked as if they consisted only of shapes randomly arranged. In a way, they were frightening, like creatures bred of the dark shadows of the cellar and never seeing the light. I was glad to escape back up the stairs and into the relative brightness of the parlour.

Now, as I sat on his bed, I thought: how like a child he is! He was babbling with excitement at being visited, like a child given a present. I asked him if he remembered the afternoon when a group of us visited him and he showed us his pictures, but he had forgotten. It was too long ago, I suppose. And I asked him if he still painted and what had become of the pictures. Had he sold them?

'Oh,' he said, 'I left them behind at the house when I came here.' He dismissed them as if they were part of something he had discarded and would prefer to forget; there had been so many pictures in the cellar, hundreds of them, and I was tempted to ask him to let me go and look at them. Who could tell? There might be a masterpiece lurking in that gloom, waiting to be discovered. I could not believe that he had left them behind, just like that. I asked him what he planned to do with them.

'Nothing,' he said. 'They weren't any good.' He did not sound regretful but, rather, relieved, as if he had rid himself of a great, unbearable burden at last.

I asked him, 'Did you think when you were young, that you would ever come to a life without painting—a canvas and brushes and paints?'

He answered simply. 'It was always only a hope, never a conviction. But hope sustained until . . .' His voice trailed away as if he no longer remembered the sequence of events.

The bare, poorly-furnished room was without books or pictures, uncurtained, with only a single window through which the morning sunlight poured bright and undiluted, a spare bed across the width of the room in a far corner, no flowers and the ceiling stained brown with water from the floor above. Yet, while I was saddened by the bare and loveless look of the room and the lonely figures of the other members of the household, the two old women in the living room and the gaunt man in the kitchen sighing over his egg as he recalled better days, as I thought about the terrible loneliness to which old age had sentenced them, I had to accept that Mr Farley was cheerful. Perhaps it was because he had never had a family; he had always been lonely and this state was not new to him. He was smiling when he began to speak.

'All those pictures,' he said, 'and, believe me, I never felt as if I had ever finished a single one of them. There was always something to be done to complete every one. So I never had any satisfaction. I would put it aside, meaning to go back and finish it, but I was never able to. Another picture would come to mind and crowd the last effort and failure out, and I never looked at that last one again; I was never able to remember what I wanted to paint.'

'It must have been like a nightmare,' I said, 'or a series of nightmares, never being able to recall the vision that started the picture.'

'Frustration it was, and confusion. That's what it was. I am glad for this peace now.' And he looked around the room, the bare and cheerless room, like a child welcoming an open space where he could run and romp.

'How do you spend your time now?' It was, all of a sudden, important for me to know.

'I look at the sea,' he said, so solemnly that I thought he was making fun of the question. But he wasn't.

'You know,' he said, 'I never knew what light was. All those years behind those trees in that dark house. The light used to trickle through the leaves, only trickle, never flow. Mark you, I used to like it, I didn't complain. I thought the gloom was pleasant. But I never knew what light was.'

'And how did you come to find out, to see the light?' I asked.

'I was lucky. When my sister died, there was no one to look after things;

I had never learned to cook. My friend told me about this place. The moment I saw it, with the light on the sea, I knew that I was not going back to that dark house.'

'So you just upped and left your pictures and the furniture and everything?'

'It was easy and, besides, what was there to wait for? They look after me very well here, the girls are kind and they leave me alone, which is a kindness. Do you understand how being left alone can be a real kindness? And, now, look, you have come to see me. You never came to the old house.'

'Don't you feel lonely here?'

'No, not lonelier than I have always felt. I have never been what you could call gregarious. And I never get tired of looking at the sea.'

He laughed, and I said goodbye and told him that I would come soon to see him again.

'When you came,' he said, 'I was going to have a shower.' He clutched his dressing gown with a dramatic gesture, like Gielgud clutching his toga in Julius Caesar. I never thought that he had such panache in his make-up. As he spoke, he was making his way to the bathroom, and by the time I reached the door and looked back to see what he was doing, he had already put me out of his mind.

When I stepped outside the front door, I found one of the old ladies pulling dry yellow leaves off a hibiscus bush in the untidy garden. She was so intent on what she was doing that she did not even reply when I said goodbye.

The bright Sunday morning glistened and the sea sparkled vast and wide and flat to the horizon.

JAN CAREW (b. 1925)

Tilson Ezekiel Alias Ti-Zek

He'd been drinking all day long with Ramkissoon, a cattle rustler from the Maichony savannahs, and Ram had the smell of fear coming off him like stench from a ramgoat. There was a quality of heaviness about Ram as if he was born with weights on his spirit. He talked heavily and walked heavily and ate and drank heavily. By sundown, when the sky had long streaks of fire and smoke stretching from end to end of the horizon, Ram was drunk and repeating the same story he'd been telling since morning.

'Boy, Ti-Zek, was cat-piss-and-pepper!' Ram's eyes were so red they looked as if he'd pasted hibiscus petals over the eyeballs.

Ti-Zek, reclining on a bed of banana leaves, said derisively, 'All-you too blasted stupid! Three grown men going to thief cattle in broad day-light from Singh ranch? All-you must've had too much bad-rum in all-you damn head. That was suicide, pardner! Don't tell me you didn't know was Buddy ranch! Government call in the guns an' yet Buddy got more guns than you got thirst for drink, and what's more he can use them. That man can hit a twenty-five cent piece at fifty yard.'

'Buddy is a douglah like you, Ti-Zek,' Ram mumbled.

'Whatever kind of blood he got in him is bad blood, an' it mix with poison. That bitch more bad than a snake in the grass.'

'Ti-Zek, tell me something, how come you get that . . . name?'

'If I tell you, you won't believe me.'

'Try me.'

'Why you never ask me this question before? I done know you gone on fifteen years, and now all of a sudden you burst the question over me head.'

'Never wanted to know before.'

'Mi mother wanted me to have a name that nobody else had. So she christen me Tilson Ezekiel.'

'And who cut it down to Ti-Zek?'

'Me self nuh!'

Ram changed the subject, and said reflectively, 'Buddy resemble you, you know, Ti-Zek. Sometimes me can't tell who is who.'

'You jumping from one thing to the other like a grasshopper in a bush fire, Ram. One or two . . . drink in you an' you can't talk sense, no more!' Ti-Zek sucked his teeth contemptuously. 'If I know Buddy, he let you get away an' he shoot them other two Unablers you had with you for sport.'

'When the bullet hit Charlie, he spin like a leaf in the wind. Charlie turn, a leaf spinning in the wind. Charlie boy, rustling was not for you, old man! Should've stick to pragging. Prags, boy, prags! The whole country livin' by prags.' Ram leant his leonine head to one side and rolled his inflamed eyes.

'And how Jag go, Ram?' Ti-Zek asked, although he already knew.

Ram pretended to be too drunk to understand the question. He didn't want to talk about Jag's death or the way he himself had escaped swimming across the Maichony river, while scores of alligators basked on the muddy banks eyeing him malevolently. Scores? Well, perhaps there were only a few, but they looked like scores.

'Jag was an ass,' he muttered. 'A real ass.'

Day cleaned with a suggestion from Ram that they do a job on Boodoo's estate together. And having made the suggestion, alcoholic fumes rose in Ram's brain like incense. He kept thinking in this state of euphoria that he should go to Arjune, the Sadu, for a good luck charm to tide him over his current spell of bad luck but Ti-Zek drove the thoughts from his mind with a burst of harsh banter.

'Do a job with you, Ram? Don't mek sport. You' brain an' you' frame too slow to keep up with me, pardner. And besides I like to work alone, all alone with my own sour self.'

'I broke, man, an' desperate, an' me chile mother facing starvation.'

'Which chile mother, Ram? I thought you lost count of the woman them who mother pickny for you.'

'You gotto help me, Zek.'

Against his better judgement Ti-Zek decided to join Ram in shifting a couple hundred coconuts from Boodoo's estate.

It was noontime. Low clouds were sifting the sunlight. The wind had vanished from the foreshore and was skulking somewhere deep in the forests. A pair of bluesakees were playing mating games in a low thicket of black sage and ants bush. They darted from one clump of bushes to the other and their wings were the colour of bluebells.

Ti-Zek and Ram had picked the dry coconuts and were peeling them on wooden spikes they had driven into the ground. They worked quickly. The job had to be done before the rangers resumed their patrols after breakfast.

But Roberts, a bitter old man and the bane of raiders, had been tipped off by the rum shop owner who had heard Ram mumbling his secrets aloud between sleeping and waking. Roberts should have retired a long time ago, but a passion for hunting men kept him alive and on the job. For him retiring to a quiet life would have been worse than death.

The first shot caught Ram in the back of the head, and falling forward, his own wooden spike pierced his throat. Ti-Zek ran bird-speed zig-zagging so that Roberts couldn't take proper aim. Two buckshot pellets caught him in the right leg, one close to the Achilles tendon and the other in the big outer muscle of the thigh. Roberts made a gesture of pursuit but soon gave up, cursing himself for his age and decrepitude. He left Ram's body on the spike and went for help. He knew that Ti-Zek was bold and vengeful.

'That Ti-Zek like a Manipuri tiger,' he said to himself as he walked away. 'You frighten him and he will take a round-about trail and come back to strike at whatever make him run away.' Ti-Zek as Roberts had suspected ran in a wide circle and returned to the spot where Ram had fallen. He was bleeding but had traced his wounds to their sources and was satisfied that they were only superficial ones.

'Jesus Christ, Ram had bad luck! Mantop was hunting him down for the whole of last month. Peculiar how Mantop does play games with some people before he snatch them, and I swear he was playing a tiger and bush rabbit game with ole Ram. Two times in three months Mantop make a pass at Ram. During September rains a boat engine explode on the Mahaica river and toss him twenty foot in the air. He had bad luck for months after that. Then Buddy shoot them two Unablers who was rustling cattle with him, and now, the third time, old man Roberts, half blind and decrepit, erase his name from the register of the living.'

Ti-Zek watched Roberts hurry away noisily with his double-barrelled shotgun cradled against his chest.

They say that Roberts can palaver with the dead, that he can gaff with jumbies on moonlight nights when he's alone in Shadowy and silent coconut groves.

Ti-Zek didn't mind ghosts. What frightened him was the thought of being caught in a web of prison and desolation by one of those unfree spirits forever hunting him down.

He suppressed a feeling of revulsion, removed Ram's body from the spike that held it fast, laid it on the ground and covered it with banana leaves. Above him the sky was the colour of a buck-crab's back—a hard metallic blue—and carrion crows were already circling, floating on air currents and tracing patterns as though invisible and deft hands were using them to write a secret calligraphy.

Ti-Zek, crouching in the shadows, waited around as long as he dared. He didn't want the carrion crows to rob Ram of his eyes, because Ram was the kind of man who always needed to see where he was going.

Long before he had stumbled into this unexpected and sudden exit of death, Ram had declared, 'Pardner, me don't want to go to Heaven. Them say the big chibat does feed you on milk and honey there. That will only be a lotta work for me man, milking cow and goat, carrying them out to the pasture, sitting up all night to protect them from vampire bat. And who goin' keep the bee hive, and gather the honey, and have bee stinging them and shutting up they eye? No, pardner, give me hell anytime! With all them friends and enemies down there, me will only have to work a two hour shift a day stoking fire.'

'So go well, Ram, I will miss gaffing with you. Remember that story you tell me 'bout this big chibat, who, when his first son born decide that the boy-chile should have the most reliable company in the world to grow up with? How this big chibat search and search and wrack he brain 'till he come up with the bright idea that the most reliable companion on this earth was Mantop? So he search out Mantop and say, "Mantop, I want you to stand godfather for me one-boy." And Mantop say, "All right, but there will come a time when I will have to come for him like everybody else." And the boy father say "Well, tha's you and he story. All-you two will have to settle that when the time come." So Mantop became godfather for the boy, and the boy become the village doctor. Now, as a doctor, he see Mantop the Reaper come for old and young, weak and strong, rich and poor, and he keep thinking, "All right, so Mantop is me' godfather. The two of us close as sweat to skin. I wonder if he will come for me the way he does come for everybody else?" So the doctor ask him, "Mantop, why don't make me you' pardner for all time?" "Can't do that," Mantop say. "Is only room for one of us in this job." So the doctor go away, and from that time he start to learn all of Mantop tricks: how to enter a house anytime of day or night. An' Mantop, seeing how smart this doctor trying to get, decide to come for him before his time was up. The night he come, the doctor get a real fright and he brain start to work overtime. When the quaking inside him abate, and he could find he tongue and give voice again he say, "Godfather, give me two more days to settle up me affairs, then you can come!" And Mantop agree. But as soon as Mantop leave the doctor get busy, and seal up every crease and crack and crevice in the house, board and bar the windows, and all he lef' open was one keyhole and he put a bottle to that keyhole and wait. Mantop come again jus' like he say, and when he see that he godson seal up everywhere he get vex like hell, and he call out, "Godson, open up this minute!" But the doc didn't answer. Well, wasn't long before Mantop find the keyhole and slip in and land right inside the bottle, and the doc jump up and seal him in, and although he cry out to make stone weep, the doc take the bottle and bury it in he back garden. Well, with Mantop gone, the doc act like he own land and sky, and he make mirth with anyone who try to stand in his way. He rob people of they land; he take 'way they wife and daughter; he properly parade himself and take advantage. But he didn't know that with Mantop gone, Time stop and wait 'till he come back so nothing new was happening day in and day out. The doc was jus' stumbling round and round, walking the same trail in circles; 'till he get fatigue. And one day, when he couldn't think of nothing better to do, he start planting vegetables in the back garden, and forking up the ground and he break the bottle that had Mantop locked up inside it. Mantop didn't wait then; he strike at once and carry the doc away.

'Well, old man Roberts give you a quick passage to the Beyond, pardner, so you an' you' friends will do shift-work stoking fire down below. Go 'long you merry way, boy! I gotto go bird-speed. I can hear them coming. At least I save your eyes, so you can see where you going. And these two buck-shot in me leg biting me. I will send message to Sister Rhona an' ask she to come and fix it. She got a healing hand, and she will boil up some bush and in no time the wound will heal.'

They came with dogs. Ti-Zek made a detour to the main canal and swam as quietly as an alligator for half a mile to ensure that the dogs would lose his scent.

Old man Roberts said, 'Eh, eh, somebody move the body.'

'Is that damn thief-man Ti-Zek,' a young ranger with muscles up to his ears said. 'I wish you caught him instead.'

'Is fifty odd years I work on this estate, boy, and in all that time there never was a thief like Ti-Zek.' Old Roberts spoke as though he had a profound respect for Ti-Zek, and this surprised the younger rangers.

The muscle-bound one said, 'Me will get him sometime, man.'

But Roberts cautioned him, 'Don't bite off more than you can chew, boy; learn the ranger work, and study Ti-Zek like a book, read every sign he lef' behind him, and if you suspect he around, every blade of grass that move might not be the wind moving it; it might be Ti-Zek waiting to ambush you. I wish I had Ti-Zek as a ranger. This estate wouldn't lose a single coconut.'

They made a stretcher out of plaited coconut branches and carried Ram's body to the threshing floor of a rice mill that had long been abandoned to rust and moss and rats and sleepy serpents. Narine walked slowly down the pathway from his house leaning heavily on a gnarled letterwood stick. He approached the corpse and prodded it with his stick, and staring ahead of him his eyes became calm and contemplative.

Here was a thief shot in the act of robbing him of the rightful fruits of the land he had inherited from his ancestors! He wished that the soul of this lost one, this spawn of Kali the Destroyer, could migrate for an eternity from the body of one wild beast to another. He stood there for such a long time that the others around him became restless and uncomfortable. Ram's brains, pouring out from the back of his head, looked like fallen petals of a yellow hibiscus, and this viscous pulp almost touched the toes of Narine's shoes.

Roberts cleared his throat loudly, and looking up from his daydream Narine ordered one of the young rangers to go and fetch the Police, 'Boy, make sure you find Inspector Gordon. Tell him that Uncle say he must come right away.'

'I will find him,' the ranger said. 'I not coming back with nobody else.'

The Inspector was a big man who walked as softly as an ocelot. He had a thick neck and the veins on it stood out like lianas; but even when he was as hearty as a red howler monkey in the mating season, one was conscious of his small eyes, and how cautious they were, and how sly and cunning they could be, and how absolutely they belied his apparent joviality. Standing beside Narine with the sun behind him, the Inspector looked like a dark boulder shielding a blade of grass.

'Gordon, I too glad to see you, man, too glad.' Narine extended a hand that was veined and fragile and trembling like a leaf in a gentle wind.

The Inspector took the small and vulnerable hand in his immense one, and declared, in a voice that sounded like the roll of drums, 'Came as soon as the boy came and told me you had some trouble here, Uncle. I was on my way to settle a disturbance in Baggotstown. Is human-beast we have to deal with these days, Uncle.'

The Inspector exchanged a few pleasantries with Roberts whose deceased wife had been a distant relative of his, and then he took out his notebook and began to question him officially. Roberts gave a rambling description of what had transpired and the Inspector, again and again, brought him back to the main point. Narine listened so impassively that the flies crawling on the face of the corpse and those on his own face seemed to be crossing the same surfaces of dead flesh.

The young muscular ranger was anxious to give his version of what had happened. He felt that he could do a much better job than Roberts, but a look from the old landowner was enough to let him know that the choices were his silence or his job.

'It's clear as rain water that Ram and Ti-Zek was working together, Inspector. Them two was always close as sweat to skin, and . . .' Roberts would have continued.

But the Inspector interrupted him, 'Leave Ti-Zek out of this, Roberts!'

'Leave him out, Inspector?' Roberts looked up, and his big veined eyes sunk in wrinkled flesh were wide open with bewilderment.

The Inspector smiled and explained patiently, 'Come, come, Roberts, a black man and an Indian joining forces to rob a notable landowner? No, sir, that's politics. My job is to uphold the law, to deal with crime. So here is what the official story will be, and this will be the whole truth and nothing but the truth et cetera: Ram was caught red-handed stealing coconuts at 10:30 in the morning of April fifth. You and two young rangers called on him to surrender, and you surrounded him. You called on him to give himself up peacefully three times. He took a few steps forward, as though he was going to comply, and then he picked up a cutlass and rushed at Ranger Telford. You shot him. With a story like that everybody comes out looking good and there's no untidiness about the affair.'

The Inspector's eyes made four with each of the rangers in turn and they nodded their agreement and lowered their heads.

'Come to the house and have a drink, Gordon,' Narine said. 'Is a long time since you come this way, man.'

'Glad to, Uncle,' the Inspector said. And when they were out of earshot of the others, he added in a low voice 'There's a nice little piece of property in Georgetown that I have my eyes on, Uncle, and I'll need a mortgage.'

'After all, is cooperation and self-help these days, Gordon.'

'So what you want us to do with the body, Inspector?' Roberts called out.

'I'll notify the hospital as soon as I get to a telephone. They'll send an ambulance. Look out for the ants and the wild dogs and the carrion crows. Don't want to spoil things for the autopsy, you know.'

Roberts watched the two walking up the pathway to the big house with its green gables and the darkness inside which often made Narine keep the lights on in the daytime, and he kept repeating under his breath: 'The wild dogs and the carrion crows and the ants!' And he said to himself, 'This is a place with vultures and creatures and things to backup the vultures. Wild dogs and carrion crows and ants and cannibal fish.'

'You said something, skipper?' the young ranger asked.

And Roberts told him that he could go home to his wife and children since they all had a hard day. 'I will keep vigil over the body,' he said. 'Never know when that ambulance will turn up.'

Darkness swallowed the sunset with a single gulp and stars scattered themselves across the skies like flocks of gilded ricebirds surprised by a scarecrow. The moon nudged its way above canopies of coconut palms and moonlight and smoke from Roberts' pipe drove away the mosquitoes singing around his grizzled head. Navy blue shadows squatted under the trees like tethered beasts. The old man, with his shotgun across his knees, listened to rainfrogs crying out to the moon and who-you birds conversing with ghosts; and every now and then he swayed and nodded drowsily murmuring strange orisons between sleeping and waking. Around midnight, he heard the chickens in his backyard coop, behind the rice mill, stirring restlessly. He stood up and shook himself and stamped the ground to banish the stiffness from his joints. Palm fronds, stirring fitfully in the wind, made rusty whispers echo in dark groves where owls and mice played secret games. As if the wind and moonlight had filled him with the breath of life again, Ram stood up, shook himself like a wet dog and began walking away. Roberts, when he recovered from the shock and amazement and fear that had overcome him called out and fired a warning shot; but Ram, looking back and covering the hole in his throat with his right hand, disappeared in the shadows.

Roberts felt himself floating down a river in his canoe until he struck a submerged log and the canoe capsized. He found himself swimming endlessly in opaque depths. When the ambulance arrived, the body had vanished and Roberts was in a coma. He never regained consciousness.

For months afterwards, the villagers kept telling stories of how this or that one had seen Ram and Roberts walking side by side, and how the two had always smiled a cunning secretive smile, and how Ram was forever covering the hole in his throat with his hand.

Sepersaud Narine died in his sleep six months later. His body, frail and floating in a sea of wild flowers, lay in state in the cool dark living room of the big house. A cluster of pandits chanted prayers to the gods and their messengers in the Hindu Pantheon who would take the soul of the deceased back into an eternal web of transmigrations.

The cremation ceremony took place on the foreshore in mid-afternoon when the tide was low and the wind was whispering requiems in the verging courida groves. The pandit intoned and the distant sea and the wind and the mourners responded. Flames from the scented wallaba pyre bent the body in two. It looked as though the corpse was sitting up, defying the fire and at the last moment trying to cheat death. But those who attended the funeral swore that they saw a hand reach into the flames, push the body backwards and hold it down until it disintegrated.

Narine's heirs, as he had stipulated in his will, recovered his ashes, and placed them in a marble urn in the centre of his seventy square mile estate. The urn was surrounded by coconut palms, ants bush, black sage and yellow cacia flowers.

The night after the urn was installed Ti-Zek drove a wooden spike close to it and carried out a ritual of stripping hundreds of coconuts so that the husks obliterated the fading wreaths piled on the ground. As Ti-Zek worked the moonlight striped the ground with shadows and who-you birds cried out malevolently to one another. He shelled the coconuts on the spike rhythmically and interspersed his actions with words: 'Uncle, is how much land a man does need after all? You had so much that from your housetop to the end of the sky a man couldn't see all that was yours, and now all you can claim is enough earth to cover your blasted ashes. You had to leave all that land, and the money in the bank badmindedness to crush other people lives in you' weak trembling hand. When Mantop come for you, in your sleep, you couldn't offer him deeds to the land or cash in the bank,'cause he is a dealer in life and death. So, Uncle, I working close to the miserable ashes they put in a stone jug, an' you can't do nothing 'bout it, an you' rangers them afraid of the moonlight and the jumbies and all them people who die on this estate with the taste of bile in they mouth and blood in they eye and emptiness in they heart 'cause they hurt so much they couldn't feel pain no more. So I taking these coconut for all them mute folk who life you squeeze like simitu on a vine when you suck out the sap and throw away the skin, them people who grey-hair they life and toil like slave to make oil from you' coconuts-them. Is only Ram and me get away from you; both of we free like the wind is free or a harpy eagle does be in the wide, wide sky, out of your reach. So let you' ashes eat all the land it can eat and never rest in peace!'

The who-you birds called out more insistently, and the estate works, listening inside their cruel huts, shivered and shut out the moonlight and the shadows and the rusty murmurings of wild palms.

The muscular young ranger who had succeeded Roberts stumbled upon Ti-Zek's handiwork on his foreday morning patrol, and making sure that his only witnesses were singing birds, he laughed until he cried.

Shadows Move in the Britannia Bar

The Britannia is old. It is hard to say which is older, the city of Port of Spain, or the rum-shop. No-one alive today can say which one gave birth to the other, the rum-shop to the city, or the city to the rum-shop. It stands at the corner of Frederick Street and the South Quay, facing the old railway station, the customs house, and the sea. It was located there for convenience, for a past which is dead, for travellers who no longer ride the railroad, for a lighthouse whose beacon is lost, and a customs house without traffic.

In an odd way, the Britannia is the womb of the past. It is the only museum that Trinidad has to offer, for the island's history is written on the rum casks, the walls, the floors, the brass spittoons and, most of all, the men who gather there, held and drawn like puppets by thin threads of time and memory.

There are those who swear by its rum, by its ancient wooden kegs whose staves and worn-down rusted hoops are held together by innumerable coats of paint. Others swear by the shadows they may hide themselves between, and still another group will tell you that the place has a strange magic, an ether that draws men out, and wraps about them a warm and immediate camaraderie. And they come, all manners of men, in search of its ether. They gather in small cliques, just large enough to house the warmth of chat and chatter. Five men, six men, one more would drown out the magic. Instinct and the essence of their topic alone will determine the size of the clique.

This was Sookoo's clique. He was perhaps just a boy when he first came in to the Britannia Bar. Today he is old. The hair on his face is thick, like grey steel wires, his crown bald, with the soft fuzz of baby's hair, and his eyes are constantly searching.

Each time the swinging half-doors of the rum-shop fly open, he looks up as though he awaiting someone. But his movements, his expressions, are from his eyes alone. They circle, they dance, they draw tightly together, and sometimes they flash. The old man had his clique about him, about five or six other habitues of the Britannia, and he was talking in his usual rolling, lilting, sometimes angry and abusive way.

'The time dat I talkin bout, all yuh fellars didn't dream to born yet. Dem was the old time days. People uses to have a kind of belief in dem days, a respec' for all what they see happen with they own two eye. What I mean to say is dat tings still happen, but is people like all yuh young fellars, is people what blind, they eye shut, it half-close. But it have something. Where? Up in the sky! Inside your belly! A man! God! It have something!

'In dem days it didn't have so much motor-car to jam up the road; Port of Spain wasn't pack-up with so much people. Trinidad? Hm! Dis island uses to be different in dem days, boy . . . different. People uses to work hard hard hard! Not like nowadays, all you hear is "Independence", "Federation", "Hilton Hotel". People askin me if I ent see how the town change up. "But look how we have six-storey sky-scraper . . . look how we have elevator in the department store . . . look how we have Woolworth five and ten." I have to laugh because I ent see nothing change. People in Trinidad stop the same way . . . chupid! It have something, and I know because I see it with my own two eye.

'One o'clock, two o'clock we leavin dem far far places in the bush to reach Port of Spain before dayclean. Nobody on the road. And dark? Pitch black! All you have is your lil hurricane lantern prop up on top your cart, and it loaded down with coals. But what good dat lamp is? Is for police nuh . . . for dem not to give you a case, lock you up for drivin without light. But where you do find police at dat hour? Dem rascals gone to catch a sleep somewhere too.

'O-ho! So you think dat is thief I talkin 'bout? Boy what thief want to hold-up coal-man? Is joke you makin. Everybody know dat a coal-man ent have a cent with he when he goin in town. Not thief man . . . not livin' people. Dem is not what I talkin 'bout—something else. It have people who could do something to you, and all-yuh young fellars can't see because you ent believe. Dat is why you ent have the respec' what we old time people have for dem tings. It have to have something. Dis world ent make out from nothing. *Somebody* . . . *something* does make it turn 'round. And I see tings dat make me know dat. And if I ent see dem, my name ent Sookoo, and I-is-a-blasted-liar-so-help-me-God. I say my name ent Sookoo and God lick me down with a big-stone if I lie! I know what I talkin 'bout and if I lie I die. I see 'nuff ting to make your blood crawl and dat ent all.

'You remember it have a fellar name Mahal?' Member how he uses to walk miles doin up he hand and foot like if he drivin motor car? The man uses to walk *quite* from Tunapuna. All the way through Curepe and St Joseph and San Juan he shiftin' gear and blowin horn . . . You tink is mad he mad? He family the same way too you know. Is somebody who make him get so. He had a sister who uses to crawl on she hand and foot like a dog, and she uses to bark like a dog too. I tellin you is something bad dat family gone and do, and somebody make dem come so. You living in Trinidad so long and you never hear about obeah? You say you *hear* but you ent *see*. Well you ent see because you ent believe, and is your own bad luck if you ent want to listen to people what see for they-self. But I know dat it have something outside there, boys, something big and strong, and I see it already.

'What I see? You ever hear about La Diablesse? Well comin in to town one night, you know when you pass police station in St Joseph it have a small cemetery bout quarter mile down the road? I turn up the hurricane lamp bright bright bright when I passin in the police station because I don't want no trouble from dem scamps. Soon as I pass dem a lil way, I turn the lamp down. The pitch-oil was low nuh . . . and I was tryin to make it last till I get in to town. The cart going crick-crack, the donkey going clip-clop clip-clop. Now I say to myself, now is the time to get a lil rest . . . for the eyes you know. I hear they say after you do this coal work for years your eyes does get weak, so I say let me give dem a lil rest.

'Bam . . . I start to hear a funny kind of noise. I say, what happen at all? The donkey limpin or what? It sound like if he walkin on three foot, then it sound like he walkin on five foot. I say, man, I dreamin or what? I put my hand on the donkey back . . . to feel he nuh, to feel if he walkin even even. The donkey have he head down like he ent hear nutting. You know how animal have more sense than people? Soon as something bad come near, is dem who smell it first? Anyway, the funny noise stop and the donkey sound like if he have all he four foot an dem on the ground.

'We go a lil way, and just before we get close to the gate yard to the cemetery I see it. It took like a ball of fire what pitch-out from behind the train line and it explode! In my half-sleep I say, well it must be another cart or a car or some vehicle. But the ting remain stand-up by the gate . . . shining like a bright piece of galvanise in the moonlight. I look up to the sky, man. I say, but this is dark-dark tonight, it ent have no moon. And soon as we come up longside the cemetery gate yard, the donkey begin to bawl. I jerk the rein hard in he mouth, and the animal begin to *trimble*! *Trimblin* like if he have the fo-day-fever. And the cart? Well it jerk to a stop like if it have a *brakes* in the wheel.

'I keepin my head on all the time you know. After you travel the Eastern Main Road like a coal man for thirty years, you bound to see a lot-o-tings. But in all my days I never bounce up with anything like this. *One nice woman*! She-pretty-for-so! And she dress up in a yellow sateen dress. Dat is what I see shinin in the dark you know, she dress. And when the cart come up close-close-close, I begin to smell dis sweet ting. You know how fainty dem jadmin flowers does smell when you mash up one of the plants in the bush? Well, is just so I smellin dis fainty smell. Well I thought it was comin from the cemetery, you know how a lot of people like to carry a wreath make up from dem flowers when they bury they dead.

'My friend . . . when I come up close close close, I hear she say, "Good night, mister. You so hurry to go to town, you ent have time to stop and talk." All this time so she stand up in front the gate-yard to the cemetery. The only movement you could see is when she take a breath, she belly and she tot-tots shining like silver under dat dress, and she have a cigarette in she hand, an she only puffin an smokin. Was a big woman you know! Is not fat she was fat . . . *nice*.

'I get down from the cart. I look below one wheel, I look below the other wheel, it ent have nuttin. But the donkey still cryin. Not a kind of loud bawlin like they does make when they hungry, but a quiet quiet kind . . . like a chile when he just wake up. And then I hear the woman say, "Have a cigarette with me nuh . . . You does smoke?"

'Boy my head have so much worries bout the coals and what time I go reach town, I just say no without even lookin at she. I come round to the front of the cart and start liftin up the donkey foot one by one to see if he have a nail or a stone dat make he walk so chupid. I look and look. I take down the hurricane lamp and start to look with dat too . . . I can't find nuttin. I was still stoopin down on the ground, and when I lift up my head, *what* I see from between the donkey foot! The woman comin cross the road to my cart. And dat is when I hear the same clip-clop clip-clop that I hearin up the road. Good ting I was stoopin down low otherwise I never see it with my own two eye . . . she have one foot like a woman, and the other like a horse.

'I say "*Oh God!* Is not a woman . . . is a La Diablesse!" And with that I run round and pick up the rein in my hand and jump up on my seat. I have a big-stick right under my seat you know, but I realise dat it wouldn't do me no good . . . not with a La Diablesse. But I ent no fool. I know I have something *better* than any big-stick. "I don't take no cigarette from no La

Diablesse!" I bawl out to she. I hear she foot you know. She make she mistake when she begin to cross the Main Road, and is then I know why I did hear dat funny sound before, like if the donkey have three foot one minute, than five foot later. But she still comin, clip-clop clip-clop, and she hips twistin up nice when she movin from one foot to the next one.

'The woman still smilin smilin and comin closer to me with the pack of cigarette open and one or two sticken out. You know how dem La Diablesse like to give a man all kind-o-ting to eat and drink and smoke? And then after the man take them and they go to a quiet lonely place together she make him lose his senses and he wake up naked next mornin in a bush full of stingin nettle? Well boy, I start to loosen-up the button of my sleeve. I ent fraid you know. I say let she come real, real close . . . then I go give it to she. So I wait till she come right close to my shoulder and I *pull up* my sleeve, and I show she *this!*

'You see it . . . you watchin it good? What the hell all-yuh pissin-tail boys from nowadays know at all? This lil box you see I have tie on to my arm make from pure silver . . . solid silver . . . solid solid silver. Any you know what kind of obeah it have inside dat? Hai-aye-aye, boy! Is obeahman *poopah* what make this for me. Nuttin in the whole world could touch me.

'I hear one loud scream from she voice and I see she turn to one ball of fire right befo me eye and it gon peltin down the road. And then I hear this ugly nasty laugh pitch up high like a fowl . . . a chicken, comin from far far down by the police station. And I could still hear it ringin in my ear up till today: "Soooookoooo . . . Sooookoooo . . . Sooookooooo, you get away this time, boy." And then dat laughin what I tellin you bout like a fowl what have a sore throat and he tryin to crow fo-day mornin.

'Oh-ho . . . so you ent want to believe me? Look how I go say it again. If I lie . . . God lick me down with a big-stone! You see? You see I still here and nuttin ent happen to me? Now you go believe? Listen! Li-sun! Li-sun nuh man. I ent drunk you know. I ent gettin light-headed like some of dem rum-suckers who can't hold they liquor. It take mo than a nip o' Black Cat Rum to make my tongue heavy; I know what I talkin bout. And you know why? Because I ent only see . . . but I *believe.* I believe dat it have something . . . something stronger than *even* this rum. Let me tell you something else. I ent see this with my own two eye; it happen to somebody else, not me, a fellar who name . . . em . . . what the hell the man name now? Look at how I does forget tings? . . . Oho, Rajan. Dat is what he name. He uses to be a coal man too, but you know how everybody gettin lectric and gas stove and nobody usin coal-pot these days? Well this man can't make a livin at the trade no mo. Soon as he stop work, he gone by he son and he say, "Well boy, I get old now, and I take care of you all your life, now is your turn to take care of me." Dat worthless son, he have kick him out the yard and they begin to fight . . . *right there*! All the neighbours comin to watch the bacchanal. Nobody put hand, nobody interfere. Is not like long-time you know. A boy never kick out he poopah in dem days. And what else? Nobody want to break the fight, all the neighbours only come to watch . . . to enjoy theyself. Anyway, the old man was a powerful fellar still. You know you does work hard when you do this coal work, liftin up them heavy heavy bag on the cart, hoisting them down to show a customer for them to inspec'? The man was powerful! He still have big big muscles all about in he arm an he shoulder. He chest was still big in dem days. He tumble dat boy on the ground and he beat him like a old snake, then he get up and he left he. But the boy only *playin* like a snake. He well coil-up when the old man bustin licks on he, and soon as he father turn he head, the boy get up and snatch a big stick and he give he father *one lick* on the head. I was right there, man. I hear the blow, the crack what the stick make when it hit the man head. And then on top of dat, the stick break . . . right in the boy hand. Must-be it was an old dry-stick . . . I would lie?

'The old man turn round and he begin to rain mo blows on he son. He say, "You want to kill me here today with big-stick? I go show you who is man . . . I go show you who is man here . . . today today!" And with every word the old man say, he give the boy another blow. And when he ask the boy if he had enough, you know what dat rascal say to he poopah? He say, "You go dead bad!" The old man hit him again . . . hard. "Dat is the thanks you get in dis world for makin children!" And when he hit dat boy again, he ask he, "Dat satisfy you? You get nuff licks? It have plenty mo where dat come from." The boy say three-four-five time, "I go work a obeah on you . . . you go dead bad!" And the old man standing up with one foot pon he chest all dis time so . . . watchin to see dat he don't make another move. "It ent have nuttin like obeah, you fool. What you think, is fraid I fraid? If you want to play *man* you want to fight like *man*, get up and let we see who is *man* . . . *today today*!" But the boy look like he get nuff blows. He fraid the old man. He wouldn't get up from off the ground. All he could say is dat he go work a bad obeah on he poopah. By this time so the father get vex because all kind o' people gang up to watch the fireworks, and it look as if he shame to make people see how he well beat he son, and he ent have no feelin's for he own chile . . . he own flesh-an-blood. So now he change he tune. He say to the boy nice nice nice, "Tell me you sorry you did lift you hand to hit your poopah what bring you in the world." You know what dat boy do? He spit on the ground an he cuss again . . . bad bad words! The old man temper *really* get hot now, but, it look like he still feeling sorry for the boy too. He take the boy hand and he twis-it behind he back. "Tell me you sorry now . . . let all these people hear you sorry dat you hit you poopah." The boy twis-up he mouth like a dry-up hibiscus flower . . . like if he tastin' something sour, and he suck he teeth makin a nasty noise. The old man twis' harder. "Say you sorry! You worthless scamp!" The boy coil round on the ground till he couldn't bear no mo pain, and then he say, "Oh God . . . Oh God—oye . . . Oh God I sorry." And then he father tell he, "Say you sorry, PA . . . PA. I want to hear you say you sorry, PA, befo I loosen you." And the boy say again, "I sorry, Pa!" *Then* the old man loosen he.

'Eh-eh! Soon as he loosen him, the boy fly pon he father . . . just like snake. And he put *one bite* on the man chest, and it begin to bleed right-there-and-then. The old man catch him by he hand again and everybody swear dat the old man go kill him dead dis time. What? No police around him! Where you could find a police? Where dem scamps hear it have a fight somewhere, they run like hell befo they get lick down too.

'The old man have the boy hand twis' . . . and it look like if the boy hand lose all the strength it have in it. But the boy ent cryin you know. He face like Mad Adam stone . . . like if he ent have no feelin's at-all, at-all. "Kiss me!" the father order he. And the boy was still layin down on the ground. "Kiss me an tell me you sorry," he poopah tell he. And when the father twis' the boy hand nuff, he well crawl up like a animal and he kiss he poopah foot. "You go work a bad obeah on me, eh! Well kiss me other foot and tell me you sorry." The boy say quiet quiet that he was sorry. "Louder! Louder! So dat dese people here could hear what the hell you sayin." The boy say he sorry again, and this time the old man drag he up by the collar, and make he stand up. "Kiss me right here where you bite me like a dog and tell me dat you sorry." But the boy hold he face bout four-five inches from the bite and he wouldn't do it. "Kiss me right here, you damn rogue. Right here where you make the blood come out . . . You did want my blood? Well taste it! You taste it befo when you did bite me, taste it again! I is you father and you want to kill me . . . ? You want to work bad obeah on me . . . come on now and kiss me on my chest, otherwise I break you hand like a dry-stick." And the old man did mean it. He did mean every word he say. He pinch the boy hand hard . . . HARD. And then the worthless scamp kiss he poopah chest and tell he that he sorry. But when he poopah loose he, he run from the yard like a mongoose peltin down in the bush bawlin out to he poopah, "You go dead bad, I goin bus' a bad obeah on you, you go dead bad!"

'Well . . . nobody see that boy face from that day, but he old man begin to take in more and more stick, and it look like if he fraid what the boy tell he. At first he didn't believe, but later people say he uses to hang around in all kind of rum-shop talkin to people like if he fraid to go home in the night.

'Another time I hear somebody say that the old man heself begin to believe the boy work a strong obeah on he, so he gone to a *more* strong obeah man to break the spell, but it look like he ent believe in the obeah man at first, so the obeah man can't do too much for him.

'And you know what the obeah man tell he? He say if that boy really mean in he heart of hearts what he say, and he go to a obeah man, that it bound to come true, that the old man go dead bad one day. The man still strong, you know. I does still see him. He lef' the coal work, he had a few shilling save up here and there, and all he could do is spend all he money on one obeah man after another. All a dem make him bring chicken, dey make him bring rum, dey make him bring goat brains, the obeah man he go to . . . they tell he the same-same thing. They will take the money first you know, then they say they can't help he because he ent believe.

'Well boys . . . I ent know what to tell you myself. But the man look like if he possess! Like if he haunted! Some people say dat he waitin . . . waitin for the day when he son go *do* for he. He turn frighten! The man turn *coward-coward*! And all the time he lookin round to see if somebody followin he. Sometimes he think dat he believe in one obeahman and he say dat things does happen . . . next day he have a lil doubt, and he start to trimble . . . trimblin like if he have the fo-day-fever, and all he could do to ease he mind is to get a nip-o-Black Cat.

'What you say there, boy? You closin shop? Alright, just let me finish tellin these boys an-dem something. Alright-alright, man! I know police go lock you up for sellin liquor after hours. You think I born yesterday? Ah me . . . is just a lil pain dat I have here in my chest. Give me a lil glass of water to drink, and I go clear out.

'Listen, boys, this man have to close up the rum-shop. He have the law to respec'! Otherwise he get in bad trouble. You can't blame a man for dat; everybody have to have something dat they must respec'! Gimmie a lil hand and let me go outside and sit down on the pavement where I could catch the sea-breeze in my lungs. That's it . . . that's it . . . easy now . . . thank you . . . thank you. Just put me down here and let me stretch out on the pavement a lil bit. I know how dis pain does come and go. I go feel better just-now . . . j-u-s-t—n-o-w.'

Sookoo was breathing heavily, with short gasps between each breath, and one of the men from the clique banged on the door of the Britannia to get some more water for him. The old man lay prone on the pavement of Frederick Street trying to reach up to rub his chest. One of the younger men helped his shaky hand to loosen the buttons of his shirt and began massaging the spot where the old man complained of feeling a burning pain. The door of the Britannia opened a crack and the other man came out with pitcher of water and a flash-light. And when the beam of the torch fell on the old man's chest, they all withdrew with a little gasp as he said his last words.

'Oh God, boy . . . you come at last? You come at last? Been waitin for you so long.'

He turned up his eyes in their sockets, and his breathing halted as he lay on the dark pavement outside the Britannia Bar. On his chest, close to the nipple of his right breast, was the scar of teeth marks, an upper and a lower semi-circle of small dark indentations punctured in his dark brown skin.

RENÉ DEPESTRE (b. 1926)

Rosena on the Mountain

Translated by Carrol F. Coates

*How beautiful are the feet of the messenger on the mountain
when he brings good tidings.*

Isaiah

1

That year I wanted to become a saint. My vocation was welling up like
water in a cistern. Leaving school one afternoon in November, I went
through the gates of Saint Martial's School and Seminary, which was run
by the Fathers of the Holy Spirit. I asked to see Father James Mulligan.
They told me to wait in the parlor because the priest had not yet finished
his classes that day. The Irish missionary had acquired the reputation of a
man of great wisdom and learning. He was teaching philosophy at the
high school on the Street of Miracles.

He welcomed me cordially and invited me to follow him into his chambers. The room had the good smell of lavender and fresh linen. The walls
were covered with bookshelves. Stacks of books also towered on his night
table and even on his prie-dieu [kneeling bench]. On the priest's desk
fresh roses from that morning adorned an orderly mess of notebooks and
folders. The sunlit branches of a tree brought the lyrical songs of birds to
the window. This was not exactly the way I had pictured the cell of a saint,
but the studious comfort and cleanliness of the room impressed me.

The minute I sat down, I began to tell him the reasons for my visit. I
explained why I was making my request to a religious order rather than to
the secular clergy. I felt destined to rise at two o'clock each morning of my
life and to utter only three words a week. My ideal would have been the
Trappists, but there was no Trappist monastery in our country. If the
world is a vale of tears, Haiti is the best watered corner on the globe. Since
I was born Haitian, sainthood seemed to me to be the only way to attract
Christ's attention to a planet without tenderness or consolation.

For more than an hour, I developed these ideas with a vehemence that

119

left my jaws aching. Father Mulligan found it admirable to respond to an inner call resounding so forcefully. He shared my opinion that the worst of misfortunes in the Americas was to be born in Haiti. He could understand why I envisioned the extreme alternative of suffering and renouncement. He added that the seditious fires burning within had not tarnished the child's candor in my features. In his eyes, my face stood out boldly from the banality of the young men in that year's philosophy class. He was happy that he could not sense in me any vendor of imported merchandise, senator, or minister of state. I was a young man in a state of revolt, called to the great adventure of the priesthood. God had planted me in this ungrateful and sterile terrain for his own purposes. As he spoke, the wrinkles at the corners of his Irish eyes took on an expression of joy.

'My son, accept the mystery and the violence of this call. Do not rush the flow of the sap. Sainthood is a tree biding its time in the Lord's eternal plan. Beware impatience! It is an arrow in Satan's bow.'

Then he questioned me about my parents and my background in Port-au-Prince.

I was the eldest of a family with seven children. Years ago, following my father's premature death, we had been left penniless. My mother tried ten other jobs and then became a seamstress. She worked at her Singer sewing machine day and night to keep a roof over our heads, feed us, clothe us, and send us to school.

In the poor section of Tête-Boeuf, our house had two rooms but no electricity or running water. Our toilet was a ditch over which there was a kind of little shack covered with haphazard planks. It was located in the courtyard with absolutely no privacy. When the ditch was full, we called the *bayakou*. These men worked up to their waists shoveling fecal matter out of the ditch. Those nights, nobody in Tête-Boeuf could close an eye. Everyone in the area waited for dawn and the departure of the truck that would take away the odiferous load. We imagined the workers with vulture wings or jackal maws. When we discovered that they were really human beings, we hurled stones, empty bottles, and epithets at them.

I ought to have become a tailor's or cobbler's apprentice long before, but my mother would not hear of this. She wanted me to get a high school diploma and go to medical school. Her fondest dream was to see me in a doctor's white smock, working in the posh sections of Port-au-Prince. In order to see it come true, she said that she would be capable of prostituting herself with the merchants along the waterfront when her sewing machine was ready for the junkyard. She repeated this with a kind of icy rage in her voice, even when there was company. It did not lower her in people's estimation since, in our area, hunger eventually drove most women to sell their bodies.

I confided to Father Mulligan that during the slow season, when my mother could find nothing to sew, she strung the family budget together by telling fortunes for masons, tinsmiths, servants, boilermakers, prostitutes, thieves, and other neighbors in Tête-Boeuf. They would come to consult her all day long. She would read the future in out-of-work hands. Sometimes she would pretend to be mounted by Vodun spirits. Her face would become long, with hardened features, and she would give advice and encouragement in a falsetto tone to the customers who listened to her in this trance-like state. As soon as they left, she broke into raucous laughter in front of us, without disguising the tears that betrayed her extreme dignity.

Each year she sent her little ones off in the *taptap* toward Croix-des-Bouquets. At a fork in the road, the bus would stop and we would cover some ten kilometers on foot to Dorelia Dantor's farm. During the two or three days that we spent with this well-known mambo, each of us received a magic bath prepared with orange leaves, holy water, jasmine flowers, barley water, rum, and powdered almonds. Dorelia would also bathe us in a mixture with garlic, chives, thyme, cassava flour, rum, salty coffee, and *bwakaka* [a Haitian tree]. She had us swallow herb teas and concoctions of various aromatic plants or she would give us a large class of castor oil that had been boiled with soap shavings. In order to make our blood too bitter for sorcerers, she fed us cockroaches fried in castor oil, spiced with garlic and nutmeg. These treatments would scare bad luck, the evil eye, and supernatural maladies out of our bodies like rabbits. On occasion, two men would grab one of us by our legs and swing us head down for a minute over a ritual fire. At that moment, the drums beat along with the chants of the *ounsi* [postulants] and the participants invoked Gede-Nibo, General Grand-Bois, Captain Maloulou, and Boumba-Lord-of-Cemeteries. These spirits were all as familiar to us as the ants and rats at home in Tête-Boeuf. The ceremony in their honor would last all night. Dressed in red, ears and nostrils stuffed with cotton, and wearing a three-horned hat of tin or a Chinese hat, Dorelia would officiate. One evening, she threw all her clothes to the devil and offered her nude body to the erect flames. Once the mystical union had been consummated, there was not a single trace of a burn on her smooth flesh.

This last account led Father Mulligan to question me about my sexual experience. Had I already committed the sin of the flesh? I told him everything I knew. I came from a background where people were generally not ashamed of their private parts nor of their ability to enjoy them to the fullest. We talked about them and used them freely. Boys and girls were proud of their penis or vagina when they discovered these organs as a source of pleasure that brought them a sense of well-being and health. Everybody quickly discovered the meaning of menstruation, rounded buttocks, breasts, and the swaying of girls' backs and hips. The same was true of the penis, testicles, erection, ejaculation, and sperm for the boys. Far from provoking guilt, this discovery brought a joyful self-confidence to both sexes. The initiation to physical relationships came about in the most natural manner through chance encounters and animated sessions of petting in the shadows of porches.

The naked truth is that, strange as it may seem, I had never yet known a woman, not in the full sense of the expression. I knew everything that you can know about the act of love. I had spied on couples making love. This spectacle had seemed quite healthy and had a beauty about it that took my breath away every time. I had tried fornicating, alone or in a group, without fear or disgust but with a kind of spontaneous delight. Like most of my friends, I had massaged my penis with cocoa butter in the hope of increasing its diameter and length. Once or twice, when I was in the country, I had tried fucking with a goat or a heifer but without much enthusiasm. In spite of these precocious experiences, I had never yet had the experience of disappearing ecstatically into a girl's vagina. If the act of love was a sin, I claimed no virtue for not having committed it. If chastity was a virtue, I was practicing it by instinct.

According to the priest, the fact that I had been wallowing in paganism for years without spoiling my innocence was proof that my calling had been sprouting in fertile terrain. When God is going to confide a great mission to one of his children, He often works deliberately to try that individual's soul and flesh in the miasma of sin. The history of the Church teems with men forced to traverse swamp after swamp without soiling their purity. This was undoubtedly what had happened to me. From now on, however, it would be necessary to break with the pagan eccentricities of Vodun and to found my destiny on chastity.

Then we talked about the practical aspects of my vocation. I was in an advanced class at Pétion Lycée, with two more years of classical studies to finish before beginning theological studies. Was I gifted in Latin? Father Mulligan grabbed one of Seneca's works and asked me to translate a passage chosen at random. The text was laced with difficult translation problems that I could not resolve, although I was one of the best students in my class. I was extremely upset, but the priest closed the book and told me not to worry. It was no secret that the pupils in Pétion did not shine particularly in Latin and Greek. The professors of that impious establishment undoubtedly had better things to do with their time. He was prepared to help me catch up and volunteered to give me Latin lessons three times a week. In fact, he had a better proposal to make: every year he spent the hot season in a retreat that the Fathers of the Holy Spirit maintained in the mountains. I could simply go with him next summer. My Latin would improve decisively and I could participate in his priestly exercises.

When I was out in the street once more, I could tell that my inner well was overflowing. *Vocatus! Vocatus!* With the Latin word, my calling resounded with fresh emotion in the Haitian night, flooding my banks, spreading its poinciana-laden branches within me.

2

One day, after lunch, all three of us were seated on the porch of a little house hidden in the lush forest, a hundred meters from Lamark Chapel. We had left Port-au-Prince a month earlier. Father Mulligan was smoking his after-dinner cigar in silence. I was helping Rosena to husk the rice in a winnowing basket.

The priest had asked the mother of one of his pupils to find a housekeeper for his vacation. The woman had sent Rosena Rozel. She was a young woman of about nineteen, half-clove, half cinnamon as far as her complexion and perfume went. She had finished her secondary schooling and, in some less stifling kingdom, her talents, beauty, and queenly bearing would have brought her a better station in life. It would have been necessary to articulate each syllable with the tongue in order to state that she was RE-SPLEN-DENT. And, once that was said, a philosophy teacher in a religious school or a future priest needed a whole string of Hail Mary's to bring his circulation back to normal.

'I was expecting someone to clean house,' said Father Mulligan. 'They've sent a lioness, a biological scandal! May misfortune befall those who create scandals.'

The scandal was there. It was breathing the same air that we did, under the same roof day and night. It was preparing our meals, washing and ironing our linens, making our beds, serving us meals and, most of the time during the week, Rosena the scandal was the only one of the faithful kneeling in the chapel as I assisted the priest in the pre-dawn Mass. At that very moment, the tiger-eyed scandal was winnowing the evening rice, shaking her shoulders and breasts above our souls cooled only by the shade of the Lord's mystical almond trees.

'Tomorrow is market day,' said the priest.

'Yes, Thursday already,' said Rosena. 'Who is going with me this time, Father, you or Alain?'

'Alain has his Latin homework. I'll go with you just like the last time,' the priest decided imperatively.

'What if we take the mule?' suggested Rosena.

'A good idea, Rosie. We could buy a stalk of aromatic bananas.'

'And maybe a kid,' suggested Rosena.

'Ah, a barbecue!'

'With yams, onions, roucou sauce, cayenne pepper!' exclaimed Rosena.

The market was about an hour's trip from the foothills where the chapel was perched. I had gone with Rosena the first Thursday after our arrival. We set out right after the Mass. We followed the peasant women who were converging from all sides of the mountain to the main path toward the market. Some were on foot, others were riding bareback on donkeys with hooves covered by dew. Along the way, buntings, wood-pigeons, and even couples of guinea fowls flew up with a whirring of wings and rustling of leaves. The mountains were slowly emerging from the shadow and unveiling here and there shacks from which the aroma and steam of the first coffee rose agreeably. We were progressing in silence at a steady pace. Rosena forged ahead undaunted, pulling me in her wake and paying no attention to the brambles that kept scratching her long, bare legs. Her strides communicated pure lyricism to her buttocks. Thanks to the host that I had swallowed a few minutes earlier, I associated those curves with some innocent design of God.

At the market, I admired her talent for instinctively selecting the best water-melon, the ripest avocados, the freshly laid eggs, the eggplants, tomatoes, and cucumbers that promised the most beautiful salads. I could also see that the vendor was not yet born who could induce Rosena to pay an inflated price for a hen or a quarter-stalk of fig bananas. We returned loaded like donkeys and were forced to rest and regain our breath as we proceeded up steep slopes in a luminescence as tawny as Rosena Rozel.

'Is it true that you want to become a priest?' she asked during one of our stops.

'Yes, I feel the vocation.'

'What's it like when somebody feels the vo-ca-tion?'

'It's like a burst of light inside. You have a taste for humble, tender things,' I answered.

'How's that?'

'You keep the spirit of childhood that most men quickly lose for the rest of their life when they become an adult. You follow God's gentle commandments night and day. You scorn the fleeting sensations of the flesh.'

'My word, you already sound like a priest in the pulpit! So God forbids you to taste a woman?'

'Yes. Chastity is a commitment that you make for life,' I replied.

'And why do our *Iwa* make love freely when they are gods too? Dambala Wédo is married, you know. He's not a black male for nothing. Agwé Taroyo's exploits on the sea are no more notorious than his oar strokes in the flesh of Ezili Freda!'

'Our *Iwa* are only concerned with terrestrial affairs. Their faith is practical. They are ambitious spirits—hard-drinking, crafty, lewd fellows. They like to eat, drink, dance, and fornicate. They forget their own souls in their revelry!'

'Has Father Mulligan stuffed your head with that nonsense? Huh? That's his affair if he wants to keep his prick in the Holy Spirit's cooler all his life! I think that our *Iwa* are right to limber up their limbs when they feel like it,' chided Rosena.

'Those are pagan words, Rosena!'

'Pagan! It feels so good to be pagan from head to foot! There's no evil in that. Look, you can feel the heat of paganism working on my flesh,' she said as she placed my hand flat on her belly. 'The soul! You can't talk about anything but that wisp of hot air! I'm not ashamed of being a woman with an oven under my dress!'

She pulled her blouse open. 'Look, why should I be ashamed of these perky breasts? And my thighs!' She pulled her skirt up to her belt. 'Do you think that they bring bad tidings to the hills?'

All of a sudden, everything had begun to spin: huge trees, breasts, sky, the joyful explosion of the mountain, paths, thighs, and solemn buttocks in the morning light. An impulse to slap Rosena on the mouth boiled inside as that rapacious rascal I had once tamed began rising inside my pants. I was nailed to the spot, fists clenched, head bowed, and tears rolled down my blushing cheeks.

'I'm sorry, Alain,' she said. 'I didn't mean to hurt you. It's stronger than I am when it hits. When I was born, somebody must have rubbed hot peppers on the soles of my feet and the hot points of my body. Forgive me.'

She came closer and dried my cheeks. Little pearls of sweat were shining on her forehead and arms. She was almost pressed against me. I could smell the aroma of cinnamon and feel her hot breath. I saw my damnation taking on the color and sparkle of her eyes. She was a satanic force of seduction, and her breasts were pulsating against my throat.

'Let's make peace, little brother,' she pouted tenderly. 'I promise never to talk that way again. Tell me, my sweet pastor, will you make peace with Rosena?'

'Yes,' I said without looking at her.

Now, she was shaking the basket and putting the husked rice onto a metal platter. That innocent chore, like everything that she did, was charged with electricity. She must have exercised her charms on him in the same way. The Thursday before, the priest had gone with her to the market. Since then, I had noticed a change in their relations. A kind of familiarity had appeared between them. He called her Rosie now. He allowed himself to make little jesting remarks on her coquetry. He paid more attention to his clothes. He no longer wore his cassock and did not roll up the cuffs of his trousers, not even when he went to cut wood. He trimmed his beard and mustache. Every afternoon, he changed shirts and sprinkled himself with lavender water after his bath. The fine wrinkles at the corner of his eyes were always smiling. He had gotten rid of his suspenders and was wearing a tobacco-brown belt and metal buckle embossed with the initials J. M. When Rosena leaned over to pour his soup, I kept waiting for the priest's eyes to light directly on her breasts. But I suppressed all these suspicions as unworthy of my piety. They kept coming back to mind even stronger. The previous night, I was awake and praying anxiously when I saw the priest get out of bed. A thin partition separated us from Rosena and we could notice every time she turned over, moved her legs, or talked in her sleep. The priest looked at me for an instant. Seeing that I was motionless, he stepped onto a chair with all the stealth of a wild-cat on the prowl and began staring over the top of the partition. After a long moment of reflection, he went back to bed and lit a cigarette. I understood why he was set on accompanying Rosena to the market once more.

After the incident with Rosena, I had hurried to confess everything to the priest the same day. He praised the arms with which my purity had held off the demonic assault on my flesh. He reproached my lack of skill, however. In the future, I should prove myself a more ingenious pastor. The soul of this kind of pagan is a skein that must be artfully unraveled. Confronted with the young woman's impious passion, I should have pretended to be seriously caught up in it in order to guide her wisely to the lap of God.

'Grace is not contagious, my dear boy,' he said to me. 'It's a matter of patience.'

God had let this diabolic dew fall on my path in order to test the quality of the grass growing in my life. I must pray lest the droplets falling from the most satanic part of the sky appear one fine morning to be a benediction! I promised to follow his advice. And then, while I was awake that night, this holy man, who perhaps had a direct line to the Mother of Christ, had gotten up with feline stealth and trembling beard to drink in Rosena's defenseless nakedness. You could bet that this Thursday would be a decisive day. The priest and Rosena would fall onto the short grass of the mountain together, one on top of the other, intertwined in a panic of the senses. Satan would winnow them like a sizzling basket of rice under the Haitian summer sun . . .

3

Several hours later, I accompanied Rosena down the steep road that led through a growth of fern to the river. She led the way. The rhythm of our descent made her thighs vibrate, which had a violent effect on my own blood pressure. I was carrying the buckets that we had to fill.

Usually, she made the trip for water alone. She would come back sparkling each afternoon, with a clean dress and without her apron. The priest would be reading his breviary on the porch while I knelt in the chapel, gazing devotedly toward the lamp on the altar. I heard some steps behind me: It was Rosena coming toward me with clacking sandals and outrageously swinging her paganism in front of the holy sacrament.

'I'm sorry to disturb you. Come help me carry the buckets.'

'Father Mulligan won't be happy if I go to the river with you. He'll scold me.'

'You and your red-haired god make my tits ache!'

'Rosena, are you forgetting where you are?'

'That's true,' she said making the sign of the Cross. 'Are you afraid of being devoured?'

'It's not that, but Father Mulligan strictly ordered me not to be alone with you.'

'Since when?'

'Since the day when you showed me your . . .'

'Imagine that! You'll go to hell because you saw my . . .'

'Rosena, not here, please!'

'Excuse me.'

She crossed herself again, kneeling this time.

'Come on, be nice. Come give Rosena a hand.'

'OK, I'll come. Wait for me a minute at the hollowed road. I'll be with you in a minute.'

'Thank you, Saint Alain of Tête-Boeuf!' (She laughed aloud in the chapel.)

Toward the river, the road dropped vertiginously as the shadows of fern closed in around us. The path took a brusque turn to the clearing at the steep bank, scattered with flat, multicolored, polished stones. The rushing stream made a hairpin turn and formed a large basin upstream. At certain places, you could lose your footing. As soon as we arrived, I bent over the water and began to fill the two buckets. Standing beside me, Rosena observed me with a suggestive glance, something like two glowing coals of searing sensuality. When I had filled both buckets, I took the handles and was ready to start back up.

'Don't you want to take a dip?' she asked.

'No, I already washed right here at four o'clock.'

'Doesn't the water tempt you again?'

'No, Rosena.'

'Will you wait for me then? Turn around. It won't take me long.'

I set the buckets down and turned my back to Rosena. I could hear her undressing behind me. A moment later, she was splashing noisily in the river.

'The water's great!'

I did not answer. I felt ridiculous and did not even feel like praying. My favorite 'Ave Maria' was stuck in my throat now, and I had a slight sensation of nausea. My blood was coursing through my eyes, cheeks, hands, and, especially, my testicles. I turned around abruptly. Rosena was standing in the least shallow part of the river, up to her calves in the water. She smiled.

'Well, little Jesus-of-Prague! Make up your mind.'

I kept quiet, without taking my eyes off her. I had never looked at anything with such amazement. My eyes were literally washing her and she made no effort to hide. I felt terribly awkward with my trembling hands and my swollen trousers. Trying to regain my composure, I bent over and picked up a little rock, pretending that I was going to throw it at her. She dove and came up several meters further away, laughing and shaking her head in defiance.

'Why don't you throw it? I'm not afraid of you.'

I held on to my pebble. My vision was blurred with shame and desire. Rosena took several steps in my direction and began to splash me with water.

'I baptize you in the name of my mouth, my breasts, and my holy spirit,' she yelled in a burst of laughter as she showered me again.

I backed up to the grass. She took several more steps. Her breasts loomed above the current. She kept coming toward the bank, still splashing water. Suddenly, at her middle, an eagle appeared with its wings deployed for battle and it was swooping down on me with the furious cries of its kind. In all my clothes, I dashed toward the flaming black triangle. I pushed Rosena over into the river. We fell onto a sandbar. We rolled in the shallow water, with our bodies, hands, and lips mingled, reaching desperately for each other like drowning people. She got up, escaped from my grasp with a jerk of her hips, and began running upstream. I ran after her, tripping in my wet shoes. I joined her beneath a canopy of silken fern where she had stretched out with her arms under her head. I threw my clothes to the four winds. I could feel her heaving buttocks between my thighs. I arched my body against hers. Rosena turned over in ecstasy and offered me her tongue, her teeth, her eyes, her ears, her dimples, her belly, and her sovereign breasts. Her long legs arched in a sunny cross over my back as her waist ineluctably became unknotted. Her mound suddenly became the foliage of sensation. It was a beautiful, muscled, bulging vulva, generous in savor and fire. I was grafted onto Rosena and her blood flowed with mine, far from the coast, blending life and death, marvelously reconciled in the dual rhythm of our breathing. We plummeted breathlessly, measuring our overheated boundaries, kneading each other, and swelling into a full, knowing, glorious fruition as we launched into a final, piercing ecstasy.

4

Father Mulligan saw a transfigured couple arriving on the plateau that evening. What we had just done must have shone so intensely on our faces that he shaded his eyes. He understood at first glance that it was not the same Rosena or the same Alain who had returned from the river.

'What happened to you?' asked Father Mulligan.

'Nothing, Father,' I answered as Rosena disappeared into the kitchen.

'What do you mean "nothing"? You're all wet.'

'I slipped into the water as I was helping Rosena to fill the buckets.'

'And the ecstasy I see on both your faces? Did the river do that to you?'

'Where did I fall?' I asked with a sinking feeling.

'You're asking me? You are betraying your vocation without shame! Rosena, come here! What happened at the river?'

'Nothing serious, Father. Alain slipped while he was helping me.'

'Is that why you both have that look?'

'What look is that?' she said innocently.

'This is too much! Should I draw you a picture? You must take me for a raving idiot. You are both dripping with sin and lies. You've just been fornicating! You're a miserable pair of fornicators!'

'It's true, Father,' I answered. 'Pardon us.'

He turned toward Rosena looking for an expression of contrition. But she kept still. Her eyes flashed anger and her breasts were more insolent than ever.

'Rosena, do you persist in lying?'

'We did nothing wrong. We made love, Father. It was good, good, good!' She closed her eyes.

'Shut up! You have sullied this boy and that's all that you can say!'

'There's nothing dirty about love,' we said.

'You treat vile fornication as love? Aren't you ashamed to profane a word so close to our Lord? You wallowed like pigs in the slime at the edge of the river!'

'That's enough!' yelled Rosena, beside herself. 'I've had it with your hypocritical raving. It's nothing but jealousy bothering you. Don't lie, Father. Do you think I haven't been aware of your strutting around like a rooster? "Rosie, this! Rosie, that!" Your eyes haven't stopped caressing my "good angel". You would have loved to be in Alain's shoes. He clipped the grass under your spurs, that's all!'

The priest was dumbstruck. Words seemed to well up into his mouth like new teeth. He glanced at Rosena and then at me, with a crazed look and dangling arms. His beard looked like the fur of a scalded cat and he seemed like a small boy holding back his tears.

'Leave me alone, please,' he finally told us.

Rosena went to the kitchen. I went out into the evening, headed for the chapel.

The next day, after the Mass, which I served without taking Communion, the priest with an apparently relaxed manner asked me to go to market in his place with Rosena. We left toward dawn, in good spirits. We walked clear to the market in silence, each of us pretending simply to watch the people we met and to note the little stirrings on the mountain. She made her purchases with determination. Before 9:00 a.m., we were ready to return. I went first and pushed the brambles out of Rosena's way. In spite of our loads and the steep road, we were making good time and breathing deeply in the shimmering daylight. We had already covered half the road, totally absorbed in watching where we stepped. Rosena broke the silence.

'Alain, let's rest for a minute.'

'Sure, Rosena dear.'

I was surprised by what I said. I put down the provisions I was carrying and turned around. Drops of sweat were rolling down Rosena's cheeks. I pulled out my handkerchief and gently wiped her face. She rested against my shoulder a minute and then changed her mind and sat down on the grass in the shade.

'We were really trotting along.'

'Like flying . . .'

'Because of what we did, right?'

' . . .'

'You're not answering.'

'Yes, love.'

She raised her eyes with astonishment. Her lips and her nostrils quivered. Her bosom was heaving beneath her dress. The serious look on her face changed bit by bit to a kind of grateful affection.

'I love you, Alain.'

A delicious aroma of Rosena-cinnamon filled my arms. We placed our bundles behind a bush and stretched out on the grass. I slipped my hand under her dress. With crab fingers and closed eyes, I caressed her from the soles of her feet to her breasts, which awakened to form distinct silhouettes. I went straight to her center. The triangle conveyed ecstasy and intimate knowledge of consummate form. This was a mill to make the blood flow, the prodigy that began life before fire and rain, before sand and wind, and particularly before any mythology had denatured the female womb into the great misshapen monsters of the species. Beneath the mountain sunlight, Rosena opened up once more. My diamond-prick sculpted the radiance of her harmonies, her curves, her golden number.

6

The evening of the same day, I found myself alone with Father Mulligan. We were reading in silence. He had Maritain's essays on *The Spirit in Its Carnal State* and I was reading the story of a little prince who had escaped from an asteroid with the help of a flock of wild birds. Rosena had already gone to bed. Since our return from the market, I had been looking for a chance to set matters right with my confessor. In his look, there was no animosity, just a virile, self-aware kindness that even seemed to be affectionately understanding toward us.

' "Scandal" won the first round,' he said.

'And I have to look out, right, Father?'

'We both have to look out. We were both in the ring, weren't we?' he replied.

'What surprises me is that I don't feel as if I've sinned. I feel as pure as before. It's as if I just sampled the tip of ecstasy. Rosena made me experience the other four-fifths of an incredible state of grace.'

'It's not right, my son, to compare grace to an iceberg. If that were the case, I would have seen two frozen statues coming back from the river. Confess that this wasn't true,' he said, laughing.

'Maybe a divine "iceberg", submerged in our blood contains the very warmth of God.'

'You are completely caught up in your fascination with evil. It's blasphemous to associate grace with a mere adventure of the flesh.'

'And yet, Father, I prayed for a long time yesterday evening. The more I asked God's forgiveness, the more it seemed to me that he was blessing me for having dipped my soul like a piece of toast in the honey of the mountain. Why should evil be more fascinating than good? Why should I have experienced Rosena like a life-giving explosion?'

'Now you are touching on one of the great mysteries of creation. Light comes from Satan, also. According to the designs of the Creator, it would be too simple if the demon always appeared with the familiar look of a minion of darkness. . . .'

'So, in your eyes, Rosena is evil incarnate?'

'I've already told you that God sometimes submits his chosen ones to the illusions of the flesh in order to test their mettle. It is all to the better if this trial has not exhausted your store of purity. But it would be a serious sin to confound Satan's brilliance with the limpid incandescence of grace!'

'I don't feel the least remorse. The little bit I felt last night was swept away this morning. God placed the pristine form of woman's sweet flesh in my hands. These hands are entranced for the rest of my days!'

'My son, you need help!'

'Help me, Father,' I replied.

'Let's go pray together.'

He got up, took the hurricane lamp and started along the path leading to the chapel. I followed him through the night. He placed the lamp at the foot of the altar and knelt. His deep voice rose with gravity and sonority as he intoned the 'Pater noster' and the 'Ave Maria'.

I responded, 'Holy Mary, Mother of God, pray for us, poor sinners, now and at the hour of our death. . . . Our Father, who art in Heaven, . . . I salute you, Mary.'

As I uttered these sacred words, tears came into my eyes. A different memory and a new piety brought the name of Rosena and our experience at the river to mind, forcibly replacing the image of the Mother of God.

'I salute you, Rosena, full of grace, now and at the hour of our death . . . .' Suddenly my voice cracked with sobs.

'Don't be ashamed of your tears, my son,' said Father Mulligan. 'They are flowing down the cheeks of the marvelous woman who is listening to us.'

He got up and I followed him. My heart was ready to burst. My legs would barely carry me. The transparent, fresh night of the mountain must be Rosena. The lactescent, starry sky is Rosena, is it not? And my pillow and sleep that night: Rosena!

7

Had anybody watched us during the following weeks, they would have thought that the peace of the Lord was reigning beneath the shady foliage around Lamark Chapel. At dawn, I continued to assist Father Mulligan at Mass. Rosena kept kneeling behind us each morning. When I changed the place of the Missal on the altar, I glanced at her and her smile told me that we were following the same religion. When I rang the bell for the consecration and Rosena piously bowed her head, I knew that the bread and wine, mysteriously changed into the body and blood of Christ by the priest, had a special savor for us like the beautiful work of our flesh. Father Mulligan observed the Mass in accordance with the most orthodox Roman rites as he unknowingly celebrated the secret rites by which Rosena and I experienced our delirious identity in love. The gods of our childhood were slyly alert behind our Christian ritual.

Once she had served breakfast, after Mass, Rosena disappeared for several hours to take care of her kitchen and housekeeping chores. Father Mulligan gave me Latin lessons in the cool shade of a tree below the porch. He was also initiating me to philosophy. He often spoke to me about a current of Catholic thought that particularly interested him at that time—neo-thomism. He was acquainted with its principal proponent, Jacques Maritain, then teaching at Columbia University and at Princeton. The priest wanted to invite Maritain to give some lectures in Haiti.

Once a week, he received his mail from the capital. He gave me commentaries on the war, which was in full swing. That summer, the big news was the English resistance to the German offensive in Libya and the admirable strengthening of the Red Army, in the Caucasus and on the Don. The communiqués also mentioned the attacks by the Japanese forces in New Guinea and the bloody stages of the campaign of Guadalcanal. Father Mulligan's passion, however, was for Free France. He never tired of talking about what had happened at the beginning of the summer in the Libyan countryside. For almost two weeks, General Charles de Gaulle's troops had heroically resisted German Stukas and General Rommel's heavy artillery.

'Beginning with Bir Hakeim, France has come back into the war in the finest tradition of its past,' he explained.

He repeated the text that the head of Free France had addressed to the heroes of Bir Hakeim: 'General Koenig, you and your troops should know that France watches you and that you are her pride.'

'You would think that this was one of Napoleon's edicts,' exclaimed Father Mulligan.

At the time, I knew nothing about the political divisions of the modern world. The familiar names of the war, Guadalcanal, Tobruk, the Dneper, Timoshenko, El Alamein, the Crimea, and Montgomery, mixed with the names of Latin authors such as Cicero, Titus Livy, and Pliny the Younger. They all took their place beside the name of the woman who was offering me an entirely different bread of life. . . .

At lunch, we ate together. Without fail, the priest and I would congratulate Rosena on her culinary ability—not the least of her talents. After lunch, we helped her with the dishes, shelling peas, peeling potatoes, cleaning the lamps, cutting wood, and other household tasks. Father Mulligan always carried his medical kit with him and he had the gravity and assurance of a doctor when he attended cases of fever, yaws, kwashiorkor, and other maladies endemic to the Haitian countryside. Rosena and I served then as his attentive nurses. We discovered the avitaminosis that affects both children and adults. We heard explanations given by the priest on rickets, scurvy, beriberi, and pellagra. When we returned to the house, we walked in silence while the beauty of the trees in which the birds chased each other singing and the joyful summer of the mountain made us bleed inwardly from the misery that left us powerless. The same disarming sadness made Father Mulligan more somber. At those times, Rosena and I felt a bit abashed at our secret celebrations.

In fact, when the priest thought that I was piously kneeling in the chapel at prayer time, I had often run top speed to join Rosena in the shade of a bush or at the river bank. We made love in dazzling harmony. As soon as we had reached climax, I ran back to kneel in the chapel.

One morning, we had taken each other standing in the kitchen. We were so ecstatic that it seemed our legs had vaporized and our bodies floated over the pots and the incandescent coals. Often toward dawn, after making sure that the priest was asleep, I slipped into Rosena's room. The silence in which we gently excited our circulation was so full, so good, so dizzy that it seemed like the very embodiment of the vagina in which my existence centered.

Once, when we had spent three days without touching each other, we made love on a pew in the chapel, feverishly blending our orgasms with the very breath of God. As for the priest, he began treating Rosena with a highly paternal respect. 'Now he knows the kindling that I am burning. He is cautious, but basically the Irish rooster in him isn't asleep,' said Rosena.

One afternoon, toward four o'clock, a peasant arrived as breathless as the horse he was riding. He had come to take Father Mulligan to a dying man several leagues from Lamark. He said that the man had lived a good, Christian life and, since he had heard of the priest, did not want to die without the final sacraments. The peasant added that if he drove his mule hard, the priest could get back before sunrise. As he was leaving, Father Mulligan took me aside and pointed out the danger I was in, remaining alone in the house with Rosena Rozel after such a torrid August day. He advised me to spend all night praying in the chapel.

'Look out, my son. The earth will be devastated this evening by the wars of the flesh. It will be an agonizing vigil!'

I promised to keep my lamp lit.

Our honeymoon began in the river. In the fantastically starlit night, we went back to the house without dressing. We had a feast of oranges, melons, bananas and other fruit brought from the market the day before. By the light of the hurricane lamps, we pushed the three beds together in order to enlarge the arena for our nuptial games. Hours later, intoxicated and fatigued from mutual delight, we fell into the sleep of children, the insane, and lovers.

We did not hear the priest come in. When I opened my eyes, I did not know how long he had been there watching us sleeping with interlocked arms and legs. The lamps were still lit. The priest's eyes were bulging out of his head and his prickly beard was darting red flames. The veins in his neck were beating, and his Adam's apple stood out like a curious erection. I grabbed a sheet and covered Rosena, who was still asleep. I got up to put on my pajamas. Father Mulligan threw himself on me. With a rough prod, he pushed me against the wall. He punched me right in the face. Then he hit me on the nose. I stifled a cry of pain.

'Stop, or I'm going to start punching, too,' I said.

He poked me in the mouth. My nose and lips were bleeding. I was reeling from more blows, but kept taking them like a fool, forgetting that I was an athlete. Finally, our struggle aroused Rosena. Seeing my disarray, she fled to the kitchen and ran back in immediately with a machete in one hand. Father Mulligan turned. Without letting go of her weapon, she threw off the cumbersome sheet. She was splendidly naked with the knife in her fist. She was staring at a precise part of the priest's anatomy. The man saw in her eyes that Rosena was determined to cut *them* off, once and for all.

'Drop your trousers,' ordered Rosena Rozel.

Like an automaton, the mesmerized priest unbuckled his belt with incredible humility. The trousers fell at his feet, baring his sturdy legs, all covered with red hair.

'Your shorts, too,' said Rosena with the same commanding tone.

He obeyed, revealing a tumescent organ that appeared pugnacious and warlike, ready to face any danger. Rosena took a step and struck with all her strength. I rushed at her, pushed her frantically into the other room, and disarmed her. Then I flew back to the missionary's aid. He was bent in two, pulling cotton out of a first-aid kit and trying to stop the bleeding from the ugly wound.

'I don't need your help,' he growled. 'Take her away! Get out of here, couple from hell!'

We dressed and threw our affairs into one packet. With tears in our eyes, we set out into the fresh, sparkling dawn.

In mid-September, I tried discreetly to get some news about Father James Mulligan from a nurse I knew in the municipal hospital. I found out that he had fallen victim to a serious accident in Lamark, where, according to his custom, he had gone for the summer. A vicious horse had given him such a violent kick on the tender parts that he was now in convalescence. At last report, he was accepting his condition philosophically.

ROY HEATH (b. 1926)

The Master Tailor and the Teacher's Skirt

The Teacher had saved enough money to treat herself to an extravagance. She shared a house in Diamond with a younger married sister and her husband and their three boy children. Lately they had also taken in a woman friend who, in exchange for looking after the children, lived there free of charge.

The Teacher's attachment to her sister's family had caused her to put off marriage to a man who had been courting her for the last nine years. The attachment had been all the stronger as her brother-in-law had been out of work; but now he was employed at the match factory in Pouderoyen and the only reason for delaying her marriage had disappeared. She was so set in her ways, however, and her procrastination had become such a natural reaction to his repeated proposals that she continued to resist.

'No, I won't ever get married,' she told herself.

And with that admission came the realization that her excessive concern with money in the bank was misplaced.

The Teacher, an extremely cautious lady, decided to wait until the object of her indulgence occurred to her, naturally as it were. If she bought a watch—her first idea—she might regret it. There were so many other ways of telling the time. She needed a pair of galoshes for the rainy weather; but galoshes were hardly an extravagance. A meal for the family at the Arapaima in town she rejected as well, since she regarded that as a transient pleasure. No, there was nothing for it but to wait.

One morning, during the August holidays, while on her way to Supply to visit another married sister, her attention was drawn to a woman of about thirty who had just got out of a taxi. She dismounted from her cycle and walked after her, resisting the impulse to say outright how much she admired her skirt. It was only when the young woman was about to turn into a yard that she plunged into what she later saw as an unforgivable indiscretion.

'Excuse me. I was admiring your skirt. Who made it for you?'

The lady smiled and told her of a remarkable tailor working in town.
'It suits you . . . Anyway, I'm sorry.'
'No! I'm glad you tell me.'
They parted, the Teacher still smarting from her boldness, and unable to look back once more at the stranger's khaki skirt.
She spoke to her sister and brother-in-law about the skirt while they were sitting on the back stairs that evening.
I've never seen any skirt like that in my life.'
'Get one made, then,' said her brother-in-law.
'I'm going to, but not just yet.'
'What're you waiting for?' her sister asked.
'I'll get it, but not yet.'
Their yard sloped down to the river, where unidentified objects were floating on the ebb tide.
'D'you think I'll ever get married?' the Teacher asked.
Neither her sister nor brother-in-law answered and all three thought it was best so.
The Teacher's sister, as impulsive as her sister was cautious, could not understand her hesitation about the skirt.
'Make the skirt,' her brother-in-law ventured. 'Get married. Lash out for once! It not goin' kill you.'
'Marrying is lashing out,' said her sister. 'But buying a skirt . . .'
Reassured that her caution was excessive, the Teacher, while pretending to give the matter thought, decided that she would buy the cloth the following day.
Mr Melville was a good tailor. He was, indeed, a fine tailor, one of the last of the master craftsmen who worked alone or with, at most, two employees. *He* had no assistants, relying only on his wife to help him with little jobs around the shop, like unstacking customers' cloth when a length went astray, or the adding up of accounts for which he had conspicuously less talent than cutting or styling.
Contemptuous of the large establishments which had sprung up in the sixties and secured their business from government departments and public corporations, he declared that he would not stoop to paying $500 to a corrupt civil servant in order to secure a large contract for 150 uniforms. What would they make of his honesty and handiwork, which would be vitiated by the meddling of many hands? No! A shirt-jac or a pair of trousers must marry the man's figure as if he were born in it. Mass production was the enemy of art and the artistic drive, and he was an artist, an artist's artist.

In spite of his acknowledged flair for judging a customer's *drift*—the word he used to describe the singularity of every individual's figure—and supreme skill in cutting, Mr Melville had begun to notice a falling-off in the demand for his work. He was not unduly worried, because the waiting list of customers was quite impressive, and their orders included seventeen shirt-jacs, five pairs of trousers and a garment of indeterminate classification which a lady customer had ordered for the first lodge meeting to initiate women members.

Whenever Mr Melville mentioned this falling-off of orders to his wife she looked at him blankly, not caring to venture an opinion. Her husband was an affable man, but he was also quick-tempered and believed not only that he was entitled to the admiration and respect of all those with whom he came into contact, but also that such esteem placed him beyond any reproach, however mild.

Mr Melville had recently bought a telephone, an unnecessary acquisition, his wife thought.

'How many tailor-shops got telephone?' she asked, breaking her rule never to criticize him.

'This is not a tailor-shop, I keep telling you, woman. Is a establishment. Tobesides it'll increase business.'

'What you want to increase business for when you don' want to take on tailors?'

Interpreting her candour as criticism he warned her to watch her tongue.

In the event, the telephone did nothing for business, which continued to decrease, slightly but noticeably.

The master tailor greeted every client with the same show of delight, even if the person had spoken to him the day before. The men he addressed as 'Brother' and slapped those of long acquaintance on the back, while the few ladies who patronized his establishment he called 'Sister' and rewarded the ones he knew well with a vigorous embrace.

'Good afternoon, sister,' he said to the Teacher who was leading her cycle over the bridge which connected the shop and pavement.

'Mr Melville,' she declared, 'You've been highly recommended. I'd like you to make me a skirt. My dressmaker doesn't work in khaki, you see.'

'No problem, sister. My wife will take your measurements.'

'Oh, I don't mind if you did,' said the young woman. 'These are modern times.'

Mr Melville duly measured his client, took her instructions and named his price. Then, examining the length of cloth she had brought with her, he declared it to be satisfactory.

'When can I come for it?' she enquired.

'Tomorrow,' he said, beaming. 'My motto is "speed and craftsmanship".'

'Alright, tomorrow, then. What time do you close?'

'At six.'

'I'll come at half-past five.'

'What a pleasant man!' the Teacher muttered as she wheeled her cycle round and set off home. 'What an extraordinarily pleasant man!'

She had decided to have two khaki skirts made and pay well, for she wanted them to last forever.

'Tomorrow! He doesn't drag his feet.'

The following afternoon she set out for the tailor-shop armed with a wicker basket to carry her brand new skirt. If the craftsman's work was as good as people said it was she would order the second skirt, which, the way things looked, she could be wearing in a fortnight's time.

'Good afternoon, Mr Melville,' the Teacher greeted the tailor, who was smiling broadly and had his right hand stretched out to receive hers.

'Good afternoon, sister.'

'I've come for the skirt.'

'Ah!' he said, without letting go her hand and beaming as broadly as ever. 'We've got a problem.'

'What?'

'It's not finished.'

'But you were positive yesterday,' the teacher protested with surprise. 'You promised.'

'Tomorrow without fail,' he assured her. 'You come tomorrow. Not at half-past five, but at any time. You want to come first thing in the morning?'

'No Mr Melville. I'll come at half-past five . . . I was planning to christen that skirt tomorrow, you know. I now have to go home and . . . Oh, it doesn't matter.'

She went off, more keen than ever to see the workmanship that would compensate her for the disappointment she felt.

'Goodbye, sister,' he said, waving at her.

His wife appeared on the bridge just after the Teacher left, in the company of their small son. The tailor came to meet them.

'What the lady want?' she asked.

'A skirt I measure her for.'

The tailor, glad of company after working all day, lifted his son above his head and began to romp with him, while his wife set about tidying up the lengths of cloth and finished garments her husband had left lying about. She then disappeared into the back room to prepare the evening meal on an ancient coal-pot she had rescued from under her house during the gasoline shortage in the middle seventies.

The following day the Teacher telephoned the tailor early in the afternoon to make certain that the garment was ready.

'No problem, sister Teacher. When you want to come?'

'We agreed on half-past five,' the teacher answered, speaking with a certain irritation for the first time.

'Right. See you at half-past five.'

She arrived promptly, dismounted from her cycle, her wicker basket dangling from the handle-bar. At the same time the Tailor's wife was leaving the shop to go and fetch her child from her uncle's home.

'It in' ready yet, you know,' she told the Teacher apologetically.

'What?' came the unbelieving rhetorical question. 'But I phoned only this afternoon and he said, "No problem". He even suggested I could come whenever I wanted.'

The tailor's wife looked away, as embarrassed as if she had been caught with her fingers in her neighbour's nut butter.

'Why not give him a week?' she suggested, examining the sky as if there was something unusual moving across it.

'A week! . . . This is unbelievable! A week.'

The last word came out so weakly the tailor's wife looked at her again, full of pity, knowing how women suffered in this world.

'A week? But I told the teachers in my school I'd be wearing the skirt tomorrow. Your husband sounded so confident. A week . . . Alright, I'll come next Thursday at the same time and I'll ring two days before.'

Dolefully she turned her cycle round and, in trying to mount it, missed her step and nearly fell.

Now, until that afternoon the Teacher had never once experienced any aggressive feelings towards anyone, not even her younger brother when they were children and he used to shoot compressed bits of paper at her. Now, for the very first time in her life she had to suppress a wild impulse to do the tailor an injury.

'Is he tetched?' she thought. 'It's only a skirt. How long does he take to make a pair of trousers!'

Finding that she had turned right instead of left and was heading for the Sawmill, she interrupted her reflections and concentrated instead on the business of getting home in one piece.

In the late hours of that fine June afternoon her placid nature reasserted itself and she was overcome with a great sympathy for the unfortunate people who lined the East Bank Public Road waiting for a taxi to take them home. *She* had a bicycle!

And with the discovery of her good fortune the Teacher berated herself for wishing to throw a brick at the tailor's shop a while ago.

'Mr Melville?'

'Ah, Teach! I recognize your voice right away. When you coming for the skirt? This afternoon?'

'This afternoon! I told your wife tomorrow. I just rang to give you time.'

'Time!' the tailor said scornfully, and blew into the receiver. 'No problem at all.'

'This afternoon then,' the Teacher declared, involuntarily smoothing the skirt she was wearing. 'Goodbye, then.'

'See you, Teach.'

The Teacher's heart was overwhelmed with Christian charity. It was lunch-time and she was telephoning from the drug-store a few doors away from St Barnabas Primary School where she worked. She smiled and thanked the dispenser for allowing her to use his telephone. Nowadays people expected you to pay for such favours; nowadays, when even small children knew the going rate of exchange for the American dollar as against the Guyanese, official as well as unofficial. He, like the tailor, was of the old school, full of courtesy and good service.

That afternoon as she led her cycle over the tailor-shop bridge, she spotted the couple's small son sitting on the counter, his features as expressionless as his mother's. His father possessed enough fire and charm for both of them, and more to spare.

'Good afternoon, Mr Melville,' the Teacher called. 'At last!'

The tailor might have been facing a ghost, for the surprise that came over him. But, recovering swiftly, he thrust out his arm and said: 'Shake hands!'

Perplexed, suspicious, the Teacher put out her hand and allowed it to be shaken by the tailor.

'You want to eat with me?' he asked, nodding towards the kitchen. 'Is pork!'

'No thanks, Mr Melville. I've come for my skirt. Is it ready?'

'Hold on . . . Cheryl! Cheryl!' he called out to his wife. 'Where's that khaki cloth for the skirt?'

His wife appeared and joined him in the search for the length of cloth his client had entrusted to his care so hopefully. They hoisted piles of garments, undid parcels, unfolded, half-bales, scattered left-overs, bent double to examine the shelves under the counter, lifted up their son to see if he was sitting on the missing cloth, bumped into each other, and even leaned out of the window in case it had, somehow, managed to slide into the gutter below.

'Ah, here it is!' the tailor shouted, rescuing a length of material beneath a heap of finished garments.

'Mine, Mr Melville,' said the Teacher coldly, 'is khaki.'

'What's got into me?' he said. 'Of course.' And so saying, he slapped his forehead so vigorously his wife looked up in alarm.

'Is this it?' she asked, retrieving the missing material from the same heap.

'Yes, that's it,' the Teacher said, as coldly as before. 'It's not done.'

'No Teacher,' declared the tailor, 'I got a problem. Is the thread. I don' have the right colour thread. But if you wait I goin' go up the road and borrow some khaki-colour thread from Tailor-Fawfee-Eye. If you wait here I'll get the thread an' do the skirt for you now. Right now! And! And you can eat with me while you wait.'

'No, Mr Melville,' the Teacher said, her fury all the more apparent from the controlled way in which she spoke. 'I will not eat with you and I will not wait. But what I do want to know is when my skirt will be ready.'

'Tomorrow . . . without fail.'

'Let us say in a month's time, Mr Melville. I will come on the seventeenth of July.'

She consulted her diary to verify that the seventeenth was indeed a weekday.

'Shake hands, Teach!' he offered.

But the Teacher turned away and went out of the shop, leading her bicycle. She was to recall later that not once had the little boy moved while his parents were turning the shop upside down. The tailor's wife, she was certain, had all but died of shame.

That evening the Teacher found she could not swallow because her saliva had dried up. She begged her sister and brother-in-law to understand that nothing was seriously wrong with her. Her saliva would start flowing again before she retired for the night, she was certain. It had happened once before, during her probationary year. A friend of hers used to break out in a cold sweat from time to time, which was much worse; but once they were qualified everything was well again.

The month passed gradually, a late June of rainy days and sullen nights and a July that could not match the summers of years ago, when you could plan a picnic with the certainty of unblemished skies. The Teacher became obsessed with her unmade skirt. No longer did she worry about what her colleagues at work thought or whether she would give Mr Melville the order for a second one. That was out of the question. After her experience she would not ask him to cut a handkerchief! Apart from her anxiety that went with the suspense of waiting, it was her unusual fantasies about the tailor which worried her. Once, in the limbo state between sleeping and waking, he approached her in his affable manner, the finished skirt held triumphantly above his head. Delighted that the business was at an end she quickly opened her purse to pay him, only to find that on looking up again the new garment had been transformed into its original state, a length of khaki cloth.

But her imagination fashioned incidents less innocent at night, soon after she dropped off. She had taken to entering his shop with her wicker basket full of bricks, with the intention of hurling them at him if he used any of the expressions she had come to detest: 'No problem', 'I've got a problem', 'Shake hands', or should he declare that the skirt was yet unmade. But to her dismay, on waking, she remembered that in her dreams she had joined the tailor in a meal during which he used the forbidden words several times without any protest on her part.

The day in July duly arrived, a day like most other days, when the sun rose at the appointed time and housewives were preparing to stand in cooking-oil lines for hours and the morning service was broadcast, like the rising sun, at the appointed time, and harassed teachers were preoccupied with bullying head-teachers and affable tailors. And the first sight that attracted the Teacher's attention as she rode by on the way to school was a heap of bricks on a building site. Not being a superstitious person, however, she rode on without seeing any significance in the unsightly mound.

That afternoon, on her way to the tailor-shop to collect her skirt she recalled the pile of bricks, which reminded her of the pile of garments under which the tailor's wife had found her length of khaki.

Once more she pushed her cycle over the bridge, her heart throbbing in anticipation.

'But where's that shirt-jac?' she heard the tailor's voice.

A tall man was standing with his hands akimbo, watching the tailor and his wife, who were engaged in a desperate search for a missing garment. Catching sight of her he lifted his hand in a gesture which said, 'Just a little while and I'll be with you.' He was not smiling. For the first time since she met him he wore the same blank expression as his wife and son. Lengths of cloth and finished garments were scattered about the counter and the cloud of dust testified to a long, persistent search. The male client stood silently, with that show of Guyanese patience which astounds even Barbadians, who are noted for their mild manners.

'It's that one,' the client said, without joy. 'The one in your hand. Give it to me, please.'

'But I'll finish it by tomorrow,' the tailor protested. 'Come firs' thing in the morning and it'll be ready.'

The man leaned over the counter, look the cloth from the tailor and, without more ado, left the shop.

'To think he did only bring me it in March!' he exclaimed, at a loss to understand his client's behaviour.

Saying this he put out his hand to shake the Teacher's.

'Teach! I'm so hot! You met my wife, haven't you?'

The women nodded, each apparently put out by the other's presence.

'Teach, I got a problem,' the tailor said, shaking his head. 'The skirt not done.'

'I don't believe you . . . Can I see it?'

'It's not done,' he repeated.

'The cloth, I mean.'

'The cloth?'

'Yes.'

Without looking down he put his hand under the counter and drew out the material.

'You haven't even started it,' she said.

'I couldn' get the thread, Teach.'

'May I have it?' she asked, without a trace of irritation in her voice.

He gave her the cloth and she took it, half reluctantly, thinking that it might be best after all to leave it in the hands of an exasperatingly unreliable craftsman than with a mediocre tailor who took Time seriously.

146

Perhaps there was a tailor, somewhere in the city, who was master of his craft and reliable into the bargain. Perhaps.

The couple stood side by side, watching the Teacher mount her cycle.

'Now you see why business falling off,' his wife ventured.

'That's what *you* say. I say people getting unreasonable. An' I tell you something I jus' notice. You so sour-faced I sure you does put off a lot of customers. You can't laugh a little? Look at me!'

GABRIEL GARCÍA MÁRQUEZ (b. 1928)

The Last Voyage of the Ghost Ship

Translated by Gregory Rabassa

Now they're going to see who I am, he said to himself in his strong
new man's voice, many years after he had first seen the huge ocean liner
without lights and without any sound which passed by the village one
night like a great uninhabited palace, longer than the whole village and
much taller than the steeple of the church, and it sailed by in the darkness
toward the colonial city on the other side of the bay that had been fortified
against buccaneers, with its old slave port and the rotating light, whose
gloomy beams transfigured the village into a lunar encampment of glowing houses and streets of volcanic deserts every fifteen seconds, and even
though at that time he'd been a boy without a man's strong voice but with
his mother's permission to stay very late on the beach to listen to the
wind's night harps, he could still remember, as if still seeing it, how the
liner would disappear when the light of the beacon struck its side and how
it would reappear when the light had passed, so that it was an intermittent
ship sailing along, appearing and disappearing, toward the mouth of
the bay, groping its way like a sleepwalker for the buoys that marked the
harbor channel until something must have gone wrong with the compass
needle, because it headed toward the shoals, ran aground, broke up, and
sank without a single sound, even though a collision against the reefs like
that should have produced a crash of metal and the explosion of engines
that would have frozen with fright the soundest-sleeping dragons in the
prehistoric jungle that began with the last streets of the village and ended
on the other side of the world, so that he himself thought it was a dream,
especially the next day, when he saw the radiant fishbowl of the bay, the
disorder of colors of the Negro shacks on the hills above the harbor, the
schooners of the smugglers from the Guianas loading their cargoes of
innocent parrots whose craws were full of diamonds, he thought, I fell
asleep counting the stars and I dreamed about the huge ship, of course, he

was so convinced that he didn't tell anyone nor did he remember the vision again until the same night of the following March when he was looking for the flash of dolphins in the sea and what he found was the illusory liner, gloomy, intermittent, with the same mistaken direction as the first time, except that then he was so sure he was awake that he ran to tell his mother and she spent three weeks moaning with disappointment, because your brain's rotting away from doing so many things backward, sleeping during the day and going out at night like a criminal, and since she had to go to the city around that time to get something comfortable where she could sit and think about her dead husband, because the rockers on her chair had worn out after eleven years of widowhood, she took advantage of the occasion and had the boatman go near the shoals so that her son could see what he really saw in the glass of the sea, the lovemaking of manta rays in a springtime of sponges, pink snappers and blue corvinas diving into the other wells of softer waters that were there among the waters, and even the wandering hairs of victims of drowning in some colonial shipwreck, no trace of sunken liners or anything like it, and yet he was so pigheaded that his mother promised to watch with him the next March, absolutely, not knowing that the only thing absolute in her future now was an easy chair from the days of Sir Francis Drake which she had bought at an auction in a Turk's store, in which she sat down to rest that same night, sighing, oh, my poor Olofernos, if you could only see how nice it is to think about you on this velvet lining and this brocade from the casket of a queen, but the more she brought back the memory of her dead husband, the more the blood in her heart bubbled up and turned to chocolate, as if instead of sitting down she were running, soaked from chills and fevers and her breathing full of earth, until he returned at dawn and found her dead in the easy chair, still warm, but half rotted away as after a snakebite, the same as happened afterward to four other women before the murderous chair was thrown into the sea, far away where it wouldn't bring evil to anyone, because it had been used so much over the centuries that its faculty for giving rest had been used up, and so he had to grow accustomed to his miserable routine of an orphan who was pointed out by everyone as the son of the widow who had brought the throne of misfortune into the village, living not so much from public charity as from the fish he stole out of boats, while his voice was becoming a roar, and not remembering his visions of past times anymore until another night in March when he chanced to look seaward and suddenly, good Lord, there it is, the huge asbestos whale, the behemoth beast, come see it, he shouted madly, come see it, raising such an uproar of dogs' barking and women's panic that even the oldest men remembered the frights of their great-grandfathers and crawled under their beds, thinking that William Dampier had come back, but those who ran into the street didn't make the effort to see the unlikely apparatus which at that instant was lost again in the east and raised up in its annual disaster, but they covered him with blows and left him so twisted that it was then he said to himself, drooling with rage, now they're going to see who I am, but he took care not to share his determination with anyone, but spent the whole year with the fixed idea, now they're going to see who I am, waiting for it to be the eve of the apparition once more in order to do what he did, which was steal a boat, cross the bay, and spend the evening waiting for his great moment in the inlets of the slave port, in the human brine of the Caribbean, but so absorbed in his adventure that he didn't stop as he always did in front of the Hindu shops to look at the ivory mandarins carved from the whole tusk of an elephant, nor did he make fun of the Dutch Negroes in their orthopedic velocipedes, nor was he frightened as at other times of the copper-skinned Malayans, who had gone around the world enthralled by the chimera of a secret tavern where they sold roast filets of Brazilian women, because he wasn't aware of anything until night came over him with all the weight of the stars and the jungle exhaled a sweet fragrance of gardenias and rotten salamanders, and there he was, rowing in the stolen boat toward the mouth of the bay, with the lantern out so as not to alert the customs police, idealized every fifteen seconds by the green wing flap of the beacon and turned human once more by the darkness, knowing that he was getting close to the buoys that marked the harbor channel, not only because its oppressive glow was getting more intense, but because the breathing of the water was becoming sad, and he rowed like that, so wrapped up in himself, that he didn't know where the fearful shark's breath that suddenly reached him came from or why the night became dense, as if the stars had suddenly died, and it was because the liner was there, with all of its inconceivable size, Lord, bigger than any other big thing in the world and darker than any other dark thing on land or sea, three hundred thousand tons of shark smell passing so close to the boat that he could see the seams of the steel precipice, without a single light in the infinite portholes, without a sigh from the engines, without a soul, and carrying its own circle of silence with it, its own dead air, its halted time, its errant sea in which a whole world of drowned animals floated, and suddenly it all disappeared with the flash of the beacon and for an instant it was the diaphanous Caribbean once more, the March night, the everyday air of the pelicans, so he stayed alone among the buoys, not knowing what to do, asking himself, startled, if perhaps he wasn't dreaming while he was awake, not just now but the other times too, but no sooner had he asked himself than a breath of mystery snuffed out the buoys, from the first to the last, so that when the light of the beacon passed by the liner appeared again and now its compasses were out of order, perhaps not even knowing what part of the ocean sea it was in, groping for the invisible channel but actually heading for the shoals, until he got the overwhelming revelation that that misfortune of the buoys was the last key to the enchantment and he lighted the lantern in the boat, a tiny red light that had no reason to alarm anyone in the watchtowers but which would be like a guiding sun for the pilot, because, thanks to it, the liner corrected its course and passed into the main gate of the channel in a maneuver of lucky resurrection, and then all the lights went on at the same time so that the boilers wheezed again, the stars were fixed in their places, and the animal corpses went to the bottom, and there was a clatter of plates and a fragrance of laurel sauce in the kitchens, and one could hear the pulsing of the orchestra on the moon decks and the throbbing of the arteries of high-sea lovers in the shadows of the staterooms, but he still carried so much leftover rage in him that he would not let himself be confused by emotion or be frightened by the miracle, but said to himself with more decision than ever, now they're going to see who I am, the cowards, now they're going to see, and instead of turning aside so that the colossal machine would not charge into him, he began to row in front of it, because now they really are going to see who I am, and he continued guiding the ship with the lantern until he was so sure of its obedience that he made it change course from the direction of the docks once more, took it out of the invisible channel, and led it by the halter as if it were a sea lamb toward the lights of the sleeping village, a living ship, invulnerable to the torches of the beacon, that no longer made it invisible but made it aluminum every fifteen seconds, and the crosses of the church, the misery of the houses, the illusion began to stand out, and still the ocean liner followed behind him, following his will inside of it, the captain asleep on his heart side, the fighting bulls in the snow of their pantries, the solitary patient in the infirmary, the orphan water of its cisterns, the unredeemed pilot who must have mistaken the cliffs for the docks, because at that instant the great roar of the whistle burst forth, once, and he was soaked with the downpour of steam that fell on him, again, and the boat belonging to someone else was on the point of capsizing, and again, but it was too late, because there were the shells of the shoreline, the stones of the streets, the doors of the disbelievers, the whole village illuminated by the lights of the fearsome liner itself, and he barely

ANDREW SALKEY (1928–1995)

A Proper Anno Domini Feeling

One time, when Anancy was really suffering bad from a proper Anno Domini feeling, like it was catching him right deep inside him plexus and thing, he start to consider himself as a traveller; and he say to himself sort of sweet and easy, 'How much I learning from travelling, though eh?'

Now, talking to youself and putting question to youself is one thing; it not too difficle. But truthful answer is a dead slow knock, in most case, and this one, here so, so slow, is nothing but pure earthworm spool, I can tell you.

Anancy wait and he wait and he wait. Not a answer is a answer.

Then, he ask himself it, again. He even talk loud, this time. And he wait.

In fact, he wait until day turn into dark night, and until dark night turn into Christmas time, and until mucho Christmas come and gone.

And then, sudden, one September day, the answer lick him sideways. When we hear it coming out of him head, he couldn't believe him ears. As a matter of story, now, he jam up him ears tight with cotton tree leaf, so that he wouldn't hear the realness of the answer, but still and all, the answer start to come through him nose.

And it sound like a actual Anancy answer, especial as how it got a nose twang helping it out.

See the answer, here so: this is what you learn, Anancy, that the world don't make f'the sake a human woman and man, and it not growing human nohow even with him living in it.

Anancy nearly fall down paralytic when he consider what him mind telling him with that saying. And he know say that the saying reaching him from a society thinker-person name H.M., in something deep he write down, in a small book, in a far north country that been going on real domineering, exploiting, penetrating and fuck up with other countries, right cross the world.

You see, as how initials go, H.M. going have to stay as plain and conceal up H.M., without it get spell out proper; but take story word for it, the

153

name true and actual, and is a name the north country did wrestle with, some years aback, when all the green youth people them did decide to rip down the temple and stop the war, over foreign.

Anyway, the answer blowing way Anancy self. He scringe up him face, as though pain lashing it two side. Then, he circle walk, little bit. After that, he stand up and he ponder and he ponder. Final thing, he say to himself, 'But stop, is that I learn after the how much and how long I been travelling?'

He nod him head, swallow hard, and say, again, 'People bad no sore, Papa D.'

So he say it, so he nod, nod, nod. Until he say this one last thing, 'World, you on you own. If is human you looking to be, don't bother with people example. It not going help you, no matter how much faith you got in them brain power and such like prettiness.'

Like it was thunder thumping up the sky belly, a big opening up there just happen, and a cloud, taking shape of history suction, call out to Anancy, 'You learning good, spiderman. Take it from you friend, me, people forgetful easy. You can always repeat and repeat on them. I do it, all the time. Them scarcely know how f'read the go-between between past scripture and present dealings. And future muchness? That book shut tight. Keep travelling, Anancy!'

And Anancy say to himself, sad no burial Sunday, 'I wonder if the world stand a chance?'

Same time as Anancy say that, a whole mountain drop down on top of him. One part bawl out, 'Is old you getting old, Anancy! That's why you feeling the world heavy no plantation on you shoulder. Bear up strong, Anancy!'

A next part of the mountain that have a nose voice just like Anancy roll over three, four, five time on the ground, and say, 'People not bad, Anancy. Them is only people. Goodness and badness not into anything. And the world? Well, that is nothing without people, and world self know so. Advice to you is this, Anancy: don't look back; walk on direct into wind face; travel far; make history with people; and dead when time come. The world human enough for now. It going even get worser.'

When I tell you that Anancy catching a *bangarangs* of worries and mix-up, I ain't telling you lie. He be nothing less than tormentation pickney.

Well, anyway, as from time, when Anancy sinking into bothers and brain pain, he usual go by Caribbea and splint up himself with her words and sea wisdom.

He buck up on her guarding the islands them, as she always doing, and he walk up to her, soft, and say, 'I come, as you know I had was to come, yes?'

'Cho, Anancy, man,' Caribbea said self say back. 'I did figure out that, long time.'

'How?'

'Well, from the time that H.M. drop them worry words on you, I know say that you was going be in spirit trouble. You mustn't take all them sayings f'true, you know. Them is statement make by north people who losing the common faith-hope-action-and-struggle bottom to them basket. Next thing, them going get up one morning and go to the seaside and want to full up the basket and empty the sea, and when that cawn happen, them going call the world bad name, and them going call people worse than bad. People not bad, Anancy. Them is just people. Out-and-out people. Them lost most of the time. Don't know who them is themself. Don't know where them come from. Don't know what them doing in the world. Don't understand life. Fraid to dead. Just people, Anancy! You not to expect goodness or badness from them. Just peopleness! Remember that, and you going learn a whole heap from travelling! Promise me, now!'

Anancy lick him top lip and promise her. Then he sit down on a dry coconut and he look tender out to sea, with plenty love in him heart.

This Caribbea pretty, though eh? he tell himself. She be one woman I respect deep. What I like about her is that she free and liberate up in her work, to depths unknown to all like a spiderman like me, that sometimes I sure she be a planet in water shape. Correct thing! That's what she be to me. A planet! And she not growing old and such like.

'Anancy?' Caribbea call out, like she teasing him.

'Yes, Caribbea,' Anancy say back, cautious.

'You got Anno Domini on you mind. Don't it?'

'I mustn't tell you lie, Caribbea. Yes, old age icicle finger touching me, too much, these last days. I don't like it. It causing me bothers.'

'Well, let it go from now, Anancy. You can hope to change most things. But, that one, you got to live with and dead and left it behind to torture trillions. Is like so, exact how that big cousin I got set up the situation in the world.'

Anancy open him eye wide. He way, 'I never know that Mother Nature be you cousin, Caribbea?'

'She's me big cousin, Anancy. All water is close relative to her.'

'So, you belong to First Family?' Anancy smiling.

'Not so I reasoning it, Anancy. I belong to I. I belong to the work I been doing, centuries and centuries. I belong to you and to all the islands them, yes. And I don't consent to class, at all, at all. Big Cousin Nature got her job cut out massive for her. We meet up, now and then, especial when she restless and considering disaster with weather, wind and water. She's a funny, contrary, contradict-up, old woman, you know. Healer and killer. And talking about Anno Domini, she is that, plus zillions on top of zillions on top of zillions.'

Anancy scratch him headside. Maybe, I not so old, after all? he reckoning fast.

Caribbea noticing that Anancy pressure dropping. She feel good. She fling a sweet wave up by him neck back, and it relax him, nice, nice.

'Remember how I always telling the islands them that hope is a green thing, Anancy?'

'Yes.'

'And how struggle even more green than hope?'

'Yes.'

'And how all we make for is struggle and more struggle and more struggle, until dead we dead?'

'Yes.'

'So?'

'So, what, Caribbea?'

'So, we know how it go. And we know what f'expect. And that is that, Anancy. Live on! Struggle and dead!'

Eh, eh, that be the total answer? Anancy asking himself. Cawn go so. It too dry. Life must have some water into it. I mean to say, people cawn just get up with problem, move out with problem, live with problem, fight back, and dead?

The dry coconut be sitting on make a rolling movement under him, sudden.

Anancy jump up, like him hear news.

The dry coconut have two brown eye, and that give it face. It roll near the water, and stop. It grin, little bit.

Anancy walk down to it. Then, he stoop down and make four eye with it.

Them stare hard into one another face.

'I small and I lost me green coat, long time, now, but I understand what old age coming mean,' the dry coconut say, after it make cautious sure say Anancy really serious by the ace staring eye he claps on it own brown eye. 'F'you one main trouble, Anancy, is that you won't glimpse the world as what it real self is. You see, spiderman, you keep making up the world in you head, every day you get up, until every night you shut eye. You is a composer of world, Anancy! It go according to you, yes? No! Not so! You wrong!'

Anancy blink must be forty-four time or more. He just cawn understand how the dry coconut getting inside him mind and kicking pupa-lick, as it like, so easy.

'How the world stay, then?' Anancy ask.

'It stay rough, Anancy. It don't got no business to smooth. World born without heart. Is only belly it have. So, it eat people. It eating you, right now. That is why Anno Domini mashing you up, present at thy table, Lawd!'

'But you wronging me, there,' Anancy say. 'I know age bound to advance like soldier into enemy bullet. I not fraid a that.'

'You cawn fool me, Anancy,' the dry coconut say. 'I feel say that you want to live, for ever, amen! Dead not into your day or night language. Is that you fighting, no?'

'I not saying that,' Anancy say, turning him left side and just in time to see Caribbea winking her eye. 'Is the world bothering me mind.'

'How it causing you bothers, Anancy?'

'It growing old but it not growing good.'

As Anancy say that, the dry coconut roll down to the water, wet up itself, spin round a few time, and roll back up to where Anancy stooping down.

Then, it say to him, 'Anancy, I like you style. You is a world dreamer, when you want. You is a world composer. You is a world conscience. You have plenty nough heart. And I hear say that you is a long-time trickster and cunny master. But guess what?'

Anancy face twitch, tight, and he say, 'What?'

And the dry coconut say, 'You don't got doubt.'

'Maybe I don't need it,' Anancy say.

'Most every total creature, under Big Cousin Nature hand, need it to live life in the world, Anancy. How come you different?'

Anancy shake him head. He trying him best to figure out this dry coconut hardness, but it beating him.

Is how come you so concrete up? Is because you drop out of the coconut tree, long ages, and lose you green, or is what? You couldn't born the way you is, now?

While Anancy asking himself those manners set of inside question, the dry coconut start a rolling movement up to the coconut tree, some yards behind Anancy.

As that going on, the dry coconut brown eye them turning round and round, and them winking at Anancy, just like how Caribbea did wink, a little time ago.

Anancy call out, 'Don't leave, yet!'

But the dry coconut moving steady, heading for the coconut tree. When it get nearish, it say, 'Anancy, I can see you trying to reach me history. Like say, you want to capture the dryness and work it out for youself. Yes? Well, you remember the story about you and Brother Crab and Mada Cantinny and the animals she fostering? You remember how you, cunny Anancy, get to find out say that Mada Cantinny name was really Mada Cantinny? Well, then, you going have to sing Mada Cantinny song, the same one she sing to find out who give way her name mongst her children them. You going have to sing to every dry coconut pickney in the land, if you want to connect up with the dryness I got as me natural self. I gone.'

Anancy watch as the dry coconut roll tight up to the root of the coconut tree, roll straight up the ladder ring them on the trunk, and roll direct inside a bunch of green coconut and lost itself, cool as dry ice.

Anancy know that the Mada Cantinny song is something he cawn sing, nohow. So, he x-out the scene. But before he leave, he turn round and see Caribbea winking sweet salt at him. Is the kind of wink that saying inside it that, don't mind, everybody get a proper Anno Domini feeling, now and then, but the thing is to keep travelling, if you is Anancy.

As Anancy passing under the coconut tree, he hear a hoarse voice say, 'Don't sorry for the world, Anancy; it dry, because is so it stay. Don't fret youself about old age grabbing you shirt tail; it come to all. And don't, don't never, *never* stop travelling. Is reach you going reach, one day. Maybe.'

PAULE MARSHALL (b. 1929)

To Da-duh, in Memoriam

'. . . Oh Nana! all of you is not involved in this evil business
Death,
Nor all of us in life.'

—From 'At My Grandmother's Grave',
by Lebert Bethune

I did not see her at first I remember. For not only was it dark inside the crowded disembarkation shed in spite of the daylight flooding in from outside, but standing there waiting for her with my mother and sister I was still somewhat blinded from the sheen of tropical sunlight on the water of the bay which we had just crossed in the landing boat, leaving behind us the ship that had brought us from New York lying in the offing. Besides, being only nine years of age at the time and knowing nothing of islands I was busy attending to the alien sights and sounds of Barbados, the unfamiliar smells.

I did not see her, but I was alerted to her approach by my mother's hand which suddenly tightened around mine, and looking up I traced her gaze through the gloom in the shed until I finally made out the small, purposeful, painfully erect figure of the old woman headed our way.

Her face was drowned in the shadow of an ugly rolled-brim brown felt hat, but the details of her slight body and of the struggle taking place within it were clear enough—an intense, unrelenting struggle between her back which was beginning to bend ever so slightly under the weight of her eighty-odd years and the rest of her which sought to deny those years and hold that back straight, keep it in line. Moving swiftly toward us (so swiftly it seemed she did not intend stopping when she reached us but would sweep past us out the doorway which opened onto the sea and like Christ walk upon the water!), she was caught between the sunlight at her end of the building and the darkness inside—and for a moment she appeared to contain them both: the light in the long severe old-fashioned white dress she wore which brought the sense of a past that was still alive into our bustling present and in the snatch of white at her eye; the

159

darkness in her black high-top shoes and in her face which was visible now that she was closer.

It was as stark and fleshless as a death mask, that face. The maggots might have already done their work, leaving only the framework of bone beneath the ruined skin and deep wells at the temple and jaw. But her eyes were alive, unnervingly so for one so old, with a sharp light that flicked out of the dim clouded depths like a lizard's tongue to snap up all in her view. Those eyes betrayed a child's curiosity about the world, and I wondered vaguely seeing them, and seeing the way the bodice of her ancient dress had collapsed in on her flat chest (what had happened to her breasts?), whether she might not be some kind of child at the same time that she was a woman, with fourteen children, my mother included, to prove it. Perhaps she was both, both child and woman, darkness and light, past and present, life and death—all the opposites contained and reconciled in her.

'My Da-duh,' my mother said formally and stepped forward. The name sounded like thunder fading softly in the distance.

'Child,' Da-duh said, and her tone, her quick scrutiny of my mother, the brief embrace in which they appeared to shy from each other rather than touch, wiped out the fifteen years my mother had been away and restored the old relationship. My mother, who was such a formidable figure in my eyes, had suddenly with a word been reduced to my status.

'Yes, God is good,' Da-duh said with a nod that was like a tic. 'He has spared me to see my child again.'

We were led forward then, apologetically because not only did Da-duh prefer boys but she also liked her grandchildren to be 'white', that is, fair-skinned; and we had, I was to discover, a number of cousins, the outside children of white estate managers and the like, who qualified. We, though, were as black as she.

My sister being the oldest was presented first. 'This one takes after the father,' my mother said and waited to be reproved.

Frowning, Da-duh tilted my sister's face toward the light. But her frown soon gave way to a grudging smile, for my sister with her large mild eyes and little broad winged nose, with our father's high-cheeked Barbadian cast to her face, was pretty.

'She's goin' be lucky,' Da-duh said and patted her once on the cheek. 'Any girl child that takes after the father does be lucky.'

She turned then to me. But oddly enough she did not touch me. Instead leaning close, she peered hard at me, and then quickly drew back. I thought I saw her hand start up as though to shield her eyes. It was almost as if she saw not only me, a thin truculent child who it was said took after no one but myself, but something in me which for some reason she found disturbing, even threatening. We looked silently at each other for a long time there in the noisy shed, our gaze locked. She was the first to look away.

'But Adry,' she said to my mother and her laugh was cracked, thin, apprehensive. 'Where did you get this one here with this fierce look?'

'We don't know where she came out of, my Da-duh,' my mother said, laughing also. Even I smiled to myself. After all I had won the encounter. Da-duh had recognized my small strength—and this was all I ever asked of the adults in my life then.

'Come, soul,' Da-duh said and took my hand. 'You must be one of those New York terrors you hear so much about.'

She led us, me at her side and my sister and mother behind, out of the shed into the sunlight that was like a bright driving summer rain and over to a group of people clustered beside a decrepit lorry. They were our relatives, most of them from St Andrews although Da-duh herself lived in St Thomas, the women wearing bright print dresses, the colors vivid against their darkness, the men rusty black suits that encased them like straitjackets. Da-duh, holding fast to my hand, became my anchor as they circled round us like a nervous sea, exclaiming, touching us with their calloused hands, embracing us shyly. They laughed in awed bursts: 'But look Adry got big-big children!' / 'And see the nice things they wearing, wrist watch and all!' / 'I tell you, Adry has done all right for sheself in New York. . . .'

Da-duh, ashamed at their wonder, embarrassed for them, admonished them the while. 'But oh Christ,' she said, 'why you all got to get on like you never saw people from "Away" before? You would think New York is the only place in the world to hear wunna. That's why I don't like to go anyplace with you St Andrews people, you know. You all ain't been colonized.'

We were in the back of the lorry finally, packed in among the barrels of ham, flour, cornmeal and rice and the trunks of clothes that my mother had brought as gifts. We made our way slowly through Bridgetown's clogged streets, part of a funereal procession of cars and open-sided buses, bicycles, and donkey carts. The dim little limestone shops and offices along the way marched with us, at the same mournful pace, toward the same grave ceremony—as did the people, the women balancing huge baskets on top their heads as if they were no more than hats they wore to shade them from the sun. Looking over the edge of the lorry I watched as their feet slurred the dust. I listened, and their voices, raw and loud and dissonant in the heat, seemed to be grappling with each other high overhead.

Da-duh sat on a trunk in our midst, a monarch amid her court. She still held my hand, but it was different now. I had suddenly become her anchor, for I felt her fear of the lorry with its asthmatic motor (a fear and distrust, I later learned, she held of all machines) beating like a pulse in her rough palm.

As soon as we left Bridgetown behind though, she relaxed, and while the others around us talked she gazed at the canes standing tall on either side of the winding marl road. 'C'dear,' she said softly to herself after a time. 'The canes this side are pretty enough.'

They were too much for me. I thought of them as giant weeds that had overrun the island, leaving scarcely any room for the small tottering houses of sunbleached pine we passed or the people, dark streaks as our lorry hurtled by. I suddenly feared that we were journeying, unaware that we were, toward some dangerous place where the canes, grown as high and thick as a forest, would close in on us and run us through with their stiletto blades. I longed then for the familiar: for the street in Brooklyn where I lived, for my father who had refused to accompany us ('Blowing out good money on foolishness,' he had said of the trip), for a game of tag with my friends under the chestnut tree outside our aging brownstone house.

'Yes, but wait till you see St Thomas canes,' Da-duh was saying to me. 'They's canes father, bo,' she gave a proud arrogant nod. 'Tomorrow, God willing, I goin' take you out in the ground and show them to you.'

True to her word Da-duh took me with her the following day out into the ground. It was a fairly large plot adjoining her weathered board and shingle house and consisting of a small orchard, a good-sized canepiece and behind the canes, where the land sloped abruptly down, a gully. She had purchased it with Panama money sent her by her eldest son, my uncle Joseph, who had died working on the canal. We entered the ground along a trail no wider than her body and as devious and complex as her reasons for showing me her land. Da-duh strode briskly ahead, her slight form filled out this morning by the layers of sacking petticoats she wore under her working dress to protect her against the damp. A fresh white cloth, elaborately arranged around her head, added to her height, and lent her a vain, almost roguish air.

Her pace slowed once we reached the orchard, and glancing back at me occasionally over her shoulder, she pointed out the various trees.

'This here is a breadfruit,' she said. 'That one yonder is a papaw. Here's a guava. This is a mango. I know you don't have anything like these in New York. Here's a sugar apple.' (The fruit looked more like artichokes than apples to me.) 'This one bears limes. . . .' She went on for some time, intoning the names of the trees as though they were those of her gods. Finally, turning to me, she said, 'I know you don't have anything this nice where you come from.' Then, as I hesitated: 'I said I know you don't have anything this nice where you come from. . . .'

'No,' I said and my world did seem suddenly lacking.

Da-duh nodded and passed on. The orchard ended and we were on the narrow cart road that led through the canepiece, the canes clashing like swords above my cowering head. Again she turned and her thin muscular arms spread wide, her dim gaze embracing the small field of canes, she said—and her voice almost broke under the weight of her pride, 'Tell me, have you got anything like these in that place where you were born?'

'No.'

'I din' think so. I bet you don't even know that these canes here and the sugar you eat is one and the same thing. That they does throw the canes into some damn machine at the factory and squeeze out all the little life in them to make sugar for you all so in New York to eat. I bet you don't know that.'

'I've got two cavities and I'm not allowed to eat a lot of sugar.'

But Da-duh didn't hear me. She had turned with an inexplicably angry motion and was making her way rapidly out of the canes and down the slope at the edge of the field which led to the gully below. Following her apprehensively down the incline amid a stand of banana plants whose leaves flapped like elephants ears in the wind, I found myself in the middle of a small tropical wood—a place dense and damp and gloomy and tremulous with the fitful play of light and shadow as the leaves high above moved against the sun that was almost hidden from view. It was a violent place, the tangled foliage fighting each other for a chance at the sunlight, the branches of the trees locked in what seemed an immemorial struggle, one both necessary and inevitable. But despite the violence, it was pleasant, almost peaceful in the gully, and beneath the thick undergrowth the earth smelled like spring.

This time Da-duh didn't even bother to ask her usual question, but simply turned and waited for me to speak.

'No,' I said, my head bowed. 'We don't have anything like this in New York.'

'Ah,' she cried, her triumph complete. 'I din' think so. Why, I've heard that's a place where you can walk till you near drop and never see a tree.'

'We've got a chestnut tree in front of our house,' I said.

'Does it bear?' She waited. 'I ask you, does it bear?'

'Not anymore,' I muttered. 'It used to, but not anymore,'

She gave the nod that was like a nervous twitch. 'You see,' she said. 'Nothing can bear there.' Then, secure behind her scorn, she added, 'But tell me, what's this snow like that you hear so much about?'

Looking up, I studied her closely, sensing my chance, and then I told her, describing at length and with as much drama as I could summon not only what snow in the city was like, but what it would be like here, in her perennial summer kingdom.

'. . . And you see all these trees you got here,' I said. 'Well, they'd be bare. No leaves, no fruit, nothing. They'd be covered in snow. You see your canes. They'd be buried under tons of snow. The snow would be higher than your head, higher than your house, and you wouldn't be able to come down into this here gully because it would be snowed under. . . .'

She searched my face for the lie, still scornful but intrigued. 'What a thing, huh?' she said finally, whispering it softly to herself.

'And when it snows you couldn't dress like you are now,' I said. 'Oh no, you'd freeze to death. You'd have to wear a hat and gloves and galoshes and ear muffs so your ears wouldn't freeze and drop off, and a heavy coat. I've got a Shirley Temple coat with fur on the collar. I can dance. You wanna see?'

Before she could answer I began, with a dance called the Truck which was popular back then in the 1930's. My right forefinger waving, I trucked around the nearby trees and around Da-duh's awed and rigid form. After the Truck I did the Suzy-Q, my lean hips swishing, my sneakers sidling zigzag over the ground. 'I can sing,' I said and did so, starting with 'I'm Gonna Sit Right Down and Write Myself a Letter', then without pausing, 'Tea For Two', and ending with 'I Found a Million Dollar Baby in a Five and Ten Cent Store'.

For long moments afterwards Da-duh stared at me as if I were a creature from Mars, an emissary from some world she did not know but which intrigued her and whose power she both felt and feared. Yet something about my performance must have pleased her, because bending down she slowly lifted her long skirt and then, one by one, the layers of petticoats until she came to a drawstring purse dangling at the end of a long strip of cloth tied round her waist. Opening the purse she handed me a penny. 'Here,' she said half-smiling against her will. 'Take this to buy yourself a sweet at the shop up the road. There's nothing to be done with you, soul.'

From then on, whenever I wasn't taken to visit relatives, I accompanied Da-duh out into the ground, and alone with her amid the canes or down in the gully I told her about New York. It always began with some slighting remark on her part: 'I know they don't have anything this nice where you come from,' or 'Tell me, I hear those foolish people in New York does do such and such. . . .' But as I answered, re-creating my towering world of steel and concrete and machines for her, building the city out of words, I would feel her give way. I came to know the signs of her surrender: the total stillness that would come over her little hard dry form, the probing gaze that like a surgeon's knife sought to cut through my skull to get at the images there, to see if I were lying; above all, her fear, a fear nameless and profound, the same one I had felt beating in the palm of her hand that day in the lorry.

Over the weeks I told her about refrigerators, radios, gas stoves, elevators, trolley cars, wringer washing machines, movies, airplanes, the cyclone at Coney Island, subways, toasters, electric lights: 'At night, see, all you have to do is flip this little switch on the wall and all the lights in the house go on. Just like that. Like magic. It's like turning on the sun at night.'

'But tell me,' she said to me once with a faint mocking smile, 'do the white people have all these things too or it's only the people looking like us?'

I laughed. 'What d'ya mean,' I said. 'The white people have even better.' Then: 'I beat up a white girl in my class last term.'

'Beating up white people!' Her tone was incredulous.

'How you mean!' I said, using an expression of hers. 'She called me a name.'

For some reason Da-duh could not quite get over this and repeated in the same hushed, shocked voice, 'Beating up white people now! Oh, the lord, the world's changing up so I can scarce recognize it anymore.'

One morning toward the end of our stay, Da-duh led me into a part of the gully that we had never visited before, an area darker and more thickly overgrown than the rest, almost impenetrable. There in a small clearing amid the dense bush, she stopped before an incredibly tall royal palm which rose cleanly out of the ground, and drawing the eye up with it, soared high above the trees around it into the sky. It appeared to be touching the blue dome of sky, to be flaunting its dark crown of fronds right in the blinding white face of the late morning sun.

Da-duh watched me a long time before she spoke, and then she said very quietly, 'All right, now, tell me if you've got anything this tall in that place you're from.'

I almost wished, seeing her face, that I could have said no. 'Yes,' I said. 'We've got buildings hundreds of times this tall in New York. There's one called the Empire State building that's the tallest in the world. My class visited it last year and I went all the way to the top. It's got over a hundred floors. I can't describe how tall it is. Wait a minute. What's the name of that hill I went to visit the other day, where they have the police station?'

'You mean Bissex?'

'Yes, Bissex. Well, the Empire State Building is way taller than that.'

'You're lying now!' she shouted, trembling with rage. Her hand lifted to strike me.

'No, I'm not,' I said. 'It really is, if you don't believe me I'll send you a picture postcard of it soon as I get back home so you can see for yourself. But it's way taller than Bissex.'

All the fight went out of her at that. The hand poised to strike me fell limp to her side, and as she stared at me, seeing not me but the building that was taller than the highest hill she knew, the small stubborn light in her eyes (it was the same amber as the flame in the kerosene lamp she lit at dusk) began to fail. Finally, with a vague gesture that even in the midst of her defeat still tried to dismiss me and my world, she turned and started back through the gully, walking slowly, her steps groping and uncertain, as if she were suddenly no longer sure of the way, while I followed triumphant yet strangely saddened behind.

The next morning I found her dressed for our morning walk but stretched out on the Berbice chair in the tiny drawing room where she sometimes napped during the afternoon heat, her face turned to the window beside her. She appeared thinner and suddenly indescribably old.

'My Da-duh,' I said.

'Yes, nuh,' she said. Her voice was listless and the face she slowly turned my way was, now that I think back on it, like a Benin mask, the features drawn and almost distorted by an ancient abstract sorrow.

'Don't you feel well?' I asked.

'Girl, I don't know.'

'My Da-duh, I goin' boil you some bush tea,' my aunt, Da-duh's youngest child, who lived with her, called from the shed roof kitchen.

'Who tell you I need bush tea?' she cried, her voice assuming for a moment its old authority. 'You can't even rest nowadays without some malicious person looking for you to be dead. Come girl,' she motioned me to a place beside her on the old-fashioned lounge chair, 'give us a tune.'

I sang for her until breakfast at eleven, all my brash irreverent Tin Pan Alley songs, and then just before noon we went out into the ground. But it was a short, dispirited walk. Da-duh didn't even notice that the mangoes were beginning to ripen and would have to be picked before the village boys got to them. And when she paused occasionally and looked out across the canes or up at her trees it wasn't as if she were seeing them but something else. Some huge, monolithic shape had imposed itself, it seemed, between her and the land, obstructing her vision. Returning to the house she slept the entire afternoon on the Berbice chair.

She remained like this until we left, languishing away the mornings on the chair at the window gazing out at the land as if it were already doomed; then, at noon, taking the brief stroll with me through the ground during which she seldom spoke, and afterwards returning home to sleep till almost dusk sometimes.

On the day of our departure she put on the austere, ankle length white dress, the black shoes and brown felt hat (her town clothes she called them), but she did not go with us to town. She saw us off on the road outside her house and in the midst of my mother's tearful protracted farewell, she leaned down and whispered in my ear, 'Girl, you're not to forget now to send me the picture of that building, you hear.'

By the time I mailed her the large colored picture postcard of the Empire State building she was dead. She died during the famous '37 strike which began shortly after we left. On the day of her death England sent planes flying low over the island in a show of force—so low, according to my aunt's letter, that the downdraft from them shook the ripened mangoes from the trees in Da-duh's orchard. Frightened, everyone in the village fled into the canes. Except Da-duh. She remained in the house at the window so my aunt said, watching as the planes came swooping and screaming like monstrous birds down over the village, over her house, rattling her trees and flattening the young canes in her field. It must have seemed to her lying there that they did not intend pulling out of their dive, but like the hard-back beetles which hurled themselves with suicidal force against the walls of the house at night, those menacing silver shapes would hurl themselves in an ecstasy of self-immolation onto the land, destroying it utterly.

KAMAU BRATHWAITE (b. 1930)

for
David Rudder

Alex Haley
20 Yrs in the US Coast Guard who died today May 92
age 70

The sea was like slate grey of what was left of
my body
& the white waves
I remember
they was like very white
on what was left of my skin
& they kept comin in at this soft swishing diagonal
against the
bow & wet metal slides of my nerves

where the US Coast Guard cutter was patrolling all
along the borders of the Mexicans & my brothers –
the what was called 'the Haitian Refugees'

//// *I write Shante Chackmul & ask*
**WHAT NAME BAHAMAS GIVE TO
HAITIANS WHO COME TO YR OUSE**

TO BEG WRUK ////

And it was not that we was goin anywhere if you
see what i mean –

i mean we was not goin anywhere although the ship
was movin

i suppose & the sea was also movin impeccable & so
were the waves

& yet in my dream it was juss like on board anyship
anytime & tide –

there was that up & down movemant & soft ooze of
things creakin & tryin to fall or actually fallin even
though evvating on board that hillslide was suppose
to be slipshape if you know what i mean

& something like bells on the horizon either still
like a sword or a razorblade of light or going up &
down slowly & soffly grey like the ship in my head

w/the nerves breaking out sibilant & white like a
long line of lip rolling softly . the side of the ship &
our feet clanging restlessly up & down the studded
metal stairs of our soft muted agony

w/that strange smell of something like hidden oil &
closed-in space & the memory of cabins of mal-de-
mac & wanting to throw-up & having to run
compulsively somewhere to scuttle it down the
hatch

& there was like nothing we cd do about anything
now that we was there in the dream of the ship
waiting as I say for these Haitian refugees in a
strange land

& i do not know why i was there –
how i came to be on board that ship – that navel of
my past w/ my nerves as I say comin & goin & my
head soffly spinnin &

beginnin to get like giddy & my heart pushin hard
against the daylight of my leafless body & swishing
for the peace & darkness & the spice of gumbo
Sundaes

since i was suppose to be a poet not a coast guard
cutter or fireman or one or two others on that
deck & standing by the railing where there was
these hard white life-savers or boys that you
pulley over yr head like tyres as you swim in the
dark or the water or
throw them screaming to someone tryin to dream or
drownin

& there was suppose to be some kind of rope or
chord/of music or an anthology called life-line
that iere had send me & gripped in yr hands when
you tossed this little white sweetie with the legend

US COAST GUARD GUTTER

stencilled upon its both sides in black on what i
suppose was suppose to be like top & bottom

US COAST GUARD GUTTER

& then

RETTUG DRAUG TSAOC SU

w/i suppose the

US COAST GUARD GUTTER

part for yr head & the

RETTUG DRAUG TSAOC SU

for yr feet or coffin

if you shd ever have to jump thru one of those
mints like on the scarlet airlines where the

HOSTESS

stand in front of evvabody else
xcept the crew

wavin she limbs about & smilin like the palmfronds &
hardthighs on some lonely or crowded
beach/noticeably absent both on ship & in the air/&
pretendin to be doin all these things w/yellow &
whistles & no pain or snarl since we are not in the
air

& my head is like getting giddier & giddier as I try
to writhe this w/the blinds down . the light & my
nerves so tight that i am kinda blind
not being able to see

SALKEY
or Sundee or the Port-au-Prince of my youth
anymore

& i often wandered what it wd really be like out
there far from my homeland on the Atlantic with ion
& only my head above the thatch roofs of the
waves & my hands lonely up

& down the rub & knub of the white ahab stump of
my elbows & no feet under the water since nobody
cd see them in that kind of gaol & sickness of the
sea & its thicknesse anyway

and as I say – not one of us knew what we was doin
there when we shd have been somewherelse writin
poetry or whatever that was

& i notice in the dream how carefully no one didnt
know where that was either/which after all is not
surprising since we had been at sea for a long time
now – ever since i had packed my suitcase before

PETIT MATIN

. high above Morne D'Estagnes in all that mist of
Kenkoff & bamboos & did not even have time to
scrape the ashes from the fireplace before I was
down the hill bound for those tuilleries behind the
Iron Market where we were to meet the man w/ the
canot 'Salvages' & i remember thinkin

SEA COME NO
FATHER SEA COME
NO FATHER

as if i was already turning the leaves of the waves
like that for a long long history time before i cd
get back to sleep & in anycase nobody had written
anything serious since Mexican died
& the Gilbertery of 1988 i think it was

because of what was being said of Omeros & TTR &
Bobby Antoni's cedar shipped Palmares poem
La Divina Pastora or whatever

So we was all standing there in that kind of windy
silence of this dream – not close together of
course since we was all artists & strangers to
each other & not soldiers or sailors or dwarfs as i
have to go on insisting even though

we were all on the same trip
as Black Stalin had said so many years before &
all on the same ship
& the same sloping deck &

there was no doubt about that since there were
ropes neatly toiled & there was the smell of cool &
salt & gun-metal oil & the first thing that shd have
warned us that something unusual was happening
outside of wherever

we shd have been writing was when Sun
Bryan
appeared on the water like a kind of living life-
buoy

but it was only his face there in the shape of a
smile or what looked like a smilin triangle made out
of tinnin as if he was the work of Murat or
Grègoire or Marèshal

or a sheet of soff metal or a lief of cardboard
more probably – painted or treated to look like
tinnin or metal or the wrok of Murat or Grègoire or
Marèshal – only – as you see – somewhat
backwrods

& he passed quite closed but swiftly by like a kind
of sea-island kite
[yes thats what it was] on what the pilot or captain or
somebody w/a microphone probably on the bridge or
up in the sky of the

riggin – though we hardly ever looked up there for
the stars/since everything was like movin so
strangely

& if/when we did

we wd find ourselves like fallin hard on the deck
or not bein able to pay our homage or balance our
bills

& pitching forward or sideways towards the railings
& the frontiers of our nation which was all we had

between ourselves & those high nervous seas out
there & the

captain was saying
(as I said)
that the Sun Bryan object
(which is how you wd have i suppose to describe it)

was on a 'starboard' course' whatever that meant
– rocking from side to side
like a cock or a pendulum/ of time as if he was
suspended from the top of his pointed head above
the water while the base of his face which somehow
– now that i think back about it & have been able to
revise & correct what i got up to write down far
too hurriedly early this morning as we went on
board the canot

& i remember feeling very cold even though we were

25

in a boat designed as the TV commentator kept

saying to carry only 14 or 15

& this kite & rockin triangle of him seemed to
contain all the rest of his body/i mean like his
mouth w/his font teeth missin as usual & his chin &

his shoulders & his shirt & chest all down to his
belt & waistbuckle & the torn dirty

trousers of the farmer
(when he chose to be a farmer that is)

& his feet like tucked & folded up under evvating
just like us on 'Salvages'/

though as i say you cdnt see them & indeed you
cdnt see nothin but this rockin & smilin triangle of
the head rollin swiftly past the Coast Guard Gutter
& like tick/tockin from side to side from the top of
the clock of his hair/
& we all locked at each other because we had
heard that

MADAME
MARGARET EUGENIA
AZUCHAR
✦ MARKETPLACE ✦

had at last gone up w/her harsp gruff whip &
chauffeur of a voice to IT or perhaps it was

Penlyne to see what was going on & to give some
kind of support & *macoute* to the farmers in
response i suppose to my telephone call years
before to her on that beach of shells where she
had been able to pick up a large pink *lambi* or conch
in her hands w/out being cut by the sharpe edge of
the *vèvè*

as had happen to me when i was a little boy on a
Bank Holiday when i was too young really to
remember anything else xcept the dunes & the
bright light on all that sand & dazzle & the red
blood from my finger blooming down into all the
coral beaches i wd ever stand on since/looking at
birds & fishes far out on the horizon

& by the time i got up there everyone was of
course talking about the visit & how good it was of
her to come even though it was clearly too late to
overstand &

everything was growing back again dark green over
all the morass & the chasm & the awesome landslipe
that had covered the golden flute of the bamboo
clump that she had never seen

so that she cd smile in the sunlight & feel it
warming her arms & her face & her dark glasses &
opening every cribbit & corner

of her skin & pouring like the waves all round her
into rocks & eddies & responding to the colour of
the daylight & the chlorophyll

so that she was able to come to a firm political
decision pretty soon after that – about commanding
heights of the economy & level playing fields & light
at the end of the tunnel

etc etc etc

& departed all our shorne hillside to the deck of
the ship where we were now passing Sun Bryan
& looking out for Mexican & the Haitian refugees

though nothing had happened as i have been telling
you for what seemed like a long long time & we had
started to relax under the tall grey pool of the
ship when someone shouted the way Sancho Panzo

must have shouted for

Columbus

on the twelve October 1492

& we all ran to the railings again since it wasnt
raining or anything like that – gripping them tightly

of course since we didnt wish to fall into what the
sailors called drink

& in anyease we were all afraid of doing so all the
time just as i noticed that when i went up to Penlyne
or tried to cross any bridge of dirt or stone at

IT

or slipped down the slopes of coffee & pimento to
one of
Neville Dawves
very early morning Jamaican poems

that i was like afeard of heights even though it was
a landscape of sounds & sweet airs that give
delight & hurt not – which we now know it wasnt –
so that i fe/fe/feared i felt
(it felt something like that)
that i wd fall & tumble down into the valley or
rather into the dark blue hole far below/which was
like the end of the story i was writing of my life or
all my life i cant remember which –

but i noticed that the railings or stations &
stanchions or whatever they are nautically called
were like made of the same material as our fingers
& the palms of our hands & the airhostesses & the

lifeboys suddenly out there in the water like flying
fish or whales or poipoises or like

land ahoy

like Guanahani or a rainbow out to sea or anything
startling & unusual that people on board the Middle
Passage rush to see to relive their limbs of what
becomes like tedium on board the bells of a ship

& each one had like a white head that flashed back
& forth to a black head just floating by in the
water & each one of them had like this great wide
open mouth crying out for their country & calling
to us across the narrow valley of water to help
them or come fish them out or unhook them as if
they was congoreels or lobsters or negatives
w/thin wet tentricles

which of course they were or had become though
we didnt know then that the Salvages had tried
climbing up one more hill just out of sight of Pt
Serene & we had gone like stumbling down into this
dark blue dungeon of sound & the water churling
into our lives like these hard hard leaves that dont
allow us to breathe or even dream ourselves out of
its convent &

as i went down into like somebody blind & convicted i
remember that it was like some dark gaoler of

183

convex was like locking us up again & again & i cd
hear the long echo/ing noise of the metal doors

clanging shut in our faces as if it was Christophe
on La Ferriîre walking the slow corridor of water

as if it was Toussaint Legba all the way out in
Napoleons jokeless island on the glacial seas of the
Jura

& we were trying to reach the lifelines that were
made of the same material as our lungs & our
fingers & our skin although we cd hardly see that
nobody had started throwing any of them overboard
to help us

dechouguet dechouguet dechouguet

& there was so much going on all above & around us
what with the ferrymen shouting & fighting for
survivors though we were all quite dead & bloated
by this time
& some of us had even started floating on our
blacks up to the surface which is when i suppose we
cd barley see

that nobody wasnt throwing no lifelines nor booies
nor anything like that towards us & in anycase i
didnt have time to think any of this down even if i cd
have in all that

crushing & crying & falling into those cul –
de-sac heights that i had always feared

but i know that they were trying to tell us –
w/their black eyes filled w/water & the wonder &
the

whole wide desert of Atacama

blowing so bleakly into their faces that they
couldnt see far less see us anymore – that we
were their brothers & fellow writers bound to us
by all kinds of ties & the content of their
character

as if we didnt remember how they had put on their
shoes that afternoon – bending down to the blue
pumps to tie the black laces to take us up to
Petionville to scroll through the markets of Limbé
& Limånade & Labasse & Petit-Goave

& see where Hector Hippolyte lived –

though of course they said nothing at all but just
went lobbying by with their heads up & down in the
corvée of water & their arms still vainly trying to

reach Miami & Judge Thomas & the US Supreme
Court & their mouths wise
open drinking dream & seawater like

⌈a crȿte-a-pierrot

all over & over & over again while we stood on the
soft hard deck of the Coast Guard
'Impeccable'/watching them poem

New York
February 1992

ANTONIO BENITÉZ ROJO (b. 1931)

Buried Statues

Translated by Andrew Hurley

That summer—how could I forget it?—after don Jorge's lessons were over for the afternoon and Honorata had pleaded with us for a while, we'd go out hunting butterflies in the gardens around our mansion, which was up on a hill in Vedado. Aurelio and I would give in to her because she had a limp on her left side and because she was the youngest (in March she'd turned fifteen), but we wouldn't give in till she begged us, so we could see her lower lip start trembling and the tears come to her eyes and her fingers start twisting at her braids—though the truth was, deep inside we liked to draw straws for the hunting horn, out at the empty dovecote, and wander through the statues with our butterfly nets at the ready, following the paths through the Japanese garden, which were paved with stepping stones and full of pitfalls under the wild vegetation that grew right up to the house.

That vegetation was the biggest threat to us. It had taken over the fence on the south-west years ago—the one facing the Almendares River, which was the wettest side, the side that gave the vegetation the greatest encouragement. The undergrowth had even taken over the plots that Aunt Esther was in charge of, and in spite of all of her and poor Honorata's efforts, it was battering at the big windows in the library and the French doors of the music room. Since that undermined the security of the house (which was Mother's responsibility), loud arguments that led to impasses would end our meals and there were times when Mother, who got terribly nervous when she wasn't 'under the influence', would put her hand on her head to signal one of her migraines and burst into tears and then threaten, sobbing, to desert the house, yield up to the enemy her part of the joint ownership of the property if Aunt Esther didn't weed out (always within an exceedingly short time) the vegetation that was overrunning the porches and that might well be a weapon deployed by those on the outside.

'If you prayed a little less and worked a little harder . . .' Mother would say as she stacked the plates.

'And if you stopped hitting the bottle for a while . . .' Aunt Esther would shoot back.

Fortunately, don Jorge never took sides; he would retreat into silence with his long gray face, folding his napkin, avoiding becoming embroiled in the family's dispute. Not that don Jorge didn't belong to the family—after all, he was Aurelio's father; he had married the sister who came between Mother and Aunt Esther, the sister whose name nobody spoke any more. But be that as it may, he wasn't a blood relation and we spoke to him with the formal usted rather than the informal tú, and never called him 'Uncle'.

It wasn't like that with Aurelio. When nobody was looking we would hold hands with him, as though he were our boyfriend, and that summer was the summer he was supposed to choose between us, since time was passing and none of us were children any more. All of us loved Aurelio for the way he carried himself, his lively black eyes and above all, that special way he had of smiling. At lunch or dinner, the biggest servings were for him, and if you could smell Mother's boozy breath above the odors of the food, you could bet that when Aurelio handed his plate toward her to be served, she would serve him slowly, her left hand grasping his against the chipped edge of the rim. But Aunt Esther wasn't far behind her—with the exact same diligence she fingered the beads of her rosary, she would grope for Aurelio's leg under the tablecloth and kick off her shoe. That was the way the meals went. Of course, he allowed himself to be loved, and if his room was next to don Jorge's, back in what used to be the servants' quarters, totally separate from the rooms we slept in, it was because that's what the Code stipulated—Aunt Esther or Mother, either, would have given him a room on any floor, and he would have appreciated it, and we girls would have loved to have him so close by, to feel that he belonged to us a little more on nights when there were thunderstorms, with all that lightning, and the house under siege.

The document that defined each person's responsibilities and listed all the duties and punishments, we called simply the Code, and it had been signed by his three daughters and their husbands back when my grandfather was alive. The patriarchal commandments were set down in the Code, and although it had to be adapted to new circumstances, it was the core and center of our firmness in the face of adversity and we were guided by it. I'll just briefly outline its details:

Don Jorge was given permanent right to inhabit the property free of charge and was recognized as a full member of the Family Council. He was in charge of provisions, military intelligence, resource management, education and cultural affairs (he had been Under-Secretary of Education in the administration of Laredo Brú), and also of electrical and masonry repairs and cultivation of the land adjacent to the north-east wall—the wall that divided our property from the big Enríquez mansion next door, which had been converted to a polytechnic institute since late '63.

Aunt Esther was charged with caring for the gardens (including the park), caring for any young or new-born animals that might need attending to, political agitation, water and plumbing repairs, the organization of religious observances, and washing, ironing, and mending clothes.

Mother was assigned to cleaning the floors and furniture, drawing up plans for defense, doing any necessary carpentry repairs, painting the walls and ceilings, performing medical services, and cooking and related work—which was what she spent most of her time on.

As for us—the cousins—in the morning we helped with the chores and in the afternoon we had lessons with don Jorge; the rest of the day was for recreation. Of course, like everybody, we were forbidden to set foot outside the boundaries of the estate. On pain of death.

Spiritual death, that is—the 'death on the outside' that awaited anyone who crossed to the other side of the wall. The ignominious path which, in the nine years the siege had lasted, fully half the family had followed.

But anyway—that summer we hunted butterflies. They would fly up from the river and flutter above the flowering vegetation, stopping at a petal here and there, or on the still shoulder of some statue. Honorata would say they cheered the garden up, that they 'perfumed' it—always so imaginative, poor Honorata—but it always disturbed me a little that they came in from outside and, like Mother, I was of the opinion they were some secret weapon that we didn't understand yet. Maybe that was why I liked to hunt them. Though sometimes they would startle me and I'd run, pushing the vegetation aside, cutting my way through it with my hands, thinking they were going to take me by my hair, my skirt (like that engraving that hung in Aurelio's room), and carry me off, above the wall and across the river.

We would catch the butterflies in nets we'd made out of old mosquito netting and put them in jelly-jars supplied by Mother. Then, at nightfall, we would gather in the study for the beauty contest—which might last for hours, because we had dinner late. We would take the most beautiful one out of the jar, empty its abdomen and pin it into the album don Jorge had given us; with the rest of them (an idea of mine for making the game last longer), we'd pull off their wings and organize races—we'd bet pinches and caresses that weren't sanctioned by the Code.

Finally, we'd put them in the toilet and Honorata, trembling and teary-eyed, would push down the handle that would start the burbling gurgle, the basso rumblings of the whirlpool that would sweep them away.

After dinner, after Aunt Esther had lodged her allegations against Mother—who'd rush off to the kitchen with the irrevocable intention of leaving the house as soon as she'd washed the dishes—we would all go into the music room to listen to Aunt Esther at the piano, where she would play her hymns in the quivering half-light of the single candelabrum. Don Jorge had taught us a little of the violin, and its strings were still intact, but the piano was so out of tune that there was no way to play along with it, so by now we just left the violin in its case. Other times, when Aunt Esther was indisposed or Mother scolded her because she'd fallen behind in the mending, we would read aloud from things that don Jorge suggested, and since he was a great admirer of German culture, hours would pass as we mumbled through stanzas from Goethe, Hölderlin, Novalis, Heine . . .

It was only seldom, very seldom, in fact, practically never (except on rainy nights when the house would get flooded or on some extra-special occasion)—that we would go through our collection of butterflies, the mystery of their wings penetrating deep inside us—the wings charged with signs and portents of what lay on the other side of the iron lances of the fence, outside the wall whose top bristled with broken bottles; and there we three would sit in the candlelight and silence, united in that shadowy dimness that masked the humidity of the walls, the sidelong glances, the wandering hands, knowing that we all felt the same thing, that we had come together in the depth of a dream as green and viscous as that river seen from the fence. And then that sway-backed ceiling, crumbling away piece by piece, leaving dust in our hair and on our most intimate gestures.

So—we collected butterflies.

My greatest pleasure was imagining that at the end of the summer Aurelio and I would finally be together. 'A disguised priest will marry you through the fence,' don Jorge would say, circumspectly, when Aunt Esther and Honorata were off somewhere else. I thought of nothing else; I dare-say it comforted me in those interminable mornings of work; Mother was deteriorating fast (besides cooking, which always took her forever, she could barely handle the washing up of the plates and silverware), so I was the one that had to slosh water over the tile floors and shake out the shabby slipcovers and keep the rickety chair-seats dusted off.

This might be a dangerous generalization, but somehow Aurelio kept us all going—his affection helped us all bear up. Of course, there were also other things at work in Mother and Aunt Esther—but how else explain the gastronomical indulgences, the exceptional attention to the most fleeting cold or the once-in-a-blue-moon headache, the prodigious efforts to keep him strong, neatly groomed, happy? . . . Even don Jorge, who was always so proper and so measured, would sometimes turn into a mother hen. And Honorata!—so optimistic, poor thing, so unrealistic, as though she weren't a cripple. But Aurelio was our hope, our sweet morsel of wishful thinking; and he was the one that enabled us to remain serene inside those rusty fence-lances, which were so beset by enemies without.

'What a beautiful butterfly,' said Honorata on that dusky evening barely a summer ago. Aurelio and I were walking ahead, on the way back to the house—he was making a path for me with the pole of the net. We turned around to look; Honorata's freckled face was skipping through the vegetation as though she were being pulled along by her braids; above her, alongside the spreading branches of the flamboyán tree that stood at the entrance to the statuary path, there fluttered a golden butterfly.

Aurelio stopped. With a broad gesture, he signaled us to crouch down in the vegetation. He moved forward slowly, net raised, left arm stretched out at shoulder level, creeping through the undergrowth. The butterfly dropped a bit, opening its enormous wings defiantly, until it was almost within Aurelio's reach, but then, darting beyond the flamboyán, it fluttered into the allée of statues. Aurelio followed it, and soon they both were out of sight.

By the time Aurelio returned, night had fallen; we had already chosen the beauty queen and were preparing her, to surprise him. But he came in serious and sweaty, saying it had gotten away, he'd been just about to snare it, had climbed up onto the wall and been *that* close—and in spite of our insistence, he wouldn't stay for the games.

That worried me. I could just picture him up there, practically on the other side, the butterfly net hanging over the river road and him—within a hair of jumping. I remember I told Honorata that I was sure the butterfly was a decoy, that we had to step up our vigilance.

The next day was memorable. By dawn the people outside were up at arms, carrying on like crazy, and they went on that way all day—they fired off cannons and their gray airplanes left trails in the sky; down lower, helicopters in triangular formation made whitecaps on the pea soup river and whipped the vegetation into a frenzy. They were celebrating something, there was no doubt about it, maybe some new victory—and us incommunicado. It wasn't that we didn't have radios, but for years we hadn't paid the electric bills, and the batteries in Aunt Esther's Zenith had turned sticky and smelled like the Chinese ointment that Mother kept in a special place in the back of the medicine cabinet. Our telephone didn't work, either; nor did we get a newspaper, or even open the letters that so-called friends and traitorous relatives sent us from outside. We were incommunicado. It's true that don Jorge carried on a trade of sorts through the fence; without that, there'd have been no way for us to survive. But he did it at night, and none of us was allowed to witness the transactions, or even ask any questions about them. Though once when he was running a high fever and Honorata was taking care of him, he hinted that the cause was not altogether lost—world-famous organizations were taking an interest, he said, in those of us who were still resisting.

That evening, after all the hullabaloo had faded away—the patriotic applause from the polytechnic people, the military music that came over the wall and its yellowed shards of glass and drove Mother crazy in spite of her earplugs and compresses—we unhooked the horn from the dusty old display of antique weaponry (don Jorge had declared a holiday) and went out hunting for butterflies. We were walking along slowly; Aurelio's brow was furrowed. That morning he had been harvesting the cabbages that grew alongside the wall, and without the requisite protection he had heard the clamor of the anthems and the feverish, unintelligible speeches at noon. He was not himself; he had refused to abide by the results of the drawing of lots and had usurped Honorata's right to assign us our territories and carry the hunting horn. We went off on our separate paths in silence—there was none of the joking of other times, because the rules had always been observed before.

I had been moving down the path that ran alongside the fence, more or less marking time till nightfall, my jar filled with yellow wings, when I sensed that something had got tangled in my hair. For a second I thought it was the gauze of the net, but when I raised my left hand my fingers brushed against something with more body, like a piece of silk, that bumped my wrist and then was gone. I whirled around and saw, hovering in midair before my eyes, the golden butterfly, its wings opening and closing just at the level of my throat—and me all by myself with my back against the wall! At first I managed to control my panic; I gripped the pole and swung it; but the butterfly dodged to the right. I tried to calm myself, tried not to think about Aurelio's engraving, and began to step cautiously backward. Slowly I raised my arms, never taking my eyes off the butterfly; I took aim and swung. But the tail of the net caught on one of the iron lances and I missed again. And this time I had dropped the rod in the undergrowth along the path. My heart was pounding so that I could hardly breathe. The butterfly made a circle and lunged at my throat. I barely had time to scream and throw myself down into the vegetation. I felt a stinging sensation on my chest and my hand came away with blood on it. I had fallen on the tin ring the net was attached to and wounded myself in the breast. I waited for a few minutes and then turned over on my back, gasping for breath. It had disappeared.

The vegetation rose all around my body—it protected me, like that Venus fallen from its pedestal that Honorata had discovered deep in the park. I lay there, as motionless as that statue, looking perfectly consciously at the dusk as it fell about me, and suddenly Aurelio's eyes were in the sky and I was looking into them quietly, watching them move down along my almost-buried body and stop at my breast, and then continue down into the stalks, conquering me in the struggle and turning into the long, painful kiss that made the vegetation shiver. Afterward, the inexplicable awakening: Aurelio on top of my body, still holding his hand over my mouth in spite of the biting, his forehead marked by my fingernails.

We went back to the house—me, without a word, disillusioned.

Honorata had seen everything from the branches of the flamboyán.

Before we went into the dining room we agreed to keep the secret. I don't know whether it was because of the looks from Mother and Aunt Esther through the steam rising off the soup, or because of Honorata's sighs all night as she tossed and turned in the sheets, but the sun came up and I realized that I didn't love Aurelio as much as I had before, that I didn't need him—not him or that nasty thing either—and I swore never to do it again until my wedding night.

The morning was longer than it had ever been and when I finished my chores I was exhausted.

At lunch, I passed Honorata my ration of cabbage (as hungry as we both always were) and stared at Aurelio icily as he told Mother that a cat from the polytechnic had bitten his hand, scratched his face and disappeared over the wall. Then came the Logic lesson. I barely heard what don Jorge was saying, in spite of the nice Latin-like words he was explaining: *ferio, festino, barroco* and some more.

'I'm exhausted . . . My back hurts,' I told Honorata after the lesson, when she wanted to go hunt butterflies.

'Come on, don't be mean,' she pleaded.

'No.'

'Sure you're not just scared?' asked Aurelio.

'No, I'm not afraid of anything.'

'Really?'

'Really. But I'm not going to do it any more.'

'What, hunt butterflies?'

'Hunt butterflies or the other thing either. I'm not going to do it any more.'

'Well, if both of you don't come I'm going to tell Mother!' Honorata suddenly shrieked, her cheeks blazing.

'I've got no objections,' said Aurelio with a grin, grabbing me by the arm. And turning to Honorata, without waiting for my reply, he said, 'Bring the nets and jars. We'll meet you at the dovecote.'

I felt confused, insulted; but when I saw Honorata walk away, limping so badly it broke your heart, I had a revelation—I suddenly understood it all. I let Aurelio put his arm around my waist and we went outside.

Submerged in the warm vegetation, we walked along in silence, and I realized that I felt sorry for Aurelio too. I realized that of the three of us, I was the strongest, and maybe the strongest person in the whole house. Funny—me so young, not even seventeen yet, and stronger than Mother with her progressively worsening alcoholism and Aunt Esther clutching at her rosary. And now, all of a sudden, stronger than Aurelio too. Aurelio was the weakest of all of us, in fact, I thought—weaker than don Jorge, weaker than Honorata; and now he was smirking, grinning lasciviously, squeezing my waist as though he'd vanquished me, never realizing, poor thing, that I was the only one who could save him—him and the whole house.

'How about here?' he said, stopping. 'I think this is the same place as yesterday.' And he winked at me.

I nodded and lay down in the vegetation. I felt him raise my skirt, kiss my thighs, but I lay there like that goddess, cold and still, letting him do it to keep Honorata's mouth shut, so she wouldn't tell the story that would make them all envious—them so unsatisfied and with the war we were fighting and all.

'Scoot a little more to the right, you two—I can't see,' called out Honorata, astride a branch.

Aurelio ignored her; he unbuttoned my blouse.

It got dark and we went back to the house, Honorata carrying the nets and me carrying the empty jars.

'Do you love me?' he said as he pulled a dry leaf out of my hair.

'Yes, but I don't want to get married. Maybe next summer.'

'But . . . you'll keep doing it, won't you?'

'All right,' I said, a little startled. 'So long as nobody finds out.'

'In that case, I don't care if we get married or not. Although the grass and weeds poke through everywhere—they're awfully itchy.'

That night Aurelio announced at dinner that he wasn't going to get married that summer, he was postponing the decision till next year. Mother and Aunt Esther breathed a sigh of relief; don Jorge barely raised his head.

Two weeks went by, Aurelio deluding himself that he owned me. I would make myself comfortable in the vegetation with my arms behind my head, like the statue, and allow myself to be touched without feeling the pain of the affront. As the days went by, I perfected a rigid pose that fired his desires, that made him dependent on me. One afternoon we were walking along on the river side of the estate, while Honorata was catching butterflies among the statues. The rains had begun and the flowers, wetted down at noon, were clinging to our clothes. We were talking about various trivial things; Aurelio was telling me that Aunt Esther had visited him the night before, in her nightgown, and suddenly we saw the butterfly. It was flying along ahead of a swarm of ordinary colors; when it saw us it made a couple of curlicues in the air and then lighted on the tip of one of the lances. It opened and closed its wings, but it didn't move from the fence-rail—it was pretending to be tired—and Aurelio, stiffening, let go of my waist so he could scale the fence. But this time the victory was mine—I lay down without a word, my skirt up around my thighs, and the situation was back under control.

We were waiting for the man because after the History lesson don Jorge had told us he was coming that night, around nine. The man had been our source of provisions for years, and he went by the name of 'the Mohican'. Since according to don Jorge he was an experienced and courageous combatant—which was hard to understand, since his house had been taken—we would welcome him as our guest after pretending to debate the question. He would help Aunt Esther exterminate the vegetation and then he would cultivate the lands on the south-west, by the river.

'I think that's him now,' Honorata said, her face pressed against the iron bars of the gate. There was no moon, so we were using the candelabrum.

We drew close to the chains that restricted access to the estate, Aunt Esther muttering a hurried rosary. The foliage parted and Aurelio illuminated a hand. Then came a wrinkled, inexpressive face.

'Password?' demanded don Jorge.

'Gillette and Adams,' replied the man in a muted voice.

'That's the password. Permission to enter.'

'But . . . how?'

'Climb the lances there, the lock is rusted shut.'

Suddenly a whisper caught us all by surprise. There was no doubt about it—on the other side of the fence, the man was talking to somebody. We looked at each other in alarm, and it was Mother that fired first.

'Who are you talking to?' she demanded, shaking off her stupefaction.

'I . . . I didn't come alone.'

'You mean . . . you were followed?' asked Aunt Esther, her voice betraying her anxiety.

'No, it's not that. It's that I . . . I brought somebody with me.'

'But good God! Who?'

'It's a young woman . . . she's just a girl, really.'

'I'm his daughter,' an exceptionally clear voice interrupted him.

We deliberated for what seemed hours. Mother and I were against it, but there were three votes in favor and one abstention—from don Jorge. Finally they dropped down on to our side.

She said her name was Cecilia and she walked with a very self-satisfied air down the dark paths. She was Honorata's age, but much prettier and without any anatomical defects. She had blue eyes and golden-blonde hair, very strange-colored; she wore it straight, parted in the middle; the ends, which flipped up, reflected the light of the candelabrum. When we came to the house she said she was awfully sleepy; she went to bed early, she said—and grabbing a candle she marched very decidedly into my grandfather's room, down at the end of the hall, as though she'd known him, and closed the door behind her. After saying goodnight to everyone (holding his hand to his chest and breathing as though he were winded, or couldn't catch his breath), the man—because I now know that he was *not* her father—went off with don Jorge and Aurelio to the servant wing. We could hear him coughing every step he took. We never found out what his real name was; the girl refused to disclose his name when don Jorge, who was always an early riser, found him next to the bed the next morning, dead and without any identification.

We buried the Mohican that afternoon out by the well next to the polytechnic, under a mango tree. Don Jorge intoned a farewell to the deceased, calling him 'our Unknown Soldier', and the girl brought out a bunch of flowers from behind her back and put it in his hands. Then Aurelio started to shovel in the dirt and I helped him set up the cross that don Jorge had made. And then we all went back, except Aunt Esther, who stayed to pray for a while.

Along the path, I noticed that she was walking in an odd way; it reminded me of ballerinas I had seen as a girl at the ballet. She seemed very interested in the flowers and would stop to pick them once in a while, holding them against her face. Aurelio was supporting Mother, helping her along (the way she was staggering was sad), but he never took his eyes off Cecilia, and he smiled idiotically every time the girl looked at him.

At dinner Cecilia didn't eat a bite; she pushed the plate away as though it made her sick and then she passed it down to Honorata, who reciprocated by complimenting her on her hair. Finally I decided to speak to her.

'Your hair is such a pretty color. Where did you find the dye?'

'Dye? It's not dyed, it's natural.'

'But that's impossible . . . Nobody has hair that color.'

'I do,' she smiled. 'I'm glad you like it.'

'Could I take a closer look?' I asked. I didn't believe her.

'Sure, but don't touch it.'

I picked up a candle and went over to where she was sitting; I leaned on the back of her chair and looked at her hair for a long time. The color was perfectly even; it didn't look dyed, although there was something artificial-looking about those golden threads. They looked like cool, cold silk. Suddenly it occurred to me that it might be a wig, so I gave it a tug with both hands. I'm not sure if it was the shriek that knocked me to the floor or the shock at seeing her jump that way, but whatever it was, there I lay in a daze at Mother's feet, watching the girl run all over the dining room (colliding with the furniture as she went), head down the hall and lock herself in my grandfather's old bedroom—all the time holding her head as though it were going to fall off; and Aurelio and Aunt Esther pretending to be so upset they were beside themselves, putting their ears to the door so they could hear her bellowing, and Mother waving a spoon around with no idea what had happened, and to top it all Honorata standing on a chair applauding. Fortunately, don Jorge was speechless.

After Mother's blubbering and Aunt Esther's long-winded reprimand, I made an honorable retreat and, refusing to take the candle that Aurelio held out to me, I groped my way upstairs in the dark, my head held high.

Honorata came in, but I pretended to be asleep, so as not to have to talk about it. Through my eyelashes, though, I watched her put the candlestand on the dressing table. I turned over on my side, to make room for her; her shadow sliding over the wall reminded me of the Games and Pastimes of the *Children's Treasure Trove*, a book by Mother that don Jorge had done the negotiations for four years earlier. Honorata's shadow made huge limping motions; back and forth it went, unbraiding her braids, opening the drawer for the white nightgown. Now it was approaching the bed, getting bigger and bigger, leaning over me, touching my hand.

'Lucila, Lucila—wake up.'

I feigned a yawn and rolled over onto my back. 'What is it?' I said as irritably as I could.

'Have you seen your hands?'

'No.'

'Aren't you going to look at them?'

'There's nothing wrong with my hands,' I said, and paid no attention to her.

'They've got . . . like . . . a stain on them.'

'I imagine they're filthy, the way I yanked on that girl's hair and shoved Mother . . .'

'But they're not filthy that way—they're *gold*,' she said, furious.

I looked at my hands and it was true—there was gold dust all over the palms of my hands and on the inside edges of my fingers. I rinsed them off in the wash basin and put out the candle. When Honorata got tired of her vague conjectures, I managed to close my eyes. I woke up the next morning late, and groggy.

I didn't see Cecilia at breakfast because she had gone off with Aunt Esther to see what they could do about the vegetation. Mother was already drunk and Honorata stayed with me to help me with the cleaning; later, we'd see to lunch.

We'd finished downstairs and were upstairs cleaning Aunt Esther's room—me dusting and shaking things out and Honorata with the broom—when somehow it occurred to me to look out the window. I stopped flicking the feather duster and contemplated our estate: to left and right, the fence along the river bank, its iron lances being swallowed by the undergrowth; closer in, beginning at the orange-flowered flamboyán, the greenish heads of the statues like the heads of drowned people, and the gray shingles of the Japanese dovecote; off to the right, the garden plots, the well, and Aurelio bending over, picking up mangoes beside the little cross; beyond that, the wall, the roof-tiles of the polytechnic and a flag snapping in the wind. 'Who in the world would break the news to the Enríquezes?' I thought. And then I saw it. It was flying very low, toward the well. Sometimes I would lose sight of it among the flowers, but then it would appear again farther on, gleaming like a golden dolphin. Now it had changed direction; it was headed straight for Aurelio, and suddenly it was Cecilia—Cecilia emerging from the big oleander bush, running across the red ground, her hair fluttering in the breeze almost as though it were floating around her head. It was Cecilia talking to Aurelio now, kissing him before she took him by the hand and walked with him down the path that led through the park.

I sent Honorata off to make lunch and I lay down on Aunt Esther's bed; everything was spinning and my heart was thumping terribly. A while later, somebody tried to open the door—they rattled and shook it for a long time—but I was crying, so I shouted that I didn't feel well, to leave me alone.

When I woke up it was dark outside and I realized immediately that something had happened. Shoeless, I jumped out of bed and ran downstairs; I made my way down the hallway step by step, nervous and scared, muttering to myself that there was still a chance, that it might not be too late.

They were all in the living room, gathered around Honorata; don Jorge was sitting on the edge of the sofa, crying softly; Aunt Esther, on her knees beside the candelabrum, was turning toward Mother, who was flailing around in her chair, unable to sit up straight; and me, unnoticed, leaning on the doorjamb, at the edge of the circle of light, listening to Honorata, watching her act it all out in the middle of the carpet and feeling weaker and weaker; and her giving all the details, explaining how she'd seen them just at dusk walking along the river road, on the other side of the fence. And at that, the wailing broke out—Aunt Esther's prayers and supplications, Mother's keening swoon.

I put my hands over my ears, I lowered my head—I thought for a second I was going to throw up. And then, through the skin of my fingers, I heard the shrieking. After that somebody fell on the candelabrum and everything went dark.

They Better Don't Stop the Carnival

Lord Invader sat on a bench underneath the breadfruit tree. He had his right leg crossed over the left knee, and his head leaned against the tree trunk. His eyes were open but he wasn't thinking about the tree at all, or whether there were any breadfruit to fall on him. What he was thinking about was one thing: would Governor Sir Hubert Young stop the Carnival?

He sat up, worried. The knocking of hammer on oil drum distracted him a little and made him even more irritated. Just imagine—Governor Young was calling on all Trinidadians to strain every muscle to help in the war effort, and yet he didn't want to give the all clear for bands to practise. Instead, he had made a statement saying that Carnival at this stage of the war was a big risk.

'What risk!' he said to himself. 'What the hell?'

The banging grew louder and he turned around and looked at the two Manette boys. They had a little wood fire on the other side of their breadfruit tree, and they both had their pans over the fire, taking them off every now and then—and knocking and denting the faces to get the sound they wanted. At other times Lord Invader would have smiled and even gone over to help them. Now, forgetting he was in their yard instead of the other way round, he said, 'Ellie man, what you and Birdie doing?'

Ellie said, 'How you mean? So we mustn't tune up?'

Lord Invader turned around, 'Well, what you tuning up for? Tell me, what you tuning up for? You read the papers?'

Ellie did not say anything, but continued. Birdie, silent as usual, was testing the notes he had already got. Lord Invader looked at them, but he saw he could not get their attention nor get them to stop. He was beginning to think, 'I'd better go'.

But go where? Go back to Carenage where he was living? And do what? Lie down on the bed and just worry? He looked across the road at the huge sward of green that was the Queen's Park Oval and there were a few cyclists riding around the track, maybe practising for some big athletic meeting that was coming up. He looked at them, but they did not hold his attention. In fact, he looked at them without even seeing them. He just kept saying to himself, 'They better don't stop the Carnival!'

Suddenly, he heard soft, flaky laughter, and looking to the other side of him at the house, he had a glimpse of Ma Manette at the window.

'Morning, Ma Manette.'

'Oh, that's you, Invader. I nearly didn't make you out.'

'I thought you was laughing at me.'

'Me? Laughing at you? What I'll be laughing at you for?'

He turned back his head, looking in complete repose.

Ma Manette said to her husband, still chuckling, 'I wish I was a calypsonian. Look at Invader. Not a care in the world. Ten o'clock in the morning and look at him. I wish a breadfruit could fall on his head!'

Old Mr Manette smiled. He went to the window, moved the curtain aside and took a little peep. Then he said, with a certain degree of certainty, 'Is a tune he composing.' The flaky laughter came again and Ma Manette quickly put her hand to her mouth. She said, 'O God, I hope he don't hear me.'

Lord Invader kept lying still, and now his eyes were closed. But he was not sleeping. In fact, although his eyes were closed, the scene before his eyes could not have been more vivid. It was the height of the calypso season and he was on stage. He was at the *House of Lords* at 100 St Vincent Street, and the applause was so deafening he had to turn away. But they wanted him to come back again, for an encore. He had had three already but they wouldn't leave him alone. And there he was, wearing his white flannel pants and his pink silk shirt, and a handkerchief round his neck. He had never heard so much applause. But what was the calypso he was singing? He was singing, *They better don't stop the Carnival!*

He turned his head the other way and said, 'Stupes'. Why should he be singing that? He didn't even want to think that such a thing could happen. Things were hard enough. There was no rice in the shops, no flour. The war was raging, and German submarines were reaping havoc in the Caribbean Sea. None of the ships could come in, and what did people have to eat? There was plantain, green fig, and mocoe; dasheen, cush-cush, potato. Or if you down by the sea, you could dig you chip-chip because it's free.

He was excited. 'That is what I should sing,' he said to himself. 'That is the rouso! That is true for 1942.'

He turned his head, and as he looked at the window, he caught Mr Manette looking at him. Mr Manette had no time to pull back in his head. Mr Manette pretended he was looking up at the breadfruit, then at the sky, then shamefacedly he said, 'Invader boy, the war look tough. Yesterday the *Evening News* said . . .' He stuttered a little bit because he did not know what the *Evening News* said yesterday. Because he did not buy a copy of the *Evening News*. Lord Invader did not even wait for him to finish. He said sharply, 'Yes. It said they want to stop the Carnival.'

'Oh, yes? It said so?' Mr Manette said, taken aback. The lady came to the window too. Lord Invader could see her head behind the curtain. All of a sudden, the banging on the pans stopped, and both Ellie and Birdie were staring at him. Ellie said at length, 'Look, Invader, if you making joke why you don't say you making joke?'

'How do you mean making joke, you mean you all don't know what happening?' He sat up, uncrossed his feet and turned round. He looked at the two young boys with their pans resting on the wood fire. He said, 'I can't believe you all ain't know this. Hubert Young come back from England yesterday, and saying in big that we can't hold no Carnival because of the war.'

'Good God!' He heard Ma Manette say.

'But the Governor was on the radio last night, too.'

'We ain't have no radio,' Ellie said. His face looked drawn. Birdie was so depressed that he just stooped over his pan and said nothing.

Lord Invader said, 'But at least things on the papers for everybody to see.' He pulled out the *Port-of-Spain Gazette* from his pocket. He said, 'Yesterday it was on the *Evening News*, and now it's on today's papers. Look. Look at the headline: "Governor May Stop The Carnival".'

'Christ!' He heard the gruff voice at the window. Looking towards the window, he said, 'Pappie Manette, it's not Christ, you know, it's Governor Hubert Young. And look,' he turned to the boys, 'this man so bold-face, he saying we must do everything to make England win the war. And I'll tell you what, he don't only want to stop the Carnival, he want you pans too. You know what he said? Look,' he held up the newspaper and read: ' "And we expect that this loyal population of Trinidad will do its bit towards winning the war. The Germans are bombing London, and there is a great loss in men and material. People are volunteering from all over the Empire. But the great need of the moment is material. Bring your unwanted scrap iron in all quantities . . ." '

'This is not unwanted. I want me pan.'

'But what you'll do with it? That's why I asked you if you read the papers. What you'll do with it if the Governor stop the Carnival?'

Ellie Manette felt deeply troubled. He said, 'They better don't stop the Carnival!'

Birdie looked around and said under his breath, 'This blasted war. If the British and the Germans want to fight for ten thousand years, let them fight, but they don't have to touch this Carnival. We didn't do them anything. If the Germans bombing London every night, it ain't have nothing to do with me. I'm here tuning up me pan for Carnival and you telling me this.'

Ma Manette did not hear the actual words, but she heard the grumbling. She called: 'Boys, don't worry. They could do what they like, but not for as long as they like. You like your steel band and you preparing for Carnival, but if Young ban Carnival, so what? I know it's hard on you. Invader could still go to the tent and sing about that. And you see him under the tree, you bet he's composing.'

Lord Invader had turned around again and crossed his leg and leaned against the breadfruit tree. He was hardly hearing what was being said. When Ellie had grumbled, 'They better don't stop the Carnival,' the words had rung and reverberated in his ears, and had bounced in all the corners of his mind, because it was exactly the same way he was feeling. After all, he thought, that is the people's bacchanal.

He lay back with his head against the tree, his eyes closed. The boys had reluctantly gone back to their pans, and were banging. Old Mr Manette was looking at the boys sadly, and at Lord Invader.

Lord Invader was in a world far removed. The sound of the pans every now and again was touching on a note, and this was forming the shade of a tune, and although in between there were discordant sounds, a little melody was oozing out of the pans and gripping on some of the words that were pouring out of Invader's head:

> *They better don't stop the Carnival,*
> *Carnival is a Creole bacchanal,*
> *They better don't stop the Carnival ...*

Lord Invader grew excited. Yes, this could be one of his numbers this year. This could be one of his great ones in the tent. They were starting the calypso season on Saturday, and apart from the one he had composed about the Yankees, this one and maybe another in the same vein could bring down the house.

He hardly heard the continued banging of the pans, for melody and words were now rushing into his head. Ma Manette came to the window several times and looked at him reclining under the breadfruit tree as if lost in a dream world. Several times, the little flaky laughter overcame her and she said to herself, 'Whether they stop the Carnival or not, you think they could stop Lord Invader? Look at him. I'm sure he composing.' She looked at her two boys tuning their drums, and she walked out into the yard.

She said, 'Ellie, what happening to you and Birdie? They ain't having Carnival this year. You didn't hear Invader? In fact, it's not he who say so, it's the papers.'

'Yes, but it say that the Governor *might* stop the Carnival. Perhaps he mightn't stop it in the end. I really wouldn't like him to stop it, not after we get the pans to this stage.'

Birdie said, 'Lord Invader is okay. Calypsonians don't have to have Carnival, they have their Calypso season. We steelbandsmen need the Carnival.'

She smiled at Birdie calling himself 'steelbandsman'. He was only fourteen. She said, 'You mean steelband *boy*. Anyway, the others mightn't come to practise tonight, if they read the news.'

Ellie said, 'Somehow, I don't think they'll stop the Carnival. It's too much of a big thing. People will riot.'

Ma Manette looked at him with horror. 'Riot? Look, if they ban Carnival, you don't go out on the street for me, please! Riot? You think the police will make joke? They'll just shoot them down.'

Lord Invader lay quietly there listening to them. He just lay still, saying nothing.

Ellie said, 'Don't worry, Oval Boys wouldn't go out on the road.' Birdie looked towards him. Ellie said, 'It's only twelve of us. It's easy meat for the police, they'll beat us with our own pan.'

'I wasn't thinking of that,' Birdie said. 'I was just thinking that if anybody want to play mas—if anybody really want to jump up—he'll have to go out in the country, you know, in some place like Princes Town, or even Mayaro.'

Lord Invader uncrossed his legs and got up from the old drum. All he said was, 'Look, I'm going, I have to go. I'll see you.'

The Manettes were taken aback. The lady said, 'What happen, Invader? We making too much noise and you composing? Why you didn't say something?'

'No, Ma Manette. No, it's not that. It's something I have to see about.'

The two young boys were flabbergasted. Mr Manette, looking out of the window, said, 'It's something he forgot. You don't know how calypsonians is?'

Ma Manette, in looking at how Invader dashed out of the yard, could not help being convulsed in laughter.

Invader took a bus to Carenage, and all the while music kept drumming in his head and words kept flowing into his mind. He had wanted another number for the calypso season and he got it. Yes, he got it. He sat on the bus and he was not seeing anything, although his eyes were wide open. The conductor had to touch him in order to collect the fare from him. In his mind, Invader was hammering the tune into shape as the words flowed. The bus rolled on, and with his head turned towards the sea, he was thinking of what Birdie had been saying; and cutting the phrases, trimming and fitting in his mind, he felt sure he had got the first verse. His eyes became more glassy and vague. His lips began moving slightly, and as his eyes closed, he did not feel the jerking of the bus for he was in the calypso tent. The melody joined with the words, and he was strutting across the stage and declaiming to hundreds of people:

> *The Governor stop our festival*
> *But some say they'll still play their Carnival,*
> *The Governor stop our festival*
> *But some say they'll still play their Carnival,*
> *So the Lord Invader went out of town,*
> *I was afraid they'd shoot me down,*
> *So I went down Carenage Water*
> *Playing hide and seek with my neighbour's daughter.*
>
> *To San Fernando ...*

The bus came to a brusque and noisy stop, throwing Lord Invader against the seat in front of him. Some of the passengers looked back and the conductor was standing in the passageway looking at him impatiently. The conductor said, 'Ain't you say you going Carenage? You sleeping, man.' Invader looked outside and saw that indeed it was Carenage. He hastened out of the bus, his guitar under his arm, his handkerchief inside the neck of his shining silk shirt. Somebody on the bus said, 'That's Lord Invader.' As the bus moved off, everybody turned back to look.

Lord Invader turned into Abbé Poujade Street, but he did not go right down. His mind was still aflame. He made for the almond tree, not far from which was the sandy coastline upon which the waves rushed up and rushed back. He could have gone home, which was the last house on the right, but he could not wait. He was afraid to lose the words which felt red hot and pouring from his mind. The melody was pressing upon him. Strumming his guitar, he found himself muttering:

> *To San Fernando I was to take the gal*
> *But down there they say they playing Carnival,*
> *Then I decided on Princes Town*
> *They say they going to play even if they shoot them down.*
> *I finally decided I could not go, and now I'll tell you in calypso*
> *That I went down Carenage water*
> *Playing hide and seek with my neighbour's daughter.*

*   *   *

Weeks went by and the calypso season was in full swing when Ma Manette, looking out of the window, saw the figure with the pink shirt and the guitar under the arm turn into the yard by the breadfruit tree. She cried, 'Invader, I want to see you.'

He went up to the house. 'Yes, Ma Manette?'

'So since you take the place by storm you don't know us again?'

Invader smiled. 'Ma Manette, you know what season this is. The fellers so busy. I have to keep up.'

'Have to keep up?' she said. She was on the steps and looking at him from head to toe. 'Look, I have the radio in the kitchen right there. I can't hear me ears for, "The Governor stop our Carnival."'

Invader laughed. He said, 'Where's the boys? How come no fire under the breadfruit tree—they ain't tuning pan?'

'Governor Young stop the damn Carnival, how they'll tune pan? They gone out somewhere. I don't know.'

'I wanted to see them. Especially Birdie.'

'I'll tell him.'

Invader pushed his hand in his pocket and took out a fancy wallet. He said, 'This Governor stopping the Carnival—me calypso—it going down good.'

Ma Manette said, 'I know it going down good.'

'It's through Birdie. You remember the day?'

'Of course I remember the day.' Ma Manette jogged her memory to try and remember what day Invader was talking about. And what happened that day. She said again, 'Of course I remember. Who you think you talking to?'

Invader said, 'Well, I want you to give Birdie this for me.' He stretched out a twenty dollar note to her. She felt so good she could hardly contain herself, but she said, 'Okay. When he comes I'll give him. But you know what he said last week, just before Hubert Young announce that he was banning Carnival? He said, "Well, Lord Invader get so popular that we better cash in on the name. *Oval Boys* is good, but it doesn't give us the pep. I mean, now it's war, that's why the Governor stop the Carnival. Look, they have a war picture called "Invaders", and Lord Invader making havoc in town. That's the name we want, *Invaders*, not *Oval Boys*." That's what he said.'

Lord Invader looked up at her, astonished. He almost could not believe it. He never had anything in his life named after him, and if his favourite steelband was going to be called *Invaders*, why, that called for another note. And it called for seeing Birdie and Ellie personally and shaking their hands.

He said, 'Ma Manette, look, I'll come back later. Tell the boys they'll see me.'

She smiled as he bolted out of the yard. She called after him, 'Where you going now? Carenage water?'

The Night Watchman's Occurrence Book

November 21. 10.30 p.m. C. A. Cavander takes over duty at C— Hotel all corrected. *Cesar Alwyn Cavander*

7 a.m. C. A. Cavander hand over duty to Mr Vignales at C— Hotel no report. *Cesar Alwyn Cavander*

November 22. 10.30 p.m. C. A. Cavander take over duty at C— Hotel no report. *Cesar Alwyn Cavander*

7 a.m. C. A. Cavander hand over duty to Mr Vignales at C— Hotel all corrected. *Cesar Alwyn Cavander*

This is the third occasion on which I have found C. A. Cavander, Night Watchman, asleep on duty. Last night, at 12.45 a.m., I found him sound asleep in a rocking chair in the hotel lounge. Night Watchman Cavander has therefore been dismissed. Night Watchman Hillyard: This book is to be known in future as 'The Night Watchman's Occurrence Book'. In it I shall expect to find a detailed account of everything that happens in the hotel tonight. Be warned by the example of ex-Night Watchman Cavander. *W. A. G. Inskip, Manager*

Mr Manager, remarks noted. You have no worry where I am concern sir. *Charles Ethelbert Hillyard, Night Watchman*

November 23. 11 p.m. Night Watchman Hillyard take over duty at C— Hotel with one torch light 2 fridge keys and room keys 1, 3, 6, 10 and 13. Also 25 cartoons Carib Beer and 7 cartoons Heineken and 2 cartoons American cigarettes. Beer cartoons intact Bar intact all corrected no report. *Charles Ethelbert Hillyard*

7. a.m. Night Watchman Hillyard hand over duty to Mr Vignales at C— Hotel with one torch light 2 fridge keys and room keys, 1, 3, 6, 10 and 13. 32 cartoons beer. Bar intact all corrected no report. *Charles Ethelbert Hillyard*

Night Watchman Hillyard: Mr Wills complained bitterly to me this morning that last night he was denied entry to the bar by you. I wonder if you know exactly what the purpose of this hotel is. In future all hotel guests are to be allowed entry to the bar at whatever time they choose. It is your duty simply to note what they take. This is one reason why the hotel provides a certain number of beer cartons (please note the spelling of this word). *W. A. G. Inskip*

Mr Manager, remarks noted. I sorry I didnt get the chance to take some education sir. *Chas. Ethelbert Hillyard*

November 24. 11 p.m. N.W. Hillyard take over duty with one Torch, 1 Bar Key, 2 Fridge Keys, 32 cartons Beer, all intact. 12 Midnight Bar close and Barman left leaving Mr Wills and others in Bar, and they left at 1 a.m. Mr Wills took 16 Carib Beer, Mr Wilson 8, Mr Percy 8. At 2 a.m. Mr Wills come back in the bar and take 4 Carib and some bread, he cut his hand trying to cut the bread, so please dont worry about the stains on the carpet sir. At 6 a.m. Mr Wills come back for some soda water. It didn't have any so he take a ginger beer instead. Sir you see it is my intention to do this job good sir, I cant see how Night Watchman Cavander could fall asleep on this job sir. *Chas. Ethelbert Hillyard*

You always seem sure of the time, and guests appear to be in the habit of entering the bar on the hour. You will kindly note the exact time. The clock from the kitchen is left on the window near the switches. You can use this clock but you MUST replace it every morning before you go off duty. *W. A. G. Inskip*

Noted. *Chas. Ethelbert Hillyard*

November 25. Midnight Bar close and 12.23 a.m. Barman left leaving Mr Wills and others in Bar. Mr Owen take 5 bottles Carib, Mr Wilson 6 Bottles Heineken, Mr Wills 18 Carib and they left at 2.52 a.m. Nothing unusual. Mr Wills was helpless, I don't see how anybody could drink so much, eighteen one man alone, this work enough to turn anybody Seventh Day Adventist, and another man come in the bar, I dont know his name, I hear they call him Paul, he assist me because the others couldn't do much, and we take Mr Wills up to his room and take off his boots and slack his other clothes and then we left. Don't know sir if they did take more while I was away, nothing was mark on the Pepsi Cola board, but they was drinking still, it look as if they come back and take some more, but with Mr Wills I want some extra assistance sir.

Mr Manager, the clock break I find it break when I come back from Mr Wills room sir. It stop 3.19 sir. *Chas. E. Hillyard*

More than 2 lbs of veal were removed from the Fridge last night, and a cake that was left in the press was cut. It is your duty, Night Watchman Hillyard, to keep an eye on these things. I ought to warn you that I have also asked the Police to check on all employees leaving the hotel, to prevent such occurrences in the future. *W. A. G. Inskip*

Mr Manager, I don't know why people so anxious to blame servants sir. About the cake, the press lock at night and I dont have the key sir, everything safe where I am concern sir. *Chas. Hillyard*

November 26. Midnight Bar close and Barman left. Mr Wills didn't come, I hear he at the American base tonight, all quiet, nothing unusual.

Mr Manager, I request one thing. Please inform the Barman to let me know sir when there is a female guest in the hotel sir. *C. E. Hillyard*

This morning I received a report from a guest that there were screams in the hotel during the night. You wrote All Quiet. Kindly explain in writing. *W. A. G. Inskip* Write Explanation here:

EXPLANATION. Not long after midnight the telephone ring and a woman ask for Mr Jimminez. I try to tell her where he was but she say she cant hear properly. Fifteen minutes later she came in a car, she was looking vex and sleepy, and I went up to call him. The door was not lock, I went in and touch his foot and call him very soft, and he jump up and begin to shout. When he come to himself he said he had Night Mere, and then he come down and went away with the woman, was not necessary to mention.

Mr Manager, I request you again, please inform the Barman to let me know sir when there is a female guest in the hotel. *C. Hillyard*

November 27. 1 a.m. Bar close, Mr Wills and a American 19 Carib and 2.30 a.m. a Police come and ask for Mr Wills, he say the American report that he was robbed of $200.00 ¢, he was last drinking at C— with Mr Wills and others. Mr Wills and the Police ask to open the Bar to search it, I told them I cannot open the Bar for you like that, the Police must come with the Manager. Then the American say it was only joke he was joking, and they try to get the Police to laugh, but the Police looking the way I feeling. Then laughing Mr Wills left in a garage car as he couldn't drive himself and the American was waiting outside and they both fall down as they was getting in the car, and Mr Wills saying any time you want a overdraft you just come to my bank kiddo. The Police left walking by himself. *C. Hillyard*

The Night Watchman's Occurrence Book

Night Watchman Hillyard: 'Was not necessary to mention'!! You are not to decide what is necessary to mention in this night watchman's occurrence book. Since when have you become sole owner of the hotel as to determine what is necessary to mention? If the guest did not mention it I would never have known that there were screams in the hotel during the night. Also will you kindly tell me who Mr Jimminez is? And what rooms he occupied or occupies? And by what right? You have been told by me personally that the names of all hotel guests are on the slate next to the light switches. If you find Mr Jimminez's name on this slate, or could give me some information about him, I will be most warmly obliged to you. The lady you ask about is Mrs Roscoe, Room 12, as you very well know. It is your duty to see that guests are not pestered by unauthorized callers. You should give no information about guests to such people, and I would be glad if in future you could direct such callers straight to me. *W. A. G. Inskip*

Sir was what I ask you two times, I dont know what sort of work I take up, I always believe that nightwatchman work is a quiet work and I dont like meddling in white people business, but the gentleman occupy Room 12 also, was there that I went up to call him, I didn't think it necessary to mention because was none of my business sir. *C.E.H.*

November 28. 12 Midnight Bar close and Barman left at 12.20 a.m. leaving Mr Wills and others, and they all left at 1.25 a.m. Mr Wills 8 Carib, Mr Wilson 12, Mr Percy 8, and the man they call Paul 12. Mrs Roscoe join the gentlemen at 12.33 a.m., four gins, everybody calling her Minnie from Trinidad, and then they start singing that song, and some others. Nothing unusual. Afterwards there were mild singing and guitar music in Room 12. A man come in and ask to use the phone at 2.17 a.m. and while he was using it about 7 men come in and wanted to beat him up, so he put down the phone and they all ran away. At 3 a.m. I notice the padlock not on the press, I look inside, no cake, but the padlock was not put on in the first place sir. Mr Wills come down again at 6 a.m. to look for his sweet, he look in the Fridge and did not see any. He took a piece of pineapple. A plate was covered in the Fridge, but it didn't have anything in it. Mr Wills put it out, the cat jump on it and it fall down and break. The garage bulb not burning. *C.E.H.*

You will please sign your name at the bottom of your report. You are in the habit of writing Nothing Unusual. Please take note and think before making such a statement. I want to know what is meant by nothing unusual. I gather, not from you, needless to say, that the police have fallen into the habit of visiting the hotel at night. I would be most grateful to you if you could find the time to note the times of these visits. *W. A. G. Inskip*

Sir, nothing unusual means everything usual. I dont know, nothing I writing you liking. I don't know what sort of work this night watchman work getting to be, since when people have to start getting Cambridge certificate to get night watchman job, I ain't educated and because of this everybody think they could insult me. *Charles Ethelbert Hillyard*

November 29. Midnight Bar close and 12.15 Barman left leaving Mr Wills and Mrs Roscoe and others in the Bar. Mr Wills and Mrs Roscoe left at 12.30 a.m. leaving Mr Wilson and the man they call Paul, and they all left at 1.00 a.m. Twenty minutes to 2 Mr Wills and party return and left again at 5 to 3. At 3.45 Mr Wills return and take bread and milk and olives and cherries, he ask for nutmeg too, I said we had none, he drink 2 Carib, and left ten minutes later. He also collect Mrs Roscoe bag. All the drinks, except the 2 Carib, was taken by the man they call Paul. I don't know sir I don't like this sort of work, you better hire a night barman. At 5.30 Mrs Roscoe and the man they call Paul come back to the bar, they was having a quarrel, Mr Paul saying you make me sick, Mrs Roscoe saying I feel sick, and then she vomit all over the floor, shouting I didn't want that damned milk. I was cleaning up when Mr Wills come down to ask for soda water, we got to lay in more soda for Mr Wills but I need extra assistance with Mr Wills Paul and party sir.

The police come at 2, 3.48 and 4.52. They sit down in the bar a long time. Firearms discharge 2 times in the back yard. Detective making inquiries. I don't know sir, I thinking it would be better for me to go back to some other sort of job. At 3 I hear somebody shout Thief, and I see a man running out of the back, and Mr London, Room 9, say he miss 80 cents and a pack of cigarettes which was on his dressing case. I don't know when the people in this place does sleep. *Chas. Ethelbert Hillyard*

Night Watchman Hillyard: A lot more than 80 cents was stolen. Several rooms were in fact entered during the night, including my own. You are employed to prevent such things occurring. Your interest in the morals of our guests seems to be distracting your attention from your duties. Save your preaching for your roadside prayer meetings. Mr Pick, Room 7, reports that in spite of the most pressing and repeated requests, you did not awaken him at 5. He has missed his plane to British Guiana as a result. No newspapers were delivered to the rooms this morning. I am again notifying you that papers must be handed personally to Doorman Vignales. And the messenger's bicycle, which I must remind you is the property of the hotel, has been damaged. What do you *do* at nights? *W. A. G. Inskip*

Please don't ask me sir.

Relating to the damaged bicycle: I left the bicycle the same place where

I meet it, nothing took place so as to damage it. I always take care of all property sir. I dont know how you could think I have time to go out for bicycle rides. About the papers, sir, the police and them read it and leave them in such a state that I didn't think it would be nice to give them to guests. I wake up Mr Pick, room 7, at 4.50 a.m. 5 a.m. 5.15 a.m. and 5.30. He told me to keep off, he would not get up, and one time he pelt a box of matches at me, matches scatter all over the place I always do everything to the best of my ability sir but God is my Witness I never find a night watchman work like this, so much writing I dont have time to do anything else, I dont have four hands and six eyes and I want this extra assistance with Mr Wills and party sir. I am a poor man and you could abuse me, but you must not abuse my religion sir because the good Lord sees All and will have His revenge sir, I don't know what sort of work and trouble I land myself in, all I want is a little quiet night work and all I getting is abuse. *Chas. E. Hillyard*

November 30. 12.25 a.m. Bar close and Barman left 1.00 a.m. leaving Mr Wills and party in Bar. Mr Wills take 12 Carib Mr Wilson 6, Mr Percy 14. Mrs Roscoe five gins. At 1.30 a.m. Mrs Roscoe left and there were a little singing and mild guitar playing in Room 12. Nothing unusual. The police come at 1.35 and sit down in the bar for a time, not drinking, not talking, not doing anything except watching. At 1.45 the man they call Paul come in with Mr McPherson of the SS Naparoni, they was both falling down and laughing whenever anything break and the man they call Paul say Fireworks about to begin tell Minnie Malcolm coming the ship just dock. Mr Wills and party scatter leaving one or two bottles half empty and then the man they call Paul tell me to go up to Room 12 and tell Minnie Roscoe that Malcolm coming. I don't know how people could behave so the thing enough to make anybody turn priest. I notice the padlock on the bar door break off it hanging on only by a little piece of wood. And when I went up to Room 12 and tell Mrs Roscoe that Malcolm coming the ship just dock the woman get sober straight away like she dont want to hear no more guitar music and she asking me where to hide where to go. I dont know, I feel the day of reckoning is at hand, but she not listening to what I saying, she busy straightening up the room one minute packing the next, and then she run out into the corridor and before I could stop she run straight down the back stairs to the annexe. And then 5 past 2, still in the corridor, I see a big man running up to me and he sober as a judge and he mad as a drunkard and he asking me where she is where she is. I ask whether he is a authorized caller, he say you don't give me any of that crap now, where she is, where she is. So remembering about the last time and Mr Jimminez I direct him to the manager office in the annexe. He hear a little scuffling inside Mr Inskip room and I make out Mr Inskip sleepy voice and Mrs Roscoe voice and the red man run inside and all I hearing for the next five minutes is bam bam bodow bodow bow and this woman screaming. I dont know what sort of work this night watchman getting I want something quiet like the police. In time things quiet down and the red man drag Mrs Roscoe out of the annexe and they take a taxi, and the Police sitting down quiet in the bar. Then Mr Percy and the others come back one by one to the bar and they talking quiet and they not drinking and they left 3 a.m. 3.15 Mr Wills return and take one whisky and 2 Carib. He asked for pineapple or some sweet fruit but it had nothing.

6 a.m. Mr Wills came in the bar looking for soda but it aint have none. We have to get some soda for Mr Wills sir.

6.30 a.m. the papers come and I deliver them to Doorman Vignales at 7 a.m. *Chas. Hillyard*

Mr Hillyard: In view of the unfortunate illness of Mr Inskip, I am temporarily in charge of the hotel. I trust you will continue to make your nightly reports, but I would be glad if you could keep your entries as brief as possible. *Robt. Magnus, Acting Manager*

December 1 10.30 p.m. C. E. Hillyard take over duty at C— Hotel all corrected 12 Midnight Bar close 2 a.m. Mr Wills 2 Carib, 1 bread 6 a.m. Mr Wills 1 soda 7 a.m. Night Watchman Hillyard hand over duty to Mr Vignales with one torch light 2 Fridge keys and Room Keys 1, 3, 6 and 12. Bar intact all corrected no report. *C.E.H.*

JOHN STEWART (b. 1933)

The Old Men Used to Dance

It had never dawned on him all through the years that Trinidad was a narrow place. Now that Simon is retired from his teaching appointment in the Miami district and is spending his days as a tourist his views have changed. When he drove around Miami going from school to school teaching, coaching, demonstrating how to play the steelpan, he dearly loved everything about Trinidad. Now, since he has toured in Vancouver and Toronto, Hollywood, and Albuquerque New Mexico, his feelings have changed.

One of the things he likes about the western places he's seen is the streets. The roads. Their spaciousness, their direct lines. Whoever laid them out did so with a large plan and clear goals in mind, the desire to facilitate great deeds and leave access to them for all who come behind. This year he's back home to tour the four corners of Trinidad, and the contrast between roads here at home and the roads on which he has toured abroad strikes him as humiliating.

Of course he's accustomed to the murderous potholes that go on for miles: all Trinidadians are, and he had more or less prepared himself to deal with that. The sharp, flat curves that invite oncoming drivers to ignore the lanes and drive a straight line, that too. The corrugated paving that shook his stomach into mild nausea at times, that too. Concrete abutments and canals where there should be shoulder, all of that. He was prepared to handle all the conditions for which Trinidad roads are well known, including the intemperate taxi drivers who overtake, stop, start, cut in oblivious to the heart-jolting jeopardy in which they place other drivers.

But here he is after five days—since he'd taken time to overnight in San Fernando, Point Fortin, Moruga, Mayaro—in the last hours of his tour, on his way to see the old house in Princes Town, and only now awakening to an impaling circumstance that must have been there before his eyes all along without his recognizing it. Too often when he got off the main road to pass through little villages and towns he decided to see for the first time he found there was simply no easy way to get through. Too often he found that the road just runs out, or that side or back streets are too thin and narrow, that they curve and twist without reason, hump and sink into open drains, slide tiredly into the muck of a pasture, or expire at the base of some concrete wall topped with barbed wire or pointed shards of broken glass ready to eviscerate the sky itself, were it so malicious as to come down any closer.

Manzanilla, Sangre Grande, Toco, Valencia, more of the same. Of course Trinidad is not a big country rich enough to afford boulevards and avenues (although one sees the sign 'avenue' often enough where there's nothing but a narrow lane) but surely we have imagination and energy aplenty (just look at carnival!), and the material (La Brea has been shipping pitch for roads to Europe and elsewhere in the world for nearly a century and the pitchlake still brims) and the manpower to conceive a plan, lay down a 'plat' for a decent network of roadways that didn't run us into unmarked dead ends or run us into fields where cows graze.

This treacherous and frustrating passageway is not the result of sporadic and self-indulgent irrationalities, however. It may seem so, but the thing happens too regular for there not to be a hand behind it all, he thinks. Our roads say, the mission here will be limited. No matter what the spirit invested in this place, the mission will be limited, the power to do things awarded grudgingly, at times suspended, or even withdrawn. The forces that carved out towns and villages in Trinidad were grudgingly awarded and suspended here and there through whimsy.

Now that he's taken time to travel through his homeland, from Cumuto, Tacarigua, Tunupuna, to Curepe, he sees the same hand mingy with space for passing, the same atmosphere armed with an aggressive narrowness. It offends him. The press of open drains and abutted concrete curbs, the unexpected ditch that must be skirted with great care between close, menacing walls offend him. Overseas the drains are all placed underground: why couldn't such care be taken here? The press of other drivers impatiently cutting and squeezing in their knowledge of the local terrain offends him. Why couldn't things be more orderly here? Why couldn't street signs be posted at a level where drivers may easily read them?

He finally finds the correct street leading back to the main road out of San Juan. And once he gets through the tangled maze of taxis, buses, trucks and vans back onto the dual highway he breathes again with ease. This is more like it. This is how it should be: dual lane space, shoulders, no concrete abutments. This is how it should be everywhere from the beginning.

He knows, he can understand. He is not a scholar but he's been a teacher and he enjoys reading history. He knows that streets in the towns of

Trinidad were not laid out with the automobile in mind. These streets were made for walking, for the bicycle, for a time when the country was a more friendly place. A jovial place, with lilies and hibiscus blossoms dancing in the breeze, and people in their graceful country walk taking time to stop here and there and talk to one another. Even from his own childhood he could remember the warmth and neighborliness of the streets in St Joseph, Barataria, Laventille, people walking to church or market, men on their bicycles to and from work, everyone with time to see and recognize each other on the road, time to stand up in the grass or in a gap and talk, time to walk or ride slowly with friends or someone who would soon be a friend. Sunday walks around the savannah, when old and young, the well-off and the poor joined in casual strolls around the bandstand. Motor car changed all that. They demand space to turn, to park, to roll past each other without bouncing. They are not made to negotiate lanes, be carried across gutters, or up the track where paved streets peter into rocky paths between the neighbors' yards. Not that he harbors any preference for the old days, he likes having the motor car. What grinds him is the slowness or absence of effort to adapt the streets themselves to civil use of the motor car. The slowness to have streets that reflect the new order—well marked and spacious, not corrugated—the deadlock this brings around every narrow town square, the tension of driving in defence against unmarked deadends.

On the dual carriage highway there is still a bicycle or two as he crosses the flat plain of Caroni. He enters the hilly terrain at the heart of the Naparima district thinking no one back then when he was young forecast the crush of squeezing, noisy, exhaust-belching machines forcing themselves into deadlock around every market center, or the hurried and careless fashion in which people shoulder by each other in their shopping. Nothing in his childhood foresaw how rusty and dilapidated shops that once housed books, and cloths, and favours of all kinds from various countries would become. Of course, there were the new buildings too. Straight-up concrete boxes with glass louvred windows. Like the new streets they no doubt were reasonably functional but they made no statement. They were no evidence that so-and-so was once here. Anybody could have thrown them up.

He had to face it now. This touring of his homeland is in no way innocent. He had come back primed to see Lloyd, and Sheila, Earl and Hugh and reconstruct the times they used to have dancing, laughing, being in the company of each other. He had come back primed to see Gregory and the boys, to play with them, and get immersed again in the sound and feeling of those days. He was hungry for the sound and feeling of those days. No denying that. He had come back exactly as they used to say islanders always come back, hungry for sweet life after all the false and shallow hurried-up living done abroad. No denying. But even so, even if he had not come back with a probably over-burdening romantic desire, there was still much here to make return a disappointment.

The young Indian family who apparently owned what used to be the ice-cream shop on High Street, once he got in to Princes Town, were not selling ice-cream and peanut punch. The small counter behind which they gathered was greasy and taken up mostly with a glass case of cooked meats. The atmosphere was strong with sweet curry. 'Can you tell me which street it is the Pompeys live on?' he asked the young girl serving as the cashier.

'Pompey? I don't know no Pompey here in Princes Town.'

'They used to live on Centenary Street. I passed by there but somebody else in the house said they had moved. You don't know the Pompeys?'

'I never hear about no Pompeys living here. The person in the house couldn't tell you?'

'Said she's just moved in and didn't know. He used to be the light-heavy weight champion of the empire.'

'No, I never hear about nobody by the name of Pompey. But let me ask.'

She went to the rear of the shop from where steam and the smells were coming, then came back. 'No. We don't know of no Pompeys. Ask next door by the bank. Somebody there might be able to help you.'

Next door at the bank the clerks were all young Indians. They had never heard of Pompey. But 'Ask the guard there by the door,' one young man with pomaded hair and an executive power tie said. 'He's an old-timer. He might know.'

And that's how a world champion ranks in the esteem of these new citizens. Something an old-timer might remember.

The old-timer at the door was not at the door. He was in a small room next to the manager's office making coffee. He was grey, tall, and had the lean hard look of a former fighter himself. 'Pompey?' he said. 'Pompey dead. You enh hear that? Pompey dead long time. You must be from away?'

'I used to live here.'

'Well you must be away long time because Pompey dead and bury so long, plenty young people nowadays don't even know nothing about him.'

He did not ask about Gregory.

Market Street was crowded, with vendors and shoppers locked in a haggling noise he didn't want to hear. It grated against the two solos he carried in his head. He had two. One for Gregory, and one for himself saying maybe thanks to this place where he had first learned to hear and reach the big pulse, the heart that was in everybody. That's what drummers do. Reach the big heart in everybody. And he had learned that here, in a place less noisy, crowded and complacent.

The old men used to dance outside the rumshop near the warden's office. And Gregory was their favourite drummer. Gregory had the gift, they used to say, and when he played, if you were man you knew there was nothing you couldn't do. He used to watch Gregory play, watch the old fighters dance, and feel the awesome stir that made their faces sweet and fierce at the same time. 'Bois!' he could still hear the voices, the solemn, chanting men's voices singing their best to tame the drums and in absolute self-confidence sending their own exclamations to the sky, 'Bois!'

He had two solos, one for Gregory, one for the boy who had never left this town of sloping yards with their flower gardens, zaboca, teke, and mora trees, and the rolling fields of sugar-cane covering the distance. This boy in him who had come home to find the market square a muddle with small heaps of white chicken feathers, broken boxes and stale produce in the drains, and vendors crowded everywhere, their cloths spread in the street itself, all hawking the same tomatoes, melongene, bhodi, ochro, pumpkin, bananas, spices. No one offered flowers. And the haggle of voices was no chant. No one seemed the least bit concerned with the sky, and he reasoned with the boy inside that this was so because times change, things change, people change, all in time becomes the jettison of a drama taking place somewhere else. He reasoned with the boy.

AUSTIN CLARKE (b. 1934)

Leaving this Island Place

The faces at the grilled windows of the parish almshouse were looking out, on this hot Saturday afternoon, on a world of grey-flannel and cricket and cream shirts, a different world, as they had looked every afternoon from the long imprisonment of the wards. Something in those faces told me they were all going to die in the almshouse. Standing on the cricket field I searched for the face of my father. I knew he would never live to see the sun of day again.

It is not cricket, it is leaving the island that makes me think about my father. I am leaving the island. And as I walk across the green playing field and into the driveway of the almshouse, its walkway speckled with spots of tar and white pebbles, and walk right up to the white spotless front of the building, I know it is too late now to think of saving him. It is too late to become involved with this dying man.

In the open verandah I could see the men, looking half-alive and half-dead, lying on the smudged canvas cots that were once white and cream as the cricketers' clothes, airing themselves. They have played, perhaps, in too many muddy tournaments, and are now soiled. But I am leaving. But I know before I leave there is some powerful tug which pulls me into this almshouse, grabbing me and almost swallowing me to make me enter these doors and slap me flat on the sore-back canvas cot beside a man in dying health. But I am leaving.

'You wasn't coming to visit this poor man, this poor father o' yourn?' It is Miss Brewster, the head nurse. She knew my father and she knew me. And she knew that I played cricket every Saturday on the field across the world from the almshouse. She is old and haggard. And she looks as if she has looked once too often on the face of death; and now she herself resembles a half-dead, dried-out flying fish, wrapped in the grease-proof paper of her nurse's uniform. 'That man having fits and convulsions by the hour! Every day he asking for you. All the time, day in and day out. And you is such a poor-great, high-school educated bastard that you now acting *too proud* to come in here, because it is a almshouse and not a *private ward*, to see your own father! And you didn't even have the presence o' mind to bring along a orange, not even one, or a banana for that man, *your father!*'

She was now leading me through a long dark hallway, through rows of men on their sides, and some on their backs, lying like soldiers on a battle field. They all looked at me as if I was dying. I tried to avoid their eyes, and I looked instead at their bones and the long fingernails and toenails, the thermometers of their long idle illness. The matted hair and the smell of men overdue for the bed-pan: men too weary now to raise themselves to pass water even in a lonely gutter. They were dying slowly and surely, for the almshouse was crowded and it did not allow its patients to die too quickly. I passed them, miles out of my mind: the rotting clothes and sores, men of all colours, all ages, dressed like women in long blue sail-cloth-hard shirts that dropped right down to the scales on their toothpick legs. One face smiled at me, and I wondered whether the smile meant welcome.

'Wait here!' It was Miss Brewster again who had spoken. She opened the door of a room and pushed me inside as you would push a small boy into the headmaster's office for a caning; and straightway the smell of stale urine and of sweat and faeces whipped me in the face. When the door closed behind me I was alone with the dead, with the smells of the almshouse.

I am frightened. But I am leaving. I find myself thinking about the trimmed sandwiches and the whiskey-and-sodas waiting for me at the farewell party in honour of my leaving. Something inside me is saying I should pay some respect in my thoughts for this man, this dying man. I opened my eyes and thought of Cynthia. I thought of her beautiful face beside my father's face. And I tried to hold her face in the hands of my mind, and I squeezed it close to me and kept myself alive with the living outside world of cricket and cheers and 'tea in the pavilion'. There is death in this room and I am inside it. And Cynthia's voice is saying to me, Run run run! back through the smells, through the fallen lines of the men, through the front door and out into the green sunlight of the afternoon and the cricket and shouts; out into the applause.

'That's he laying-down there. Your father,' the voice said. It was Miss Brewster. She too must have felt the power of death in the room, for she spoke in a whisper.

This is my father: more real than the occasional boundary hit by the cricket bat and the cheers that came with the boundary only. The two large eyeballs in the sunset of this room are my father.

'Boy?' It was the skeleton talking. I am leaving. He held out a hand to touch me. Dirt was under his fingernails like black moons. I saw the hand. A dead hand, a dirty hand, a hand of quarter-moons of dirt under the claws of its nails. ('You want to know something, son?', my godmother told me long ago. 'I'll tell you something. That man that your mother tell you to call your father, he isn't your father, in truth. Your mother put the blame of your birth on him because once upon a time, long long ago in this island, that man was a man.')

I do not touch the hand. I am leaving this place.

And then the words, distant and meaningless from this departure of love because they came too late, began to turn the room on a side. Words and words and words. He must have talked this way each time he heard a door open or shut; or a footstep. '. . . is a good thing you going away, son, a good thing. I hear you going away, and that is a good thing . . . because I am going away . . . from this place . . . Miss Brewster, she . . . but I am sorry . . . cannot go with you . . .' (Did my mother hate this man so much to drive him here? Did she drive him to such a stick of love that it broke his heart; and made him do foolish things with his young life on the village green of cricket near his house, that made him the playful enemy of Barrabas the policeman, whose delight, my godmother told me, was to drag my father the captain of the village team away drunk from victory and pleasure to throw him into the crowded jail to make him slip on the cold floor fast as a new cricket pitch with vomit . . . ('And it was then, my child, after all those times in the jail, that your father contract that sickness which nobody in this village don't call by name. It is so horrible a sickness.') . . . and I remember now that even before this time I was told by my mother that my father's name was not to be mentioned in her house which her husband made for me as my stepfather. And she kept her word. For eighteen years. For eighteen years, his name was never mentioned; so he had died before this present visit. And there was not even a spasm of a reminiscence of his name. He was dead before this. But sometimes I would risk the lash of her hand and visit him, in his small shack on the fringe of Rudders Pasture where he lived out the riotous twenty-four years of middle life. ('Your mother never loved that bastard,' my godmother said.) But I loved him, in a way. I loved him when he was rich enough to give me two shillings for a visit, for each visit. And although my mother had said he had come 'from no family at-all, at-all', had had 'no background', yet to me in those laughing days he held a family circle of compassion in his heart. I see him now, lying somewhere on a cot, and I know I am leaving this island. In those days of cricket when I visited him, I visited him in his house: the pin-up girls of the screen, white and naked; and the photographs of black women he had taken with a box camera (because 'Your father is some kind o' genius, but in this island we call him a blasted madman, but he may be a real genius'), black women always dressed in their Sunday-best after church, dressed in too much clothes, and above them all, above all those pin-ups and photographs, the photographs of me, caught running in a record time, torn from the island's newspapers. And there was one of me he had framed, when I passed my examinations at Harrison College. And once, because in those days he was my best admirer, I gave him a silver cup which I had won for winning a race in a speed which no boy had done in twenty-five years, at the same school, in the history of the school. And all those women on the walls, and some in real life, looking at me, and whispering under their breath so I might barely hear it, 'That's his *son!*'; and some looking at me as if I had entered their bedroom of love at the wrong moment of hectic ecstasy; and he, like a child caught stealing, would hang his father's head in shame and apologize for them in a whisper, and would beg the women in a loud voice, 'You don't see I am with *my son*? You can't behave yourself in his presence?' And once, standing in his house alone, when he went to buy a sugar cake for me, I was looking at the photograph of a naked woman on the wall and my eyes became full of mists and I saw coming out of the rainwater of vision my mother's face, and her neck and her shoulders and her breasts and her navel. And I shut my eyes tight, tight, tight and ran into him returning with the sugar cake and ran screaming from his house. That was my last visit. This is my first visit after that. And I am leaving this island place. After that last visit I gave myself headaches wondering if my mother had gone to his shack before she found herself big and heavy with the burden of me in her womb. ('Child, you have no idea what he do to that poor pretty girl, your mother, that she hates his guts even to this day!') . . . and the days at Harrison College when the absence of his surname on my report card would remind me in the eyes of my classmates that I might be the best cricketer and the best runner, but that I was after all, among this cream of best blood and brains, only a bas—) '. . . this island is only a place, one place,' his voice was saying. 'The only saving thing is to escape.' He was a pile of very old rags thrown around a stunted tree. Then he was talking again, in a new way. 'Son, do not leave before you get somebody to say a prayer for me . . . somebody like Sister Christopher from the Nazarene Church . . .'

But Sister Christopher is dead. Dead and gone five years now, 'When she was shouting at the Lord one night at a revival', my godmother said.

'She's dead.'

'*Dead?*'

'Five years.'

'But couldn' you still ask her to come, ask Miss Christo, Sister Christopher to come . . .'

There is no point listening to a dying man talk. I am going to leave. No point telling him that Sister Christopher is alive, because he is beyond that, beyond praying for, since he is going to die and he never was a Catholic. And I am going to leave. For I cannot forget the grey-flannel and the cream of the cricket field just because he is dying, and the sharp smell of the massage and the cheers of the men and women at the tape, which I have now made a part of my life. And the Saturday afternoon matinees with the wealthy middle-class girls from Queen's College, wealthy in looks and wealthy in books, with their boyfriends the growing-up leaders of the island. Forget all that? And forget the starched white shirt and the blue-and-gold Harrison College tie? Forget all this because a man is dying and because he tells you he is going to die?

Perhaps I should forget them. They form a part of the accident of my life, a life which—if there were any logic in life—ought to have been spent in the gutters round the Bath Corner, or in some foreign white woman's rose garden, or fielding tennis balls in the Garrison Savannah Tennis Club where those who played tennis could be bad tennis players but had to be white.

Let him die. I am leaving this island place. And let him die with his claim on my life. And let the claim be nailed in the coffin, which the poor authorities for the poor will authorize out of plain dealboard, without a minister or a prayer. And forget Sister Christopher who prefers to testify and shout on God; and call somebody else, perhaps, more in keeping with the grey-flannel and the cream of the cricket field and Saturday afternoon walks in the park and matinees at the Empire Theatre. Call a canon. Call a canon to bury a pauper, call a canon to bury a pauper, ha-ha-haaaa! . . .

Throughout the laughter and the farewell speeches and the drinks that afternoon, all I did hear was the slamming of many heavy oak doors of the rectory when I went to ask the canon to bury the pauper. And I tried to prevent the slamming from telling me what it was telling me: that I was out of place here, that I belonged with the beginning in the almshouse. Each giggle, each toast, each rattle of drunken ice cubes in the whirling glass pointed a finger back to the almshouse. 'Man, you not drinking?' a wealthy girl said. 'Man, what's wrong with you, at all?' And someone else was saying, 'Have any of you remember Freddie?' But Briggs said, 'Remember that bitch? The fellar with the girl with the biggest bubbies in the whole

Caribbean? And who uses to . . . man, Marcus! Marcus, I calling you!
God-blummuh, Marcus we come here to drink rum and you mean to tell
me that you selling we *water*, instead o' rum?' And Joan Warton said, 'But
wait, look this lucky bastard though, saying he going up in Canada to university! Boy, you real lucky, in truth. I hear though that up there they possess some real inferior low-class rum that they does mix with water.
Yak-yak-yak! From now on you'd be drinking Canadian rum-water, so
stop playing the arse and drink this Bajan rum, man. We paying for this,
yuh know!' I was leaving. I was thinking of tomorrow, and I was climbing
the BOAC gangplank on the plane bound for Canada, for hope, for school,
for glory; and the sea and the distance had already eased the pain of conscience; and there was already much sea between me and the cause of
conscience . . .

And when the party was over, Cynthia was with me on the sands of
Gravesend Beach. And the beach was full of moonlight and love. There
was laughter too; and the laughter of crabs scrambling among dead leaves
and skeletons of other crabs caught unawares by someone running into
the sea. And there was a tourist ship in the outer harbour. 'Write! write,
write, write, write me everyday of the week, every week of the year, and tell
me what Canada is like, and think of me always, and don't forget to say nice
things in your letters, and pray for me every night. And write poems, love
poems like the ones you write in the college magazine; and when you write
don't send the letters to the Rectory, because father would, well . . . send
them to Auntie's address. You understand? You know how ministers and
canons behave and think. I have to tell father, I have to tell him I love you,
and that we are getting married when you graduate. And I shall tell him
about us . . . when you leave tomorrow.' Watching the sea and the moonlight on the sea; and watching to see if the sea was laughing; and the scare-
crows of masts on the fishing boats now lifeless and boastless, taking a
breather from the depths and the deaths of fishing; and the large incon-
gruous luxury liner drunk-full of tourists. And all the time Cynthia chatting and chattering, '. . . but we should have got married, even secretly and
eloped somewhere, even to Trinidad, or even to Tobago. Father won't've
known, and won't've liked it, but we would've been married . . . Oh hell,
man! this island stifles me, and I wish I was leaving with you. Sometimes I
feel like a crab in a crab hole with a pile o' sand in front . . .'

'Remember how we used to build sandcastles on bank holidays?'
'And on Sundays, far far up the beach where nobody came . . .'
'Cynthia?'
'Darling?'

'My Old Man, my Old Man is dying right now . . .'

'You're too philosophical! Anyhow, where? Are you kidding? I didn't even know you had an Old Man.' And she laughs.

'I was at the almshouse this afternoon, before the party.'

'Is he really in the almshouse?'

'St Michael's almshouse, near . . .'

'You must be joking. You *must* be joking!' She turned her back to me, and her face to the sea. 'You aren't pulling my leg, eh?' she said. And before I could tell her more about my father, who he was, how kind a man he was, she was walking from me and we were in her father's Jaguar and speeding away from the beach.

And it is the next day, mid-morning, and I am sitting in the Seawell Airport terminal, waiting to be called to board the plane. I am leaving. My father, is he dead yet? A newspaper is lying on a bench without a man, or woman, Something advises me to look in the obituary column and see if . . . But my mother had said, as she packed my valises, making sure that the fried fish was in my briefcase which Cynthia had bought for me as a going-away present, my mother had said, 'Look, boy, leave the dead to live with the blasted dead, do! Leave the dead in this damn islan' place!'

And I am thinking now of Cynthia who promised ('I promise, I promise, I promise. Man, you think I going let you leave this place, *leave Barbados*? and I not going be there at the airport?') to come to wave goodbye, to take a photograph waving goodbye from the terminal and the plane, to get her photograph taken for the social column waving goodbye at the airport, to kiss, to say goodbye and promise return in English, and say '*au revoir*' in French because she was the best student in French at Queen's College.

A man looks at the newspaper, and takes it up, and gives it to a man loaded-down as a new-traveller for a souvenir of the island. And the friend wraps two large bottles of Goddards Gold Braid rum in it, smuggling the rum and the newspaper out of the island, in memory of the island. And I know I will never find out how he died. Now there are only the fear and the tears and the handshakes of other people's saying goodbye and the weeping of departure. 'Come back real soon again, man!' a fat, sweating man says, 'and next time I going take you to some places that going make your head *curl*! Man, I intend to show you the whole islan', and give you some dolphin steaks that is more bigger than the ones we eat down in Nelson Street with the whores last night!' An old woman, who was crying, was saying goodbye to a younger woman who could have been her daughter, or her daughter-in-law, or her niece. 'Don't take long to return back, child! Do not tarry too long. Come back again soon . . . and don't forget that you was borned right here, pon this rock, pon this island. This is a good decent island, so return back as soon as you get yuh learning, come back again soon, child . . .'

The plane is ready now. And Cynthia is not coming through the car park in her father's Jaguar. She has not come, she has not come as she promised. And I am leaving the island.

Below me on the ground are the ants of people, standing at an angle, near the terminal. And I can see the architect-models of houses and buildings, and the beautiful quiltwork patches of land under the plough . . . and then there is the sea, and the sea, and then the sea.

Victory and the Blight

Victory didn't even good open his barbershop when Brown reach to play draughts, with him a stringy bushyhead fellar who Victory see once or twice about the town. Right away Victory face changed. To have draughts playing in the barbershop before he began working was sure to blight him for the rest of the day. And to make it worse, the fellar with Brown was a stranger. As he was thinking how to tell this to Brown, Pascal came in and sat down for a trim. Though now, technically, he was about to work, Victory still had this feeling that Brown and his pardner bring with them a blight to his barbershop this Saturday morning.

'The draughts board underneath the bench,' Victory said, with stiff aloofness, not even looking at Brown. 'When you finish with it, put it back where you get it.'

Brown didn't even hear him, he was so busy introducing the pardner who had come in with him. 'This fellar new up here. He working on the farm, with Walker and Carew and them.'

Victory looked at the fellar, not wanting to appear to be interested.

'My name is Ross,' the newcomer said. 'From Arima.'

'And the man you looking at,' said Brown, 'is the great Victory. If you want to get the run of this town, stick close to him. Sports, fete, woman, Victory is the boss.' Pointing to the photographs on the wall, Brown added, 'You see him there on the wall? Tell me which one you think is him?'

The fellar named Ross stood before the photographs, cut out from magazines and framed and his eyes went over Joe Louis and Jack Johnson and Sugar Ray Robinson and Mohammed Ali, and over the West Indies cricket team with Worrell and Weekes and Walcott and Sobers and Hall and they came down to the Wanderers cricket team, the team with Rupert and Manding and Hailings and Slim and Cecil and the Ramcharan brothers and to Penetrators football team with Berris and Mervyn and Campbell and Bass and Jacko and Breeze, and then he pointed to a photograph with Victory in a blazer, standing in the back row of the Wanderers team.

'That is the year they went to Tobago,' Brown said in a kind of glee. 'And that one,' he said pointing to the photograph of a young muscular fellar on a rostrum receiving a trophy from a middle-aged white woman, 'Tell me, who that is?'

'That is you?' the fellar named Ross asked.

'Fifteen years ago,' said Victory. 'Victor ludorum. Hundred, two hundred, long jump, high jump. That is the Warden wife giving me the prize.'

'Didn't know he was an athlete too, eh,' Brown said gleefully. 'I tell you the man is everything.'

Slightly appeased Victory took up the cloth to put around Pascal's neck to keep the hair off his clothes. He shook it out, flop, flop, flop, went around behind Pascal and fit it over him, then he pinned the cloth at Pascal's neck. Brown, in the meantime, had picked up the draughts board and was moving out the bench so he and his pardner could sit astraddle for their game.

'And don't block the door,' Victory said. 'And that bench. One of the legs ready to fall off. People sit down on that bench like they riding a horse.'

Brown and his pardner were setting up the knobs.

'Wait,' Victory said. 'You better wait 'till I start to trim this head before you move a knob. I really don't want a blight to fall on me today.'

'Okay, chief,' the fellar named Ross said.

'Chief?' Victory looked directly at him. 'I thought Brown tell you my name.'

'Okay, Victory,' the fellar named Ross said.

Victory had his scissors at ready; but, now, Pascal was fiddling with the cloth pinned at his neck. 'If it too slack,' Victory cautioned, 'hair will get on your skin.'

'Too tight,' Pascal said.

Without another word Victory unpinned the cloth, slackened it and pinned it again. Somehow he felt today wasn't going to be his day.

'How you want your trim?' he asked, clicking his scissors over Pascal's ear.

'Clean it,' Pascal said.

Victory paused, 'Think a clean head will suit you?' Then, he chuckled, 'Look at the nice head this man have to take a good trim and he telling me clean it.' He chuckled again, the chuckle turning to a smile, the smile widening his lips, swelling his face, 'Like you want to put me out of business. Like you want me to leave this trade and go and drive taxi or something.' He clicked his scissors again, faster this time, 'Clean it, you say?'

'Okay. Trim me how you want,' Pascal said. 'My head is in your hands.' He was laughing too.

'Trim you how I want?' Victory stopped his scissors. 'I can't do that.

Your head is not my head. I here to do as the customers say. If you say clean, is clean. I would clean it.' A seriousness was creeping into his voice, 'Look, I have one of those machines here that you could just plug in . . . they call it a clipper. I could just plug in the clipper and put it on your head and bzzz! Just like that, and all your hair gone. But, I don't call that barbering. Barbering is playing music. Everything have to flow. Things have to fit.'

'Victory, just give me a good trim, not too low,' Pascal said, trying with a light tone to ease the heaviness of the mood he felt descending.

Victory started his scissors clicking again, but did not touch it to Pascal's head, 'No. Serious. I mean it. I could just plug in that machine, that clipper and put it on your head, and you will give me the same three dollars and bzzzz! Your head will be clean.' He touched the scissors to Pascal's hair, 'Everything in the world losing taste, everything quick, quick, quick. . . . And you know how I get this clipper? A pardner send it from the States for me. The latest. You know who send it? Rupert, the fast bowler from Wanderers. He gone up there in the States and see this clipper and he say, "Victory will like this" and he send it for me.'

'How long he away now?' Pascal asked.

'Four, five years. Last time I hear about him he was living in New Jersey. I always wonder why he send me the clipper.'

'Maybe he didn't like how you used to trim him,' Brown said.

After the laughter, the barbershop was filled with the sound of the clicking scissors, with Brown and the fellar named Ross intent on their game.

'Those was the days when Wanderers was Wanderers,' Brown said. 'This barbershop was the centre. On a Saturday morning you couldn't get in. All the young teachers and civil servants lined up to talk cricket and boxing and waiting to trim. Those days real draughts used to play, with Castillo and Cecil and Mr Arthur leaving Libertville to clash with Paul. Now Paul, too, gone away.'

'The worst thing this government do is to allow people to go away,' Victory said. And he swung the barbering chair around to get to tackle the other side of Pascal's head.

Tugging at the cloth pinned loosely at his neck, Pascal held up a hand to stop Victory, 'You know this thing kinda slack.'

'Hair scratching your skin,' Victory said with undisguised triumph, and began to unpin the cloth once more. 'Pascal, you know what wrong with you. You always feel it have an easy way in everything. Some things aint have no short cut. You just have to do them. No short cut,' he said, tightening the cloth at Pascal's neck, and pinning it.

Suddenly there was an uproar from the draughts game. 'Come and see how this man dead and he don't know! Come and see play!' Victory couldn't believe it. It was the fellar named Ross making this big uproar. The first time this man step into my barbershop, and not even for a hair cut and hear the noise he making, Victory thought, stopping his barbering to allow Pascal to see the position of the game.

Brown countered well, they swapped a few knobs and the tension eased. Victory clicked his scissors and Pascal settled back in the chair.

'So, Victory, what is going to happen to your side now?' Pascal asked, idly. With Victory working on the front of his head, he was looking at the photographs on the wall.

'Which side?' Victory answered.

'You know who I mean, Wanderers. Your side.'

'Wanderers is not a side. Wanderers is a club. A club is not a side. A side is when you pick up eleven fellars to play a match and next week you have to look to pick up eleven fellars again. A club is solid. It is something to belong to.'

'What going to happen to your club when all your players gone away?'

'All? All the players?'

'Well, the stars. Prince, your fast bowler going to Canada. Murray going. Ali gone to the States.'

'Who else going?' Victory asked. He didn't like this talk.

'Is your club. You should know.'

'What you want us to do? They going to study. They have to think about their future. They have to get their education. Just now, just from the fellars who leave and go away from Cunaripo and they come back with their BAs and MAs and Ph dees they could run the government.'

'I wish I was one of them going,' Brown said. He was relaxed now. Ross had miscalculated.

Victory was ready now to clean the edges of Pascal's head with the razor. Quickly, he lathered the shaving brush and brushed it across the edge of hair he was going to remove, then, tilting the chair, bending at the knees, he swept the razor in brisk, deft strokes at the base of Pascal's head and behind his ears, nobody saying anything, Pascal sitting very still. Then Victory attacked the head once more with the scissors; then, with a powder puff, he puffed some white powder over the places where he had wielded the razor. He took up a comb and handed it to Pascal. He was going to do the final shaping of the hair now.

'Comb out your hair,' he said to Pascal. 'Wait. Is so you does comb your hair?' he asked, seeing Pascal combing from back to front.

'I combing it *out*. I usually comb it backwards.'

'Well, comb it backwards, just as you does comb it when you dollsing up.' Watching Pascal comb his hair, Victory continued talking. 'You build a club to last, to stand up. They say nothing can't last in Cunaripo. They say we can't build nothing. And you build a club and next thing you know, bam! fellars you building it with gone away.'

'What you want them to do?' Pascal asked.

'You think I going to stay here just to play cricket?' Brown said.

'*Just?*' Victory asked. '*Just* to play cricket? How you mean *just* to play cricket? What you think put us on the map, make us known in Pakistan, England, Australia? You all don't know what to care about?'

'You have to be able to afford to care,' Brown said. 'How you expect a fellar like me scrambling for a living, to care about cricket?'

'And how you will care about anything? Somebody will pay you to care? They will give you money and then you will care, eh, Brown? Money will make you care?' Victory had stopped work on Pascal's head.

'I would go away to better my position,' Brown said. 'Not because I don't care.'

'Betterment? By the time you come back you stop playing cricket, you seeing 'bout wife and children, you get fat. It was like if you was never here. Sometimes I look through the scorebook and see the names of players who used to play: Bridges, Kedar, Housen, Francis, Lee, Bisson, Griffith. Was like they was never here. Maybe the government should give a subsidy to care, eh, Brown, eh?'

'Is not the going away,' the fellar named Ross said.

Victory turned upon him, 'Is not the going away? Wait! You come in this barbershop a stranger and making more noise than anybody and now you telling me "is not the going away"?'

'Is not the going away,' Ross said, holding his ground in the now silent barbershop, 'What it is? Is what they do while they here. . . . I see Housen. I see him play in Arima and I see him play in 'Grande. I remember him like today, and is how long ago I see him play? He bring an excitement, a magic, a life. You see him on the field and you see life. You see yourself. Is like that, I miss a man like Housen. I glad he was here.'

The silence deepened in the barbershop.

'Is true, Victory,' Pascal said. 'I play against him once. He playing for Dades Trace, I playing for Colts, and when he finish bat . . . I mean, when we at last get him out, the whole field was clapping, not because we out him, because of the innings he play. Is true. The man coulda bat.'

Victory spun the chair around and crouched and looked at Pascal's head, then he spun the chair again and looked at the head as a surveyor looking for an angle. Then he rose up.

'So you does play cricket?' Victory asked, turning now to the fellar named Ross, his scissors clicking once again. 'What you do? Bat? Bowl?'

'Open bat and bowl medium pace. Inswing mostly, but now and again I does get one to move away.'

'Ross, you say your name is? From Arima. It had a fellar used to work with the electricity company. Gerome Ross. Tall, kinda good looking, always with his hair cut neat and his moustache trimmed?'

'Gerome? That is my first cousin.'

'When he was up here, he was my good pardner. Neat, clothes always sharp, dressed to kill when he playing cricket, but he couldn't play fast bowling. Bounce one at him and he start to dodge away. Rupert used to have him hopping. What about him?'

'He get kinda fat,' Ross said.

Victory looked down at his own middle, 'Just now I have to start some jogging. Or maybe start to referee some football. Pascal, you don't remember Gerome? Coulda kick a football *hard*. Goalies used to cry when they see him coming.'

Brown had been studying the draughts board and now, as if he had the whole game worked out, he pushed a knob and said to Ross, 'Your play.'

Victory finished touching up Pascal's head, went around behind him and unpinned the cloth, taking it off carefully so that the hair wouldn't fall on Pascal's clothes. He brushed the tufts of cut hair off the cloth into a heap on the floor, then went to the door and holding the cloth with two hands dusted it out, flap, flap, flap, then he began to fold it. When he turned it was to see Pascal standing in front the mirror looking at his head admiringly.

'You still think I shoulda clean it?' Victory asked, still folding the cloth.

Pascal turned his head this way and that. Then a smile broke onto his face, 'How much I have for you?'

'The price ain't gone up,' Victory said.

As Pascal put his hand in his pocket, Brown let out a big exclamation and slapped a knob down on the draughts board, same time springing to his feet just as the legs of the bench gave away, upsetting the whole game, but not before Ross, with a quickness that amazed Victory, had leapt from the falling bench. Victory thinking, yes, he's an opening bat in truth.

'I tell you,' Victory said sternly. 'I tell you the legs of that bench not good. I don't have money to pay compensation when somebody break they back. People sit down on that bench like they riding a horse. Brown,' he said, his tone changing, 'You better come tomorrow with your hammer and fix that bench before somebody get kill.'

Ross had moved to the mirror and was looking at his head. Then he lowered himself into the barbering chair, 'You think you could give me a trim, Victory? I does really trim in Arima, but I going to be up here now.'

'How you want it?' Victory asked, picking up the cloth once again.

'Now,' said Ross. 'It mustn't be too low. Cut down the sides, level off the back, and leave my muff.'

Victory unfolded the cloth, went to the doorway and dusted it out, flop, flop, flop, then he came around behind Ross to pin the cloth around his neck, 'And, you know,' Victory said as he drew the ends of the cloth securely around Ross' neck, 'When you step through that door this morning, I sure you was a blight.'

MARYSE CONDÉ (b. 1937)

The Breadnut and the Breadfruit

Translated by Richard Philcox

I met my father when I was ten years old.

My mother had never uttered his name in my presence, and I had ended up thinking that I owed my life to her unbending will-power alone. My mother walked staunchly along life's straight and narrow path. Apparently she only strayed once to follow the unknown face of my father, who managed to seduce her before handing her back to a life of duty and religion. She was a tall woman and so severe she seemed to me to be devoid of beauty. Her forehead disappeared under a white and violet headtie. Her breasts vanished in a shapeless black dress. On her feet were a pair of plimsolls carefully whitened with blanc d'Espagne. She was laundress at the hospital in Capesterre, Marie-Galante, and every morning she used to get up at four o'clock to clean the house, cook, wash, iron, and goodness knows what else. At twenty to seven she would open the heavy doors after shouting:

'Sandra! I'm off!'

Twenty minutes later, our neighbor Sandra hammered on the dividing wall and yelled: 'Etiennise! Time to get up!'

Without further ado I would sit up on the mattress that I laid out each evening beside my mother's mahogany bed and reflect on the sullen day that lay ahead. Monday, Tuesday, Wednesday, Friday, and Saturday were as alike as two pins. Things were different on Thursdays and Sundays because of catechism and Sunday school.

So when I was ten my mother bent her tall figure in two and came and sat down opposite me.

'Your father's a dog who'll die like a dog in the trash heap of his life. The fact is I have to send you to the lycée in Pointe-à-Pitre. I haven't got enough money to put you in lodgings. Who would lodge you, come to that? So I shall have to ask him.'

235

In one go I learned that I had passed my entrance exams, that I was going to leave my island backwater, and that I was going to live far from my mother. My happiness was so overwhelming that, at first, words failed me. Then I stammered out in a feigned sorrowful tone of voice: 'You'll be all by yourself here.'

My mother gave me a look that implied she didn't believe a word. I know now why I thought I hated my mother. Because she was alone. Never the weight of a man in her bed between the sheets drawn tight like those of a first communicant. Never the raucous laughter of a man to enlighten her evenings. Never a good fight in the early hours of the dawn! Our neighbors in tears would walk around with bruises, bumps, and split lips that spoke of pain and voluptuousness. But my mother, she modelled herself along the lines of Saint Thérèse de Lisieux and Bernadette Soubirou.

At that time—I'm talking about the end of the fifties—the town of Capesterre numbered a good many souls, how many I don't know exactly. Everything seemed drowsy. The teachers who had us recite 'the River Loire has its source in the Mont Gerbier-de-Jonc', the priests who had us stumble through 'One God in three distinct persons', and the town crier beating his drum 'Oyez, oyez!'

Only the sea, a crazed woman with eyes of amethyst, leapt in places over the rocks and tried to take men and animals alike by the throat.

Three times a week a boat left Grand Bourg, Marie-Galante, for the actual island of Guadeloupe. It was loaded with black piglets, poultry, goats, jerricans of 55% rum, matrons with huge buttocks and children in tears. One late September morning my mother made the sign of the cross on my forehead, kissed me sparingly, and entrusted me and my few belongings to the captain. Hardly had we left the jetty on which the crowd grew smaller and smaller than my joy gave way to a feeling of panic. The sea opened up like the jaws of a monster bent on swallowing us. We were sucked into the abyss, then vomited out in disgust before being dragged back again. This merry-go-round lasted an hour and a half. Women with rosaries in hand prayed to the Virgin Mary. Finally we entered the mauve waters of the harbor with Pointe-à-Pitre shining as a backdrop.

I spent three days without seeing my father, who was away 'on business' in Martinique. In his absence I got to know my stepmother, a small woman draped with jewelry and as rigid as my mother, as well as my half-sister, who was almost blonde in a pleated skirt. She ignored me disdainfully.

*

When he leaned against the door of the cubby hole I had been allotted in the attic, it seemed to me that the day began to dawn on my life. He was a fairly dark-skinned mulatto whose curly hair had begun to grey. A web of wrinkles surrounded his dark grey eyes. 'What a damned Negress your mother is, even so!' he laughed in a sparkle of teeth. 'She didn't even tell me you were born and now point blank she writes to make me "face up to my responsibilities". But I have to admit you're the spitting image of your father!'

I was terribly flattered I resembled such a handsome gentleman! Etienne Bellot, my father, came from an excellent family. His father had been a public notary. His elder brother had taken over his father's practice and his sister had married a magistrate. When at the age of twenty he had failed part one of the baccalauréat for the fourth time he had the brilliant idea of getting Larissa Valère, the only daughter of the big ironmonger on Market Square, with child. He was married off therefore in great pomp at the Cathedral of Saint Pierre and Saint Paul, four months before his daughter was due to be born, then appointed to replace his father-in-law who was getting on in years. Not for long! It was soon discovered that the daily takings of the ironmongery, substantial as they were, vanished into thin air among the men with whom he lost at cards in the bars of the Carenage district, the women he bedded just about everywhere, and the professional cadgers. Larissa therefore took her seat at the till and stayed there from that day on.

I was not the only illegitimate child of Etienne's, even though I was the only resident one. Oh no! After Sunday school there was a stream of boys and girls of every age and every color who came to greet their begetter and receive from the hand of Larissa a brand new ten franc note that she took out of a box specially reserved for this purpose. The stream dried up for lunch and siesta only to resume in greater force from four o'clock in the afternoon until night fall. My father, who never moved from his bed on Sunday, the Lord's Day, kept his bedroom door firmly closed, never letting a smile or a caress filter through.

In fact nobody found grace in his heart except for Jessica, my almost blonde half-sister whose grey eyes, the very image of her father's, seldom looked up from her twopenny novels. I soon learned that one of Etienne's mistresses had maliciously struck Larissa down with a mysterious illness that had laid to rest two other legitimate children—both boys—and that Jessica was the couple's greatest treasure.

Larissa must have been very lovely. Now gone to seed, there remained the fern-colored eyes behind her glasses and teeth of pearl that her smile sometimes revealed. The only times she left the house were to sit straight-back at the till or to go to confession or mass. Up at four like my mother, Larissa, who had three domestics, would let no one iron her husband's drill suits, shirts, underwear, and socks. She polished his shoes herself. She prepared his coffee and served him his breakfast, the only meal he took at a fixed time. All day long he came and went, and his place remained set for hours on end while the ice turned to water in the little bucket next to his glass where the flies drowned themselves in despair. When he was at home, somebody would be waiting for him in the sitting room, on the pavement, at the wheel of a car, and he would hurry off to some mysterious rendezvous from which he returned late at night, always stumbling on the fifth stair that led to the first floor. I don't quite know how he became interested in me. For weeks he scarcely gave me a look and found it quite natural for me to be treated hardly better than a domestic, clad in Jessica's old dresses, wearing a worn-out pair of sandals and studying from her old books that were literally falling to pieces. On Sundays when Larissa was doing the distribution she used to give me two ten franc notes and I went to the 'Renaissance' to watch the American films in technicolor.

One day I was sitting in the yard studying for a poetry recitation. I remember it was a poem by Emile Verhaeren:

> Le bois brûlé se fendillait en braises rouges
> Et deux par deux, du bout d'une planche, les gouges
> Dans le ventre des fours engouffraient les pains mous.

He loomed up beside me amidst a warm smell of rum, cigarettes, and Jean-Marie Farina eau de Cologne and tore the book from my hands.

'For God's sake! The rubbish those people teach you! Do you understand anything?'

I shook my head.

'Wait there. I've got just what you need.'

He plunged inside the house, stopping Larissa who was already busy laying the table: 'No, honey dear, I've no time to eat.' Then he came back brandishing a little thin book: 'Now read that instead!' Larissa intervened and firmly took it out of his hands: 'Etienne! Don't fill that child's head with rubbish!'

I never did know what book my father wanted me to read, but strangely enough, from that day on the ice was broken. He got into the habit of stopping in the dining room near the corner of the table where I did my homework and leafing through my books, commenting: 'The Alps! What's got into them to teach you about the Alps? I bet you don't even know the names of the mountains in this country of ours?'

'There's the Soufrière!'

'All right, next Thursday I'll take you to the Soufrière. We'll leave as soon as it's light. I'll take Jessica along too. It will do her good to get away from the twopenny romances by Delly and Max du Veuzit! Larissa, you'll prepare a picnic hamper for us.'

Larissa did not even bother to reply and went on checking the cook's accounts. 'A bunch of mixed vegetables for the soup. A bunch of chives. A box of cloves.'

I did not hold it against my father for not keeping his promises or for not turning up for his appointments. He was usually fast asleep when we were to leave at dawn. Or else he did not come home until midnight when we were supposed to go out in the evening.

No, I did not hold it against him.

If it had not been for him I would never have dreamed, imagined, hoped, or expected anything.

If it had not been for him I would never have known that mangoes grow on mango trees, that ackees grow on ackee trees, and that tamarinds grow on tamarind trees for the delight of our palates. I would never have seen that the sky is sometimes pale blue like the eyes of a baby from Europe, sometimes dark green like the back of an iguana, and sometimes black as midnight, or realized that the sea makes love to it. I would never have tasted the rose apples after a swim down by the river.

He actually only took me out once. One Saturday afternoon Larissa and Jessica had gone to pay a visit to the family and I was languishing away with one of the girl domestics who was as scared as I was in this old wooden house where the spirits were simply waiting for nightfall to haunt our sleep. My father burst in and stared at me in surprise.

'You're all alone?'

'Yes, Larissa and Jessica have gone to Saint-Claude.'

'Come with me.'

A woman was waiting for him on the other side of the Place de la Victoire: jet black with her lips daubed bright red and loops dancing in her ears.

'Whose child is that?' she asked in surprise.

'It's mine.'

'Larissa is really going too far. It wouldn't kill her to buy two yards of cotton! Look how the child's got up!'

My father looked at me and perhaps saw me for the first time in my

Cinderella rags. 'You're right,' he said, puzzled. 'How about buying her a dress at Samyde's?'

They bought me a salmon taffeta dress trimmed with three flounces that clashed with my plimsolls which nobody thought of changing. While we walked along, the woman undid my four plaits greased with palma-christi oil that were knotted so tightly they pulled back the skin on my forehead, and rearranged them in 'vanilla beans'. Thus transfigured, I took my seat in the motor coach, *Mary, Mother of All the Saints*, that rumbled off to Saint Rose.

Sabrina, who was heavy with child through the doings of Dieudonné, master sail-maker, was being married off. The priest, who was a good old devil, had closed his eyes to the bride's 'hummock of truth' and agreed to give the nuptial blessing.

The wedding ceremony was being held in a spacious house circled by a veranda and built somewhat negligently amidst a tangle of bougainvillea and allamanda a few feet from the sea that gave a daily show under the sun. A table several feet long had been set up under an awning of woven coconut palms stuck here and there with little bouquets of red and yellow flowers. In each plate the women were arranging piles of black pudding, as big as two fingers, together with slices of avocado pear. A band was already playing under a tree and the flute of the hills answered the call of the *ti-bwa* and the *gwo-ka*. I did not mix with the group of children as I thought their games quite insipid. I preferred to listen in on the conversation of the grown-ups whose coarse jokes I guessed without understanding them. That's how I found myself beside my father whose tongue had been loosened by too much rum:

'We don't get two lives Etiennise. Down there under the ground there are no wooden horses and the merry-go-round has stopped turning. We're all alone, cramped in our coffins, and the worms are having a feast day. So as long as your heart keeps beating make the most of it. Don't take any notice of people who say: "Ah, what a bitch life is! A crazed woman who knows neither rhyme nor reason. She hits out right, she hits out left, and pain is the only reality." Let me tell you, that woman. . . .' Unfortunately somebody intervened and I never knew the end of the story. When my father returned his mind had turned to other things.

'My parents used to tell me: "We are mulattoes. We do not frequent niggers." I never understood why. My best friends are niggers you know. The first woman I made love to was a negress. What a woman! Ah, what a woman! When she opened her legs she swallowed me up! Your mother was the same. What a woman! Mme Delpine recommended her to Larissa for the ironing as she did wonders with her instruments. And not only with them, believe me! Unfortunately, she had a serious frame of mind. Father Lebris had filled her head with all sorts of tomfoolery about Mary and virginity. She used to sleep in the attic. The afternoon I set upon her like poverty laying hands on the pauper she was reading "The Imitation of Our Lord Jesus Christ." You should have heard her beg me: "Let me be, Monsieur Etienne, God will punish you. Let me be!" You bet if I let her be. . . .'

And instead of rebelling against the calvary of my poor ravished albeit raped mother, I uttered a raucous laugh. I laughed chickenheartedly.

'Each time it was one hell of a job. I'm sure it was all pretense and she enjoyed it as much as I did. And then one morning she disappeared. Without a word of explanation. Without even asking for her wages. Larissa was furious. . . .'

Another crime to add to my list: I showed no signs of pity for my mother; neither for the terror of her discovery and her flight to her native island nor for the family lamentations, the neighbors' malicious gossip, and that pathetic gesture to cover my illegitimacy, the name of Etiennise, daughter of Etienne.

When we got home on Sunday around three o'clock in the afternoon, Larissa, who had never raised a hand against me, gave me a thorough beating, claiming that I had lost my best school dress. I know what infuriated her, it was this growing intimacy with my father.

My mother saw it immediately. Hardly had I set foot on the jetty where she was waiting than she ran her eyes over me significantly and said: 'You're very much his daughter now!'

I didn't answer. I spent the Christmas holidays barricaded behind the hostile silence that I had raised between us, the unjust cruelty of which I only understood too late, much too late.

I didn't realize to what extent she was suffering. I didn't see the taut features of her face droop and slacken. The wheeze in her respiration, keeping back the grief, escaped my attention. Her nights were wracked with nightmares. In the mornings she would plunge into prayer.

The intimacy with my father soon took an unexpected turn from which I obviously did not dare shy away. He entrusted me with little notes to hand to all the girls at the lycée who had caught his eye.

'Give this from me to that little yellow girl in the fourth form.'

'And this one to the tall girl in the second form.'

It soon became a genuine commerce of billets-doux. You would never imagine how ready they were, these young girls from a reputable family seen at church on Sundays, closely chaperoned by father, brothers, and mother and stumbling with beatitude on their return from the altar, how ready they were to listen to the improper propositions of a married man with a reputation.

I devised a daring technique. I would approach the coveted prey while she was chatting with her classmates in the school yard. I would stand squarely in front of her and hand her the note folded in four without saying a word. Somewhat surprised, but unsuspecting, she would take it from me, open it, start to read and then blush deeply as far as the color of her skin would let her. My father did not exactly treat the matter lightly:

My little darling,
Ever since I saw you on the Place de la Victoire I have been madly in love with you. If you do not want to have a death on your conscience meet me tomorrow at 5 p.m. on the second bench in the allée des Veuves. I'll be waiting for you with a red dahlia in my buttonhole. . . .
Waiting for an answer in which I hope you will accept.

The effect of such an epistle was radical. Before class was over the victim would hand me a folded sheet accepting the rendezvous.

While I was in form three a new pupil arrived, Marie-Madeleine Savigny. She had just arrived from Dakar where her father had been a magistrate and her African childhood had given her an aristocratic languor. She called her sandals 'samaras' and her mother's domestics 'boyesses'. Every able-bodied man in Pointe-à-Pitre was eaten up with desire for her, and my father more than the rest.

When I brought her the traditional billet-doux she cast her hazel eyes over it and without a moment's hesitation tore it up, scattering the pieces of paper at the foot of a hundred-year old sandbox tree. My father did not consider himself beaten. With me as the go-between he returned to the attack the next day and the next. By the end of the third week Marie-Madeleine had not given an inch while my father was an absolute wreck. Back home on time he would be watching for me from the balcony and then rush down the stairs as impetuous as a teenager.

'Well?'

I shook my head. 'She won't even take the letter from me.'

His face dropped and he became the outrageously spoiled little boy he had once been. He had been his mother's favorite, his grandmother's; his father's sisters and his mother's sisters, who showered him with kisses, turned a blind eye to his caprices and called him voluptuously 'Ti-mal'. In June Marie-Madeleine caused a stir by not entering for part one of the baccalauréat. A few weeks later we learned she was to marry Jean Burin des Rosiers, the fourth son of a rich white creole factory owner. Great was the stupor! What! A white creole to marry a colored girl? And not even a mulatto into the bargain! For although he was a magistrate, Mr Savigny was but a common copper-colored nigger! As for the mother, she was half-coolie! Such an event had not occurred since 1928, the year of the terrible hurricane, when a Martin Saint Aurèle had married a Negress. But the family had turned their backs on him and the couple had lived in poverty. Whereas the Burin des Rosiers were welcoming their daughter-in-law with open arms. The world was completely upside down!

Everyone had just regained their calm when Marie-Madeleine, who no longer needed to lace herself up in corsets, exhibited at least a six-month-old belly in her flowing flowery silk dresses.

My father joined in the rush for the spoils. In the middle of a circle of lecherous listeners I heard him recount, without ever trying to deny the fact, how he had tasted Marie-Madeleine's secret delights but unlike Jean had not let himself be caught red-handed.

I spent an awful summer holiday on Marie-Galante. Since I was soon to enter the lycée in the rue Achille René-Boisneuf and take physics and chemistry with the boys, my mother got it into her head to make me a set of clothes. She went down to the Grand Bourg where she bought yards and yards of material, patterns, marking crayon, and a pair of tailor's scissors. . . . Every day when she came back from the hospital there were the unending fitting sessions. I could not bear the touch of her fidgety hands and her grumbling: 'This side hangs all right. Why doesn't the other side do the same?'

On Sunday, August 15, I refused to accompany her in the flared dress she was so proud of. She looked me straight in the eyes: 'If you think he worships you why doesn't he pay for your dresses?'

It was true that for the three years or so I had been living with my father I had never seen the color of his money, except for Larissa's two little brand-new notes. I was doomed to gaze from afar at the books in the bookshops, the perfume in the perfume shops, and the ice creams at the ice-cream parlor.

Whenever she had the opportunity, my mother sent me two or three dirty banknotes with a note that always read: 'I hope you are keeping well. Your affectionate maman, Nisida.'

I was thus able to buy my exercise books and pens and fill my inkpot with blue ink from the seas of China.

When school started again in October my father stopped his traffic of billets-doux. I felt so frustrated, deprived as I was of my mean little mission as a go-between, that I would have gladly drawn his attention to the pretty chicks (that's how he used to call them) who scratched around untouched in the school yard. I soon discovered the key to the mystery. He had fallen head over heels in love with the very pretty wife of a Puerto-Rican tailor by the name of Artemio who had opened his small shop on the rue Frébault. Lydia was a righteous woman. Or perhaps quite simply she did not like my father. She talked freely to her husband of these constant advances that troubled her, and the husband, hotheaded as Latins are wont to be, resolved to give the brazen fellow a lesson he would not forget. He hired the services of three or four bullies, one of whom was a former boxer nicknamed 'Doudou Sugar Robinson'. They lay in wait one evening for my father while he was striding across the Place de la Victoire and left him lifeless at the foot of a flame tree. Around midnight Larissa was presented with an inert, bloodstained body. Transfigured, she swooped down on her husband, who was finally at her mercy. For weeks it was a constant traffic of herb teas, poultices, frictions with arnica and pond leeches destined to suck out the bad blood. Once the doctor had turned his back carrying off his sulfanilamides, in came the *obeah* man with his roots. Every Sunday after the high mass the priest popped in to describe the flames of hell to the notorious sinner.

My father never recovered from this misadventure. In his enthusiasm, Doudou Sugar Robinson had fractured his eyebrow, crushed his nasal bone and broken his jaw in three places. All this knitted together again very badly and the good souls of Pointe-à-Pitre shook their heads: 'God works in mysterious ways! And he used to be such a handsome man!'

But above all, it was his pride and his morale that took a beating. My father realized he had become a laughingstock. He became easily offended and susceptible. He quarrelled with his best friends. He lost that vitality that had made him so popular with the ladies. He became sad, vindictive, and whimpering.

As for me, with the typical cruelty of teenagers, I hastened to keep my distance from the hero who was no longer a hero and who shuffled around harking back to his former conquests. I began to look at him in a new light. What exactly was he worth?

I was pondering upon this when I learned that my mother had been taken to the hospital.

Less than one year later she died of cancer, having hidden the first symptoms from everyone.

VELMA POLLARD (b. 1937)

Altamont Jones

'Ef you dont want to live here you can blasted well leave, you know!'

Her voice was high-pitched and tuneless. Somehow I felt this was a beginning, not an ending, so I slackened my pace.

'Every night you come een ere wid you face mek up like you smell someting ar you jaw puff out like frag a go chin cucubeh. Mi tiad fih look pan sour face. A bet a no so you sour up wen you a gaah upstairs Maas Isaac shap to dat dyam red gal!'

I couldn't hear any response. I knew there was none. I couldn't see anything, so I couldn't judge the sourness of the face. But everything seemed clear to me. He was trying to be good tonight. He had come home. He hadn't gone to the damn red girl. He had hoped to be greeted with a smile and perhaps a hot meal and eventually to improve on the awful mood he had brought from the job.

I could imagine the man establishing a mental distance between himself and the tirade. My mind flashed back to a Canadian city, a bus stop on a cold pavement and a woman, dancing round an impassive man, pointing her index finger in his face and screaming angrily in French while he stared stonily into space. This local counterpart was probably staring into space and focusing totally on the red girl. She wasn't pretty; cute perhaps, but not pretty. She never even offered him anything to eat. She would offer him a cigarette, his brand, and curl up in a chair across from him. Come to think of it there was never a bite of food in sight. He could have a cup of coffee if he wished, nothing else. Perhaps she always ate before he came; perhaps she ate in a restaurant; he didn't know and he didn't care. He went to her for peace and he got it. He wouldn't pretend he didn't get anything else . . . but so what? No big deal! The big deal was her silence, like a cat; even her slippers were soft so when she moved about, the few times she moved about, it was soundless and unobtrusive.

'Yes, you nat answerin,' the high-pitched female voice continued. 'I know dih trick; so dat everybody will seh I am a virago an you are a nice quiet man. All dih same you cyan fool dem; far everybady know seh saafly rivva run deep; ih hih, deep an dutty!'

A short, plumpish man with a round face that registered no emotion at all, entered the bar and sat on a stool two places from mine. I hate the flavour of beer but I like the degree of absolute coldness only a cold Red Stripe can reach; colder than any rum or scotch on any number of rocks; so I downed my beer not tasting it, but letting each gulp idle in my throat and clutch at it inch by inch in the descent. I wasn't watching the man. At least I hadn't set out to watch him; but you can't help noticing a fellow who sits facing you in an early Friday night bar. We were sitting each a stool away from the corner so he was literally facing me. By the time I was halfway through my beer he had consumed three drinks, Black Seal, on the rocks.

I saw the glass move forward again; then it was empty in two gulps. I remembered how Philip Chin had died when I was in short pants and how we had heard that Black Seal, straight, had caused his palate to slip down his throat; clearly this man had no palate. The face across from me was becoming reddish, a sort of purple, like a ripe kidney mango; vestiges of Massa or Busha somewhere were discernible now. The eyes across from me were taking on a faraway look; the kind of look you think you would see in your own eyes if you tried to watch the effect of a spliff in a mirror. Suddenly, the man slid off the stool, slammed the glass now empty for the fifth time, on the counter and shouted, 'Mr Abrams!'

The bartender spun round, obviously taken aback.

'Yes, Mr Jones?' Thus the bartender managing to maintain an even tone.

'Mr Abrams!' the man repeated, responding, it seemed, to a conductor on an invisible podium and not to the bartender's alertness.

'Do you think I should slept upstairs wid dat dam red gal?'

'Well . . . arm . . . arm . . .' stammered the bartender, scratching his head with his free hand.

'Do you think,' interrupted the man, the voice of his impatience rising, his hand slamming the glass on the counter so it would surely break; 'I should slept upstairs with that dam red girl?'

'Mr Jones,' the bartender recovered himself, 'that's a decision you have to make for yourself; me nor nobody . . .'

'Before I slept upstairs,' Mr Jones interposed, responding again to his invisible conductor; 'wid dat damn red gal, I prefaaaaaaar to slept with my wife . . .'

I like to think I mind my own business, but I was so sure the earlier monologue I had overheard was a prologue to this that I paid for my beer and left
the shop as soon as I decently could. I gathered nothing from the sniggers
of the few other men scattered about in the bar. Perhaps I hadn't paid
enough attention to their faces; perhaps I was too distracted by the the-
atrical quality of the whole affair.

The rumshop was at the corner of Chain and Grange Streets. It wasn't
difficult to spot my friend. He was waddling up the street as he had waddled from the shop, blessing now the right side, now the left side of an
invisible aisle with his tread. I followed at a discreet distance. About six
corners up the road, near the spot I recognized, he opened a gate and
almost fell over a large suitcase just inside the gate. I turned left on that
corner and I could see, clearly written in white letters on the suitcase,
ALTAMONT JONES. No lights were on in the house. The street lights gave
a vague and general yellowness to everything. Mr Jones took high, slow
steps along the concrete path, trudged up three steps and banged on the
door. And the echo of his fists came back to him. In my mind, I pictured a
large woman, twice his size, amply endowed with breasts and hips, waiting
in the darkness with a whip in her hand, swinging the leather end slowly,
apprehensively.

Mr Jones descended the steps carefully, shuffled along the walk, picked
up the suitcase, stepped out the gate and closed it behind him. The street
lights were few and far between. The street was an endless stretch of yellowness. Mr Jones bent his head and seemed to will himself to drag his
suitcase up the street. I couldn't see a face in the house but I felt that a large
woman was somewhere pressing her nose against a window pane watching a weak, drunken man drag his suitcase away.

I started to follow again, discreetly, till Mr Jones dropped the suitcase
with a thud and sat upon it. His shoulders began to shake violently. The
man was weeping, there, sitting on all his earthly belongings, a few corners
away from his house. He was weeping like a frightened child. Now that
he was free, he surrendered himself completely to his emotions. I couldn't
tell whether it was anguish or relief that possessed him. Perhaps someone
had made a decision for him, one he had put off making himself over
and over again; perhaps he felt naked and vulnerable in the fullness of his
freedom.

The street seemed unreasonably empty. It was too late for one crowd
too early for the other and it was not a popular street. It didn't lead to any
centre. If anyone in any house knew what was happening, a great show of
diplomacy was being made.

THEA DOELWIJT (b. 1938)

In Foreign Parts

Translated by James Brockway

They were in a foreign, sunny country, but the people there spoke the same language as they did, so it did not strike anyone how strange they were. People did look at Alena, but, after all, she has beautiful long brown hair and when she walks, m-mmm, when she walks you want to go to bed with her. Alena, however, doesn't want to go to bed with anyone—only with Orlo.

They were living in a strange house with lots of rooms in it where Alena played lots of roles, with Orlo as her sole audience. She made strange clothes, which she showed off to him like a fashion model; she prepared strange dishes, which she served up to him like a servant-girl. Orlo never saw Alena—he didn't want that—as a charwoman, a washerwoman, a gardener-woman.

Both of them liked her role as a lover best of all, yet Orlo saw her less and less in bed. For many nights now Orlo had been meditating. Tonight too. He clapped his hands together but did not see the mosquito that had been circling round for some time fall to the ground. They won't get the better of me, the mosquito thought, grimly. He dived under the table and landed on Orlo's big toe. God, what a thirst I had, he thought in between two sips.

Orlo wrinkled his nose. He thought of rats which sometimes die a sudden death, in a gutter or in the middle of some backyard. The stench they carry about with them their whole life long rises up in all its triumph after they die screaming with laughter at the people who scurry past, retching—forbidding them to think for one moment: poor, dead rat.

Rats, Orlo thought, look at you with eyes full of hate and loathing, just as you want to look at them. Strange. In the twilight this evening a rat had been sitting in the pouring rain in the middle of the road and Orlo had braked for him. Orlo didn't understand a bit of it.

Oh, how glad I am, the rat thought, when it finally began to rain. He had been waiting for it from five o'clock on. He jumped up and scurried out of the gutter. He hadn't been sitting in the rain for two minutes when he saw the light coming at him. For a moment he thought of going on quietly sitting there, but he knew he ought not to kid himself; he knew he had to be off.

'Mi Gado, mi Jesus, mi Masra, mi T'ta,' he cursed as he raced away. 'One can't even have a quiet bath nowadays.' Orlo lifted his leg and scratched his big toe. Mosquitoes were the very devil, mosquitoes were the first creatures he had learned to kill. You get like that in a strange country; even though you feel quite at home, you act differently all the same, until you no longer know who you were and who you are. What then?

'You must decide,' Alena said. 'It was you who wanted to come here.'

'Yes, but you can say something too, can't you?'

'You never do what I want anyway.'

'That's not true. If you say you want to leave, then we will.'

Alena smiled. 'Darling,' she said, 'it's your problem. If you want to stay here, I'll stay too. If you want to go away, I'll go with you. You'd go alone otherwise.'

Shbap! A beetle in the ashtray. I smoke too much, thought Orlo, looking at the beetle, which kept colliding with a cigarette stub.

I mustn't panic, thought the beetle, but I must get out of here, in a hurry. Seen from the air, it had looked like a nice quiet little spot, with a few white hills; now he was here he was almost choking to death. I don't understand a thing about it, he thought, and I don't want to understand a thing about it either. Ow! he biffed his head against a bauxite wall.

'Stupid,' said Orlo, and he held out a matchstick towards him.

My God, the beetle thought. This is the end. He pulled in his legs and went rigid with mortal fear.

'Come on, get a hold on it and then I'll pull you out.'

Orlo gave the beetle a little push with the matchstick, which rolled him over on to his back. The beetle screamed blue murder, but Orlo didn't hear. 'Sorry.'

Orlo pushed the beetle back on to his feet with the matchstick. Now! the beetle thought, and made a run for it. Ow! Another wall.

'Calm down now, you'll never get out that way!' Nothing for it then.

Orlo got hold of the beetle by his back between thumb and forefinger and put him on the table.

The beetle had lost all sense of direction. Instead of flying away he crept under some papers where he began to feel so stifled that he could not hold back a shriek of alarm. Orlo lifted up a sheet of paper.

Where am I now? What's going on now? the beetle wondered, at his wit's end. He crept into a newspaper. Do as you like then, Orlo thought and forgot his existence.

He sat suddenly silent and tensed, listening intently. He would do that on an evening, several times. He was trying to identify the exotic sounds of this country. If he didn't succeed, he grew afraid, although he didn't, of course, know why. He didn't care what might become of him, but nothing must happen to Alena, though he didn't know how Alena would manage, if anything happened to him.

All the houses in the neighborhood are dark after ten o'clock. Friends don't usually come along after ten o'clock.

After ten o'clock the night beasts gather together to whistle *tori* to each other, the whole night through. Orlo had never seen them, the beasts of the night. They probably don't even exist; they probably only have to whistle to show how quiet the night is. And perhaps, too, they only have to whistle and whisper to camouflage the strangest and most menacing noises.

Whatever is the matter with me? Orlo wondered. He wished he didn't keep seeing the dog's corpse before him all the time. He had good eyes for discovering corpses along the road (chunks of bloody, stinking flesh) and quickly looking the other way. That *was* a dog, his eyes saw, and that a cat, and these are insides, intestines, and actually, actually we haven't seen anything at all, his eyes said.

But yesterday they really had seen something and that's why now Orlo didn't merely see the trees, staring like inquisitive women neighbors at the man at the open window, not merely the drawing of the clown on the wall, who didn't respond to his feelings of solidarity, not merely all the things which made him feel at home in this room. Now he saw as well the legs of the dead dog, pointing up to the sky, its bloated body, the black gash in its throat where it had bled to death, the dead eyes at the side of the road.

A cockroach glided across the wall. Orlo jumped up, his slipper in his hand. He hated the idea of them sometimes invading his room, even if Alena did keep the house so beautifully clean—that he knew. He struck out. What lousy luck, thought the cockroach, as it fell to the ground.

Orlo struck again, too hard. The cockroach's stomach split open and a dirty-white, sticky mess poured out of it. He didn't want to see it. 'Alena, come and sweep something up!'

'What is it?'

'Sweep that up!'

'Why don't you do it yourself?'

Orlo didn't reply. He went and sat down at his table again, his head between his hands. He listened to Alena. That was that. Don't think about it.

'I'm going to bed. I'm tired. Are you going to sit here much longer?'

Orlo stood up and flung his arm round Alena.

'I'll take you to bed and come along later.'

In the bedroom Orlo saw that a moth had hanged itself.

'What a shame,' Alena said. 'He's worn himself out flying around.'

'Not at all. Look, there's the little bench he's kicked away. He's committed suicide.'

For two days and one whole night I've tried to live, the moth thought. And now I've had enough. He looked about him and suddenly caught sight of the thread the spider had left dangling. Is that an omen? He flew up to it but swerved aside at the last moment to the top of the mirror. Now I can still go in any direction I choose. I can go to the left and to the right, upwards and downwards. I can even still fly out of the window, if I want to. But to the left and the right, as the moth knew, are walls on which they'll shortly be spraying a deadly poison. Up there the light drives me frantic and down there there'll be some silly dog that'll snap at me without meaning or wanting to. That'd be a senseless sort of death. And if I fly out of the window, I shall immediately dash into another room where light is burning, shriek with enthusiasm, shout for joy that I've found the answer at last . . . only afterwards, pretty soon afterwards, to start thinking and doing the same things all over again. I'm not all keen on things any longer, thought the moth. He picked up a small bench and flew towards the spider's thread, and making a loop in it, put his head inside. Then he kicked the bench away.

'Dodo!' Orlo cried. 'Come to bed!'

The dog crept under the bed.

'Shall I use the Flit spray?'

'Oh, leave it,' said Alena.

'Sleep well then.' Orlo kissed Alena on her eyes, her nose and then lightly on her lips.

'Don't be too late.'

Orlo did not reply, turned off the light, and peered into the dark hall (the light had gone again) stretching out as though it were God. He pulled the bedroom door to behind him and whispered angrily to the hall:

'Act naturally, why can't you? You're nothing very special. Agreed, you're long and lofty, but you belong to me and so you will remain. Without me you're powerless.'

The hall stared gloomily ahead as Orlo entered the kitchen and went up to the ice-box. Now, I have to take the beer bottle out first and then get hold of the cola bottle. He ran his fingers through his hair in irritation: it takes too much time, we haven't got all night. He tugged the bottle of cola clumsily over the top of the beer bottle and crossed to the sink.

Plop! said a couple of frogs. They've grown smaller still, Orlo thought. But I can't prove it.

He went to his room, picked up a magnifying glass and followed the frogs with it as they leaped away from him, up against the kitchen walls and into dark hiding places. Orlo removed his glasses and laid them on his left arm.

'Just look,' he said softly (Alena didn't have to hear it). 'Even you will see that there's nothing to be seen . . .'

He made the glasses grow bigger and smaller with the magnifying glass. Suddenly he shivered. I'm an intermediate station. How nasty and hot that was, the frog thought, jumping into a cup.

Rum in the glass, the tray of ice cubes at last wrested loose and under the tap, ice cubes in the glass, a dash of cola.

God, what a thirst I had, Orlo thought in between two sips. He lifted an ice-cube out of the glass and wiped it across his clammy forehead. A feeling of cramp shot across his belly. I'll have to go to the lavatory when I should be studying frogs. Strange, that they should be getting smaller. Where have I left that magnifying glass? Where are my glasses? Oh, leave it—lavatory first. Seated on the pot, he stared down at the floor where a number of ants were busy with the job of living. Orlo narrowed his eyes a little and looked down at his bare feet (he would always kick off his slippers when on the lavatory) which formed part of the ants' landscape. They haven't any notion that they're crawling over the feet of a lifesize human being. To them I am enormous, to them I am immense, infinite; to them, Orlo thought, I am God. He nodded at them. I am your God, he whispered. No reaction. The ants went on crawling about as though He didn't exist. They did not know Him, they did not see Him, they did not recognize Him, they did not even recognize His little toe.

Orlo lifted up his feet and dangled them above their heads like a threatening thundercloud. After this, he had to devote all his attention to his own needs for a while, and he forgot the ants and plumped his feet down on the floor without thinking. He looked upwards and listened to the bats as they led a life all unknown to him under the roof. Why were they chasing about like that now?

When he looked down again the ants had disappeared. There was just a small black spot moving across the floor. Again he narrowed his eyes—I'm a shortsighted God—and then discovered that he was looking at the corpse of a small, shriveled-up fly which was being pushed along by a small black ant. He's sweating like a navvy out in the midday sun. It's too crazy for words.

'You'll never manage that on your own. Hey!'

Suddenly Orlo saw another ant a little further off. That's all absolutely wrong too—that's not the way things should be in My Kingdom.

'Go and give your comrade a hand,' He commanded. 'Can't you see him struggling away there?'

The ant looked the other way. Oho! We're having none of that! Orlo leaned over and intervened with a Divine finger. He gave the ant a push and all but crushed him to death. 'Sorry.'

Then of one of His fingers He made a wall over which no ant could climb. The ant swerved aside, still didn't want to go to his colleague's aid. Orlo didn't give up. He placed His finger in front of, at the side of, behind the ant, showing him in this way where a job of work was awaiting him. It mustn't go on for too long, Orlo thought.

'Get a move on!'

The ant, however, had other ideas in mind, other things to do and tried, with an angry expression on his face, to go his own way.

'Goddammit!' Orlo picked up the ant carefully—yes, carefully—between His thumb and forefinger and put him down next to his sweating comrade.

'Cooperation,' Orlo whispered, 'makes things so much easier.'

Something cracked, something got broken, something was crushed fine. The ant with the dead fly looked up, vexed.

'Mi Gado,' he sighed, 'that on top of everything else! Now I've got a casualty to look after too!'

'Just let me lie here,' groaned the injured ant.

'Are you crazy? Of course, I'll help you. Can you stand on your feet? What happened actually?'

'I've no idea,' said the injured ant. 'No idea.'

I'm the Benevolent God, Orlo thought as he pulled the chain. Suddenly everything is clear. It is finished. In bed he drew Alena close to him. 'I love you.'

'What's the matter?' Alena asked sleepily.

Orlo laughed. He felt good. 'We could easily go home for a while, you know,' he said.

'What?'

'Shall we go home?'

They were in their own country, but it was a strange, cloudy land. They spoke their own language, yet people noticed how strange they were.

People often looked at Alena, but, after all, she has beautiful long brown hair and when she walks, m-mmm, when she walks you want to go to bed with her. Alena, however, doesn't want to go to bed with anyone—only with Orlo.

They were living in a strange hotel with lots of rooms in it where people lived whom you never saw. The few you encountered in the corridors or on the terrace could only whisper. Alena lay in bed the whole day long under blankets of orange wool. Orlo still thought them endearing blankets, because under them during the first nights she had acted her role as a lover so well—better even than usual.

Their friends from former days had come to visit them only during the first days. They laughed, because Orlo and Alena felt cold while the sun was shining. Now the sun was not shining anymore.

In those first days they had gone into the wood. Arms round each other, Orlo and Alena had said how beautiful the brown leaves were and how strange it was that here you didn't need to be afraid of anything.

They spread out a coat on the moss and lay close to each other. But Orlo had not felt at home, he didn't recognize the sounds anymore, the leaves spoke a different language, the wind in the trees sounded strange. He sat up.

'Do come and lie down,' Alena said.

'I can hear something.'

Alena laughed.

'I have to protect you, don't I?' said Orlo. He picked up a twig and broke open the soil with it.

'What are you doing?' Alena asked sleepily.

'I'm looking for ants.'

'Be glad there aren't any here.'

'Here too there are ants. I'm sure. Before they were here too.'

'We've picked a nice spot,' Alena said. 'Do come and lie down again.'

Orlo remained sitting up.

'What's wrong now?'

'I want ants!' Orlo snapped at her.

Alena sat up too and flung her arms round Orlo's neck. 'Aren't you pleased we're here? Do you want to go back?'

'I don't know,' Orlo said. 'I don't know.'

'We've got to get used to it,' Alena said. 'We've got to get used to this country again, to the people, to everything. After a while everything won't seem so strange anymore. After a while we'll have friends again, after a while we'll live normally again.'

But it had grown colder and colder and Alena had stayed in bed longer and longer. She did not play roles anymore.

Orlo always wore a thick coat and a woollen scarf. Dressed like this, he would sit meditating, days and nights at his desk in the hotel room, staring at strange walls. He ordered strange drinks, listened to strange sounds. He was never really afraid anymore.

Animals he no longer saw, not live ones, not dead ones.

Never once did he know he was God. Many a night a strange mist hung in the air, and the trees were unrecognizable.

won, or at least, that's what we thought then, before we sensed your true intentions, the ability with which you had been manipulating us so that we began to merge, so that we began to fade into each other like an old picture lovingly placed under its negative, like that other distressed face we carry deep down, that one day will surface when we stand in front of that mirror someone removed from the wall.

When all is said and done, this doesn't seem so strange, it is almost necessary that everything should have happened the way it did. We, your lover and your wife, have always known that a prostitute hides beneath the skin of every lady. It is apparent in the way they slowly cross their legs, rubbing themselves lightly with the silky insides of their thighs. It is apparent in the way they get bored with men, they don't know what we go through, plagued by the same man for the rest of our lives. It is apparent in the way they jump from man to man on the tips of their eyelashes, hiding a swarm of green and blue lights in the depths of their vaginas. Because we have always known that each prostitute is a potential lady, drowned in the nostalgia of a white house like a dove that will never be held, of that house with a balcony of silver amphoras and plaster fruit garlands hanging over the doors, drowned in the nostalgia of the sound of china when invisible hands set the table. Because we, Isabel Luberza and Isabel la Negra, in our passion for you, Ambrosio, from the beginning of time, had been growing closer; had been blessing each other without realizing it, purifying ourselves of everything that defined us, one as a prostitute and the other as a lady. So that in the end, when one of us won over the other, it was our most sublime act of love.

You were to blame, Ambrosio, no one could know for sure who was who until today. Isabel Luberza, collecting money to restore the plaster lions of the town square that had stopped spurting colored water from their mouths, or Isabel la Negra, preparing her body to receive the semen of the rich boys, the sons of those friends of yours that entered my shack every night with their shoulders drooped timidly, dragging their desires like pigeons dying of consumption, famished in front of the banquet of my body; Isabel Luberza, the Auxiliary Lady of the Red Cross or Elizabeth the Black, the president of the Young Lords, affirming from her platform that she is the proof in flesh and blood that there was no difference between those of Puerto Rico and those of New York because they had all been united in her flesh; Isabel Luberza collecting funds for Boy's Town, City of Silence, Model City, dressed by Fernando Pena with long white lambskin gloves and a silver mink stole or Isabel the Slavedriver, the exploiter of contraband Dominican girls put on the shores of Guayanilla; Isabel

Luberza the Popular Lady,[3] the companion of Ruth Fernández, singing the soul of Puerto Rico in political campaigns,[4] or Isabel la Negra, the soul of Puerto Rico made into a procuress, the Queen of San Antón,[5] The Cunt of Chichamba, the sharpest-shooting whore in Barrio de la Cantera, the harlot of Cuatro Calles, the fuck of Singapur, the flirt of Machuelo Abajo, the sharpest streetwalker of all Coto Laurel; Isabel Luberza, the one who raised young pigeons in La Sultana cracker tins on the roof of her house to make broth for the sick townspeople, or Isabel la Negra, of whom it never could be said that she cared one way or the other because she was neither fish nor fowl; Isabel Luberza the cake baker, the knitter of little cloud colored booties and blankets, the embroiderer of trutrú,[6] around the little collars of the little gowns made of the finest linen, those made to order for the babies of the Alumnae of the Sacred Heart; Isabel the Rumba Macumba Candombe Bambula;[7] Isabel the Tembandumba de la Quimbamba,[8] swaying her okra flesh through the lighted Antillean street, her grapefruit tits sliced open on her chest; Isabel the Second, Queen of Spain, patron of the most aristocratic street in Ponce; Isabel the Black Lady, the only one ever bestowed with the order of the Saint Prepuce of Christ; Isabel, sister of Saint Louis, King of France, town patron of Santa Isabel, lulled for centuries under the blue Tits of Doña Juana;[9] Isabel Luberza the Catholic Lady, painter of the most exquisite amulets of the Sacred Heart, dripping through its side the only three divine ruby drops capable of detaining Satan; Isabel Luberza the saint of Oblates, carrying a tray served with her pink tits; Isabel Luberza the Virgin of the Thumb, thrusting her thumb piously through a little embroidered hole in her gown; Isabel la Negra, Brincaicógelo Maruca's[10] only girlfriend, the only one who ever kissed his deformed feet and washed them with her tears, the only one who danced with the children to the rhythm of his cry Hersheybarskissesmilkyways, through the burning streets of Ponce; Isabel the Black Pearl of the South,[11] the Queen of Saba, the Queen of Sheba, the Chivas Regal, the

---

[3] Refers to being a supporter of the Popular Democratic Party in Puerto Rico.

[4] Popular singer who is also an active member of the Popular Democratic Party.

[5] Reference to the home of the *plena* and Isabel la Negra.

[6] Embroidery done by the Sisters of Charity.

[7] Line from the poem 'Majestad negra' written in 1934 by Luis Palés Matos.

[8] Ibid.

[9] Reference to two breast-like mountains near a town called Juana Díaz.

[10] Folkloric character from Ponce; famous for selling candy and being friendly with children.

[11] A reference to Ponce, which is called The Pearl of the South.

Tongolele,[12] the Salomé, spinning her belly in gyroscopic circles in the eyes of men, shaking for them, from immemorable times, her multitudinous cunt and her monumental ass, spreading misfortune on all the walls, through all the streets, this confusion between her and her, or between her and me, or between me and me, because as time passed, from loving her so much, from hating her so much, it became more difficult for me to tell this story, it became harder to differentiate between the two.

So many years of anger stuck like a lump in my throat, Ambrosio, so many years of painting my fingernails while walking towards the window to see better, of always polishing them with Cherries Jubilee because it was the reddest color in those days, always with Cherries Jubilee while I thought of her, Ambrosio, of Isabel la Negra, or perhaps I had already begun to think of myself, in that other identity that had begun to grow in me like a cyst, because, to start with, it was strange that I, Isabel Luberza, your wife, with such refined tastes, would like that shrill and gaudy color that only Negroes like. Following one by one, the contours of the white moons at the base of my fingernails, brushing carefully the dainty hairs of the brush around the little edge of my almond-shaped fingernails, around the edge of the cuticle that always stung a bit at the contact with the nail polish because while trimming them, my hand always slipped a bit, because as I saw the defenseless and soft skin between the tips of the scissors, I would always get angry and couldn't help but think of her.

Sitting on the balcony of this house that now will belong to both of us, to Isabel Luberza and to Isabel la Negra, of this house that will now become part of the same legend, the legend of the prostitute and the lady. Sitting on the balcony of my new brothel without anyone suspecting, the balustrade of long silver amphoras now painted shocking pink, aligned in front of me like happy phalluses, the white plaster garlands adhered to the façade, that gave the house that romantic air and a feeling of excessive respectability as in wedding cakes, that sensation of being covered by a cakey icing, stiff like the skirt of a debutante, now painted in warm colors, in chartreuse green with orange, in lilac with dahlia yellow, in those colors that invite men to relax, to let their arms slide limply down their sides as though they were navigating on the deck of some white transatlantic liner. The walls of the house, white and powdery like the wings of a heron, painted now a bottle green, a transparent green so that when we stand, you and I, Ambrosio, in the main hall, we will see what is happening in each room, we will see ourselves unfold into twenty identical images, reflected

---

[12] Vedette dancer from the 1950s.

on the bodies of those who will rent these rooms to have in them their indifferent orgasms, completely absorbed in spite of our presence, repeating with their bodies, one after another, to the end of time, our ritual of love.

Sitting on the balcony, waiting for them to enter this house to whisk her away, sitting there while waiting to see her take that path to the grave that was destined to be mine but that now will belong to her, to the sacred body of Isabel Luberza, to that body which nobody had ever seen exposed to this day in the smallest sliver of her white buttocks, in the most tenuous shavings of her white breasts, her chaste skin that had protected her flesh, now snatched away from her, renounced at last that virginity of a respectable mother, of a respectable wife that had never before stepped into a brothel, that had never before been slandered in public as I have been so many times, that had never before left uncovered, food for the ravenous eyes of men, any part of her body except her arms, her neck, her legs from the knee down. Her body now naked and tinctured in black, her sex covered by a small triangle of amethysts, including the one the bishop had worn on his finger, her nipples trapped in nests of diamonds, fat and round like chickpeas, her feet stuffed into shoes of red rime, with twin hearts sewn on the tips, the heels still dripping some drops of blood. Finally, dressed like a queen, dressed as I would have, if it had been my funeral.

Waiting to rub on her cheeks, when she sways underneath a mountain of rotting flowers, her perfume Fleur de Rocaille, with which I anointed my body, her powder, Chant D'Aromes, with which I whitened my breasts and that now silently trickles down the wrinkles of my belly, my hair, a cloud of smoke around my head, my legs, smooth like the nuptial sex of a sultana. Waiting with her dress of silver lamé, covering my shoulders with folds, spilling down my back like a cape of ice that shines with a furious midday light, my throat and wrists tightened by threads of diamonds exactly as then, as when I was still Isabel Luberza and you, Ambrosio, were still living, the town emptying itself into the house to attend the parties, and I standing next to you like a sprouted jasmine clinging to the wall, yielding my perfumed hand to be kissed, my small creamy hand that had begun to be hers, Isabel la Negra's, because since then I felt a tide of blood rising from the base of my fingernails, soaking my insides with Cherries Jubilee.

It wasn't until Isabel la Negra lifted Isabel Luberza's door knocker and pounded three times that she feared for the first time, that what she was doing wasn't sensible. She had come to talk to her about the business of the house they had both inherited. Ambrosio, the man they had lived with when they were young, had died many years ago, and Isabel la Negra, out of consideration for her namesake, had not decided till then to claim her part of the house, although she had already efficiently invested the money her lover had left her. She had heard that Isabel Luberza was crazy, that since the death of Ambrosio, she had locked herself up in her house and would never go out, but this never came to be more than a rumor. She thought that so many years had gone by of their being rivals, that all resentment would now be forgotten, and that their immediate needs would facilitate a sensible and productive dialogue between the two. The widow was surely in need of rent money that would assure her a peaceful old age, and this would perhaps motivate her to sell her half of the house. On her part, Isabel la Negra thought that she had plenty of reasons for wanting to move her brothel there, although she didn't understand some of them very clearly. The business had been so successful, that it would be necessary to expand it. Isabel was convinced that it would be convenient to take it out of the slum because in the slum it lost prestige and even gave the impression of being an insalubrious business. But the yearning to own that house, of sitting out on the balcony behind the silver balustrade, beneath that façade laden with baskets of fruit and garlands of flowers, answered to a profound nostalgia that had become more inflamed over the years: the desire of finding a substitute in her old age, for the memory of that childhood vision, which visited her whenever she walked past that house, barefoot and dressed in rags, the vision of a man dressed in white linen, standing on that balcony, next to a blond woman, incredibly beautiful, wearing a dress of silver lamé.

It was true, she was now a self-made woman, and she had reached an enviable status in the town, even in the eyes of those society women whose families are ruined and are now only left with the empty pride of their names, but who haven't even enough money for a little trip to Europe once a year as I do, or for wearing the latest fashions as I always do. But still, despite the satisfaction of knowing that her social endeavors were recognized, her fundamental importance in the economic development of the town as the recipient of numerous prestigious appointments, such as president of the Civic Ladies, of the Altruists, of the Junior Chamber of Commerce, she felt that there was something missing, that she didn't want to die without having made at least the attempt to realize her chimera, that caprice of a fat and rich lady, of imagining herself, young again, dressed in silver lamé and sitting on that balcony, clinging to the arm of the man she also had loved.

When Isabel Luberza opened the door, Isabel la Negra felt her knees weaken. She was still so beautiful that I had to lower my eyes, I almost didn't dare look at her. I felt the desire to kiss her eyelids, tender as the flesh of a new coconut, bevelled into almond shapes, I thought of how much I would have liked to lick them to feel them tremble, transparent and slippery, over the balls of her eyes. She had braided her hair about her nape, as Ambrosio had told me. Her overly sweet perfume, Fleur de Rocaille, brought me back to reality. Above all, I needed to convince her that I sought her friendship and her trust, that if it was necessary I was willing to admit her as a business partner. For a moment, seeing her looking at me so intently, I asked myself whether she was crazy as people said, if she truly thought she was a saint, if she lived truly obsessed, as Ambrosio would tell me smiling, with the idea of redeeming me, submitting her body to all sorts of absurd punishments that she offered in my name. But it doesn't matter. If the rumor was true, it would work in my favor since she has shown me some affection. After looking at me for another moment, she opened the door and I entered.

Entering the house I couldn't help but think of you, Ambrosio, of how you had me locked up for so many years in that shack of planks with a zinc roof, condemned to passing the days milking the cream out of the little rich boys, of the sons of friends that you brought me so that you can do them the favor Isabel, so that you will open for them the canned desires that those poor fellows bring, damn it Isabel, don't be like that, you're the only one who knows, you're the one who does it best, we can only do it with you, nibbling on them like pieces of quince or guava paste, smacking my cheeks, forehead, mouth, eyes with their silky penises to excite them, for sure you can son, why can't you, let yourself go that's all, as though you were sliding down a hill, down a mountain of soapsuds without stopping, pissing on them so that they could come, so that their fathers could sleep peacefully at last because the sons they had born had not turned out to be sissies, had not turned out to be little saints with porcelain splintered butts, because the sons they had borne were the sons of Saint Dagger and Saint Iron, but they could only bring them to me in order to prove it, kneeling in front of them like a priestess officiating at my sacred ritual, their hair blinding my eyes, lowering my head until I feel the sheathed penis like a lily inside my throat, being careful of squeezing too much with my man-pruning legs, taking infinite care of not squeezing my lips too much, devouring them like lotus pistils with my unsatiable mouth. Thinking that it wasn't for them that I was doing what I was doing but for myself, to pick up something very old that leaks down in bittersweet rivers behind my throat, to show them that real women are not sacks that are left impaled against the bed, that the most macho man is not the one that allures the woman but who has the courage to let himself be allured, showing them how to share pleasure with me, hidden in my brothel, where no one will know that they have let themselves be made, that they have been putty in my hands, so that then they can, pompous like roosters, delight the little white girls, those blobs of custard that rich girls probably look like in bed, because it is not proper for a good girl to thrust her pelvis, because good girls have vaginas of polished silver and bodies of carved alabaster, because it isn't right for good girls to mount on top and gallop for their pleasure nor for the pleasure of anyone, because they couldn't have learned to do any of this with good girls since it would not have been proper, they wouldn't have felt themselves to be machos, because the macho must always take the initiative but someone must show them the first time and that is why they go to Isabel la Negra, black like the grounds on the bottom of a coffee pot, like the mud at the bottom of the gutter, rolling themselves in the arms of Isabel la Negra as though they were whips of mud, because in the arms of Isabel la Negra everything is allowed, sonny, nothing is forbidden, the body is the only eden, the only fountain of delights, because we know pleasure and pleasure makes us into gods, sonny, and although we may be mortals, we have bodies of gods, because for a few moments we have robbed them of their immortality, only for a few moments, sonny, but that's enough, that's why we don't care if we die. Because here, hidden in the arms of Isabel la Negra no one will see you, no one will ever know that you also have the weaknesses of a man, that you're also weak and can be at the mercy of a woman, because here, sonny, rooting in my armpit, sticking your tongue inside my sweaty vulva, letting your little mute nipples be sucked and letting them be slapped by mine that really can nourish, that really can, if they want, give you sustenance, here no one will know, here no one will care if you're another whimp, shit-scared with fear in my arms, because I am no more than Isabel la Negra, the scum of the earth, and here, I swear by the Holy Name of Jesus that is looking at us, no one will ever know that you also wanted to be eternal, that you also wanted to be a god.

When you started getting old, Ambrosio, luck turned in my favor. You could only feel pleasure while seeing me in bed with those boys that you brought to me all the time and then you began fearing they would see me secretly, that they would pay me more than you did, that I would abandon you forever. Then you had the notary come and you edited a new will benefitting equally your wife and myself. Isabel la Negra remained looking at the sumptuously decorated walls of the living room and thought that the house was perfect for her new Dancing Hall. From now on forget the five and ten cent whore house, the in and out for a buck, the kings that come and go leaving us behind, always poor. Because while the Dancing Hall remains in the slum, no matter how marvelous it may be, no one will want to pay more than ten bucks a night. But here in this house and in this neighborhood everything would change. I could hire a couple of young chicks that will help me out and charge fifty bucks a fuck or nothing. In this house there would be no more old whores, no more dry mush, no more clitorises wrinkled like orange seeds or irritated like rusty salt shakers, it would be the end of croton coituses in cockroach infested cots, it would be a house of double egg mousse and no more. Isabel Luberza approached Isabel la Negra without saying a word. She had stretched out her arms and placed her fingertips on her cheeks, touching her face as though she were blind. Now she takes my face in her hands and kisses me, and then begins to cry. God damn it, Ambrosio, you had to have a heart of stone to make her suffer the way you did. Now she takes me by the hand and stares at my fingernails polished with Cherries Jubilee. I'm surprised to see she has painted her nails in the same color. At first, Ambrosio, I couldn't understand why you left Isabel la Negra half of your inheritance, half of this house where you and I had been so happy. The day after the funeral, when I realized the whole town had found out about my disgrace, and I was being slandered to bits, I walked through the streets hoping everyone would die. It was then that everything began to change. Isabel la Negra had torn down the shack where you visited her and with your money built her Dancing Hall. Then I thought of what she had meant to us, the final sum of our love, and I could not accept what she had become.

Because it was clearly said by Saint Paul, Ambrosio, adultery is one thing when it is carried out with modesty and moderation, and another when it is public pandering, a rape of coin machines and neon lights. It is clearly said by him in his Epistle to the Corinthians, if a woman's husband is unfaithful to her for another woman, let him beware of committing an even greater sin by remaining with a prostitute rather than with an ordinary woman. And the woman, in turn, by remaining faithful to her duties as a wife and mother, her lily-white skin mortified, her roots submerged in suffering as on the edges of a placid lake, exhales the ineffable perfume of a virginal spirit that rises and soars to the clouds, pleasing Our Lord infinitely.

The first years of our marriage, when I realized the relationship that existed between you two, I felt like the unhappiest woman on earth. I cried so much it felt as though coramine had been injected into my eyelids, and they trembled like red fish over the balls of my eyes. When you came to our house I knew immediately that you were coming from hers. I knew by the way you placed your hand on my neck, by the way you slowly moved your eyes over my body like satisfied flies. It was then I was most careful with my satin slips and my French lace underwear. It was as though you carried her memory mounted on your back, tormenting you with arms and legs, hitting you without compassion. Then I would stretch out on the bed and let myself be made. But I would always keep my eyes wide open and look over your shoulders as they bent down over and over again, so as not to lose sight of her, so that she would not think that I was giving in to her, not even by mistake.

I then decided to win you over in other ways, through means of that ancient wisdom I had inherited from my mother and my mother from her mother. I began placing your napkin in a silver ring next to your plate, sprinkling drops of lemon juice in your water goblet, spreading your linen myself on sheets of zinc, burning hot from the sun. I placed on your bed the sheets still warm from drinking sunlight, white and soft underneath my hand like a smooth lime wall, spreading them inside-out and then folding them right-side out and thereby releasing, to delight you when you lie down, a dissipation of variegated roses and butterflies, the amorous threads of the most tenuous rose color, a refined sugar tint that would remind you of the lineage of our surnames, checking well to see if the vine of our initials was always under your forearm, so that it would awaken, with its delicious light silkworm touch, the sacred fidelity of our union. But everything was fruitless. Daisies thrown to the pigs. Pearls to the muck-heap.

This was how, through the years, she began turning into something like an evil necessity, a tumor that we carry in our breast and cover with our softest flesh so that it won't be bothersome. It was when we sat at the table that I felt her presence. The porcelain plates emanated a creamy peace from their bottoms, and the drops of sweat that covered the goblets of chilled water, suspended in the heat like fragile tits of ice, seemed as though they would never slide downhill, as though the cold that kept them poised on the glass, the same as our happiness, would remain there, balanced forever. I would then think of her obstinately. I wanted to build her features in my imagination in order to have her sit at my side at the table, as though in some way she made possible that happiness that had brought us even nearer together.

In those days I imagined her to be bewitchingly beautiful, her skin so absolutely black as mine was white, her hair braided into a thick rope, fat and stiff, falling to one side of her head, when I wrapped mine, thin and ductile like a watch-chain about my neck. I imagined her teeth, large and strong, rubbed daily with the white flesh of soursop to whiten them, hidden behind her thick lips, reluctant to show themselves unless it were a lightning of authentic happiness, and then I thought of mine, small and transparent like fish scales, showing their edges over my lips in an eternal polite smile. I imagined her eyes, soft and bulging like hicaco seeds, placed inside that yellowish egg white that always surrounds Negroes' eyes, and I thought of mine, restless and hard like emerald marbles, enslaved from day to day, coming and going, measuring the level of flour and sugar in the jars in the pantry, counting over and over again the silverware inside the coffer in the dining room to be sure none were missing, calculating the exact amount of food so as not to have leftovers, so I can lie down peacefully tonight thinking I have fulfilled my obligations, that I have protected your fortune, that I have been useful for something other than being the doormat you used this morning to clean your shoes, the body where you scrubbed your penis quickly to have an almost pure orgasm, as clean as a butterfly's, so different from those you have with her when the two of you wallow in the mud of a slum, a fertile orgasm that deposited in my womb the sacred seed that will carry your name, as it should always be between husband and wife, so I can lie down tonight thinking that I am not a grey rag doll stuffed with tapioca, conformed to the shape of your body when you lie beside me in bed, so I can think that I have been your dear little woman, as it should be, economical and clean but above all a model of honesty, the peaceful tabernacle of your pink penis that I always carry inside, a hole sewn and tightened with one hundred thread.

In this way we had reached, Ambrosio, without your knowing it, an almost perfect harmony among the three. I, loving her more and more, began mortifying my flesh, at first with small and insignificant actions, to make her return to the good path. I began leaving the last teaspoon of meringue on my plate, to run a belt over my raw skin, to close my umbrella when I went walking through the streets so that my skin would be scorched by the sun. That skin that I had always protected with long sleeves and high collars because it is credible proof of my pedigree, evidence that in my family we are white on all four sides; my skin of bridal satin, of lime milk spilling out of my low neckline and arms. Exposing myself like that, for her sake, regardless of what people say, of have you seen how toasty so and so is getting with old age, poor dear, they say it leaps backward, that the blood always comes out in the end.

With time, however, I realized that those sacrifices were not enough, that in some way she deserved much more. I imagined her then in the cot with you, adopting the most vile positions, letting herself be teased all over, letting herself be fucked in front and from behind. In some way I enjoyed imagining her like that, made into a broth of honey, letting you do things to her a proper lady would never allow. I began castigating myself harshly, imagining her drowned in that corruption but always forgiving her in each cup of boiling coffee I drank so that my throat would break out into blisters, forgiving her with each fresh cut on my fingertips that I cured slowly with salt. But you threw everything to waste Ambrosio, you destroyed everything with one blow when you left her half of your inheritance, the right of being an owner, the day she desired, of half of this house.

It wasn't until a moment ago, when I heard the knock on the door, that I knew I still hadn't lost the game. I opened the door knowing it was her, knowing from the beginning what would happen, but at the sight of her I felt for a moment bereft of all strength. She was exactly as I had imagined her. I felt an irresistible desire to kiss her thick eyelids, half-closed over those soft pupils without luster, to press tenderly the balls of her eyes with the tips of my fingers. She had loosened her braid in a triumphant mane of smoke that ballooned on her shoulders and I was surprised to see how little she had aged. I almost felt a desire to forgive her, thinking of how I had loved you. But then she began to sway her hips in my face, balancing herself back and forth on her red heels, her hand on her waist and her elbow extended to leave uncovered the smelly hole of her armpit. The interior of that triangle was embedded in my forehead in one blow and I remembered everything that had made me suffer. Beyond the angle of her arm I could see clearly the door of her cadillac still open, a piece of navy blue with gold buttons on the chauffeur's uniform. It was then I asked her to come in.

I knew from the very beginning why she had come. She had already succeeded in replacing me in all the town activities that I had presided over with you, holding on to your arm like a sprouted jasmine clinging to the wall. Now she wants to keep this house, she will grab on to your memory like a vine of leeches until she has taken it all, until she has finished sucking the powder of your blood with which I have coloured my cheeks every morning after your death. Because until now, on her account, I haven't yet understood all this suffering, all the things that have tormented me, but obscurely, as though seen through a darkened mirror, but now I will see clearly for the first time, now I will confront at last that face of perfect beauty with the face of my sorrow in order to understand. Now I approach her because I want to see her face to face, see her the way she really is, her hair no longer a cloud of smoke, rebelling around her head, but thin and ductile, wrapped like an antique chain about her neck, her skin no longer black, but white, spilled over her shoulders like burning lime milk, without the least suspicion of a coloured leap, swaying myself now back and forth on my red heels, through which come down, slow and silent like a tide, that blood that was rising from the base of my fingernails from so long ago, my blood soaked with Cherries Jubilee.

E. A. MARKHAM (b. 1939)

Mammie's Form at the Post Office

She remembered it just in time and panicked; but there must be a way of getting the money there today. Her children were heartless, telling her it wasn't necessary: they had no respect for the dead.

At the Post Office, she went to the wrong end of the counter, and felt a fool when they directed her to the right queue, as if she couldn't read; so she tried to explain. There were a lot of openings but most of them said CLOSED, so she had to join a queue. It embarrassed her that all these Post Offices now had bullet-proof glass shutting out the customer: really, it was offensive to treat people like this—she was almost beginning to feel like a criminal. She thought of Teacher Tudy's Post Office at home where people from the village would come and stand in the yard with their back to the Stables (which Tudy had converted to a garage) while their names were read out from the dining-room door. Of course, Mammie never had to stand in the yard; she would either send over Sarah or Franco; or if she didn't think of it, Tudy would put the letters aside, and probably bring them over herself the next night. Queuing behind the bullet-proof glass, Mammie couldn't help feeling that she'd been reduced to standing with her back to Teacher Tudy's Stables, waiting for her name to be called out.

When it was at last her turn, she told the boy behind the counter that she wanted to send some money to the West Indies, she wanted to send $100 home. But the boy pretended he didn't understand what she was saying, and then asked if she wanted to send money ABROAD. She had to correct him and tell him she was sending her money HOME: that's where she was from. She was indignant that first they treated you like a foreigner, and then they denied you your home. He was just a child, and she wondered why they didn't have anyone bigger who could deal with the customers and understand what they wanted. She wanted to send $100 home.

'D'you want to send dollars?'

'Yes. Yes. A Hundred.'

'$100. To the West Indies.'

'To Murial.'

'Yes. Not sure if you can do that, actually. Look, I'll just . . .'

'And I'm in a hurry.'

He was just moving off, apparently to look for something, and stopped. 'Look, I've just got to check on this, all right?'

'Yes. Go ahead. As long as it gets there in a hurry.'

'You'll have to send it by Telegraph in that case. Can you . . . Just hang on . . .' He reached under the counter and took out a Form. 'I'll just go and check on the rates. If you'll just fill out this meanwhile.' He slipped the Form under the bullet-proof glass, and told her to fill out both sides.

Mammie took the Form and started searching for her glasses. And after all that, the Form didn't make sense. It was all to do with people sending money to Bangladesh and Pakistan, and not one word about the West Indies; so the young fellow must have given her the wrong Form.

When he came back—with a big book—Mammie returned the Form and asked for one for the West Indies; and he said it didn't matter: West Indies was the same as Bangladesh. It was the first time in her life she'd ever heard anyone say that the West Indies, where she was born and grew up and where all her family came from and where her mother and the rest of her relations died and were buried, was the same as Bangladesh which was somewhere in India, where the people were Indian, and she'd never set foot in her life. But she kept all this to herself, and filled out the Form nevertheless.

She put down Murial's name. Murial didn't live in a 'Road or Street'; she lived in the village (she had a lovely house in the village), so Mammie had to leave out that line and go right on to 'Village or Town' and 'Country of Destination' having again left out 'District, State, or Province'. While she was doing this, someone pushed her to one side as if she was a beggar, and took her place; but she wasn't going to argue with any of them.

On the other side of the Form, she had to make a decision. Murial wasn't a DEPENDANT, so that took care of that. She was tempted to sign her name under PURPOSE OF PAYMENT, but the money had nothing to do with:

a) for goods imported into the UK up to £50 in value . . . subject for the possession of an import licence if necessary;

b) of subscriptions and entrance fees to clubs/societies other than for travel services up to £50 per year per club/society;

c) of maintenance payments under Orders of Court;

d) in settlement of commercial and professional debts up to £50 (See paragraph below).

She was sending the money to repair her uncle's headstone and to weed the family plot. As Murial was kind enough to look after her affairs at home, Mammie thought it might upset her if she sent the money as PAYMENT, for Murial wasn't someone she employed, Murial was a friend. So in the end, she entered it under CASH GIFT.

The boy took the Form and said she'd have to send it in Pounds, and they could change it at the other end. That was all right. Then he started filling out another Form, checking with his book, and showing it to the man working next to him, so that the whole world would soon know her business. Then he looked up and smiled at her, and asked if it was urgent.

The boy was a fool, she had already told him it was urgent.

'Then, that'll be . . . £45.50 plus THREE and SEVEN TWENTY. That would be . . . £55.20. O.K.?'

He was crazy. She had £30 which was plenty. He was joking.

'You joking?'

'Sorry . . . ?'

'Last time it cost only £24. Or Twenty Three.'

Then he said something that she didn't really follow. So she asked him to repeat it, because then he'd surely find out his mistake.

He was treating her like a child now. 'That'll be £45.50 for the $100. And there's THREE POUNDS charge for sending it urgently. You want it urgent, don't you . . .'

'Yes. Yes.'

'. . . and then there's the message, and that's going to cost you another . . .'

'Cut it out. Cut out the message.' The message wasn't important. The message itself was all right, the message was free. But . . . Mammie wanted the message out.

He read as he crossed it out 'THIS IS TO WEED THE HEADSTONES.'

'Not weed. To weed the *graves*.'

'Yes, well it don't matter now, I've crossed . . .'

'It *does* matter. I'm not illiterate. You can't weed the headstones, you repair them.'

'It doesn't cost any more, it's the address that's expensive. Look, do you have to send it . . . It'd be cheaper by *Telegraph Letter*.'

'Will it get there today?'

His friend, working next to him made a comment and laughed, but the young lad himself didn't laugh. He came very close to the glass and she didn't like his look.

'It'll get there in a few days. I mean, it's not exactly *urgent*, is it?'

'All right, all right.'

'You'll send it the cheaper way?'

'It's all right, I'll go to another Post Office.'

This time he was very rude.

'It didn't cost so much last time,' Mammie wasn't going to be defeated. But by then he was dealing with another customer, complaining.

She was too busy to go to the other Post Office now; she had to go home to put on the dinner, in case anyone dropped by; she had to look after the living as well as the dead *the quick and the dead*: she smiled to herself. The joke pleased her. It occurred to her then that at the Post Office she had just said 'Dollars' to the young lad; she didn't specify West Indian Dollars which were only about Four Shillings and Twopence, which would be less than 25p in the new money (at least, that's what it was in the old days). Last year, it had only cost her £24 to send the money to Murial. At the other Post Office. This year, she was prepared to allow for another £4 for inflation and for Telegraphing it . . . Unless the boy was talking about some other dollar; but he must know she was West Indian, even though he wasn't qualified to work behind the bullet-proof glass. But what could she do; she was tired: her mother would have to wait another day, choking in grass.

MYRIAM WARNER-VIEYRA (b. 1939)

Passport to Paradise

Translated by Betty Wilson

Eloise was a strong countrywoman, tireless and carefree as a carnival night. At thirty, she had a lovely family: four boys and four girls who were bursting with health. Her pregnancies had never stopped her from doing her work. She did not suffer from any of the usual discomforts other women experienced. Florette, her eldest, now almost nine, was already her mother's right hand. Eloise took her last baby, just three months old, to the field with her every day, in a basket which she carried on her head securely balanced on a *cotta* of rolled-up rags. She put down her baby in the shade, where she could see him, under the watchful eye of one of the bigger ones, who had been given this task, and attacked her work.

Their cane crop had all been harvested the day before, so that day she had begun to weed her vegetable garden. As she always did, she sang one of the old tunes which came from deep in her memory to keep time with her hoe as she dug up the weeds. She loved her man, her healthy children, her clean house; she was blessed with the strength and the courage to work. For her that was what happiness really meant.

Eugenio had just delivered his last cartload of cane to the Derousier factory. He would still have to wait several days before he could exchange the slip he had been given for a few banknotes which would be barely enough to wipe out his debts at the store and allow the family to eke out their meager existence by the grace of God, until the next crop. He was tired. At forty, he had spent thirty years at hard labor in the fields, and *clairin*, that clear liquid which he constantly consumed, was certainly partly responsible for his being old before his time. But *he* did not know that. Besides, his physical weariness did not dampen his zest for life. His wife's good planning and her enthusiasm for work relieved him of all domestic chores. He loved her very much, but he was also a man with a craving. A fervent disciple of the god *Tafia*, he had, as a final will and testament, asked his wife Eloise to put a little flask of this firewater in his coffin, whenever he was ready to depart from this world.

That day Eugenio stopped in front of Miss Adelaide's rum shop at about five o'clock. He shouted 'whoa' to his two mules and jumped down from his cart to have a few drinks with his regular companions before dinnertime. He rarely remembered the taste of this meal, because by then he was usually drunk enough to sleep with his eyes wide open on a pile of stones. 'Trouble don't set like rain.' He had hardly had time to swallow his first drink when an altercation broke out between two men. Eugenio, who was still quite sober, unlike the others, attempted to calm them down but to no avail. The quarrel grew louder and louder and they came to blows. The first was fatal; a bottle split open a skull; Eugenio's. He sank silently to the ground, died with one last hiccup, blood smelling of rum trickling from his mouth . . .

Eugenio's friends gave him a memorable wake, their favorite liquid flowed freely . . .

The next day, very, very early, Eloise dispatched a friend and neighbor to see 'Monsieur le Curé', their village priest, to ask him if he would kindly come and bless the body. She did not have the wherewithall to give him a first-, second-, or even third-class funeral. Still, as a believer it was very important to her for the body to be blessed, and for the priest to recite one of his prayers in Latin, the key that would open the gates of heaven.

The neighbor came back with the priest's reply, as serious as it was unjust: Eugenio, a notorious alcoholic, living in sin, had died without going to confession. No act of contrition, no absolution, no extreme unction, no benediction.

When she heard the news, Eloise felt the blood rush to her head. A multicolored veil, mostly red and black, blinded her vision. For a moment she could not even speak. Her man was going to burn in hell, not because of his sins, but because he was poor and black. The rich *békés* of the land openly kept several concubines; their skins and their eyes had the greenish tint of the absinthe which they drank like coconut water and which aged them as rapidly as the cartman's white rum. Yet, when one of them died, he was given the grandest of funerals. The whole clergy, in their robes, walked in procession before the hearse with crosses and banners. Masses sung in Latin were celebrated for months on end for the repose of their souls . . .

Faced with Eloise's deep depression, Eunice, her neighbor, remembered a stranger who had recently arrived from Asia. Everyone in the marketplace said he possessed the power to make amulets which were passports to paradise. You had only to lay the charm on the chest of the deceased and he was sure to go to heaven. Eloise was ready to try anything to save her man's soul, even if she had to give hers to the devil in exchange. She gave

Eunice her most valuable possession, a ring that Eugenio had given her on the day that they had set up house together, ten years before.

Eunice set off in search of the magician, and one hour later she brought back the precious viaticum. It was a piece of goatskin on which there were strange markings, Chinese or Arabic characters, to the two women it was one and the same. Eloise kissed the sacred parchment, and entrusted it with her love as well, to go with the beloved on his journey. She placed it on Eugenio's bosom, under the only white shirt he had ever possessed in his whole life. At that moment she experienced the relief of having done her duty and she felt almost happy. Eugenio's soul would fly up to paradise in spite of the curé and on the day of her death, she would be reunited with him on high . . .

A week after the burial, the whole village in the little commune of Grand-Font-de-Sainte-Agnès learnt with great consternation that the vendor of tickets to the Great Beyond had been arrested by the police for fraud. A word which no one knew and which they had trouble pronouncing. It came out as flowd, frowd, frode, flawed. To cut a long story short, a high-up civil servant came from town and questioned the man about his powers. Of course, it had not occurred to anyone that to prove a crime had been committed it was necessary to demonstrate that the merchandise sold, in this case talismans, was useless. *That*, no one could prove, and no departed had come back to complain that the gates of heaven had remained closed to him. Therefore, for want of tangible evidence, there being no criminal act, they were obliged to release the prisoner. All the humble people in the village applauded heartily. The stranger set himself tirelessly to the task of giving every person in the village his celestial safe-conduct, ready for the moment of departure. Those who by day loudly proclaimed their disbelief, by night slunk along the fences secretly to procure their amulet, in order to hedge their bets. Even the *quimboiseur*, after invoking the gods of Africa, thought it prudent discreetly to get himself this additional assurance of a good seat on the sailing ship for the great voyage back to Guinea.

The last I heard, our Merlin of the islands was mixing lamb's blood with China ink to increase the effectiveness of the heavenly passport. The only dissatisfied people in the village were the members of the clergy, because, needless to say, now not a single soul came to ask them to say masses for the dead.

Heaven open to everybody and sin gone out of use. . . . Man's imagination can certainly go to unfathomable depths!

CLYDE HOSEIN (b. 1940)

Morris, *Bhaiya*

Morris was an island in a sea of Indians. He spoke Hindi even better than his canecutter father who had left him the house and land, the copy of the Ramayana wrapped in red silk, and the Matchless motorcycle he had found abandoned in a field at an edge of Enterprise estate at about the time Morris dropped out of fifth standard to become an apprentice mechanic in Frankie's Garage.

After ten years Morris had felt confident enough to leave Frankie's and start his own business in his backyard. Unable to induce auto owners to use his services, he took in radios, bicycles, and clocks for repair, rather as his mother had once taken in clothes for washing from the Seven Days Adventist congregation in nearby Kora.

It took Morris five more years to gain the money for the parts to make the cycle serviceable and the use to which it was first put demonstrated how naturally the son had progressed in the footsteps of the father as a straddler of two worlds.

The news had reached Morris the day the Matchless had at last started that Surujpat, his neighbour and best friend, had been injured in the canefield to which he had gone to work at dawn. Morris had leapt on the cycle and spluttered to the school where Pat's wife, Girlie, vended her wares. She had sat side-saddle, her *orhani* flying in the wind as they bumped along palmiste-lined Enterprise Road to the burnt field.

Arriving there they had found that a cart had taken Pat to Kora, and tearing along the Kora Road they caught up with the weary mule, with whose driver Morris had sent Girlie back home, and, tying his semi-conscious, bleeding friend to the pinion with a borrowed rope, Morris had sped along the horse-dunged lanes to Kora Health Centre, where, had it not been for Morris' Masonic membership, the government doctor might have left Pat to bleed on the steps alongside the burn-victim who had camped there groaning in pain.

The gash stitched and dressed, the arm in a sling, Morris had driven Pat back to Enterprise, getting away just in time to return to Kora for the evening practice with the Back Street Boys steelband in which Morris was the percussion bamboo beater.

Into the steelband and the Masonic Lodge—to which he had been introduced by Schoolmaster Bryce—Morris had entered with a sense of necessity of which he was not yet convinced; for, as Miss Jenny, the only other African living in his quarter of Enterprise, had kept telling him, it was time he asserted himself and did things that were decidedly African. 'Otherwise,' she had warned, 'you'll end up just like Theophilus Cudjoe, your Indianized father, cutting cane with the coolies and dead to we own things, like steelband, Saturday night dance, carnival . . . Who knows, you might meet up with your *doux-doux* at Kora Adventist Church!' She had said this with a sense of cultural identity though she herself lived a life to fit smoothly into the ethnic situation.

But when it came to beating a drum Morris by far preferred the *tassa* strung around his neck and in his hands the two sticks flying upon the taut goatskin while the circular wooden base rested on his thighs as he walked in the Husain procession with the Muslim drummers behind the men who pulled through the streets on wooden dollies the *tajiahs* with their exquisitely beaded archways, minarets, and domes.

At first he was glad that Miss Jenny had got Schoolmaster to inveigle him into the Masonic Lodge but after he had penetrated its mystery he found that he favoured the Ramayana readings in the temple and the holy food passed from hand to hand in the silent simple grace of joy. No secret handshake gave him such deep pleasure as the ceremonial Hindu and Muslim weddings to which he was often invited and he would sit before his banana leaf plate, upon which servers ladled generous helpings of rice, *karhi*, and curried mango, and reach out and take handfuls of paper-thin *parata* roti that came apart at his touch, and, as he chewed and chatted with the circle of eaters, he would watch the wedding cook roll another bread and call his assistant to manipulate the sheer size of it to throw it accurately on the huge baking stone over the pit of the wood fire.

This was Enterprise and this was his kind of life. He was comfortable and he had his friends around him, chief of whom were Surujpat and Girlie.

But then an insistent wind, hot and close, blew across the island. It came rushing down from Port of Spain over the green fields and through the palmiste trees of Enterprise. It brought fiery words.

And months later, even before the election campaigns had formed up, Morris had grown uncomfortable, puzzled by the distance that his friends gradually had put between themselves and him. Even Pat was scarce, hardly coming to his gallery to look across the hibiscus hedge to the centre room, the toolroom, where Morris worked at his repairs while he discussed with Pat the news that came over the Pye radio he, Morris, had bought from Frankie when he had left the garage.

Now at his toolroom window Morris watched Pat, his cutlass and *boley* water gourd in hand, crossing the savannah on his way home from cutting cane. Pat stopped among the goats Girlie had tied to iron stakes she had driven into the grass before she had gone to sell *channa,* mango *amchar,* and pickled *pommes cythères* under the almond tree in the schoolyard.

Along the bank, through the cashew patch and vegetable garden, Pat drove the six bleating animals and when he arrived at the water barrel outside the kitchen, Morris called over the hedge, 'O Pat, what you think of this news? More killing in Kenya, they bombing down the forests. Plenty elephants and rhino but they still can't get Kimathi!'

'I don't business too much with Africa,' Pat replied as he tied the goats to the mango that overhung the thatched kitchen and went in.

Morris tried to recall what he had done to offend Pat. He could not understand why his friend was giving him the cold shoulder. Why, for weeks, had Pat not come over to listen after Morris moved the tuner through the shortwave bands and found among the myriad South American stations an English or American voice that told them what was happening in the world.

The Saturday night chat was something special; the precedent was set even before Morris had acquired the radio. During the war he had read Pat the newspapers and together they strained with the Allies against the Axis. They compared Paton and Zhukov, MacArthur and Montgomery. They knew all about Stalingrad and Timoshenko. They danced in the streets on VE Day.

Later, there had been no more stalwart a supporter than Morris for the Indian National Congress' cause for *Swaraj,* for the Mahatma and Jawarhalal who often languished in jail, and for their followers who fell under the *lathis,* hooves, and boots of the imperial guard.

In the inevitable celebration of Indian independence in 1947, Morris, with half of Enterprise armed with drums and a harmonium, had gone up to Port of Spain. He was one of ten Africans who danced under the tricolour with Asoka's wheel in the centre and shouted with the multitude, the men in dhotis or their best parson's grey, the women in hastily-made or mothball-smelling saris, till the name of freedom echoed in the hills over the Queen's Park Savannah.

Morris closed his eyes and saw the younger man he had been, bending his knees with every accent of the drum over the singing and shouting that were to continue even after they had got off the train and alighted in the cabs that brought them clip-clopping down Enterprise Road.

Miss Jenny woke him from his reverie.

'When you taking down that?' She bit her jet lip and pointed to the red and white *jhandis* Morris flew at the side of his house.

'Why?' His mind was still on Pat.

'You don't see what's happening? You dead or what? Didn't the Party man come and see you?' She flashed her golden smile to tell him her salvo was entirely for his benefit.

'I didn't care for what Johnson had to say,' he said.

'What about your neighbours, eh?' She raised her chin at Pat's half-wood, half-mud house.

'Well, to tell you the truth, like they vex with me or something.'

'Aha! I tell you man, these coolies out for themselves. They want to take over Trinidad.'

Morris laughed. He had heard that statement in many guises before.

'You laughing eh, but look around. See how they stick with one another. They minding cow and goat, but what you and I have? They planting rice, cane, vegetable garden. They have shops and parlour; don't talk about gas station and theatre and anything to do with motor car. Look at Frankie, he Indian . . .' Her eyes followed Girlie walking home, in the tray balanced on her head some unsold *channa* twists and *pommes cythères* in the large bottle. Miss Jenny said, 'Hello, hello Neighbour. Sun hot for so, eh?'

Girlie turned her entire body to control the weight on her head and said redundantly, 'You finish sell before me?'

'Yes Neighb,' Miss Jenny said, 'you know how children love sweetie?'

As Girlie walked away Miss Jenny continued where she had left off. 'Singh have grocery, Patel have jewellery store, they Indian. All them creole people in Kora renting house and room from Indian. Wait and see, a lot of these coolies here will get rich and go to join the others in Kora. And build big house. And buy big car and truck.' She fumed with the fire of conviction. 'That's what the Party opening up we eyes to! Too long we sitting down on we tails and falling behind!'

She went with the iron he had repaired for her promising to pay him, 'Month-end'. Morris sighed and wished he had never heard of the election.

There had been one general election before, in 1946, when the Colonial Office introduced universal suffrage. Morris had not voted.

'Who you voting for Morris, *Bhaiya*?' Pat asked.

Morris, Bhaiya

'I don't think I taking on this one either.' Dressed in his dhoti, his Nehru cap at a jaunty angle, Morris had met Pat on the way to Macuum's house where the prayer meeting was being held.

Macuum made his *puja* offering to the god of truth and after the thanksgiving the pundit waved the sacred *tulsi* leaf, blew the conch shell, and began to read the Gita. Morris listened to the lyrics whose beauty and wisdom lifted him and brought him into visions so that he shared with Arjuna the crisis of soul that gave him his understanding of harmony.

Pundit Tilak read Vedic scriptures and Pat's lips moved with the priest's, 'Let us leave here those who are evil-minded, and cross over to powers that are beneficent . . .'

And then Tilak was saying, 'Just as in those days the Rig Veda tells us, "The evil-doing Dasyu is around us, senseless, keeping false laws, inhuman," the Dasyu, the enemy of us Aryans, would destroy our language, our culture, our heritage. Look around you and see the Dasyu. See how the Vedas, the Gita, the Ramayana stand in danger!'

Morris flinched in horror when he heard the mouth that had praised the ways of harmony and mental advancement instructing the gathering to vote for the Indian Party. He did not wait for the ceremonies at the end of the prayers, but, taking his *prasadi* sweetmeats in the little brown paper bag Mrs Macuum offered, began to walk home, his spirits low.

All at once music filled the air. He saw behind him, rounding the corner from the railway station, a motorcade at the head of which was a Land Rover. The loudspeaker mounted on its roof now vented the voice of the man in the passenger seat, 'Vote Manohar Lakhan! Vote the Indian Party! . . . the Party that stands for democracy! . . . the Party that will not bring in the small islanders to swamp you out of your land! Ladies and gentlemen, let us speak sincerely. Search your mind and cast your vote wisely!'

Young men in cars behind slapped their doors and drummed on the roofs. Crowds of children ran out and lined the road.

The drivers began to honk as they did at weddings. Morris stood on the grass verge.

Suddenly a driver said, 'What this *karpar* doing in dhoti?' Laughter flowed down the line. His passenger said, 'Ai nigger-man, why you not in John-John with the other monkeys beating old iron and jocking!'

'And climbing lamppost!' the driver added.

Rum talking, Morris thought and he hoped that that particular car would roll past and he would be rid of the one troublemaker who, like in everything else, led others like sheep to all sorts of indignities.

But the car stopped. The driver put out his oil-slicked head and, to the now stirred-up mass behind him, said, 'Look at this *lund*, let's . . .' The loudspeaker blasted music that drowned the obscenity.

Morris held his ears for the volume and saw the two men leap out of the car. They held the brooms as lances as they came at him.

'Clean sweep,' the driver said.

One man lunged and Morris felt the broom's sharp coconut ribs. He saw blood-shot eyes, gold-toothed mouths, a flask of rum carried like a Hollywooden six-gun. He raised his arms and tried to ward off the longer straw broom that now swept his chest. His thoughts raced: how should he extricate himself? He was not going to lose his dignity if he could help it.

'Clean sweep,' one man said.

'Ai, leave that man alone!' No one seemed to hear Pat who had burst from the crowd.

From the back seat of a car a gangling youth, cutlass in hand, emerged.

Angry voices reared above Pat's protests and the music. Morris began to run.

He looked back to see them laughing; some holding their sides, their mouths opened to the ground; some waved their brooms.

After the motorcade had gone, Pat went into Morris' yard and found him sitting on a bench surrounded by tools and tins of oil, his hands in the cycle's engine.

'Don't mind them fellars,' Pat said, 'they drunk.'

Morris' nostrils flared; two bulbs at the end of his flat nose. He tossed his head as if to aright his kinky muff: a sure sign that he was angry.

'Drunk with ignorance,' Morris finally said.

'It's what your Doc say, man, brother.' Pat sat on the nearby stairs and contemplated his toes that stuck out of his sabot. 'The man get up in Woodford Square and say all kind of things about the Maha Sabha. It's that what making them people in the motorcade mad.'

'What you talking about? . . . The Doc only quoting Nehru. Nehru say the Maha Sabha in India is a bunch of fanatics who fight up with Gandhi. Over here the Maha Sabha *is* the Indian Party and they don't care one damn about nationalism. Wasn't nationalism what Gandhi and Nehru get jail for?' Morris turned back to the cycle and uncoupled a hold-down bolt.

They sat in silence save for the clack of the palmiste branches above them.

Pat surrendered to the cool wind his close-cropped salt-and-pepper head. He held it at the parietal bone and chin and cracked his neck. He said, 'Yes, but the African Party going to bring communism to Trinidad. I care two hoots, yes, about them Russians taking over . . . You don't see how your Doc want to change up the school? . . . He want to bring in all kind of new book and train teachers to brainwash little children. Then he forcing birth control down people throat. All that is Red tactics; is a good thing the Yankees have they base here, *oui.*'

Morris sucked his teeth and dropped a spark plug into a tin. 'We don't have high science in Trinidad, but the Doc study in the States, man, *the Kremlin* of science. He live in England too, so he should know about population control. As for education, you want children to read only, "Dan is the man in the van," and "Twirly and Twisty were two screws?"'

'So you not voting, eh?'

'You damn right! Indians surprise me . . .' He gave his attention to the blaring horns. Through the hedge they watched the motorcade return, this time at a faster speed, the men in the cars holding their brooms down on the road and shouting, 'Clean sweep! Clean sweep!'

'They right,' Morris said. 'Indian Party going to sweep the polls here; after all, Enterprise is ninety-five per cent Indian.'

'African Party bound to win in John-John,' Pat retorted.

'With all the high teaching of the Gita and the Ramayana behind it, Indian Party should show more class,' Morris said. 'Africans can't remember Africa. Look at me!'

Pat got up, drawing the tails of his shirt into a knot, neighbourhood boys having raided Girlie's clothesline and cut off the buttons to swap in games of marbles, and said 'Communism, that's what this talk of nation going to bring.'

Morris could have quoted to the contrary from the newspaper clippings he kept; from Nkrumah, Cesaire, Nehru, from the Bandung conference reports. But deep down he was no longer convinced of what was said. All he really wanted was to be left alone. He was glad when Pat went.

The election had come and gone. African Party, with the support of Indian Muslims, won thirteen of the twenty-four seats, forming the new government that faltered for lack of experience.

Morris met Schoolmaster at the weekly meeting of the Lodge. The talk was all about the attacks of Opposition, Church, and press on the African Party, and the intransigence of the Indians.

'These coolies want a lash in their arse,' Schoolmaster said.

'The licks we give them at the polls have them "*basourdi*",' Luther Rawlins said.

'We will give you our business,' Hector Buckmyre told Morris.

And though, true to their word, Kora Africans brought their bicycles, radios, and clocks, his earnings for their repair fell short of his usual income. Morris saw that he would have to find a new way of earning his living. But that realization remained purely intellectual; saddened by the charge and countercharge of recalcitrance and the threats that flew around him, he shrank into himself. Often he looked up to the rainy-season skies and imagined the pall to be the bitter words that had floated up from below.

As the months went by political gossip and altercations dwindled in incidence and importance. The calypsonian philosophy, 'All ah we is one,' took hold and spread like wildfire through the cosmopolitan population that also included Syrians, Europeans, Chinese, and a host of interracial combinations.

Girlie took Morris *dhal puri* and curried shrimp. Macuum went over to chat and carried a bowl of *paynoose*. Morris ate the beestings in the yard while they talked to Pat across the hedge and Macuum kept saying, 'This is the *seventh* time that blasted cow put down.' Mobarak invited Morris to help build the *tajiahs* and beat the tassa drums.

But in spite of what seemed a return to sanity, Morris could not purge his mind of the pollution that had soiled him. One day he put on his Nehru cap and dhoti. The folds of the gown flapped at his sides as he rode the Matchless past the sugar factory, far into the bamboo and through the coconut groves before he stopped at the sea.

Across the bay dots of Kora fishermen bobbed on the shimmering turquoise. Nearer, the swamp lay drowned in the blood red of flamingoes. Fork-tailed flycatchers came winging in to roost in the mangrove trees.

The steamy air redolent of crushed grass made just a ripple over the surface of the sea. Above an orange mountain of jagged clouds, in a swirl of salmon, the evening star came out.

The beauty of the earth pained him deeper than he could bear and he knew he had to save himself; the time had come for change.

The drone from the underbrush and the trees brought to his lips a *jog* made famous by wandering Indian minstrels, so that the crickets accompanied him as there poured from him the song of the outward poverty of God, who, an ascetic, naked and penniless, roams the earth.

Seated on the cycle, he felt his spirit coil like a snake and reach up in a whiplash of energy above the now ochre clouds to the worlds above him to which he might escape; some place where true freedom—freedom from the negativity of wrath and loathing—reigned.

He was in that mood of self-discovery when he walked behind the *taji-*

ahs, the tombs of Hassan and Husain. The drumsticks flew in his hands, zinging the goatskin with an outburst of uncontrollable joy.

It had come as a shock to Pat when the truck arrived and the men loaded it with Morris' possessions. Pat had kept walking behind the hoisted furniture and boxes saying, 'You're a real serious man, Morris, *Bhaiya*,' or, 'You really going? Where you going man?'

That had been more than a year before. And only once had Morris returned; the day he had shown the house to the couple who had come from Grenada and who, with their seven children, had since set themselves up in the clouds, avoiding Pat and Girlie and the other neighbours like the plague.

It was Ramlila time again. Pat sat watching the window across the hibiscus. He thought he heard. 'O Pat, what you think of this news?' His mind went into convolutions as he pictured the *deyahs*, the small earthen crucibles, their wicks flaming in oil, standing on the steps and around Morris' house to light the way of God as He came out of banishment from the forest.

Girlie said, 'But you don't know town, man; you will get lost!' But Pat did not hear her. Something had gone out of his life that he could not explain. After work he was going into Port of Spain.

In the field, one by one, he seized the cane stalks. Through the mass of leaves burnt to soot he delivered a diagonal blow at the root; then he lopped off the still partly green head and threw the stalk into the heap behind him.

The cane stumps almost bored into his calloused soles and through his torn, floppy hat and khaki shirt the sun beat harder and harder as it rose straight up. The weight of the cutlass hurt his swinging arm.

He drank the cool water from his *boley* that he had hung from a nearby tamarind tree and walked home, tired not only by work but also by the excitement of the trip ahead.

In an hour he was on the train.

The telephone wires, from which blackbirds whirled, flew behind him. The coconut trunks spun in the groves. The gravel along the track strobed with the speed and the wooden third-class carriages clattered over the points and clanked along bridges that spanned the streams. Occasionally, he considered his new Bata *washecongs*, the white canvas sparkling with Blanco; they were a good buy.

Jerningham Junction, Cunupia, St Joseph. Station after station, halt after halt, and finally the train steamed into Port of Spain.

Pat smoothed his going-out white drill pants, spat on the handkerchief on which he had been sitting and wiped the spot where his shoe had been scuffed.

He followed the sprinkle of passengers and came to a ticketing hall, then to a piked fence beyond which cars and buses whizzed on a wide street. When he reached the sidewalk, all his fears returned. He ran back to the railway guard and confirmed the time the last train would be returning south. He asked the ticket clerk the way to Old St Joseph Road.

The crowd, the jumbled overhead wires and the traffic created an atmosphere of commerce that cowed him. He inched along a street of shops, skirting drunks, and taxi drivers playing draughts beside their half-filled cars, till he came to the Cathedral of the Immaculate Conception. Its size and Gothic design astonished him; he gawked. He asked further directions from a man on a bicycle.

He passed the statue of Columbus and saw the policeman standing in front of the huge ochre-washed building; Besson Street Police Station, the landmark for which he was looking.

A bit further on he saw the house: the fifth from the rum shop, with the galvanized iron fence along its narrow yard.

At the jalousied door, he called, 'Good evening!'

He stood back. The gutter, filled with tins, chicken droppings and orange peel, gave up its stench.

'Evening!' he said at the jalousied window.

When still no one answered he went to the side and peered over the galvanized iron gate.

A head appeared at the window he had just left. The man called into the house, 'Anybody expecting a coolie man?'

'I looking for Mr Morris,' Pat said.

'Oho!' The man scrutinized Pat with a squint. 'Push the gate.'

The fence made private a stony courtyard between the house and the next. On a pile of bottles surrounded by mossy bricks a wash of faded cotton clothes lay in the sun. Behind the wash, steps of stride-wide tiles led up to the latrine and, on a gradient even steeper, an abandoned house leaned down.

To that structure a band of children, shattering the late afternoon, ran from the voice that had shooed them from the doorway of the dark room at the back of the rotting house to which Pat had come.

The form that now filled the doorway put up a hand to the glare and stood at the edge of the gloom.

'Pat?'

'It's me Morris, *Bhaiya*.' Pat went forward in fear and not without pity, for he had known the man in an air-filled house where light gave substance to his face.

'O Pat, man Jeez!' Morris said. 'Come in.' He stepped back and held out a chair with a torn cane seat and cast his eyes around as if he wished to see as Pat did: the tools upon the table, the shirts and underwear hanging from the line across the room, the cast iron pan on the coalpot on its stand.

'I'll be getting out of here soon,' Morris said.

In the shafts of light from door and window they sat facing each other.

'How's Girlie?' Morris asked.

Pat stared at Morris' drawn face and glanced out of the window at the stripped Matchless in the damp yard before he replied, 'She well, yes. When you coming down to Enterprise?'

He hoped Morris would say he was fed up with Port of Spain and would be returning to Enterprise for good.

Morris said, 'Time is the problem. I have work up to my throat. I holding a good job now, with McEnearney. Learning all about Ford cars.' He went to the table and switched on the Pye. He opened the flask and, pouring two rums, handed one to Pat.

'Stay the night,' Morris said, 'you must stay the night. Plenty room,' and he waved his arm at the sagging mattress. 'We have a lot to talk about.'

Pat unburdened himself of his great load. 'Man, I hear they going to let we go. They bringing in harvester and thing to reap the cane.' His eyes narrowed. He sniffed and said, 'But I will manage. I will plant garden. I will buy a cow. I will mind myself and Girlie.'

Another rum loosened their tongues. The past unravelled.

The threatening-to-orange light drew Pat out of the lost world into which he had sunk. With deep regret he said, 'The train leaving half past five.'

'I'll walk with you,' Morris said. They had one for the road.

On the way out they passed the children at the gate and Pat saw other lives, as if by the covering of their nakedness, strangely subdued. The children stood in print dresses and shirts, some outsized, some artfully darned, and stared at Pat. A few boys wore no pants; the girls giggled.

It seemed that he and Morris had exhausted their memories. Dodging the evening traffic, they did not speak.

'Regards to Girlie,' Morris said over the whistle of the *Lady Bede Clifford*.

Pat watched Morris wave until the bend of the track shut him from view.

WILLI CHEN (b. 1941)

Trotters

Bent like her walking stick, Ma Abdool lived a frugal life, balancing her budget like the basket atop her head that floated precariously with straggly bundles of yellowing chive and pale ochroes which like her dry self had long passed the age of slime. Yet she planted, the only way she knew of, for a small income so meagre at times that, after Choy Wing closed his shop, she would blow out her flambeau, knot the coins with her orhini, raise her eyes to the dark heavens as if in supplication, and walk the tired road home.

Zobida, her new daughter-in-law, bright eyed but plump and smooth like 'bigan', lived with her. She cooked and kept house, collected coconut husks and, whenever the wind littered the yard, bent with one arm behind her back, the other rotating in rapid arcs with her cocoyea broom, heaping up the trash that went up later in dry leaf smoke.

Late one afternoon, Ma Abdool returned from selling.

'You na cookam yet, gul. And night done come.'

'Mai, ah done put the water to boil.'

'Wata . . . wata . . . what you make am?'

'Mai, Azard say he goh take some soup tonight.'

'Soop . . . soop. We is creoni? Only creoni does drinkam soup.'

'But Ma, it still have piece a sada roti.'

'Bete, I wantam choka, too. See you have am damadol and chonkay it.'

Azard worked in the sugar estate. When he married Zobida, two of his best friends boycotted the wedding. They listened to the rumour that Zobida was 'dougla', even though the bride's parents denied it. Later, many times sitting on the doorstep, as he rummaged her head on his lap, he would stop for long moments, his fingers probing the strands of hair behind her ear, and watch their natural curl as he thought of black pepper grains. He wondered what brand of lice fed on 'dougla' heads, but musingly smiled for he had loved Zobida and that was what counted.

She was so different from other Muslim girls. He liked the way she carried the pitch oil pan of water on her head, her thick calves bouncing along the railway road like cork balls, her splayed toes stubby like a moro-coy's. But most of all, it was her waist—rounded and moulded—rotating in that flawless rhythm as she walked, dizzying his head until his heart was seized by joyous palpitations.

Azard knew of the mild bickerings at home. That clash between the old world philosophy and the challenging horizons of anticipated resistance. The strong-willed hard-core precepts clashing against the liberal exuberance of new world ethics. Yet he loved them both: the caring mother and the loving wife.

He sweetened their lives with brown sugar, cane syrup, and at times molasses he brought home in his food carrier, and had more than once intoxicated them with puncheon rum spirited away from the sugar estate distillery in his bamboo walking stick. He was a panboiler assistant. He would pass the gateman after work, head aloft, walking briskly, the small parcels of brown sugar concealed, tied around his calves under his baggy pants.

'Gul, I don't know how we goh make out nah; Ma doh eat this and you doh like dat. This kinda thing could drive a man crazy. Just now we goh have two pots in this house, one for you and one for she.'

'You think is dry baggee I go eat every day, Azard. You, yuh self. I want solid food. I doh want anybody to call me like Ma, mangy Madinga,' Zobida replied.

'I know, I could see for myself but you know how them old people accustom to they own diet,' Azard said.

'Since I small, I know baggee bound to be on the table. But I used to like Johnny bake. Ma used to cook roti, but I always used to ask her to make a fat one for me. And was chocolate tea with fry fish and salt beef,' Zobida answered.

'So, is true you have a liking for creole food?' Azard asked.

'Why not, and that is good food, too? Food without grease is like grass for cow.'

Azard's suspicion of Zobida's blood strain continued to grow. Not only because of the physical attributes of her buxom body, but also her flair for cooking exotic, greasy dishes.

Tonight it was soup time. Ma Abdool leant her stick in a corner and gently placed her basket of unsold provisions on the floor. She took an enamel cup of water and gargled, spitting expertly out into the yard. Azard brought her roti on a plate and she sat alone near the doorway.

'Try some soup Ma, the choka ent hot yet,' Zobida said.

Zobida stirred the iron pot. The smells of boiling plantain and yams that came back from the market and long dumplings she had kneaded out of flour and cornmeal were strong. For added taste she had included coconut milk, pigeon peas and, secretly, her own concoction.

Azard took his simmering bowl and sat at the table; Zobida's share was the largest. They ate under the kerosene lamps, cooling the food by blowing on the hot viscous pottage.

Ma Abdool sipped, watching in the dim light the bluish tinge of molten eddoes floating in her colourful enamel bowl. She sat, as always, on the floor, hunched up like a relic, the curve of her bony chest depleted, her bowl of soup on a bench.

The flickering kerosene lamp threw large shadows on the walls. Azard's silhouette assumed a giant torso, Zobida's a shapeless heap. At the family meal only the smattering of lips broke the silence. The soup went down well, Zobida went back to the pot and poured out generously again, taking time to share with her husband.

Ma Abdool enjoyed her portion; the dumplings were lumpy but tasty. She went through them with stubborn gums and munched, relishing the taste.

Then suddenly she held her jaw and called out in pain.

'O Gard, stone, Beta.' Ma Abdool held her face with both hands, rose towards the doorway, but changed her course and came back to the table.

'Mai, what wrong?' Zobida asked.

Azard looked at his mother, putting down his own spoon. A chunk of cassava filled out his cheeks.

Ma Abdool held something in her hands which she brought towards the lamplight and then threw them on the table. They rolled across the table like dice and Zobida pushed a plate to cover them. But Azard, observing her quick movements, gently pushed her plate aside and picked up the bits of bone and brought them nearer to the lampshade, examining them as Zobida held her breath.

'What that, Beta?' Ma Abdool asked innocently.

Azard scrutinized the pieces of bone in the palm of his hand.

He placed them in Zobida's hand and looked at her long and hard.

Ma Abdool looked into her son's eyes then shifted her gaze to Zobida's face. Mother and son awaited an answer.

'Is meat bone,' Zobida said at last.

Azard, wanting to confirm the discovery further, kept staring at her.

'What kind?' he insisted.

'Trotters,' she answered.

'Trotters. What is dat?' Azard asked.

'I hear people by the market does call it so.'

'Trotters, what you mean by trotters? You does buy from that Potogee man? That you put in the food?' Azard asked.

Ma Abdool continued looking at them. Her heart skipped a beat. A smile escaped Azard's face, his eyelashes rose surreptiously.

'What that, Beta?' she enquired tremblingly.

'Nothing. Is beef bone. Let me see if they have more.' He assured her, turning to stir her soup, laughter choking in his throat. Ma Abdool felt relief.

'Chotters is beef bone, Beta?' Ma Abdool still asked the inevitable question.

Azard never answered his mother. He turned away from her, gave out a throttled, piggy grunt and sought refuge from his mother across the table. But Zobida was looking intently at her own soup, her lips churned, making slurping noises, hiding a smile.

Azard thought about the rumour that kept his friends away from his wedding and he became more convinced than ever that the rumour might be true.

'To hell with them,' he thought to himself, again almost blurting out aloud. He loved Zobida and that was that. After all, she was his wife and if she wanted to eat pig foot at times, why not? That was her own business. And who cared whether she was Dougla, part Creoni, or even a full blood-ied Creole. Azard probed into the murky depths of his own bowl. Pushing eddoes, cush-cush, and dumplings aside, he searched until he found a knuckle, lifted it into the chasm of his mouth, gnawed into gristle and bone and, savouring the crumbled morsel, turned and winked at his wife.

As for Ma Abdool, she resumed her position at the doorway and abandoned her plate and roti on her bench. She stooped over her bowl, smattered her lips and called out to Zobida.

'Beti, yuh haveam any more chotters?'

The Conversion of Millicent Vernon

In the distance, the bell from the Lutheran church started to sound. A minute or so later it was joined by the lugubrious, deeper bell of the Anglican church. For a while these two bells limped along together, out of step, and then the high sweet chimes of the Catholic church rang out, intermingling with them and confusing the difference between all three.

Millicent Vernon, a light-skinned girl of eighteen leaned her elbows on the rail of Canje Bridge and stared dejectedly into the brown creek waters. Selma, her friend, stood with her back to the rail jutting out her pointy breasts like an old poster of Jane Russell she had once seen and spitting the stones from purply-black jamoon fruit into the road.

'Oh God, Selma, is how I goin' get money to fix me teeth?'

'Write your cousin in England and beg her the money. You know how we Guyanese like to beg.' Selma gave a malicious smile.

The two girls turned and began to stroll back to New Amsterdam. A carload of boys in an ancient jalopy passed them, whooping and hollering in the early evening light. Selma threw them one of her sultry, haughty looks as she strutted along in her skin-tight, shiny blue pants, slapping at the sandflies as they bit. Millie wore a white blouse and red shorts. Her long legs turned to gold in the evening sunlight. Somewhere, in the bush alongside the creek, a keskidee bird was calling.

On their right, set back off the road in a patch of land that seemed a wilderness, stood the rambling ramshackle madhouse. From one of the upper storeys, as they passed, came the sound of a woman's voice screaming like a cat:

'Bring me something, please. Bring me something, please.'

The girls shrieked and ran.

It was dusk as the two girls walked into the centre of town. People stood in knots outside in the warm night air, lounging against the wall of a rum shop, liming, passing the time of day. Flambeaux, lit by the street-vendors, flickered on trestle tables lighting the meagre range of buns and peanuts and sweets. It was a ghost town in more ways than one. In this place the ghosts walked openly and brazenly in the streets. The blue eyes of a Dutch planter looked enquiringly out of the black face of the local midwife; the wrists of an Indian indentured labourer who had died a hundred years earlier were the same wrists that twisted brown paper round the peanuts Millie bought at the stall. Mr Chan's face had skipped down the centuries, travelling through Demerara and all the way to Panama and back before arriving to peer anxiously from the doorway of his restaurant on this, the main thoroughfare of New Amsterdam. With each decade the genetic kaleidoscope shifted and a greater variety of ghosts appeared, sometimes as many as four or five mischievously occupying one body. Jumbie people. That is the best way of describing the population of New Amsterdam, capital of Berbice county. Jumbie people.

There had been no electricity for four weeks. Apart from Mr Chan's restaurant which had its own generator, the only illumination in the street came from the pots of fire on the vendors' tables, an unstable flickering light that cast weird shadows on the moving faces. Millie was trying to dislodge the crunched peanuts from the cavities in her back teeth when Selma whispered in her ear:

'See Mrs Singh over there?' Millie glanced at the full bosomed Indian woman examining sandals at a stall. Selma continued:

'She can't get children.' Selma's eyes were small, hard and black as ackee seeds. 'They say that after she marry, her pussy stop being sweet and creamy an' it start to spout ammonia and acids. Then it start to talk an' say rude tings an' her husband too frighten to go near her.'

At that moment, Mrs Singh looked up straight into Millie's eyes. Millie felt herself flushing.

'Good evening, Millie.' She called across. 'Say hello to your mother for me.'

'Yes, tank you, Mrs Singh.'

Selma continued relentlessly:

'Anyway, her husband send her to see an Indian obeah man and he tell her she must take an image of Mother Cathari—that's the evil one of seven Indian sisters—and keep it under her pillow and then her pussy will stop talkin' and spittin' poisons and she can get children.'

'Shhhhh. Selma you wicked.' Millie looked troubled. Her mother had tried to stop her seeing too much of Selma but as she lived next door, it was impossible. When Millie asked why, her mother had replied grimly:

'Because that girl don' give satisfaction, that's why.'

Millie and Selma walked in silence to New Street where they lived.

'Bye, Selma.' Selma climbed gingerly the disintegrating wooden steps of the one-storey house on stilts. When she reached the top she turned and waved like a film star on the steps of an airplane, before vanishing into the dark, rotting timber jaws of the house.

Millie hung around on the steps of her own house. How could she tell her mother that she needed one hundred and fifty dollars to save her teeth? She went in. Her mother bent over the sewing machine working by the light of the kerosene lamp. Granny slept in one of the threadbare armchairs, her bad leg thick and swollen like a turtle's leg resting on a stool.

'Millie, quick, come watch this rice for me while I fetch the washing.' Christine, her sister, stood by the stove in a loose blue tee-shirt and brown corduroy pants. She sniffed under her arm:

'Phew! I'm rank,' she said. Her four-year-old daughter, Joanne, chattered at her side. Christine bent over to fasten the child's ribbon:

'If you lose this ribbon you can't get another and it's no more party time. Understand?'

Millie poked at the rice to stop it catching at the bottom of the pan. She turned to tell Christine what the dentist had said about her teeth but Christine had already disappeared down the back steps into the yard. A minute or two later she returned, arms full of washing, prattling in her shrill voice:

'Well, Millie girl, they tell me at work today that another one of that family in Fyrish drop down dead. That makes twelve altogether. You know how it start?'

Millie took the boiling corn off the stove and put the curry back on the burner. She shook her head disinterestedly at the question. Christine was the only one of the family with work—as a clerk in the bauxite factory:

'Well. This boy in Fyrish left his girlfriend with their baby and went away to Miami. When he came back he say that he goin' marry another girl an' he call this new girl his fiancée. The baby-mother sent this new fiancée a custard block and soon she dead. Then the boy dead. At first they think is the girl do it. Then she dead too. All the family keep dying. They call in a big obeah man—the very best from Surinam. They call him Jucka. Whatever it is he do, it can't work. Cousins, aunties, one by one they keep dying. A policeman try to call at the house but when he reach the door he start shakin' and he turn and run. The house is empty. Fowls and goats left to run loose. Nobody enters.' Christine had taken over from Millie's half-hearted efforts at the stove and was banging pots and shifting the steaming pans onto the sideboard as she spoke:

'Now they say is Bakoo do it.'

'What's a Bakoo, Mummy?' enquired Joanne.

'It's a thing they keep in a bottle,' replied Christine, warning Millie with a look that the conversation should stop.

The meal was served. Millie's two elder brothers emerged from the back bedroom which they shared. Mrs Vernon took her place at the head of the table. Behind her head on the blue-painted wooden wall hung an anaemic picture of Christ. Strung below that on a nylon thread was a row of faded Christmas and birthday cards. Mrs Vernon said grace. The family bent their heads:

'For what we are about to receive, may the Lord make us truly thankful. Amen.'

The meal consisted of half a piece of bad corn each. Rice. Curry without meat. Some pieces of black pudding. A salad made from tomatoes and cucumber. Millie toyed with her corn. Just as she was about to mention her teeth, Mrs Vernon started up in her twittering voice:

'That sewing machine can't mend. The timing belt is gone. The Lord knows what will happen. The council has written to say if we don't pay the back taxes on the house they goin' put it up for sale. Fitzpatrick, Colin, you must go to Georgetown in the morning and look for work there if you can't find it here. You can stay with Uncle Freddie.'

'Don' fret. We find the money somewhere.' Colin was always full of empty promises.

'Joanne,' Christine lifted her daughter down from the stool, 'run to the Chinee and beg a piece of ice for Granny's drink.'

Millie left the table. She took a candle and went to inspect her teeth in the cubicle that passed for a bathroom. Inside, there was a corroded tin bath and an ancient cranky shower attachment. No water. The water in the town had been turned off for nearly three weeks apart from the standpipe in the back yard. People put out pots and pans to catch water when it rained. Millie wrinkled her nose at the sour stench. She took the piece of broken mirror from the ledge and examined her teeth. In the uneven light from the candle she could just see the holes in the bottom back teeth. More serious was a brown patch, the beginning of a cavity in one of her top teeth right at the front. She felt sick. She practised smiling without showing her teeth. Underneath her feet, a hole in the floorboards allowed a glimpse of the ground below. Avoiding it, she slipped through the back way into the kitchen, scooped a cup of water from the big pan and returned to the bathroom to scrub her teeth obsessively. There was no toothpaste. Toothpaste and soap were in short supply in New Amsterdam.

The boys had dissolved into the dark night. The family sat in the living area lit by the kerosene lamp. Four wooden pillars supported the sloping eaves of the house. Pictures of Christ adorned the walls. The nylon curtains tied with plastic hair-bows hung still in the airless night. Nobody spoke. Christine was dabbing methylated spirits on Joanne's mosquito bites. Millie hoicked her legs over the arm of the chair. She could wait no longer. Her voice was croaky:

'Mummy, I went to the dentist today and he say I goin' lose my teeth unless I can give him one hundred and fifty dollars to save them.'

Mrs Vernon frowned:

'Oh dear, oh lor'. Millie I don' know what you goin' do. All I can think you must do is go to church and pray and by the grace of God, He will help you. I can' help you.'

Millie wished she'd never asked.

'That's all right, Mummy. I goin' write to Evangeline to see if she can send the money.'

'If you write to Evangeline,' said her mother, 'ask her please if she could send me a timing belt with thirty-five links for a Singer sewing machine, model 319.'

That night, Millie could not sleep. She shared her bed with her mother. Her tossing and turning eventually obliged Mrs Vernon to get up and sprinkle her with holy water to let her sleep. In the morning, the sound of her mother sweeping woke her. Quickly, she dressed, plaited her hair and hung the mosquito net on the nail in the rafter overhead. Then she fetched a pen and paper and sat on the edge of the bed. The floorboards felt warm under her toes. She puckered her forehead and bit the end of the pen, staring unseeingly at the socks and panties hung on a wire across one corner of the room. Then she began:

17 January, 1987

My dear cousin Evangeline,

How are you? I do hope this letter reaches yourself in the pink of health. As for me I'm fine.

Evangeline, as you know I am not working yet and things are very tough in the home at present. Evangeline, I would be very thankful if you could send me some money to get my teeth done. My teeth has started to decay. I would be glad if you could send whatever you could afford. I know you would understand the situation, if I delay until next year I would lose my teeth completely, for when I went for the examination of my teeth the dentist told me, by the next two months if I don't fill them I would lose them. I would hate to lose them.

Do you remember I told you I was waiting on my advanced typewriting results? I was successful but there is no jobs.

Evangeline, I am enclosing a dollar bill wrapped in carbon paper to give you an idea how to post the money.

It cannot be detected that way.

Care yourself, I would always remember you in my prayers.

Your loving cousin, Millie.

P. S. Please send mummy a timing belt (35 links) for a 319 Singer machine.

After she had dropped Joanne off at school, Millie ran back down Main Street and cut up through King Street to the Strand, her thick plaited pony-tail leaping and flying behind her. The morning sun was extraordinarily bright, its corona dancing in circles. As yet there was not much heat. She flew past clumps of banana trees that leaned their tattered leaves over fences like common gossips. She posted the letter, turned round and bumped slap into Mad Max Marks:

'Poop me loops, sister Millie.' The mulatto's green eyes sauntered lasciviously down her slim body and up again to her neck. 'That's a pretty necklace.' Millie's hands leapt up to where her blue necklace was fastened at the back:

'How much will you give me for it?' He scratched his ginger hair:

'Three dollar. Pity it ain' green. Green is obeah colour. People pay more for green.'

She gave him the necklace and put the money down the front of her blouse. It's a start, she thought, for my teeth money.

Millie rounded the corner of New Street. Outside her house two women were arguing. One of them was Selma's mother. A small group had gathered to watch as the two women circled each other in the yard:

'Yuh lie! Yuh mad! If you lay one finger on my chile again I goin' box you upside down.'

'Is your chile put grease on the wall,' screamed Selma's mother, 'an' it spoil my pants. I give him one big lick an' he deserve it.'

'That wall is 'e father's property. 'E can do what 'e like with it. 'E put grease there to stop you sittin' an' limin' 'pon it.'

''E's a dutty little scunt.'

Before they could exchange blows, Selma's eleven-year-old brother shot out of their house calling for his mother:

'Mummy come, quick quick. Sometin' happenin' to Selma.'

Selma's mother spat at the neighbour, tossed her black curls and waddled as fast as she could up the stairs and into the house.

'Wha'appenin', Jonjo?' Millie was curious. The boy's eyes had widened with fright:

'Selma catch some kinda fit. She on the floor wrigglin' like a bushmaster snake an' she can just grunt. An' a whole heapa spit comin' outta she mouth.' He ran back in the house.

Millie could hear muffled thumps from inside. Seconds later he re-emerged taking a flying leap down the stairs and swerving to avoid Millie. Without stopping he shouted:

'Mummy says I must fetch Mr Evans from the Backdam.'

Apprehensively, Millie watched his bare heels kicking up behind him as he ran. Mr Evans was an obeah man. She trailed up the stairs to her house, part of her wanting to stay outside and see what went on, part of her frightened by it. In the cool, dark interior, Mrs Vernon was fixing her hat ready for a church meeting. She had heard Jonjo's shouted remark:

'Millie, don' business with those people. They deal with their troubles their own way. We is Catholics remember.'

'What does that mean, exactly?' Millie asked, truculently.

Mrs Vernon looked nonplussed:

'It means we go forth and do the best we can,' she said vaguely. 'Come to church with me now to say some prayers and maybe God will help you.'

'No tanks, Mummy. My throat is hurtin' me. I stay here.'

Mrs Vernon descended the stairs. Her small head poking out of the big frilled collar of her dress and her springy step made her look like a turkey.

Millie went into the kitchen and cut a piece of cornmeal pone. Then she took up position in her bedroom and watched from the window.

Shortly, Mr Evans appeared marching purposefully towards Selma's house. He was a short, stocky black man of about forty, his dark suit buttoned up at the front despite the heat. His white shirt bit into his thick neck. Under one arm he carried a briefcase, like an accountant. Behind him, Jonjo hopped nervously from side to side as if he were herding a great bull up the street. Millie knelt on the bed to see them enter the house. The door slammed shut behind them.

Millie explored her teeth with her tongue. If Mr Evans was as powerful as people said, perhaps she should ask him for help. She wondered how much he charged. Then she slipped off the bed and opened the ill-fitting bottom drawer of the chest quietly so Granny wouldn't wake. In a cardboard box at the back were several hundred dollars saved by her mother to pay back taxes on the house. Five thousand were owing altogether. Millie took out fifty and stuffed them down the front of her blouse. The room was hot and stuffy. For a while she sat on the bed staring into space. Then she heard a noise. She looked out of the window to see Jonjo being sick over the side of his steps. She ran down and beckoned to him from the shadows of her own bottom-house:

'Pssst. Jonjo. Wha 'appenin' in there?' Jonjo looked subdued as he approached wiping his mouth with the back of his hand:

'Mr Evan took a spirit out of Selma.'

'Did you see him do it?' The boy nodded and came and crouched on the ground in the shade under Millie's house. He started to describe what had happened in a monotonous little voice:

'First he did light a sulphur candle. Then 'e lock the door and block up the key-hole with a rag. Then 'e look for all the cracks in the windows and block them up too. All the time, Selma gruntin' like a hog in a cart.'

Millie tried to imagine Selma like that—Selma, who always managed somehow to emerge from that black pit of a house immaculately turned out, smart as paint. Jonjo continued:

'Then he put healin' oil on she hair and knotted the hair so the bad spirit can' get out that way. 'E pour oil in she ears too. Then 'e question the spirit an' ask it why it troublin' Selma. Thas when I start feel sick but they wouldn't let me open the door and come out in case it got out with me. So I jus' sit under the table an' cover me eyes wid me hands. When I peep out, 'e holdin' a bottle to Selma's ear. 'E said some things and call the spirit into the bottle an' Selma start to jerk. Then 'e put the stopper on the bottle. Thas when they let me out. I hear him tell Mummy 'e goin' put it in cement and throw it in the river.'

'How is Selma?' Millie needed to know for sure if this business worked.

'All right. I tink she sleepin'.'

Jonjo wandered off a little dazed. Millie waited nervously for Mr Evans to come out. It was mid-day. The heat was unbearable. Not many people were out. Eventually, the door of Selma's house opened just long enough to let Mr Evans out before banging shut again. He paused to wipe his brow and the back of his neck with a white handkerchief, then set off down the street. Millie followed him. Across Main Street. Past the church. Up Crab Street and through a network of little streets that led down to the

Backdam. Once or twice Millie tried to call out to him but her voice wouldn't work.

He lived at the end of a row of old slave logies on the Backdam. She did not want to enter the house. People said the walls were covered in chicken blood and the tap dripped human blood. As he reached his front door, Millie managed to call out:

'Mr Evans.' He turned. 'Mr Evans can you help me please?'

'Come in, chile.' He went in through the door. She had no choice but to follow him.

The tiny room was spotlessly clean and neat as a pin. From an armchair in the corner an old black woman, smoking a clay pipe, nodded and smiled. Mr Evans put down his briefcase, lowered himself into the other armchair and leaned back expansively like a bank manager greeting a client:

'What can I do for you?' Millie's lips felt dry and split:

'I ain' havin' no luck an' me teeth need to fix. I gat fifty-three dollars. Can you help me, please?' Her voice sounded like a goat bleating. He regarded the young girl, beads of sweat on her upper lip:

'You tink someone is doin' you harm?'

'I don' know,' said Millie miserably.

He rose suddenly and went over to a small cupboard. Out of the cupboard he took four eggs intricately tied with black thread:

'I tell you what you must do. See these eggs? Put these eggs under where you sleep tonight and bring them back to me in the morning. That way we find out something.' He pocketed the money Millie offered and muttered a polite goodbye.

Excitedly, she picked her way past the sluggish waters of the Backdam, holding the eggs carefully.

That night, after dark, she crept down and placed the four eggs by the timber post directly under her bedroom. She glanced over at Selma's house. It was ominously quiet. She covered the eggs with an upturned colander so that no animal could get at them and placed a tin can on top of the colander so that she would hear the noise if somebody tried to move it. In the morning she was up, dressed and out before her mother had stirred. The eggs were still there.

Mr Evans was yawning and rubbing the sleep from his eyes as he took the eggs from Millie. There was no sign of the old woman. He broke the eggs one at a time into a shiny aluminium pot. In each egg there shone a glistening sharp needle. Mr Evans pointed them out to Millie:

'Someone put these under where you sleep to do you harm. The eggs has sucked them up in the night. Your luck will change up now.'

Millie hovered in the doorway. It didn't seem enough. She wanted him to do something more. Sensing her dissatisfaction, he added: 'One more ting. Next time you pass a Congo pump tree—mek sure seh you touch it. Lay your hands 'pon it. Wish and pray to it. Good mornin'.'

Millie returned home with a feeling of anti-climax in her stomach. Her teeth were no nearer being fixed and she had taken her mother's money and spent it. Over the next few days she had a gnawing fear that her mother would count the money and find some missing. She became irritable and grumpy. She kept examining her teeth in the mirror. One day she met Jonjo in the street and asked him about Selma.

'She OK now. 'Cept she don' speak no more.'

Millie fretted and fretted. Finally, she went down with a full-blown fever. Her throat was painful and swollen. Her mother fluttered over her with prayers and rubbed her neck with camphorated oil at night. Over a fortnight passed.

On the first day that she felt properly well, Millie sat out on the front steps. It was cloudy. She was still weak. Her mother brought her out a warm cherry drink and some pieces of sugar cane stripped and cut in three-inch lengths. She bit into the woody stem and sucked the sweet juice letting it run down the back of her throat. At first she did not see it. A piece of tooth sticking in the sugar cane. Then she gave a cry and put her hand to her mouth. She picked out the piece of jagged tooth, dashed the plate away and ran to the mirror with her hand still over her mouth. What she saw was like looking into the gates of hell itself. There was a gaping black hole where half her front tooth had come away.

She was running. Down Main Street. Past King Street. Out of the town. Somewhere where nobody could see her. The bush. She wanted to hide deep in the bush, pull it round her. Thunder rumbled over the creek. A short burst of rain made her shelter under the wooden porch of a house. Then she was running again. Instead of going over Canje Bridge, she plunged down the banks towards the creek itself. Crying now, she stumbled along the muddy tracks by Canje Creek. Turkey grass and razor grass slashed at her legs. The piece of tooth remained clenched in her fist.

She came to an enclosed patch of land, bound on one side by the creek and on the other three sides by a tangle of tall bushes, bamboo, cane, and wild eddoe plants. Someone had set fire to it to clear the land for planting. Everything was charred and burnt. The blackened stumps of one or two trees stuck up out of the scorched trash on the ground, a burnt mess of coconut leaves and awara tree leaves; a desolate, incinerated place. Millie flopped down on a boulder. After a while the crying stopped, leaving a dull sensation of misery. She stared at her wet brown feet in their flip-flop sandals. The luminous orange nail varnish that someone had told her punks wore in England was flaking off her toes. She bent down and fingered the leaves of a sleep-and-wake plant that had sprung up by the boulder. The leaves curled up slowly as she touched them. The massy protuberance on the tree trunk next to her was an ants' nest, so she moved to another rock. There she stayed, motionless, head bowed. An hour passed. Tree-frogs were croaking after the rain. Raindrops glistened on the wild eddoes. Slowly, the sun travelled across the sky, gleaming balefully now and then from behind great grey clouds. A chicken-hawk flew down onto one of the burnt tree stumps. It surveyed the scene, turning its head sharply this way and that, then flapped off over the bushes.

It began to grow dark. The waters of Canje Creek turned a glittering black. Millie shivered at a gust of wind. She got up slowly like someone stiff with rheumatism. Putting the fragment of tooth in her pocket, she bent and plucked some black sage to use as soap. She crushed it in her hand and trod through the marshy undergrowth at the creek's edge. There, she freshened her hands with the soapy substance from the plant and rinsed her face and hands with creek water. As she turned to clamber back, she looked up and drew in her breath with a gasp.

On the opposite side of the patch of land stood a gigantic Congo pump tree, its black silhouette outlined sharply against a moving backdrop of grey clouds. The tapering trunk lacked all foliage until the very top where the branches splayed out flat as a pancake. Mesmerized by the sight, Millie's eyes remained fixed on the magnificent, stately tree. It was without doubt the king of trees, ancient and powerful. It was as though it had sprung up behind her while her back was turned at the creek. Her heart was thumping. The wind rustled the bamboo and cane hedges as she ran across the burnt scrub to place her hands on the cool trunk. She bent her head back to look up once more at the top of the tree and went giddy at the dizzying height of it. Leaning her cheek against the trunk she prayed and wished for everything to come right. After two or three minutes, she fished the piece of tooth out of her pocket, scratched away some earth from the base of the tree and buried it.

Without a backward glance and feeling more at peace than she had for weeks, Millie left the patch of land and walked home.

Christine, hands on hips, waited for her at the top of the steps:

'Is where you been, Millie?' her shrill voice scolded. 'You din' pick up Joanne from school. Two hours she waitin' there. Mummy had to leave her church meetin' to fetch her an' the teacher sittin' there with a face like a squeezed lime.'

Millie opened her mouth and showed Christine the gap-tooth. Christine was shocked into silence and then remembered:

'Oh, there's a letter for you from England.'

Millie opened the letter and screamed with joy. Folded in carbon paper just as she had instructed were two United States twenty dollar bills, enough to pay the dentist's bill and replace her mother's money. She flung her arms round Christine, who reeked of onions, and they danced together on the greyish floorboards. In the bedroom doorway, Mrs Vernon stood smiling, flourishing a letter of her own:

'Praise the Lord,' she said. 'The timing belt is on its way.'

As Mrs Vernon said grace that evening, Millie cast a sly look up at the pale, impotent picture of Christ on the wall. She knew without a shadow of doubt that it was the Congo pump tree that had worked her good fortune. Mrs Vernon brought out the bottle of Banko that was kept for special occasions and proposed a toast thanking the Good Lord for their fortune. Millicent Vernon raised her glass and pledged her secret allegiance to the Congo pump tree.

OLIVE SENIOR (b. 1941)

Do Angels Wear Brassieres?

Beccka down on her knees ending her goodnight prayers and Cherry telling her softly, 'And Ask God to bless Auntie Mary'. Beccka vex that anybody could interrupt her private conversation with God so, say loud loud, 'No. Not praying for nobody that tek weh mi best glassy eye marble.'

'Beccka!' Cherry almost crying in shame, 'Shhhhh! She wi hear you. Anyway she did tell you not to roll them on the floor when she have her headache.'

'A hear her already'—this is the righteous voice of Auntie Mary in the next room—'But I am sure that God is not listening to the like of she. Blasphemous little wretch.'

She add the last part under her breath and with much lifting of her eyes to heaven she turn back to her nightly reading of the Imitations of Christ.

'Oooh Beccka, Rebecca, see what yu do,' Cherry whispering, crying in her voice.

Beccka just stick out her tongue at the world, wink at God who she know right now in the shape of a big fat anansi in a corner of the roof, kiss her mother and get into bed.

As soon as her mother gone into Auntie Mary room to try make it up and the whole night come down with whispering, Beccka whip the flashlight from off the dressing table and settle down under the blanket to read. Beccka reading the Bible in secret from cover to cover not from any conviction the little wretch but because everybody round her always quoting that book and Beccka want to try and find flaw and question she can best them with.

Next morning Auntie Mary still vex. Auntie Mary out by the tank washing clothes and slapping them hard on the big rock. Fat sly-eye Katie from the next yard visiting and consoling her. Everybody visiting Auntie Mary these days and consoling her for the crosses she have to bear (that is Beccka they talking about). Fat Katie have a lot of time to walk bout consoling because ever since hard time catch her son and him wife a town they come country to cotch with Katie. And from the girl walk through the door so braps! Katie claim she too sickly to do any washing or housework. So while the daughter-in-law beating suds at her yard she over by Auntie Mary washpan say she keeping her company. Right now she consoling about Beccka who (as she telling Auntie Mary) every decent-living upright Christian soul who is everybody round here except that Dorcas Waite about whom one should not dirty one's mouth to talk yes every clean living person heart go out to Auntie Mary for with all due respect to a sweet mannersable child like Cherry her daughter is the devil own pickney. Not that anybody saying a word about Cherry God know she have enough trouble on her head from she meet up that big hard back man though young little gal like that never shoulda have business with no married man. Katie take a breath long enough to ask question:

'But see here Miss Mary you no think Cherry buck up the devil own self when she carrying her? Plenty time that happen you know. Remember that woman over Allside that born the pickney with two head praise Jesus it did born dead. But see here you did know one day she was going down river to wash clothes and is the devil own self she meet. Yes'm. Standing right there in her way. She pop one big bawling before she faint weh and when everybody run come not a soul see him. Is gone he gone. But you no know where he did gone? No right inside that gal. Right inna her belly. And Miss Mary I telling you the living truth, just as the baby borning the midwife no see a shadow fly out of the mother and go right cross the room. She frighten so till she close her two eye tight and is so the devil escape.'

'Well I dont know about that. Beccka certainly dont born with no two head or nothing wrong with her. Is just hard ears she hard ears.'

'Den no so me saying?'

'The trouble is, Cherry is too soft to manage her. As you look hard at Cherry herself she start cry. She was never a strong child and she not a strong woman, her heart just too soft.'

'All the same right is right and there is only one right way to bring up a child and that is by bus' ass pardon my french Miss Mary but hard things call for hard words. That child should be getting blows from the day she born. Then she wouldn't be so force-ripe now. Who cant hear must feel for the rod and reproof bring wisdom but a child left to himself bringeth his mother to shame. Shame, Miss Mary.'

'Is true. And you know I wouldn't mind if she did only get into mischief Miss Katie but what really hurt me is how the child know so much and show off. Little children have no right to have so many things in their brain. Guess what she ask me the other day nuh?—if me know how worms reproduce.'

'Say what, maam?'

'As Jesus is me judge. Me big woman she come and ask that. Reproduce I say. Yes Auntie Mary she say as if I stupid. When the man worm and the lady worm come together and they have baby. You know how it happen?— Is so she ask me.'

'What you saying maam? Jesus of Nazareth!'

'Yes, please. That is what the child ask me. Lightning come strike me dead if is lie I lie. In my own house. My own sister pickney. So help me I was so frighten that pickney could so impertinent that right away a headache strike me like autoclaps. But before I go lie down you see Miss Katie, I give her some licks so hot there she forget bout worm and reproduction.'

'In Jesus name!'

'Yes. Is all those books her father pack her up with. Book is all him ever good for. Rather than buy food put in the pickney mouth or help Cherry find shelter his only contribution is book. Nuh his character stamp on her. No responsibility that man ever have. Look how him just take off for foreign without a word even to his lawful wife and children much less Cherry and hers. God knows where it going to end.'

'Den Miss M. They really come to live with you for all time?'

'I dont know my dear. What are they to do? You know Cherry cant keep a job from one day to the next. From she was a little girl she so nervous she could never settle down long enough to anything. And you know since Papa and Mama pass away is me one she have to turn to. I tell you even if they eat me out of house and home and the child drive me to Bellevue I accept that this is the crosses that I put on this earth to bear ya Miss Katie.'

'Amen. Anyway dont forget what I was saying to you about the devil. The child could have a devil inside her. No pickney suppose to come facety and force-ripe so. You better ask the Archdeacon to check it out next time he come here.'

'Well. All the same Miss Katie she not all bad you know. Sometime at night when she ready to sing and dance and make up play and perform for us we laugh so till! And those times when I watch her I say to myself, this is really a gifted child.'

'Well my dear is your crosses. If is so you see it then is your sister child.'

'Aie. I have one hope in God and that is the child take scholarship exam and God know she so bright she bound to pass. And you know what, Miss Katie, I put her name down for the three boarding school them that furthest from here. Make them teacher deal with her. That is what they get paid for.'

Beccka hiding behind the tank listening to the conversation as usual. She think about stringing a wire across the track to trip fat Katie but she feeling too lazy today. Fat Katie will get her comeuppance on Judgement Day for she wont able to run quick enough to join the heavenly hosts. Beccka there thinking of fat Katie huffing and puffing arriving at the pasture just as the company of the faithful in their white robes are rising as one body on a shaft of light. She see Katie a-clutch at the hem of the gown of one of the faithful and miraculously, slowly, slowly, Katie start to rise. But her weight really too much and with a tearing sound that spoil the solemn moment the hem tear way from the garment and Katie fall back to earth with a big buff, shouting and wailing for them to wait on her. Beccka snickering so hard at the sight she have to scoot way quick before Auntie Mary and Katie hear her. They think the crashing about in the cocoa walk is mongoose.

Beccka in Auntie Mary room—which is forbidden—dress up in Auntie Mary bead, Auntie Mary high heel shoes, Auntie Mary shawl, and Auntie Mary big floppy hat which she only wear to wedding—all forbidden. Beccka mincing and prancing prancing and mincing in front of the three-way adjustable mirror in Auntie Mary vanity she brought all the way from Cuba with her hard earned money. Beccka seeing herself as a beautiful lady on the arms of a handsome gentleman who look just like her father. They about to enter a night club neon sign flashing for Beccka know this is the second wickedest thing a woman can do. At a corner table lit by Chinese lantern soft music playing Beccka do the wickedest thing a woman can do—she take a drink. Not rum. One day Beccka went to wedding with Auntie Mary and sneak a drink of rum and stay sick for two days. Beccka thinking of all the bright-colour drink she see advertise in the magazine Cherry get from a lady she use to work for in town a nice yellow drink in a tall frosted glass . . .

'Beccka, Rebecca O My god!' That is Cherry rushing into the room and wailing. 'You know she wi mad like hell if she see you with her things you know you not to touch her things.'

Cherry grab Auntie Mary things from off Beccka and fling them back into where she hope is the right place, adjust the mirror to what she hope is the right angle, and pray just pray that Auntie Mary wont find out that Beccka was messing with her things. Again. Though Auntie Mary so absolutely neat she always know if a pin out of place. 'O God Beccka,' Cherry moaning.

Beccka stripped of her fancy clothes dont pay no mind to her mother fluttering about her. She take the story in her head to the room next door though here the mirror much too high for Beccka to see the sweep of her gown as she does the third wickedest thing a woman can do which is dance all night.

Auntie Mary is a nervous wreck and Cherry weeping daily in excitement. The Archdeacon is coming. Auntie Mary so excited she cant sit cant stand cant do her embroidery cant eat she forgetting things the house going to the dog she dont even notice that Beccka been using her lipstick. Again. The Archdeacon coming Wednesday to the churches in the area and afterwards—as usual—Archdeacon sure to stop outside Auntie Mary gate even for one second—as usual—to get two dozen of Auntie Mary best roses and a bottle of pimento dram save from Christmas. And maybe just this one time Archdeacon will give in to Auntie Mary pleading and step inside her humble abode for tea. Just this one time.

Auntie Mary is due this honour at least once because she is head of Mothers Union and though a lot of them jealous and back-biting her because Archdeacon never stop outside their gate even once let them say anything to her face.

For Archdeacon's certain stop outside her gate Auntie Mary scrub the house from top to bottom put up back the freshly laundered Christmas Curtains and the lace tablecloth and the newly starch doilies and the antimacassars clean all the windows in the house get the thick hibiscus hedge trim so you can skate across the top wash the dog whitewash every rock in the garden and the trunk of every tree paint the gate polish the silver and bring out the crystal cake-plate and glasses she bring from Cuba twenty-five years ago and is saving for her old age. Just in case Archdeacon can stop for tea Auntie Mary bake a fruitcake a upside-down cake a three-layer cake a chocolate cake for she dont know which he prefer also some coconut cookies for although the Archdeacon is an Englishman dont say he dont like his little Jamaican dainties. Everything will be pretty and nice for the Archdeacon just like the American lady she did work for in Cuba taught her to make them.

The only thing that now bothering Auntie Mary as she give a last look over her clean and well ordered household is Beccka, dirty Beccka right now sitting on the kitchen steps licking out the mixing bowls. The thought of Beccka in the same house with Archdeacon bring on one of Auntie Mary headache. She think of asking Cherry to take Beccka somewhere else for the afternoon when Archdeacon coming but poor Cherry work so hard and is just excited about Archdeacon coming. Auntie Mary dont have the courage to send Beccka to stay with anyone for nobody know what that child is going to come out with next and a lot of people not so broadmind as Auntie Mary. She pray that Beccka will get sick enough to have to stay in bed she—O God forgive her but is for a worthy cause—she even consider drugging the child for the afternoon. But she dont have the heart. And anyway she dont know how. So Auntie Mary take two asprin and a small glass of tonic wine and pray hard that Beccka will vanish like magic on the afternoon that Archdeacon visit.

Now Archdeacon here and Beccka and everybody in their very best clothes. Beccka thank God also on her best behaviour which can be very good so far in fact she really look like a little angel she so clean and behaving.

In fact Archdeacon is quite taken with Beccka and more and more please that this is the afternoon he decide to consent to come inside Auntie Mary parlour for one little cup of tea. Beccka behaving so well and talking so nice to the Archdeacon Auntie Mary feel her heart swell with pride and joy over everything. Beccka behaving so beautiful in fact that Auntie Mary and Cherry dont even think twice about leaving her to talk to Archdeacon in the parlour while they out in the kitchen preparing tea.

By now Beccka and the Archdeacon exchanging Bible knowledge. Beccka asking him question and he trying his best to answer but they never really tell him any of these things in theological college. First he go ask Beccka if she is a good little girl. Beccka say yes she read her Bible every day. Do you now say the Archdeacon, splendid. Beccka smile and look shy.

'Tell me my little girl, is there anything in the Bible you would like to ask me about?'

'Yes sir. Who in the Bible wrote big?'

'Who in the Bible wrote big. My dear child!'

This wasn't the kind of question Archdeacon expecting but him always telling himself how he have rapport with children so he decide to confess his ignorance.

'Tell me, who?'

'Paul!' Beccka shout.

'Paul?'

'Galations six eleven "See with how large letters I write onto you with mine own hands".'

'Ho Ho Ho Ho' Archdeacon laugh.—'Well done. Try me with another one.'

Beccka decide to ease him up this time.

'What animal saw an angel?'

'What animal saw an angel? My word. What animal . . . of course. Balaam's Ass.'

'Yes you got it.'

Beccka jumping up and down she so excited. She decide to ask the Archdeacon trick questions her father did teach her.

'What did Adam and Eve do when they were driven out of the garden?'

'Hm,' the Archdeacon sputtered but could not think of a suitable answer.

'Raise Cain ha ha ha ha ha.'

'They raised Cain Ho Ho Ho Ho Ho.'

The Archdeacon promise himself to remember that one to tell the Deacon. All the same he not feeling strictly comfortable. It really dont seem dignified for an Archdeacon to be having this type of conversation with an eleven-year-old girl. But Beccka already in high gear with the next question and Archdeacon tense himself.

'Who is the shortest man in the Bible?'

Archdeacon groan.

'Peter. Because him sleep on his watch. Ha Ha Ha.'

'Ho Ho Ho Ho Ho.'

'What is the smallest insect in the Bible?'

'The widow's mite,' Archdeacon shout.

'The wicked flee,' Beccka cry.

'Ho Ho Ho Ho Ho Ho.'

Archdeacon laughing so hard now he starting to cough. He cough and cough till the coughing bring him to his senses. He there looking down the passage where Auntie Mary gone and wish she would hurry come back. He sputter a few time into his handkerchief, wipe his eye, sit up straight and assume his most religious expression. Even Beccka impress.

'Now Rebecca. Hm. You are a very clever very entertaining little girl. Very. But what I had in mind were questions that are a bit more serious. Your aunt tells me you are being prepared for confirmation. Surely you must have some questions about doctrine hm, religion, that puzzle you. No serious questions?'

Beccka look at Archdeacon long and hard. 'Yes ,' she say at long last in a small voice. Right away Archdeacon sit up straighter.

'What is it my little one?'

Beccka screwing up her face in concentration.

'Sir, what I want to know is this for I cant find it in the Bible. Please sir, do angels wear brassieres?'

Auntie Mary just that minute coming through the doorway with a full tea tray with Cherry carrying another big tray right behind her. Enough food and drink for ten Archdeacon. Auntie Mary stop braps in the doorway with fright when she hear Beccka question. She stop so sudden that Cherry bounce into her and spill a whole pitcher of cold drink all down Auntie Mary back. As the coldness hit her Auntie Mary jump and half her tray throw way on the floor milk and sugar and sandwiches a rain down on Archdeacon. Archdeacon jump up with his handkerchief and start mop himself and Auntie Mary at the same time he trying to take the tray from her. Auntie Mary at the same time trying to mop up the Archdeacon with a napkin in her mortification not even noticing how Archdeacon relieve that so much confusion come at this time. Poor soft-hearted Cherry only see that her sister whole life ruin now she dont yet know the cause run and sit on the kitchen stool and throw kitchen cloth over her head and sit there bawling and bawling in sympathy.

Beccka win the scholarship to high school. She pass so high she getting to go to the school of Auntie Mary choice which is the one that is furthest away. Beccka vex because she dont want go no boarding school with no heap of girl. Beccka dont want to go to no school at all.

Everyone so please with Beccka. Auntie Mary even more please when she get letter from the headmistress setting out Rules and Regulation. She only sorry that the list not longer for she could think of many things she could add. She get another letter setting out uniform and right away Auntie Mary start sewing. Cherry take the bus to town one day with money coming from God know where for the poor child dont have no father to speak of and she buy shoes and socks and underwear and hair ribbon and towels and toothbrush and a suitcase for Beccka. Beccka normally please like puss with every new thing vain like peacock in ribbons and clothes. Now she hardly look at them. Beccka thinking. She dont want to go to no school. But how to get out of it. When Beccka think done she decide to run away and find her father who like a miracle have job now in a circus. And as Beccka find him so she get job in the circus as a tight-rope walker and in spangles and tights lipstick and powder (her own) Beccka perform every night before a cheering crowd in a blaze of light. Beccka and the circus go right round the world. Every now and then, dress up in furs and hats like Auntie Mary wedding hat Beccka come home to visit Cherry and Auntie Mary. She arrive in a chauffeur-driven limousine pile high with luggage. Beccka shower them with presents. The whole village. For fat Katie Beccka bring a years supply of diet pill and a exercise machine just like the one she see advertise in the magazine the lady did give to Cherry.

Now Beccka ready to run away. In the books, the picture always show children running away with their things tied in a bundle on a stick. The stick easy. Beccka take one of the walking stick that did belong to Auntie Mary's dear departed. Out of spite she take Auntie Mary silk scarf to wrap her things in for Auntie Mary is to blame for her going to school at all. She pack in the bundle Auntie Mary lipstick Auntie Mary face powder and a pair of Auntie Mary stockings for she need these for her first appearance as a tight rope walker. She take a slice of cake, her shiny eye marble and a yellow nicol which is her best taa in case she get a chance to play in the marble championship of the world. She also take the Bible. She want to find some real hard question for the Archdeacon next time he come to Auntie Mary house for tea.

When Auntie Mary and Cherry busy sewing her school clothes Beccka take off with her bundle and cut across the road into the field. Mr O'Connor is her best friend and she know he wont mind if she walk across his pasture. Mr O'Connor is her best friend because he is the only person Beccka can hold a real conversation with. Beccka start to walk toward the mountain that hazy in the distance. She plan to climb the mountain and when she is high enough she will look for a sign that will lead her to her father. Beccka walk and walk through the pasture divided by stone wall and wooden gates which she climb. Sometime a few trees tell her where a pond is. But it is very lonely. All Beccka see is john crow and cow and cattle egret blackbird and parrotlets that scream at her from the trees. But Beccka dont notice them. Her mind busy on how Auntie Mary and Cherry going to be sad now she gone and she composing letter she will write to tell them she safe and she forgive them everything. But the sun getting too high in the sky and Beccka thirsty. She eat the cake but she dont have water. Far in the distance she see a bamboo clump and hope is round a spring with water. But when she get to the bamboo all it offer is shade. In fact the dry bamboo leaves on the ground so soft and inviting that Beccka decide to sit and rest for a while. Is sleep Beccka sleep. When she wake she see a stand above her four horse leg and when she raise up and look, stirrups, boots, and sitting atop the horse her best friend, Mr O'Connor.

'Well Beccka, taking a long walk?'

'Yes sir.'

'Far from home eh?'

'Yes sir.'

'Running away?'

'Yes sir.'

'Hm. What are you taking with you?'

Do Angels Wear Brassieres?

Beccka tell him what she have in the bundle. Mr O'Connor shock.

'What, no money?'

'Oooh!'

Beccka shame like anything for she never remember anything about money.

'Well you need money for running away you know. How else you going to pay for trains and planes and taxis and buy ice cream and pindar cake?'

Beccka didn't think about any of these things before she run away. But now she see that is sense Mr O'Connor talking but she dont know what to do. So the two of them just stand up there for a while. They thinking hard.

'You know Beccka if I was you I wouldnt bother with the running away today. Maybe they dont find out you gone yet. So I would go back home and wait until I save enough money to finance my journey.'

Beccka love how that sound. To finance my journey. She think about that a long time. Mr O'Connor say, 'Tell you what. Why dont you let me give you a ride back and you can pretend this was just a practice and you can start saving your money to run away properly next time.'

Beccka look at Mr O'Connor. He looking off into the distance and she follow where he gazing and when she see the mountain she decide to leave it for another day. All the way back riding with Mr O'Connor Beccka thinking and thinking and her smile getting bigger and bigger. Beccka cant wait to get home to dream up all the tricky question she could put to a whole school full of girl. Not to mention the teachers. Beccka laughing for half the way home. Suddenly she say—

'Mr Connor, you know the Bible?'

'Well Beccka I read my Bible every day so I should think so.'

'Promise you will answer a question.'

'Promise.'

'Mr Connor, do angels wear brassieres?'

'Well Beccka, as far as I know only the lady angels need to.'

Beccka laugh cant done. Wasnt that the answer she was waiting for?

Goodbye Mother

Translated by Jo Labanyi

1

'Mother's dead,' says Onelia, emerging into the sitting room where we're grimly waiting to take turns at her sickbed. *Dead* she repeats flatly and emphatically. The four of us gape at her, unable to take it in, struck dumb all of a sudden. Solemnly, we line up and file into the big bedroom where she is

2

lying stretched out on the bed; her long body covered up to the neck by the majestic quilt we jointly stitched, under her strict instructions and scrutiny, as a triumphal offering for her last birthday . . . Stiff, for the first time in her life not moving, not watching us, not motioning to us, she lies there. Stiff and white. The four of us tiptoe gingerly over to the bed and stand in silent contemplation. Ofelia bends over her face. Odilia and Otilia, falling to their knees, clasp her feet, while Onelia, going over to the window, gives full vent to her despair. I draw closer to inspect her hard-set features, her tightly pressed lips drawn out in a rictus; I make as if to stroke her face but I'm afraid the sharp edge of her nose will cut my hand. 'Mother, Mother,' Otilia, Odilia, Onelia and Ofelia start to chant. And shrieking and sobbing they circle round her, beating their breasts and brows, tearing their hair, crossing themselves, genuflecting, round and round and round

3

till I too, moaning and pummelling my chest, am drawn into the procession. Utterly disconsolate we continue to wail and gyrate round Mother's body throughout the evening and night, till dawn breaks and it's daylight and still our moans go on. Each time I go past the bedhead I scrutinize her face, which seems to get progressively longer and stranger, till by the following nightfall (which finds us still howling and gyrating) I can hardly recognize her. A ghastly sort of pained, frightened (and frightening) expression has taken possession of her features. I glance up at my sisters.

But they, undaunted, unflagging, go on wailing and circling her body, oblivious to the process of change. Mother, Mother, they tirelessly chant, as if possessed, transported into another world. And I follow their gyrations—as another night falls—unable to take my eyes off those ever more discoloured features . . . Mother stripping corn husks, giving out the daily round of orders, filling the night with the smell of coffee, handing round coconut balls, promising we'd all go into town next week: is this the Mother I see before me? Mother tucking us up tight before blowing out the oil-lamp, standing under a tree pissing, riding home in the rain with a bunch of fresh-cut bananas, is this the Mother I see now? Mother summoning us to lunch from the hallway, tall, starched and smelling of herbs, is this what she is now? Mother gathering us together at Christmas time, is this her now? Mother carving the sucking pig, serving the slices of meat, pouring the wine, passing the sweetmeats . . . is this her? Mother (our eyes glued to her) opening up the trapdoor and handing down from the loft an array of walnuts, marzipan, candies, and dates . . . Is this her? Is this her? Is this her stretched out on the bed before us (it's dawn again), slowly swelling, starting to stink?

4

And, as we keep going round and round, it occurs to me that it's about time we buried her. I break the circle and, slumping down by the closed window, beckon to my sisters. Still wailing, they cluster round me: 'We know how you feel,' Ofelia says, 'but you mustn't give in. You mustn't let your emotions get the better of you. She'd never forgive you . . .' 'Come on,' says Odilia taking me by the hand, 'come with us.' Otilia grasps my other hand: 'She needs us at her side now more than ever.' And so I'm back in the circle, like them wailing, beating my breast with both fists and at times holding my nose . . . And so we carry on (and another night falls). Imperturbable, they halt the procession from time to time to plant a kiss on Mother's disfigured face, clasp one of her bloated hands or smooth back her hair, straighten the folds of her dress, polish her shoes and pull the majestic quilt, now plagued by a swarm of flies, up over her body . . .

Taking advantage of this ritual preening, I too stop as my sisters, engrossed, comb her hair for the umpteenth time, tie a shoelace that has come undone as her feet start to swell, struggle to button up her blouse which her now gigantic bosom keeps popping open. I think, I murmur, head bowed,

5

the time has come to bury her.

6

'Bury Mother!' Ofelia exclaims, while Otilia, Odilia and Onelia look on with an identically shocked expression. 'What's come over you? The thought of burying your own mother . . . !' The four of them glare at me so fiercely that for a moment I think they're going to tear me to pieces. 'Now that she's closer to us than ever! Now that we can stay by her side night and day! Now that she's more beautiful than ever!'

'But haven't you noticed the smell, the flies . . . ?'

'How dare you suggest such a thing!' Onelia snaps in my face, flanked by Otilia and Odilia.

'What smell?' says Ofelia. 'How can you bring yourself to say that Mother, our beloved Mother, smells?'

'And who decides what's a good smell and what's a bad smell, anyway?' Ofelia asks. 'Can you say what the difference is?'

I'm lost for words.

'Look at him,' Ofelia goes on. 'The traitor! A traitor to his own mother! To whom we owe everything! To whom we owe our very existence! Unforgivable . . . !'

'Never has she smelt more sweet,' Onelia insists, inhaling deeply.

'What a wonderful, wonderful smell!' Otilia and Odilia chant ecstatically. 'Exquisite!'

They all inhale deeply, glowering at me.

I go over to where Mother is lying; waving aside (for a minute) the clamouring cloud of flies, I too take a deep breath.

7

We are the flies,
delectable and pure
Come and adore us!
Our marvellous bodies are perfectly proportioned
giving us access to any occasion or place.
Funeral or coronation,
wedding cake or bleeding entrails,
there you will find us
cheekily buzzing and flitting, partaking of the spoils.
No festivity do we spare.
No environment do we spurn.
No morsel do we shun.
Watch how we gracefully glide over field and garden
doomed to a fleeting existence.
And yet nothing can stop us

from settling where we like:
on a queen's arse,
on the dictator's nose,
on the fallen hero's wounds, on the suicide's spattered brains.
Oh come and adore us!
See how prettily we dance, dart and fornicate on the tombs of the gods of old,
on the rostrum of the latest leader,
swamping the ringing speeches,
soaring above the bowed heads bullied into submission, slipping in between the bound hands bullied into applauding their own prison sentence.
Look at the fancy coils and carefree whirls we trace over the sea of skeletons whitening the desert, over the lolling, purple tongue of the latest victim of the gallows—you!
Look at us buzzing in the ears of the man patiently waiting his turn in the queue—you?
In the same breath we drink the warm blood of the latest martyr and feast on the tender heart of the adolescent shot by the firing squad.
Earthquakes,
explosions,
ice ages and thaws,
ends of eras,
the rise and fall of tyrants.
And we buzz on glorious and undeterred.
Can you name one execution, one massacre, one funeral, one disaster, one holocaust, one single memorable event in which we have not played a part?
Watch me go from the dung-hill to the rose.
Look at us on the imperial brow and on the foetus abandoned in the wood.
In the hallowed halls of the gods I drink my fill and hold my sway
with the same ease as in the seedy prostitute's haunt.
Oh, name one flower that can vie with us in greatness (in beauty).
Watch as, after savouring with equal relish the national hero, the intellectual and the delinquent, we soar heavenward—pure, calm, and regal—to eclipse the sun with our glory.
I challenge you:
Name one flower, just one, that can vie with us in splendour, in greatness—in beauty.

8

Now the swarm of flies is hovering over Mother's mouth which—as she enters her second week as a corpse—is gaping grotesquely while a greyish liquid oozes from her dilated eyes and nostrils. Her tongue, which has also swollen monstrously, lolls out of her mouth (for some inexplicable reason the flies suddenly take off). Her neck and brow are also horribly swollen, making her hair stand out at right angles to her ever more taut skin.

Odilia comes close and gazes at her.

'Doesn't she look lovely!'

'Doesn't she,' I reply.

We all draw round to admire her.

9

She's exploded. Her face had gone on growing till it turned into an amazing balloon, and now it's burst. Her stomach, which had risen so high that the bedspread kept slipping off, has also burst open. The accumulation of pus sprays us with its intoxicating perfume. The excrement accumulated in her bowels also spatters us. The five of us inhale ecstatically. Hand in hand we start to circle round her once more, gazing at the strings of mucus and pus hanging from her gaping nostrils and from her jaw which has now fallen apart. And her yawning stomach, which has turned into a simmering morass, starts to emit the most exquisite vapours. Fascinated, we all gather round to watch the spectacle that is Mother. Her intestines bubble and splutter in a series of explosions; the excrement dribbles down her legs—which have also started to bubble and splutter—mingling with the vapours given off by the murky orange-and-green liquid oozing from every pore. Her feet, which have also turned into shiny balloons, burst open inundating our lips as we avidly devour them with kisses. Mother, Mother, we chant as we circle round and round, intoxicated by the exhalations from her heaving body. In the midst of this apotheosis Ofelia suddenly pauses, gazes radiantly at Mother for a few seconds, goes out of the room and

10

here she is back again, brandishing the huge kitchen knife only Mother could (and did) use. 'Now I know what to do!' she cries, interrupting our ceremony. 'Now I know what to do. At last I've deciphered her message . . . Mother,' she goes on turning her back on us and drawing closer, 'here I am, here we are, steadfast and true, ready to obey your every command. Happy to have devoted ourselves and to continue to devote ourselves to you alone, now and for ever . . .' Odilia, Otilia and Onelia also draw near and fall on their knees by the bed, moaning gently. I stay standing by the window. Ofelia ends her speech and goes up to Mother's side. Clutching the huge kitchen knife with both hands she plunges it up to the hilt into her own stomach and, in a frantic flurry of twitching limbs, falls on the sprawling, teeming morass that is now Mother. Otilia's, Odilia's and Onelia's moans rise to a rhythmic crescendo that is intolerable

11

(for me, the only one listening).

12

The wondrous perfume of Mother's and Ofelia's rotting bodies transports us. Both of them are crawling with glistening maggots, and we are riveted to the spot by the spectacle of the transformation process. I look on as Ofelia's corpse, by now in an advanced stage of decomposition, merges with that of Mother to form a single festering, murky mass whose fragrance permeates the whole atmosphere. I also observe the covetous look in Odilia's and Otilia's eyes as they gaze at the heaving mound . . . The odd beetle scuttles in and out of the cavities in either corpse. Right now a rat, tugging at the wondrous heap with all its might, has made off with a piece of flesh (Mother's? Ofelia's?) . . . As if acting on the same impulse, obeying the same command, Otilia and Odilia fling themselves on the remains and—both at the same time—grab the kitchen knife. A brief but violent battle ensues over Mother and Ofelia, sending the magnificent rats scurrying for cover and making the beetles retreat into the mound's innermost recesses. With a deft forward lunge Odilia seizes control of the knife and, clasping it with both hands, makes ready to plunge it into her bosom. But Otilia, breaking free, snatches the weapon away from her. 'How dare you!' she screams at Odilia, stepping on to the heaving mound. 'So you thought you could join her before me, did you? I'll show her I'm the most devoted of the lot.' Before Odilia can stop her, she plunges the knife into her breast and falls on to the heap . . . Whereupon Odilia, in a frenzy, pulls the weapon out of Otilia's chest. 'You selfish bitch! You always were a selfish bitch!' she shrieks at her dying sister. And plunges the knife into her heart, dying (or pretending to die) before Otilia, whose body is still twitching. Both of them eventually expire on top of the mound, locked in a final, furious embrace.

13

We are the rats and the beetles.

Mark our words:

the rats and the beetles.

So come and adore us.

Come and bow down before us,

the only true gods.
Sing hymns of praise to my beetle's body,
a body that in need can feed off its own body,
Dark or light, wet, dry or rough: all paths are ours.
I crawl along the ground but if required I can also fly.
If part of my body gets broken off, it can easily be replaced.
I am self-generating and self-sufficient.
Living off putrefaction, we know the world will be ours for ever.
Liking to build our homes in dark, filthy crannies, we cannot be elimi-
nated from a world made to our measure.
As for us rats,
no praise is high enough for us,
no hymn worthy to be sung in our honour.
Our eyes can see in the dark:
the future is ours.
We can live anywhere,
we have seen all the hells on earth.
There is no sacred text that does not mention us nor apocalypse where we
do not appear.
We frequent churches and brothels, the cemetery and the theatre, the
teeming city and the primitive hut.
We can swim in rushing waters,
we can disappear into the air.
The world is ours from pole to pole.
We bring life to the castle,
wonder to the graveyard,
we rule the rafters,
we tunnel underground and bring comfort to the prisoner.
We accompany the condemned man both before and after his execution
(living with him, eating with him and then eating him).
We are never still. In sumptuous coffers, in cardboard boxes, on board ship
or in the coffin, we march ever onwards.
We are an image of the universal and the eternal.
So we ask not for a crown, which after all is transient,
nor for a nation or a continent, both of which can disappear.
We lay claim to the universe regardless of progress or decay, which is to say
that we lay claim to eternity.
I challenge you to name a dove or rose, a fish, eagle or tiger that can boast
such talents or make such claims. I challenge you to name any other creature deserving of such epithets.

I challenge you.

As for us beetles, sublime winged creatures that can live underground, in a latrine or in a turret,

we also challenge you to name one flower, one beast, one tree, one god who can equal our greatness and endurance—our capacity for life.

Give us snow or fire,

give us flood or boundless desert.

Put us in solitary confinement or in a crowd.

Subject us to health campaigns or air raids.

Set us on a mountain, on the hard tarmac, in a sealed pipe, in a ruin, in a palace or in a pantheon,

in a bottomless pit:

Oh name me one rose,

but one rose

that can eclipse my glory.

Name me one rose,

but one rose.

14

The fragrance of the rotting bodies of Mother, Ofelia, Odilia, and Otilia wafts far and wide, turning the whole area into a delectable wasteland as the horrid birds, the hideous butterflies, the fetid flowers, the pestilent herbs and shrubs, along with the loathsome trees, have vanished or shrivelled up, dying or beating a hasty retreat, shamed (rightly) into submission. Goodbye to all such foul, feeble frivolities. To a vile, idle, unjustifiable landscape. And now the whole area is a magnificent expanse alive with an incredible clamour: the incessant scuttling of rats and beetles, the gnawing of maggots, the tireless hum of iridescent swarms of flies. Swaying to this unrivalled music, intoxicated by this marvellous perfume, Onelia and I go on circling round the enormous mound, and if (just occasionally) we look up it is to contemplate the unstoppable flood of magnificent creatures coming to pay their spontaneous homage: rats, mice, and other rodents, splendid outsize beetles, lithe relucent worms. We've thrown open the doors to give them easy access. And still they keep coming. Hordes of them. Whole battalions of them. They mill round our feet in an exuberant, surging tumult, proceeding on to the giant heap over which they swarm to create a mountain in perpetual motion. A dense, billowing, rising, spreading cloud. Constantly changing shape in a singular swaying, shifting, restless, muted frenzy. The grand apotheosis. In homage to Mother. On account of and on behalf of Mother. The grand apotheosis. With Mother at the centre of it all,

15

reigning supreme, acknowledging the tribute. Waiting for us.

16

And to join You we go, Onelia and I; still possessing enough energy (no doubt thanks to Your inspiration) to struggle towards the mound and, jubilantly, offer ourselves up. Onelia laboriously clears a pathway through the swarm of sublime creatures. Pushing aside the busily gnawing rats and mice, scattering in all directions flies and beetles which immediately re-settle on the spot, plunging her hands into the swirling mass of maggots, she manages to recover the kitchen knife. She eyes me warily in case I try to grab it from her. She lets out a little squeal of triumph and, without further ado, falls on to the teeming mountain. The stately beetles, the splendid rats, the sublime scented maggots rearing and writhing majestically instantly swallow her up.

17

We are the maggots
Come and worship us.
Come and bow down humbly before us, supreme rulers of the universe, with due reverence, pomp and circumstance heed our brief but indisputable oration:
Centuries and centuries of toil: all for our benefit.
Millennia and more millennia: and all for our benefit.
Infamous and treacherous deeds,
pride and ambition, castles, towers, royal insignia,
skyscrapers, pageants and
air raids
        bomb blasts,
one swindle after another: all for our benefit.
experiments, congresses,
infiltrators,
slaves and new forms of slavery, elections and other abominations,
coronations and self-investitures,
revolutions and revolutions betrayed:
crucifixions, scourges, purges, and expulsions: all for our benefit
For just one minute halt your crowing, your bowing and scraping, your toasts and your condemnations, and pay us the homage we deserve.
Admire
our magnificent figures. We are philosophy, logic, physics and metaphysics. Moreover we possess an admirable ancient skill: the art of slithering.

How can we be mutilated when we have no limbs?

Who would think of banishing us when we are the lords of the subsoil?

Who would want to gouge out our eyes when we have no need of them?

If we are cut in half we reproduce ourselves.

Who can give us a sense of guilt when we know that in the dustbin of history all bodies taste the same and all hearts stink?

What god can damn us (much less destroy us) when damnation is our reason for existence, when

destruction is what gives us life? How can we be devoured if, after they have devoured us,

we shall end up devouring the devourers?

Fly, beetle, rat: no matter how great your triumphs, they end at the point where I begin to tunnel my way to power.

How can you destroy me if destruction is the source of my supremacy?

Where can you run to that my legless, wingless body will not find you,

where my armless body will not embrace you,

where my mouthless body will not eat you?

Surrender then, surrender.

       I heard you compare yourselves

to roses and to gods.

Do I have to compare myself to such shortlived creatures in order to sing my praises?

Frankly I loathe hackneyed comparisons, easy victories, foregone conclusions.

So away with you till the moment of sacrifice,

carry on with the circus, keep dancing and prancing,

make merry, hang someone, go for each other's throat.

Invent new swindles and take advantage of old ones,

mortify your neighbour and, if you get the chance,

             get fat

                 get fat

                     get fat.

The supreme irony: although of all the creatures in the world you and I are the only ones that can be quite certain we'll meet again, I can't in all honestly say *see you later.*

18

The moment has come. The big moment when I must join Mother. Must? Did I say *must?* Want to, *want,* that's the word. And now at last I can by plunging into the seething mass of vermin . . . *vermin?* How can such a word have escaped my lips? Can my mother, my beloved mother, that heaving mound, be called *vermin*? Is vermin the word for those sublime creatures awaiting me, to whom I must sacrifice myself? But what am I doing saying *must* again? How can I be so unworthy, how can I forget that it's not a matter of duty but an honour, a spontaneous gesture, a privilege . . . Clutching the huge knife in my hands I circle the funeral mound which heaves and contracts and palpitates under the sea of vermin . . . That's the second time I've caught myself saying *vermin*! How can I stand here without ripping my tongue out? The overpowering joy of knowing that soon I shall form part of that fragrant heap is evidently making me talk gibberish. Quick, I mustn't (mustn't?) waste another minute. Every passing minute is a mark of my cowardice. My sisters have all joined Mother already, in a marvellous symbiosis. And here am I still circling the funeral mound clutching the kitchen knife in both hands, too much of a coward to plunge it into my chest in one bold thrust. What are you waiting for? I halt next to the sacrificial victims. But what am I doing calling them *sacrificial victims*? So then, I halt beside the mound composed of my beautiful, sweet, selfless, slaughtered sisters. But what villainy is this? How can I use a word like *slaughtered*? I halt beside the mound composed of my four joyfully offered-up sisters. I grasp the knife as firmly as I can and raise it to my chest. I press it against me. But it won't go in. All these weeks of circling the mound without anything to eat must have sapped my strength. But I've got to go through with it. I've got to try again. I've got to make an end of it . . . I go into the sitting room which is likewise permeated by the fragrance of Mother and of my sisters. I open the door into the hall, which had blown shut. I place the knife between the frame and the door, pulling the latter to so that the blade is left firmly wedged in place, sticking out at a right angle ready for me to hurl myself on to it and impale myself without any need for muscle power. Just like a character I once saw in a movie I sneaked off to see in town without Mother knowing . . . I remember exactly what happened: the character placed the knife between the frame and the door. He pulled it to. And then he committed suicide by hurling himself on to it. Without, of course, leaving his fingermarks on the weapon . . . What was the film called? And what was the name of the star . . . ? The beautiful woman accused of the crime . . . was she his wife . . . ? But what am I doing thinking of such trivia when Mother is next door in the bedroom waiting for me. Calling me to join her and all my sisters. I must go . . . Ingrid Bergman! Ingrid Bergman! Now I remember . . . That was the star's name. But what is all this, what on earth are you saying? Ingrid Bergman! Ingrid Bergman! But how dare you utter such words . . . ? I open the door and the knife falls to the ground. Outside, beyond the dusty expanse that once was the farmyard and corral—our land—a clump of trees stands out faintly against the distant skyline. I turn round for a moment. Inside I can hear the assorted vermin gnawing away. I go back to contemplate the scene . . . Ingrid Bergman! Ingrid Bergman! I shout the words still louder, drowning the crunching and munching of the rats and other creatures. Ingrid Bergman, Ingrid Bergman, I keep on shouting as I rush out into the open and run across the corral, across the vast expanse of flattened earth till I reach the edge of the wood . . . The stench of the trees fills me with delight; so too the putrescence of the grass in which I roll. Ingrid Bergman! Ingrid Bergman! I'm intoxicated by the rank scent of the roses. I'm an irremediable degenerate. I can't resist the open countryside's corrupting influence. Ingrid Bergman! I flagellate myself, I beat my breast. But I stagger on through the wood, hurtling into the tree trunks, clutching at the leaves, inhaling the fetid fragrance of the lilies of the valley . . . I get to the sea and, stripping off all my clothes, breathe in the salt air. Naked I plunge into the waves which must surely smell nauseous. I forge my way through the no doubt pestilent foam. Ingrid Bergman! Ingrid Bergman! And I dive headlong into the translucent white—stinking?—surf . . . I'm a traitor. A confirmed traitor. And happy.

Ballad for the New World

The snapshot in the old family album shows an all-American-kinda-looking guy. We were in the shadow of America a long time, a long time. '. . . rum and Coca-Cola . . . working for the Yankee dollar.'* Nineteen forties, nineteen fifties, the decades get mixed up: Jitterbug, Rock-and-Roll at the Empire Cinema, the Globe, Radio City 12.30, Rivoli in Coffee Street San Fernando.

Hollywood.

Was there anything for him then? His mother took him out of school. He worked the boats at night: Import/Export down by the wharf. Did he have a time? I wanted to know, to trace the regret, the anger, the wish to die—young.

The snapshot shows him in white T-shirt, beige slacks. Were they T-shirts then? and slacks? We called them pants. They called them pants too. (The Americans.) He was slim with short hair like young guys now: fresh-faced, frightened, looking brave and startled; looking for a new world. Dark. He lifted weights. The white T-shirt tight at the muscles on his arms. He rode a motor-bike. I, small, rode pillion fast down the pond stretch with the wind and him and my arms around his waist. He had a dog, Mutt, from the *Mutt and Jeff* comic strip; a squirrel all day long in his pocket, on his shoulder, running over his neck, nuzzling in his chest. He had a parrot in a cage on the back verandah. One day, it flew off to the swamp and didn't come back. Next to his bed he had other cages with two rabbits, an agouti and a small mongoose. He rode horses out of the sugar-cane estate yard, cantering the traces with Baboolal, the young East Indian boy. He used to lie on top of his bed, on top of the counterpane with his arms behind his head cocked on the pillows, thoughtful, looking at his menagerie on the sill of the Demerara window with one leg drawn up and the other lying out. Resting, he dreamt of horses in the dawn with Baboolal.

When he started lifting weights he began to broaden. In this other snap-

---

* Lord Invader, 'Rum and Coca-Cola' 1943.

shot he is definitely short next to his taller brother and his even taller friend, but here on the steps of the bungalow with Mutt he is the all-American-kinda-looking guy.

We weren't American or English. We were French creoles. But—that was fading away. That was fading away fast in the yellow and wrinkled faces of the aunts and uncles embayed in the wickerwork chairs on the wide verandahs who talked of the 'good old days', those old-time days in the cocoa hills. And, now they say, 'When cocoa was king', looking at the state of the island, hardly even remembering. Nowadays some of the children from the families marry coloured people and people who aren't Catholic.

Independence was in the air.

Independence had always been in the air, was always in the air. Not the open-door-the-British-Foreign-Secretary-held-open-kinda   independence. No.

Freedom

Riot

   and

Affray

Stamping feet on the asphalt-pitch road.

'What is that noise? Shut the door, girl. Close the windows.'

That noise on the other side of the fence we were trying to shut out.

And, we had had the war too. It had come and gone: Germans, Japs. Black guys went to war for King and Country far away, white fellas too. The West Indian Regiment. Now we've got war memorials like exclamation marks. I remember a pink dirty crushed ration card on the shelf in the pantry which we had to show the commisserie man to get sugar, rice, and coconut oil. In the streets the calypsonians were singing 'Chiney never had a VJ Day', and in dark places where the sun shone hot and strong, in red dirt backyards with governor plum trees, music came from dustbin covers, and oil drums were fashioned and tempered in that same fire behind the fence we were trying to put out.

Now I think of it no one ever told me when I was small, smaller than him in the snapshot, that six million people had been gassed by civilized Europeans. Only, on Good Friday, at the Mass of the Pre-Sanctified, we said special prayers for the conversion of pagans, heretics, and Jews. And, during the Stations of the Cross, I wondered why the Barbadians had nailed Jesus to the cross.

On the radio in the drawing-room: 'Hiroshima . . . Nagasaki . . .'

'We will have to pay for this,' his mother said when she heard the news.

'We'll have to pay for this.' Hiroshima, Nagasaki. Far away headlines in *The Gazette.*

We were in the shadow of America a long time, a long time. Like under a big umbrella.'. . . rum and Coca-Cola . . . working for the Yankee dollar'.

You see, you start telling the story about a guy and then you get to telling the story of a time, a place, a people, and a world. Then I start getting into the story. Well I made that choice early. I remember him well, the all-American-kinda-looking guy on the steps of the sugar-cane estate bungalow with Mutt his dog. Broad shouldered, his stare holds Baboolal: the white French creole with the Indian boy.

It was one night out on the sugar estate . . .

He was still at home, lifting weights under the house in the afternoon. He was the last of the boys to leave home. That's what she (my, and his mother, she who said, 'We will have to pay for this') always said: 'He was the last of the boys to leave home', with that look in her eyes which knew that we all had to go eventually and leave her alone with her husband. It wasn't true that he had been the last of the boys to leave. I was. But for her there were always the boys, my sister, and me. So, he was the last of the boys to leave. Then she had me to speak to, had me there, not like a child but more like a lover, a changeling companion, a mirror, a fairy child, a Peter Pan— but that's another tale. Then I left and she and her husband were alone and she was always wanting us to come back, looking out of the window down the gravel road. He always did, dropping in with the jitney to do a message, carrying something, have a coffee with her at the edge of the dining-room table, pulled by her, she listening, reaching out to touch his arm on the table with raised veins, listening, feeling proud. When he came, there would have to be a leg of lamb and macaroni pie. She wouldn't have siesta if he was going to drop in for tea, or might. She would bake a sponge cake and be tired in the evening and have to have a whisky and soda. He would have a slice of the cake for her sake between cigarettes and black coffee, not tea. She would look at him with half a look of owning and half a look of relinquishing and then call him over to the side of the drawing-room to have a talk about his job. He marvelled, we all did, how she could talk of cars and mechanics when it was cars and mechanics, and later about oil derricks, bits, blow outs, and cementing. Then she would let him go to his father on the verandah. She liked the idea that her boys were close to their father. It was just an idea. The man said little and the boys were left yearning and looking elsewhere, dreaming the dream of their ancestors, El Dorado. His memory was the dawn, horses and Baboolal.

. . . But maybe it was on one of those nights when he had already left home and there was a leg of lamb and macaroni pie. Out of the blue he bet me I would not run down into the yard in the dark, down behind the hibiscus hedge into the savannah and touch the trunk of the big silk cotton tree under which a coolie man was buried and a jumbie lived. If I did he would take me to the pictures there and then, night-time pictures there and then, that night. He bet it not as a threat or something to demean me, that I might not be able to do, but rather as a warm reaching-out challenge to my boyish youth and his own, spoken across the wide polished oval dining-room table like a mirror for us to see ourselves and the servants passing out and coming in through the pantry door when my mother rang the little brass bell. He spoke it with affection and warmth and with an endless desire for adventure. 'Come, boy, let we go.' He wanted me to have an adventure and he wished to be the one to offer it. I leapt out of my chair and went out into the dark, not pretending, through the hibiscus hedge, across the gravel road, down into the gully and the savannah to the base and trunk of the silk cotton tree where the coolie man was buried and my heart jumping for the jumbie that might be. I touched the tree. I did what he had said and ran all the way back up to the bungalow, up the back steps, through the pantry. There, I had done it, and off, at once, because we were late and my mother said that we wouldn't make it on time. We went to the cinema. Theatre.

Time would stop for us in the jitney round the bend by Palmiste where the bull gouged out the overseer's stomach in the savannah, over the pot-holed roads, through the kerosene flambeaux-lit villages, through the dark to the Gaiety Theatre in Mucurapo Street, warm and alive with talk, car horns, roast corn, peanuts, and channa from vendors with tin stands lit by flambeaux burning through perforated holes made with an ice pick in an old biscuit tin. Palms warm with hot groundnuts in small brown-paper bags, throwing the shells on the ground. Night-time theatre.

My memories kept by a memory of him. I longed for him on a horse, held in front, too small to straddle the strong back, to rub those sweating flanks, with him and Baboolal's thin brown legs flying in the wind.

It was a double: *The Wild One* with Marlon Brando, and *Rebel Without a Cause* with James Dean. Looking at the snapshot it is James Dean who was always young that I remember. I remember his chiselled cheekbones, his sad soft eyes dreaming of an early death: and him in the snapshot, his sad soft eyes, sitting with Mutt on the steps of the bungalow.

They were all of a time, mixed up in memory. A decade of heroes and gods. Brando, James Dean, and a little later Elvis. He of the snapshot liked Frank Sinatra, and Frankie Laine singing 'I believe'. Singing, 'I believe in every drop of rain that falls', and 'When you hear a new-born baby cry, I believe'. Mario Lanza's 'Ave Maria'. He tried to crack the glass in the bathroom window like him when he took a shower.

We weren't American, but we lived in the shadow of America a long time, a long time . . . 'Working for the Yankee dollar'.

Hiroshima, Nagasaki. Like a big parasol.

'They will have to pay for this,' she said.

Yes, gods: Brando, Dean. The way they walked. The way they talked. Bigger than life on the big screen: John Wayne, Errol Flynn, Rock Hudson, heroes of the 12.30 matinée. Heroes for him in the snapshot, for the black tess on the pavement, the badjohn on the sidewalk under the rum shop. Like them he had an odyssey weaving the gravelled traces with his motor-bike, skidding the corners at the Wallerfield American Base Camp in the motor-car rally on two wheels, the white promise of the carnival-queen beauty-show cat walk screaming at the curb, shaking their pony tails.

Twice they woke her, madonna mother, prayer of rosaries and novenas for her boys all night, while her husband snored forgetting that he had begotten sons. In the next room in the troubled house her débutante daughter asleep under the picture of guardian angels set in battle array. Twice they woke her, his pardner messenger at the front door with the news. His car was in the ravine. He had been snatched from death, tugged to life with a string of rosary beads, whispered novenas and ejaculations to Saint Christopher.

She had kept on believing; so had he.

'He is a religious boy. He has a natural religious feeling. He always prays. Always thinking of God. The Man Upstairs he calls Him. If I think of any of my boys being religious I think of him. He used to wake early and take me to the First Friday morning mass. He always had his rosary in his pocket. He had a strong sense of right and wrong. Always went to confession and communion, a religious boy, pious. Used his missal.'

That was her creed. Although they always, the boys, followed mass from the back porch of the church and smoked cigarettes during the sermon leaning up against their cars in the churchyard. But, they were the boys. I, blent with her in prayer, kneeling side by her under the statue of Saint Thérèse of Lisieux, The Little Flower. Taking it all in.

You try to put it all down before it passes away. Sing the ballad for the heroes of the new world. Heroes of the dawn, he and Baboolal.

Do you remember that James Dean walk? The way he kicked a stone in *East of Eden*? The way he hung his head and the way he suddenly bounded out of himself up the stairs to find his mysterious mother? The way he would hold back, hang back in there, inside himself with his sad soft eyes dreaming of an early death, and then hit out, want to hit someone, hit himself, pound the ribs of the house with his fists? He was like that, a badjohn. He had to hit someone. He would have to cuff someone down.

There was this mixture in him of sadness and softness, tenderness and hardness all blent in one, this religious boy who was the last of the boys to leave home. I see him now, he begins to change '. . . rum and Coca-Cola . . . working for . . . the Yankee dollar.' Grog.

White shirt, collar, and tie when he used to sell motor-cars in San Fernando for his uncle. He quit that. He had to make more money. He had to prove himself otherwise he would have to hit somebody. Big car time. Cocoa and sugar dead. Motor-cars
oil
the decades pass.

Now Texaco is written where the British Oil Company used to be. The history book says they sucked the orange dry.

Later in his khaki pants, unshaven, bare-backed, brow stained, smelling of cigarettes and black coffee, rum, his hands smelling of oil, we would go for a drive alone to see where he worked. Alone, driving through the bush to the clearing in the forest where the oil well stood, the derrick pumping out oil, piping stacked on the sides. I learnt about drilling a hole, cementing, bits, blow outs, and the whole adventure, the whole far-flung adventure of his—American, British, French, Dutch, Spanish here again for El Dorado the sixteenth-century myth.

There was no stopping him. He said it himself, 'I am a self-made man.' He still liked to ride his motor-bike for the hell of it, back from the beach with a carnival queen riding pillion in the dusk, in the amber of the dusk and rum. Madonna mother prayed all the while for him and the parish priest came to bless the office when he formed his own company and hanged the picture of 'The Sacred Heart' over his desk.

He went from there to become a millionaire. He made himself, he said, and said it again, 'I'm a self-made man,' forgetting (if he ever knew) what whiteness meant. What did it cost him? He had collected houses, cars, companies, registered companies.

The story begins to fade as I begin to lose him as he enters dreams, his hallucinations, *folies de grandeur*, the old madness of the ancestors of the savannahs of Monagas, the pampas of Bolivar. They dreamt of horses and the building of large houses and eternal gardens, dreaming of a grandeur they thought they once had.

He lost his James Dean rebel smile. His broad shoulders caved in. His sad soft eyes stared blindly without anger or dreams.

'If only Baboolal could see me now. If only Baboolal could see me now . . . If only he could see this lake with ice, this land with conifers,' (the dream of Christmas in a tropic mind). 'Baboolal never see ice, except he see it by the USE ICE factory San Fernando roundabout, or shave ice on the promenade.'

It all came rushing back, this ballad for the heroes of the new world as we sat in a little Spanish restaurant in the old world.

'I going away,' he said.

'Go to a hot country,' I said.

'Maybe hot, maybe cold,' he said.

I paid the cheque (unusually) for the last time.

As he stares now through amber at the green dream of green canefields in the sun, he remembers the East Indian boy Baboolal barebacked with him on horses cantering the gravelled traces.

If Baboolal could see him now, I thought.

'. . . rum and Coca-Cola, down Point Cumana . . . working for the Yankee Dollar.'

ANA LYDIA VEGA (b. 1946)

Eye-Openers

And for to make you the more merry,
I myself will gladly ride with you.

Geoffrey Chaucer, *Canterbury Tales*

An explosion of red clouds lighted the sky and the shadows of yagrumo trees lay in long slanting lines across the Guavate Forest when our driver made the disturbing confession that he could barely keep his eyes open. 'Talk, ask riddles, tell jokes,' he entreated, rubbing the merry eyes that looked at each of us in turn in the rearview mirror. The radio, that last resort of drivers lulled in the arms of Morpheus, was broken. It was life or death: we either gave him his dose of Eye-Opener Tonic or the *público* would take a short-cut to eternity.

There was a brief silence that seemed to drag on forever while one of us could screw up our courage to break the ice. Fortunately, the passenger from Maunabo, loose-tongued even under less demanding circumstances, moistened his lips and took the plunge:

'In the town where I live, out near the lighthouse, down by Cape Malapascua, there once lived a man that had thirty-seven children, all of them by different mothers. I don't know what that man had between his legs, but whatever it was, apparently the Virgin Mother herself couldn't have resisted it.'

The narrator paused, to await his audience's reaction. You could have cut the silence with a knife, and the faces looked as though they'd been cast in cement. I turned my head toward the window to hide my sinful grin. When the driver gave a good hearty laugh to celebrate the minor sacrilege, the storyteller plucked up his courage and continued on:

'Yessir. *BIG* family this guy had himself. And a good husband and father he was, too. So nobody would get their feelings hurt, he took turns sleeping one night in each different house.'

The driver snickered again, but this time he had company—a retired schoolteacher type in a dark suit coat.

'But the best part was that this man's wives were all just as happy as

333

could be with this arrangement, and it was them that worked out the calendar for where this man would sleep each night. Why, if one of them had to run some errand or something, one of the other ones would take care of the children for her. You'd've thought they were Mormons!'

The driver's hilarity was irresistible. The other passengers laughed just to hear the driver's asthmatic wheezes. I must confess that I personally didn't think that last part was so funny.

'Things were going just fine for this fellow. He worked hard farming and such, and he'd do part-time jobs in town whenever he got a chance to, and with the help of God and that flock of wives of his and his Uncle Sam's food stamp program, he pretty much kept food on the tables and clothes on the backs of everybody in those thirty-seven houses.'

A charismatic lady wearing a white habit tied at the waist by a rope with red balls on the end couldn't contain her indignation.

'Very nice! He didn't have to change the dirty diapers or peel the plantains for the *tostones* . . .'

'Now don't get yourself all worked up there, ma'am,' the Maunabo man said gently. 'You'll see what happened to this gentleman in a minute. Good things don't last, and when they do . . . well, as the old saying goes, It's a mighty good wind that blows nobody ill. As I was saying: Like any good citizen, this man filled out his income-tax form every year and paid his taxes. And every year the list of dependents this fellow claimed on his tax form got longer and longer. At first, the income-tax people let it slide, but when things in the government started getting bad economically speaking—or started getting worse, rather—one of the inspectors they've got there, a real little hornet of a fellow that had ambitions to rise in the government as a reward for the way he squeezed the good honest hardworking folks out of their hard-earned money, this little inspector-fellow sent this man a letter. "You must present," read the letter, or words to that effect, "a birth certificate or evidence of baptism and social security number for each dependent claimed." What a problem, ladies and gentlemen, because neither he nor his wives had ever bothered to register those children—not in town at the Registry Office and not at the church. And can you imagine what that man would've had to go through at this stage of the game to get that flock of thirty-seven Christian children all registered at once—and with two weeks to go before April 15 at midnight, when that income-tax form has to be postmarked or else? I'll tell you, if it was me, I'd take out a loan even if I had to be in debt up to my ears for the rest of my life before I'd voluntarily get myself into such a mess of red tape as that . . .'

'So what did he do?' the kid with the Walkman asked. When he'd seen everybody laughing he'd taken off his earphones, and now he was hooked on reality.

'A lawyer-friend of his told him to obey the law, that was the best thing he could do, but this fellow had neither the time nor the patience for that route. Several nights he lay in his bed cogitating, and then all of a sudden the light dawned. The next day he went over to this car dealer's place in Maunabo—the dealer it seems owed him a favor—and he reserved himself three vans—those big ones they're using these days to ferry kids to school in, with the doors that slide on the outside? He reserved himself three of those vans and he found himself two out-of-work *público* drivers, and him driving one van and these two other guys driving the others, they went from house to house picking up children of all sizes and colors. There were kids in those vans from little tykes two years old to big husky eighteen-year-olds. The kids, imagine, they had themselves a ball. They rode along singing songs and yelling dirty words out the windows at people along the highway. The other two drivers drove through the mountains like a bat out of hell—they couldn't wait to get rid of those holy terrors they had for passengers. But this fellow I'm telling you about just drove along like he was out for a Sunday drive in the country, smiling to himself and humming.

'When they came in sight of that big new Treasury Building, there at the entrance to Old San Juan, this fellow motioned the vans over to the side of the road, got out, and went from van to van with their instructions: "When we get there, I want you children to get out of the vans with me, and then I want you to get up those stairs you're going to see inside there, and I want you to make all the racket you can . . . I want you to make the biggest fuss these people ever saw, and if anybody says a word to you about hushing or behaving yourselves, you tell them to talk to your daddy—I'll be right there with you. Everybody understand?" Did they understand? Is the pope Catholic? Those poor people in the Treasury Department didn't know what hit 'em. When that flock of kids erupted through the front door of the building, it was a wonder the roof didn't cave in. You'd have thought it was an earthquake. And their daddy behind them, just smiling to himself.'

The driver's belly was rising and falling, brushing the steering wheel with every new gale of hilarity. We passengers couldn't wait to hear what . . .

'Yessir, ladies and gentlemen—this man walks up to that little inspector-fellow's desk as calm as you please, and that gang of young heathens right behind him. Those kids were into everything, opening and closing drawers, poking around in the wastebaskets, picking up telephones, sharpening pencils, everything they could think of, and you could hear the noise all the way to the Plaza Colón.

'So anyway, the man says to that inspector, as meek as can be, "Here are those thirty-seven dependents you were asking me about, mister. If you want to get a piece of paper we can write their names down for you . . ."

'The little inspector-fellow looked at him a minute. He didn't know what to say. And those children still opening and closing drawers and stapling papers together and playing tag around the desks in the office . . . Finally the inspector stands up, straightens his tie a little, and goes off to find his supervisor, to see if he couldn't get him out of this fix. And those kids running after him, jumping around and doing cartwheels and pinching him on the rear. The supervisor comes out about then, and he goes berserk—within ten minutes he'd lost his voice from yelling at those infidels to keep quiet and settle down, and finally he threatened to call security if this fellow didn't get out of there that minute, himself and his thirty-seven wild animals. No sooner said than done, don't you know. Still yelling and jumping around and screaming like a pack of banshees, they were down those stairs and out of the building.

'As a reward for how well his kids had behaved themselves, this fellow took 'em all to McDonald's in Puerta de Tierra before he trucked 'em back to Maunabo. That was ten years ago. And this fellow is still making out his list of dependents every March, and to this day the Treasury Department hasn't even *thought* about bothering him again. As the saying goes, "You want to be real careful what you ask for, because you might get it." '

There was applause from the driver and the retired schoolteacher. The storyteller from Maunabo smiled contentedly, and said now it was somebody else's turn.

Surprisingly, it was the kid with the Walkman that stepped in next.

'In Arroyo, where my grandmother lives, there's been all these fires. There's been businesses, cane fields, houses burned to the ground, and there's even been some women that've poured gasoline all over themselves and set themselves afire. My grandmother says it's the curse of this sailor that got sick on a boat one time, he got sick with something real contagious, I don't remember exactly what she said it was, and the crew put him off in a little boat and set him on fire.'

'When he died?' the Maunabo man, a little confused by this last part, asked.

'That's the point, dude, they *torched him*, get it? They. Burned. Him. Alive.' The kid pronounced each word separately and very, very carefully, as though he were talking to a lip-reader. He was a little upset that nobody had gotten the point of the story.

The brevity of the story was a disappointment to the driver; again he threatened to fall asleep if we couldn't do better than that. The charismatic lady took up the challenge next.

'I'm from Arroyo too, and it's a fact—you'd think fire had something against my poor hometown. This story I'm about to tell happened quite some time ago. I'm not going to mention any names, in case some of you know the people—down in Arroyo, everybody is related to everybody else, or about to be.

'What happened was that sometime around the turn of the century a widow lady from the Canary Islands came to Arroyo to live. This woman had a grown son and a lot of money. Pretty soon what was bound to happen happened, and this son fell in love. He fell in love with a nice girl from there that he'd met in town, and he decided he wanted to get married. Only problem was, the girl's skin was a little darker than his. Well the mother wouldn't hear of it, and not only because of the girl's color—truth was, no girl was going to be good enough for her boy. And in order to keep 'em from having that wedding she even got sick and everything. But the son stood his ground, and since he was of legal age there wasn't much the mother could do about it. Finally one day he gets tired of waiting for his mother to change her mind, and he grabs that dark-skinned girl and they go talk to the priest and the next day she had a wedding ring on her finger. They went off to live in a little house he'd rented right there in town. Now this young man was a good son, and he would visit his mother every week, regular as rain. She'd open the door to him, but she wouldn't let her daughter-in-law so much as set foot on her porch. She wouldn't give that girl the time of day.

'Well, as time went on, the son and his new wife discovered that with the blessing of God they were going to have a baby. It was born as white as the father, but even so, the grandmother refused to even look at it.

'Then about a year after the baby was born, strange things started happening in the son and daughter-in-law's house—keys would disappear, the water would turn itself on and off, smoke would come up out of the toilet . . . One night a pack of big black dogs got into the yard and barked all night. Things were getting ugly. So finally the girl sent for the priest. The priest said two or three *dominus vobiscums* in the living room, the bathroom, and each bedroom and sprinkled holy water all through the house. But that same night those black dogs were back again, and the bed shook, and all the shutters in the front room opened and closed all by themselves.'

The narrator had lowered her voice, which accentuated the sinister atmosphere of her story. All of us, including the driver, were leaning toward her, not wanting to miss a word of the tale. Night had fallen now, and the air on the highway through the forest was cool. I surreptitiously rolled up the window beside me, in case some venturesome spirit should take a mind to join us.

'The girl then sent for her aunt, who had the understanding. And that black *espiritista* no more than walked through the front door into the living room when the light fixture came crashing down from the ceiling and landed practically on top of her. "*Ay Santa Marta!*" she says, looking around warily, "the evil work is in this house," and she starts trying to find it. She looked high and low—she practically turned that house upside down hunting for the thing that was causing all this trouble. But she looked and she looked and she still couldn't find the lock of hair or whatever it was anywhere. So she took up one of those spirits that's loose just about anywhere and she took it up and it began to speak out of her mouth. "Your mother-in-law has done this," the spirit says to the girl, "she's the one that's doing this to you, and until you find the thing that's doing it, the spirits she's set on you will never leave you in peace." '

'What they ought to have done is send a couple of guys over to that mother-in-law's house to teach her not to meddle in other folks' business,' pronounced the driver, though he had his fingers crossed, just in case.

'Or put a spell on her that was bigger than the one she put on *them*,' said the retired schoolteacher type, who not for nothing was from Guayama, which anyone will tell you is the witching capital of Puerto Rico.

'Anyway, that night, when the widow's son found out about all this, naturally he refused to believe it. How could such a thing be? His mother, such an upright, Catholic woman . . . But his wife was convinced, and she refused to sleep another night in that house until the spell had been found and undone. She stood her ground, too, so finally her husband promised her that the next day he'd find them another place to live. Meanwhile, they went to bed, scared to death, and it took them hours to ever get to sleep. Along about morning, they suddenly woke up to the smell of something burning. The smell was strong, too. He ran to find out where the fire was, and she had her housedress about halfway pulled on, when they heard the baby crying. So the girl, dressed in nothing but her nightgown, ran into the child's room. And there—*ay Virgen del Carmen*, it gives me goosebumps just to think about it—she found her baby on fire, like some human torch lying there under the mosquito net.'

Thank goodness we'd gotten onto the expressway by now, so the lights of the cars helped not only light the way but dispel our fears a bit as well.

'What happened to the widow? Did they get her for it?' the driver demanded, unconsciously taking out his vengeance on the accelerator.

'What happened to somebody didn't happen to the widow, it happened to the poor daughter-in-law. The widow accused her of murdering the child, and since the old lady had money and lots of connections, she fixed things so her daughter-in-law was carried off to San Juan and locked up in the lunatic asylum.'

The retired schoolteacher then asked the question we had all been silently asking:

'And what about the husband? Didn't he do anything?'

'Yes, of course he did,' she said, with a gesture of disgust. 'He went back to the Canary Islands with his mother . . . just so you'll see how false and cowardly some men are.'

The moral of the story aroused protests from some quarters—the four representatives of the male sex, who were in the majority in the car. The retired schoolteacher was determined to save the honor of his sex, and no better way could he find than to take up the challenge with a further tale:

'In a town on the south coast whose name I do not wish to remember, there was a businessman with a great big elegant house sitting beside his store, which was right near a fire station. His wife was elegant, also—a tall, white-skinned foreign lady with blue eyes. She was very lovely, but she was a little, you know . . .'

The charismatic lady pursed her lips in preparation for the expected offense to her modesty; the driver, as was his wont, noisily greeted the possibility.

'. . . too hot to handle . . . One man was not enough for her, shall we say. Or two. Or three. Or four. Her poor husband had horns growing every which way out of his head—he looked like one of Santa Claus's reindeer. Of course, he didn't even realize he was being . . . *cuckolded*, I believe, is the polite name for it, since he was a little . . . you know . . . slow on the uptake himself.'

The driver now was choking with laughter, the Maunabo gentleman joined in, and the lady from Arroyo opened her eyes and took a deep breath. The kid with the Walkman winked at me enigmatically; I had no idea how to take that.

'The wife's taste leaned to firemen, of all things. And since she had them right there at hand, you see, why every night she'd give her husband a cup of linden tea sugared with two or three sleeping pills, and while he lay there snoring she'd spend the night putting out fires.'

'Good god!' the charismatic lady muttered softly, and looking for moral reinforcements she cast her irate eye on me. I didn't know whether to look serious or just get it over with and laugh out loud, so I sat there with a sort of half-smile on my face, looking wholly idiotic.

'The husband's friends found out what was going on, of course, and they alerted the guy so he could take patriotic action. The fellow thought about it a good long time, because it was hard for him to believe that his beloved wife was cheating on him with half a battalion of firefighters. One night he decided to just *pretend* he was drinking the linden tea his wife always fixed him, and so he just lay there awake studying the ceiling for a long time, *pretending* he was asleep. Pretty soon he heard sounds in the room next door, so he got up, sneaked out the back door, went around the house, and crossed the street and found himself a lookout behind a tree. What he saw was a whole parade of firemen in and out of his house, so finally he woke up to what had been going on all this time. But he controlled himself—he waited for the last one to come out before he did anything. Then he crossed the street and went back in the house.'

In spite of the narrator's perverse sense of storytelling, the story had us all by the throat. Even the charismatic lady was holding her fire so that we could come more quickly to the ending.

'Those who were there say that husband was like a madman. They say his face was purple with rage. He threw open that door, stalked into the bedroom, grabbed his wife by the hair, dragged her out onto the porch, and threw her out in the street as naked as the day she was born.'

Now nobody was laughing. The abruptness of the finale had taken our breath away.

'So you see, missus,' said the narrator without missing a beat, 'we men may be false, but women can be a whole lot falser yet.'

'Those that are, are,' intoned the man from Maunabo in a conciliatory tone of voice, 'but most women are truer than we men, you know, my friend, as my mother is, and I imagine your own.'

The sentimental evocation of our mothers calmed tempers a bit. The latest storyteller, in fact, was rendered so tender-hearted that he did not even realize that his mother's purity had been called, ever so delicately, into question.

'There's more to the story than that,' said the charismatic lady suddenly, and we all turned to look at her. 'You haven't told but one side of it. You've made that poor woman sound like the villain.'

Eye-Openers

The man from Guayama opened his eyes wide and shrugged his shoulders in a guise of total innocence. But the lady in the habit was adamant. She looked him straight in the eye and crossed her arms censoriously.

'Then *you* tell the story, you tell it,' urged the driver, his tired eyes taking on new light. The lady considered the invitation, hesitated a few seconds, and then without further ado launched herself into the tale, her fingers fiddling with the rope-ends at her waist, her eye set on the window.

'What happened was that this businessman we were talking about was no saint himself. His idea of fun was to take the ignorant young girls from the countryside around there and carry them to a house of ill repute there used to be in town and have his way with them.'

The phrase made the kid with the Walkman smile. But he contritely lowered his eyes when my gaze met his.

'That place was famous for the parties they used to have there—the most degenerate men along the whole southern coast with their mistresses and whores and scarlet women. Orgies was what they had there, orgies that'd put the Roman emperors to shame.'

'Well, now . . .' murmured the schoolteacher, who was beginning to be distressed by the turn the story was taking. The charismatic lady, though, was not so quick to relinquish the floor.

'The wife, of course,' she forged on, 'knew nothing about any of those shenanigans. The whole world knew what was going on, but since her husband kept her all shut up in that great big house of theirs all the time, with no family and no friends, there was no way for her to hear anything about is. So about that time a pretty young girl comes to work in the house. This husband of hers had sent the girl supposedly to help out. The girl was polite and obedient, a real nice girl, and the wife was delighted.

'One day, as she was cleaning, this young maid stuck her hand back behind a bookcase in the room the husband used for an office. And what did she put her hand on, behind a false wall, but a whole stack of books all wrapped up and tied with a cord. Since the poor girl didn't know how to read, she didn't realize she'd come across a collection of dirty books— every one of them, every single one, on that Index, that list the Catholic Church keeps of forbidden books. But she did know how to look at pictures, and since the books had gotten her curiosity up, she started thumbing through one particular big thick album that she found sticking out between two smaller books. Imagine the look on that poor innocent young girl's face when she sees what's in it—all these photographs of the husband and his filthy friends doing terrible things with little girls twelve and thirteen years old, and with negro women and even with animals, oh my God . . .'

'Those orgies must have been something,' said the driver, fascinated, and nobody dared to laugh.

'She didn't want to get into trouble, so she kept her mouth shut about what she'd found. *To each his own, I guess,* she thought. But God works in mysterious ways, and what happened was that this businessman we were talking about, he'd had his eye on this girl he'd brought in to help his wife around the house, and around this time he begins to fondle her a little bit every time she'd get within reach. At first she tried to brush his hand away, like this, you know, not too much fuss about it, but the man kept on and kept on, and he'd watch and try to corner the girl whenever he could. The night he tried to get into her room, she drew the line. She packed up her things and the next morning she went in to say goodbye to the wife. But the truth was, she liked the wife, the wife had been real good to her, so when she opened her mouth to tell her she was leaving, she broke out crying like a nine-year-old child. The wife didn't know what to think, of course, so she started asking questions. And she kept asking questions until finally the girl told her the truth. The woman didn't want to believe her, of course, but the girl took her by the hand and led her into the husband's office and showed her the false wall and the album of dirty pictures and everything.'

After the requisite pause to let her words take effect, the charismatic lady couldn't resist hammering in one last nail:

'So you see,' she said, smiling, 'how the story changes depending on who's telling it.'

The man from Guayama, though, was not altogether abashed.

'I hope you'll forgive the question,' he said, in a tone entirely too polite for the moment, 'but where exactly did you get that version of the story?'

Surprisingly, it was the driver that came to the lady's aid.

'From the same place you got yours, and did anybody ask *you* how you came by it?' And he broke the tension with one of his inimitable bursts of laughter.

A comfortable silence fell over us. The driver, as he shepherded us along the Caguas highway, looked bright-eyed and awake now. We'd soon come to the exit for Río Piedras. I knew that by all rights my turn had come, but fortunately the trip was almost over. Then just as I thought I was safe, the voice of the man from Maunabo checked me:

'Well, young lady, aren't you going to tell us a story?'

The driver and the other passengers joined in. But I shook my head and began trotting out my entire arsenal of cheap excuses—I didn't have anything interesting to tell, life in San Juan was so boring, nothing ever happened, and of course we were coming to the plaza now and we'd all be getting out and going our own ways, so I really didn't have time to tell one. But everyone was so insistent that finally I even had to claim I had a sore throat. Suddenly turning up the volume on his Walkman and blasting us with the latest hip-hop hit, the kid with the Walkman came to my rescue. So with youth arrayed against them, the older folks from the south coast finally stopped insisting and resigned themselves to traveling the last short stretch of the trip in silence.

In the plaza at Río Piedras, the goodbyes took a while. People introduced themselves to each other (by name, I mean, at last) and shook hands warmly. The man from Guayama, who turned out to be a fireman and not a retired schoolteacher, drew us a map on a napkin so we could all get to his house sometime. The driver even gave us his card, and he told us several times not to hesitate to call him the next time we wanted to 'go down that way'.

'Next time, have a cup of coffee before you leave,' suggested the charismática lady, picking up a box, tied all round with twine, that smelled deliciously of ripe mangoes.

The driver laughed one of his unmistakable laughs again.

'Goodness gracious,' he said, 'that's just a trick of mine to get to hear people tell stories . . .'

I walked down Georgetti toward my apartment, and I hadn't got far before I had the eerie sense that someone was following me. Given the all-too-real possibility of a mugging to welcome me to the metropolitan area, I turned around, only to discover that it was the kid with the Walkman. I thanked him for coming to my rescue in the *público* and we walked on together toward Ponce de León. He told me he went to the university days and sold ice cream nights in Los Chinitos.

'Come in sometime and have an ice-cream courtesy of the management,' he said, this time with a less ambiguous wink. And then, just as we were about to part —

'Hey, listen, what do you do? Do you work here, or what?'

I just smiled, coyly waved goodbye, and kept walking. I didn't want to break the magic of the moment. My head was full of words, and I could hardly wait to sit down at my typewriter and roll in that first piece of paper.

Sunday Cricket

Look man, is a hard ting wen is Easter Sunday, West Indies battin, an yuh wife decide dat de whole family have to go to church. Nat only de West Indies battin, but dey look like dey set to win de series. Englan go one up in de firs tes, de secon wash out, de third we scrape troo wid a draw by de grace of God rain. I say God save Englan so often dat is high time likkle blessing fall pon we. De fourth, we win, wid a much questioned wicket wen dem say Richards pressure de umpire. Doah I watch it, I cyaan really say wedda de man out or not, I is nat im bat so I cyaan say wat touch mi, but ah do know dat de umpire was already walkin away from behin de stumps as it was de end of de over, wen Richards run dung pon im an im half turn back an raise de finger. An yuh should see Ambrose face, im nuh so hard yet dat im face doan show surprise an doubt no matter wat im body appealin for.

Well dat gone. We win, but nat wid no sweetness fi me. Dis laas tes now, dis is serious business. Yes, we all have a betta feeling fi de England team since dem get rid a de racis dem an even have tree West Indian pon dem side. Despite all dis doah, we still can't lose we pride so much as to mek Englan beat we.

All dat aside, today is de third day a de laas test an bwoy, we battin sweet. Englan all out fi 260 an Haynes an Greenidge nearly pass dat. Nat a man nat out, imagine, an yuh wife insisting yuh have to go to church because is Easter Sunday.

Now yuh probably wonderin why I tek up Bredda B case so, but bein a woman who love her cricket, is a dilemma I well understan. Bredda B is mi neares neighbour an is him I get a answerin moan from wen a fella out or a joyful shout wen ah holla cross, 'Bredda B, yuh see dat cover drive!' Add to dat de fac dat I promise my madda sincerely to accompany her to church dat very same Sunday. I mek dat promise long before I know de date dem fi di game an she wearin a look pon her face dat say life goin to be well miserable for a lang time if ah change mi mind. Nothin like bein comrades in sufferin to create a likkle sympaty.

De final woe of de mawnin never befall we until, in we own separate house, we each tryin to find de earplug fi we transistor radio. Sister B mussi did know wat Bredda B was plannin because all de corner dem dat im would usually put de ear plug dat would change de radio into a walkman was well empty. As to me, it was jus caylissniss.

We was two sorry an dutiful people as we set aff to church dat mawnin, already a few minutes late. At de laas moment ah decide to push de likkle radio in mi bag anyway. Ah don't say a ting to Bredda B as im might go smile too broad an mek im wife suspicious. We reach, an tek we usual seat in de back bench while my madda an im wife head towards de choir.

Well bwoy, de firs ting get we vex is wen we see who come out to lead de service. Now, we was sure it had to be Pastor or some visiting dignitary fi dis special day, but nuh same ole Bredda Kelly who we all know since we goin to Sunday school. To put it to de bes compliment we can find, de man is barely literate. Im can read yes, but de way im string im words together an de lengt a time im tek to figure out de nex one, we done lose all sense about wat gone before. Yuh all know how bible haad fi mek sense of already. Nat to mention, dem set a mike in de pulpit, but im so short nat even im breat can ketch it, so we dung a back can hardly hear a ting.

Now if Bredda Kelly did have a bit of drama to im, yuh know, a likkle grunt here or dere like im in pain or a hop skip an jump an den pounce dung hard pon de bible, it would did keep we more activated. But Bredda Kelly, im talk like im constipated.

I grimacin to myself doah Bredda B tekkin it all in stride. Dat only mean dat since de bes course nuh wan possible an de secondary course a wash out, im tek de third course which was, im resort to sleep. Im head was back pon de bench an im mout wide open.

I dere, itchin fi di radio, but tryin to tek Bredda Kelly wid more patience dan God give Job. Yuh see, ah have reason to believe is I who cause it.

I don't really come to church every Sunday, but Pastor an I talk frank. Ah was active as a teenager but yuh all know dat is wen de affairs of de worl get really interesting. But dat is anadda story. However, since ah come home dis time from my wanderins, Pastor aks mi if ah wouldn like to tek up mi membership again. Ah had to explain dat if ah should tek dat course of action ah would lose out on mi ministry wid de yout in particular since right now ah could sit down an have a real progressive an spiritual discussion about every subjec under de sun wedda dem was drinkin a likkle rum or smokin some good bush.

To give Pastor full justice, im see de point an did admit dat de church get really conservative an if im was to practise de ministry like Jesus, de very member dem would criticise. Im aks mi if ah was comin to church de nex

Sunday, which wasn't no special day, an ah tell im ah only comin if is im preachin but ah really nat goin to sit down an listen to some sleepy borin member who lackin in any kine of inspiration. I don't feel dat de number of years yuh spen in church qualify yuh to preach. I believe in callin, an who call to tek up collection or repair de bench is nat necessarily who call upon to preach de word of God. Pastor never agree wid dat; im say is de word important, nat who preachin it.

So wen I see Bredda Kelly tek de pulpit, ah say to miself, bwoy, Pastor pull a faas one to teach mi a likkle humility. Dat would mek mi laugh on anadda day for ah enjoy Pastor sense a humour, but nat on a Sunday wen ah give up some brilliant stroke play in wat look like a record breakin openin paatnership an a winnin West Indies team.

So dere we was, de backbenchers, one sleepin, one bored, an Bredda Kelly ramblin on in between de song dem dat always start too high fi my medium key voice. Ah couldn't help feelin dat de spirit in Recreation Groun in Antigua mus be a lot more suitable to de idea of de risen Lord dan de feelin in dis church. Dis feelin more like Good Friday.

It was right in de middle of dat thought dat Bredda B let out a loud half cut off snore an mi see im wife eye searchin im out. Jus as de choir singin 'up from de grave he arose', Bredda B voice ring out, loud an clear, 'dem drop im, man, im get a life!'

Yuh should see Sista B face swell up, an as to how she red already. De whole set a young people side a we bus out wid laugh an den ketch demself quick an push dem yeye back eena dem hymnbook. Bredda B don't know a ting, im head jus rock to de adda side an im silent again. Bredda Kelly cyaan do more dan gwaan wid de service.

I feel so relieve wen I hear Bredda Kelly announce dat is nat him preachin de sermon, is Bredda Jerry. Now Bredda Jerry have nuff energy an can guarantee fi wake up de people dem, plus, im use to play cricket nuff before im meet de Lord an have to give up im Sunday. Well, im tek de pulpit an tings staat to heat up. Immediately im call a chorus an han start clap an cymbal soun up.

Dis is a fairly new ting in Baptis church. Troo de older generation of de membership is fram a likkle higher up de social order, dem use to show dem status by refusin to clap han an play cymbal. Dat did leave to de Pentecostal dem where de poorer people go. It seem to me dat troo dem did only have few member lef who was all ready to move on to heaven, dem decide fi lively up wid some riddim an try bring een some young people. It workin too.

Church staat swing. Bredda Jerry get een pon im sermon an even

Bredda B staat rock likkle bit eena im sleep, open one eye an drif aff again wid a timely 'Amen'.

Wen Bredda Jerry reach de risen Lord now, im tell de whole church fi stan up an say, 'Praise de Lord'. De church shout 'Praise de Lord'. Bredda Jerry say 'Wave yuh han in de air an say Tank yuh Jesas'. De church raise dem han an say 'Tank yuh Jesas'. Bredda Jerry say 'Yes, yes, bredrin an sistrin, we have a saviour. It is nat de empty grave dat is important today, dat could have been a samfie man trick, a Nansi game. What is important today is de Risen Lord, de Risen Lord. He is our hero an He is here. Mek we clap we han an give a roun of applause to de Risen Lord.'

De whole church give a firm an loud clap han. Is dis rise Bredda B, im jump up quick, like im late fi heaven, clappin im han an hollerin out 'Im mek a double century or im out?'

As soon as dis come out im mout, de laughin bus out fresh from de back an de vex face dem turn roun from de front. Sista B put dung her hymn-book an staat head out troo de side door so can come een troo de back door fi im. My madda face tight like no joke cyaan mek fi at leas a year.

Is Bredda Jerry save de day, ah have to give it to dat man. Im answer Bredda B right back. 'Out? Out? Nooooo . . . Not out, never out. We have a openin bat dat never out. None like Him been aroun for centuries. An church, if yuh have Him on yuh side yuh cyaan lose, no, yuh cyaan lose. My openin bat, your openin bat. Mek Im lead dis team today. Jesus! What is His name? . . . Jesus! Caall on His name . . .'

De whole congregation bawl out, 'Jesus'. All de backbencher dem come een, 'Jesus'.

Bredda B, wide awake now, breathe out in sheer relief as im wife stop at de doorway an head back to de choir jus as Bredda Jerry raise de final song.

> *Up from de grave He arose*
> *wid a mighty triumph o'er His foes*
> *He arose a victor from de dark domain*
> *An will live forever wid de saints to reign.*

We voice lif up like we was ready to over run a pitch.

> *He arose He arose*
> *Hallellujah, Christ arose.*

Me an Bredda B let out a sigh of relief an we really did mean dat final 'Amen' fah we know how often we go dung into terror wid we cricket, collapse afta a good start into de grave, but we always rise again, hallellujah, always to rise again!

ASTRID ROEMER (b. 1947)

The Inheritance of my Father: A Story for Listening

Translated by Hilda van Neck-Yoder

On a pine worktable lies a yellowed photograph, two wrinkled airplane tickets, several airmail envelopes, letters, and a stamp album. There is also a red Walkman with several cassettes next to it. A black tape recorder is set to record. The child of a mother who will be forty tomorrow begins to speak out loud.

Before the summer vacation of this year, I had never seen my grandma. Yet I knew exactly what she looked like, from a photograph, of course.

In the picture, she wears a huge, wide skirt almost to her feet, made of very stiff material that stands straight out. Around her head, she wears a scarf with pointed corners made of the same material as the jacket. Her neck is covered with necklaces. Many bracelets decorate her arms. With her glasses and a twig of flowers in her hand, my grandma looks just beautiful—always smiling, in a frame on the television.

I also know my grandma from the letters she writes. Once a month an envelope with beautiful stamps drops onto the floor in our hall. The stamps are for my album, and later, my mother says, I may also have the letter. She always reads the letter out loud. There is always something for me in the letter. Then my grandma wants to know how I am—in grammar school and in Sunday school. And she always writes, that, in the picture, I look just like my father, and how much she longs to see me.

That is what she always tells me when my mother calls her: 'Bonkoro my half-breed, I would love to see you yet before I die.' And then she starts to talk slowly in a language I cannot understand and then she suddenly cries. It always goes like that. Then I give the telephone back to Mama. Then she begins to talk loud and fast. Sometimes Mama cries too.

I think that Grandma does not like it that we live so far away from each other. We live a plane trip of nine hours and almost three thousand guilders per person away from each other. And that is terribly far away, you know.

One night I wake up and hear my father talk real loud in a language he always uses when he is excited. Because I do not hear the voice of my mother, I go to the living room. Papa is on the phone, naked, and Mama is on the couch in her nightshirt, with a cigarette. Quietly, I sit down next to her and together we look at my father. I can see him clearly in the dark even though his skin is almost black. His upper body is long and his legs are bony and thin, just like mine. He has no mustache and no beard, and I know that he has invisible curly hairs on his chest and arms. That is what I was thinking while I sat next to Mama and felt how tightly she pressed me to her.

I do not know why he suddenly threw down the phone and with long strides sat down next to us—in silence. I do not think that he had seen me, for suddenly he looked at me, shocked. I remember that I looked down immediately and became a little afraid. I had never seen him naked and I was embarrassed. He too. He got up, left, and returned in his housecoat and turned on the lights. It was almost three o'clock in the morning.

'My mother is going to be eighty years old this summer and she especially wants to see you.'

He talked and he talked, a little rough, and my heart pounded terribly. I believe my body trembled too. Not that I was shocked, but my father had never talked with me about the country of his birth in a way that made me sad.

While he was talking like that, Mama became very quiet as if she were no longer there. First Papa looked only at me, but then he talked, looking at the floor, and suddenly he stood up, with his back to us telling us how much he loved his country. He said: 'Every time I see you, my child, I miss my mother in a way that tears my heart apart.'

Then Mama began to cry real loud, and I became even more nervous. In the middle of the night they started to quarrel, and it was frightening: Mama kept getting redder and redder, and Papa turned blacker and blacker. I screamed that they should stop: Otherwise I would leave them and never come back. It seemed as if I was the cause of everything—everything.

After that night I began to think about everything, about who my parents were, about my mother, about where my father is from, about what I am, about who we are together. Often it makes me sick. It is as if I have to throw up but cannot. When we three are eating. I look carefully at the people who are my parents and then it starts. Then I hate rice and cauliflower and how Mama talks to Papa and how Papa looks at Mama. Then I hate meat and fish and how they worry about my appetite.

Then I hope that some day I will puke so much that the whole table and their faces will be covered with the mess. In bed, I keep wondering why my father had not just stayed in his own country—then he would never have met my mother; then I would not be there. And I would not have all that fuss from my mother's family, of how brown I am, and how blond I am becoming.

Because those two could not care less about that, their own fights are loaded with the nasty words that people yell at me in the street—honky, nigger, and the whole alphabet of insults. That is why I never complain to them about what happens to me outside; like lumps of oatmeal I keep swallowing all this teasing, bah!

But that night made everything worse. I really understood what my father meant when he said that he has been living here for twenty years and that he has married a woman of this country and that his child is born here but that they still want him to return to the land of his birth—as soon as possible. And after that night I am ashamed to be the child of a woman with blond hair and grey eyes and a voice that sounds just like that of people who are not black. Believe me, I longed for a mother with a scarf on her head and a skin so dark that I never would have to be afraid at night again that the sun would ever burn me.

A musical instrument is taken out of a drawer of the pine worktable, also some pages of sheet music. The volume of the tape recorder is adjusted. The child of the mother who will be forty tomorrow begins to play the flute with her eyes wide open—so that the frightening dreams mask themselves as a fairy tale.

In a country where the sun is so close that everyone can touch it, in a country where everything is green, and the corn constantly waves to the heavens, in a country where pumpkins glitter like clumps of gold on the ground, in a country where the wind awakes the morning with giggles and the rain hums the night to sleep, in a land where clothes are made of pieces of cloud and jewelry of drops of stars, in a country where beetles, donkeys, elephants, lions, rhinoceroses, serpents, hawks, dolphins, and herrings crawl over each other around everywhere and no one, no one knows who all this belongs to and how that all came about—in that country lives a young girl in a place that even the wind cannot reach. She has no name—

she has no family—and she was so full of life that even the bees and ants admired her. Boys daydreamed about her. Men stayed in love with her. Girls wanted to know her. Women talked all the time about a voice whose song could destroy unhappiness and happiness—because the girl had a voice! When her songs sounded over the valley, the wind encircled the trees to keep the leaves from moving and the water no longer ran in the rivers—it danced. As soon as a child could not sleep, its mother would hum the song of the girl; as soon as a man and a woman got into a fight over who was boss, their children would begin to sing the song of the girl; even when someone had died, people would sing her song around the grave.

One day, the people of the country were startled by a curious sound. Everyone kept very quiet and although it was incredibly early in the morning, the chickens did not cluck and the birds did not chirp. Everyone listened to the deafening gargle as if hundreds of giants were rinsing their throats.

Just as suddenly as the sound appeared, it disappeared. Children, women, men—they threw themselves again into the bustle of the day with a hug here and a snarl there. Only the girl kept waiting, living in a spot that even the wind could not reach. She knew that that sound was the sorrowful song of the mountains. The earth was about to explode and mudslides would cover everything.

Because the mountains began to bray more threateningly, people became afraid. They knew the earth could suck in their lovely country so that afterwards no one would know what lay under the boiling mud. That is why they went to the girl who could subdue the wind with her voice and keep the waters in check. They took her along and left her alone with her songs at the foot of the mountains. And the girl sang. And the mountains became quiet. And she sang and she sang without noticing that she slowly changed into a mountain. When she realized what had happened, she screamed so loudly that the earth tore open. Hundreds of butterflies burst out, flashing like fireworks. Like shells covering the beach, the butterflies attached themselves to the land.

This dream did not always end so full of color. Sometimes instead of butterflies loads of mud burst out of the earth. Then my screams would awaken my parents and my arms would flay about as if wasps were attacking me. Mama would bring me sugar water to drink, and Papa would ask me to cut out the stories about the land of his birth. But I kept on dreaming—the dream became a fairy-tale garden in which I found myself more and more. With every thing I did, I kept thinking of the mountains, of the greenery, the butterflies, and the girl without a name. I was unfriendly, cold, short. I ate poorly and I slept badly.

Slowly it dawned on my parents that I wanted to go to my Grandma for almost three thousand guilders and a nine-hour flight.

The weeks just went by. The airmail became more urgent; more and more the telephone rang in the night.

My mother was the first to give in; I was allowed to go with or without my father to the birthday of my Grandma. She would stay home. She did not want to run the risk of being treated like an undesirable stranger in his country or by his family. There were dreadful discussions between my parents, sometimes even in the car in the middle of a traffic jam. For me the days of insecurity became days of exuberance. Days of pain followed when Mama began to pack my suitcase with much care. Never had I spent a summer without her.

At first it felt weird to be sitting alone with my father in the airplane. He looked truly handsome in his light summer suit. Moreover, he had not dyed his grey hair black because Mama had asked him not to. She had driven us to the airport and had said a friendly goodbye, long before it was time to go to the departure hall. It had hurt to see her walk away alone, not turning around again, disappearing among the people. Goodbye Mom, my eyes said, while my hand grasped my father's—come along Dad! I knew that we were flying away from the country of my mother and—to rid me of my frightening dreams—toward the country of my father. With a head full of plans and all wound up because almost everyone on the plane had plenty of pigment—and because of how they talked and laughed, joked and played—I saw that my father cried when the plane took off. In between sleeping and being awake, I listened to pieces of conversation that I did not understand. Almost everyone spoke in their own language. Only my father's baritone sounded familiar. Moreover, via my Walkman, I heard my mother say: 'My darling, whatever you may experience in your fatherland, do not forget that there is also a woman who has given you a motherland!'

I decided to become a pilot—taking off, flying-flying, descending, from country to country, touching the earth and slicing the sky—north, south, east, west.

Next to the pine worktable is a large kit. It has to become a passenger plane. The hands that hold the recorder now pick up the kit. The stop button is being pushed in. Just a few moments for some dreams about the future. Just a moment. Tomorrow a mother is turning forty and her present has to be revealing. The child pushes the stop button back out.

I do not remember much about the first days in the country of my father's birth. It is as if so much happened at the same time that I barely can retain anything—like a dizzying ride in a race car at the fair.

The whole family had come out to get us. And there were so many kinds of faces of so many kinds of races with so many kinds of voices in so many kinds of languages and of all ages and sizes. This welcome took days, and for days I did little but mumble my name and gasp for air whenever I would disappear in an embrace.

But the dream about the earth bursting with butterflies and about mountains spitting mud did not return. And when my mother called Papa and me after one week, we could at least tell her that I did not wake up screaming at night anymore. The opposite: Dead tired, I would fall asleep early in the evening, and my father had trouble getting me out of bed in the morning before breakfast.

We were staying in a large hotel. There was a bar and also a swimming pool. And there was a strange shopping center. There was also an underground garage where the car was that my father had rented. But a day would fly by so quickly that neither the bar nor the swimming pool nor the shopping center would notice us. Already at breakfast Papa would be picked up and we would be driven to different faces once more. And the fun they always had together—my father and his friends and his relatives! But he would never lose sight of me; I always had to sit next to him. And with an arm around my shoulders he would explain to everyone who wanted to hear that he had returned to the country of his birth especially to give me a chance to really learn to know him. Then everyone would be silent for awhile until he would raise his glass and pronounce: 'For thirty years my heart has remained in this country, amen!'

One night I awoke bathed in sweat. I had dreamed about mountains that threw up wasps and that I had to run away real fast because they were buzzing after me. It was cool in the room and the sound of the ventilator was irritating. I got up to turn it off and to get a drink of water when I discovered that my father was not in his bed: It was quarter to one in the morning.

I quietly took a shower, got dressed nicely and took the elevator to the bar. Immediately I saw him, sitting there, not on a barstool like most of the men, but at a table—with candlelight. With him was a woman. They were looking at each other, and I believe they did not say anything. They only stared and remained silent.

Frozen, I stopped in my tracks and did not know what to do. To return to my room was impossible because I had accidentally locked the door. And my father and the woman were so incredibly beautiful together that I could not keep my eyes off them—ach, ach. He let her drink from his wine glass, and she took his hands by the wrists, and they got up slowly and started to dance. There were other people dancing by the bar, but everyone turned around when my father put his arms completely around the woman. Silently and passionately, they moved with the music. With my heart throbbing in my throat I watched until they danced away.

Then I ran, first to the swimming pool, then to the bathroom. But because there were too many people I sneaked into the restaurant. I sat down at the table where we always have breakfast. I wanted to call to Mama, really. But when I opened my mouth there was a wave of warmth— puke on the white table cloth, puke on the plates. And suddenly every- where the voice of my Grandma: 'Bonkoro, I want to see you so badly before I die.'

My God, when I saw my father again, I was lying in a strange bed. A friend of Papa, who everyone called 'datra', stood next to my bed. She was wear- ing a doctor's coat and wiped my face with something wet.

'I want to go away!' I kept yelling, and I realized that I was crying. My father asked 'datra' to leave us alone. Shaking her head, she left. Then I really let my tears come; my body shook with sobs, but I did not dare tell what I had seen that night. I kept looking at my father; I did not mention my mother. I hoped that he would understand that it was he who had to tell me something. But he kept silent, silent, and only tried to hold my hand. I kept pulling my hand away; I was beginning to loathe him.

All those quarrels with my mother and all those letters from Grandma were about something that I slowly began to understand. And I knew then for the first time that it certainly had a whole lot to do with me.

When he started to talk he talked to me like a spoiled child. He promised me all kinds of things: airplane trips to Indian villages, boat trips to water- falls, camping among the Maroons. But that caused me to gag again, and so the doctor had to come again with her wet cloths, and my father had to stand at the end of my bed again—watching. Ach-ach, I could see from his eyes that he did not understand why I begged him not to leave me for a moment.

*

The Inheritance of my Father: A Story for Listening

There I was, as they say, in my father's country, in a hospital bed recuperating from what everyone called 'adjustment problems'. For the rest of our vacation I was not allowed to drink water from the tap, and of course no lemonade or fruit juices. And what was definitely worse: I was subjected to a tasteless diet. Furious, I listened to all that, and staring straight ahead of me I nodded in agreement. After all, I was almost thirteen—sensible enough to take the opinion of adults into consideration. Moreover, all that throwing up had weakened me considerably. And everything-everything had disturbed the intimacy with which my father and I had begun our journey.

There I was, just lying in a room listening to my Walkman, and he was just sitting there with his nose in a magazine.

But what I am going to say now, I know as well as the nose on my face. It is as if I made it up, but believe me it happened just like that.

Listen—my father falls asleep with his head a little to the right, the paper in his lap, the magazine on the floor, really snoring. I am leaning against some pillows in bed, and I am just rewinding the tape to listen to my mother saying, 'My darling, whatever you may experience in your fatherland, do not forget that there is also a woman who has given you a motherland!'

I hear my mother's voice clearly, and I see my father's face clearly, and I wonder why we still have not gone to Grandma. Suddenly the door swings open and there she is—my Grandma. She is dressed just like in the picture on top of the television—only she is leaning on a cane. Her skin color is even blacker than that of my father, and she has dull grey hair, frizzy at the temples.

One step at a time she approaches. Her cane makes a regular ticking sound, but it is as if my heart is throbbing. Beside my father she stands still. She bends a little to have a good look at my father's face; she only does that for a moment while her cheeks are trembling vehemently. Then very softly she calls his name and Papa wakes up, startled. His chair falls, and he lets it lie to look at his mother with the same look, the same trembling cheeks.

That took much too long—really, much too long. Finally he said, 'Ma, you could have waited until I was ready to come and see you.' But his mother turned around and commanded: 'Boy, tell the doctor that the child is going with us—right now.'

Above the pine worktable is a bulletin board. The child of the mother who is going to be forty tomorrow looks at the eyes of Michael Jackson, at the breasts of Madonna, past the clothes of Prince. Suddenly, she rips the poster in the middle from the board. On this spot she puts a postcard of an Aucaner woman. The woman smiles to the photographer.

My Grandma does not live in the city. She lives along a kind of country road—miles and miles outside the capital. The rented car of my father could not even get to her house. Walking and dragging our suitcases, we reached the house; it is built on knee-high stone corbels, is made of wood, and on the outside it looks old and weathered. Around the house everything is real green: trees, bushes, grass. And dogs—she has too many. A red stairway took us into the living room full of shiny furniture, copperwork and the air of ripening bananas. I saw them hanging on a hook in the kitchen—in bunches.

An ancient man who lives with her shook our hand silently; his eyes glittered behind his bushy eyebrows. There were several fat women sitting on their haunches, and a man with dreadlocks brought our luggage to a bedroom.

My father did not say much; he listened and smiled, nodding from one to the other. The women wanted to embrace him, and he allowed that, laughing loudly. I was sitting on his lap; my anger had actually almost disappeared. Nobody talked to me. They talked about me and looked at me. When Grandma finally sat down with us she did not wear her scarf. She was dressed like a lot of the women I had seen—a cotton dress and a small belt. Her legs were very thin, and her feet were real skinny in her slippers. She had a potion for me to prevent fainting. She fed it to me one spoon at a time. Willingly, I swallowed this because it did not taste bad and smelled like her—like fruit. Ach-ach, I immediately loved her, so totally different from my Grandma in my mother's country. And only after a night together with her would the first day in the land of my father's birth begin.

Ouma, as everyone called her, thought that I had the look of somebody wise enough to know what the adults were discussing. She did away with my father's objection by saying: 'Everything that our eye looks at on this plantation and everything our ear hears on this plantation and everything our hand touches on this plantation is my grandchild's, and therefore my grandchild has to learn our secrets as well.'

After she said that, I went for walks early in the morning to survey the estate. But neither my eye nor my ear nor my hands could reach far enough to know what Ouma meant. However, I really felt wealthy—a large landowner—and I sent a postcard to my mother with a noble title in front of my name—as a joke, of course!

Henri, as she called my father, walked around the whole day in miserable, short pants—barefoot. He did all kinds of jobs for his mother. After a few days, with has beard and mustache, he looked as wild as all the other men. Ach, how wonderful it was to take a bath in the afternoon with buckets full of ice-cold well water. To eat hot meals with so many people out in the fresh air, to listen to each other's stories, to sleep on the wooden floor.

Far too often I was thinking about my mother and how she would really have enjoyed this—just like me, she was crazy about the wilderness. Finally I realized what had brought her and my father together, even though it remained hard to figure out that they stayed married because of me. But there was not much time to worry. Ouma's eightieth birthday was coming, and that is the reason I had down to this country. Therefore no one heard me complain about frightening dreams, about feeling sick, and about my parents. Everyone saw me walking around singing loudly, along with my Walkman. Ouma toned down the excitement of the people around her. On the day of her birth, she only wanted to have a church service and some live music. No dancing, no masses of people. The kitchen should be well provided but not overflowing. Also they should prepare for a lawyer to come to the house and for a special medicine man.

Because she was used to having her orders followed precisely, she quietly went around the house doing her own things the week of her birthday—as if there was nothing special happening. As long as they did not bother her, those that loved her were allowed to make preparations, and thus they fixed up the house on the outside and did some painting on the inside. Her girlfriends polished the wooden furniture even more, and the copperwork could compete with the sun.

During that time, my Grandma demanded all my attention. She showed me her koto-dresses, her jewelry, her Bibles, her money, and she said again-and-again that that would be mine—from now on. She noticed that I did not know what to do with my inheritance because she was still very much alive and because my father was her only child. But as soon as I started to talk about her son, she would silence me. I had to wait patiently for the presence of the lawyer and the medicine man. My father told me that the first one would come from the city, but that the medicine man had to travel for days before he would get to Ouma. And he, too, kept silent as soon as I started about the possessions of his mother.

On the pine worktable stands a wooden drum. It is an apinti-drum from a country that is nine-flight-hours and almost three-thousand-guilders-per-person away from here. She pulls the drum out with her legs. The gold-brown fingers of the child of the mother who will be forty tomorrow drum on the tightly drawn animal skin. Dark sounds well up. The recorder shuts off. The tape is being turned over to arouse the memories with fast drumming.

On a Thursday morning, four days before the celebration, the medicine man announced himself. With a following of three people he arrived on the estate of Ouma. His arrival created considerable excitement. The huts in which he and his helpers were going to stay had to be completed in a great hurry. Three of them were being covered with roofs made of palm leaves. One for him, one for his co-workers, and one for his hocus-pocus. My friend with dreadlocks explained that to me patiently and also why it would be better if I would stay away from the huts.

Therefore I took care of the dogs—washing, combing, feeding. And I was so busy doing that that I did not notice that they were constantly talking about me.

Until, Ouma called me one afternoon just after I had bathed. In the hut of the medicine man were my father and also Ouma's ancient friend. It was a strange get-together, but I was not afraid. Papa was there and my grandma, and even though I could not understand them—with them nothing could happen to me. I had to sit on a kind of bench and do exactly as the medicine man told me. Hold a gourd with water in the palm of my hand while my father talked to me and we looked at each other. At that moment I heard from the mouth of my father that he had to hand over his right to his inheritance because he had turned his back on his mother for almost thirty years, because he was married to a woman of another race, because he had no other descendants but me. My father spoke slowly, clearly, and quietly; he kept looking at me and his eyes looked terribly loving. I heard his mother choke back her tears.

That night we four ate a meal that the medicine man had prepared. I ate too much and too fast. Everyone had nodded to me encouragingly. I was even allowed to drink alcohol if I wanted to. My father poured me a little ginger wine. The medicine man constantly mumbled things I could never understand.

This event has attached itself to my memory as a mysterious experience—together with the secret of the plantation that my grandma revealed to me at the end of the dinner, without witnesses. It was a command that changed me from a child into an adult, from one moment to the next.

When the lawyer came on Saturday afternoon, I was therefore less tense. Even though I did not have to sign anything, he showed me the documents and read out loud with a melodious voice what the inheritance meant. My father had to sign for me because I was under age. After the papers had finally disappeared in big envelopes and the lawyer sealed some of these with a red seal, the champagne exploded.

I was being congratulated on my inheritance in all kinds of ways. Ouma and the people who were always with her sang to me about strength and wisdom—it made me so shy. Maybe it was the alcohol that flowed so generously that loosened their tongues. Ouma started to sing with a croaking voice. Giggling, Papa began to talk about his youth: Like in a poem, he began to describe the daughter of the minister whom he had loved so much that he left his mother and his country forever when her parents refused to give their daughter to the son of a common woman. I listened to him and became afraid when he suddenly did not laugh but burst out in tears, when he told how he had danced-and-danced with her, every night in the bar of the hotel. He got up and stood next to his mother and announced that he had wanted to marry a woman of his own people so badly and that he had wanted to give her dozens of heirs if only that miserable father of the woman of his dream had not constantly been waving the Bible at his daughter: after that, his hatred for everything that had to do with the church had only increased; he had missed his mother so much in all these years that all his dreams had been filled with pain.

Amen-Amen-Amen-Amen, everyone called around him and his mother kept singing with her eyes on her son—slowly and full of moaning.

Gulfs of tenderness, warm as blood, pushed through my whole body, when my papa came to me and lifted me up above his head and laid me down at the feet of his mother.

Everyone joined my grandma and the singing became more intense; happiness and sorrow had joined together.

Champagne sprayed on the floor. Glasses were filled. I heard how too many dogs cried.

The man who was going to lead the church service was small and lively. He was dressed in pearl white, just like Ouma who stared intensely in front of her. She was eighty years old now and was still alive—thank God. That was what I heard everyone say. For her that was not enough of a reason to invite guests and to be cheerful, she told me on that Monday morning.

The church service was intended to ask for a blessing on the covenant that was settled between Mrs Helena, Mr Henri, and their heir. That is the way the minister put it, and in a full voice he started to read the story of the prodigal son. Although there were more and more people and more and more flowers in the living room, I began to feel more and more alone. My father was sitting there with his head raised. He only looked at his mother and probably was not aware that the tears were running down his nose. He had shaved himself neatly and was very well dressed. I saw that many women could not keep their eyes off him during the service. None of them, however, was the woman with whom I had seen him dancing that night, so full of love.

Ach-ach, even though he does not really love my mother, my father at least loves his own mother and me, I consoled myself blubbering.

While everyone closed their eyes for prayer, I slipped outside. I walked on to the path along the estate that is mine. With every step I repeated the secret of its soil: Only the person who joins someone of the original African race will have a fertile life on this plantation because too much African blood still breathes in her soil.

On the road I met musicians with drums, laughing black men in native dress, and women who were dressed wondrously, carrying flowers to my grandma. Their husbands, in dark suits, were walking along humming.

Further-further I walked, against the stream of people, just to be alone. But I was not alone. In my thoughts an image of a woman grew: thick blond hair and deep-grey eyes—my own sweet-sweet mother. I suddenly longed for the smell of our house—furniture polish—and how Mama laughs, with her mouth open, and how she always-always waits for Papa with our evening dinner, and how she never-never goes visiting without Papa, and how she watches the news—smoking—and how she embroidered my sheets—with clovers. My thoughts of my mother were like crumbs of happiness that I stepped on with my own shoes as if they were firecrackers. Around me they exploded: Even if I had to suffer my whole long life, all my heart and all my body would belong to a black person—just like you Mama, Amen!

Chased by my own words and pursued by doubts, I ran back to the church service. Too many dogs of Ouma had followed me like friends.

The Inheritance of my Father: A Story for Listening

On a pine worktable there is a yellowed picture, two wrinkled airplane tickets, several small envelopes, letters, and a stamp album. There is also a red Walkman with some tapes next to it. A black recorder is being turned off. The child of a mother who will be forty tomorrow begins to cry out loud. Luckily the present is finished.

JAMAICA KINCAID (b. 1949)

Blackness

How soft is the blackness as it falls. It falls in silence and yet it is deafening, for no other sound except the blackness falling can be heard. The blackness falls like soot from a lamp with an untrimmed wick. The blackness is visible and yet it is invisible, for I see that I cannot see it. The blackness fills up a small room, a large field, an island, my own being. The blackness cannot bring me joy but often I am made glad in it. The blackness cannot be separated from me but often I can stand outside it. The blackness is not the air, though I breathe it. The blackness is not the earth, though I walk on it. The blackness is not water or food, though I drink and eat it. The blackness is not my blood, though it flows through my veins. The blackness enters my many-tiered spaces and soon the significant word and event recede and eventually vanish: in this way I am annihilated and my form becomes formless and I am absorbed into a vastness of free-flowing matter. In the blackness, then, I have been erased. I can no longer say my own name. I can no longer point to myself and say 'I'. In the blackness my voice is silent. First, then, I have been my individual self, carefully banishing randomness from my existence, then I am swallowed up in the blackness so that I am one with it . . .

There are the small flashes of joy that are present in my daily life: the upturned face to the open sky, the red ball tumbling from small hand to small hand, as small voices muffle laughter; the sliver of orange on the horizon, a remnant of the sun setting. There is the wide stillness, trembling and waiting to be violently shattered by impatient demands.

('May I now have my bread without the crust?'
'But I long ago stopped liking my bread without the crust!')

All manner of feelings are locked up within my human breast and all manner of events summon them out. How frightened I became once on looking down to see an oddly shaped, ash-colored object that I did not recognize at once to be a small part of my own foot. And how powerful I then found that moment, so that I was not at one with myself and I felt myself separate, like a brittle substance dashed and shattered, each separate part without knowledge of the other separate parts. I then clung fast to a common and familiar object (my lamp, as it stood unlit on the clean surface of my mantelpiece), until I felt myself steadied, no longer alone at sea in a small rowboat, the waves cruel and unruly. What is my nature, then? For in isolation I am all purpose and industry and determination and prudence, as if I were the single survivor of a species whose evolutionary history can be traced to the most ancient of ancients; in isolation I ruthlessly plow the deep silences, seeking my opportunities like a miner seeking veins of treasure. In what shallow glimmering space shall I find what glimmering glory? The stark, stony mountainous surface is turned to green, rolling meadow, and a spring of clear water, its origins a mystery, its purpose and beauty constant, draws all manner of troubled existence seeking solace. And again and again, the heart—buried deeply as ever in the human breast, its four chambers exposed to love and joy and pain and the small shafts that fall with desperation in between.

I sat at a narrow table, my head, heavy with sleep, resting on my hands. I dreamed of bands of men who walked aimlessly, their guns and cannons slackened at their sides, the chambers emptied of bullets and shells. They had fought in a field from time to time and from time to time they grew tired of it. They walked up the path that led to my house and as they walked they passed between the sun and the earth; as they passed between the sun and the earth they blotted out the daylight and night fell immediately and permanently. No longer could I see the blooming trefoils, their overpowering perfume a constant giddy delight to me; no longer could I see the domesticated animals feeding in the pasture; no longer could I see the beasts, hunter and prey, leading a guarded existence; no longer could I see the smith moving cautiously in a swirl of hot sparks or bent over anvil and bellows. The bands of men marched through my house in silence. On their way, their breath scorched some flowers I had placed on a dresser, with their bare hands they destroyed the marble columns that strengthened the foundations of my house. They left my house, in silence again, and they walked across a field, opposite to the way they had come, still passing between the sun and the earth. I stood at a window and watched their backs until they were just a small spot on the horizon.

I see my child arise slowly from her bed. I see her cross the room and stand in front of the mirror. She looks closely at her straight, unmarred body. Her skin is without color, and when passing through a small beam of light, she is made transparent. Her eyes are ruby, revolving orbs, and they burn like coals caught suddenly in a gust of wind. This is my child! When her jaws were too weak, I first chewed her food, then fed it to her in small mouthfuls. This is my child! I must carry a cool liquid in my flattened breasts to quench her parched throat. This is my child sitting in the shade, her head thrown back in rapture, prolonging some moment of joy I have created for her.

My child is pitiless to the hunchback boy; her mouth twists open in a cruel smile, her teeth becoming pointed and sparkling, the roof of her mouth bony and ridged, her young hands suddenly withered and gnarled as she reaches out to caress his hump. Squirming away from her forceful, heated gaze, he seeks shelter in a grove of trees, but her arms, which she can command to grow to incredible lengths, seek him out and tug at the long silk-like hairs that lie flattened on his back. She calls his name softly and the sound of her voice shatters his eardrum. Deaf, he can no longer heed warnings of danger and his sense of direction is destroyed. Still, my child has built for him a dwelling hut on the edge of a steep cliff so that she may watch him day after day flatten himself against a fate of which he knows and yet cannot truly know until the moment it consumes him.

My child haunts the dwelling places of the useless-winged cormorants, so enamored is she of great beauty and ancestral history. She traces each thing from its meager happenstance beginnings in cool and slimy marsh, to its great glory and dominance of air or land or sea, to its odd remains entombed in mysterious alluviums. She loves the thing untouched by lore, she loves the thing that is not cultivated, and yet she loves the thing built up, bit carefully placed upon bit, its very beauty eclipsing the deed it is meant to commemorate. She sits idly on a shore, staring hard at the sea beneath the sea and at the sea beneath even that. She hears the sounds within the sounds, common as that is to open spaces. She feels the specter, first cold, then briefly warm, then cold again as it passes from atmosphere to atmosphere. Having observed the many differing physical existences feed on each other, she is beyond despair or the spiritual vacuum.

Oh, look at my child as she stands boldly now, one foot in the dark, the other in the light. Moving from pool to pool, she absorbs each special sensation for and of itself. My child rushes from death to death, so familiar a state is it to her. Though I have summoned her into a fleeting existence, one that is perilous and subject to the violence of chance, she embraces time as it passes in numbing sameness, bearing in its wake a multitude of great sadnesses.

I hear the silent voice; it stands opposite the blackness and yet it does not oppose the blackness, for conflict is not a part of its nature. I shrug off my mantle of hatred. In love I move toward the silent voice. I shrug off my mantle of despair. In love, again, I move ever toward the silent voice. I stand inside the silent voice. The silent voice enfolds me. The silent voice enfolds me so completely that even in memory the blackness is erased. I live in silence. The silence is without boundaries. The pastures are unfenced, the lions roam the continents, the continents are not separated. Across the flat lands cuts the river, its flow undammed. The mountains no longer rupture. Within the silent voice, no mysterious depths separate me; no vision is so distant that longing is stirred up in me. I hear the silent voice—how softly now it falls, and all of existence is caught up in it. Living in the silent voice, I am no longer 'I'. Living in the silent voice, I am at last at peace. Living in the silent voice, I am at last erased.

The Walk

Faith reached up and unbuttoned the apron at the back. Let it drop to the front. Reached back and loosened the knot at her waist. Pulled off the apron and dropped it on to the barrel behind the door. She slumped on to the bench just inside of the kitchen door. She looked across at the fireside, at the scattered bits of wood, at the ashes cold and grey around the wood. Her eyes moved automatically towards the coal-pot, where a yellow butter-pan rested on partly burnt-out coals. She wondered whether Queen had prepared anything. To tell the truth, she was too tired to really care. She turned and looked at the bucket of water on the dresser, at the two pancups hanging from a nail above it. She took a deep breath, released it and let her head fall forward on to the rough board of the kitchen table.

'Oh God ah tired!' For a few moments, Faith remained like that, letting her body savour what it was like to be sitting down, letting it relax. And then her bottom registered that there was something hard on the bench. Faith's hand found the pebble, removed it. She sat up with a sigh and threw the pebble through the window over the shelf. Faith looked down at the floor. Yes. Queen had scrubbed it. A good child, when she put her mind to it.

Faith leaned back against the brown board of the partition and closed her eyes.

'Queen! Queenie oh! Bring some water give me!'

Queen came running. 'Mammie I didn't hear you come, non! And I look out the back window and I see light in the Great House still, and I see a lot of cars go up, so I say they having party, and . . .'

'All right. All right!'

Faith held the pancup with both hands, drinking the water in great gulps.

'Ah! Dat good! You boil de cocoa tea?'

'Yes, Mammie.'

'The lady pay me dis evening. I want you to go up for me tomorrow mornin.'

Queen sucked her teeth. 'Mammie I . . .'

'You what?' Faith sat up, her eyes demanding the response they defied her daughter to make. 'Look, child! If you know what good for you, move out of me eyesight, eh! You have to go up for me tomorrow and pay de society, an Cousin Kamay have the little pig mindin so I could turn me hand to something. I want you to pass and see if it drop already. You remember de house where I did show you Cousin Sésé daughter livin?'

'De house wid de green gate and the yellow curtain in the window?'

'So if they change de curtain you won't know de house?'

'Ay! Yes, Mammie, it have a big mammie apple tree in the yard.'

'Right. Pass there and tell Cousin Sésé daughter, Miss Ivy, I ask if de message ready already.'

'Yes, Mammie.'

Faith looked at her daughter standing beside the bucket of water, at her bony, long-legged frame in the baggy dress. She sighed. It would be a long walk, but Queen was used to it. She wished she didn't have to take the child away from school to make these errands, but what with living so far away and not being able to get a job nearer to the family! And she *must* pay the society. If she dropped down tomorrow morning, what would happen to Queen? A person must make sure to put by a little. You never know when you time would come without warning! And if the pig drop now, she could sell one and have enough to at least buy a little bed. And perhaps she might even be able to take out a better susu hand. Anyway, don't count you chickens! Just hope for the best. Just hope!

'Don't drink too much water, Queen. Next thing you know, you playin baby give me an wetting you bed. Is time for you to go an sleep. You have to get up early. You drink the coraile bush for the cold?'

'Yes, Mammie, an I make some bakes and put in de safe.'

'Good. That good. You a real help to me, yes. I don't know what I would do without you, child! Take de small lamp an go inside and sleep. Leave de masanto here for me. What light you sit down inside there with? You have a candle?'

'No, Mammie, I was just sitting down looking out of the back window at the Great House lights.'

'Sitting down in the dark, Queen? Why you didn't take the small lamp all the time?'

'Was only for a little while, yes, Mammie, after I finish clean up the kitchen.'

'All right, go on! Go on and get ready for bed!'

Queen took the lamp and walked out of the kitchen door. For just a moment she glanced to the left, at the quiet, dark outline of coconut trees.

But she didn't like the way the coconut trees rustled, and besides you could never trust a sudden breeze not to put the lamplight out.

Queen climbed the two wooden steps into the house, placed the lamp on the shelf and prepared for bed. She was thinking of the following morning's walk as she pulled the pile of bedding from under the sofa in the corner and spread it out. Queen did not like having to walk all the way to River Sallee. The road was long. She was always afraid to walk that long road. Queen stood for a long while staring at the lamp. She looked at the partition above the lamp, at the picture which had written on it, *God Save Our Gracious King*. Thrown over the top of this picture was her mother's chaplet, the cross resting on the king's forehead. Queen wasn't really *seeing* the picture. She was thinking. Wondering who and who was going to make that walk to River Sallee with her tomorrow morning. Who else was going up? In her hand was the old, torn dress that her mother no longer wore and which she was about to spread out on the floor over the other things already there. Queen walked to the door, her dress band trailing. She had already undone the fastener at the back, and the dress was drooping, baring one bony shoulder.

'Mammie! Cousin Liza goin up tomorrow too?'

'Yes. She goin to call for you early in the morning. You say you prayers yet?'

'No Mammie. I goin an say it now.'

Queen changed quickly, knelt down, bent her forehead to touch the sofa, and prayed aloud: 'Gentle Jesus meek and mild, look upon a little child!'

She lifted her head and looked at the crucifix over the bed. 'Papa God, help me to grow up into a big strong girl for me please. God don't let me die tonight or any other night please. Bless Mammie and Cousin Dinah and Maisie and Mark. Make the walk tomorrow not hard please and don't let me and Cousin Liza meet anything in the road. Bless Cousin Liza too and let me have a lot a lot of money when I get big please God. Amen.'

Still on her knees, Queen lifted her head.

'Good-night, Mammie.'

'Good-night, chile. Turn down de lamp low.'

'You not goin an sleep now, Mammie?'

'Yes. I just takin a little rest fus.'

'Well come and rest inside here, non, Mammie.'

'Queenie hush you mouth an sleep now. You pray already. Stop talkin like dat after you pray.'

About an hour later, Faith, having eaten some of the bake from the safe and allowed the day's weariness to seep from her body through the boards to the still, hot air outside, walked heavily up the two board steps and into the house. There was some noise as she passed briefly through the watching darkness; a cat scuttling, perhaps, a dog scratching, a frog hopping by. Faith didn't look around. She hardly heard them. The sounds of darkness were always with her. Nothing strange.

Her young Queen was fast asleep, mouth slightly open, left hand thrown wide and resting on the floor outside the bedding, the cover partly twisted around her waist. The mother stood staring for a moment, then stooped to straighten the piece of bedding which served as a cover and pulled it up over her daughter's body. She turned to the sofa, then sank to her knees and bowed her head. Faith spoke no words aloud. She talked silently to the Lord. Her last waking thoughts were, Today is the madam party. I wonder if Mr Mark suit . . .

When Cousin Liza pounded at the door on that February morning in 1931, it was still the time of day when everyone whispered. Dark and cold in the kind of way it never was when the sun came up. It was still the time that the trees claimed as their own as they whispered secrets against the sky. They whispered something when Cousin Liza knocked, and she looked around nervously, but they became silent then.

The walk from St David's to River Sallee was a long and arduous one. It was best started early. Queen was still half-asleep when they left. But the way Cousin Liza walked, sleep didn't stay around for long. It departed with a frown and an irritated yawn. Wide awake after the first few minutes, Queen pushed the straw hat more firmly on to her head, held the cloth bag securely on her shoulder, and kept running to keep up.

Cousin Liza had planned to start at five a.m. She must have made a mistake, though. Day was a long time coming, and the trees and the shadows and the frogs shouting in the drains kept insisting that it was still their time. They had been walking for more than two hours when the first glimmers of dawn appeared. At one time they had passed a house in which a light burned brightly. The man inside may have seen them, for the door was open. Into the darkness he shouted, 'Wey dis two woman goin at this hour?' and his feet pounded on the floor as though he were coming out to get them. If she had known who he was, Cousin Liza wouldn't be afraid, but you never knew with people who were up that late. They could be doing all sorts of things with the supernatural. So Cousin Liza pulled Queen and they pelted off down the road, feet flying on the broken pavement. After this, Queen was afraid, for she realized that Cousin Liza, too, talked with fear.

At one point, when they got to a place where the road forked in three directions, Queen did not find it strange to see a cock standing in the middle of the crossroads. She was accustomed to fowls. It was only when she felt Cousin Liza jerk her towards the drain that she froze. They passed in the drain at the side of the road and walked without looking back. Cousin Liza did not have to tell Queen it would be dangerous to look back. She *knew*! Queen's whole body was heart. It pounded with a painful thump that resounded in her steps. Her bare feet felt neither the stones in the road nor the effect of the miles. Suspended in a twilight between conscious thought and puppetry, she knew neither where she was nor where she was going to. And worse was yet to come.

They were making their way through a track in Hope, St Andrew's, which could cut down on the distance to Grenville town, when Queen pulled convulsively on Cousin Liza's hand. Liza's twenty-eight years on what she knew of earth had not given her the fearlessness that Queen expected her to possess. Queen stood, one hand now on top of the straw hat the brim of which framed her round face, the thick black plaits sticking out on both sides, the other hand lifted towards the distance. Liza froze. With a taut, tense movement she boxed down the child's shaking finger.

'Don't point,' she whispered hoarsely. 'Bite you finger,' she remembered to add.

On the hill next to the gravestone, something moved. No house was in sight. Above the watching women, the branches of the trees leaned across and linked leaves, touching each other caressingly in the stillness of the morning. The thing moved again. A pale light from a wandering, waning moon flashed across it and the thing bent towards them, beckoning, encouraging them forward. Queen's arms were thrown around Liza and she clung tightly, mouth open, the breath pushed from her throat to her lips in audible sobs, eyes wide with terror. Liza, body and hands hard with fear, held on to the child. She uttered no prayer with her lips, none in her heart. Her whole body was a throbbing prayer. Papa God! Papa God!

Whatever it was was quiet now. Still, no longer beckoning. The leaves above, too, had stopped their furtive caressing. Liza's feet moved. One quiet dragging step. Two, the left foot following because it couldn't go off on its own in a different direction. T-h-r-ee. Queen's body, with no will or separate identity of its own, did whatever Liza's did. The thing bent towards them. Queen screamed. With sudden decision, Liza dragged Queen along the edge of the track. And as this living fear drew level with the taunting thing above, it stopped in unbelief.

'Jesus!' said Cousin Liza. 'Jesus!'

The plantain leaf bowed again.

Queen, sobbing now with the release of terror, clung to Cousin Liza's hand and was dragged along the track. Her destination was daylight. It was only when the sky lightened and she could hear cocks crowing and see people moving about in the yards that she became once more a conscious being. She started to feel tired and told Cousin Liza that she wanted to rest.

They had been walking for seven hours and were in Paradise with the sun blazing down upon their heads when the bus from St David's passed them on its way to Sauteurs. Queen ate her coconut-drops and stretched out her tongue at the people looking back from the back seat of the bus. Years later, an older Queen learnt that the threepence she and Cousin Liza had spent to buy things to eat along the way could have paid a bus fare. Even though she had known then, the knowledge would have been of little use. Faith would have called her damn lazy if she had suggested going by bus.

'Liza, girl, you must be tired. How you do? Come, come, come girl. Come an sit down. Queenie, child, me mind did tell me you mother would send you up today.'

Cousin Kamay accepted their arrival as a matter of course.

'Constance, put some food in the bowl for Cousin Liza. Go in the kitchen an see what you get to eat, Queen. It have food dey. Help youself to what you want. How you mother?'

'She well tanks.'

'Well tanks *who*?'

'She well tanks, Cousin Kamay.'

Cousin Kamay watched her. 'Hm! You gettin big! These children nowadays you have to keep a eye on them yes. Go an see what you get to eat!'

The journey was over. In two days' time, after being about her mother's business, eleven-year-old Queen would leave again with Cousin Liza or whoever else happened to be making the trip to St David's. The one thing that remained to haunt her was the knowledge that the return trip would have to be made in darkness, when the sun was down, and when those who had to walk always made their journeys.

EDGARDO SANABRIA SANTALIZ (b. 1951)

After the Hurricane

Translated by Beth Baugh

I

After the hurricane, the house and the whole immense—and hours before—green and raised area of the coconut grove would appear completely desolate, covered with fish. One would see octopus, squid, and cuttlefish tentacles hanging from the cornices, opalescent, moist with a gentle teary lustre that would form slow phosphorescent puddles on the floor, a large curtain in tremulous tatters of stalactites in the round—as if the roof—or what remained of the roof—were melting beneath the hot grey mist that would still fall. Through the enormous hole between the tiles, through the unprotected shattered glass windows, torrents of spray would have burst, devastating everything, pulverizing the little fragile objects, pulling the heavy mahogany furniture from the floor in whirlpools and making it sail with the lightness of rafts from room to room, dragging some things forever, driving out others—pictures, carpets, an old pendulum clock—that would then be found kilometers away on the boundaries of the coconut grove, ornamenting the countryside. It would prove to be almost impossible to walk through the salons and to climb the stairs with all the sargasso tangling the feet, with all the moving water making it slippery: it would be easy to discover sea horses and starfish, purple or cinnamon-colored crabs of elusive and exquisite forms, conches, snails, minuscule fishes sparkling like gems in the drawers, within armoires and trunks, adhering to the backs of chairs, tables, and mattresses. One would find everything that could contain any volume of water—bathtubs, kettles, sinks, vases—in ebullient precipitation, overflowing with groupers, snappers, sturgeon by the dozens, sifting and showing an inanimate and perfectly circular eye for one, two seconds on the surface of that sea that would dazzle with its scanty proportions and absence of sand. Outside, looking from the detritus-filled terrace in the direction of the beach, not even a trace would be seen of the stone barrier that used to separate the sand from the smooth terrain of emerald grass in which the house was set. Only stretches of a filth of weeds mixed with sand and palm fronds, gravel, split coconuts: the avenue that would open the tottering rows of coconut palms would signal the passing of the Great Wave that came from the ocean in the most extreme moment of the cyclone.

When Acisclo Aroca returned from his hurried flight his eyes filled with tears of grief and consternation, and he had to cover his nose with a handkerchief against the stench of rotting shellfish that was beginning to spread all over, as was the black cloud of flies. It had been a sudden unavoidable flight, principally determined by the fact that Acisclo lived alone, almost never seeing anyone in a house that could have comfortably held an entire army: at the last minute, the horizon now filling with monstrous clouds, some fisherman from around there remembered him and gave warning. He hadn't time to take anything with him, even less to secure the windows or to gather up what loose things remained here and there. He escaped because he saw in the fisherman's terrified look—sweaty below the growing, pressing shadow—that what he was saying was true: 'Leave, or you won't wake here tomorrow!' Now, facing all this, he understood that the fisherman had been right. But he wasn't thanking him, he would have preferred a thousand times more to disappear with his possessions than to face what he was seeing. Nevertheless, at the crucial moment he didn't believe so much destruction was possible. He thought on his life, and that it was better to run the risk of some adequately reparable destruction than to lose the only thing that couldn't be replaced. Never had the idea of a similar devastation passed through his mind, that in one night what had taken him so many years to construct had been demolished.

Acisclo Aroca will walk alone through the ruins of his house. With his rubber boots he will move dead fish, fragments of tile, remains of objects. He will recognize them if he pays careful attention to retain some trace or appearance of yesterday. Painstakingly, he will travel from one room to another, from the first to the second floor, stopping now and then to bend over and pick something from the floor, and to contemplate it in his fingers, stupefied, as if he were dealing with a prehistoric tool or with something he might have seen in his childhood and that he just now came to remember. It's not possible, he will murmur, lost, as if he carried a useless compass in the middle of an infinite forest. In the last room he will turn in circles, already tired of the chaos, and he will begin the path again. Suddenly though, he will turn aside towards the terrace with the speed of someone heeding a summons. Going out into the afternoon air, Acisclo will look as though he has aged ten years. To the left, out of the corner of his eye, before finally orienting his vision in that direction, he will be able to make out the silver-blue luminosity of the swimming pool.

It looks to have suffered the least destruction of his property. Branches, leaves, and every kind of debris had accumulated around the spotless surface of the turquoise oval, creating the impression that the wind had refrained from flinging anything in or that someone had taken charge of cleaning any residue from the water. The pool reflects the platinum light of the huge clouds the hurricane has left behind; the mist (now tenuous, invisible) dots the smooth water, filling it with microscopic waves that break in concentric circles, as though created by the almost weightless alighting of an insect. Acisclo can't take his eyes off it. Time passes by him unnoticed. When he comes to (moving has broken the enchantment) he discovers that there is a burning elliptical sun floating between a tight string of clouds and the coconut palms that have remained standing: the ellipse of fire threatens to singe what remains of their lopped-off crowns. Again he turns his attention to the pool. When he focuses his gaze he notices, astonished, that his strange hours-long intoxication was in no way one of sight, but rather one of sound, a suspension such that he seemed to be seeing within sound. What he has been hearing is a sort of song, he doesn't know for certain if he can call it that, but he can't think of any other word to describe it. It is a song. The most inconceivably beautiful voice that he has ever heard in his life. Singing. The most extraordinary and supernatural music that human ears have heard.

Then he would see her for the first time. A barely perceptible agitation (not of breeze or lagging raindrops) at the center of the oval. A rising, fountainlike tremor. And suddenly the head crowned with orange coral would emerge, and then the thick, greenish, mossy hair, braided with pearls and covering her shoulders, her back, her breasts, each one in turn veiled by a clinging star stone. She would be looking directly at the terrace, inexplicably immobile in the deepest part of the pool, half submerged in the water that would now have taken on a pewter tone, gilded from the waist up by the slanting glare of late afternoon. She would no longer be singing (yes, it was she who was singing!) but the face turned towards him would be as wondrous as the voice. Never in his life would Acisclo Aroca forget that vision. A little while would pass before he asked himself what the woman was doing there, and seconds later the thought of having been conscious of the song long before she emerged would make him tremble.

Even though he climbed downstairs as quickly as the debris permitted, upon drawing near to the pool he didn't see the woman anywhere, neither in nor out of the water. Night had already almost fallen, the oval was a limitless eye with a half-closed eyelid, falling, hiding the diaphanous, sapphire-colored iris. Acisclo went around the pool several times, stopping when he called out—as if movement would have impeded the use of his voice—and then did the same thing around the structure of the house, finally arriving at the boundary where the entanglement of the bent, split, unearthed trunks of the coconut grove began. She couldn't have gone so soon, without leaving so much as a trace of her damp footprints. Unless . . . it had all been his imagination. But that was impossible, he had heard her, he had distinguished her so clearly! Where was she? How was she able to disappear like that? He approached the pool again. He then remained very quiet, his five senses concentrated on the dark and serene water. He was unconsciously moving his lips, as if counting the minutes a person is capable of withstanding a deep dive. Nothing happened. Now the oval looked like an eye that had hypnotized him. For an instant he believed he had fallen and was sinking—the moon had just risen and its reflection colored the air blue with the weightlessness of the ocean bottom. Suddenly the pool was a mirror through which clouds passed and stars swam. Drained, Acisclo moved back and sat in the grass, supporting his back against the trunk of some tree that had lost its branches in the night. His head nodded sleepily. The distinct, resurgent song, spreading as if exhaled from the heart of an opened and deadly flower (the song that he would have heard, had he been more awake) finished by lulling him to sleep.

Then he will see her again. He will find himself still reclining against the tree, dozing off; an unexpected splash will make him raise his head. She will be there. Appearing beyond the marble border of the pool, observing him with eyes like drops of the bluest ocean on earth. Acisclo will not dare to move, for fear that she will submerge and never rise again. The coral will shimmer under the moon, over her hair braided with pearls that will radiate an arcane inner light. Perhaps he will say (whisper) something like who are you, but he won't hear himself pronounce a single word. Later, when he makes a deliberate attempt to speak, she will draw back suddenly as if driven by his voice. She will swim in wide expert circles, with the undulating skill of a fish, her arms at her sides, her raised head leaving the green-white wake of her skin mingled with foam. A second before she disappears in the water, he will make out the sweeping iridescent tail. Without knowing how he got there, Acisclo will find himself on his knees at the pool's edge, leaning over the subtle reflection of his searching face. It will seem to him that centuries have passed before an almost imaginary fluctuation on the surface finally reveals itself, followed by the more fleeting representation of a figure hurriedly sliding by. Swift as lightning he will shoot out his arm, catch and remove something. When he takes the string of pearls from the water, their lustre will illuminate his face. Acisclo Aroca wakes up. In his hands he discovers the string of pearls gleaming in the sun.

II

The truck reappeared as soon as the sun set, bursting into the plaza from some street through which the nocturnal wave of murkiness and stars advanced. At once it proceeded to circle the tree-lined rectangle a number of times—secret, stealthy—like an animal searching for somewhere to rest. The old men sitting in a row on the long half-moon-shaped concrete bench turned their heads in time to see it make its slow entrance. It passed in front of them (its dark blue brimming with shoals of luminescent decal art) and, turning off the headlights in the very center, stopped to one side of an arbor blown over a short while before by the hurricane. It was the same enormous, outlandish truck that had gone through the pueblo that afternoon, deafening everyone with its loudspeaker (as the crow flies, or from the top of the belfry, it would have been easy to follow it by ear through the maze of streets). It was a navy blue truck, covered with decals of fish, that ended by circling around and around the plaza, from where the echo reverberated, moving away through the series of side-streets that fed into it. Then the truck had gone into one of them and disappeared, creating an unusual momentary silence everywhere, as if it had robbed the entire village of sound. Now it was here again, and a man got out, who seemed with his glance to take in the atmosphere of the public park and the white and gravid heights of the temple, dotted with already sleeping doves. He moved towards the back part of the vehicle and struggled with the doors for a while: from inside he brought out several bolts of a greyish material that he unrolled on the ground. In about half an hour the bolts proved to be canvas, forming a small tent attached to the truck. The entrance to this sort of country house was covered with an arch of multi-colored lightbulbs that, once turned on, outlined three shining words: THE BEAUTIFUL MELUSINE in the black air of the night. At once the man went inside like a mollusk into the shell, and he didn't show himself again until the town clock struck eight. By then the line of spectators already extended several times around the square of the plaza.

Upon entering they are received all of a sudden by a man who holds a kind of large money-box in his hands (like the ones held in churches by those wooden surplice-clad altarboys with lifelike gaze and the size of an eleven-year-old child) in which the cost of admission is deposited. Crammed into the space behind the man a dolphin-print curtain reveals, when moved to one side, another space, six times larger and filled with chairs—some twenty in all—which face an opening with no canvas: there the back of the truck shows its closed doors. A single lightbulb hangs from the tent like an enormous drop of honey ready to fall on the audience. Once the seats are all occupied, the man appears and stops further entry into the tent by zipping the curtain shut. Then he turns and passes through the curving border of light outlined on the dirt floor. He walks to the front, faces the public, and begins to speak with an impassive expression in which it is impossible to detect any sentiment or thought, as if he spoke in a dream, or like someone who was releasing words from the ungraspable interior of a memory or a vision. He reaffirms what the loudspeaker had proclaimed earlier (that they are present for a fantastic, incomprehensible, unforgettable spectacle), but on his lips, the assertion had lost that quality of coarse clamorous propaganda, turning instead into a smooth dreamlike recitation. He says they are going to come face to face with a being of fable, a glorious sea creature of which the world has heard tell since the beginning of time, although no one has ever, ever seen her. Only now, thanks to the formidable power of the whirlwind that whipped the island weeks before, had she been torn from the icy shadowy abyss in which she reigned and dragged towards the coast where he himself had the fortune to recover her. They, those who listened to him that night, were the first human beings to set eyes on Melusine. 'Here she is,' he concludes quickly. . . . He turns his back to the wall of the auditorium and heads towards the truck and opens the doors wide. One, two, three lights go on in rapid sequence, aiming towards the interior where something glazed, sparkling, green-in-blue flashes, framed by strips of gleaming nickel. No sooner does the blindness dissipate than, one by one, they begin to glimpse, peering in, amazed at the proportions of the giant fish tank.

III

From time to time he would ask himself amazedly if what was happening was real. Had he torn away those pearls that illuminated his fingers with a lustre that stayed in his nails? Contemplating the pearls, had he perceived the control he could attain and thanked his luck which, along with desolation, had sent him relief? Had it actually occurred to him to sell them (although he saved three or four so as not to lose influence over her), acquire the truck and have the colossal fishtank lodged in the cargo area? Afterwards had he really cast the net into that caricature of an ocean (to which she surely must have acclimated herself by now, resigned, reduced to going around in circles like an ornamental fish in its aquarium), to catch the fish that he never imagined in his dreams, a fish of queer unattainable beauty that existed nevertheless because he carried it (carried it?) there in the back, in dark murky water, stirred by the countless jolts and bumps of streets and roads, plowing through the swell of the mountains, from village to village behind the demolition spread by the hurricane? Did he now habitually park the truck at night on the outskirts of the villages, withdrawing into jungles of yagrumos and bamboo, and shut himself up in the back, seated between the bolts of canvas, opposite the gleaming fishtank? Did he then awaken quite numb and open up to the breeze, to the first light of the morning, disoriented, surveying the sky full of birds, the vegetation, astonished that the world was not submerged, that it didn't partake of the water except for a short while, when it rained; that it was inhabited by people (of which he, unfortunately was one) who fled, opening parasols and umbrellas, or who feared drowning in rivers or in the sea. Was it true that he avoided stopping twice in the same village, because he had realized that those who entered to see her left with their gaze turned in upon themselves, flickering in short bursts, and that with enraptured faces they asked to see her again as if inside they had surrendered the power, the will that they had exercised over themselves minutes before? And was he filled with fear because he knew (knew?) from his own experience the irreconcilable consequences that a second examination of the roseate, phosphorescent breasts (as if made of the most downy sand of the ocean depths); of the scaly hip, embellishing the silvered water in a dancing boil of swishing tail; of the voice, whose echo could take over and settle forever in the hearer's soul could bring? But he would know that he wasn't dreaming when what would happen happened.

That night, for the first time, he recognizes the three men. He has already visited almost all the towns on the island, he has spent weeks going through cities neighborhood by neighborhood. Thousands of people have filed through the tent, casting short, perplexed looks at the crystal coffer of his treasure; it is frankly impossible to remember so many faces of women, children and men. But he identifies these three as the three that he has seen the day before yesterday and yesterday (yes, it's them, that's all there is to it!) entering and leaving during the stops he has made in the last two towns. The great numbers of people, the severe exhaustion that he has already begun to feel—months of travel which have raced by like so many hours, all of it indistinct: alone, driving, making stops, setting up the tent, taking it down and driving, solitary apostle of something that doesn't know (does it?) for certain what it is, impelled by the unshakable incandescence he harbors—perhaps these are the reasons he hasn't taken notice of them. Three big brown guys with black moustaches, mustard colored teeshirts with stains of sweat at the armpits and greasy mechanic's overalls. He trembles from head to toe. He decides to take drastic action: when he comes to the end of that group, he announces to the large line of customers still remaining that the show has been cancelled. The customers protest but they finally disperse, seeing that the man has begun to dismantle the tent. That night, instead of following the planned route, he travels in the opposite direction towards a tiny village in the mountains, far away and not easily accessible. But on the following night, when he opens for spectators, the same three men appear, and this time their swollen lips break into sarcastic little smiles as they avidly pay their entry fee. Now the persecution is a certainty. As best he can, he cancels the show once again and leaves the village after driving about the deserted streets a dozen times to assure himself that no one is following him. That night he hides the vehicle on a road funneled into the brush and shuts himself up in the back to contemplate the fishtank with sponge-like eyes that want to drink in all the water. When he notices the morning light penetrating the crack between the doors, he stands up and opens them. At the very instant he jumps to the ground he hears a motor starting and turning, discovers through the dustcloud it is making the truck moving off. After a second of paralysis he gives chase, but he is unable to catch up. The mermaid thrashes her tail in the silvery water, frightened by the giddy vision of the countryside and that man, ever smaller, waving his arms like an octopus. The man hears bursts of laughter mixed with the dust and monoxide which he breathes while crying out and gasping.

He will know he wasn't dreaming when he finds himself alone on that back road. He will know definitely that it wasn't a hoax, that the creature enclosed in the fishtank was superhuman, when he no longer feels the influence of her presence. It will be as if he himself were a being who spent hundreds of years submerged under the sea, and who someone suddenly took from the water. During the unbearable minute of suffocation another type of world will enter through his terrified and incredulous eyes, a world which, no sooner than he discovers it, annihilates him. He will take a few steps as if trying out the impossible sense of balance coming from this pair of extremities that have replaced his tail. He will open his mouth but rather than bubbles a shout will come out: Melusine. He will begin to run again. Melusine. At some moment on the road he will trip and fall on his face in the dust: four pearls will come rolling out of his shirt pocket. They will roll towards the grass like luxurious insects that he will start trapping. With the four of them in the palm of his hand, a lunatic giggle will escape him. The polished luminescence will make him happy, their possession will show him the way, finding her is inevitable, nothing else can happen while he has them. He won't know the time that has passed walking, sleeping beneath the trees, eating fruit and roots, asking all if they have seen a truck of such and such appearance. Slowly he will go, descending the mountains towards the sea. The sea. His hopelessness will be so great when he faces it that he will hurl the pearls over the precipice. He will regret this immediately. Looking over the rocky edge he will see the truck, smashed at the foot of the precipice, at the very edge of the water where the waves are soaping with foam the already rusting body.

The back doors were open, one hanging by the top hinge, the heavy panes of glass of the fishtank crushed, and nothing inside, not a trace of her ever having been there. The same thing in the front seats of the truck. The men had disappeared, perhaps the undercurrents had dragged the bodies (how were they going to survive a fall from such a height?) and they would now be three skeletons at the bottom of the ocean, their flesh food for the fish, sea-moss, and coral beginning to colonize the bones, schools of fish swimming through the ribcage of each one. The truck was pushed nose-first into the waves, up to the shattered windshield. Acisclo sat in the sand, distressed and worn out. His eyes wandered from the shore to the horizon, from the horizon to the shore, while he called to her with his mind, not wanting to think about the overturning and the violent impact of the fall. The whole rig, months and months of effort lost as if the hurricane had struck again. But nothing was as important to him as the fact that she had disappeared. What was he going to do now? How was he going to be able to live without her company? He would have preferred to find her dead to not knowing where she was. Suddenly he began to crawl around the beach: the pearls, the pearls, if he found them it could be that . . . But he didn't see them anywhere. He had thrown them in an attack of frustration, never imagining he would find what he was seeking at the very edge of the sea. No, he couldn't see them, couldn't find them. He was an enormous and absurd baby clambering from one side to the other and wailing. After a while he went back to sitting and remained immobile for a long time. The waves wet his heels, there were shadows of seagulls sliding in circles over the sand. When his hope was at the point of evaporating he thought he saw something shiny carried in and out by the surf. He jumped and rolled until enclosing it in his fist. He felt something take hold of his wrist below the water. When he pulled, the milk white, delicate hand emerged, grasping him with the virulence of a giant clam. At first he tried to free himself, but gave up when in front of his head—which now floated in the sea up to his chin—appeared that magnificent head that looked at him, laughing. It didn't even cross his mind to shout when a second hand gripped his other wrist with equal force. He felt the viscous tail striking against his legs while she maneuvered into the sea. Then, with his ears already plugged with water, he heard the song, bidding him welcome.

PATRICK CHAMOISEAU (b. 1953)

Red Hot Peppers

Translated by Barbara Lewis

When she arrived from the hilly region of Martinique's Morne-aux-Gueules, Anastasia made Mom Gaul's spirits soar. The old woman dropped her basket of weariness and pulled laughs and smiles from a forgotten place in her head. Feeling as soft as the heart of a coconut, she hugged Anastasia every day and murmured to her: My child, *ichewe mwen*, this is where you belong . . .

At that time Mom Gaul was selling potato curls fried in rape oil to support herself. The old woman spent her days tending four oil-filled cauldrons while Anastasia peeled the potatoes. At night they put on fresh clothes. Mom Gaul wore a long-sleeved blouse and a starched skirt that had been ironed so often it was shiny. Each of them carried a bucket of fries as they followed the set course that Anastasia made through the center of town. Mom Gaul knew in advance where to sell her fries, and before refilling any orders, she made sure she collected a deposit from every single bar in town.

The purple sky was alive with fireflies when they walked through the park. Couples were relaxing in the fresh air under the tamarind trees. Children darted between the carts of the peanut vendors, delighting in their newfound freedom on the noisy paths. Mom Gaul and Anastasia walked slowly along the boardwalk, inhaling deeply and breathing in the salt spray from the nearby sea. They sold their fries to young girls lingering around the bandstand, their heads filled with dreams of passion, their hearts open.

So life wove itself without too much sparkle or misery through the days of the two women, around the nasal voice of Ching the Chinaman who dispensed sacks of potatoes and a ready smile for faithful clients. Anastasia forgot Morne-aux-Gueules, her friends Fefee, Ti-Choute, and the others. With the earnestness of a single woman, she became completely absorbed in her new life selling fries. It wasn't long before she developed into a full-breasted, beautiful young girl, with just enough quiver and excitement under her skin that love, always on hand, merely waited to deal her its cards of joy and pain.

Mom Gaul suffered with her back. Sometimes it got so bad Anastasia would have to go to the market by herself. She took on Mom Gaul's rhythm and her short, heavy steps, her rollicking Barbadian saunter, and even, to some extent, her silhouette, which curved like a coconut palm in the wind. Completely baffled by this pretty flower who walked just like an old sorceress, the young men never talked to her of love, dances, or strolls, and never noticed the sway in her hips. This pattern was broken one evening. Zozor Alcide-Victor, a clear-skinned mulatto with curly, impeccably groomed hair, had limpid eyes that missed nothing, and on rainy days, they reflected the dark green color of dame-jeanne bottles of rum.

Ladies and gentlemen, Zozor Alcide-Victor was the product of a clandestine love affair between a Syrian and his servant. When the Syrian community heard that someone in their group was having conjugal relations with a Negress, they put him on solemn notice during one of their gatherings around a huge radio transmitting programs in Arabic. They threatened the expectant father with a boycott that would force him to sell off his stock and close his store. Terrified, the father of Zozor Alcide-Victor rushed to the woman whose ears he had been filling with promises of undying love, giving her instead the usual excuse. 'No, the child can't bear my name, but I won't neglect him, you can be sure of that. I'm his father, and may Allah punish me if I ever forget him.'

After a lonely year, sustained by bitterness and the public dole, and taking full measure of Allah's indifference, Zozor Alcide-Victor's mother had to rely on a bottle of acid and a pair of scissors to recall the worthless father to his promises if not his responsibilities. The Syrian community saw the damage to their obedient brother and put their heads together around the mighty radio. They found a solution to the problem that risked drawing the spotlight of unwelcome attention to their comfortable and prosperous existence.

So despite the absence of his father, from his infancy Zozor Alcide-Victor had a fabric store located near the marketplace, between China's Place and Ching the Chinaman. This windfall allowed him to spend his obligatory school years snoring beside his inkwell, beyond the reach of the marvels of French culture. Without this boon, he would have had to beg bread from the dogs. With the revenue from his store placed in trust, he set about his noisy, even licentious life, the cause of sentimental suffering for women of every hue. He counted 1,807 Negresses, 650 mulattoes, 400 chabines, numerous quadroons, albinos, and half-blooded Indians, two Chinese, and an entire regiment of octoroons among his conquests. He was already notorious when he emerged from under the shadows of the bandstand, where he loitered in the fresh air, to make his advance toward Anastasia and her studied way of walking.

Zozor Alcide-Victor bought her whole bucket of fries in one stroke and then with a lordly hand gave them all away to the children. He said two words to her, maybe four, and kept her company for about five hundred yards. Then he bowed graciously, expressing his distress about having to leave so quickly but assuring her they would see each other again very soon. All this was accomplished with such ease, aplomb, smiles, and modulated tones, such tentative brushings with the tips of the fingers, such liquid looks capturing glints of moonlight, and a volley of such precise French that Anastasia felt queasy right down to the tips of her toenails for the next few days. That evening, when she realized he wasn't waiting for her near the bandstand, an intense and inexpressible bitterness overwhelmed her. (Oh, you young girls all dewy with anticipation, you sweet and innocent blossoms of morning, yes, you tender shoots eager to grow: your harvest is not an arching toward the sky, but a thrust of the knife. Beware, beware of love!)

Anastasia lost her taste for life. The cauldrons no longer amused her. The glistening fries nauseated her. Mom Gaul's banter bored her. So she wrapped herself in a sweet and dreamy melancholy. Understanding nothing, the old woman thought she was in the clutches of some spell, and took pains to fortify her blood. She sought recourse in a suitable countercharm after she saw Zozor Alcide-Victor headed straight for them one evening in the park. He offered a conquering hand to Anastasia, whose sturdy legs crumbled under her in an excess of emotion. Mom Gaul understood immediately! Zozor Alcide-Victor held the young girl up as he questioned the old woman who was looking at him pointedly: Was she in pain . . . ? The evidence was plain. The seducer was sure of his victory, but Mom Gaul's hostility forced him to make the purchase of two bags of fries, a show of hasty homage before he disappeared quickly into the shadow of the bandstand.

His reappearance sent Anastasia even deeper into melancholy. The old woman ministered to her loss of appetite and weight and faded complexion, resistant to cup after cup of lemon balm tea. All to no avail. Whenever she went to sell, Mom Gaul avoided the park. But her back began to bother her again, and she had to resign herself to sending Anastasia to the market alone. With the same wisdom that denies rivers the power to carry away what fate holds, she said without illusion or conviction: Don't go near the park. The young girl stayed away the first two nights. On the third night, annoyance numbed her defenses and drew her steps to the forbidden place. Zozor Alcide-Victor, handsome, smiling, and available, found her there, just as in the worst Italian novels. Seeing her alone and trembling, he pulled out his repertory of great stories, his tales of heroism during the state of emergency and the hours of alarm, which permitted him one, two, three, to lure the love-blind girl under the tamarind tree where he regularly carried out his impromptu seductions. He thrilled her with unsuspected joys and strange pangs and sent her soaring to unprecedented heights, adding his tribute of moans and impossible tears to the pleasure.

Later, Mom Gaul saw her on the doorstep looking like a bird disoriented by the rain, her eyes misty and her body limp, and she knew that the inevitable had happened. She inveighed against her with bitter words, comparing her to Saint Peter's women, good-time girls for sailors temporarily in port. Anastasia said nothing. For days, she said nothing. Shut like a shell around the happiness she had discovered, she paid no attention to the old woman's distress. When the market day ended, Anastasia headed straight for the park, passing half the night there, and then she returned home looking more foggy than a road in the Red Hills. One night, Mom Gaul followed her and surprised Zozor Alcide-Victor, who already had his arms open to his new conquest.

'You no-good dirty pig of a monkey dog, why don't you leave my little girl alone?'

No stranger to this kind of aggression, the seducer calmly faced Mom Gaul and let loose a tirade of incomprehensible French that froze her on the spot. Then he left quietly, Anastasia hanging on his arm, heading for the aphrodisiac shade of his usual tamarind tree.

This episode widened the gap between the two women. They didn't even look at each other any more. Anastasia stopped fixing the potatoes altogether. Mom Gaul lost her smile, her wrinkles reappeared, and she resumed her habit of selling alone. The little shack began to resemble a hole containing two male crabs. This marred the new happiness of Anastasia to such an extent that Zozor Alcide-Victor noticed and solved the problem. It wasn't really a problem, he said, it's only a matter of getting a new place to stay. I'll find one for you . . .

That's how Anastasia left Mom Gaul. She paid the rent on her shack by selling a rainbow of desserts at the end of her street. During recess at the

Perrinon school she set her tray before the gates, and the kids danced around her. In time, Mom Gaul forgot her bitterness. She paid frequent visits to the former light of her life. At first she brought casseroles, knives, sheets. Then she came just to talk, for friendship, and stayed, dreading the return to her newly dull shack. She also avoided Zozor Alcide-Victor, who came often, apparently devoted to his new conquest . . .

Pepi also loved Anastasia and wasn't at all discouraged by the news of a love affair between these two beautiful people. He held on tight to his first crazy hope. Smelling of cologne, he called on Anastasia regularly, on Sunday and during the week, at night and at noon. He brought litchi nuts, mangos, and other delicacies. When he showed up on her better days, he managed to get one or two smiles from her. But in the marketplace, Pepi seemed as cloudy as a mountain top. His eyes never rested anywhere. He often remained immobile, victimized by his dreams. Mom Eli, his mother, teased him: 'What's her name, son?' His visits began to bore Anastasia. She no longer smiled and refused his fruits, finally suggesting gently that he shouldn't come any more. What would the neighbors think, and what if Zozor . . . ?

Pepi's dreams faded for the second time. He started to drink alone, at any hour, without the slightest thirst, and he began to stagger in the alleys, singing profane songs about Saint Peter that upset Mom Eli and offended some of the female vendors who were Christian. Neglecting his duties at work, he unfurled a stream of nonsense words, and ended his days sprawled out on the widest sidewalks. We thought it was all over for him when he stopped changing his overalls, darkly stained with vomit and the filth of the gutters. In the worst moments of his delirium, he camped under Anastasia's window, singing love couplets at the top of his voice to the girl who eluded and afflicted him.

One day she came out, took him by the hand, and, bracing him, led him into her house. She cleaned his face with a cloth dipped in cologne and hot water, smoothed his hair which had grown to twice its usual length, and refreshed his body. She wrapped him in a clean sheet and then washed his clothes. He was in ecstasy, letting Anastasia take charge of him while he followed her movements with a dazzled gaze. She spoke to him gently, and ironed his shirt and pants dry. Pepi bent his head, hypnotized. She dispelled his alcoholic fog with salted coffee; then suddenly he fell asleep across the chair. She had to wait for Mom Gaul to come in order to get him into bed. Instead of the usual aimless talk during their evenings together, the two women now took hold of the lover sleeping off his rum. They woke him up for a bowl of thick soup and two dried sardines.

Mom Gaul left, and Pepi and Anastasia remained face to face, eyeing each other from behind the steam rising out of their bowls. He might have embraced then and there the one who consumed his soul. Her gestures were full of gentleness, and her look compassionate. But destiny was pitiless, and the old hall began to creak with Victor's dancing step. When her seducer opened the door, Anastasia was already shooing Pepi out with both hands. In his perpetual rum fog, Pepi walked right into ruin, explaining incomprehensible things to the angels. It wounded us to see him mumbling to himself when things were slow at the cash register.

He was wrenched from passion's abyss when Mom Gaul died suddenly. The old woman's lifeless body was found sitting up very straight behind her buckets, drawing everyone into a net of sadness. Her skin had the gray ashiness of volcanic debris. Pepi came to his senses. He took her in his arms and carried her to her shack across town. He was busy at the side of Anastasia, Bidjoule, and Mom Eli, taking papers to town hall, finding a coffin. At the wake, his eyes never rested on Anastasia, praying silently. Two days after the funeral, taking up his wheelbarrow again and returning to work, he climbed to the top of the fountain, compelling the market to silence while he cried out:

'Mom Gaul, despite the misery you suffered, your eyes never lost the radiance that comes with appreciation and an understanding of life and all growing things . . .'

Hearing this homage, we all began to flood the earth with our tears— Bidjoule alone had dry eyes.

Even today, despite the pain and trouble that these memories excite, we still see the good times we enjoyed after the war, and a nostalgic wave washes over us. That was a damn good market season! We took pride in our work and we were the best, Didon, Sirop, Pin-Pon, Lapochode, and Sifilon, and despite our graying hair we all thought we were indestructible. Bidjoule had so much vigor and so did Pepi, this great laborer with whom we identified. Seeing him overcome the fatality of his monstrous father and that impossible love for Anastasia proved he was solidly planted in life, hard and resistant as barwood. True, there was some bitterness in his look, one or two wrinkles in his forehead, but at noon in the market, he displayed his astonishing energy in the midst of the peasant women and in the furor of work—he was royal. We did not yet know that suffocation was pressing down on him, and on us too.

Something terrible happened to remind us of the wages and the wonders of time: Mom Eli was reading the newspaper, and began to moan, 'Oh my

God, Oh my God!' Fearing some awful news about Pepi, we rushed in screaming: BLASTIT! . . . the only worthwhile exorcism we had against destiny.

'Anastasia is in jail!' cried our queen, powerless.

We had only suspected Anastasia's agony, but we saw it all very clearly when Mom Eli spelled out each word in the article. We knew that Zozor Alcide-Victor had given her quite a bit of attention at first. Then he had made himself as scarce as a piece of meat in wartime. Patiently, the faithful woman would wait for him, her shoulder pressed against a corner of the window, softly kneading a wad of sweet dough. Driven by nagging desires, her seducer would appear only to spread her flat against the kitchen table, between bits of eggshell and dustings of flour. Then he promptly disappeared without saying where he was going or when he would return. Weeks would then pass. The old hallway no longer reverberated with the tiptap of his nimble foot.

Because of her constant heartache, Anastasia began to resemble a dull, dry coconut, something that stunned us all. Fighting apathy, she lost herself as she made the cakes and numbed her mind with the nonstop motion required to fix her desserts. Preserving the green papayas didn't take as much concentration as she focused on the process, but it was only by exerting herself regularly and meticulously over the pots that she staved off her distress. The days began to repeat themselves: anxious waiting by the window, selling at the school gates, and the staccato appearances of Zozor Alcide-Victor, who grabbed her without saying anything. On Thursday night, she would slip into red shoes splashed with white flowers and go sniff the park's night air. She would forget herself in the sharp odor of the fallen tamarinds and prowl around the tree where the man who had crushed her heart conducted his sacrifices.

Soon she started living like a recluse without even the desire or courage to appear in the sunlight. Her shutters stayed closed. Her hair came out in clumps. Her beautiful plum-skinned complexion grew as dull as avocados picked in the rain. She no longer chased the dust from her hut but made her desserts mechanically, watching them pile up in the corners of her two rooms, smelling of rancid sugar and attracting ants and flies. From then on, her life transpired completely in her head, where she had Zozor all to herself. She imagined him always present and extremely attentive. That's why she spoke in such a soft voice, and smiled so often as if in the throes of a private joy.

The wretched woman's decline didn't at all affect Zozor Alcide-Victor, recent devotee to strange pleasures, who smoked *ganja* from Guyana and indulged himself in the peculiar pleasures of sodomites. Anastasia was now turned on her stomach under his assaults and this filled her with shame. Consumed by this new craving, the man who dominated her heart pushed her face against the kitchen table sticky with sugar or into the corrupted sheets on the straw mattress, depriving her of the sight of his beautiful face, radiant with the sacred pleasure she gave him. That was the worst. That was the one frustration that sealed the destiny of the Syrian bastard, proving that one can trifle with a monkey but can only go just so far.

One day, at the end of one of Victor's long absences when her inner sun had eclipsed under the incessant rain, Anastasia slid a kitchen knife into her blouse as soon as the bastard's step resounded in the hall. As usual, he burst into the room like a gust of wind, then, after pushing her over on her stomach, penetrated his love slave. He came quickly, reciting an Arabic poem during his orgasm. Sitting on the bed while Anastasia cleaned herself up, he sanctimoniously smoked a cigarette which gave him time to gather his strength for a second go-round. He was enjoying the languor of his muscles, and didn't notice Anastasia's fixed stare or her robotic way of walking as she approached him. She had almost touched him when he pushed her away with his hand, thinking she was already begging for another ride: Come on, Anastasia, you can wait a minute, can't you? . . . At the first blow, the knife sank behind his left clavicle. The second grazed some ribs and pierced his lung. The third severed his carotid artery. When the fourth blow disemboweled him, he was dead. At least that's what the medical expert said later in the report presented before the court.

She was imprisoned in the women's section of the main penitentiary. The police had discovered her lovingly curled around the bastard's body, singing softly in his ear the same Creole lullabies that old women croon to sick children. Anastasia was put into solitary confinement and watched over by a female guard dressed in white. The guard knitted doilies that she sold to her friends to tide her over the difficult times at the end of the month. the prisoner learned how to make Caribbean baskets, a now forgotten art. The empty little section surrounded by deserted cells added an unreal echo to their voices. The woman on night duty came at seven. The two women ate together by the light of the bulb in the little dining area. Anastasia might just as well be there as somewhere else, what did it matter?

Pan for Pockot

The black fist punched the flour-sack curtain. Then the black, emaciated face was shrieking, 'Stop beating that pan, Pockot. You want to deafen me and Mister Harris? Night and day you playing that Jerusalem song as if you want the saints in heaven to hear you.'

Lady Emelda broke out into coughing. 'This dust giving me asthma.'

From the bedroom, adjoining the kitchen, Mister Harris was also heard to cough. He was a retired engineer, whose meagre pension assured him lodging in this shack of Corbeaux City.

'Pockot,' she called hoarsely, 'just now you has to go to work in the grocery across the city.'

The boy, somewhat tall for sixteen, removed the pan from around his neck, and thrust two sticks tipped with red rubber into his rear pocket.

Lady Emelda quietly marvelled at the creation of her son. Three months ago Pockot was hammering away at the oildrum, brought back from the smoking dump. Squatting before blue-green flames he tapped out day-by-day circles, ellipses, and ovals, upon which from memory he impressed thirty-two distinct notes.

With hammer and punch he dotted the shapes containing the quavers, semi-quavers, and demi-semi-quavers. He was the creator of the Ping Pong, the smallest but sweetest of the other tuned oildrums—the bass, the cello, and the guitar. The schoolmaster was outraged; he flogged the boy for sacrilege, for reproducing those notes of his piano on some rusting pan! Pockot was expelled from the school.

Already he bore a stigma: before his birth Lady Emelda had stabbed the man alleged to be his father.

Yet somehow Lady Emelda had found her son a job in a grocery operated by a Portuguese gentleman, one of her former patrons at the city's Breakfast Shed where she had been a prosperous food-vendor.

'Ah,' she sighed, gazing out at the smouldering dump.

'That day when I see the boy sawing that oildrum in two, I say he was making he poor mammy a washtub. But the boy just like his good-for-nothing father who used to collect free oildrums from British and American ships and sell them to steelband leaders for big profit.'

Mister Harris coughed.

Lady Emelda shouted, 'Boy, go throw 'way these crab-back before they stink up the place. I already late making Mister Harris callaloo.'

Sadly she recalled, 'Is my sins I paying for. But only the Lord know I didn't mean to . . .'.

She saw herself again the prosperous but lonely food-vendor listening to the short stevedore, thumping his thigh with a bar of newsprints. Despite the scars about his face, Lady Emelda had yet found him more pleasing than either Mister Harris or her Portuguese patron.

So, one wet afternoon, she let herself be coaxed down to the wharf. The tide was out. Along the blue-warped carpet of mud, slimy stumps with dark-grey oysters dotted the shoreline. Lady Emelda shivered; the air smelled. Scores of tiny crabs and swollen fish lay lifeless in the mud. The darkening sky with the red blur of sun dipping down behind the blue haze into dark blue waters awed her. She would have turned back but onwards the stevedore had coaxed. Soon the scarlet ibis, those lively, red-plumed birds, would be feeding freely among the mangroves, unaware of squatting tourists taking snapshots of them.

Lady Emelda had groaned aloud. Whorls of sandflies hovered over her. Even the newsprints under her were damp.

Next morning, the rascal stevedore was taunting her about the scarlet ibis. The next moment, food-vendors—women supporting lovers or parasitic husbands—were shrieking with petrified patrons. Newsprint damp with blood shrouded the collapsed form. The woman was promptly dismissed from the Breakfast Shed. Six months later in court only Mister Harris was there for her; he signed the bond for the pregnant Lady Emelda.

'This ungrateful boy, beating that blasted pan just to drive out Mister Harris from the shack—where is he?' she asked of the two corbeaux fluttering down. 'Ah, Pockot deafening you birds too.'

Mister Harris coughed.

The two carrion-birds darted off from the tree outside her kitchen window. The wind with stench had winnowed the skeletal branches of most of its leaves. At the roots garbage mounted about the trunk shorn of its bark. Fierce pariah dogs combated among themselves for skeletons of fish sucked dry or bones already scraped of their meat.

Lady Emelda regretting her son's birth: 'I should of toss the child in the dump. Just another roasted stray-dog they would think the next morning. Or shove the bastard in a floursack and throw it in the Dry River on a rainy day.'

Seeing Pockot emerging from the blacksage bushes, she sighed, 'My cross, my cross . . .'.

Pockot marched in with the pan on his head.

'Always be grateful to you boss. Nobody decent does hire anybody from this slum. But you mammy promise the Potogee you giving up that pan and planning to take up some decent instrument like a guitar or something . . .'.

Lady Emelda thought she heard coughing from the bedroom.

Loudly she reminded—'You hear last night with you own two ears how me and Mister Harris quarrelling the same bitter quarrel about that pan.'

It was always Mister Harris's conviction that the pan was like an African drum, transmitting sounds for violence. He was quick to mention how ready panmen during Carnival celebration crashed those oildrums on rival bands. The bevelled edges were like meat cleavers which with knives, ice-picks, and painted cutlasses, panmen gashed, stabbed and hacked away at their rival steelbands. It was a worse experience for doctors— sewing up stomachs, stitching arms, legs, and faces. For the police, steel-band violence was worse than revolutions.

'But that pan still keeping Pockot out of mischief,' was all Lady Emelda meekly argued.

Pockot was not clipping clothes-lines or filching undergarments left overnight soaking in oildrums of soapy water. He did not rustle up scrub-boards or furniture neglected just for a moment in broad daylight. He was not looting, like other young men around, throwing rocks at the train, or stripping cars of parts. He was not rustled up like the others for the recent robbery of a cloth-pedlar in Corbeaux City. Didn't even Mister Harris himself testify that at the time of the robbery Pockot was playing 'Jerusalem, the Golden' outside the shack?

While she combed his hair, Lady Emelda warned, 'You don't get rid of that pan, Mister Harris threat'ning to leave.' She sniffed his kerchief. 'Who give you that sweet perfume? Oh, Lawd, I hope you not mixed-up with some loose woman already.'

She rasped at his chin with a rough hand. 'You face smooth like bottle. You not man yet, boy.'

The cathedral bell, and briskly she shoved him through the doorway, watching him trotting down the dirt-lane, empty except for pariah dogs. Shortly Pockot was spanking the paved sidewalk of the city. A donkey-cart with coconuts had sunk into the molten asphalt.

A whip checked Pockot.

'You want to help, slum-thief, you thiefing bitch! I just see you come out from that slum. You think I forget how you panmen picked me clean of all my cloth like corbeaux.'

Pockot escaped amid the jeering from pedlars, congesting the sidewalks. He fled down a quiet street lined with wooden warehouses exuding the smell of crushed coffee. He entered a small square with an effigy of Christopher Columbus. A richer sort of beggars promptly reached out empty hats. One was with text: 'He that giveth to the poor, lendeth to the Lord.'

Pockot turned out his pocket. But he would return with his pan and play for them 'Jerusalem, the Golden'.

Their scorn drove him off. Confused, he avoided noisy, congested streets, and soon was striding briskly through Woodford Square. Hordes of preachers and political prophets shouted for his attention. Loiterers, occupying the octagonal bandstand where steelband competitions were held annually, seemed to jeer at him. Ragged mendicants unshaven for months regarded the boy with sudden hostility. They dug their arms into tarred bins for bits of food or ransacked piles of leaves fallen from the large flowering trees, shading the square.

A preacher, yet without text, pointed his staff at Pockot. He threatened fire and brimstone if his daily ration was not met. But the boy, hearing the cathedral bell, bolted for the grocery. Just then the half-crazed preacher found a text: 'The wicked flee when no man pursueth.'

Ten minutes late, Pockot was pleading with the Portuguese proprietor.

'Praying in church, eh?' he repeated. 'Well, the radio just announce some rogue was in the cathedral and emptied the box for the widow's mite.' He shook the ash from a fat cigar. 'Before my customers see two pan sticks in your pocket or before you empty my cash register—here's your pay and get your backside out of my premise—quick sharp,' shoving a small brown envelope into the boy's hand. 'Tell your mother, boy, I owe her nothing more.'

Directly Pockot headed for the Dry River, a concrete waterway winding through the city and emptying itself in the sea not far from the city dump. Sometimes there were rich finds of coins, cutlery, combs, or bright buttons along the river bed. Eddo bushes sprouted in the wavy silt where a crab or two could be found. But the brief fruitless search ended with rain clouds breaking malevolently above him. The slightest rainfall brimmed this river. Pockot imagined the slum-dwellers already fishing out bits of furniture, derelict motor-parts, and parts of houses long fallen into deep disrepair that the river had ripped away from the poorer part of the city.

Frantically he was dashing from tree to tree in the dismal downpour.

His canvas shoes squelched and he thought about his new pair next to his ping pong pan under the canvas cot in his room.

'Not even a sheet of newspaper over you head, boy? Come shelter,' invited the deformed vendor, lifting a gunny sack of her makeshift shed. 'You want to ketch pleurisy or what?'

The cathedral bell gonged. The woman made a sign of the cross, reaching for her rosary, garlanding an upright with a cardboard placard. The charcoal letterings—oranges 1 per five, 2 for nine—challenged the boy's scant arithmetic.

The vendor, spotting the two sticks through the wet clothing, shuddering and stealthily crept a hand for her knife.

But Pockot wanted two oranges. Skilfully the woman dislodged two peeled oranges, one from either end of the base of the pyramid.

'Salt?' she queried, without enthusiasm, stating curtly, 'They is fresh oranges too. I peel them first thing this morning. I don't sell stale things like other people.' She flourished the knife.

Pockot deposited ten cents in her wet palm. She kept her eyes on him while she lifted a penny with her toes from an enamel plate under her bench.

The quote 'He that giveth to the poor . . .' was cut short.

The knife was flashed. 'Police! Police!'

Pockot, scampering away, saw the penny rolling ahead of him and slotting into a crack in the pavement.

'You fresh, forward bastard—trying to buy me with a penny. That sweet smell don't fool me. I old enough to be you mother. Beside I have a man, don't mind I does feed and clothe him.' The vendor was shouting as if there were an audience, 'You panmen wouldn't just let a poor widow earn a mite in a decent way, eh?'

Pockot might have flung himself into the swirling river. But many melodies were swirling in his brain, which he must play along with 'Jerusalem, the Golden' for those beggars. Those melodies would be the choice of calypsonians, too, and, during the carnival celebration, steelbands marching throughout the island would beat out his composition as the most popular road-tune for dancing crowds, tourists and natives alike.

The dark sky had made the day seem almost evening to him. Hungry, Pockot paused before a hooded stall. A pale, dyspeptic man in a black raincoat promised instant virility with his oysters and homemade peppersauce. He enticed the shivering boy with a sample, while an aged woman, reeking with perfume, winked enticingly at him. The vendor, splitting an oyster and squirting yellowish sauce from a green bottle, urged, 'Try this free one, boy, and if the old, fresh-up bitch don't bawl out, I pay you.'

The prostitute pushed Pockot off the sidewalk. 'The boy ain't have no hair yet.' A taxi beamed into view, the headlights revealing thin strokes of rain. The horn resonated through his head. 'You see a coffin you like, boy!' Amid the jeering Pockot galloped for home.

Lady Emelda had just bolted her kitchen window. 'Boy, I was just wondering who so damn foolish to be running through this wet rain. You want a good pneumonia to put you in the grave. I can't even afford a candle, much less a coffin.'

The boy's sudden entrance had forced Mister Harris to scurry back into his bedroom. Pockot dropped the pay-packet on the kitchen table. The mother promptly busied herself counting the earnings by the drooping flames of a kerosene lamp. Her regret was not being able to buy the length of polka-dot cloth from the pedlar robbed and beaten one bright day in Corbeaux City. But it was high time she shed her floursack dresses. About to ask her son if he had ever spotted that cloth-pedlar, Mister Harris coughed aloud.

'Ay, ay, boy, is it me who late cooking or what?' realizing Pockot had come back much too early. But caught up in her counting, she thought, 'Maybe the boss give the boy time off to bring home the pay for his mammy.' Then, she put before him a hot cup of bush tea, her antidote for pneunomia or pleurisy, reciting, 'I remember the Potogee boss, boy. He had one big appetite. And so every day I uses to give him double servings of peas and rice and full up his glass with cold drinks, sorrel, and sea-moss. Kind deeds does pay. Look today how he gone and give you a good job.'

Pockot shoved aside the bitter bush tea.

Twice then Mister Harris coughed.

Smoked coiled about the roof, leaking heavily now so that Lady Emelda hurriedly had to arrange pots and pans about the warped flooring. The wind drove water through gaping cracks in the plywood partitions. Pockot saw vermin crawling out from under the scruffed linoleum.

'What wrong you do, boy?' she exploded. 'Whole day my eyes blinking. Last night that bad dream about floods . . .' She brought the pay envelope even closer. 'I hope my eyesight good enough—but a whole ten cents missing.'

The boy merely glared towards the bedroom.

'Boy, you didn't empty the Potogee man cash-register? Answer me.'

She splashed the tea across the table. She stamped and kicked over the water receptacles already brimming over. 'So bam!' she snapped her fingers. 'Just like that you lose the job . . .'

Mutely, he avoided her glare.

'You ever does know what you mammy do to get you that job? I beg and beseech on these knees. Nobody want a slum boy to touch their grocery. They don't want to carry home lice and jigger in their groceries. These city folks think rat and cockroach follow people like Pied Pipers from this slum behind God's back. And after I give my honest word you not a pan-beating bastard like the others, the Potogee boss still remembered after all these years the kindness of this same Lady Emelda. . . . Ah, Pockot, you was my cross from the day you born.'

She dashed into his room. On re-entering the kitchen, she almost cracked his rib with the pan.

'This pan is the cause of all troubles. Your trouble, my trouble, and Mister Harris trouble. This pan is your original sin.'

Pockot hid his face but his ears seemed to have felt pain each time the crooked crowbar punctured the pan. Her aim was haphazard, but in the next few minutes Lady Emelda had gouged almost all thirty-two notes of the Ping Pong pan.

'It done,' she cried, clanging the bar upon the disfigured pan. 'Mark my word, boy, you going to end up in that same dump where you pick up this stray pan.'

No coughing came from the bedroom.

Turning to Pockot, she ordered—'Go.'

He sensed her helplessness when she whispered, 'Mister Harris don't want you to eat he food no more . . . .'.

Even faster than from the grocery Pockot fled from the shack. He was running through the rain as though chased by many demons.

'Go join those panmen and end up in jail,' she hoarsely shouted.

Steelband men in Corbeaux City ferociously protected their tent, housing their tuned oil-drums. But in the darkling afternoon the boy had crawled undetected into the tarpaulin tent and lay gasping on the wooden platform.

The tent was warmer than the shack. Pockot must have fallen asleep, for shortly he was awakened by the sound of a siren. Some stray cinder from the city dump finally must have set ablaze those shapeless shacks of Corbeaux City. But then he felt something cold against him, some flea-ridden bitch also seeking warmth.

All around the faces of pans gleamed as though to be recognized by him. Pockot knew each by name: bass, cello, guitar, and tenor or ping-pong pan. The bass, created from a full-size oildrum with bottom removed, boomed three or four full notes. These blended with the five or six notes of the cello fashioned from a smaller oildrum, and played in pairs as a rule. Smaller than the cello but larger than the tenor, the guitar pan—also played in pairs—produced as many as fourteen distinct notes.

But none except the tenor pan with its thirty-two notes existed for Pockot at that moment. He himself was its creator. He removed it from its metal stand, adjusted its canvas strap around his spindly neck, and felt the bevel cool against his aching stomach. With his pair of rubber-tipped sticks he plied its surface, teasing out note after note.

After a while he was beating louder and louder as though to muffle the memory of his own pan. In the dimness of his tears he saw the grocery battered into pulps. The next moment the littered lane became clearer and from the darkened doorway of his shack he saw Lady Emelda hovering over the form of Mister Harris, shrouded with newsprint. His mother was brandishing a bloody knife, and calling for him. . . .

Just then, Pockot felt something at his feet. But there was no malevolence in the snap of the flea-ridden bitch who, roused by the pan, weakly shook itself, and limped out of the tent.

Alone, Pockot Wilberforce wept aloud. Perhaps for the first time he was hearing his own voice which a man first of all must recognize if indeed he is to be free. Playing 'Jerusalem, the Golden', the boy, as though liberated at last, wept even louder as he unwound his triumph on the pan.

MAKEDA SILVERA (b. 1955)

Caribbean Chameleon

Yard. Xamaica. Jamdown. Jah Mek Ya. JA. Airport. Gunman, mule, don, cowboy, domestic, refugee, tourist, migrant, farmworker, musician, political exile, business exile, economic exile, cultural exile, dreadlocks, locks-woman, fashion-dread, press-head, extension hair, higgler.

Leaving the Caribbean for the North Star.

Tourist with straw baskets, suntan, skin peeling, rum-filled stomach, tang of jerk pork Boston-style. Lignum vitae carvings, calabash gourds, a piece of black coral, earrings out of coconut shell. Not to forget the tonic juices to restore nature—strong-back, front-end-lifter and put-it-back. A little ganja, lambsbread, marijuana, senseh, collie weed, healing herbs, mushrooms; you can get anything, no problem, as long as there are U.S. dollars.

Dried sorrel, fried sprat, bottles of white rum, mangoes, gungo peas, coconut cakes, scalled ackee, cerasee bush and single Bible. Reggae on cassette tapes.

Travellers dressed to kill.

Woman in red frock, red shoes, red extension hair, black skin.

Dreadlocks, Clarke's shoes, red, green and gold tam, smoking on last spliff.

Cowboy in felt cap, dark glasses, nuff cargo round neck to weigh down a plane.

Woman in black polka dot pant suit. Black winter boots high up to knees, drinking one last coconut water.

Tourist drinking one last Red Stripe beer inna sun hot.

Leaving the Caribbean for the North Star.

Back to work, to winter, snow, frostbite.

Theatre, live at the airport. Older woman bawling, young bwoy whining and pulling at woman in red frock. 'Ah soon come, ah only going for a week. Yuh bawling like me dead.'

'Forward to di Babylon lights,' utters dreadlocks in Clarke's shoes.

'Cho, a tru certain tings why ah don't shot you. Yuh a push up life, yuh waan dead? Bumbo claat, watch weh yuh a go,' cowboy demand.

'I was in di line before you,' answer woman in polka dot pant suit.

'So wah? Yuh want to beat me?' bulldoze cowboy.

'No, but ah only asserting mi rights.'

'Cho, gal, a fight yuh want? Mi will box yuh down. Mi a di baddest man around. Step aside.'

'Gwan bad man, gwan before di plane lef you.'

JA customs officer has eyes deep in passport, behind desk, trying to figure out whether dis is a banana boat passport or what.

'Well praise the Lord for a nice holiday, tomorrow back to work.' Woman in black polka dot pant suit talking to herself.

'Ah, a well-spent vacation. Why do they want to leave?' tourist wonders.

Airport personnel hard at work. Bag weigh too much. Too much clothes, too much food, too much herbs, too much souvenirs. Too much sun packed in suitcase and cardboard boxes.

Temper crackle in dis small island. Sufferation pon di land. Tribulation upon tribulation. Some cyaan tek di pressure. Chicken fat, pork fat fi dinner. Badmanism reign, rent a gun, like yuh rent a car. Gunshot a talk, cowboy, dons, police and soldier tek over di streets. Woman have fi tek man fi idiot—learnt survival skills. Man tek woman fi meat—ole meat, young meat, sometimes ranstid.

Destination America. Destination Britain. Destination Europe. Destination Canada. Destination foreign land.

Fasten seat belt. Iron bird tek off. Fly over di Caribbean sea. A site of Cuba, di Cayman Islands. Plane get cold. Goose bump rise. Blanket pull closer to skin.

Approaching the North Star. Atlantic Ocean, flying high over sea. Goodbye May Pen Cemetery, goodbye gunman, murderers step aside, goodbye dead dogs in gully, rapist, womanbeater, police, soldier, cowboy, Northcoast hustler, goodbye.

Fly higher, iron bird. Away. Goodbye.

Goodbye sunshine, warm salty sea, music with di heavy drum and bass. Goodbye mama, baby, little bwoy, goodbye, no tears, a jus' so. Wah fi do?

Woman in polka dot black pant suit. Work tomorrow. Department clerk. Live-in domestic to work under North Star. Praying that in five years, no more kneeling to wash floor, no more scrubbing clothes, replace that with washing machine, vacuum cleaner. Lady in red to seek better life, tell Immigration is holiday. Send for little boy and older woman when life tek. Dreadlocks leaving the sunshine, collie weed, 'just for a time, just for a time, Babylon force I,' him tell himself. Cowboy cool, cowboy determine,

'Foreign land, north light, fi me and you, anyone, land of opportunity, to buy di latest model gun, to slaughter di baddest bwoy.'

Goodbye slave wage, stale food, ranstid meat, tear-up clothes, rag man, tun' cornmeal, dry dust.

Music soft, no heavy drum and bass. Missing home already. Complimentary drink sweet, though, another Chivas on the rocks, another Courvoisier, cyaan buy dem a Jamdown. Plane get colder. Drinks warm up body.

Woman in black polka dot pant suit close eyes, shut out her job in di North Star. Walk baby in pram. No matter what weather. Snow high. Shovel it. Walk dog. Feed the baby. Feed the mother. Feed the father. Clean up after. Wash the clothes. Iron some. Fold up the towels and sheets. Vacuum the carpet. Polish the silver. All in the name of a honest day's work.

Plane fly low. North Star light pretty, shining all over di land. Immigration. Line long. Which one to enter. Woman or man. White or Asian. Black or white.

'Where have you been?' 'Where have you been?' 'How long was your stay?' 'Purpose of your visit?' Tourist, white, safe every time, unless foolish to take a little collie weed, a little spliff. Woman in red pass through, safe, can't touch it. Dreadlocks just coming to play music at stage show, no rush to live here, in a Babylon. Safe. Cowboy visiting mother, polite, nice smile, dress good, stamp in book, gwan through, 'Three weeks you say?' Safe. Woman in black polka dot pant suit. 'Where you been to?' 'Jamaica.' 'Reason?' 'Vacation.' 'Vacation? Family?' 'No. I stay in a hotel.' 'Why a hotel?' 'What yuh mean, sir?' 'Why a hotel if you were born there?' 'Because, sir, I go on a vacation. What yuh saying, sir? Black people can't tek vacation in dem own homeland?' 'What items did you bring back?' 'Two bottles of rum, sir, di legal amount, fry fish and cerasee bush for tea.' Officer slap ink stamp in the passport. Conveyer belt. Round and round. Lady in black polka dot pant suit pick up luggage. Show stamped card. Over there. Same questions. 'How long were you out of the country?' 'Two weeks.' 'Purpose?' 'Vacation, mam.' 'Where did you stay?' 'Kingston, mam.' 'Did you stay with family?' 'No mam, I visit dem, but I stay in a hotel.' Suspicion. 'Hotel?' 'Yes mam.' 'Take off your glasses, please.' Officer look lady in black polka dot pant suit up and down. 'What date did you leave Canada for Jamaica?' Woman in black polka dot pant suit start breathing hard. 'I have me landed papers right here.' 'Open your suitcase, please.' Suitcase get search. Hand luggage search. Handbag search. Sweat running down woman black face. Line long behind her. Officer call for body search. Woman in black polka dot pant suit trembling. Head start itch. Line longer. Black and white in line. Woman in black polka dot pant suit sweating with embarrassment. North Star cold. But sweat running down her face. Line behind long-long. People tired of waiting. Impatient wid her, not wid di Immigration woman. 'What you looking for, mam?' Question to hands searching. Ripping through suitcase. Disorder among di sorrel. Rum. Fruits. Fry fish. Routine, routine. Passenger behind getting vex wid her. Too much waiting. Lady in black polka dot pant suit try to calm nerves. Think bout work. Up at 5 a.m. Feed di baby. Walk di dog. Put out garbage. Cook di breakfast. Clean di house . . . Anyting . . . to take away dis pain. Dis shame. But not even dat can take it away. 'What you looking for? WHAT YOU LOOKING FOR?' Woman in black polka dot pant suit gone mad. Something take control of her. Black polka dot woman speaking in tongues. Dis woman gone, gone crazy. Tongue-tie. Tongue knot up. Tongue gone wild. 'WHAT YOU LOOKING FOR? Yes, look for IT, you will never find IT. Yes, I carry through drugs all di time. But you will never find it. Where I hide it no Immigration officer can find it. Is dat what yuh want to hear?' Woman in black polka dot pant suit talking loud. Black people, Jamaican people in line behind. Dem close eyes. Look other way. Dem shame. Black polka dot woman nah get no support. Hands with authority. Hands heavy with rage. Tear away at suitcase. Throw up dirty drawers. Trying to find drugs. Only an extra bottle of white rum. Polka dot woman mad like rass. Mad woman tek over. Officer frighten like hell. Don't understand di talking of tongues. Call for a body search in locked room. Black polka dot woman don't wait. Tear off shirt. Tear off jacket. Tear off pants. Polka dot woman reach for bra. For drawers. Officer shout for Royal Canadian Mounted Police to take mad woman away. 'TAKE HER AWAY. TAKE HER AWAY.' Take this wild savage. Monster. Jungle beast. 'AWAY. Arrest her for indecent exposure.' Woman in black polka dot pant suit foam at the mouth. Hair standing high. Head-wrap drop off. Eyes vacant. Open wide. Sister. Brother. Cousin. Mother. Aunt. Father. Grandparent. Look the other way.

Jesus Christ. Pure confusion at Pearson International Airport.

The cock crowing once, twice.

A World of Canes

We begin with love? Doudou, I ain't know what we begin with. What you call that? *Bullying.* You call that bullying. We begin with bullying, meet up with little love. Maybe little bit. Una could suppose.

I could remember the first time. I did had but thirteen years then, and Berry, he did had about sixteen. Thirteen and sixteen, two children, nothing more. We wasn't nothing more than two children then. I did just finish at the elementary school. I got to look for work now. I can't go at high school, ain't got nobody to send me at high school. Buy me books and different things. I got to look for work. So my grandmother, she arrange for me to go by a woman does do needleworks. I go by this woman to learn the needleworks from she, Mistress Bethel. But to get from Sherman to Mistress Bethel house now, I got to pass crossroads, you know, got to pass *he* house, where he living, this Berry. Well that ain't nothing. Ain't nothing in that. I ain't fraid for the man, I ain't thinking nothing about the man. I just keeping to myself, go long about my business. My grandmother, she buy couple dresses for me, you know, to go at needleworks, I press them and I make them neat and thing. So I walking, my little bag, my clasp and my earring. Looking pretty, real pretty now, and I pass this Berry sitting relaxing pon he gallery. Big wide porch front the house. Well this Berry stand up and he watch at me, you know, ogle me every time whilst I pass. I was thinking, *What this man watching at you for? What he watching at you for like that?* But he ain't tell me nothing, and I ain't saying nothing to he neither.

Then one time I had to go up crossroads in the night, there where he was living. I had to go up with a cousin of mine to meet with she friend. She friend uses to work at this shop, grocery shop, selling groceries. This shop close at seven o'clock, you know seven o'clock *dark.* This girl *fraid* to walk home by sheself come seven o'clock. So we gone to meet with she, you know, keep she with company. We leave home about six, six o'clock come already you can't *see* you hand front you face. So we gone over. We making plenty noise, bunch of we walking together must be about five-six, we going over to bring my cousin friend. You know must be two-three miles from Sherman to crossroads, but all is canes. Canes canes and more canes. That place. And so dark. So we got to pass by this man house, coming *and* going.

When we get there now, when we approaching this Berry house, you know he got a lot of little pups. Lot of little pups. Like he had a slut-dog or something, uses to got pups all the time. And he just keep the pups, raise up the pups. But anyway, he must be had about a dozen pups. We did frighten enough for them dogs, oh yes, but long as he there, you would think, *Well he would call them back. If he there he would call them back, them dogs ain't going be out in the road.* Well anyway you more scared of he than the dogs. You prefer the dogs to he! Cause you could ring a rock in the dogs, you could do that, but you couldn't ring a rock in *he.* He more dangerous than the dogs! So we approaching now, little before where the house is. I see he light on, I say, cause we uses to call he *the beast,* that's the name we did call he by. I say, 'The beast, the beast light *on.*' So we, we shut we mouth now, easy, we passing to this side he living to this side, you know how *frighten* we is for he? Oh, yes! And he there *a-waiting.* The beast there a-waiting we.

We going quiet now we tipping, we tipping so silent them dogs can't even hear. All in a sudden I feel somebody grab on me, my arm, grab my arm tight tight. I say, '*Wha?*' When I look, is the beast-*self* grab me. I say to myself, *Oh my Jesus what this man want with you now? What he going do with you now?* He make the rest a sign like that, he fist in the air. You know, *go-long! get!* So they all gone a-running. They take-off! Gone a-running and left me, poor me, left me there with this beast, this trap-man. I say, *My sweet Jesus don't let this man kill me! Don't let this man murder me tonight!* I say, and I talking up aloud to he now, I say, 'What you? What you *want* with me?' He did pushing me forward, shoving me like that, big tall redman. You know, red-skin negro and tall. He say, 'Una walk. Una just walk. Or I going let go *all* these pon una.' This time he got he pockets full with bombs, *full.* Cause it was getting to November now, Guy Fawkes time. And you know before Guy Fawkes they does start to selling the rockets, and the starlights, and the bombs and different things. Well we got to settle for little pack of starlights, maybe a bandit, pack of bandit, but this Berry, he got the works. He aunt bring it from town for he. This Berry got he pockets *full* with these bombs. You know the bombs you does hit down? The ones with the flint? When you hit them down that flint hit you all up in you foot. And I did frighten for them things so *bad,* so *harsh!* I say, 'What you going do with me? When them children come back, you would let me go home? You would let me go home with them?' Cause I know they had to come back going the next way. He say, 'Don't ask me nothing. Don't ask me what I going do with you, you just wait and see.' I say, 'If you kill me they would find me tomorrow, and them children know you is the body carry me!' I start to wriggle now, wriggle-out, he say, 'Don't you wriggle neither. Don't you wriggle neither or you going wriggle in two of these. *In* you backside I going put two of these bombs!' Bombs with the flint, oh my Jesus that thing does hurt so, scorch you all up in you foot.

I just want to get way. I did fraid so bad when them other children leave me, and I just want get home. I say, 'What you going do better start doing now, cause it getting late.' He say, 'Got to do in the patient.' I say, '*What?*' He say, 'Got to do in the patient now.' I say, 'You, you wouldn't patient with me already! What you going do, do *now*. And let me go. Cause when them children reach home they would tell my grandmother where I gone, and she would call police pon you!' He say, 'I ain't killing nobody.' I say, 'Look how you got me holding! I ain't give you consent to touch-up me!' He was walking me straight, direction of them canes. So we reach in the dark now, this where the canes start. He say, 'Stop.' I say, 'What you stopping for? You going shoot me?' He say, 'You see I got gun?' I say, 'I ain't know what you got, nor I ain't *want* to know neither.' He say, 'You know what I want.' I say, 'I ain't know what you want, and you better, you better don't *touch* me!' He say, 'You done touch already.' I say, 'Done touch already, but never by no vagabond like you. Never by no beast!'

Cause, doudou, I didn't had much of experience, not much, but I had enough to know sex is the firstest thing they does go for. The firstest thing. I accustom to that already. But truth is, I didn't think that's what Berry did want from me. I didn't think that for minute, not one second. Amount of bright-skin girls going at the high school would give he that? And anyway you don't does fraid for that. You more fraid for he to do you some *meanness*, cut you up beat you. Cause you know them people with money, always want to beat up the poor ones like that. They always doing like that. Berry say now, 'You going give me trouble tonight?' I say, 'I ain't going to give you no trouble. But if I give you anything, make this the first and the last. Cause me and you ain't no company.' He say, 'Oh, yes. You very easy to say make it the first and the last. You want to get way.' I say, 'Yes, I want to get way.' He say, 'Why you want to get way from me?' I say, 'You is no good, you does beat up people, you unfair!'

Well we reach in the canes now. Deep in the deep of them canes. I can't see where I going, just walking in the blind wherever he push me, shove me. I say to myself, *Ain't no cause to fight he. Big tall red-man. Just let he do what he want, then you could go home.* So then, then he stop. He lie me down, lie me down in them canes. You know, things happen, he just do he business and that is that. Wasn't no pain, that terrible pain searing. Wasn't nothing. Nothing to not-like nor like neither. Just what you got to put up with. What you got to bear. And you getting accustom to that already anyway.

So he finish, he get up, I get up, I want run now. But still he holding me, holding my arm. He say, 'Where you run and going?' I say, 'I going home.' He say, 'You expecting to go cross that road by youself?' I say, 'More happy going by myself than going with you.' He say, 'After what happen you ain't trust me?' I say, 'No. That could happen to anybody. That ain't nothing. That's just something *got* to happen.' He say, 'You's a stupid woman.' Just like that. I say, 'Well I like to be stupid.' That's all I did answer he, 'Well I just like to be stupid.'

So we walk. We walk in them canes, he holding my arm. He ain't saying nothing, nor I ain't saying nothing neither, only, 'When I get home I going tell my grandmother, that's all.' He say, 'Well you tell you grandmother and let *all* you cousins hear what you do, then you name going be out in the street. Ain't nobody would bother with me, but they all going talk about *you*.' And that's the truth. Cause you know when a girl do anything like that, when people hear, they call you *nasty*. Oh Lord they does call you so bad! You got to keep that thing in the secret. I say, 'But if I don't tell them, if I don't tell nobody, *you* would tell them. You would tell them cause you's a *slut*.' He say, 'You ain't got nothing to say to hit me with, who you calling a slut?' I say, 'You.' Just like that. He say, 'When I going see you again?' I say, 'You ain't *never* going see me again. Never. Me and you ain't no company.' I say, 'Why *me*? All we going up crossroads together, other girls there and thing, why me? Why you *picking* pon me? Is cause my family can't, cause we can't come up? Cause we poor?' He say, 'It ain't money. It is people. People. You understand?' I say, 'That ain't true you know better than that. You and me ain't no company. And you ain't *never* going see me again.' He say, 'When you going up crossroads tomorrow, going at needleworks, you stop me from seeing you. Try and stop.' I say, 'All right, see you tomorrow. Just let me go home, and I would see you tomorrow.'

So he left me go now, left my arm go. I run home. I gone. And I ain't tell nobody, not my grandmother nor nobody. I too shame to tell. I *can't* tell. Just like he say, I can't afford for my name to be out in the street. I just go to the pipe for water and I bathe. I bathe and I scrub that piece of soap so hard, wash he out from my skin. Next morning I got to go at needleworks, I play sick. I tell my grandmother something, my belly bad or something. I play sick for two weeks. Cause, doudou, I ain't going back at needleworks for he to hold me again. Mistress Bethel send to ask my grandmother what happen with me, how I just start out and learning the needleworks so good and thing, what happen that I stop so quick? My grandmother say I claim sick, but she ain't know what happen, cause I ain't sick. She did know wasn't nothing wrong with me. Onliest thing is, I can't *tell* she that. How I fraid to go at needleworks cause fraid for this man to hold me again.

I get a job ironing out the clothes with my Uncle Arrows. He father is Mr Bootman the Panama Man, and Mr Bootman got he business to wash out the clothes for the sailors. Sailors that come in off the ships. American and English ships. Cause whole lot of American and English ships uses to come in in Corpus Christi then, come in from the war. Mr Bootman would pick up the nuniforms from off the ships in the harbor, and he bring them back in he car for Arrows to wash them out. So Uncle Arrows would mind the machines turning to wash and dry the clothes, but then he got to iron out the seams. I tell he I could do that. I say, '*Chups!* Arrows, man, I could do that!' Was one of them heater-irons he had, you know, the kind with the coals. So pon my way in the morning I just buy up two pound of coals, light the coals, and when them catch up good, cover it down. Cover that iron down tight tight. Cause it could go a long time like that. That's one them *big* iron I could tell you, with handle, and *heavy*. I could scarce even pick up that thing. Doudou, you know the amount of pants and thing I scorch and had to throw down in the toilet before my uncle miss them, and Mr Bootman!

So I ain't seeing Berry again. Must be about three-four months. I ain't going at crossroads so ain't *got* to see he. But this Berry making it he business to come in now, come in by Sherman where I living. He get to know a fellow name of Lewey, this Lewey live facing my grandmother house. So Berry, he would come early pon evenings, you know, cook and different things with Lewey. They playing draughts and thing. Making a racket. But still I ain't had no confrontation with the beast as yet, not since the first time. I didn't even uses to be at home most the time pon evenings.

Cause my grandmother, she uses to go at church regular pon evenings. Church meeting, or choir practice, something so. You know she always doing something in that church. My grandmother go with she boyfriend, Lambert, and I uses to go with them and visit with my cousin whilst they in the church. Cause my cousin living cross from the big Baptist church, and I could visit with she. So when ten o'clock come, and my grandmother and Lambert going home, they call me out from my cousin house, I just run and catch the bike and I go long. Cause Lambert uses to drive bicycle, and he would, you know, put my grandmother to sit pon the front, pon the crossbars, and he riding the pedals and they going long like that.

So I there talking with my cousin, it getting late, past ten now, and I hear, *glerring! glerring!* Lambert pon he bell. My grandmother call, 'Time to go home!' I was just waiting to hear she voice, and I bawl, 'I coming!' and I run out to catch, you know, hold the fender and running behind. I ain't notice nothing particular, my grandmother sitting pon the crossbar, she wearing she broad-hat that she uses to wear at church, and Lambert driving the pedals. Onliest thing is, they moving a speed tonight, *fast*, but I could run fast too, so I just catch the fender and running behind. Quick now Lambert shift in the dark. Shift in the dark quick quick like that, dark of them canes side the road. I say to myself, *This very strange, that he shifting in the canes? What Lambert going in them canes for?* Because una could suppose maybe my grandmother want to use the toilet, you know, something like that. But una ain't thinking nothing particular, just hold pon that fender and running behind. All in a sudden I notice, I say, *Well my grandmother looking very big tonight. She looking very big and tall tonight.* When Lambert stop, and my granny hold, hold pon my arm tight tight. Doudou, when I look up in my granny face, I see this vagabond. Is Berry *self* dress up ganga! And there driving the bike is he friend Lewey. I say to Berry, 'Wait! Is you, you again!' Berry was wearing he own grandmother broad-hat, he had on this wig that he get from some place. He got on earrings, and bracelet, rings pon he fingers. He wearing he grandmother long-dress, oldfashion long-dress with them big pump-sleeves, big apron, so that could fit he like that. Big tall red-man like he, dress up in he grandmother clothes *ganga!*

Well I say to Lewey now, cause I know Lewey he living cross the street from me, I say, 'Lewey, man, why you drive this man bike for me to hold on like that? You know I ain't want nothing to do with this beast.' Lewey say, 'He pay me to do it. He give me money pay me and you know with money, anything goes. You *know* that!' Berry jump off the crossbar now and Lewey gone, was Berry bike Lewey did driving. Lewey gone and he take off like that, left me there with this vagabond. I think to myself, *This man gone and hold you again? You got to go through this thing again?* I say, 'I ain't talking with you. Ain't talking with you no matter *what* you do me.' He say, 'Wait! I go through all this to get to you, dress up myself in ganga, and you ain't going talk with me?' He say, 'You think that I would go through all this, and let you go so easy?' This time I thinking, *Well you can't fight with he, big tall man like he, and strong.* I say, 'Talk then. Talk then what you want cause I can't fight with you.'

So then he talk talk talk. He talk. But I ain't answering he nothing. I ain't speaking a good time. Last I say, 'You does bully everybody to talk with you like this?' He say, 'No. I don't does bully people.' I say, 'Well what you doing with me now then? You don't call this bullying? This is bullying, this ain't love.' He say, 'I does feel something for you.' I say, 'Well I ain't feel nothing for you. I just feel when I look in you face hatred like I want *kill* you! Or you going kill me!' He say, 'You just keep quiet, or let me cuff you in you mouth.' I say, 'I know you going cuff me in my mouth that's all you could do is cuff.' He say, 'Why you keep telling me them things? Why you keep telling me them things make me mad, and running from me? Why you keep running from me for?' So I say, 'I fraid for you to cuff me.' He say, 'Not so easy. Not so easy.' I say, 'What you going do with me now?' He say, 'I ain't going do nothing more than I ain't do already.' So I say, say like the last time, 'Well you just do it quick and let me go. Cause onliest thing I want is to get way from you.' He didn't answering nothing to that, and I didn't talking nothing no more neither. He just pushing me walking through them canes, push me deeper in them canes. So now I thinking, *Well look, you could just give up. Cause he so tall, and strong, you can't do nothing to get way from he.* And plus I was thinking, *Well if he could put heself so low, so low as that to dress up heself as woman, dress up heself as ganga, only to get to you, maybe something there? Maybe something there in that?*

Then he lie me down again pon some dead canes, he find someplace soft in them canes for we to lie. Now he start to feeling me up, but not so rough, more gentle this time, and I kind of relax. I say, 'Leastest thing you could do is take off that wig. That broad-hat and them earring. You look like a *fool*.' He did embarrassed now, so he take off he ganga-clothes, he start up again. I just relax more into it, don't fight with he too much, and I did start to like it this time. You know, he was feeling me up but gentle, gentle now, and I just go soft inside. Down there. I just go all to waters. Deep blue and purple warm *wistful* waters, and he raise up and he go inside, he, whole of he warm deep inside, and I just melt down soft into it like that. Easy. Not fighting now. And it did feel good this time. And he did know I was liking it too.

When he finish, you know, he laugh and thing, I laugh, I feeling good now. Not so bad. We talk and thing, we laugh little bit, he ain't holding me no more but I ain't running neither. We say, well he ask me if I want to go in town. I say, 'No. I can't go in town. I ain't got no money to go in town. What little few cents I could catch from the ironing got to give my granny. Or take and buy the things that I need. I ain't got no money to go in town. You know how it is?' He say, 'Well I could give you money to go in

town. You could be my girlfriend.' I say, 'Don't you, don't you *laugh* at me!'
He say, 'Ain't laughing at nobody.' I say, 'You and me is different kind of
people. Where you come from and where I come from is different kind of
people. So you got to look for you kind of people, and I got to look for my
kind of people. That's just the way.' He say, 'Who is my kind of people?' I
say, 'People that got money. Got education. People that go at high school
and got car and big house and thing.' He say, 'It don't be money. It *don't*. Is
just people, understand?' He say, 'Just let we, just tell me if you would be
my girlfriend, and you could see me. I ain't want to dress up in ganga-
clothes all the time to come looking for you.' Well I laugh at that. I just *had*
to laugh at that. He laugh too. We laugh so hard! We laugh till we belly
hurt. Now we ain't saying nothing a time. A long time. Just sitting there in
the silent. Listen in the silent to them breeze brushing through the canes,
all them canes a-creeking, *kerrack, kerrack-kak*, and smelling green, and
earth wet. And feeling the cool. Feeling far off. Like we did far off from
everybody. Last he say, 'Man, do, say something!' I say, 'All right. All right
then. I could be you girlfriend. You ain't got to walk behind me dress up
ganga, but you, don't you *bully* me!' He say, 'I ain't going bully you. I ain't.
You going see. I going be all right.' So then we, we do it again. He ain't hold
me this time and I ain't run this time neither. We do it again and I hold *he*.
Hold on tight to melt in them warm, wistful waters. And I did like it good
enough this time.

So he tell me where to meet he and I go. We meet. Time to time. You
know, I still did doubt, I still did had it pon my mind. I ain't in love with the
man so good as yet. But then he did behaving heself ok. The beast did
behaving heself ok. I start to like he. Well, *more* than like, and he too. Time
come when I just couldn't miss he out from my eyesight. Nor he couldn't
miss me out from he eyesight neither. We did going together, a time, we go
in town a Saturday evening, take in a picture-show, things like that. And
we go in the canes, always in the canes.

But then my grandmother get to find out, find out about we. Sweet
Jesus! My grandmother give me so much of *struggle*, so much of struggle
over this man. Tell me I hang my hat too high, and when I go to reach it
down it going fall and hit me pon my head. I trying to come up too much,
I should mind my station. All them kind of thing. My grandmother say,
you know, he too big for me and thing. And then he father get to find out,
Berry father did. Well he was more worse than my grandmother. He tell
Berry I ain't no good, no class, I ain't no class for he. Berry father say I's
low-down people, call me monkey, molasses-monkey, all them kind of
thing. Oh Lord we get the *works*. So much of struggle. He get it from he

side and I get it from my side. When I go in the canes at night with Berry, my grandmother shut me out the house. Lock me out. I got to sleep under the cellar. You know that house was standing pon posts, groundsills, and underneath open. We call that the cellar. And that place so damp, and so cold. When I sleep under the cellar my eyes swell up. Catch cold in my face.

So when Berry come to see me the next morning, he bathe and dress and walk over to see me, come from crossroads, you know I can't come out. My eyes swell too much! And then my little cousin, my little cousin Clive run out and he say, 'She sleep under the cellar last night!' Thing like that. I can't see Berry no more, I too shame. But then one time Clive run out and he tell Berry, 'She sleep under the cellar last night and she face swell!' But Berry call me still. He call me to come out and he standing there waiting till I come. He say, 'You must *tell* me. When she shut you out like that.' I say, 'What I going tell you? I can't go telling you things that happen to me about my family. I got to *bear* with it. Cause you and me ain't no company.' I say, 'If you treat me bad, kick me or anything so, you know what they going say? They going say how I *deserve* that. How I hang my hat and thing. And they going be right. I can't bring my troubles before you. Cause I ain't got no *right* to be with you!' Berry just stand there and he shaking he head, say, 'Just you tell me when she shut you out. Just you tell me so.'

We meeting in the canes about every night now, sexing all the time, and feeling good. Reach a point we ain't want to go home not for nothing, he to hear from he father, me from my grandmother. One night we stay out most the whole night, and didn't get scarce no sleep neither. That morning I scorch up must be about a dozen the sailor pants. You know I was working two heater-irons now, two going at the same time, steaming up, ironing out the seams. I smell this thing scorching and I turn round, I throw off the iron quick quick and sprinkling water pon this pants, time as I turn round again, *next* pants a-scorching. On and on again and again till I must be scorch up about the entire American Navy! Me one. And is not Uncle Arrows come in that morning to find me, is *Mr Bootman the Panama Man*. When that Mr Bootman the Panama Man come in to find me with all these sailor pants a-scorching, near went after *me* with them iron! He say, 'Man, you know who nuniform this is? You know who nuniform you got the privilege to hold in you hands? This garment near *sacred*. You don't play with Uncle Samson like that already!' I just take-off and I running. Take-off and I ain't looking back.

Now I got to find more work. I say to myself, *What you could do? Ain't nothing you could do.* So then I watch at my grandmother. She does work estate, work in the fields doing labor. Not cutting canes. She work pulling grass, pulling grasses from between the canes, keeping the canes clean. So I say to myself, *You strong as she. You could do that good as she.* I ask my granny, 'I want to help you in the field.' Granny Ansin say, 'I ain't want you coming behind me. I ain't want you nowhere *near* behind me. I ain't even want you in my house!'

But I go behind she still. I was thinking, *Them's the whitepeople canes. Them don't belong to she. I got as much right to work them canes as she.* So I follow behind, and when she look back, I dodge in the canes. I watch at she how she doing, and I doing just the same, and when she look back I dodge in the canes again. Time as lunch come I near fall down about four times. That work so *hard*! I so tired, and mouth so dry! But I keep on. I just keep on the whole day. When I reach home that evening. Well Ansin, she reach before me, and when I reach home Ansin was there waiting, she say, 'Girl, you look like a ghost, you turn black like a ghost. Look you face black already and you turn more black still, black like a ghost!' She say, 'You go outside and you bathe before you come in here.' I say, 'I too tired to bathe. I going rest awhile, and when night come I would bathe.' Ansin say, 'You get pay?' I say, 'No.' She say, '*What?*' I say, 'Ain't sign so ain't get pay. Ain't nobody tell me to sign.' Granny Ansin say, 'Girl, I ain't know if you more black or more stupid. I ain't know *what* you is.' I say, 'Well you don't worry cause I know what I is. I is human being. And tomorrow morning I going sign and I going get pay.'

So things carry on like that. I work two weeks and then I rest awhile. Cause that's hard work you working them canes, you can't go like that all the time. I rest and I work some more. They pay me sometimes three dollars, three-fifty for two weeks. That can't buy you scarce nothing that three-fifty. Maybe couple yards of cloth to make a dress. Jar of cream, Pons cold cream, something like that. Two weeks for jar of cream. But that's the only work you could get, so you got to do it. Berry, he ain't want to hear nothing about me working in them canes. Cause that's poor people work, that's the work for poor people. And plus, he know when I in the canes working all the day like that, I ain't going back in the night. I say, '*Chups!* Man, next thing I be *living* in them canes.' I say, 'I tired, man. I too tired!' But he know I still like it good in them canes. Like it good enough.

Then one time my grandmother went pon excursion, church excursion. You know how the church have excursion to visit some other church and thing? We call that mission day. Well this mission day was my grandmother turn to cook. You know, preacher give she money to make the picnic. So my grandmother bake and cook and all kind of thing, and she make this big picnic basket for this excursion. *Big* basket. I wasn't going, but I tell my grandmother that I would carry the basket for she, with all these cokes and food and different things. I know me and Berry would get chance to be together the whole day cause my grandmother ain't going be there. I say, 'Ansin, let me carry the basket. This a big basket, and I could carry it I stronger than you. Let me carry the basket up the hill.' So she say I could carry the basket. I raise it up pon my head to carry, we walking with them other women going up crossroads to catch the bus. I tell my grand-mother, 'You go-long. Go-long up in front and catch the, you know that bus would come soon so you go-long and catch and I would come up fast behind.'

So I walking long and I reach up my hand throwing out the cokes now, two for him and one for me. I throw out some sandwich, about six-eight sandwich, cakes, about three different kind of cakes I throw out, coconut cakes and chocolate, different fruits and thing. He did hiding in the canes, following behind me but sticking to the canes, and when I throw out, he just run and he collect-up. The things I throwing out. One time like my grandmother, like she catch me, she wait for me to come up and she say, 'What happen with you? You very far back.' I say, 'Feel so *tired*.' She say, 'You go-long home! Give my basket and you go-long home.' I say, 'No. I going carry it to the bus.' Cause I did feel so shame now to give she back that basket. She say, 'I feel something going happen with you today. I got a pre-sentiment for that.' I say, 'Ain't nothing going happen with me. You go-long have youself a nice time in the picnic.' Anyway, bus come, my grandmother gone, she climb up in the bus and she gone. Ain't even notice the basket empty. Near empty. But when this man come out the canes now! So many things I throw out, near about *everything* was in that basket. Well we running we can't scarce carry all this food and cokes and different things, can't scarce wait to get weself inside them canes. So then we sit down and we start and we eat. We *eat eat eat*. Eat cakes and different things, eat banana, we must be eat about six banana each. Now we take a break and we do little something, we do little something and then we eat some more, eat some sandwich and drink a coke, take a break and do little something more, eat some more, eat a coconut cake, or chocolate, off and on and off and on like that *whole* morning long. My sweet Jesus *that* was picnic we make that day! We did start from early morning, about eight o'clock, we doing just how we feel. *Everything!* So reach now about two o'clock, I say I going home and bathe and change, he say he going home and bathe too, and he would meet me back there in the canes about four o'clock.

413

So I going home now, but before I go and bathe I pass by a friend of mine cause I did feel so *thirsty*. After we eat so early and so much, eat till all finish, cause we ain't stopping till ain't nothing more to eat. So this girl-friend of mine, where she living had plenty coconut trees, *tall* coconut trees. Coconut trees with water-coconuts. Them trees so tall the coconuts stand and get big big, you know everybody fraid to pick them coconuts cause they fraid to climb up so high. But doudou, this day I feeling I is boss. I is *boss*, and I going climb up them tree. I put this big ladder up in the tree, and I start to climbing up in that tree till the ladder get a belly like, a belly of sinking, but I keep climbing. I keep climbing, and just when I get at the center, just when I reach in the center of that belly, *plaks!* the ladder break, and all I know now is I flying. Doudou, I *flying!* Flying through the air. Ain't even know when I hit, when I hit the ground. Cause all I could remember is that flying.

When I wake up must be about three-four days later. I ain't even know how I reach in the bed. All I know is my body so stiff, so stiff. I couldn't even raise up my head off the pillow. But he come and he stand pon me. Berry did. He come and he stand pon me every day, and soon I start to feeling better, getting back pon my feet. You know he bring eggs, and malt, iron, build back up my nerves. He buy block of iron, you know that black thing? He just chip off some in the milk, and milk start and turn just like iron. Taste, *shew!* real bad, but it good for you, good for the nerves. I lie there in the bed, he looking down pon me, I looking up pon he face, I say to myself, *Well let you look and he real good now. Look at he good, cause you only ever see this rat mostly in the night, darkness of them canes.* And he was hand-some too. He with he long nose, and them freckles on it. That man hand-some in truth. Then my grandmother, one morning she come to me and she say, 'Like he a nice boy. Like I did treating he wrong.' I say, 'I know he gavering nice to me. He gavering nice to me a time.'

So I start to getting back pon my feet now. Everybody saying like I preg-nant and gone up in that tree cause I gone crazy, I want to throw the child. Berry father say I did want to kill myself, cause I pregnant and he family don't like me. Say he feel sorry, he feel sorry for doing that. But truth is, I wasn't pregnant then. I sure about that. I sure I wasn't pregnant then. Cause that come *after*. Maybe about three, that came about three-four months after the tree. After that fall. And when I start and find myself pregnant now, when I find myself now with baby in truth, doudou, that's when everything turn to bad. Not for Berry. He did happy enough. For everybody else. Granny Ansin and he father. For them two things turn straight to bad.

My grandmother turn bad pon me again. Treat me so harsh. Worse even than when she uses to lock me out the house, and I got to sleep under the cellar. Worse even than that. Then one day I went up crossroads, catch the bus, and Berry father hold me front everybody. Hold me and curse me front everybody. Say, 'I would give you one kick in you belly kick that child through you mouth! Get you whoreself way from my son!' Say worse than that. Oh my Jesus I did feel so *bad*, so shame. And, doudou, I did crying. I cry so much for that. I say to myself, *Lord, what I gone and do? What I gone and do to get this?* I tell Berry, I say, 'Look, man, you just go about you business, and forget, let me go about my business.' Berry say, 'You can't tell me that. You *can't*. Cause that what you got in you belly that belong to me too. We just got to make out. We just got to make out together.'

So Berry gone now and he apply for fireman. Gone and apply for fire service. You know you got to sit exam to do that, cause that's government thing. So Berry sit exam and he come out all A's. All *A's!* Cause he very very smart, he very smart and he could write so *pretty*. They tell he he come out all A's. So he gone and he drop from the high school, cause he going join in the fire service now. Hat and cape and everything. We find weself this little house to rent. Pay down the first month. Six dollars. Only a little one-room board-house, but it got in the bed, and two chairs, and little table.

We had it plan. How we did do. You know Berry gone and he buy the bucket, water bucket, and I gone and I buy you the cup. Little white metal cup for you. And little spoon. Cup and spoon and water bucket. And we own house to live in. Doudou, that afternoon we did think we own the sky! We own the sky and earth both, so much of things we had! So next morning when Ansin go in church, and Berry father out driving the bus, we move in all we things inside the house. Yesterday. That was only yesterday we movin' here. Seem like a month! This little house. But, doudou, ain't so small. Cause you know what you daddy tell me? He say, 'Vel, the thing I like mostest of this house is the yard.' I say, '*Yard?*' I say, 'Onliest thing we got for yard is the street. Pothole and puddle!' Berry say, 'I talking about the *back* yard. You ain't notice the back yard?' he say, 'We got the whole world of canes for we back yard.'

The Waiting Room

There are waiting rooms everywhere—at hospitals reeking of disinfectant and cold methylated smell of sickness; at prisons stinking of urine, sweat, and human despair; at government offices humid with the thick moisture of bureaucratic boredom punctuated by the click-click of typewriters and chewing gum; at police stations rank with violence; at bus stations; . . . everywhere. And then there is this one.

Its walls are pristine, painted a brilliant white, the benches inside arranged like pews in a church. No plants or flowers relieve the glare. No paintings on the wall welcome the faithful believers.

To this place comes the hopeful, the hopeless, the meek, the proud, the rich, the poor, the intelligent, the dull, the hustlers, the pimps, the whores, the educated and the unschooled, and the dreamers. Especially the dreamers.

To this place came Elisa Barker, creole, light brown, with good hair (her mother was Mestizo with some Welsh blood, somewhere). She was temporarily huffed by the guard at the gate who apologetically asked her to open her expensive white leather handbag before he cruised something that looked to her like a gun detector over her body. He had not touched her. In fact, he had acted with the utmost propriety, but still Elisa felt disturbed. It annoyed her. She had not been prepared for it. Usually it was her privilege to sweep regally past such persons like maids, guards, secretaries, et cetera, but the man had insisted. That insistence alone had surprised her, had made her hesitate and her momentum had been lost. She had become angry at the guard's searching of her bag, but she carefully controlled herself. Recovering her poise, she stepped confidently into the waiting room.

Everyone turned to look at her. She ignored the stares. She was used to it. As she had fastened the thick gold chain around her neck, before she had left the house that morning, she had stared into the mirror, candidly assessing her features. Her freshly permed hair lopped elegantly around her shoulders. Her makeup was fresh and sophisticated. She had good white teeth, a straight nose, a mouth full of promise, and a body rounded in all the right places. Behind her she had seen the man she was married to, thirty years older than she was. She didn't care what people said. It was her business if she didn't love him. Living in the big house with gables on Southern Foreshore, with a maid and her own car, she had become Mrs Barker and she was already beginning to forget that she had ever been anything else.

She found a place next to a woman who reeked of what smelled like kush-kush. Elisa wrinkled her nose and pulled a glossy Glamour magazine from out of her bag. She leafed through the pages, pretending to read. She felt totally at a loss. She had asked none of her friends for advice. They were her husband's friends anyway; they all had travelled abroad before and Elisa was secretly ashamed of the fact that she had never been to New York, or L.A., or Chicago. Her neighbour, Mrs Collins, a Belizean girl married to a Brigadier in the British Army, had even been to Wales. She had told her husband nothing either. She felt she had captured him by being bold, aggressive, and self-confident. She felt he had assumed that her sophistication came from having travelled abroad, and she did not want him to find out that she had hardly ever left Placencia, her tiny hometown village, before she met him. She had learnt about the world from working with tourists, from her friends who had travelled, and from anybody else she could. Besides, Elisa knew she was smart. She had always been.

She got bored leafing though the magazine and taking a deep breath, she ventured to look up, wanting to see what the other people were doing. To her chagrin, everyone else seemed to know what was going on, what was to be done. She felt foolish, her poise slipping. Someone touched her arm and she jumped. It was the woman to her left, the one who smelled of cheap perfume. Elisa tried not to look as annoyed as she felt.

'You get your form yet?' the woman was asking kindly, pointing to the counter where secretaries buzzed importantly to and fro.

'Oh, thank you' Elisa answered politely. 'I was just waiting until I caught my breath.'

'I know,' the woman nodded understandingly. 'Right so me stay when I come here. Frighten.'

Elisa did not answer, she only smiled a small superior smile as if fear had never occurred to her. She picked up her magazine again, hoping to discourage further conversation. When she felt sufficiently safe she put her magazine away and rose purposefully, heading for the counter. She observed the secretaries on the other side of the clear glass wall and she knew they observed her. Yet it was a full five minutes before one of them came to attend to her.

When the secretary reached the counter, Elisa began haughtily: 'I'd like a form for a visa please.'

To her indignation the woman looked, did not answer but made a bored gesture with a perfectly manicured fingernail in a downward motion. Elisa stopped, puzzled. Then she noticed a small hole in the glass pane. It was at her waist level. She realized she had to bend down and speak through the glass pane. It was an ignominious position to be in. She felt that everyone was staring at her jutting behind as she awkwardly placed herself to speak through the hole. The bending motion made her well arranged hair flop forward and by the time she had finished speaking her blouse had risen to reveal her belly button. To top it all, the secretary did not bend down likewise to answer her query about the form. After Elisa repeated her question twice, the woman merely pointed unsmilingly to a notice posted just a little above Elisa's head.

Elisa read the notice, feeling even more of a fool. It gave clear instructions about just what was to be done with the forms which lay in a neat pile to the extreme left of the counter. Picking up two, she stepped back to her seat. There, she quickly filled in the form. Luckily she had brought along some pictures. She handed in the form with the pictures and then sat down to wait. After the first twenty minutes she could no longer keep up the pretense of reading the magazine, nor did she want to doze and miss her name. Besides, the hard wooden bench was beginning to make her bottom ache. She got up and walked to the back of the room where she leaned against the wall, observing the people around her.

The room was full. Most of the people sat quietly looking anxious, speaking to one another now and then. There was a subdued buzz as mothers hushed children, as comments were passed from one person to another. There were mainly creole people in the room and most of them were women. Every so often she heard something indistinguishable over the microphone and then one of the persons seated would rise and go to the cubicles which stood like telephone booths in the corner. Sometimes a whole group rose in a body to the cubicle and hovered around. The persons took five minutes, sometimes longer, but everytime they returned Elisa watched their faces for smiles or vexation or disappointment and depending upon what she saw she knew whether it had been a 'Yes' or a 'No'. After standing there for more than an hour watching the many who returned, she saw that only a few had been chosen. Elisa began to feel the beginning of the tension which gripped everyone else in the room. Suppose she didn't get it? It was the first time that thought had even crossed her mind. She had never even dreamed that she would become like people she heard about. Those who didn't 'get through' who had to go 'through the back', the victims of elaborate schemes who sometimes ended up in a Mexican jail.

She watched a fat black woman with a greasy curly afro dressed in a bright flowered dress, white pumps and stockings, and three gold chains around her neck come back from the cubicle, failure and disappointment etched in every line of her face. She looked as if she wanted to cry. The woman went to where she had left three children on the bench and was collecting them when another woman, three benches behind her, hailed.

'Miss June? How it gone? You get through?'

Miss June sucked her teeth and shook her head. She slowly sat down, tired.

'Ay, Ruthie girl, dem people hard, dem hard.'

The woman called Ruthie moved from where she was to sit beside her.

'You mean you never get it?'

'Dat's right.'

Ruthie looked bewildered.

'But how? I mean you have bank statement and invitation letter and everything!'

'Ruthie girl, I could have all the money in the bank and all the invitation letter in the world and the man still would give me hard time. I don't know, de man look me straight and tell me he don't think I will come back.'

'But he facey.'

'Dat is not the word for it. If me never bring up good and have respect for authority me would tell him some tings dat would make him change colour. Him had the guts to tell me that I going there to work, dat plenty woman dat go visit never come back. My poor daughter work hard 'cross there to send plane ticket and bank statement for nothing. NOTHING!'

'After you travel so far!' Ruthie exclaimed sympathetically.

'I wake up four o'clock dis morning Ruthie, catch the Corozal bus, me and the children, to come here.'

'And de children? What he say 'bout dem?'

'Well, don't ask about dat! As far as he concern de mother must bring dem in and you know Maybelle in Chicago.' She paused and sighed heavily. 'The poor girl did only want to see them. This last one, Charlie was only three months when she left. I raise all three for her. Now, I think dey need dem mother.'

'True, well she have to get fix up or send for dem through de back.'

'Must be. But she never want it dat way. Ay but what vex me is how dis same man give Catherine, my cousin, who have no bank statement and five children over dere illegal. She get.'

'Girl, dis place, it's your luck.' Then she lowered her voice and Elisa had to strain to hear.

'I hear you could go down to Stann Creek and get dat lady to bathe you and say prayers. It take three days.'

'Ruthie, you think dat work? I never hear 'bout dat. I must try it.'

Miss June stood up.

'O.K. den Ruthie. I will see you a next time. I wish you luck!'

Elisa had edged herself up to the two women and had heard the last part even though they spoke in low confidential tones. What she heard did not make her feel any better. She looked at her silver watch. Half an hour more had passed. She paced the floor, walked the length of the room and looked at mug shots of men wanted by the FBI, her tension increasing.

'You get through Hortence?' she heard an old lady sitting at the back ask a woman who was dressed in the uniform of one of the banks. The one called Hortence nodded, smiling.

'Thank God,' replied the other, adding quickly, 'What you get?'

Like two conspirators they bent down and whispered so that Elisa could not hear anymore.

After the one called Hortence had left the building, Elisa heard the woman with whom Hortence had been whispering turn to her neighbour and say:

'That's my neighbour you know. A nice girl. She work at Bank. She get Multiple Indefinite.'

'What! Dat good' exclaimed the other, a clear note of envy in her voice. 'I hope they don't give me no trouble.'

'Dis your first time?' asked Hortence's neighbour.

'Yes, I have all my children over dere. L. A. I was just waiting till my last grandson dat I raising for my daughter finish high school over here so she could get him over, den I go with dem.'

'Dat's good girl. I going to Chicago to my son. I hear it cold over dere but girl, I can't take Belize no more. Things too expensive here man. And the little money you make could hardly stretch. My daughter-in-law tell me dat de chicken over dere is 99¢ a pound. You believe dat? And she tell me you could get de best clothes and shoes 'pon sale cheap, cheap, cheap. She just bought a home over dere. She say she not coming back here.'

'Girl, dat good. Belize is not the same quiet place it use to be one time. You hear what all those aliens doing up north? I hear they shoot some

Indian man three weeks aback. Now dey come and grow up all de weed. Dey soon take over Belize.'

'Dat's why I going, before dat happen.' Hortence's neighbour's friend laughed. Elisa, listening keenly to the exchange got caught up in it and did not hear when the metallic voice called her name. The name was repeated and when no one moved someone in the front row called out:

'Elisa Barker, who dat?'

In a nervous rush Elisa picked up her bag from a chair and walked quickly to the cubicles, her high-heeled sandals making a staccato sound on the tiled floor.

She went to the only empty cubicle and putting her bag down on the counter she took a deep breath before smiling brightly at the person on the other side.

'Hello. I'm Elisa Barker.'

The man did not smile back. He examined something he held in his hand and on closer look she saw he was holding the card she had filled out earlier.

'Yes ma'am. So you want a visitor's visa?'

'Yes sir' she replied, completely taken aback by the cold impersonal tone. She looked at his left hand and saw a thick wedding ring.

'You are married ma'am?'

'Yes sir.'

'Are you living with your husband?'

'Of course! We just got married a year ago!' Elisa replied indignantly. The man raised his head from his examination of the form and gave her a cynical smile.

'What is your occupation ma'am?'

'I'm a housewife.'

'Did you have any skill or training of any sort before you got married ma'am?'

'Well, I. . . . I . . . used to work in a hotel.' Elisa stumbled.

'Where?'

'In Placencia. I was the receptionist.'

'I see. About how long ago was that ma'am?'

'About two years ago. Then I got married.'

'Have you worked since then?'

'No sir, I haven't.'

'What is your purpose for visiting the United States ma'am?'

'I'm going on holiday.'

'And who will be funding this trip?'

'My husband.'

'What does your husband do ma'am?'

'He has a business.'

'Can you tell me what his annual income is.'

Elisa was at a loss. She rubbed her hands together.

'I . . . I don't know. He doesn't discuss those things with me.'

'Can you tell me what sort of business he does?'

'I tell you I don't know. He doesn't discuss his business affairs with me.' Her voice was agitated.

'Okay,' he replied airily, as if it had never mattered in the first place. Elisa felt the back of her neck knot with the tension.

'Let's see,' he continued, after checking the form again.

'Do you have your bank statement with you?'

She nodded the negative.

'No? How about your bankbook? No?'

He sat back.

'Ma'am, there are a lot of young women, just like you who come in here everyday and try to convince us that we should allow them a visa to visit. What they really want to do is go to the United States, find a job, and work to support their families here in Belize. They say they are single, when they aren't, or vice versa. They say they are married when they aren't. You put me in a difficult position. You don't have a job to come back to. You say you are married but I need proof that your husband is here and that you are living together. Neither do you have children to come back to. Do you have relatives in the U.S.?'

'Yes, a great deal.' Elisa answered eagerly, glad that at last she could show something positive.

'Close relatives?'

'Yes sir, my mother and my two sisters are there.'

'O.K. Please wait a minute' he replied. Then rising from his seat, he went behind to the office section. Elisa remained, twisting her handkerchief nervously. She began to wish she had never come. But she did want that visa. She would not be one of those who walked through those doors with the stamp of failure. At least the man was trying to help.

The man had returned.

'Ma'am' he sighed and ran his arm through his thin corn-coloured hair. 'Our records show that both those persons you mention received visas to visit for one month and now are there for almost three years. I'm sorry but that doesn't help your case.' Now there was an air of finality about him that

Elisa didn't like. She felt he had made up his mind. Still she decided to give another try. She drew a deep breath to let the panic subside.

'Sir' she began, swallowing hard, feeling the tension stretch from her neck to her forehead and the sweat gather in her armpits.

'I can assure you that unlike other women who may have come here before telling lies about their marital and financial status, I am above such things. My mother and sisters have, I must admit, done something wrong but must I be punished for that? Ever since childhood I have longed to visit the United States because I have heard about the wonderful country it is. It's true that I don't work, but I don't have to. My husband is well off. And even if I don't have my own bank account, I have my own car. It's right outside if you care to look.' She could not help the pleading note on which she ended her little speech.

'The man was silent for a while. Then putting down his pen with a stroke of finality, he stood up.

'Ma'am, what proof can you show me that you will not become a charge on the Government of the United States?'

She was silent.

'Ma'am, I'm afraid I can't grant you a visa without proof of your financial status. I will place your application on record and . . .'

'But I can get it!' Elisa interrupted desperately. 'Today, this afternoon. It's no problem.'

She reached out instinctively with one hand to try and touch his arm in appeal but her hand was stopped by the dividing glass; her wedding ring making a loud smack.

Both she and the man stood silently looking at where she had knocked the glass. She heard the noise lull in the waiting room and she knew that the others in there behind her had heard the sound and were looking on interestedly, hoping for a dramatic scene. Elisa felt the blood rush to her head in shame. She looked down at her hands fighting tears.

'I'm sorry ma'am' she heard the man repeat in an expressionless voice. 'As soon as you have the required proof you may bring it in to us and we will review your application. Good morning.'

Elisa did not move. She felt dazed. Only when the man pulled the microphone to his mouth and announced the next name did she remove her bag from the counter and walk towards the glass door. With an effort she kept her head high and looked neither left nor right. But as she passed, she heard Hortence's neighbour whisper loudly to her newfound friend:

'See what I tell you. She no get through.'

Canada Geese and Apple Chatney

Bai dhem time something else—rough—rough like rass. And was no laughter. Yuh want hear about dhem time? Leh me tell yuh. And don't bother with Writerji. He's mih friend but remember he's a writer. He change-up everything, mix-up people and place so nobady could tell who is who, and what what. And if yuh ain't know, all sound like true. But dhat is because Writerji good. Well he always good. Yuh see dhat story about running from immigration officer which set in New York. Dhat same thing happen here in Toronto to he. And was he, me, and Hermit sharing a apartment at the same time. Yuh know how Anand get dhat name Writerji? Is me give he, me and Hermit. Ask Hermit when yuh see he.

And dhat bai Hermit is something else. A holiday—was Christmas. Just the three ah we in the apartment. Snow like ass outside. Prem and Kishore invite we over but Hermit old car ain't starting, and anyway too much snow. And Prem and Kishore ain't gat car—dhey living in the east end, somewhere behind gaad back near Morningside. In dhem days, once people know yuh illegal, nobady want see yuh, nobady invite yuh at them house. Even yuh own relative—people come hey and change. Money, money, money. Mih own uncle don't call me. And when he ass going to UG he staying at we place, five years—mih mother neva tek a cent from he. When yuh illegal everybady think yuh want money, or something. Yuh don't let people know you situation—yuh laugh outside. So is just dhe three a we. Snow tearing tail and we putting lash on some Johnnie Walker Black Label. Hermit bring out he big tape and we playing some Mukesh and Rafi. Suddenly the tape finish. Is a eerie silence. Fat snow flakes khat khat khat on dhe window pane.

Suddenly Hermit seh, 'And Writerji—a hope yuh ain't turn out like Naipaul. Yuh see how he write *Miguel Street* and *Biswas*. Mek a mockery a everybady, mek a mockery a dhe culture . . .'

'Ah, come on, Hermit. Naipaul nat so bad. He write fiction, stories. And stories are more than just the truth, more than just a little lie. And we more

424

critical than Naipaul. Remember how we say dhat all pandit ah bandit! What more derogatory than that.'

'But we say it as joke!'

'Same thing with Naipaul!'

'Anyway, mek sure yuh ass don't write nothing about me.'

'He gat to write about something, Hermit,' I teasing Hermit, 'and what you gun do if he write about you?' Since Guyana we calling he Hermit because he like a bookworm, always reading when yuh miss he. Was dhe same thing here. When he come home and after he eat, he head straight fuh he room and read. Sometimes he look TV with we.

'Well, we friends a lang time, since high school, but don't do dhis to me. I serious. Don't let me recognize anything about me.' Man is like dhe cold come inside the apartment. Hermit serious, real serious. Rare thing for Hermit. Since I come to Toronto, only one time I see he so serious and angry. I tell you, dhem quiet people, yuh could neva tell. Funny how we always teasing he about he hook nose and he long hair since school days. Anybady with a joke about finding anything, is Hermit nose could find it. Anybady want string to tie anything, is Hermit hair. Talk about bird, is description by length and curve of beak—like Hermit beak-nose. When yuh can't find anybady—dhey gaan into seclusion like Hermit. But Hermit always laugh. Dhis time Hermit serious.

That other time was a month or two before. We gaan up Jane Street to see Hetram but Hetram ain't home yet. So Hermit seh let we say go across to the Jane-Finch Mall at dhe McDonald's. Buy coffee and some chicken burger or something—he paying—and check out the girls. Funny thing about Hermit was he like spend a lat a time by heself but when he come outside is like he can't get enough of people, place, things. And he pleasant and outgoing. If a nice chick pass, Hermit lose shyness. He gan straight up to she and tell she she nice, sometimes mek a date with she or something. Was a Sunday and dhe mall full because of the flea market. McDonald's full too. So Writerji and me go and hold a table while Hermit in the line. Me and Writerji surveying everybady else. Suddenly a little commotion start up before the cashier. Hermit and a dread squaring off. Me and Writerji run up.

'Listen, man. I'm in this line before you. Yuh just want to come from nowhere and get infront me!' Hermit voice not loud but like a spring, one hand in he jacket pocket. Well, yuh know Jane-Finch area. Plenty West Indians, plenty Jamaicans with dhey drugs and crime and bullying people like dhey own dhe whole place. We think Hermit holding he wallet because of pickpocket.

'Listen—I gettin serve now, coolie bai.'

'Not before me, *rass*-ta.' Hermit deliberately breaking up the word. The dread black like tar and about four inches taller than Hermit, long dreadlocks and one a dhem green and red cap with Selassie picture. Hermit about 5′ 9″, not exactly short, he hair long like a yogi, and he skin fair. A odd contrast and similarity.

'I gettin serve now or is shooting.'

'Not before me, *rass*-ta.' Hermit turning squarely to dhe dread and straightening and suddenly smiling, 'friend I is a peaceful man—like Gandhi—you know Gandhi. Believe in non-violence. But lil advice from me; when yuh talk about shooting yuh should gat a gun in yuh hand first. I know people—nat me—who would shoot yuh dhe moment yuh talk about shooting. I know people—nat me—who would shoot yuh cunt dead, now, if yuh talk another word.' I getting coldsweat hearing Hermit. He ain't afraid though, he smiling. And I thinking, praying that the dread and he partner ain't start shooting fuh truth. I think we dead. Well, is Jane-Finch Mall and a whole crowd a Jamaicans suddenly stan up behind dhe dread. Just Hermit and me and Writerji near he. Dhem Indians and white people stay right at dhem table like sheep. Everything happening like lightning.

'Next cashier open here,' a supervisor said, smiling and breaking the tension. 'May I help you here, sir', she said pleasantly. She just open a cashier near the dread. Nothing like a pretty white girl to disarm a dread! Dread turn to she with a swagger and smiling like Hermit ain't exist. Later when we in the car driving home Writerji burst out, 'Hermit, I think we dead, man. Nearly piss mih pants.'

'Nah. He just bluffing.'

'What if he tek out a gun?' I ask.

'If he only put he hand in he coat pocket, I woulda shoot dhe bitch. An he know it.'

'With what?'

'This.' Hermit reach into he jacket and tek out a small blue automatic gun.

'Yuh mean yuh holding that thing all dhe time? How lang yuh gat this, man!' Writerji tek the gun and examine it fine fine.

'When I first come to this country.' Man, I in shock. I live with Hermit for six months and neva know this. But Hermit in Canada six years before me. And he live in Montreal most a dhe time. Same time I come from Georgetown, same time he come down from Montreal. Dhem Frenchie racial, he seh, and dhem want dhem own country. Like if dhem own anything. Is thief, they thief dhe land from dhem Amerindians—and don't matter Frenchie lose dhe 1980 referendum. Next time round and next time. Toronto tame compared to Montreal. . . .

Well, me and Writerji remember this incident and the gun same time, and how Hermit cool like cucumber and scared a nobady. Suddenly Writerji smile. 'Hermit—relax, my friend. Ah know yuh hungry. Well, this meat defrost. I will cook some—curry?'

'Nah, how about some bunjal geese,' Hermit laughed, 'and a bake one—come, I'll come and help you. Put on dhat Sundar-Popo tape, Jones.' Hermit turn to me a bit unsteady. He nicknamed me Jones because I see Jim Jones when he first land in Guyana, and because I went and see he fraud miracle in Sacred Heart Church lang before all them murders. Well, I start one big laugh. And Hermit start laughing too.

I tell yuh, times was tough. Hermit just come down from Montreal—he just get he landed and want make a new start—he give too many false name and false social insurance number in Montreal, and dhem Frenchie getting more racial—I coming up from GT and illegal, then baps, Writerji landing down on we. See how things happen! Remember dhem time when government thugs try to break up we meeting at Kitty Market Square and dhey get beat up and run in the police station for help. Was me, Cuffy and Akkara, and some other bais from Buxton. They shoot Akkara in dhe gardens and seh he had gun fuh overthrow dhe government, and dhey beat up Cuffy in he garage and put a AK-47 in he car trunk and seh he about to resist arrest, that he commit suicide in jail. All this just after Rodney assassination. Well, I ain't wait around. Them days yuh didn't had to get visa to come to Canada. Next flight I in Toronto. But mih uncle and he wife meking all sort a remark. If I bathe two times a day—that was a summer hotter than anything in Guyana—they complaining I bathe too lang and too often, I go to the toilet too often—is money water cost. This nat Guyana! Yuh pay fuh water here! Well, a meet Hermit in Knob Hill Farms one day and he seh he gat same prablem, he went through same thing—leh we rent a two-bedroom. I ain't gat no wuk yet, you know. He seh, man, no problem. He get a social insurance number and a name fuh mih. Some Indian name. The man dead and one a Hermit girlfriend get the name and number. Frank Sharma. See how Frank stick. All yuh must be think that I change mih name, become Frank instead of Ramesh because I want become Canadian duck. Nah. This coolie ain't shame he name. Anyway I Frank Sharma now. And frighten like ass when I go any place to wuk and I gat to say I name Frank Sharma. I trembling but trying to look bold, hoping I ain't say meh real name.

Yuh think is three cents we go though! Well, I ain't gat no wuk yet and Hermit just pick up a thing in a factory. Although he just get he landed, money still small. Almost a month and I ain't get nothing, then I walk in a factory at Steeles and Bathurst desperate—and get tek on. The supervisor want a forklift operator. Man, I neva drive a donkey-cart yet, much less forklift. I tell the man, with experience, I could manage dhe forklift, anything. Lucky for me the forklift break down, and the forklift driver who didn't show up, turn up next day. The supervisor find wuk for me packing boxes. And next two weeks, bam, Writerji turn up in the apartment lobby. He dhe last man to land in Canada before Canadian immigration decide yuh gat to get visa from Guyana, too much Guyanese fulling up Toronto. We bunking on dhe ground, can't afford a bed or even mattress, in a room and squeezing cents. Hermit trying to get a name and number for Writerji.

Well, Writerji waiting fuh he name and number but he ain't wasting time. He want learn about Toronto and Canada. He find library and reading up about Canada, about trees and birds. Whenever we go out anyway he pointing out birch, spruce, oak, cedar, weeping willow, pussy willow, ash, he pointing out bluejay, redstart, sparrow, starling, cardinal. He teking walk in park—yuh want know which park? Is at Eglinton and Jane street—Eglinton Flats. Autumn coming and Writerji want experience Canadian fall—colours radiant over all dhem trees. Geese coming in to land sweet sweet like plane. Every afternoon he coming home and writing poems. A night he writing a poem and suddenly he buss out one big laugh. He seh we thinking money scarce and cutting we tail and food all over dhe place. All them geese nice and fat, heading south fuh winter. He seh if is Guyana yuh think all them duck could deh so nice and lazy all over dhe place, preening themself like majesty and nobady own them, and people starving? And other people feeding them bread and fattening them up fuh we!

He seh why we don't catch some a dhem geese and stock up for winter. Them geese heading south to get away from the cold and now is dhe right time. And he tell we how in England dhem bai do dhe same thing and some Trini writer name Selvon write about this thing in a book call *The Lonely Londoners*. Hermit remember he hear this someway but he laugh and seh nobady neva write this—and how he know? Tell yuh the truth, I see them geese and I thinking same thing—how dhem bais in Guyana woulda done wuk them down.

'Is how I know? I'm a writer man!'

'So Hermit is Gandhi like Gandhiji and yuh is Writer—like Writerji,' I buss out one laugh.

Well, Hermit still ain't believe that this thing write down, so Writerji and we gone to St Dennis library near Weston Road and Eglinton corner and he get Hermit to borrow *The Lonely Londoners* and *Ways of Sunlight* by Sam Selvon. As soon as we get home he find the page and start read how hunger washing Cap tail and Cap decided to ketch seagull and eat them. We laugh good. And dhat is how he get dhe name Writerji. From dhat night we call he Writerji. But he done plan this thing. We could buy expire bread, and night time head down to Eglinton Flats Park. Them geese sleeping right next to a little culvert and all over the grass behind them trees. Two a-we could catch ducks and one man swipe dhe neck. Hermit get excited. He want try this thing. Well, is me and Hermit end up catching all them ducks and geese. I holding them and Hermit swiping them neck. All Writerji doing is holding bag and keeping lookout. Just like he since schooldays. He always thinking up something and me and Hermit doing the wuk. A trunk full a ducks in large double garbage bags. We skin them when we get home. Writerji saying we ain't stupid like Cap and we dispose of them feathers and skin real good. Nobody could catch we. Well them geese taste good.

Hermit seh next weekend let we take some fuh Prem and Kishore. They apartment overlooking Morningside Park and them maple trees flaming with colours. Writerji want tek a walk in the park and see this thing near. I want see too—was mih first autumn—but I playing I ain't care before them bai start laugh at me and call me Newfie and Pole and Balgobin-come-to-town. Writerji ain't care about who laugh he, he want see this thing close, hold them leaves. So we laughing he, asking if he really want size up more geese because it gat geese in that park. We teking a drink on a picnic table in the park and Writerji disappear. Next thing he coming back with he hand full a them small sour apple. He can't believe all them apple falling on the grass and wasting. People wasteful in Canada, he muttering over and over. Writerji want help to pick some nice green apple on them tree. Why? He thinking just like how yuh use green mango, or bilimbi, or barahar to make achaar and chatney, why not green apple. And right then mango scarce in Toronto, cost a fortune. Them days was not like nowadays when you gat West Indian store every corner. Them days you only get fruits from the West Indies when anybody coming. But that apple chatney taste good with them geese we bring for Prem and Kishore. Writerji didn't make no chatney though. He gat all dhem ideas but is me, Hermit, and

Prem and Kishore in they apartment making apple chatney! Not three cents dhat bai Writerji.

Anyway just after new year Hermit get a number for Writerji and same time a Vietnamese girl get pregnant and quit. So I talk to dhe boss and Writerji get tek on. Well, is a factory making knockdown cardboard cartons up in Concorde by Steeles and Bathurst and is winter. We getting up five in the morning to reach for seven. Writerji get easy job. How he manage I ain't know. See, I working on line. As fast as them boxes come off the line we gat to pack them on a crate. Yuh ain't even gat time to blow you nose or scratch yuh balls. If you tek a break while machine working, cardboard pile up on you. Bai, we only glad when machine break down every other day so we get an extra half hour or hour break. And them thing heavy. All Writerji gat to do is move them crates and strap them cardboard tight. Is not easy work but he could control things at he own pace. Dhe man whistling and singing while he working as though nuthing bother he. Lunch time he finding time to talk with them Vietnamese girls. Since I working in dhat factory them Vietnamese don't mix with nobody. At break time at nine they sit in a group one side in the factory, lunchtime they sit there, and afternoon break they sit there. Them two Vietnamese men watching Writerji carefully but soon he gat them girls laughing, and they saying hello now when they passing, and he know all they name. Writerji dressing smart and comb he hair everytime he go to the toilet, soon he in the office talking to dhe payroll clerk, Annette, who uncle own dhe factory. She really pretty and she rarely come into the factory until Writerji start talking with she now and again during lunchtime. The office mek with plexiglass and them office people could see everything happening in the factory. Soon she lending Writerji book. He just smiling when I ask he and saying is just literature. He trying to catch up on Canadian Literature.

Don't let mih tell yuh, dhem white man in the factory vex. They gat all them forklift and checker and loader and supervisor and manager jobs but Annette ain't bothering with dhem. Lunchtime and break time them bigbais alone in the lunch room. Only Ravi with them. Ravi come from Sri Lanka and he is senior floor hand—them supervisor give he order and he give we order. And he feel superior. He working there long and feel he is white man too. He don't mix with we. All them floor hands Guyanese or Trini Indians, Sri Lankans or Vietnamese—and it look like everybody refugee. Soon the foreman start finding extra work for Writerji. As soon as Writerji finish strapping, he gat to come and help we on line, help with the forklift, clean up the factory floor, help with checking, help with dhis and dhat. Writerji still smiling but he hardly talking to Annette except when he gat to go and collect he paycheque from she every Friday afternoon. She and he talking on phone night-time, and weekend she coming for Writerji and they going for lunch or dinner. Writerji ain't going no place except work if he ain't get car. April coming and every morning at dhe bus stop Writerji grumbling about dhe blasted Canadian cold—and how dhe blasted foreman picking on he.

This lunchtime Writerji just done eating and he can't bear it. He walk straight in dhe office and give Annette a book, and spend two minutes chatting with she. And everybody could see what happening with dhem. Is love like first time. As soon as he come out dhe office and sit down next to me, the foreman come out the lunch room.

'Anand—this lunch room need cleaning and sweeping. Go and give it a clean out.'

'I'm on lunchbreak now Tony.' Writerji sounding sharp and everybody listening. The factory silent, nat a machine working. You know how in a factory everything close down because everybody get break same time.

'Well, things slack now. . . .'

Writerji cut him off and speaking louder. 'Listen, Tony, I said I'm on my lunch break. Talk to me after my break. Do you understand simple English?'

'You Paki teaching me about English?'

'I'm not a Paki. See, you don't even know geography!'

'All right, smart ass. Clean and sweep this lunch room after break—here's the broom.'

Writerji jump up and I get up too. I thinking he gun knock the foreman. 'Let me tell you something, Tony. You can take that broom and shove it. I don't eat in that lunch room. Let the pigs who eat in there clean it up.'

'You're fired, man. You're fired.'

Writerji laugh loud and touch he waist. 'O course I'm fired! Jealous son-of-a-bitch! And you think I'm scared, yeh! I had enough, yeh! I quit anyway, yeh!' He imitating the Canadian accent perfect perfect. I want laugh, but I thinking about meself so I hold in till Tony rush to the office. Writerji pick up he things and walk to dhe office, everybody watching as he bend down and whisper something in Annette ear and kiss she cheek. And she get up and follow he to dhe door. Night time Writerji tell me and Hermit he thinking about heading for New York. Same time Hermit lawyer just file my papers and he seh things look good fuh mih so I holding on. Writerji seh he ain't able with this cold and stupid Canadians, and he jus call he cousin in New York. New York warmer and things easier. The biggest joke is that he cousin give he two names in Toronto to contact in the 'backtrack' ring to smuggle he across dhe border and one a dhe people is Hermit self!

Well, next day late winter storm—one foot snow and cold cold. Minus fifteen degrees and with wind chill like minus thirty. Confusion on dhem road. People hardly go to wuk. I stay home. Writerji said he cut right card. He going to New York, he ain't staying for next Canadian winter. Two days later, is Friday, and everything running. Temperature warm up to minus two and road salted and clear, sunshine. Friday afternoon after work Annette come and she and Writerji gone out. Dhe man feel free like a bird. He stap grumbling about Canadian cold now he decide to head south. Half past five and place dark already. Me and Hermit done eat and looking news when, bam bam bam on dhe door. We think Writerji come back, forget he key or something. Is good thing is Hermit open dhe door. Two immigration officer get tip that an illegal alien name Anand living here. Man I nearly get heart attack. Hermit checking dhem ID and talking to them officer like is he own buddy and he invite them officer in for coffee—cold night for this work, he telling them. Hermit say is just the two a-we live there. He show dhem ID and tell them how lawyer file paper fuh me. I not working, he say, just waiting for my case, and he send me for mih passport and immigration papers. I sweating and praying dhat Writerji don't turn up then. After he tell dhem I ain't working I feeling better. I afraid I might say something wrang.

Finally them officer gone—apologize to we, man them men nice and pleasant and apologize. Hermit seh when dhem gane, don't let them smile fool yuh. Well, is time to move Writerji. When Writerji come home is late. We looking TV and waiting fuh he but is he and Annette come in quiet quiet. Writerji laugh when he see we up. Well, we gat to wait till next morning. We done know why dhem come in so quiet quiet like fowl thief. We mek excuse and hustle to bed closing we room door and left them on dhe settee.

Next morning Writerji blue when we give he dhe lowdown. He seh he certain is Tony. Yuh think Writerji would lie low after this! Dhat bai now get bad to go out. And Annette teking day off from work. . . .

Yuh think is lil story we go through nuh. When Writerji ready fuh leave, is how you think he cross the border. Well, a gun tell you, but still secret. Yuh think Writerji can write dhis? Is in a container truck. Special container, forty-foot container. Them bai moving genuine shipment of furniture and personal effects to the States. Yuh know people always moving back and forth to States legally. A separate section in dhe front of dhe container conceal real good—double wall—to hold four people. That is how. Can't give more details as dhem bai still using dhe route. And Hermit seh less I know, less I talk. Well he didn't figure on Writerji. Writerji disappear underground in New York and is years we hear nothing about he. Next thing we know is novel out set in Guyana, and then dhem 'Underground Stories' by a writer name S. T. Writerji! He mixing up place and incident between New York and Canada—who can tell what is what? But them thing real and only we know who is who. Writerji send Hermit book to mih house. When Hermit, Lena, and them children come over Hermit quiet quiet. Is summer and we barbecuing in the backyard and dhem children running around, just like now. He find a corner and read that book right out. Nat a man disturb he. Lena surprise but nat me, dhat is dhe Hermit I know. When he done he shake he head and come over and tek a drink. Ask Lena and Katie. We drinking in mih house. Tears run down he eyes. No, that bai nat like Naipaul, he seh. He mek we proud! Dhem days, dhem days right hey, mixup and sanaay, sanaay good like rice and daal, and nice hot seven curry with hot chatney. I read dhat book out, right out dhe night before, and was same way I feel. Hermit tek a next drink—I gat a special bottle 12 Year Old Demerara Gold—and he come and sit next to me. Ask he when yuh see he. And he point to dhe front page. Writerji mek dedication—

To Hermit and Jones

—and he seh, 'dhem days, bai, dhem days is something else. See what we gain from dhem!' He close dhe book—just so and tears run down he face. Ask he, ask Hermit when yuh see him, ask him about dhat, about Writerji, about we.

My Brother's Keeper

When Papa dead, I cry till I almost vomit. I never know I would miss him that much because I used to never see him plenty, even when him was alive. I used to see him during Christmas when him would come back from Belle Glade in Florida. I can't even remember him face. I remember that him was a tall, bowlegged man who used to make some chaka-chaka sound when him eat. So when Ma tell me that Papa dead in a car accident in Miami with some woman, and that me have a little brother name David, I couldn't believe it. But when Ma tell me that the boy was going live with me and share my bed. I know I was going hate the boy even before I meet him.

I don't like hating people, but when him step in through the door with him new bag, new shoes, new shirt, and new pants, and me sit down there in the living room, barefoot and tear-up, tear-up, I hate him even more. Worse, him was wearing the watch that Papa did promise to give me the last time him leave at Christmas.

Papa did say as soon as him get back to America, him would send the watch to me in the mail. Him say him would wrap it up tight tight so them thiefing people at the post office wouldn't take it out and keep it for themself.

Now the watch wasn't a fancy watch with gold or anything like that. It was just a regular Timex, but it had a calculator and timer and a whole heap a thing me would never use. But nobody else on the block, not even Richard Chin Sang, who used to get me in trouble with Ma, and who used to think that him was better than everybody else, including me, had one. I ask the boy for the watch, and explain to him that Papa did promise the watch to me, and that him should just hand it over to me there and then. You know what that little idiot have the nerve to say? No. I did feel like to just box him over him head, and take it way, but I never want to get into any more trouble with Ma, so I just let it be. It was then I decide, fly high, fly low, I was going to get that watch. Papa did say it did belong to me. It was mine.

So the boy start to unpack and everybody start to make a fuss over him like him was Marcus Garvey son. I couldn't believe the fuss that them was making over that little red 'kin boy. It was like Ma never realize that the only way that him could be my brother is that Papa was sleeping with another woman, probably the woman who him dead with. And from the look of that boy, it was probably a white woman. I guess it never sink in, for if anybody did do that to me, orphan or no orphan, him would be out in the street.

But that is Ma problem and where me an she different. She always take up these hardluck stories and trying to save people and change the world. That is why her brother, Uncle George, living with us. Him used to own a bar down in Papine till him drink off all the profit. Now, everyday him getting drunk. So when the boy take out a present for him and it was a bottle of Johnny Walker from the States that him aunt, who couldn't take care of him any more, send with him, eye water start to run down the man face and him say, 'This is a good boy, Doreen. A good boy. David, I want you to stay out of trouble and don't follow that little hooligan over there. I love you boy. I love you.'

Uncle George would love anybody who give him a drink. That old rum-head fool will say anything for a Appleton and when thing get bad, bay rum. But the boy take him serious and start to hug the old rum head. And Uncle George hugging him back and bawling. Everybody forget that is me always have to fetch Uncle George, sometime in the worse bar in Kingston, clean him up, and take him home.

Then the boy start to take out all the trophy him win in school in Miami. Basketball trophy, baseball trophy, football trophy, and Uncle George, who start the bottle already, rubbing the boy head and saying, 'Doreen, this boy is a athlete!' And Ma put all the trophy on the dresser. My dresser. Then Ma begin to cry and say how strong him was and that Papa was strong too. She hug the boy and leave me in the room with the trophy. I feel like break every single trophy on the dresser, but I know if I did ever do that it wouldn't be Ma who would beat me, it would be Uncle George and him beat hard. Since the last time him beat me, I never want him to beat me again. And especially when him drunk, which is all of the time. Ma you can fool with a little scream, but with Uncle George you could bawl and scream as loud as you want, '*Lord, Lord, Lord God! Stop! I not going do it again. I not going do it again. I promise. I promise. I promise you. I promise you I won't do it again. I going dead now, I going dead. Lord, Lord, Lord God, Lord God!*' him wasn't going stop until him was done. And then dog eat you supper.

So I just look at the trophy them and pass aside. All them trophy. Me never get a trophy in my life for nothing. The one thing that me know me can do good is bird shooting, and you don't get trophy for bird shooting. Plus Ma make me stop because one time I kill a mockingbird. Now I was only trying to help because every morning, before she had to go to school, she would wake up and say how this mockingbird was waking her up at five o'clock in the morning and that she couldn't get a good night sleep. So I wake up early one morning and as the bird open him mouth, baps, him dead. So I walk into the kitchen big and broad with the dead bird, but Ma start to cry and give me this long speech how I was wicked to shoot a bird during mating season and that God was going to punish me and I was going to hell. She made me feel so bad. All I wanted to do was help her, but it never worked. But that is just how Ma is, you can never understand her.

Even my father could never understand her and that is why him leave the last time. I know she did really love him, but I know that they was married because of me. How I know is one time Papa and Ma get into a big fight and Papa lick Ma.

Well, she phone Uncle George and him come to the house with him gun. Them have a few words and Papa say something and then Uncle George say something.

Then Papa say him would never marry Ma if it wasn't for me. And then Uncle George slam the door and I think him pull the gun. That is how I find out that I was a bastard.

Anyway, *that* bastard was back here in my room, and Ma was running her hand through him hair and saying how straight it was and how him was so light skin. Uncle George was patting him on the shoulder and looking at him teeth.

Uncle George don't have a teeth in him head. Him lose all of them by fighting and the rest of them rotten out and him have to pull them. But this boy did have all him teeth, and some with gold fillings too. That impress Uncle George. Me, I lose two in a fight, and I never been to a dentist, though me is sixteen years old. I don't think I ever going to one.

Ma hug him again and say she was going to fix dinner and if him did like chicken. Him say yes and Ma just wrap him up in her bosom and give him that smile that you couldn't help but smile. But I never smile. I just show him where him could put the rest of him things. Uncle George say I was jealous, but what did that old rumhead know?

One thing I can say about the boy though, him was hard to fool. Him wasn't like me cousin, Owen, from the country who me did lock in the closet. I tell Owen it was a elevator and him believe me. As him step inside,

I just lock the door and keep him in there for about a hour until Uncle George hear the knocking and run come inside the room. I let out Owen right away. When I see Uncle George, I tell him we was just playing, and I guess him never feel like beat me that day, and him believe me. But this one you couldn't fool. I try, but it never work. Him was smart. Him was dangerous.

So I leave him in the room and run down the street to meet my friend over by the park. As I jump over the fence, I hear these footstep behind me. I chase the boy back to the yard. I tell him that him couldn't come because him was wearing him new shoes. Him say the shoes wasn't new, them was six months old. Real American. I tell him that him couldn't come and play and wear the watch, for it could break. Him say it was shock proof. I tell him that him would have ask Ma first before him leave, and it was then him have the gall to call my mother, my own mother, 'Ma', to my face. I tell him there and then that she was my mother. She wasn't him mother. Him did have a mother of him own, and that whoever she was and wherever she was, him should go find her. I tell him if him ever call her Ma in front of me again, I don't care what Uncle George would do to me, I was going to beat the shit out of him.

Him walk off and start to bawl, but I never care, for him wouldn't be trailing me all around the place, so that all my friend would laugh after me.

When I get back home that night though, it was bangarang. Ma start to give me a long speech about how I must think about my little brother feelings and after what I learned in Sabbath school about Cain and Abel. She go on for about a hour about the Sabbath school business. Sabbath school. I only used to go there to please her because she always talking about how she going to dead and how she want me to grow up to be a good man. Good man, good woman. Them things dead from the start. She is a good woman and look where it get her. A little elementary schoolteacher in Back O' Wall or whatever they call it now. Good woman. The only thing that worth is a whole heap a pain and a little boy following you around the place and asking questions about, 'What's this?' and 'Why do they call it that?' while all you friend laughing after you. Which is what I have to put up with because Ma say so. What nearly kill me, though, is that she say him could call her Ma if he wanted to. She say it. I hear it from her own mouth. But I take one look at him and him never do it in front of me.

So the next day me and him was walking down the street and him start telling me story about how Papa take him to Disney World, how Papa this and how Papa that, and I never want to hear it. And then him tell me how Papa dead and how him cry and cry, and him glad that I was him brother.

And that was why him want to keep the watch because it remind him of Papa. It was then I know how much I hate him, for nobody could love Papa like me.

When we get to the park, I tell him to keep him mouth shut. I never want my friend to find out that him was me brother. But as we step through the gate, Richard Chin Sang say, 'Who that with you, Umpire?' Umpire is my nickname, but that is another whole long story. Before Richard could finish the question, the little idiot shout out, 'I'm his brother.'

Well, everybody start to laugh because him never look anything like anybody in my family and Richard say him must be a *jacket*. Richard did want to change my name from Umpire to 'Three Piece Suit and Thing'. 'And Thing' would be David.

But Richard wouldn't have him way. Me and him did fall out from the time him try to tell a lie on me and it backfire. Richard used to thief for nothing. One day me and him was in the staff room at school and him thief ten dollars from a teacher purse. Them find out that it was only me and him who was in the room that morning, so it must be one of us. Richard say him don't need the money for him bring at least thirty dollar to school every week. And him pull out the thirty dollar.

So everybody say it must be me. I nearly end up with a caning because everybody know I used to get into a whole heap of fight and they say I was a troublemaker. Now I couldn't get a caning, for if you get a caning they call your house. Then I have to go home to face Uncle George and get another whipping. So I take everybody to the other end of the school where I know Richard used to hide all the things him used to steal. When they open the locker, comb, toothbrush, chewing gum, even somebody slide rule fall out. He never need them, but him thief them. So they suspend him from school, and when him get home, him father beat him so hard him never come out for three week. It was from then me and him never get along. So the truth come out, but it never set me free. Even my friend Peter from up the road did try to call me, 'Three Piece Suit' because him did know I couldn't get into any more fight. But I tell him if he ever called me that, I would tell Laura Spenser father what them was doing at the Christmas fair behind the Ferris wheel. I had to threaten all of them like this, for I know everything about all of them, but they don't know a thing about me. I always make sure people owe me, not me owe them or them have anything on me. Just because I can't fight anymore, don't mean that anybody can take steps with me. I keep everything to myself, but this little idiot was going to mash up everything. I never like that.

But him did have some use. In time we teach him how to play cricket and football. Him call it soccer. Teaching him to play cricket was a joke. The boy lick four runs, drop the bat and start to run like him hear news. We just tell him to pick up the bat, and tell him that it wasn't baseball him was playing. We teach him how to hold the bat, to dip and score runs. It did take time, but him learn.

But the best thing was all them trophy that him did get from basketball. Him never play football good, so we put him in the goal. Papa, now that was a goalkeeper. From the ball land in him hand, that done. Him catch it. From that day on, Richard Chin Sang and him friend never score a goal on we. We beat them team ten games straight. That never happen before. Every Saturday them used to just win all the games and send we home with a bus ass. But when we start to win, them did want stop play with we, but them soon realize that if them did really want a good game of football, even though them never like we, them would have to play against we. Now, don't get me wrong, is not that I did start to like the boy, but we was winning, and that make a difference.

So when we start win all the game, everybody else start to like him. Sometime I wish them did call we 'Three Piece Suit and Thing'. But all of them forget. People have short memory, especially when them is your friend. Peter even wanted to call David, 'Little Umps' but I put an end to that too. I wasn't sharing my name with him.

But everything broke loose one evening after a football game. I had to go help Uncle George get home. Him was drunk again. And it was a bar way down in Hermitage. So I had to get him and clean him up. When I finally find him, it was about seven o'clock and by the time we get home it was eight-thirty. Just as I finish clean him up and put him in the bed, Peter little sister run inside the house and tell me that David in a fight with Richard. I just take me time, for I know David couldn't take on Richard and win. Him was finally going get the bus ass that him should get from the first day him step inside my house.

By the time I get to the park, Richard was holding the boy like a piece of stick and licking the boy in him face. Well, sooner or later the boy would have to learn, and I wasn't going to get into any fight for him. If I was going to get in a fight, it would be my fight. And whoever I fight would have to be worth the beating I would get when I go home. This boy wasn't worth it.

When Richard see me, him stop and pretend like nothing was going on. But when him see that I wasn't going help the boy, him lick the boy so hard I feel it down to me shoes. Is then I find out what the fighting was about. Richard hold him and say, 'See, I tell you, him afraid of me. Him not going fight for you. Him don't even like you.'

'I still say,' David was shouting, 'he can beat you up any day.'

The little idiot. Him was fighting to defend me name. Some people never learn. You shouldn't say things, even if they true, if you can't back them up with your fist. Richard throw him down on the ground and kick him in him side. Now that wasn't right. Beating up somebody is one thing, but when you kick them on the ground is another. But it wasn't my fight.

Then Richard tear off the watch off David hand and was going crush the face with the heel of him shoes, and David bawl out, 'I'll give you the watch, Paul. But don't let him break Papa's watch.'

And as Richard foot come down, the boy dive underneath it and take the heel in him chest. Him really did love Papa.

Well, before Richard know what happen, I sucker punch that Chinee boy so hard, him was seeing Chop Suey. Him stagger for about two yard and then I lick him cross him face with my fist. Him get a good blow to my face and bloodup me nose. But I kick him in him seed and him fall down and then start to run to him yard, bawling like a dog and saying him was going call me house and tell them what I do to him.

Is then I know I dead. Uncle George was going beat me this time. I was dead. I couldn't hide my nose with the blood; it was all over my shirt. Even if I could bribe David not to tell—although I never know with what, I never have anything on him—Richard was going to tell him father. Then him father would call my mother and embarrass her with, 'What kind of wild animal you have there in your house that you calling your son? If you see what he do to my son and bla, bla, bla, bla, bla.' I might as well run away from home.

I pick him up off the ground and clean him up. I help him wash him face with the hose near the badminton court. It was the first time I see him face. Him look at me and say, 'I hope Ma doesn't beat you too hard when we get home.'

I almost forgive him for calling her Ma that time.

'Here, take this,' him say and try to give me the watch. I couldn't take it. The boy earn it. I push him hand away and tell him to keep it. As we was walking home though, I ask him if I could borrow the watch every now and then. Maybe I could borrow it for the Christmas fair, if I was still alive. Him say yes and as we turn the corner, I look on the verandah and I see Uncle George, drunk and holding onto one of the column with one hand and the belt in the other. I know I was dead.

I couldn't run away, I never have anywhere else to go. And if I run away, I would have to come back, and the beating would still be waiting on me. I would probably get it worse then. I couldn't do a thing. I could only hope that him was too drunk to stand up and that him would fall asleep or throw up before him finish. But what if him remember that him never finish tonight and start on me tomorrow morning?

David see the look on me face, and run straight up to the verandah. Him start to cry and say how if it wasn't for me how them was going to mash up Papa watch. And him tell some lie about what them was calling Ma, all kind of bad word me never know the boy know. Then him say that Richard and him friend was running joke about Uncle George, that him is a rum head and how me rescue him from Richard and three of him friend. Three of him friend! The boy was good. It did sound so real. Me was there and even me did start believe it. The boy put on one show. Uncle George drop the belt, hug me and say, 'For the first time, you do good, boy. You do good.' Ma kiss me, rub me head, then take him inside. And all the while him smiling and winking with me. I couldn't believe it. It end up that me owe him. The little idiot save me.

Private School

It was the roaches that had caused the disgrace.

'I hate them, I hate them, I hate them,' Denise whispered to herself as she sat on a gravestone in the cemetery. She hated the roaches even more than she feared the duppies who she knew roamed the cemetery at nights. Everyone in her neighbourhood had seen at least one duppy, but never in the daytime; like roaches, the duppies shunned bright light. If it had been dark, Denise would not have dared to set foot in this place of tumbledown headstones and dry red earth. But the blaze of the morning sun was enough to keep all but the stupidest of duppies underground. Denise herself was already sweating in her gaberdine blue uniform.

She pulled several comic books out of her bag—*Archie*, *Peanuts*, *Tarzan*—and settled down in a corner of the cemetery, staying far away from the cotton trees which she knew duppies especially liked. When she finished the comics, she wandered round, reading the words on the headstones.

It was the third school-day that she had spent in the cemetery, and like the previous two times, she went back home at about 1.30 in the afternoon, taking the key from under the mat and letting herself into the two-room house, which stood in a big yard full of other two-room wooden houses. She ate the left-over cornmeal porridge from that morning then pulled a book from the mahogany bookcase (her mother's pride and joy) to pass the time. She had read *Black Beauty* before, but she started it again, feeling the familiar rage against the people who were going to mistreat the horse.

Her mother returned home from work around six o'clock that evening and asked what she had done at school that day.

Denise mumbled something about arithmetic.

'Mr Benny said you came home early.' (Mr Benny lived in the two rooms at the front of the yard.)

'Yes, Mama. Miss Maude let us out early because she had a headache.' Denise felt her stomach hurting as she told the lie, but she didn't know how to tell her mother what had happened. She pretended to do homework while her mother cooked green bananas and callaloo with saltfish on their little kerosene stove.

'I'm glad to see you doing your homework already,' her mother said. 'Miss Maude is a good teacher. Nearly everybody who go to that school pass their common entrance and go to high school. You only have one more year, and then it's your turn.'

Denise said nothing. She hated Miss Maude as much as she hated the roaches. It was funny; lizards didn't bother her, even the biggest of green lizards who stuck their tongues out and had been known to jump on people. Nor did rat-bats who sometimes flew into the house, seeming to dive right at you. Her mother always said they brought good luck while the other people in the yard swore that the bats were flying duppies—they always showed up soon after someone in the neighbourhood died, or was killed.

But Denise only had to see a roach to get panic-stricken. Her mother knew about Miss Maude's roaches but she thought Denise could put up with them for the sake of a good education. Once she got to high school she would forget all about them.

Before dinner was ready, Denise went to one of the two bathrooms in the middle of the yard and took her evening shower, closing her eyes against the whip of the cold water. She wished she was brave enough to run away and stay forever in the cemetery, until her mother realized how much she hated Miss Maude's school. But then her mother would be alone and she didn't want that either. She stayed in the bathroom until her mother shouted for her to come and eat. It was a quiet dinner; Denise couldn't think of a word to say and her mother seemed worried about something.

Later, while her mother ironed clothes, Denise read in bed, her face inches from the book because of the dimness of the lightbulb. She finished *Black Beauty* by the time her mother turned off the light but she couldn't sleep as she thought of the roaches. It was because of them that Miss Maude had embarrassed her in front of the whole class.

Miss Maude's Private School had no flushing toilet, just a pit toilet, something that Denise had thought existed only in her mother's day. Her mother had talked about them, about how her father (Denise's grandfather) had spent weeks digging one, and he dug it so deep that it never filled up. It had been the best pit toilet in the village where Denise's mother grew up. But all her life, Denise's mother had hated the smell, and when she moved to Kingston, she made sure she lived in a place which had toilets you could flush. The yard where they lived had two toilets, each with a chain that you could pull, and everyone took care to leave the bowls white and clean. A dirty toilet could be the cause of loud cuss-cuss among people in the yard, but that had happened only once or twice.

At Miss Maude's Private School, the toilet was at the very back of the premises, about sixty feet from the classroom, but you still had a clear view of it from the classroom windows. It was built of wood with a rickety door and inside was a wooden box erected over a deep dark pit. The top of the box had a round opening over which you sat. It stank, although Miss Maude—a tall gangly woman who inspired terror in the 28 children whose parents paid her five shillings a month for schooling—often poured Dettol disinfectant down the darkness. The children were not allowed to say the words 'pit toilet'; they had to say 'outhouse'.

Denise's constant nightmare was that she would fall into the pit of the outhouse, and she knew how far the plunge would be. She'd once dropped several lighted matches into the hole and something had caught fire a long way down. She'd had to pee quickly to put it out.

Her dread of the toilet grew when she found out about the roaches who lived there. As soon as she shut the door and the darkness engulfed her, she could hear them crawling about. When the door was open, she saw how fat they were. Some of the boys at Miss Maude's school made a sport out of stepping on them, and the 'plop' and white pus made her sicker than seeing the healthy roaches crawling around.

She had tried not to use the toilet, so that by the time she got home at 3.30, she'd be in agony from the cramps in her belly. When she couldn't control herself, she asked to be excused from the classroom and urinated in the yard, hoping no one would look out and see her. Sometimes though Miss Maude conducted the class outside, under a tamarind tree, and then Denise would hold herself tightly, trying not to cry. But four days ago her control had cracked, causing Miss Maude to do what she did best—public shaming.

That day Miss Maude had been teaching the class outside, barking on and on about learning to spell right while Denise's need to go to the toilet grew along with her fear.

'Who is going to win the Spelling Bee for me this year?' Miss Maude asked. 'Jennifer, come up here. Spell buffalo.'

While Jennifer spelled, forgetting one 'f' and cowering under Miss Maude's scorn, Denise whispered to her best friend in the class, an Indian boy named Ian, to stand up and shield her. They were both sitting in the last row of the semicircle of children.

Ian stood up and Denise stooped behind him and felt her belly empty like a burst tyre. Miss Maude saw her.

'What are you doing back there,' she hollered, causing the rush of brown liquid to soil Denise's socks and shoes.

'Come up here.'

As Denise dragged herself to the front of the class, Miss Maude screamed, 'You nasty little creature. Imagine defecating in front of a boy!' Denise had actually stooped behind Ian, but she couldn't find the words to point that out to Miss Maude.

'Take your bag and go home right this minute,' Miss Maude spat at her. 'Tell your mother I want to see her tomorrow.' Denise left without looking at Ian and took her long walk home, imagining swarms of flies following her, buzzing with news of her nastiness. She didn't tell her mother what had happened but spent the next days pretending to set out for school and passing the time in the cemetery three streets away from their yard. She had made up her mind to spend her life doing that rather than return to Miss Maude's Private School.

But what if her mother found out and made her go back? Denise's whole body burned anew with shame. She slept in fits, slipping in and out of a nightmare where all the rooms in the yard were in flames and some-one, Mr Benny from the front rooms, was crying 'help me lawd help me'.

The next morning, Denise noticed that her mother's face looked more tight and tired than she had seen it in a long time. Her mother was a tall, fine-boned, black-skinned woman with short hair and full lips. But what people noticed right away were her eyes—big, kind, and thoughtful as if she was concerned about everyone. People said Denise looked just like her mother except for the eyes. 'That is a determined little girl,' Mr Benny always said. 'She going go far.' Denise didn't know what he meant.

This morning her mother's eyes held fear. She kept sighing as she pre-pared breakfast. When Denise asked, 'what happen, Mama?' her mother shook her head. 'Mister Man giving me trouble at work. I think he want to fire because he in money difficulties.' She always called her boss 'Mister Man' although his name was Jackson. He was an accountant and she worked as his office maid.

'Denise, you have to get a good education so you can do better than me, you hear?' her mother said as she gave her her school-bag and waved her off.

This time Denise by-passed the cemetery and walked as far as the gate to Miss Maude's private school. She stood outside watching the other chil-dren enter, waiting until Miss Maude rang the bell for them to gather in the classroom.

When all the children were inside and only Miss Maude stood in the yard still ringing the bell, Denise slowly approached the tall wiry woman. Miss Maude stopped ringing and stared at her. Denise forced herself to look in the woman's stern eyes.

'Can you please take me back, Miss?'

'Where's your mother?'

'She gone to work. She 'fraid that they going to fire her and I don't want her to worry 'bout me. Please, Miss.'

Several emotions went across Miss Maude's face. Almost absent-mindedly, she rang the bell once more. Then she said, 'Spell buffalo'.

'B-U-F-F-A-L-O,' Denise recited.

'Mmmm. I don't want any more defecating in this yard. Do you understand?'

'It was only because I 'fraid of the roaches,' Denise said, her voice breaking.

'What roaches?'

'In the pit . . . in the outhouse.'

'Roaches don't bite,' Miss Maude snapped. 'Anyway, I'll buy some Baygon. Spell "Mississippi".'

'M-I S-S-I S-S-I P-P-I,' Denise sang. It was one of the first words her mother had taught her to spell. It was so easy.

'Mmmm. Go inside,' Miss Maude said, ringing the bell once more.

Nineteen Thirty-Seven

My Madonna cried. A miniature teardrop traveled down her white porcelain face, like dew on the tip of early morning grass. When I saw the tear I thought, surely, that my mother had died.

I sat motionless observing the Madonna the whole day. It did not shed another tear. I remained in the rocking chair until it was nightfall, my bones aching from the thought of another trip to the prison in Port-au-Prince. But, of course, I had to go.

The roads to the city were covered with sharp pebbles only half buried in the thick dust. I chose to go barefoot, as my mother had always done on her visits to the Massacre River, the river separating Haiti from the Spanish-speaking country that she had never allowed me to name because I had been born on the night that El Generalissimo, Dios Trujillo, the honorable chief of state, had ordered the massacre of all Haitians living there.

The sun was just rising when I got to the capital. The first city person I saw was an old woman carrying a jar full of leeches. Her gaze was glued to the Madonna tucked under my arm.

'May I see it?' she asked.

I held out the small statue that had been owned by my family ever since it was given to my great-great-great-grandmother Défilé by a French man who had kept her as a slave.

The old woman's index finger trembled as it moved toward the Madonna's head. She closed her eyes at the moment of contact, her wrists shaking.

'Where are you from?' she asked. She had layers of 'respectable' wrinkles on her face, the kind my mother might also have one day, if she has a chance to survive.

'I am from Ville Rose,' I said, 'the city of painters and poets, the coffee city, with beaches where the sand is either black or white, but never mixed together, where the fields are endless and sometimes the cows are yellow like cornmeal.'

The woman put the jar of leeches under her arm to keep them out of the sun.

447

'You're here to see a prisoner?' she asked.

'Yes.'

'I know where you can buy some very good food for this person.'

She led me by the hand to a small alley where a girl was selling fried pork and plantains wrapped in brown paper. I bought some meat for my mother after asking the cook to fry it once more and then sprinkle it with spiced cabbage.

The yellow prison building was like a fort, as large and strong as in the days when it was used by the American marines who had built it. The Americans taught us how to build prisons. By the end of the 1915 occupation, the police in the city really knew how to hold human beings trapped in cages, even women like Manman who was accused of having wings of flame.

The prison yard was as quiet as a cave when a young Haitian guard escorted me there to wait. The smell of the fried pork mixed with that of urine and excrement was almost unbearable. I sat on a pile of bricks, trying to keep the Madonna from sliding through my fingers. I dug my buttocks farther into the bricks, hoping perhaps that my body might sink down to the ground and disappear before my mother emerged as a ghost to greet me.

The other prisoners had not yet woken up. All the better, for I did not want to see them, these bone-thin women with shorn heads, carrying clumps of their hair in their bare hands, as they sought the few rays of sunshine that they were allowed each day.

My mother had grown even thinner since the last time I had seen her. Her face looked like the gray of a late evening sky. These days, her skin barely clung to her bones, falling in layers, flaps, on her face and neck. The prison guards watched her more closely because they thought that the wrinkles resulted from her taking off her skin at night and then putting it back on in a hurry, before sunrise. This was why Manman's sentence had been extended to life. And when she died, her remains were to be burnt in the prison yard, to prevent her spirit from wandering into any young innocent bodies.

I held out the fried pork and plantains to her. She uncovered the food and took a peek before grimacing, as though the sight of the meat nauseated her. Still she took it and put it in a deep pocket in a very loose fitting white dress that she had made herself from the cloth that I had brought her on my last visit.

I said nothing. Ever since the morning of her arrest, I had not been able to say anything to her. It was as though I became mute the moment I stepped into the prison yard. Sometimes I wanted to speak, yet I was not able to open my mouth or raise my tongue. I wondered if she saw my struggle in my eyes.

She pointed at the Madonna in my hands, opening her arms to receive it. I quickly handed her the statue. She smiled. Her teeth were a dark red, as though caked with blood from the initial beating during her arrest. At times, she seemed happier to see the Madonna than she was to see me.

She rubbed the space under the Madonna's eyes, then tasted her fingertips, the way a person tests for salt in salt water.

'Has she cried?' Her voice was hoarse from lack of use. With every visit, it seemed to get worse and worse. I was afraid that one day, like me, she would not be able to say anything at all.

I nodded, raising my index finger to show that the Madonna had cried a single tear. She pressed the statue against her chest as if to reward the Madonna and then, suddenly, broke down and began sobbing herself.

I reached over and patted her back, the way one burps a baby. She continued to sob until a guard came and nudged her, poking the barrel of his rifle into her side. She raised her head, keeping the Madonna lodged against her chest as she forced a brave smile.

'They have not treated me badly,' she said. She smoothed her hands over her bald head, from her forehead to the back of her neck. The guards shaved her head every week. And before the women went to sleep, the guards made them throw tin cups of cold water at one another so that their bodies would not be able to muster up enough heat to grow those wings made of flames, fly away in the middle of the night, slip into the slumber of innocent children and steal their breath.

Manman pulled the meat and plantains out of her pocket and started eating a piece to fill the silence. Her normal ration of food in the prison was bread and water, which is why she was losing weight so rapidly.

'Sometimes the food you bring me, it lasts for months at a time,' she said. 'I chew it and swallow my saliva, then I put it away and then chew it again. It lasts a very long time this way.'

A few of the other women prisoners walked out into the yard, their chins nearly touching their chests, their shaved heads sunk low on bowed necks. Some had large boils on their heads. One, drawn by the fresh smell of fried pork, came to sit near us and began pulling the scabs from the bruises on her scalp, a line of blood dripping down her back.

All of these women were here for the same reason. They were said to have been seen at night rising from the ground like birds on fire. A loved one, a friend, or a neighbor had accused them of causing the death of a child. A few other people agreeing with these stories was all that was needed to have them arrested. And sometimes even killed.

I remembered so clearly the day Manman was arrested. We were new to the city and had been sleeping on a cot at a friend's house. The friend had a sick baby who was suffering with colic. Every once in a while, Manman would wake up to look after the child when the mother was so tired that she no longer heard her son's cries.

One morning when I woke up, Manman was gone. There was the sound of a crowd outside. When I rushed out I saw a group of people taking my mother away. Her face was bleeding from the pounding blows of rocks and sticks and the fists of strangers. She was being pulled along by two policemen, each tugging at one of her arms as she dragged her feet. The woman we had been staying with carried her dead son by the legs. The policemen made no efforts to stop the mob that was beating my mother.

'*Lougarou*, witch, criminal!' they shouted.

I dashed into the street, trying to free Manman from the crowd. I wasn't even able to get near her.

I followed her cries to the prison. Her face was swollen to three times the size that it had been. She had to drag herself across the clay floor on her belly when I saw her in the prison cell. She was like a snake, someone with no bones left in her body. I was there watching when they shaved her head for the first time. At first I thought they were doing it so that the open gashes on her scalp could heal. Later, when I saw all the other women in the yard, I realized that they wanted to make them look like crows, like men.

Now, Manman sat with the Madonna pressed against her chest, her eyes staring ahead, as though she was looking into the future. She had never talked very much about the future. She had always believed more in the past.

When I was five years old, we went on a pilgrimage to the Massacre River, which I had expected to be still crimson with blood, but which was as clear as any water that I had ever seen. Manman had taken my hand and pushed it into the river, no further than my wrist. When we dipped our hands, I thought that the dead would reach out and haul us in, but only our own faces stared back at us, one indistinguishable from the other.

With our hands in the water, Manman spoke to the sun. 'Here is my child, Josephine. We were saved from the tomb of this river when she was still in my womb. You spared us both, her and me, from this river where I lost my mother.'

My mother had escaped El Generalissimo's soldiers, leaving her own mother behind. From the Haitian side of the river, she could still see the soldiers chopping up *her* mother's body and throwing it into the river along with many others.

We went to the river many times as I was growing up. Every year my mother would invite a few more women who had also lost their mothers there.

Until we moved to the city, we went to the river every year on the first of November. The women would all dress in white. My mother would hold my hand tightly as we walked toward the water. We were all daughters of that river, which had taken our mothers from us. Our mothers were the ashes and we were the light. Our mothers were the embers and we were the sparks. Our mothers were the flames and we were the blaze. We came from the bottom of that river where the blood never stops flowing, where my mother's dive toward life—her swim among all those bodies slaughtered in flight—gave her those wings of flames. The river was the place where it had all begun.

'At least I gave birth to my daughter on the night that my mother was taken from me,' she would say. 'At least you came out at the right moment to take my mother's place.'

Now in the prison yard, my mother was trying to avoid the eyes of the guard peering down at her.

'One day I will tell you the secret of how the Madonna cries,' she said.

I reached over and touched the scabs on her fingers. She handed me back the Madonna.

I know how the Madonna cries. I have watched from hiding how my mother plans weeks in advance for it to happen. She would put a thin layer of wax and oil in the hollow space of the Madonna's eyes and when the wax melted, the oil would roll down the little face shedding a more perfect tear than either she and I could ever cry.

'You go. Let me watch you leave,' she said, sitting stiffly.

I kissed her on the cheek and tried to embrace her, but she quickly pushed me away.

'You will please visit me again soon,' she said.

I nodded my head yes.

'Let your flight be joyful,' she said, 'and mine too.'

I nodded and then ran out of the yard, fleeing before I could flood the front of my dress with my tears. There had been too much crying already.

Manman had a cough the next time I visited her. She sat in a corner of the yard, and as she trembled in the sun, she clung to the Madonna.

451

'The sun can no longer warm God's creatures,' she said. 'What has this world come to when the sun can no longer warm God's creatures?'

I wanted to wrap my body around hers, but I knew she would not let me.

'God only knows what I have got under my skin from being here. I may die of tuberculosis, or perhaps there are worms right now eating me inside.'

When I went again, I decided that I would talk. Even if the words made no sense, I would try to say something to her. But before I could even say hello, she was crying. When I handed her the Madonna, she did not want to take it. The guard was looking directly at us. Manman still had a fever that made her body tremble. Her eyes had the look of delirium.

'Keep the Madonna when I am gone,' she said. 'When I am completely gone, maybe you will have someone to take my place. Maybe you will have a person. Maybe you will have some *flesh* to console you. But if you don't, you will always have the Madonna.'

'Manman, did you fly?' I asked her.

She did not even blink at my implied accusation.

'Oh, now you talk,' she said, 'when I am nearly gone. Perhaps you don't remember. All the women who came with us to the river, they could go to the moon and back if that is what they wanted.'

A week later, almost to the same day, an old woman stopped by my house in Ville Rose on her way to Port-au-Prince. She came in the middle of the night, wearing the same white dress that the women usually wore on their trips to dip their hands in the river.

'Sister,' the old woman said from the doorway. 'I have come for you.'

'I don't know you,' I said.

'You *do* know me,' she said. 'My name is Jacqueline. I have been to the river with you.'

I had been by the river with many people. I remembered a Jacqueline who went on the trips with us, but I was not sure this was the same woman. If she were really from the river, she would know. She would know all the things that my mother had said to the sun as we sat with our hands dipped in the water, questioning each other, making up codes and disciplines by which we could always know who the other daughters of the river were.

'Who are you?' I asked her.

'I am a child of that place,' she answered. 'I come from that long trail of blood.'

'Where are you going?'

'I am walking into the dawn.'

'Who are you?'

'I am the first daughter of the first star.'

'Where do you drink when you're thirsty?'

'I drink the tears from the Madonna's eyes.'

'And if not there?'

'I drink the dew.'

'And if you can't find dew?'

'I drink from the rain before it falls.'

'If you can't drink there?'

'I drink from the turtle's hide.'

'How did you find your way to me?'

'By the light of the mermaid's comb.'

'Where does your mother come from?'

'Thunderbolts, lightning, and all things that soar.'

'Who are you?'

'I am the flame and the spark by which my mother lived.'

'Where do you come from?'

'I come from the puddle of that river.'

'Speak to me.'

'You hear my mother who speaks through me. She is the shadow that follows my shadow. The flame at the tip of my candle. The ripple in the stream where I wash my face. Yes. I will eat my tongue if ever I whisper that name, the name of that place across the river that took my mother from me.'

I knew then that she had been with us, for she knew all the answers to the questions I asked.

'I think you do know who I am,' she said, staring deeply into the pupils of my eyes. 'I know who *you* are. You are Josephine. And your mother knew how to make the Madonna cry.'

I let Jacqueline into the house. I offered her a seat in the rocking chair, gave her a piece of hard bread and a cup of cold coffee.

'Sister, I do not want to be the one to tell you,' she said, 'but your mother is dead. If she is not dead now, then she will be when we get to Port-au-Prince. Her blood calls to me from the ground. Will you go with me to see her? Let us go to see her.'

We took a mule for most of the trip. Jacqueline was not strong enough to make the whole journey on foot. I brought the Madonna with me, and Jacqueline took a small bundle with some black rags in it.

When we got to the city, we went directly to the prison gates. Jacqueline whispered Manman's name to a guard and waited for a response.

'She will be ready for burning this afternoon,' the guard said.

My blood froze inside me. I lowered my head as the news sank in.

'Surely, it is not that much a surprise,' Jacqueline said, stroking my shoulder. She had become rejuvenated, as though strengthened by the correctness of her prediction.

'We only want to visit her cell,' Jacqueline said to the guard. 'We hope to take her personal things away.'

The guard seemed too tired to argue, or perhaps he saw in Jacqueline's face traces of some long-dead female relative whom he had not done enough to please while she was still alive.

He took us to the cell where my mother had spent the last year. Jacqueline entered first, and then I followed. The room felt damp, the clay breaking into small muddy chunks under our feet.

I inhaled deeply to keep my lungs from aching. Jacqueline said nothing as she carefully walked around the women who sat like statues in different corners of the cell. There were six of them. They kept their arms close to their bodies, like angels hiding their wings. In the middle of the cell was an arrangement of sand and pebbles in the shape of a cross for my mother. Each woman was either wearing or holding something that had belonged to her.

One of them clutched a pillow as she stared at the Madonna. The woman was wearing my mother's dress, the large white dress that had become like a tent on Manman.

I walked over to her and asked, 'What happened?'

'Beaten down in the middle of the yard,' she whispered.

'Like a dog,' said another woman.

'Her skin, it was too loose,' said the woman wearing my mother's dress. 'They said prison could not cure her.'

The woman reached inside my mother's dress pocket and pulled out a handful of chewed pork and handed it to me. I motioned her hand away.

'No no, I would rather not.'

She then gave me the pillow, my mother's pillow. It was open, half filled with my mother's hair. Each time they shaved her head, my mother had kept the hair for her pillow. I hugged the pillow against my chest, feeling some of the hair rising in clouds of dark dust into my nostrils.

Jacqueline took a long piece of black cloth out of her bundle and wrapped it around her belly.

'Sister,' she said, 'life is never lost, another one always comes up to replace the last. Will you come watch when they burn the body?'

'What would be the use?' I said.

'They will make these women watch, and we can keep them company.'

When Jacqueline took my hand, her fingers felt balmy and warm against the lifelines in my palm. For a brief second, I saw nothing but black. And then I *saw* the crystal glow of the river as we had seen it every year when my mother dipped my hand in it.

'I would go,' I said, 'if I knew the truth, whether a woman can fly.'

'Why did you not ever ask your mother,' Jacqueline said, 'if she knew how to fly?'

Then the story came back to me as my mother had often told it. On that day so long ago, in the year nineteen hundred and thirty-seven, in the Massacre River, my mother did fly. Weighted down by my body inside hers, she leaped from Dominican soil into the water, and out again on the Haitian side of the river. She glowed red when she came out, blood clinging to her skin, which at that moment looked as though it were in flames.

In the prison yard, I held the Madonna tightly against my chest, so close that I could smell my mother's scent on the statue. When Jacqueline and I stepped out into the yard to wait for the burning, I raised my head toward the sun thinking, One day I may just see my mother there.

'Let her flight be joyful,' I said to Jacqueline. 'And mine and yours too.'

Biographical Notes

MICHAEL ANTHONY (b. 1932, Trinidad). After a rural childhood Michael Anthony worked for some years in an iron foundry at the Pointe à Pierre oil refinery. Nursing an ambition to become a writer he migrated to England in 1954 where he lived until 1968 when he left to live in Brazil. He returned to Trinidad in 1970 and worked for many years with the National Cultural Council. He has published eleven books of fiction, including the story collections *Cricket in the Road* (1973) and *The Chieftain's Carnival* (1993, both Longman). In 1996 he published the historical novel *In the Heat of the Day* (Heinemann).

ROBERT ANTONI (b. 1957, Trinidad). Teaching now at the University of Miami, Robert Antoni maintains strong family links in Trinidad and the Bahamas. He has published two highly acclaimed novels, *Divina Trace* (Robin Clarke, 1991) which won the 1992 Commonwealth Writers' Prize and *Blessed is the Fruit* (Faber & Faber, 1998). He also co-edited the anthology *The Archipelago: New Caribbean Writing* (A special issue of the journal *Conjunctions*, no. 27, Bard College, Annandale-on-Hudson.)

REINALDO ARENAS (1943–90, Cuba). Despite coming from a poor rural background Reinaldo Arenas studied at Havana University and later worked in the National Library. At odds with the regime both politically and on account of his open homosexuality, he was expelled from Cuba in 1980 and lived in New York city until his death, from AIDS, a decade later. He published more than a dozen books, many of which are available in English translation, including a highly acclaimed autobiography, *Before Night Falls* (Viking, 1993). His fiction includes the novel *Farewell to the Sea* (Penguin, 1987; orig. pub. 1982).

ANTONIO BENÍTEZ-ROJO (b. 1931, Cuba). After a varied career in Cuba which included periods spent as a journalist, a government statistician, and as Director of the Centre for Caribbean Studies at the Casa de las Americas, Benítez-Rojo defected to the USA in 1980. He is currently Professor of Latin American and Caribbean literature at Amherst College, Massachusetts. Several of his books are now available in English, including the important critical study *The Repeating Island* (Duke Uni. Press, 1996) and his collection of stories *A View from the Mangrove* (Faber, 1998).

JUAN BOSCH (b. 1910, Dominican Republic). After more than twenty years in exile during the regime of the dictator Trujillo, Juan Bosch returned to the Dominican Republic in 1961 and was elected President. He was overthrown by a military coup the following year and went into exile once more. He returned in 1965 and has lived on the island ever since. Bosch is the author of two novels and of numerous political, sociological, and historical works, but is most famous for his short stories, the first collection of which appeared in 1933. His stories are greatly esteemed in the Spanish-speaking world, and collections have been published in French and German, but few have appeared in English.

KAMAU BRATHWAITE (b. 1930, Barbados). One of the great poets of the Caribbean, with more than a dozen collections of poetry to his credit, Brathwaite is also a historian, a teacher, and an important cultural critic. His work has always challenged conventional genre boundaries and in recent years has moved towards a more narrative format, exploiting the expressive possibilities of the 'Sycorax video style' he employs in his collection of *DreamStories* (Longman, 1994) from which 'Dream Haiti' is taken.

JEAN 'BINTA' BREEZE (b. 1947, Jamaica). Best known as a poet and actress, Jean 'Binta' Breeze has a well-deserved reputation as an inspirational performer of her own work. She came to prominence as one of very few female dub/reggae poets, but quickly moved on to explore more varied modes of tale-telling. She has published three collections, most recently mixing poems and stories in *On the Edge of an Island* (Bloodaxe, 1997).

G. CABRERA INFANTE (b. 1922, Cuba). After growing up in the Cuba of the dictator Batista, G. Cabrera Infante—who knew both Che Guevara and Fidel Castro personally—settled as an exile in Britain. Recognized now as one of the most original of Latin American writers, several of his novels are available in English, including *View of Dawn in the Tropics* (Faber, 1988) and *Infante's Inferno* (Faber, 1984).

JAN CAREW (b. 1925, Guyana). After his schooldays in Guyana Jan Carew studied at universities in the USA, Czechoslovakia, and France. Author of six novels—most famously *Black Midas* and *The Wild Coast* (both published in 1958)—he has also written plays, poetry, and criticism as well as many memorable short stories. He now lives in the USA where he is Professor of African and American Studies at Northwestern University.

ALEJO CARPENTIER (1904–83, Cuba). Born and educated in Havana, Alejo Carpentier lived for many years in France and then Venezuela but returned to Cuba after the revolution. He held various offices in the Cuban government in the 1960s and later acted as the Cultural Attaché at the Cuban Embassy in Paris. One of the major Latin American writers of the century, Carpentier has published many novels and collections of stories. Much of his work is available now in English translation (as well as in more than twenty other languages) including *Explosion in a Cathedral* (Penguin, 1971), *The Kingdom of this World* (Penguin, 1975), *The Lost Steps* (Gollancz, 1956), and *The Chase* (Deutsch, 1990).

PATRICK CHAMOISEAU (b. 1953, Martinique). The author of four novels, Patrick Chamoiseau came to international prominence when his most recent novel,

Biographical Notes

Texaco (1992), won France's most prestigious literary prize, the Prix Goncourt. Following the acclaim for *Texaco* several of Chamoiseau's books have been translated into English, including *Texaco*, which was published by Granta in 1997.

WILLI CHEN (b. 1941, Trinidad). A successful businessman in San Fernando, running a bakery and printworks, Willi Chen is also an accomplished artist and has won national prizes for his poetry, drama, and short stories. He published a collection of stories, *King of the Carnival* (Hansib) in 1988, which has been widely raided by anthologists.

AUSTIN CLARKE (b. 1934, Barbados). After leaving his 'island place' to study economics in Toronto in 1955, Austin Clarke has worked as a journalist and broadcaster and taught in various US and Canadian universities. He has published six novels and four collections of stories, including *Nine Men Who Laughed* (Penguin, 1986) and *There Are No Elders* (Exile Editions, Toronto, 1993). His other works include the autobiography *Growing Up Stupid Under the Union Jack* (Mclelland and Stewart, Toronto, 1980).

MERLE COLLINS (b. 1950, Grenada). An inspirational performer of her own work, Merle Collins has published two novels, most recently *The Colour of Forgetting* (Virago, 1995), two collections of poems including *Rotten Pomerack* (Virago, 1992), and a collection of stories, *Rain Darling* (The Women's Press, 1990). After teaching for some time at the University of North London she presently teaches literature at the University of Maryland in the USA.

FRANK COLLYMORE (1893–1980, Barbados). Actor, teacher, poet, and editor as well being the author of many short stories, Frank Collymore was a key figure in the development of modern West Indian literature. He edited the literary journal *BIM* through four decades. His *Collected Poems* was published in Barbados in 1959 and a *Selected Poems* in 1971. His stories were collected posthumously in *The Man Who Loved Attending Funerals* (Longman, 1993).

MARYSE CONDÉ (b. 1937, Guadeloupe). Regarded by many as the Caribbean's leading female writer, she grew up in Guadeloupe and later in Paris. She lived for many years in West Africa and much of her writing explores connections between Africa and the Caribbean. She has published eight novels and collections of stories and has won many important literary awards in France. Much of her work is now available in English translation, including *A Season in Rihata* (Heinemann, 1988; orig. pub. 1981) and *Windward Heights* (Faber, 1998; orig. pub. 1995).

EDWIDGE DANTICAT (b. 1969, Haiti). Edwidge Danticat was brought up by an aunt until she could be reunited with her parents in the USA at the age of 12. She studied French Literature at Barnard College and holds an MFA from Brown University. Her first novel, *Breath, Eyes, Memory* (Abacus, 1994), was widely praised. She has also published a collection of stories (*Krik Krak*, Abacus, 1996). She now lives in New York.

Biographical Notes

RENÉ DEPESTRE (b. 1926, Haiti). Poet, essayist, and educator. He lived in Cuba as an exile from the Duvalier regime for many years and was one of the founders of the Cassa de las Américas publishing house. Best known as a poet, his works include *A Rainbow for the Christian West* (Red Hill Press, 1972), the novel *Festival of the Greasy Pole* (University Press of Virginia, 1990), and a collection of stories, *Alleluia Pour une Femme-Jardin* (1981). He now lives in France.

THEA DOELWIJT (b. 1938, Holland). Her father was from Surinam and Thea Doelwijt lived there for most of her adult life, before returning to Holland in the mid-eighties when the political situation deteriorated under the military regime. She has published a novel, *Wajono*, several plays and edited the anthology *Kri, Kra*. Only a few of her stories are translated into English.

ZOILA ELLIS (b. 1957, Belize). After studying at the University of the West Indies in Jamaica and at the University of Sussex in the UK, Zoila Ellis returned to Belize, where she practises law. Several of her stories have been anthologized and she has published one small collection locally, *On Heroes, Lizards and Passion* (Cubola Publications, 1988).

ROSARIO FERRÉ (b. 1938, Puerto Rico). Established now as one of Puerto Rico's leading authors, Rosario Ferré began writing after an inspirational encounter with the Latin American writers Mario Vargas Llosa and Angel Rama while she was a graduate student in the 1960s. A poet, novelist, and essayist, as well as an accomplished writer of short stories, Ferré writes in both Spanish and English. Her novel *The House on the Lagoon* was shortlisted for the National Book Award (Abacus, 1995).

ROY HEATH (b. 1926, Guyana). His much-admired autobiography of his youth in colonial British Guiana, *Shadows Round the Moon* (Collins, 1990), ends with Roy Heath's departure for Britain at the age of 23. He has lived in London ever since and published nine novels, including *The Murderer* (Allison & Busby, 1978) which won the *Guardian* fiction prize and most recently *The Shadow Bride* (Flamingo, 1988) and *The Ministry of Hope* (Marion Boyers, 1997).

CLYDE HOSEIN (b. 1940, Trinidad). Clyde Hosein has worked in advertising, and as a journalist and broadcaster. He lived in London for some time and published a collection of stories, *The Killing of Nelson John* (London Magazine editions, 1980). He returned to Trinidad before moving to Toronto where he now lives.

C. L. R. JAMES (1901–89, Trinidad). A great Caribbean man of letters—historian, philosopher, critic, and novelist—but C. L. R. James is perhaps best known for his writing on cricket—particularly his wonderful *Beyond a Boundary*, first published in 1963. He published an important novel, *Minty Alley*, in 1936 (republished by New Beacon Books in 1971 and still in print) and short stories in *The Beacon*. In 1992 Blackwell published *The C. L. R. James Reader*, edited by Anna Grimshaw, which includes examples from across the full range of his work.

Biographical Notes

ISMITH KHAN (b. 1925, Trinidad). After working for some time as a journalist on the *Trinidad Guardian* Ismith Khan migrated to the USA where he has lived ever since. He has published three novels, *The Jumbie Bird* (Longman, 1985; orig. pub. 1961), *The Obeah Man* (Tsar, 1995; orig. pub. 1964), and *The Crucifixion* (Peepal Tree, 1987), and a collection of stories, *A Day in the Country* (Peepal Tree, 1987).

JAMAICA KINCAID (b. 1949, Antigua). One of the most original and controversial of West Indian writers in English, Jamaica Kincaid has published four novels— most recently *The Autobiography of My Mother* (Plume/Penguin, 1997), two non-fiction studies, *A Small Place* (Virago, 1988) and *My Brother* (Vintage, 1998), and a collection of stories, *At the Bottom of the River* (Farrar, Straus & Giroux, 1983). She now lives in the USA.

EARL LOVELACE (b. 1935, Trinidad). After a childhood spent in Tobago and Port of Spain Earl Lovelace studied and later taught in the USA for some years. He has lived most of his working life in Trinidad, including a period as Writer in Residence at the University of the West Indies. He has published five novels, including the much acclaimed *The Dragon Can't Dance* (Longman, 1981; orig. pub. 1979) and, most recently, *Salt* (Faber, 1987), a collection of plays, *Jestina's Calypso* (Heinemann, 1984), and a collection of stories, *A Brief Conversion* (Heinemann, 1988).

ROGER MAIS (1905–1955, Jamaica). An unconventional and controversial figure in his lifetime—he was imprisoned by the colonial authorities during the Second World War for writing a newspaper feature regarded as seditious—he published three important novels exploring Jamaican identity and spirituality, *The Hills Were Joyful Together* (1953), *Brother Man* (1954), and *Black Lightning* (1955) (all now published by Heinemann). A collection of his stories, *Listen, the Wind*, was published by Longman in 1986.

E. A. MARKHAM (b. 1939, Montserrat). Since the mid-1950s E. A. 'Archie' Markham has lived mainly in Britain and Europe, but also worked for some time in Papua New Guinea. He has published several collections of poetry, including his *Human Rites: Selected Poems 1970–82* (Anvil Press Poetry, 1984) and *Misapprehensions* (Anvil, 1995), and two collections of short stories, *Something Unusual* (Ambit Books, 1986) and *Ten Stories* (PAVIC, 1994). He has also edited important anthologies of Caribbean writing, including *The Penguin Book of Caribbean Short Stories* (Penguin, 1996).

GABRIEL GARCÍA MÁRQUEZ (b. 1928, Colombia). After a childhood spent on the Caribbean coast of Colombia, Márquez worked for some time as a journalist, travelling widely in Europe and America before publishing the novel which made his name, *One Hundred Years of Solitude* (Picador, 1978). In 1982 he was awarded the Nobel Prize for literature. *The Fragrance of the Guava*, a collection of conversations between Márquez and the Colombian journalist Plino Apuleyo Mendoza, was reissued by Faber in 1998.

Biographical Notes

PAULE MARSHALL (b. 1929, USA). Born of Barbadian parents in New York she has spent long periods living in the Caribbean. She has published four novels, most recently *Daughters* (orig. pub. 1991, Serpents Tail 1992), a volume of novellas, and a collection of stories, *Reena* (Feminist Press, 1983). A selection of her work was published by Virago as *Merle, a novella and other stories* in 1985. Paule Marshall has taught creative writing at several US universities.

ALECIA MCKENZIE (b. 1960, Jamaica). After growing up in Kingston, Jamaica, Alicia McKenzie studied at US universities and did postgraduate work in journalism at Columbia University in New York and went on to write for several national and international newspapers. Her first collection of stories, *Statellite City* (Longman, 1993), won the Commonwealth Writers Prize for first book in the Caribbean/Canada region. She now lives in Belgium and teaches at the Free University of Brussels.

PAULINE MELVILLE (b. 1941, Guyana). Well known as an actress, both on stage and film, Pauline Melville has published a collection of stories, *Shapeshifter* (The Women's Press, 1990) which won the *Guardian* Fiction Prize, and a novel, *The Ventriloquist's Tale* (Bloomsbury, 1997) which won the Whitbread Prize for first novel.

ALFRED MENDES (1897–1991, Trinidad). After fighting in Europe in the First World War, Alfred Mendes became—with C. L. R. James and Albert Gomes—an active member of the *Beacon* group in Trinidad in the 1920s and 1930s. In the early 1930s he settled in New York, where he published two novels, *Pitch Lake* (1934) and *Black Fauns* (1935) (both republished by New Beacon Books in the 1980s). He returned to Trinidad in 1940 but later settled in Barbados, where he died in 1991.

V. S. NAIPAUL (b. 1932, Trinidad). Author of a dozen works of fiction, including collections of stories, and almost as many non-fiction travelogues and histories. V. S. Naipaul is regarded as one of the major writers of our time. His great novel *A House for Mr. Biswas* (1961), reimagines much from his own childhood and family history in Trinidad, while his collections that include short stories are *Miguel Street* (1959), *A Flag on the Island* (1967), and *In A Free State* (1971). (All these titles—and many others—are presently in print from Penguin Books.) His work has won many major prizes and he was knighted in 1990.

SASENARINE PERSAUD (b. 1957, Guyana). An outspoken critic as well as a prolific author, Sasenarine Persaud has published three books of poetry, including *Demerary Telepathy* (1988), and two novels, most recently *The Ghost of the Bellows Man* (1992), all published in the UK by Peepal Tree Press. He has lived for some years in Canada and his award-winning collection of stories *Canada Geese and Apple Chatney* will be published there in the autumn of 1998.

GEOFFREY PHILP (b. 1958, Jamaica). After growing up in Kingston, Jamaica, Geoffrey Philp graduated from the University of Miami. He now lives in Miami. He has published two collections of poetry, including *Florida Bound* (Peepal Tree

Press, 1995), and a book of stories, *Uncle Obediah and the Alien* (Peepal Tree Press, 1997).

VELMA POLLARD (b. 1937, Jamaica). Senior Lecturer in Language Education at the University of the West Indies in Jamaica. She has published two collections of poetry, most recently *Shame Trees Don't Grow Here* (Peepal Tree Press, 1992), a novel, *Homestretch* (Longman, 1994), and two collections of stories, *Considering Women* (The Women's Press, 1989) and *Karl and other stories* (Longman, 1994). The novella 'Karl' won the Cassa de las Americas prize in 1992.

JEAN RHYS (1894–1979, Dominica). Jean Rhys was a rather mysterious figure and the mystery extends even to her date of birth; scholars now seem to favour 1890 but Rhys herself insisted it was 1894, and that is good enough for me. After spending her childhood in Dominica Jean Rhys came to Europe in her teens and never returned to live in the West Indies, though her imagination seems to have been haunted by that island upbringing. She published five novels—most famously *Wide Sargasso Sea* in 1966—and several collections of short stories in her lifetime. A selection of her stories with distinctively Caribbean themes was published as *Tales of the Wide Caribbean* (Heinemann, 1985).

ASTRID ROEMER (b. 1947, Surinam). Surinam's best-known contemporary writer, though only a fraction of her work is available in English translation, Astrid Roemer has written numerous books of poetry and fiction as well as many plays for stage and radio. She now lives in Holland.

ANDREW SALKEY (1928–95, Panama). Born of Jamaican parents in Colon, Panama, Andrew Salkey grew up in Jamaica before migrating to Britain in the early 1950s where he established himself as an all round man-of-letters, working in journalism and broadcasting as well as publishing several novels, collections of poems, travelogues, and editing important anthologies of Caribbean writing. His stories are collected in *Anancy's Score* (Bogle l'Overture, 1973) and *Anancy Traveller* (Bogle l'Overture, 1992). For the last two decades of his life he taught literature at Hampshire College, Amherst, in Massachusetts.

EDGARDO SANABRIA SANTALIZ (b. 1951, Puerto Rico). Regarded as one of Puerto Rico's most original new voices, Edgardo Sanabria Santaliz has published one collection of stories, *Delfia cada tarde*, and published stories in various US magazines.

LAWRENCE SCOTT (b. 1943, Trinidad). Having left Trinidad in his early twenties, initially to train as a Benedictine monk, Lawrence Scott then decided to settle in England and write. He has published two novels, the highly acclaimed *Witch-broom* (1993, Heinemann) which was short-listed for the Commonwealth Writers Prize and more recently *Aelred's Sin* (Allison & Busby, 1998). He published a collection of stories, *Ballad for the New World* (Heinemann, 1994), and a selection of his poems was included in the anthology *Caribbean New Voices* (Longman, 1996).

He now combines writing with teaching English at City & Islington College and creative writing at the City Literary Institute.

LIONEL SEEPAUL (b. 1955, Trinidad). After studying for a degree in English at Laurentian University in Ontario, Lionel Seepaul taught in high schools in Trinidad and Canada. His stories have been widely published in prestigious journals and anthologies but have not yet been collected. He presently lives in Vancouver.

SAM SELVON (1923–94, Trinidad). Perhaps *the* master storyteller of the Anglophone Caribbean tradition, Sam Selvon began writing as a young journalist in Trinidad but his career really blossomed after he migrated to London in the early 1950s. Author of ten novels, a volume of plays, and a collection of short stories, *Ways of Sunlight* (Longman, 1973; orig. pub. 1957), he is best known for his classic novel of West Indians in exile *The Lonely Londoners* (Longman, 1972; orig. pub. 1956). He spent the last fifteen years of his life in Canada but returned to Trinidad just before he died.

OLIVE SENIOR (b. 1941, Jamaica). After studying journalism in Canada and Britain Olive Senior was editor of the *Jamaica Journal* for several years. Her publications include works in social and cultural history, but in recent years she has concentrated on her fiction and poetry. She has published two collections of poetry, most recently *Gardening in the Tropics* (McClelland & Stewart, 1994), and three books of stories, including *Summer Lightning* (Longman, 1986) which won the Commonwealth Writers Prize and her most recent collection *Discerner of Hearts* (Bloodaxe, 1995). She now lives in Canada.

MAKEDA SILVERA (b. 1955, Jamaica). Co-founder and managing editor of the *Sister Vision: Black Women and Women of Colour Press*, Makeda Silvera is an important figure in the Caribbean literary renaissance that has been happening in and around Toronto through the last decade. After a childhood in Jamaica she emigrated to Canada when she was 12 and has lived there ever since. She has published several books on aspects of black cultural experience in Canada as well as two collections of stories, most recently *Her Head A Village, and Other Stories* (Press Gang Publishers, Vancouver, 1994).

JOHN STEWART (b. 1933, Trinidad). Leaving Trinidad in 1955 to study in the USA, John Stewart went on to become a Professor of English at Ohio State University. His literary publications include a novel, *Last Cool Days* (Andre Deutsch, 1971), and a collection of stories, *Curving Road* (University of Illinois Press, 1975).

ANA LYDIA VEGA (b. 1946, Puerto Rico). A professor of French and Caribbean literature at the University of Puerto Rico, Ana Lydia Vega has published three collections of stories including *Encancaranublado y Otros Cuentos de Naufragio* (1981) which won the Casa de las Américas prize. In 1985 she was named author of the year by the Puerto Rico Society of Authors.

Biographical Notes

ERIC WALROND (1898–1966, Guyana). After a childhood spent in several Caribbean territories Eric Walrond went to New York to study in 1918. Like his West Indian compatriot Claude McKay he was associated with the cultural excitement of the Harlem Renaissance in the 1920s and his collection of stories, *Tropic Death*, was published in 1926 to wide critical acclaim. He settled in Britain shortly after the book's appearance but, strangely, never published anything else.

MYRIAM WARNER-VIEYRA (b. 1939, Guadeloupe). Myriam Warner-Vieyra has lived for many years in Senegal in West Africa, where she works as a librarian and researcher at the University of Dakar. She has written two novels, both translated into English, *As the Sorcerer Said* (Longman, 1982) and *Juletane* (Heinemann, 1987), and a collection of stories, *Femmes Echouées* (Présence Africaine, 1988).

JOHN WICKHAM (b. 1923, Barbados). After a career in the World Meteorological Organisation which took him to Europe for several years, John Wickham followed in the footsteps of his father, the famous journalist Clennell Wickham, and became literary editor of *The Nation*, one of the major newspapers of Barbados, in 1979. His short stories have been widely anthologized and he published the collection *Discoveries* (Longman) in 1993.

Suggestions for Wider Reading

Anthologies, particularly major collections such as this one that, bearing the imprint of the 'Oxford Book of . . .' will be read—no matter how loud the editors' disclaimers—as definitive or at least 'representative', are always problematic, controversial, and incomplete. Indeed from the informed reader's perspective, one of the pleasures of an anthology is in arguing with the editor's selections—who is omitted, which stories should represent which writers, is there 'fair' representation of authors by—in the Caribbean context particularly—gender, age, ethnicity, island/territory, language, exiles as against stay-at-homes, etc. I can anticipate already the letters we will get from some outraged reader/writers, the scorn of some reviewers with ethnic/gender/nationalist axes to grind! Even were the editors really exercised by such considerations—and all of them have some merit— the space available would never be enough. So while we have been very conscious that in such major projects the editor's real, and most frightening, power is the power to exclude, finally we have to make our choices and stand by them.

We felt it was important that we foreground what we have tried to do with this anthology, not so much to deflect critical blame but in order not to mislead those new readers we hope to draw to the region's literature. In making our selections we wanted to do justice to each of our 'generations'—we could easily have filled many more of the pages of the anthology with stories drawn from any of those periods, but that would obviously have been to distort the overview we set out to try to provide. The process of cutting stories out from our original 'long list' was particularly painful in regard to the middle generations—not to have stories by John Hearne, George Lamming, John Figueroa, Vic Read, Edgar Mittelholtzer, Wilson Harris, among others, really hurt! But it was not only that period which had to be pared down, we wanted very much to include one of Claude McKay's stories from his collection *Gingertown* in the 'pioneer' section. McKay is one of the most important writers of that period, albeit better known for his poetry and novels than for his short fiction and most often associated with the writers of the Harlem Renaissance in New York—the city he settled in after leaving Jamaica as a young man. But if we included a story by McKay, which of those other pioneers should we leave out? Already we had had to accept that we could not make room for Phylis Shand Alfrey or H. G. de Lisser or Alfred Gomes. And at the other end of the collection the selection of the stories in the section given over to the contemporary period perhaps caused us most heart-searching of all—so many interesting writers and fine stories we wanted to include—Tony Kellman, N. D. Williams, Kwame Dawes, Nirmilah Maharaj, Earl McKenzie, Erna Brodber, Rooplal Monar, Neil Bissondath, Kevin James, Opal Palmer Adissa, Heather Campbell, Marlene Nourbese-Philip, and many others. Of course, this does not begin to address the many writers in the other language traditions we could not include. We rehearse all this mechanical detail here in order that any new reader of Caribbean writing will understand just how partial even such a generous selection as this is will inevitably be, given the richness of the Caribbean short-story traditions. We hope that such readers will go on from this selection to read more widely in Caribbean literature, particularly the short story, and to that end have listed below other anthologies of short stories, both of English language stories and work from the French, Spanish, and Dutch traditions in translation. Also listed is a selection of books of stories by writers in English whose work is not included here, and a brief list of relevant critical studies, so readers working through those resources will be properly equipped to construct their own anthology and to argue with ours!

ANTHOLOGIES

West Indian Stories, ed. Andrew Salkey (Faber and Faber, 1960).

Stories from the Caribbean, ed. Andrew Salkey (Elek Books, 1965).

West Indian Narrative, ed. Kenneth Ramchand (Nelson, 1966).

Caribbean Literature, ed. G. R. Coulthard (University of London Press, 1966).

Latin American Writing Today, ed. J. M. Cohen (Penguin, 1967).

Writers in the New Cuba, ed. J. M. Cohen (Penguin, 1967).

From the Green Antilles: Writings of the Caribbean, ed. Barbara Howes (Souvenir Press, 1967).

Cuban Short Stories, 1959–1966, ed. Sylvia Carranza and Maria Juana Cazabon (Book Institute Havana, 1967).

Caribbean Prose, ed. Andrew Salkey (Evans Brothers, 1967).

Political Spider, ed. Ulli Beier (Heinemann, 1969).

New Writing in the Caribbean, ed. A. J. Seymour (Carifesta Publications, 1972).

Caribbean Stories, ed. Michael Marland (Longman, 1978).

From Trinidad: An Anthology of Early West Indian Writing, ed. Reinhard W. Sander (Hodder and Stoughton, 1978).

Commonwealth Short Stories, ed. Anna Rutherford and Donald Hannah (Macmillan, 1979).

The Spanish American Short Story, ed. Seymour Menton (University of California Press, 1980).

Heritage, ed. Esmore Jones (Cassell, 1981).

West Indian Stories, ed. John Wickham (Ward Lock Educational, 1981).

Best West Indian Short Stories, ed. Kenneth Ramchand (Nelson, 1982).

An Anthology of African and Caribbean Writing in English, ed. John Figueroa • (Heinemann/The Open University, 1982).

Ambit: Caribbean Special Issue, ed. E. A. Markham (no. 91, 1982).

Contemporary Women Authors of Latin America, ed. Doris Meyer and Margaret Fernandez Opmos (Brooklyn College Press, 1983).

The Caribbean, special issue of *New England Review and Bread Loaf Quarterly*, vol. vii, no. 4 (Summer 1985).

Suggestions for Wider Reading

Facing the Sea, eds. Anne Walmsley and Nick Caistor (Heinemann, 1986).

The Sun's Eye, ed. Anne Walmsley (Longman, 1989).

Her True-True Name: An Anthology of Women's Writing from the Caribbean, ed. Pamela Mordecai and Betty Wilson (Heinemann, 1989).

The Faber Book of Contemporary Carribbean Short Stories, ed. Mervyn Morris (Faber and Faber, 1990).

The Faber Book of Contemporary Latin American Short Stories, ed. Nick Caistor (Faber and Faber, 1990).

Caribbean New Wave: Contemporary Short Stories, ed. Stewart Brown (Heinemann, 1990).

When New Flowers Bloomed: Short Stories by Women Writers from Costa Rica and Panama, ed. Enrique Jaramillo Levi (Latin American Literary Review Press, 1991).

The Penguin Book of Latin American Short Stories, ed. Thomas Colchie (Penguin, 1991).

Green Cane and Juicy Flotsam: Short stories by Caribbean women, ed. Carmen C. Esteves and Lizabeth Paravisini-Gebert (Rutgers University Press, 1992).

Columbus' Egg, ed. Nick Caistor (Serpents Tail, 1992).

22 Jamaican Short Stories, ed. Kim Robinson and Leeta Hearne (Kingston Publishers, 1992).

New Writing from the Caribbean: Selections from The Caribbean Writer, ed. Erika J. Walters (Macmillan Caribbean, 1994).

Cowboys, Indians and Commuters: The Penguin Book of New American Voices, ed. Jay McInerney (Penguin, 1994).

If I Could Write This In Fire, ed. Pamela Maria Smorkaloff (The New Press, 1994).

Ancestral House: The Black Short Story in the Americas and Europe, ed. Charles H. Rowell (Westview Press, 1995).

Caribbean New Voices, ed. Stewart Brown (Longman, 1995).

Hispanic American Literature, ed. Nicolas Kanellos (HarperCollins, 1995).

Rhythm & Revolt: Tales of the Antilles, ed. Marcela Breton (Plume, 1995).

The Archipelago; New Caribbean Writing, ed. Robert Antoni and Bradford Morrow (special issue of Conjunctions, no. 27, 1996).

The Penguin Book of Caribbean Short Stories, ed. E. A. Markham (Penguin, 1996).

Caribbean Writing, Special Issue of the *Mississippi Review*, ed. Michael Mays, vol. 24, no. 3 (1996).

The Voice of the Turtle: An anthology of Cuban Stories, ed. Peter Bush (Quartet Books, 1997).

COLLECTIONS OF STORIES

Opal Palmer Adisa, *Bake-Face and other Guava Stories* (Flamingo, 1986).

Louise Bennett, *Anancy and Miss Lou* (Sangsters Bookstores, Jamaica, 1979).

James Berry, *Anancy-Spiderman*, Walker Books (London, 1988).

Neil Bissoondath, *Digging Up the Mountains* (Andre Deutsch, 1986).

Suggestions for Wider Reading

Dionne Brand, *SanSouci and Other Stories* (Williams-Wallace, 1988).

Wayne Brown, *The Child of the Sea* (Inprint Publications, Trinidad, 1989).

Timothy Callender, *It So Happen* (Heinemann, 1991).

Hazel D. Campbell, *Singerman* (Peepal Tree Press, 1992).

A. M. Clarke, *The Black Madonna* (Typographics Ltd., Port of Spain, 1985).

Cyril Dabydeen, *Jogging in Havana* (Mosaic Press, 1992).

Albert Maria Gomes, *All Papa's Children* (Cairi Publishing, 1978).

Lorna Goodison, *Baby Mother and the King of Swords* (Longman, 1990).

June Henfrey, *Coming Home and other Stories* (Peepal Tree Press, 1994).

Kevin Christopher James, *Jumping Ship* (Ballentine Books, 1992).

Claude McKay, *The Passion of Claude McKay: Selected Prose and Poetry 1912–1948*, ed. Wayne Cooper (Shocken Books, 1973).

Earl McKenzie, *Two Roads to Mount Joyful* (Longman, 1992).

Rooplal Monar, *High House and Radio* (Peepal Tree Press, 1991).

Seepersad Naipaul, *The Adventures of Gurudeva* (Heinemann, 1995).

Hazel Palmer, *Tales from the Gardens and Beyond* (Sister Vision, 1995).

Althea Prince, *Ladies of the Night* (Sister Vision, 1993).

Noel Williams, *The Crying of the Rainbirds* (Peepal Tree Press, 1992).

CRITICAL READING

Edward Baugh, ed., *Critics on Caribbean Literature* (Allen and Unwin, 1978).

Antonio Benítez-Rojo, *The Repeating Island: The Caribbean and the Postmodern Perspective* (Duke University Press, 1996).

Stewart Brown, ed., *The Pressures of the Text: Orality, Texts and the Telling of Tales* (Centre of West African Studies, University of Birmingham, 1995).

Wilfred Cartey, *Whispers from the Caribbean* (Centre for Afro-American Studies, University of California, Los Angeles, 1991).

Carolyn Cooper, *Noises in the Blood: Orality, Gender and the 'Vulgar' Body of Jamaican Popular Culture* (Warwick Caribbean Studies, Macmillan, 1993).

Daryl Cumber Dance, *New World Adams* (Peepal Tree Press, 1998).

Carole Boyce Davies and Elaine Savory Fido, eds., *Out of the Kumbla: Caribbean Women and Literature* (Africa World Press, 1990).

J. Michael Dash, *Literature and Ideology in Haiti 1915–1961* (Barnes & Noble, 1981).

Kwame Dawes, *Natural Mysticism* (Peepal Tree Press, 1998).

Glyne A. Griffith, *Deconstruction Imperialism and the West Indian Novel* (The Press, University of the West Indies, 1996).

C. L. R. James, *The C. L. R. James Reader*, ed. Anna Grimshaw (Blackwell, 1992).

Louis James, ed., *The Islands in Between* (Oxford University Press, 1968).

Renu Juneja, *Caribbean Transactions: West Indian Culture in Literature* (Warwick Caribbean Studies, Macmillan, 1996).

Bruce King, ed., *West Indian Literature* (Macmillan, 1995).

Evelyn O'Callaghan, *Woman Version: Theoretical Approaches to West Indian Fiction by Women* (Warwick Caribbean Studies, Macmillan, 1996).

Suggestions for Wider Reading

Kenneth Ramchand, *The West Indian Novel and its Background* (Heinemann, 1993).

Gordon Rohlehr, *The Shape of that Hurt and other essays* (Longman Trinidad, 1992).

—— *My Strangled City and other essays* (Longman Trinidad, 1992).

Dennis Walder, *Post-colonial Literatures in English* (Blackwell, 1998).

Anne Walmsley, *The Caribbean Artists Movement, 1966–72* (New Beacon Books, 1992).

Publisher's Acknowledgements

Michael Anthony, 'They Better Don't Stop the Carnival' from *The Chieftain's Carnival* (Longman, 1993), reprinted by permission of Addison Wesley Longman Ltd.

Robert Antoni, 'A World of Canes' from *Blessed is the Fruit* (Faber and Faber, 1998), by permission of the author.

Reinaldo Arenas, 'Goodbye Mother' from Nick Caistor (ed.), *The Faber Book of Contemporary Latin American Short Stories* (Faber, 1989).

Juan Bosch, 'Encarnacion Mendoza's Christmas Eve', translated by Dr John Gilmore, by permission of Dr John Gilmore.

Kamau Brathwaite, 'Dream Haiti' from *Dreamstories* (Longman, 1994), reprinted by permission of Addison Wesley Longman Ltd.

Jean 'Binta' Breeze, 'Sunday Cricket' from *On the Edge of an Island* (Bloodaxe, 1997), reprinted by permission of Bloodaxe Books Ltd.

Jan Carew, 'Tilson Ezekial alias Ti-Zek' , first published in *New England Review/ Bread Loaf Quarterly*, 7/4, (1985), reprinted by permission of the author.

Alejo Carpentier, 'Journey of the Seed' from J. M. Cohen (ed.), *Latin American Writing Today* (Penguin, 1967), translated by Jean Franco.

Patrick Chamoiseau, 'Red Hot Peppers' from *Chronique de sept misères* (Éditions Gallimard, 1986), © Éditions Gallimard 1986, and from Marcia Breton (ed.), *Rhythm and Revolt: Tales of the Antilles* (Plume Books, 1995), translated by Barbara Lewis, reprinted by permission of Éditions Gallimard and the University of Nebraska Press.

Willi Chen, 'Trotters' from *King of the Carnival* (Hansib, 1988), reprinted by permission of Hansib Publications.

Austin Clarke, 'Leaving this Island Place' from *When He Was Free and Young and Used to Wear Silks* (House of Anansi Press, 1971), copyright 1971 by Austin Clarke, reprinted by permission of the author.

Merle Collins, 'The Walk' from *Rain Darling*, first published 1990 by the Women's Press Ltd., 34 Great Sutton Street, London EC1V ODX, reprinted by permission of the Women's Press Ltd.

Frank Collymore, 'Some People are Meant to Live Alone' from *The Man Who Attended Funerals* (Heinemann, 1993), reprinted by permission of Heinemann Educational Publishers, a division of Reed Educational & Professional Publishing Ltd.

Maryse Conde, 'The Breadnut and the Breadfruit', from *Callaloo*, 12/38 (Winter 1989), 135–51, copyright © The Johns Hopkins University Press, reprinted by permission.

Publisher's Acknowledgements

Edwidge Dandicat, '1937' from *Krik? Krak!* (Abacus Books, 1996), reprinted by permission of Abacus Books and Soho Press Inc.

René Depestre, 'Rosana on the Mountain' from Charles M. Rowell (ed.), *Ancestral House* (Westview Press, 1995).

Thea Doelwijt, 'In Foreign Parts' from Marcia Breton (ed.), *Rhythm and Revolt: Tales of the Antilles* (Plume Books, 1995), translated by James Brockway.

Zoila Ellis, 'The Waiting Room' from *On Heroes, Lizards and Passion* (Cubola Productions, 1988), reprinted by permission of Cubola Productions and the author.

Rosario Ferré, 'When Women Love Men' from *The Youngest Doll*, copyright © 1991 by the University of Nebraska Press, reprinted by permission of the University of Nebraska Press and Susan Bergholz Literary Services.

Roy Heath, 'The Master Tailor and the Teacher's Skirt' from *Colours of a New Day: Writing for South Africa* (Penguin, 1990), reprinted by permission of the author.

Clyde Hosein, 'Morris, *Bhaiya*' from *The Killing of Nelson John*, first published in *London Magazine*, 1980, reprinted by permission of London Magazine Editions.

G. Cabrera Infante, 'The Doors Open at Three' from *Writes of Passage* (Faber & Faber, 1993), reprinted by permission of Faber & Faber Limited.

C. L. R. James, 'Triumph' from Andrew Salkey (ed.) *Stories from the Caribbean* (Elek Books, 1965), copyright C. L. R. James, reproduced with permission of Curtis Brown Ltd., London, on behalf of the Estate of C. L. R. James.

Ismith Khan, 'A Day in the Country' from *A Day in the Country and Other Stories* (Peepal Tree Press, 1994), reprinted by permission of Peepal Tree Press Ltd.

Jamaica Kincaid, 'Blackness' from *At the Bottom of the River*, copyright © 1983 by Jamaica Kincaid, reprinted by permission of Farrar, Strauss & Giroux, Inc. and Random House UK Limited (Vintage).

Earl Lovelace, 'Victory and the Blight' from *A Brief Conversation* (Heinemann, 1988), copyright Earl Lovelace, reproduced with permission of Curtis Brown Ltd., London, on behalf of Earl Lovelace.

Roger Mais, 'Red Dirt Don't Wash' from *Listen the Wind and Other Stories* (Longman, 1986), reprinted by permission of Addison Wesley Longman Ltd.

Gabriel García Márquez, 'The Last Voyage of the Ghost Ship' from *Leaf Storm*, translated by Gregory Rabassa, copyright © 1972 by Gabriel García Márquez, reprinted by permission of HarperCollins Publishers, Inc. and Jonathan Cape Ltd.

E. A. Markham, 'Mammie's Form at the Post Office' from *Something Unusual* (Ambit Books, 1986), reprinted by permission of the author and Ambit Books.

Paule Marshall, 'To Da-Duh, In Memoriam' from *Merle and Other Stories* (Virago, 1985), copyright 1985 by Paule Marshall, reprinted by arrangement with Writers House LLC as agent for the proprietor.

Alecia McKenzie, 'Private School', copyright Alecia McKenzie 1998, reprinted by permission.

Publisher's Acknowledgements

Pauline Melville, 'The Conversion of Millicent Vernon' from *Shape Shifter*, first published 1990 by the Women's Press Ltd., 34 Great Sutton Street, London EC1V 0DX, copyright © Pauline Melville 1990, reprinted by permission.

Alfred Mendes, 'Pablo's Fandango' from *Pablo's Fandango and Other Stories* (Longman, 1997), edited by Michèle Levy reprinted by permission of Addison Wesley Longman Ltd.

V. S. Naipaul, 'The Night Watchman's Occurrence Book' from *A Flag on the Island* (Penguin Books, 1969), copyright © 1967 V. S. Naipaul, reprinted by permission of Penguin Books Ltd. and Viking Penguin, a division of Penguin Putnam Inc.

Sasenarine Persaud, 'Canada Geese and Apple Chatney' from *Canada Geese and Apple Chatney* (Tsar Publications, 1998), reprinted by permission of the author and Tsar Publications.

Geoffry Philp, 'My Brother's Keeper' from *Uncle Obadiah and the Alien* (Peepal Tree Press, 1997), reprinted by permission of Peepal Tree Press Ltd.

Velma Pollard, 'Altemont Jones' from *Karl and Other Stories* (Longman, 1994), reprinted by permission of Addison Wesley Longman Ltd.

Jean Rhys, 'Pioneers, oh, Pioneers', from *Sleep it Off Lady* (Penguin Books, 1976), copyright © Jean Rhys, 1976, reprinted by permission of Penguin Books Ltd. and the Wallace Literary Agency, Inc.

Astrid Roemer, 'The Inheritance of My Father: A Story for Listening' from Charles M. Rowell (ed.), *Ancestral House* (Westview Press, 1995), translated by Hilda van Neck-Yoder.

Antonio Benitéz Rojo, 'Buried Statues' from *The Voice of the Turtle* (Quartet Books, 1997), originally published in Spanish as *Estatuas sepultadas*, copyright © Antonio Benitéz Rojo, translation copyright © Andrew Hurley, reprinted by permission of Quartet Books Ltd.

Andrew Salkey, 'A Proper Anno Domini Feeling' from *Anancy Traveller* (Bogle L'Ouverture, 1992), reprinted by permission of Bogle L'Ouverture Publications Limited.

Edgardo Sanabria Santaliz, 'After the Hurricane', first published in *New England Review/Bread Loaf Quarterly*, 7/4, (1985), reprinted by permission of the author.

Lawrence Scott, 'Ballad for the New World' from *Ballad for the New World* (Heinemann, 1994), reprinted by permission of Heinemann Educational Publishers, a division of Reed Educational & Professional Publishing Ltd.

Lionel Seepaul, 'Pan for Pockot' from Erika J. Walters (ed.), *New Writing from the Caribbean* (Macmillan, 1994), first published in *The Caribbean Writer*, reprinted by permission of the author.

Sam Selvon, 'The Cricket Match' from *Ways of Sunlight* (Longman, 1957), reprinted by permission of Mrs Althea Selvon.

Olive Senior, 'Do Angels Wear Brassieres?' from *Summer Lightning* (Longman, 1986), reprinted by permission of Addison Wesley Longman Ltd.

Publisher's Acknowledgements

Makeda Silvera, 'Caribbean Chameleon' from *Her Head a Village* (Vancouver: Press Gang Publications, 1994), reprinted by permission.

John Stewart, 'The Old Men Used to Dance' from *Looking for Josephine* (Tsar Publishers, 1998), reprinted by permission of the author and Tsar Publications.

Ana Lydia Vega, 'Eye Openers' from *True and False Romances* (Serpent's Tail, 1994), copyright © 1994, reprinted by permission of Serpent's Tail, London.

Eric Walrond, 'Drought' from *Tropic Death* (Boni & Liveright, 1926). Copyright 1926 by Boni & Liveright, Inc., renewed 1954 by Eric Walrond. Reprinted by permission of Liveright Publishing Corporation.

Miriam Warner-Veiyra, 'Passport to Paradise' from Carmen C. Esteves and Lizabeth Paravisini-Gebert (eds.) *Green Cane and Juicy Flotsam* (Rutgers University Press, 1991).

John Wickham, 'The Light on the Sea' from *Discoveries* (Longman, 1993), reprinted by permission of Addison Wesley Longman Ltd.